CRITICAL THINKING

CRITICAL THINKING

Consider the Verdict

Sixth Edition

Bruce N. Waller
Youngstown State University

PEARSON

Boston   Columbus   Indianapolis   New York   San Francisco   Upper Saddle River
Amsterdam   Cape Town   Dubai   London   Madrid   Milan   Munich   Paris   Montreal   Toronto
Delhi   Mexico City   Sao Paulo   Sydney   Hong Kong   Seoul   Singapore   Taipei   Tokyo

Editorial Director: Craig Campanella
Editor in Chief: Dickson Musslewhite
Executive Editor: Ashley Dodge
Editorial Project Manager: Kate Fernandes
Director of Marketing: Brandy Dawson
Senior Marketing Manager: Laura Lee Manley
Production Liaison: Barbara Reilly
Operations Specialist: Christina Amato
Manager, Text Rights and Permissions: Charles Morris
Cover Manager: Jayne Conte
Cover Designer: Suzanne Behnke
Cover Image: tlegend/Shutterstock
Media Director: Brian Hyland
Media Editor: Rachel Comerford
Media Project Manager: Barbara Taylor-Laino
Full-Service Project Management: Shiny Rajesh, Integra Software Services Pvt. Ltd.
Printer/Binder: LSC Communications
Cover Printer: LSC Communications
Text Font: 10/11 New Baskerville

Library of Congress Cataloging-in-Publication Data
Waller, Bruce N.,
  Critical thinking : consider the verdict / Bruce N. Waller. — 6th ed.
    p. cm.
  ISBN-13: 978-0-205-15866-9 (alk. paper)
  ISBN-10: 0-205-15866-8 (alk. paper)
  1. Critical thinking.   2. Verdicts.   3. Logic.   I. Title.
  BC177.W3 2012
  160.2'434—dc22
                                            2011010803

www.pearsonhighered.com

Student Edition ISBN-10:   0-205-15866-8
                ISBN-13: 978-0-205-15866-9
À la Carte Edition ISBN-10:   0-205-15881-1
                ISBN-13: 978-0-205-15881-2

Contents

Preface

Critical thinking is a valuable skill: whether you are deciding which courses to take or career to pursue, what toothpaste to use or what stocks to buy, which candidate to vote for or which cause to support, which reports to believe or what claims to reject, critical thinking can be very useful. One of the most important places for careful critical thinking is the jury room. Serving on a jury is one of the most significant and basic ways that citizens actively participate in their government, and jury service makes strong demands on citizen-jurors. Jurors must set aside any biases and judge the issues fairly; they must reason carefully about what laws are involved and how those laws apply to the specific case at hand; they must evaluate testimony and weigh both its accuracy and its relevance; and they must give a fair hearing to both sides, distinguish sound from erroneous arguments, and ultimately reach a just and reasonable conclusion. The courts offer fascinating cases for examination and analysis, and the courts have long grappled with many of the key issues in critical thinking: questions about burden of proof, legitimate analogies, distinctions between relevant and irrelevant reasons, question-begging arguments and unfair questions, the weighing of testimony (including expert testimony and appeals to expert authority), the distinction between argument and testimony, the legitimate and illegitimate use of ad hominem arguments.

The courtroom demands a high level of critical thinking skill, and it is also a fascinating place for studying and developing the key skills of critical thinking: determining exactly what the conclusion is, and who bears the burden of proving it; separating false claims from reliable information; setting aside irrelevant distractions and focusing on the question at issue; and distinguishing between erroneous and legitimate arguments. The skills that make you an effective juror will also make you an intelligent consumer, an effective planner, and a wise citizen.

The sixth edition of *Critical Thinking: Consider the Verdict* uses the jury room as the focus for developing basic critical thinking skills, but it does not stop there. Those skills are also applied to the various arguments and issues that arise in our daily lives as consumers, students, planners, and citizens. While the courtroom and the jury room are valuable laboratories for learning and testing and applying critical thinking abilities, those abilities must also be exercised when reading editorial columns, debating social issues, making intelligent consumer choices, working effectively at a career, and fulfilling one's responsibilities as a thoughtful critical citizen of a democracy. Thus, most of the exercises and examples are drawn from advertisements, social debates, political campaigns, editorials, and letters to the editor. Critical thinking skills are valuable in the jury room, but they are also valuable in the classroom, the boardroom, the laboratory, and the grocery store.

Critical thinking is often regarded as an adversarial process, where the stronger arguments triumph over the weaker. Adversarial critical thinking is common and is often valuable: Cases in court usually proceed through an adversarial process, and that can be a useful way of bringing out both strong and weak points in the arguments presented. But not all critical thinking follows the adversarial model, and the sixth edition of *Critical Thinking: Consider the Verdict* gives careful attention to the contexts when *cooperative* critical thinking may prove particularly useful. Several factors enhance effective cooperative critical thinking, and several argument fallacies are especially damaging to a cooperative critical thinking process. Both the promise and the pitfalls of cooperative critical thinking are examined in this new edition.

The sixth edition of *Critical Thinking: Consider the Verdict* contains a number of important changes and additions.

- Extensive new discussion of cooperative critical thinking (as distinguished from adversarial critical thinking), and examination of its special strengths and the contexts in which it is most effective.
- New and updated exercises and examples in every chapter.
- A new section on definitions, including examination of misleading definitions.
- Extensive new material on statistical fallacies and deceptions.
- A new section on the importance of scientific integrity and scientific cooperation.
- Additional new exercises in the special-review sections (the sections of cumulative exercises).

Critical Thinking: Consider the Verdict, sixth edition, provides a solid introduction to critical thinking; Chapters 18 and 19 offer introductory instruction in symbolic logic. Those two chapters are self-contained, and you may do either or both at any point in the course, or skip them altogether. The boxed exercises and examples throughout the text are not essential to understanding the chapters, but they do present interesting material and challenging questions. You can skip them, but you'll miss a lot of the fun.

Support for Instructors and Students

The moment you know. Educators know it. Students know it. It's that inspired moment when something that was difficult to understand suddenly makes perfect sense. Our MyLab products have been designed and refined with a single purpose in mind—to help educators create that moment of understanding with their students. The new MyThinkingLab delivers **proven results** in helping individual students succeed. It provides **engaging experiences** that personalize, stimulate, and measure learning for each student. And, it comes from a **trusted partner** with educational expertise and an eye on the future. MyThinkingLab can be used by itself or linked to any learning management system (LMS). MyThinkingLab—the moment you know.

Instructor's Manual with Tests (0-205-15875-7)**:** For each chapter in the text, this valuable resource provides a detailed outline, list of objectives, and discussion questions. In addition, test questions in multiple-choice, true/false, fill-in-the-blank, and short answer formats are available for each chapter; the answers are page referenced to the text. For easy access, this manual is available at www.pearsonhighered.com/irc.

PowerPoint Presentation Slides for Critical Thinking: Consider the Verdict (0-205-15877-3)**:** These PowerPoint Slides help instructors convey critical thinking principles in a clear and engaging way. For easy access, they are available at www.pearsonhighered.com/irc.

MyTest Test Generator (0-205-15878-1)**:** This computerized software allows instructors to create their own personalized exams, edit any or all of the existing test questions, and add new questions. Other special features of the program include random generation of test questions, creation of alternate versions of the same test, scrambling question sequence, and test preview before printing. For easy access, this software is available at www.pearsonhighered.com/irc.

Acknowledgments

I have received help and encouragement from many quarters. The first edition of the book was completed while I was teaching at Elon College, and my colleagues and students there were generous in their support and aid. John G. Sullivan read several drafts of the book, and provided insightful, challenging, and constructive criticism—while making my work environment congenial and refreshing, and vastly extending my intellectual horizons. Anne Ponder read early drafts of several chapters, and her comments and criticisms were invaluable. Barbara Plumblee was wonderfully patient in convincing my computer to cooperate with me. Tom Henricks offered much excellent advice and many words of encouragement, while regularly thrashing me at tennis. Teresa LePors, the omniscient reference librarian, found the answer to every question I posed. Gayle Fishel helped tremendously with design and structure of the book and suggested ingenious ways of organizing examples. Lillian Pollock was astoundingly efficient in the laborious task of securing permissions to reprint.

George N. Schlesinger encouraged me to write the book, gave helpful guidance throughout, and contributed delightful examples. Allen Belsheim read the entire manuscript of the first edition, and made excellent suggestions for improvements.

All the later editions have been completed while teaching at Youngstown State University, and my colleagues at YSU have built a wonderful collegial working environment. Tom Shipka's enthusiasm for the project has been constant, and as a remarkably efficient department chair he smoothed my path in innumerable ways. Since my misfortune of becoming department chair (following Tom's retirement), Tom has been a generous and wise source of counsel. Brendan Minogue, Charles Reid, Larry Udell, Stephanie Dost-Barnhizer, Jeff Limbian, Andrew Stypinski, and Martina Haines have used the book in their classes, and their suggestions for improvements have been particularly useful. The YSU reference librarians answer all my questions and make it look easy. Our student workers, Hannah Detec, James Hamilton, and Gina Ponzio, have provided cheerful help on many of the exhausting details. Our department secretary for several years, Joan Bevan, was remarkably efficient and unfailingly cheerful; I owe her a special debt for making my first years as department chair run so smoothly. Mary Dillingham, one of the few people in the world worthy of replacing Joan, has carried on a great tradition of efficiency and dedication; she is the essential element in the smooth functioning and congenial atmosphere of the department. Many other friends and colleagues at YSU have given aid and advice, and have been generous in both intellectual stimulation and warm friendship; special thanks to Nawal Ammar, Chris Bache, Cynthia Brincat, Walter Carvin, Vince Lisi, Sarah Lown, Mustansir Mir, Deborah Mower, Bernie Oakes, Dan O'Neill, Gabriel Palmer-Fernandez, Mark Shutes, Charles Singler, Donna Sloan, Linda "Tess" Tessier, Alan Tomhave, Mark Vopat, Homer Warren, Victor Wan-Tatah, and Robert Weaver.

My students at Youngstown State University have been of enormous help in the preparation of the later editions. They have been kind enough to point out—often with admirable candor—the flaws and difficulties of earlier versions; but of even greater benefit has been their enthusiasm for the book: the times they have told me of actually enjoying the reading of a textbook and sharing the book with their friends and families, their fascination with many of the exercises, and most of all their reports of successful analyses of deceptive advertisements, of political speeches, and of attorneys' arguments during subsequent jury duty. A number of students brought me examples from their own reading and experience, and many of those examples are incorporated into the later editions.

My friend Jack Raver has frequently been helpful as a computer consultant, and is one of the most enthusiastic, energetic, and joyful arguers I have ever encountered. Lia Ruttan has been a wonderful source of fascinating cases and examples, particularly from the Canadian courts. Richard White has given me many very helpful ideas, especially in the area of cooperative critical thinking in special courts. Lauren Schroeder and Fred Alexander have been particularly helpful on arguments and issues related to politics and the environment.

Special thanks to all the wonderful people who helped in putting together the photographs for the cover and to accompany the exercises: Judge Lou D'Apolito who allowed us the use of his courtroom; two fabulous photographers, James Evans and Carl Leet; Gabriel Palmer-Fernandez and Deborah Mower, who played the roles of attorneys; Homer Warren, who looked wonderfully judicial; and all the jury members (many of whom are current YSU students, together with my long-suffering sons and lovely daughter-in-law)—Russell Waller, Adam Waller, Robyn Repko Waller, Zach Robbins, Cary Dabney, Amanda Benchwick, Sarah Lowry, Rebecca Soldan, William Soldan, Gary Davenport, Heather Carbon, and Mary Dillingham.

I also benefitted from thorough and insightful review of this edition by Victoria Rogers, Indiana University–Purdue University Indianapolis; Eli Kanon, University of North Florida; Glenn Sanford, Sam Houston State University; Jean Miller, Virginia Tech; Chris Cayton, Portland Community College and from excellent suggestions made by reviewers of earlier editions: Richard McCarty, Michael A. Principe, and Joan Esposito. My editors at Pearson, Nancy Roberts and Kate Fernandes, have been everything any author could ask for in editorial guidance and cooperation: it has been a genuine pleasure to work with them. Shiny Rajesh, the project manager for this edition, is meticulous, professional, and unfailingly cheerful, and she smoothed the path of taking the book from rough draft to finished text.

My wife, Mary, has advised on every aspect of the work, made many suggestions for exercises and improvements, and her constant affection and support have been invaluable. My sons, Russell and Adam, have read sections of the book, discussed many of the examples with me, offered valuable suggestions, and have been the great joys of my life.

CRITICAL THINKING

1

❖ ❖ ❖

Introduction

You evaluate arguments and assertions every day: when choosing your breakfast cereal, evaluating reports on the effects of the caffeine in your coffee, reading your morning paper, deciding how to cast your vote. And occasionally you will consider arguments while serving on a jury. In the performance of your jury duty you will be expected to weigh evidence, consider competing arguments, reason carefully, and decide impartially. Some of your fellow jurors may disagree with your conclusion, so you must be able to evaluate their arguments and argue cogently for your own conclusions. So as we practice critical thinking, we'll examine a wide variety of courtroom and jury arguments: arguments that are interesting, important, and instructive. But we'll also study political arguments, advertisements, scientific claims, and a wide variety of other contexts where critical thinking skills are valuable.

CRITICAL THINKING IN EVERYDAY LIFE

This book pays close attention to jury deliberation, but it is not exclusively or even primarily concerned with courtroom reasoning. Jury deliberation is profoundly important, but it is only a tiny fraction of the critical reasoning you must do. Every day you are bombarded with advertisements, and to find any helpful substance in them you will have to critically winnow out masses of chaff. You are a citizen in a democratic society, and thus it is your responsibility to carefully and rationally evaluate the policies and programs of your local, state, and federal government and to vote intelligently (and perhaps campaign) for the candidates you consider most capable. You encounter advertisements, the evening news, news magazines, opinion journals, scientific reports, editorials, textbooks—all making claims that are sometimes contradictory and sometimes slanting the material presented. Sorting these out, distinguishing fact from speculation, and weighing competing theories and interpretations require the same reasoning skills that are required of an effective and responsible juror.

The subject of this book is critical reasoning in all its applications. The only way to be effective at jury reasoning is to be good at reasoning, and good reasoning requires practice. It is not something that can be turned on and off like a politician's charm. Critical thinking cannot be hoarded for use exclusively in the jury room. Use it or lose it.

A Strong-Willed Jury

In New South Wales, a defendant was charged with the theft of several cows. The jury finished their deliberations, and returned to the court with this verdict: "Not guilty, if he returns the cows." The judge was outraged, and ordered the jury back for further deliberations. The jurors, deeply offended, soon returned with a new verdict: "Not guilty, and he doesn't have to return the cows."[1]

PLAY FAIR

The first requirement for examining arguments intelligently—whether as a voter, a consumer, a reader, or a juror—is to be fair in your evaluations. Bias and prejudice close minds and stifle critical inquiry; the first task in good critical reasoning is to eliminate such bias.

At some point you will be in the jury box, and before the jury is impaneled you will be asked a few questions: perhaps by the judge; by the district attorney, and by the defense counsel if it is a criminal case; by lawyers for the plaintiff (the person suing the defendant) and for the defendant in civil suits. The idea is to seat a fair and impartial jury. This process is called the *voir dire*. (*Voir dire* is French, meaning "to see, to speak." However, *voir* is a corruption of the Latin *verus*, meaning "true"; thus the original meaning is "true talk."[2]) The *voir dire* process is supposed to detect any bias or narrowmindedness among potential jurors.

If the defendant is your lover, or if you will lose money if the plaintiff wins, or if the defendant recently ran off with your spouse, then it might be more difficult for you to remain completely impartial in considering the case. If from reading newspaper reports you have formed an unshakable conviction concerning the guilt or innocence of the accused, you will not be an open-minded juror.

Smart Jurors

Philadelphia Assistant District Attorney Jack McMahon advises rookie prosecutors on selecting a jury:

My opinion is you don't want smart people [on the jury]. Because smart people will analyze the hell out of your case. They have a higher standard. They hold you up to a higher standard because they're intelligent people. They take those words "reasonable doubt" and they actually try to think about them. You don't want those people. You don't want people who are going to think it out.[3]

SEATING A JURY

How far should the *voir dire* process go? That question is raised by the increased use of jury selection specialists, who use sophisticated techniques in an effort to discover which jurors are most likely to favor which side. A defendant being charged with drunken driving might wish not to seat a teetotaler or a juror whose child was recently killed by a drunk driver. But not all cases are so obvious. For example, in the famous trial of the "Harrisburg Seven" in 1971–1972 (in which Philip Berrigan and six other antiwar activists were charged by the federal government with conspiring to kidnap Henry Kissinger and blow up heating tunnels in Washington, D.C.), a group of social scientists did extensive research on the attitudes of the population around Harrisburg, Pennsylvania, from which the jury pool would be drawn. They discovered important information for the defense. For example, while one might expect college-educated persons to be sympathetic to the antiwar defendants, that was not the case in Harrisburg. As Jay Schulman, who directed the research, states, "Contrary to what our lawyers expected, college-educated people were not likely to be liberal in Harrisburg. Liberal college graduates, it seems, leave Harrisburg for other places, and those who stay support conservative norms."[4] Thus the defense was alerted to be cautious of college graduates. (That does not mean that in 1972 all college graduates in Harrisburg were conservatives. It means only that Harrisburg college graduates were more *likely* to be conservative, and thus more likely to be unfavorably disposed toward the defendants.)

Jury Research: Eliminating or Selecting Bias?

Is the use of social scientists to investigate potential jurors a good thing? It is certainly legal, but that is not the question. Does it make a fair trial more likely, or does it subvert justice by unfairly "stacking" the jury? That is a hotly contested issue. Opponents of jury selection specialists claim that they rig juries to reach verdicts on the basis of the jurors' biases rather than on the basis of the evidence and the arguments. Those who favor the use of social scientific research during *voir dire* claim that it is essential in order to avoid seating prejudiced jurors who cannot weigh the case fairly. After all, prejudiced jurors cannot always be exposed simply by asking a few questions during *voir dire*. (Suppose a potential jury member is asked by the lawyer for a black defendant: "Do you know of any reason why you cannot consider this case honestly and fairly?" The potential juror is not likely to respond: "Yes, I do; I have an irrational prejudice against blacks." In fact, those who are prejudiced are often unwilling to admit their prejudice even to themselves: "No, I'm certainly not prejudiced against blacks; why, some of my best friends are black; I just don't want them moving into my neighborhood.") Detecting biased and unfair jurors is not an easy task. Not every prejudiced person has beady eyes and wears a hood.

There are obviously some serious problems in current methods of jury selection. Procedures that exclude certain segments of the population—for example, systematically excluding blacks from criminal juries through use of peremptory challenges—are unfair. Such abuses are too frequent and are sometimes systematic.

Baseball and Juries

Bert Neuborne, legal director for the American Civil Liberties Union, claims that in New York City during the 1950s (when New York had three major league baseball teams—the Yankees, the Dodgers, and the Giants), lawyers used a quick and easy method for selecting jury members:

> As Neuborne tells it, attorneys needed only one question: "What baseball team do you root for?"

Yankee fans, the defense dismissed; Dodger fans, the prosecution dismissed. Giant fans were acceptable to both sides because, Neuborne says, they were "the only reasonable people in town."[5]

A handbook used in 1973 in Dallas County, Texas, gives the following instructions for criminal prosecution attorneys:

> You are not looking for a fair juror, but rather a strong, biased, and sometimes hypocritical individual who believes the Defendants are different from them in kind, rather than degree; you are not looking for any member of a minority group which may subject him to oppression—they almost always empathize with the accused.[6]

But it is essential in a fair trial that at least some members of the jury be able to empathize with the accused. Imagine how you would feel as a criminal defendant if all members of your race or ethnic group or political party or religion or socioeconomic group were systematically excluded from the jury that tried your case: It would hardly be a "jury of your peers."

Keeping Women in the Kitchen, on the Pedestal, and off the Jury

In 1966, the Mississippi Supreme Court (in *State* v. *Hall,* 187 So.2d 861) ruled that women could legally be excluded from Mississippi juries, for these reasons:

The legislature has the right to exclude women so they may continue their service as mothers, wives, and homemakers, and also to protect them (in some areas, they are still upon a pedestal) from the filth, obscenity, and noxious atmosphere that so often pervades a courtroom during a jury trial.

In short: It's for your own good, girls.

IMPARTIAL CRITICAL THINKING

The point of this chapter is that in your deliberations you must try to approach the case with an open mind, free of bias and favoritism. There will be those who wish to exploit your fears and prejudices and preconceptions: unscrupulous advertisers who play on our fears of social stigma to sell us overpriced and often unnecessary "remedies" for bad breath, body odor, and the terrors of "flaking and itching"; politicians who pander to our fears to sell us dubious foreign policies; and lawyers who hope that prejudices will substitute for arguments. It requires constant vigilance to avoid substituting our biases for rational reflection, but it is essential to do so if we are to reason well—in the jury room and the laboratory and the marketplace and the voting booth.

It is natural to feel a special sympathy with those who have similar goals and interests. Thus if you are a feminist liberal arts major at the old home state university, you may feel predisposed toward a defendant who is a feminist liberal arts major at the same school. That may be a natural tendency, but it is not a fair one. There may be some rotten apples even among the feminist liberal arts majors at state university, and the defendant may be one of them. It may also be difficult to be fair and impartial toward a defendant who is your exact opposite: a hard-nosed businessman who thinks the arts are a waste of time and that a woman's place is in the home. You may not feel sympathetic toward such an individual, and you wouldn't want to be stuck with him at a small dinner party. But if you are to consider the issues clearly, you must try to set aside that distaste. The issue is the person's guilt or innocence of some specific charge, and that has nothing to do with whether you like or dislike the defendant.

The same objectivity is required as you listen to the lawyers in the case. The district attorney may be a pompous ass and the defense attorney a great human being. That is irrelevant to which side has the stronger case, and you must set aside such personal likes

---

The Courtroom Is Not a Singles Bar

Ideally, jurors should start from a presumption of innocence, but without any bias for or against the defendant; and try to remain neutral until all the evidence is heard. One Canadian juror, Gillian Guess, failed to maintain that neutrality. During the course of a murder trial in which she served as a juror, she began sleeping with the defendant. She was later sentenced to 18 months in prison for obstruction of justice.

and dislikes in order to deliberate justly and accurately on the merits of the argument. Difficult as it may be, it is vitally important to separate argument sources and styles from argument content.

ADVERSARIAL CRITICAL THINKING

Critical thinking is a useful weapon. People sometimes speak of skill in critical thinking as "verbal self-defense," or learning "how to win arguments." And since you are daily bombarded with arguments from advertisers and politicians, and often by arguments designed to deceive rather than enlighten you, learning how to protect yourself against misleading claims and flawed arguments is a very valuable skill. Effective argument and the effective critical analysis of argument can also serve a more positive function. Under the *adversarial* system of justice—practiced in Great Britain, the United States, Canada, Australia—lawyers on either side present arguments, and from that tough argumentative contest the truth emerges: or at least, such a struggle, when it functions well and both sides are represented by honest and skillful advocates, is often our most effective means of seeking the truthful outcome. From the local courthouse to the Supreme Court, both sides present their strongest *arguments* and probe for weaknesses in their opponents' arguments, and—if all goes well—from this contest the truth eventually emerges.

In some ways science is also an adversarial system. Scientists present their theories and the evidence in their support; and other scientists challenge those theories and seek evidence to refute them. Karl Popper, one of the great twentieth-century philosophers of science, saw this as the basic method of science: present bold theories, expose those theories to scrutiny and criticism from scientific adversaries, and through this method we develop *better* theories. Indeed, Popper thought that often the best scientific work was done when strong theoretical conjectures were refuted by powerful opposing arguments. A similar process often occurs in philosophy: Philosophers present their theories and arguments, and those theories and arguments are subjected to examination and criticism—criticism that often finds flaws in the proposed theory and results in better theories and better arguments.

The contest between adversaries—whether in the courtroom, the laboratory, or the philosophy seminar—is often a valuable method for seeking better theories and finding the truth. But the adversarial process is *not* a no-holds-barred, eye-gouging, ear-biting, anything goes brawl. Or at least, it *should* not be, and—when it works effectively—it is not. To the contrary, for the adversarial process to work well, it is essential that both sides play fair and behave respectfully. Sadly, the adversarial system does *not* always function well; and when it does not, that is usually because one or both sides have corrupted the process, and the contest is not fair. Suppose you have a small software development company, and you have developed a really innovative program that is a big improvement in some area of computer use, and that is likely to be very profitable for your company. A software giant comes in and steals your innovation, and sells it as their own. You hire a lawyer and sue the company that stole your product; and in a fair adversarial process, the evidence will come out, both sides will present their cases and their arguments, and you will win your case and recover damages. But the software giant has enormous funds at its disposal, while you have very little money. If their lawyers file motion after motion and cause one delay after another, then the legal costs for both sides will become enormous—costs the large corporation can easily afford, but costs that soon take all your money and force you to drop the suit. That sort of tactic destroys the effectiveness of the adversary system. Or suppose you are a poor person who is charged with a capital offense, such as murder. You cannot afford an attorney, so the state will appoint one for you. Unfortunately, in some cases, the state appoints a defense attorney for you who is grossly incompetent: in Texas, there have been several cases in which defendants were "represented" by attorneys who showed up drunk, or who actually slept through much of the trial. When one adversary is impaired or incompetent or asleep, it is hardly surprising that the "adversary system" fails to function properly (and it is hardly surprising that a number of criminal convictions in Texas have been overturned by later tests of DNA evidence). As Samuel R. Gross states, "The American system of adversarial justice is predicated on the assumption that both sides are competently represented and have adequate resources to present their cases. That assumption is often false."[7]

And, of course, there are other ways the adversary system can go wrong: if the jury is racially prejudiced, or the judge is biased, or the evidence is falsified, or a juror is bribed, then the adversary system cannot work well. But that is not because the adversarial process is flawed, but because one or both of the adversaries break the rules. A baseball contest is a good way of determining which team is actually better—but not if one side bribes the umpire, and not if one side can afford top quality equipment while the other side uses equipment that is falling apart. The adversarial process can also work well in science, but that requires that the adversaries play by the rules. If someone falsifies research, or covers up adverse results, then the scientific adversarial process can break down: just as the adversarial process breaks down in criminal trials when there is perjured testimony or one side has an incompetent attorney, and just as civil adversarial processes break down when one side subverts the system by expensive delaying tactics.

For the adversarial process to work well, both sides must play by the rules. That is hardly surprising: it is true of almost any contest. A football match is a good way of determining which team is superior— but not if the referee is bribed, or the star player on one team has been paid to throw the game. But for the adversarial process to work at its *best*, more is required than simply adhering to the rules; in addition, both sides must be respectful of their opponents and of the process itself. When civility breaks down, the adversarial process suffers. That doesn't mean that the adversaries should be less energetic in their efforts to present the strongest case possible, and to find and exploit the weaknesses in the positions of their opponents. But such efforts should be consistent with being respectful toward one's opponent. The importance of respect and civility in the adversarial process is perhaps best observed in the British courts. There is a long and glorious tradition of debate and adversarial contest in the British courts; and it is there that the importance of civility and personal respect is quite clear; indeed, sometimes the tradition of civility is so strong it seems almost quaint. As the judge enters the courtroom, all present rise to show respect: a tradition that is found in many courts, following the British model. But in the British courts, the judge then bows to the barristers, the barristers bow to the judge and to each other. Barristers address one another as "my learned friend," and when one barrister rises to make an objection, the other immediately sits down; when the barrister has made his or her objection, the opposing barrister may then rise and offer arguments in response to the objection; but they would never stand and both talk at once. Remarks addressed to "the learned judge" are often preceded by "if your Lordship (or Ladyship) pleases." The barristers and the judge all wear white wigs and gowns, and with all the bowing and the very formal address—"My learned friend appears to have forgotten the evidence given this morning; perhaps I might refresh his memory"—may appear quaint; and indeed, if you ever have a free day in London, a visit to the Central Criminal Courts is wonderfully entertaining, and a better show than the changing of the guard at Buckingham Palace. But quaint and a bit old-fashioned as this elaborate formal courtesy may appear, it serves a very important function in the British adversarial system. It is a powerful reminder that the advocates must present their best arguments, and be zealous in looking for flaws in the opposing arguments; but that such a process need not and should not involve attacks on the person giving the arguments. And if the process is to work well, both sides must be attentive to opposing views, and neither distort nor misrepresent them in attempting to refute them. The elaborate courtesy and deep tradition of civility is not merely a quaint British tradition; instead, it is a vital element of an adversarial process that functions well, and that is genuinely interested in seeking the truth. Anyone who remembers or has seen clips of the O.J. Simpson criminal trial will recall the constant sniping and insulting and bickering between the prosecution and the defense; and it is clear that the atmosphere of incivility and hostility was a burden on the entire trial process. Whatever one thinks of the outcome, the nasty atmosphere and personal animosity in evidence at the trial—not to mention the media circus—made it difficult for anyone to feel confident that justice had been done. Sometimes civility is strained, but the forms are generally maintained in the U.S. Senate: "Will the gentleman yield for a question? Will the gentle lady allow a comment?" In an era of political grandstanding, it seems almost quaint, like the wigs and the robes worn by the barristers (lawyers) and judges. But this elaborate courtesy also serves an important function.

Cooperative Critical Thinking

Adversarial critical thinking —when both sides play fair and play nice—can be a very valuable way of finding the truth and testing theories and trying out ideas: valuable in determining guilt or innocence in the courtroom, valuable for testing theories in the sciences, valuable for trying out new ideas and examining old beliefs in dorm room debates. But valuable as adversarial critical thinking is, the adversarial approach is not always best. *Cooperative* critical thinking is also valuable, and in some contexts is much more useful. Consider some rather homely examples of effective cooperative critical thinking, offered by legal scholar and legal ethicist Carrie Menkel-Meadow:

> . . . consider two sisters, who both seem to be fighting about a single orange, when one really desires the fruit for eating and the other the rind for cooking. Or, from my own personal experience, when, with a single piece of chocolate cake left, I wanted the icing (frosting) and my brother desired the cake, demonstrating that a horizontal, rather than a vertical, cut of the cake would maximize both of our desires. . . . [8]

Obviously not all problems yield such neat cooperative solutions; but by focusing on finding common grounds and shared interests, it is often possible to reach a conclusion in which no one *loses*, and everyone comes away satisfied. Notice that the solutions gained through cooperative critical thinking are not always *compromises*. In the example above, Carrie and her brother might have reached a *compromise* by splitting the piece of chocolate cake in half, leaving neither very satisfied; by considering carefully what each really desired, and how those desires could best be met, they found a solution that met the goals of both.

Carrie wanted frosting, and her brother wanted cake. By considering the problem cooperatively, they found a solution that worked for both of them. That brings out the crucial first step in effective cooperative critical thinking: getting clear on *exactly* what goals are in play. Getting clear on the goals is vital, but it isn't always easy. Carrie wants the piece of chocolate cake, and so does her brother. But in fact, that's not quite accurate. Carrie wants the chocolate *frosting*, while her brother wants the chocolate *cake*. Only by examining more critically their actual goals can cooperative critical thinking be successful. Of course, sometimes the goals are basically incompatible: Her brother wants to eat the entire piece of chocolate cake, frosting and all; and Carrie wants to eat the entire piece of chocolate cake while her brother watches and suffers, because she is angry at him for reading her diary. But perhaps even then careful consideration of goals can result in a favorable outcome for everyone: what Carrie really wants is an apology from her brother, and for her brother to understand that such an invasion of personal privacy is wrong, and a commitment that he won't do it again. In that case, it's not impossible that both might have their real wishes fulfilled. But again, that requires looking very carefully at what their real goals are: in her justifiable anger at her brother, she desires to get even with him; getting beyond that anger, and thinking carefully, she may gain a clearer understanding of what her own desires really are.

Adversarial critical thinking is often beneficial, but in the case of the chocolate cake cooperative critical thinking is likely to prove more helpful. In an adversarial contest, the arguments would probably turn on questions of fairness: who got the last piece of the last cake, who ate the most of this cake, who asked for the piece of cake first. Such arguments might eventually lead to a result, especially if mom is acting as judge and jury. But the loser is likely to feel resentful, and the winner may not get what he or she really wants: Carrie's brother gets the cake, but he has to eat through all that frosting to get to the part he really likes. The cooperative solution would have been better for everyone, including the winner of the adversarial contest.

The benefits of cooperative critical thinking are not limited to settling sibling disputes over a last piece of chocolate cake. The legal community has come to recognize that while the adversarial system is often a good way of resolving conflicts and finding truth and protecting individual rights, it works better in some settings than in others; and in those other settings, cooperative critical thinking has proved its worth. In the traditional adversarial divorce proceeding, lawyers for both sides battle to win everything they can for the party they represent: the house, the bank accounts, the retirement accounts, the dog, the kids. If I can get 100% of the bank accounts for my client, then I am a more successful and satisfactory adversarial advocate than if I only get 60%; and if I can get sole custody of the kids for my client, then that's a better adversarial outcome than joint custody. But is that really the best outcome? Assuming that both parents love their children, and are reasonably good parents, that is very unlikely to be the best outcome for the children. In fact, it is unlikely to be the best outcome for my client, when my client steps back from the adversarial conflict and carefully considers what he or she really wants: because what my client is likely to want most of all is an outcome that is best for the children, the children who are loved by both my client and my client's former spouse. Thus in many areas—particularly in domestic disputes involving children—courts have set up special alternative ways of handling conflicts and problems. Rather than adversarial procedures, these alternatives are likely to involve cooperative processes, often with the help of counselors.

In adversarial critical thinking, my goal is to present my own position in its most favorable light, probe your argument for weaknesses, reveal the flaws in your views, and establish my position and my arguments as superior: and to the victor, the spoils. In cooperative critical thinking there is still serious sustained inquiry, but the goals are different. Rather than trying to find weaknesses in your position, I am trying to find ways in which our positions can be reconciled. And rather than trying to gain all the spoils for myself, I am seeking a way that everyone can benefit. Which form of critical thinking is better? That's not a very helpful question: it's like asking which game is better, chess or tennis. They are quite different, and both are very useful in different contexts and for different goals.

Adversarial and cooperative critical thinking are quite different methods of thinking critically; but to practice either method effectively, two things are essential. First, whether the process is adversarial or cooperative, the most important step is being clear and precise on *exactly* what is at issue, what is the question. If you are evaluating an argument, you cannot begin to determine whether that argument is good or bad until you know what the argument is supposed to be proving. An argument that establishes that coal is a plentiful and cheap source of energy will be useless if the real issue is whether burning coal increases the danger of global warming. Consider an argument that Jane *might* have murdered Allen, that we cannot rule Jane out as a suspect in the murder: that argument will be useful if the question is being discussed by detectives investigating the murder; however, it will be useless if the district attorney presents the same argument to the jury in Jane's murder, where the question at issue is whether there is proof beyond a reasonable doubt that Jane did the foul deed. And if we are thinking cooperatively about where we should go to dinner, it's important that we each consider what our goal really is: is my main concern to save money, or eat healthy, or make my ex jealous by being seen with my new lover. So adversarial or cooperative, the vital first step in successful critical thinking is being clear on exactly what is at issue.

There is a second important element to good critical thinking, useful whether the context is adversarial or cooperative: be *respectful* to others. Whether the process is adversarial or cooperative, good critical thinking is best accomplished in an atmosphere of respect and civility. That is obvious enough when we are dealing with cooperative critical thinking: after all, cooperative critical thinking can hardly flourish in an atmosphere of distrust and disrespect. But it also applies, and is just as important, when the critical thinking process is adversarial. An attack on your opponent's character, or distortion and misrepresentation of your opponent's arguments and position, is unlikely to succeed in convincing that person of the wisdom of your arguments. And if your goal is to uncover the *truth* through this adversarial contest, then defaming your opponent and misrepresenting your opponent's arguments are not promising procedures. Of course if you are not in pursuit of truth, but instead want to bluster and swagger—the sort of thing you can hear any day on talk radio—then abuse and distortion are excellent for your purposes. But such slogan-shouting "argument" rarely qualifies as thinking, much less *critical* thinking.

Both adversarial and critical thinking are useful in many contexts. If the family is deciding where to go on vacation, then—so long as the atmosphere remains cordial—adversarial critical thinking may be a useful way of carefully and critically examining each of the options under consideration. A cooperative approach could also work, of course, with careful consideration of all the interests and desires that are in play, and a cooperative effort to find a destination that satisfies everyone's real preferences.

In criminal court proceedings, the style of argument is generally adversarial; in domestic court, cooperative procedures may be in place. What about in the jury room? Suppose we are members of the jury in a criminal case: the defendant has been charged with burglary, we have heard the evidence and the arguments and the judge's instructions to the jury, and now we have arrived in the jury room to consider our verdict. Will our deliberative process be adversarial or cooperative? In most movies and dramas about juries, the style of argument is clearly adversarial. Perhaps the most famous dramatic re-creation of jury argument was the film *Twelve Angry Men*, starring Henry Fonda. The film is a bit dated—thankfully, few juries are now made up exclusively of men—but it clearly shows an adversarial argument within the jury room: some jurors argue the case for conviction, while others argue for acquittal; they present their best arguments, and attempt to refute the arguments of the other side. But while real juries often use adversarial critical thinking to reach their verdict, others adopt a more cooperative approach. Two leading researchers on juries, Neil Vidmar and Valerie P. Hans, contrast the "verdict-driven" approach (which is more adversarial) to the "evidence-driven" style of deliberation (which is more in line with the cooperative):

> Once the leader is chosen, the jury embarks on deliberating about the case. They begin in different ways; their choice of how to begin can relate to the jury's ability to reach a verdict. Some juries start by taking a formal vote, either through a show of hands or a secret ballot. In one approach, labeled the "verdict-driven" deliberation, jurors then align themselves with those who are on the same side and talk about the evidence that supports the verdict favored by their faction. In verdict-driven deliberations, polling tends to be frequent.
>
> In contrast, in an "evidence-driven" deliberation, jurors tend to embark on a general discussion of the testimony, the facts, and their meaning. Rather than offer only the facts supportive of their preferred verdict, jurors tend to talk about all of the evidence as they collectively aim to develop a common story of the events. . . .
>
> The verdict-driven style tends to be faster but also is more likely to lead to a situation in which the jurors cannot agree on a final decision.[9]

Which approach is better for jury deliberation? I don't know. The fact that one approach is more likely to lead to a hung jury does not necessarily count against it: after all, a hung jury is certainly better than a mistaken verdict. Which approach is actually better is a difficult question to test, and at this point there is no convincing research on that issue. Both approaches can work effectively. My guess is that which approach works better may depend on who happens to be on the jury. But whichever approach a jury adopts, they will certainly perform better if they look closely at the conclusion at issue: for example, the question at issue in a criminal trial is *not* whether the defendant has been proved innocent, but whether the prosecution has offered *conclusive proof* that the defendant is guilty as charged. And whichever approach the jury adopts, adversarial or cooperative, they will deliberate more effectively if they remain civil and respectful.

The cooperative approach is usually confined to civil and domestic issues, but some Aboriginal peoples in Canada have attempted to apply their community-based nonadversarial approach to the resolution of criminal cases. Starting from a common commitment to healing the community after a crime has been committed, these groups see the adversarial system as an impediment to that healing. Rather than focusing on who is guilty and which side wins, the emphasis is on what went wrong in the community and how it can be fixed, on reintegrating the offender into the community, and on healing the victims, the offender, and the community.[10] It is a very different process from the adversarial contest of most Western criminal proceedings, but it has some distinct virtues. The Canadian Aboriginal approach to justice focuses on the deeper source of the problem, and seeks a problem resolution that repairs the damage to the community and prevents further difficulties. In contrast, most Western court systems impose penalties but do nothing to solve the root of the problem. Trying to reduce crime by imposing stiff criminal penalties has been an obvious failure: Among Western industrialized countries, the United States has by far the highest prison population and is the only country imposing the death penalty, and it also has a huge lead in the amount of violent crime.

Critical thinking is important in adversarial settings, but it is more than just a sword for subduing your opponent and winning your argument. Critical thinking is also valuable in determining exactly what the problems are, exploring the various possibilities for resolving them, examining the effects of the alternatives, and arriving at the best solution for all concerned. Whether truth is sought by combat or cooperation, critical thinking plays a vital role.

Exercise 1-1

1. Suppose that you are the attorney for the defense, and your client is a 30-year-old black man who works as a tax accountant for Dow Chemical. He has been accused of assaulting a man in a tavern; he claims that he was defending himself from attack by a drunken and aggressive patron of the bar (a 60-year-old white bricklayer). What questions would you ask potential jurors during *voir dire*? (Be sure that you phrase the questions in such a way as to get genuine answers.)

2. You are the district attorney, and you are prosecuting a case in which a man—the president of a small business—is accused of assault and attempted rape. His secretary made the charges, claiming that the man assaulted her and attempted to rape her one evening when they were working late in the office. What questions would you ask potential jurors during *voir dire*? What questions would you ask if you were attorney for the *defense*?

3. In the two cases above, do you think you would be a fair and open-minded juror? If you were *those defendants*, would you be satisfied to have someone like yourself seated on the jury?

Exercise 1-2

Two women are charged with murder. Sarah is college-educated and works for an accounting firm. She is 26 years old, of mixed race, and recently divorced. Allison is an old college friend. She is 27, Irish-Italian, single; she completed 3 years of college, and now works as a sales representative for a publishing firm. Sarah and Allison had gone to a local tavern for drinks, and were there from 10:00 to 11:00 P.M. While standing at the bar, they began talking with Robert and Jay. Robert is African American, 25 years old, and recently separated; he drives a truck for a package-delivery company. Jay, Robert's friend and coworker, is Polish American: At the time of his death, he was 26, married, and had a 2-year-old daughter. When Sarah and Allison left the tavern, Robert and Jay followed. The defendants claim that Jay asked them for a ride, and when Sarah and Allison refused, he became verbally abusive. Sarah became frightened, and took a pistol from her purse, which she handed to Allison. When Jay advanced toward Allison, she shot him twice. The first bullet grazed his arm, and the second entered his heart, causing his death. Robert agrees that Jay was angry, but claims that his friend did not threaten the women, and that the shooting was unjustified. The defense claims that this was a justified homicide, with the women acting in self-defense. The prosecution is charging both women with first-degree murder (though the jury may consider lesser charges).

Don't consider whether Sarah and Allison should be acquitted or found guilty: For that, you would have to listen carefully to the whole trial. Rather, imagine that you are seating a jury. You are *not* an advocate for either the prosecution or the defense; instead, your goal is to seat the best possible jury you can assemble—the *fairest* and most *reasonable* and *just* jury you can get. Describe your *ideally just* jury for this case.

Exercise 1-3

There are two major views of the ideal jury (i.e., an ideally *fair* and *just* jury). The contemporary view is that we should strive to seat jurors who are intelligent but who know *nothing whatsoever* about the case that they will be hearing (thus ensuring that everything they know about the case will come from evidence presented at the trial). The earlier view was that jurors should be intelligent, well-informed members of the community in which the alleged crime occurred. A juror should not be the brother of the accused nor the sister of the victim; but if the juror knew the setting in which the crime occurred and perhaps knew some of the witnesses (and also knew how reliable—or unreliable—those witnesses might be), then that would make them better jurors (rather than automatically disqualifying them, as would almost certainly happen today). At the very least, good jurors were expected to know about community events, and be well informed about current happenings in the community (which of course would likely include knowing of crimes that had been committed and people who were suspected).

1. Some people claim that the traditional model worked well in earlier times, in settings of small towns and shared community knowledge, but that this model does not work well in our contemporary society. *Are* there any factors in *contemporary* society (e.g., societal diversity, or the *ways* people gain information, or the anonymity of urban life, or whatever) that make the older model *less* attractive for contemporary justice?
2. If your goal is to seat the ideal *fair* jury for a trial today, which model of the ideal jury would you follow? Or would you favor a *different* model altogether?
3. Imagine you were trying to seat the ideally *fair* jury for a highly publicized case: the O. J. Simpson murder trial. *Who* would you select as the members of your ideal jury? Is your answer closer to the *contemporary* model (jurors with no prior knowledge of the case) or the *traditional* model (jurors who are well informed about community events, who have received considerable information about the case, and have discussed it with their friends and colleagues)?

Exercise 1-4

1. Lawrence Kohlberg was a twentieth-century psychologist who conducted research on moral development, tracking the developmental stages of moral development in a large group of children in the Boston area, following them from their early years (some as young as 7) well into adulthood. In his studies Kohlberg often posed moral dilemmas to his subjects, and asked what they would do and why. One such dilemma was the story of Heinz: A man named Heinz has a wife who needs a drug to save her life, but Heinz cannot afford to buy the drug from the druggist, and the druggist will not give Heinz the drug. Should Heinz steal the drug for his wife? When confronted with this dilemma, some of the subjects thought about it, then gave an answer: Heinz should steal the drug, or he should not. But others wanted more information before deliberating about the case: Had Heinz attempted to negotiate with the druggist? What sort of person was the druggist? Wasn't the druggist concerned about saving the life of Heinz's wife? What was the relationship between Heinz and his wife? Does the demand for *more detail* correspond to an inclination

toward one or the other style of critical thinking? That is, would those taking a *cooperative* approach to this dilemma be more likely to ask for more details than would adversarial critical thinkers? Or vice versa? Or would the style of critical thinking make no difference to the amount of detail desired?

NOTES

[1] This example is taken from Barbara Holland's very entertaining brief history of trial by jury: "Do You Swear that You Will Well and Truly Try?" *Smithsonian*, March 1995, pp. 108–117.

[2] This information is from Seymour Wishman, *Anatomy of a Jury* (New York: Times Books, 1986), p. 65.

[3] McMahon's remarks were taken from a 1987 videotape for training prosecutors; as quoted in a story from the *Philadelphia Inquirer,* April 1, 1997.

[4] Morton Hunt, *New York Times Magazine,* November 28, 1982, p. 82.

[5] Paula DiPerna, *Juries on Trial* (New York: Dembner Books, 1984), p. 151.

[6] Quoted in Paula DiPerna, *Juries on Trial* (New York: Dembner Books, 1984), p. 154.

[7] Samuel R. Gross, "The Death Penalty in the United States," in *Adversarial versus Inquisitorial Justice,* edited by Peter J. van Koppen and Steven D. Penrod (New York: Kluwer Academic/Plenum Publishers, 2003).

[8] "Is the Adversary System Really Dead? Dilemmas of Legal Ethics as Legal Institutions and Roles Evolve," p. 103.

[9] Neil Vidmar and Valerie P. Hans, *American Juries* (Amherst, NY: Prometheus Books, 2007), p. 14.

[10] Brian Donohue describes this approach to justice in "The Third Solitude: Making a Place for Aboriginal Justice," *Canadian Journal of Native Studies,* Vol. 17, no. 2 (1997), pp. 315–328.

INTERNET RESOURCES

The website for the National Center for State Courts is *www.ncsc.org.* Click on Information and Resources, then Topic Categories, then Jury to find an abundance of interesting research reports on juries.

The Justice Information Center is at *www.ncjrs.gov.* The site is operated by the National Criminal Justice Reference Service. In addition to a vast number of good files, it has an extensive and well-organized directory of links to other relevant sites.

The website *www.bastionlaw.ca* is maintained by the Bastion Law Corporation of British Columbia. It is a user-friendly site for information concerning Canadian legal issues. Go to *www.bastionlaw.ca/index.asp* and click on Criminal Law and Procedure to find informative and readable material on criminal trials and the role of juries in Canada.

The Virginia Judicial System includes on its website an "Answer Book for Jury Service." While aimed at Virginia jurors, it provides good general information concerning jury service. It is clearly written, well organized, and quite thorough, and it includes a brief but clear glossary of legal terms. The Answer Book for Jury Service is at *www.courts.state.va.us/citizens.html.* Click on jury service.

The Jury Rights Project contains a number of files on the history and importance of juries; you can find it at *www.levellers.org/jrp.*

Douglas O. Linder, of the University of Missouri–Kansas City Law School maintains a fascinating site on famous trials in history; you can spend hours there. Go to *www.law.umkc.edu/faculty/projects/ftrials/ftrials.htm.*

www.oyez.org is a wonderful website on the U.S. Supreme Court, including both oral arguments and written verdicts, along with photos of the justices and the courtroom, and even some photos of the private chambers of some of the justices.

The Innocence Project—at *www.innocenceproject.org*—has a treasure trove of information on trials, especially on ways that trials can go wrong and lead to the conviction of innocent persons.

ADDITIONAL READING

A superb book on juries and the jury system is Valerie P. Hans and Neil Vidmar, *Judging the Jury* (New York: Plenum Press, 1986). It provides an excellent history of the jury system as well as a careful yet readable examination of many important issues related to the jury system (including jury selection techniques, jury competence, and jury nullification of the law). The book is particularly well documented, and the notes provide a useful guide to further material. A more recent book by the same authors, *American Juries* (Amherst, NY: Prometheus Books, 2007), discusses more recent questions concerning the jury system, as well as giving additional history of the jury system and its development.

Paula DiPerna's *Juries on Trial* (New York: Dembner Books, 1984) contains interesting information on jury selection as well as other related topics.

For a well-written and fascinating study of the jury system that covers both its history and present circumstances, see William L. Dwyer, *In the Hands of the People: The Trial Jury's Origins, Triumphs, Troubles, and Future in American Democracy* (New York: St. Martin's Press, 2002).

An excellent psychological study of the jury that gives empirical answers to a number of questions about the jury that were previously only the subject of speculation is a book by Saul M. Kassin and Lawrence S. Wrightsman, *The American Jury on Trial: Psychological Perspectives* (New York: Hemisphere Publishing, 1988).

A detailed study of the techniques of jury selection—which ranges from *voir dire* techniques to body language to interaction among potential jurors—is *Jury Selection*, by V. Hale Starr and Mark McCormick (New York: Little, Brown, 1985).

Stephen J. Adler's *The Jury: Disorder in the Court* (New York: Doubleday, 1994) gives good illustrations of some of the difficulties facing juries, and includes interesting comments on the use of social science techniques for selecting jury members.

A profound yet very readable examination of the jury is *We, the Jury: The Jury System and the Ideal of Democracy*, by Jeffrey Abramson (New York: Basic Books, 1994). If you wish to take a serious look at some of the basic issues concerning the jury system—including jury nullification, the requirement of jury unanimity, scientific jury selection, and the basic question of whether the jury system should be preserved or abandoned—this is the best contemporary book on the subject, and the many fascinating cases and lively style make the book fun to read.

For those who would like to study some important instances of critical thinking in famous cases, Peter Irons has written a wonderful and very readable book that explores 16 twentieth-century cases decided by the U.S. Supreme Court. The book not only examines the reasoning behind the decisions, but also presents the stories of the people whose court challenges led to the Supreme Court cases: courageous but little-known people like Lloyd Barenblatt, who was imprisoned for challenging the frightening power of the House Un-American Activities Committee during the height of the McCarthy era; and Daisy Bates, who braved mob violence, death threats, drive-by shootings, and bomb attacks in her struggle for civil rights in Arkansas. See *The Courage of Their Convictions: Sixteen Americans Who Fought Their Way to the Supreme Court* (New York: Penguin Books, 1988).

There are many good books on critical thinking (often called "informal logic"). Douglas N. Walton has written extensively on the subject; see his *Informal Logic: A Handbook for Argumentation* (New York: Cambridge University Press, 1989); and the second edition of *Informal Logic: A Pragmatic Approach* (New York: Cambridge University Press, 2008).

For some interesting articles on the adversarial system (with comparisons primarily to the inquisitorial system, rather than the cooperative system), see *Adversarial Versus Inquisitorial Justice: Psychological Perspectives on Criminal Justice Systems*, edited by Peter J. van Koppen and Steven D. Penrod (New York: Kluwer, 2003).

▶ Read the Document on mythinkinglab.com

Deborah Tannen, *The Argument Culture*. Deborah Tannen is a professor of linguistics at Georgetown University. Much of her work (including her book, *The Argument Culture*, from which this passage is drawn) focuses on how language can be used to increase hostility, as well as to promote cooperation and understanding. In this passage, she notes the strong tendency to frame our social issues in warlike or competitive language. If instead of framing the severe drug problem as a "war on drugs" we conceptualized it as a "search for workable solutions," would we be likely to approach the problem differently?

Deborah Tannen, *The Argument Culture*, p. 26. When we are in an adversarial framework, we tend to assume that there are two opposing sides to an argument; Deborah Tannen counsels that sometimes it is useful to challenge that assumption.

Deborah Tannen, *The Argument Culture*, p. 354. Deborah Tannen notes that when we are engaged in an adversarial argument, and eager to *win* an argument, it is very difficult to listen carefully to the views and arguments and concerns of our opponent.

"Changing a Man's Mind." This is a reminder of the importance of genuinely appreciating and understanding the views of those who oppose our arguments and beliefs.

Gerry Spence, "The Lock." Attorney Gerry Spence demonstrates the value of seeking common ground as a starting point for discussion and argument.

2

❖ ❖ ❖

A Few Important Terms

((•⃞ **Listen** to the **Chapter Audio** on **mythinkinglab.com**

ARGUMENTS

Before we plunge into examining arguments, evaluating commercials, debating social issues, and reaching verdicts, it will be helpful if we are all using the same terms, and we all agree on what those terms mean. We'll be concerned with *arguments*. An *argument* offers a *conclusion* and supports that conclusion with *reasons* (premises). Not every set of sentences is an argument. In fact, arguments constitute a comparatively small—but very important—part of our daily discourse. So the first task is distinguishing *arguments* from explanations, reports, contracts, ceremonies, questions, instructions, promises, pleas, curses, prayers, poems, exhortations, songs, and sweet talk. (Those are not always mutually exclusive categories. A prayer might contain an argument—to God—in the hope of convincing God to water the drought-stricken crops. A poem might be an argument in verse: Bob Dylan's song "Hurricane" argues that the boxer Reuben "Hurricane" Carter was unjustly convicted of murder. But usually prayers and poems and songs—and pleas and contracts and instructions—are not arguments.) An *argument* involves giving reasons that are supposed to support a certain conclusion. In an *argument* a set of *statements* is arranged in such a way that one is supposed to follow from the others.

STATEMENTS

So what is a statement? The term is used in many different ways: "His statement was false." "Senator, could we have a statement?" "Those orange shoes really make a statement." We will be using it in a more specific manner: A *statement*—sometimes called a *proposition*—is a claim that is true or false; that is, a *statement* has a *truth value*. A statement is expressed in a sentence, but not all sentences are statements. ("Please close the door" and "Did you enjoy the play?" are both perfectly decent and honorable sentences, but they are not *statements,* since they make no claims and are neither true nor false.) While a statement is expressed in a sentence, it should not be regarded as equivalent to a particular sentence. For example, this sentence—"The defendant struck Ralph"—expresses a statement, but the same *statement* could be expressed with many different sentences: "Ralph was struck by the defendant," "The defendant hit Ralph," "The man seated at the table struck the man in the witness box," and so forth. In addition, the same statement might be made in sentences in many different languages. Furthermore, while the same statement can be expressed with many different sentences, a single sentence can—in different contexts—express different statements: "I saw her" expresses an enormous variety of different statements, including Wendell saw Rachel, Wendy saw Vanessa, and Arthur saw the *Titanic*.

We shall be concerned primarily with statements: claims that are true or false. Premises and conclusions—the basic elements of arguments—are statements.

Exercise 2-1

For the following, tell which are statements and which are *not* statements.

1. Please close the door.
2. If you don't close the door, the dog will get out.
3. Read Chapter 3 before the next class.
4. Why is the sky blue?
5. Mushrooms are the summer homes of elves.
6. Go to hell!
7. I *did* see an extraterrestrial.
8. Don't rush! Think through each question before answering.
9. Let's go Mets! Let's go Mets!
10. The Mets will definitely win the World Series next year.
11. Who was the Republican vice presidential candidate in 1964?
12. Eat your vegetables.
13. The 2010 Winter Olympics were held in Vancouver.
14. The 2010 Winter Olympics were held in Miami.
15. What is your favorite ice cream flavor?
16. Earth is the only place in the entire universe where life exists.
17. Why are there no penguins in Lake Erie?
18. There was a conspiracy to kill President Kennedy.
19. Joe believes there was a conspiracy to kill President Kennedy.
20. I believe there was a conspiracy to kill President Kennedy.
21. Sal loves Sharon.
22. I love you.
23. Either there will be a reduction in air pollution or we will suffer severe global warming.
24. I hope we can reduce air pollution significantly during the next decade.
25. Add more chocolate chips to the cookie dough.
26. The cookies will taste better if you add more chocolate chips.
27. These cookies taste awful.
28. Did you make these cookies?
29. Our Sun is one of the smallest stars in this galaxy.
30. Drive carefully, and watch out for ice patches and potholes.
31. The Loch Ness Monster really exists, and is a descendant of the brachiosaurus.
32. Are there any clear photographs of the Loch Ness Monster?
33. Bill Clinton is the only U.S. president who has played the saxophone while in office.
34. Don't play poker with penguins.

35. All penguins cheat at poker.
36. Every human being has lived many past lives, though very few human beings are consciously aware of their past lives.
37. Jupiter has the most moons of any planet in our solar system.
38. What is the tallest building in Pennsylvania?
39. This is a very tough exercise.
40. Do *not* look at anyone else's paper.
41. How many stars are in our galaxy?
42. Critical thinking students study an average of 6 hours each day.
43. The Steelers will win the Super Bowl in 2025.
44. Global warming will cause catastrophic problems in the United States, and especially along the East Coast.
45. Jupiter is not the largest planet in our solar system.
46. There is a damaged alien spacecraft in a top secret military aircraft storage building near Las Cruces, New Mexico.

Premises and Conclusions

Arguments are made up of *premises* and *conclusions*. The conclusion is what the argument is trying to prove. Premises are the reasons given for the conclusion, the statements made in support of the conclusion. (The American spelling is "premise"; the British spelling is "premiss.") It is not always easy to distinguish premises from conclusion. Sometimes the conclusion is at the beginning of the argument, sometimes at the end, and occasionally it is stuck in the middle. There are a few words or phrases that usually indicate premises and others that usually signal conclusions. Premises are often preceded by words such as *since, due to the fact that, because.* And conclusions are frequently signaled by such words as *therefore, hence, it follows that, so, consequently.* Attention to such words and phrases may be helpful, but they are not always used and are certainly not a perfect guide to premises and conclusions.

The following arguments all have the same conclusion. Notice that the conclusion occurs at different points in the various arguments and that sometimes there are words to indicate the premises and conclusion and sometimes there are not.

> There were three eyewitnesses, and they all were certain that the woman they saw running from the bank was the defendant. So the defendant must be guilty.
> Of course the defendant is guilty. You could tell by her weak chin and beady eyes.
> No other woman was near the bank at the time, thus the defendant must be guilty of the crime. Besides, her alibi was very weak.
> Since her fingerprints were found in the bank and the money was found near her car, the defendant must be guilty.

The arguments above are relatively simple: a premise or two, and a conclusion. Arguments are often much more complex. A newspaper editorialist may offer several different arguments for the same conclusion, or an essay may contain several arguments for several distinct conclusions. Or you may be presented with a lengthy argument that contains several subarguments; that is, in some cases there may be an argument within an argument: "We should bet on (the racehorse) General Assembly. After all, General Assembly runs very well on muddy tracks. And since it rained all morning, the track must be muddy." The overall conclusion is that we should bet on General Assembly. The premises that support that conclusion are: The track is muddy and General Assembly runs very well on muddy tracks. But there is also a *sub*argument to support the premise that the track is muddy. That subargument has as its premise: It rained all morning. The conclusion of the subargument is: The track is muddy. Thus the *conclusion* of the *sub*argument is a *premise* of the larger argument. "The track must be muddy" is prefaced by "so," which indicates it is a conclusion; only by thinking carefully about the overall argument can you tell that it is also a premise.

Exercise 2-2

Determine which of the following are *arguments* and which are not. (Don't worry about whether the arguments are good or bad; just distinguish the arguments from the nonarguments.) Then for each of the *arguments*, state the conclusion.

1. If the moon is made of green cheese, then there are mice on the moon. The moon is made of green cheese. Therefore, there are mice on the moon.

2. I solemnly swear to tell the truth, the whole truth, and nothing but the truth.

3. Raspberry Surprise ice cream has big chunks of real fruit! What a combination! Rich ice cream with delicious fruit; it's my all-time favorite ice cream.

4. Wheaties®[1] is a nutritious cereal. After all, Mary Lou Retton appeared in Wheaties advertisements, and Mary Lou Retton is certainly healthy; so Wheaties must be nutritious.

5. Requirements for this course include three exams and two papers. You must pass at least two of the three exams in order to pass the course, and you must make a B or better on both papers in order to make a B or better in the course.

6. Last summer Joe promised Sarah he would be faithful to her, and he cheated on her. Last spring he made the same promise to Veronica, and he cheated. This past winter he promised to be faithful to Joan, but he ran around on her. And last fall he pledged to be faithful and true to Ann, and he broke that pledge. So now Joe is telling you that he's going to be faithful to you; but listen, that man's going to cheat on you.

7. The team with the best pitching always wins the World Series. So the New York Mets will win the World Series, since the Mets have the best pitching.

8. The Yankees won the World Series when they had the best pitching staff in baseball; the Dodgers won the World Series when they had superior pitching; and when the Cardinals won the World Series they had the best pitching. So the team with the best pitching staff wins the World Series.

9. When you are cooking fettucine alfredo, be careful not to overcook the pasta. If the pasta is overcooked, it will stick together, and the sauce will not spread evenly over the pasta. Also, I recommend that you serve a green salad with the fettucine, and be sure to have plenty of red wine.

10. All professors own private jets. My critical thinking teacher is a professor; therefore, she must own a private jet.

11. Three reliable witnesses saw the defendant in New York just one hour before the murder took place in Los Angeles. There's no way the defendant could be guilty of the murder. Besides, the defendant had no reason to kill the guy—they were good friends.

12. You guys charged too much for fixing my car. It only needed new spark plugs, which are fairly inexpensive and are easy to install. So I don't think I should have to pay this outrageous repair bill.

13. I am not paying that repair bill! I may have to hire a lawyer, I may have to call the state attorney general's office, maybe my credit rating will be ruined, perhaps they'll sue me. I don't care what happens; I'm still not paying.

14. I like the way the Modern Jazz Quartet plays. They have a cool, tight, almost dispassionate style. It projects a sense of tremendous energy being held tautly in check. And the drums, bass, vibes, and piano work together so perfectly that sometimes it is impossible to tell where one stops and the other starts.

15. To be successful in your critical thinking course, it is important to do as many exercises as possible. It would also help a lot to read the chapters in the text, perhaps even a couple of times. And attending class regularly wouldn't hurt.

16. Last year there was an increase in gasoline prices in July, and there was also an increase in July the year before that, and the year before that: in fact, every year of the last decade there has been a significant jump in gasoline prices during the month of July. So you can expect to pay more for gasoline this year in July.

17. When hitting a baseball, you should start with your back elbow up; then swing down. Keep your back foot stationary, and don't lunge at the ball, and be sure to follow through with your swing. And above all: Keep your eye on the ball.

18. If the recession continues, then there will be fewer jobs next year. And the recession is continuing, so clearly next year there will be fewer jobs.

19. All Cleveland Browns fans hate the Steelers. So Brenda must hate the Steelers, because Brenda is certainly a Cleveland Browns fan.

20. This year North State University had a tuition increase, and there was also a tuition increase last year, and the year before that, *and* the year before that. So very likely North State University students will be hit with another increase in tuition next year.

21. Look, this is really simple. Either we are sure beyond a reasonable doubt that the defendant is guilty, or we have to vote not guilty. Now obviously we can't be sure beyond a reasonable doubt that he is guilty, since the only witness admitted that he was drunk and isn't sure what he saw. So we have to vote not guilty.

22. If federal disaster relief had been well organized, then effective aid would have reached New Orleans immediately after Katrina passed. But in fact effective aid did not reach New Orleans until long after Katrina passed. So obviously federal disaster relief was not well organized.

23. I love Cajun music. It has a simple beat, but it's always great for dancing—especially at a Cajun street dance, when you mix plenty of wine with the music. If you have a great Cajun fiddler, who keeps a steady rhythm with the fiddle, and you throw in a good accordion player and maybe a guitar, you can dance till dawn. You haven't partied until you've danced all night to a Cajun band down deep in the Louisiana swamps.

24. Sharon must be tall. After all, Sharon is a basketball player, and all basketball players are tall.

25. If you believe in democracy, then you should vote. And of course you do believe in democracy, so therefore you should vote.

26. Please don't miss class on Friday. We'll be studying ad hominem arguments, and that's one of my favorite topics, and I would be really disappointed if no one was here to discuss ad hominem arguments with me.

27. If a wealthy country like the United States does not provide decent health care for *all* its citizens, then there should be major reform in its health-care system. So clearly there should be major reforms of our health-care system, because the United States does not provide decent health care for all its citizens.

Premises and conclusions are statements. They make claims, and they are either true or false. But while the premises and conclusions of arguments are true or false, *arguments* are not true or false. Instead, arguments are *valid* or *invalid, sound* or *unsound, strong* or *weak, cogent* or *uncogent.*

Evaluation of an argument comprises two distinct and essential considerations. First, do the premises support the conclusion? Second, are the premises true? Start with the second consideration: Are the premises *true?* The most obvious way that an argument can go wrong is by having *false* premises. "You should immediately send $10 to Reverend Megabucks, because God commands it, and if you break God's commandment God will cause blight on your crops, flat tires on your cars, fumbles by your running backs, and holes in your socks." Well, if true, that might provide some reason for coughing up a sawbuck to the Rev; but before we wonder about whether the conclusion really follows from the premises, we should first question whether the premises are actually true. Since they are not, the argument is no good—it is *unsound*—whether the premises adequately *support* the conclusion or not.

Now we come to the trickier part of evaluating arguments: Even if the premises are true, *do* they provide the right sort of *support* for the conclusion? Does the conclusion really "follow from" the premises? That is a *separate* and distinct question from the question of whether the premises are true. After all, an argument with all true premises may fail to support its conclusion; for example:

> The defendant is named George; *George* starts with *g,* and *guilty* starts with *g;* therefore, the defendant is guilty.

And an argument with false premises may strongly support its conclusion:

> If there are dinosaurs on the moon, then Earth is the largest planet; there are dinosaurs on the moon; therefore, Earth is the largest planet.

So in addition to asking whether the premises are actually true, we must *also* ask, Do the premises provide the right sort of support for the conclusion?

We'll look further into the questions of how premises support conclusions, and whether in a particular argument the premises provide the right sort of support for the conclusion. But first it is important to note that there are *two different ways* that premises can support conclusions, and those two ways mark out *two different types* of arguments. The two different types of arguments are *deductive* and *inductive*.

DEDUCTIVE AND INDUCTIVE ARGUMENTS

What are the differences between a deductive and an inductive argument? There are several, but they all stem from this key difference: *Inductive* arguments go *beyond* the information contained in the premises; inductive arguments make a *projection* based on given information. *Deductive* arguments draw out the implications of the premises; they draw conclusions that are already contained in the premises. So what you must look for in deciding whether an argument is deductive or inductive is the relation of the premises to the conclusion. If the premises are used as a base from which the conclusion makes a *projection*, then the argument is inductive; if the conclusion is purportedly drawing out implications contained in the premises (rather than going beyond the premises), then the argument is deductive. (Obviously, a deductive argument may contain a premise or premises that were established *inductively*. In determining whether an argument is deductive or inductive, the question is not how the *premises* are supported; rather, the question is how the premises are related to the conclusion.)

Suppose that the conclusion of an argument is, The Giants will win their next home game. Would the argument for that conclusion be inductive or deductive? You can't tell. It might be either. For example, you might argue like this:

> The Giants have won all their home games for the last 2 years; so they will win their next home game.

That would be an inductive argument, which projects the result of the next game on the basis of information about preceding games. But suppose that instead the argument goes this way:

> If the quarterback for the Giants is healthy and able to play, then the Giants will win their next home game. The Giants quarterback is healthy and ready to play. Therefore, the Giants will win their next home game.

That is a *deductive* argument for the same conclusion. Consider another example.

> All college students like indie music. The students at the University of Texas are college students. Therefore, all students at the University of Texas like indie music.

That is a *deductive* argument. The conclusion simply draws out the implications of the premises. It is in fact a deductively valid argument, and if the premises are true, then the conclusion *must* be true. (How do we know that the first premise—"All college students like indie music"—is true? Perhaps it was established inductively; perhaps we determined that through asking absolutely every college student; perhaps it was given in a special revelation from God. Certainly when we are evaluating the *soundness* of the argument, it will be important to know *what* the grounds are for believing the premises and whether the premises are in fact true. But when we are trying to determine whether an argument is inductive or deductive, we are *not* concerned with how the premises are known or whether they are actually true; rather, we are concerned only with the relation between the premises and the conclusion.) Contrast that deductive argument with this inductive argument:

> We have interviewed thousands of students at the University of Michigan, Yale University, the University of Arizona, Florida State, and Bates College. All the students we interviewed like indie music. Therefore, all the students at the University of Texas like indie music.

That has the same conclusion as the deductive argument in the above example, but it is an *inductive* argument that *projects* a conclusion about students who were not interviewed (students at the University of Texas) on the basis of people who are somewhat similar to the students at the University of Texas (other U.S. college students). The moral of the story is this: In determining whether an argument is deductive or inductive, you must first determine what the conclusion is, but don't stop there. Examine the *relation* between premises and conclusion; only then can you decide whether the argument is inductive or deductive.

Exercise 2-3

For each of the following cases, first tell whether it is or is *not* an *argument*; second, for each *argument* determine whether it is *deductive* or *inductive*; third, for each of the *arguments* state the conclusion. In at least one case it may be possible to interpret an argument as either deductive or inductive.

1. All licensed physicians in the United States are medical school graduates. Ralph is not a medical school graduate, so Ralph is not a licensed physician in the United States.

2. If you want to live a long and healthy life, then you should eat lots of fruits and vegetables, and stay away from junk food and fast food. Also, be sure to get some exercise, and try to get a decent amount of sleep. And, of course, don't smoke.

3. Susan is a licensed physician, and she is a medical school graduate. Sarah is a licensed physician, and she is a medical school graduate. Sam is a licensed physician, and he is a medical school graduate. Bradley is a licensed physician, and he is a medical school graduate. And Teresa is a licensed physician, and she is a medical school graduate. Ralph is also a licensed physician, so he is probably also a medical school graduate.

4. We have interviewed 1,200 college students, and 900 of them favored 18 as the legal age for the purchase of beer.

5. We have interviewed 1,200 U.S. college students, and 900 of them favored 18 as the legal age for the purchase of beer. Therefore, a substantial majority of all U.S. college students favor 18 as the legal age for the purchase of beer.

6. We should set 18 as the legal age for the purchase of alcoholic beverages. If people are old enough to vote, then they are certainly old enough to drink, and 18-year-olds are indeed old enough to vote.

7. The Yankees won the World Series when they had the best pitching staff in baseball; the Dodgers won the World Series when they had superior pitching; and when the Cardinals won the World Series they had the best pitching. So the team with the best pitching staff wins the World Series.

8. The team with the best pitching always wins the World Series. The St. Louis Cardinals must have the best pitching, because the Cardinals won the World Series.

9. I think Jones—the key witness for the prosecution—probably robbed the bank himself, and is now trying to pin the crime on Smith. In any case, there is certainly a reasonable doubt that Smith (the defendant) robbed the bank, so we should all vote not guilty.

10. Look, I don't know about anything else, but I know for an absolute fact that Jones could never have killed anyone. So when Smith testified that Jones was the murderer, Smith must have been lying.

11. We have carefully surveyed 500 registered voters, chosen at random from throughout Ohio, on whether they favor a law making it legal for ordinary citizens to carry concealed weapons. Of those surveyed, 320 opposed legalizing concealed weapons, 140 supported legalizing concealed weapons, and 40 were undecided or had no opinion. So obviously most of the registered voters in Ohio are opposed to legalizing concealed weapons.

12. We had a great camping trip. The weather was warm during the day and nice and cool during the evening, just right for a cozy campfire. The nights were so clear, you could almost reach out and touch the stars. And late at night, warm in our sleeping bags, you could hear loons calling on the lake, and owls calling from deep in the woods. It was perfect.

13. Mighty Casey will almost certainly strike out. For the bases are loaded, and Mighty Casey struck out the last time he batted with the bases loaded, and he struck out the time before when he batted with the bases loaded; and, in fact, the two times before that he struck out when the bases were loaded.

14. Either the Chicago Cubs or the New York Mets will win the World Series. The New York Mets obviously will not win the Series, since they have had lots of injuries, and their pitching and fielding have both been weak. So the Chicago Cubs will win the World Series.

15. When examining arguments, the most important thing to do is this: First, pick out the conclusion. After you have the conclusion clearly stated, then you should examine the structure of the argument, and pick out any assumptions made by the argument. Next, you should look for any fallacies committed, and the last step is to determine whether the premises are true.

16. In the last five World Series, the team that was at home for the first game won the Series. Therefore, the Toronto Blue Jays are a good bet to win this World Series, since they are the home team for the first game.

17. All U.S. citizens have a right to vote in presidential elections. Joan Jakobovitz is a U.S. citizen; so Joan Jakobovitz has a right to vote in the presidential election.

18. There are currently three major danger areas for the outbreak of war: the Middle East, Eastern Europe, and the border between India and Pakistan. Perhaps the most dangerous of those areas is Eastern Europe, though there are certainly serious dangers elsewhere around the world.

19. Last quarter there were 18 students in the critical thinking course who never missed a class, and they all passed the course. The quarter before that, 16 students attended every class, and all of them passed also. So if you attend every class this quarter, you will pass the course.

20. Ladies and gentlemen of the jury, this is a simple case. Clearly Selena Skowron is not guilty of robbing the Detroit National Bank. The Detroit National Bank was robbed at noon on March 3, 1996. If Selena Skowron was in Cleveland at noon on that day, then she could not be guilty of robbing the Detroit National Bank. And she certainly was in Cleveland at noon of that day, as was proven by the testimony of four reliable witnesses.

21. All students who are registered at the university have a right to use the university library. So Alice Andrews has a right to use the library, because she is a registered student at the university.

22. Bruce has been late for class every day since the semester started. So he will probably be late for class again tomorrow.

23. If Joan is a student at Ohio State, then she hates Michigan. Joan is a student at Ohio State. Therefore Joan hates Michigan.

24. Last year all of the critical thinking exams were really hard. And that year before that, all the critical thinking exams were brutally tough. In fact, for the last ten years every critical thinking exam has been very hard. So very likely the next critical thinking exam will be a hard one.

DEDUCTION, VALIDITY, AND SOUNDNESS

Deductive arguments are supposed to draw conclusions that are already contained in or directly implied by the premises. If a deductive argument is correctly structured, then the truth of the premises will *guarantee* the truth of the conclusion. If that is the case, then the deductive argument is *valid*. So the *definition* of a *valid* deductive argument is:

> *If* all its premises are true, then its conclusion *must* be true.

Notice the italicized words: *if* and *must*. They are essential. First the *if*: We are not saying that a valid argument *does* have all true premises; it may or may not. Rather, *if* all the premises are true, *then* the conclusion must be true. *Must* be true. It is not enough for the conclusion to just happen to be true. Its truth *must* follow from the truth of the premises;

the truth of the premises must make it *impossible* for the conclusion to be false; the truth of the premises is *inconsistent* with the falsity of the conclusion.

Obviously the actual truth or falsity of the premises is an important matter, and we shall certainly return to it. But first we want to know whether the premises, *if* they are true, will prove the conclusion true. Consider this example:

> If the moon is made of green cheese, then there are mice on the moon.
> The moon is made of green cheese.
> Therefore, there are mice on the moon.

That's not much of an argument: It has a false premise, a false conclusion, and besides, it's rather silly. But it is a deductively *valid* argument, because *if* the premises were true, then the conclusion would also have to be true. That's what it means for an argument to be deductively *valid:* If the premises are all true, then the conclusion must be true. Or put another way, it is impossible for all the premises to be true and the conclusion false. And if it is possible for the premises to be true and the conclusion false, then the argument is deductively *invalid.*

In a valid deductive argument, the truth of the premises guarantees the truth of the conclusion. But notice that that is the *only* guarantee that validity gives you; in particular, if a valid argument has *false* premises, then the validity of the argument does not guarantee that the conclusion will be false. Of course it *may* be false, but it *may* also be true. For example, consider this argument:

> All turtles are good jumpers.
> Michael Jordan is a turtle.
> Therefore, Michael Jordan is a good jumper.

That is a *valid* argument; the truth of the premises would guarantee the truth of the conclusion. *All* the premises are false: Not *all* turtles are good jumpers (Ninja turtles may be, but they are the exception), and Michael Jordan is *not* a turtle. But the conclusion is still quite true: Michael Jordan is indeed a good jumper.

The validity of deductive arguments depends entirely on their *form.* Consider the two arguments we just examined. The first (about the moon mice) has this logical form:

> If G, then M.
> G.
> Therefore, M.

The second (about jumpers) has this form:

> All T are J.
> M is a T.
> Therefore, M is a J.

Both argument forms are *valid*; it doesn't matter what you substitute for G and M or for T and J and M, they will *still* be valid.

> If gold grows on trees, then farmers are rich.
> Gold does grow on trees.
> Therefore, farmers are rich.

> If the defendant is charged with a criminal offense, then the defendant has a right to legal counsel.
> The defendant is charged with a criminal offense.
> Therefore, the defendant has a right to legal counsel.

All kings are jealous.
William is a king.
Therefore, William is jealous.

All whales are mammals.
Shamu is a whale.
Therefore, Shamu is a mammal.

All of those are valid arguments. In each argument, *if* all of its premises are true, then its conclusion *must* be true.

But obviously not all of those arguments are good arguments; for though they are valid, some have false premises. So there are two conditions that a good deductive argument must meet: It must be valid, *and* all of its premises must actually be true. When a deductive argument meets *both* those conditions, we say that it is a *sound* argument. If an argument fails on either count—if it is invalid or has one or more false premises, or both—then it is *unsound*.

INDUCTION, STRONG ARGUMENTS, AND COGENT ARGUMENTS

You have used inductive arguments all your life. When you awaken on a frosty January morning to see snowdrifts outside your window, you pull on a wool sweater and a heavy coat. This is a snowy January day, and so it will be cold outside. Such is your conclusion, if you think about it at all. But why didn't you put on your sandals and your short-sleeved shirt with the pink flamingos? That is, why were you so sure—by looking out the window of your warm bedroom and seeing snow—that the snowy day really was cold?

That's a silly question. But it's a silly question only because we take inductive arguments for granted. You've gone out in the cold snow many times before, so you concluded—quite reasonably—that this snowy day would also be cold. That is good inductive reasoning. (It's not very *profound* or difficult inductive reasoning, but it is accurate.)

A friend tells you about a new film. She likes it very much, and strongly recommends that you see it. Since in the past the two of you have agreed on movie evaluations, you conclude that you will probably enjoy this film.

You are meeting a friend for lunch. Over the years you have had a standing luncheon engagement with him for every Friday at noon, and every time your friend arrives about 12:15. So you wait and go to the restaurant about 12:15, confident that your friend's tardiness will continue. Again, that is good inductive reasoning. Of course your friend may surprise you and arrive at 12:00 sharp. That's the way it is with inductive arguments. Even though the argument is a good one, the conclusion is never more than *very probable*.

Another example was first proposed by the British logician Bertrand Russell. A turkey is living quite contentedly on a farm. Every morning the farmer comes out to the barn and brings corn, to the turkey's delight. The turkey reasons inductively that since for many past mornings the farmer has brought corn, this morning the farmer will again bring corn. But on one final occasion—perhaps Christmas morning—the turkey follows that good inductive argument to a fatally false conclusion. The late turkey used a fairly good inductive argument with true premises: Every past morning the farmer has brought corn; therefore, the farmer will bring corn this morning. How might the turkey have *improved* that inductive argument?

The unfortunate turkey was probably not in a position to gather much additional information. But what sort of information would have been useful to him, would have allowed him to develop a better inductive argument? For one thing, the turkey does not have a very broad range of information to work from: He knows only about his own relation to the farmer. The turkey might have checked around: What happens to other animals that have been in similar relations with the farmer? The pigs, for example, might have told the turkey some hair-raising (or feather-raising) stories about pigs in similar circumstances. Such further information might have allowed the turkey to draw a more accurate conclusion. On the other hand, had the turkey talked to Fluff the cat or Spot the dog, the information gained might well have led the turkey to be even more confident of the farmer's continued goodwill. Obviously this induction business is important for all of us, turkeys and otherwise—but it can be rather tricky. So it is not enough to merely gather information; we must decide what similarities are and are not relevant.

In analyzing deductive arguments, we applied two standards. Deductive arguments are *valid* or *invalid,* and they are *sound* or *unsound.* A deductive argument is *valid* if the truth of its premises *guarantees* the truth of its conclusion; that is, if all its premises are true, then its conclusion *must* be true. If a deductive argument is valid, *and* all its premises are *actually true,* then the argument is *sound. Validity* is concerned with the relation between premises and conclusion, leaving aside the question of whether the premises are actually true; *soundness* brings in the question of the actual truth of the premises. It's useful to have corresponding standards for evaluating *inductive* arguments. But obviously we can't just use the terms we applied to *deductive* arguments, because they won't fit. In a *valid* deductive argument, if the premises are true the conclusion *must* be true. But because inductive arguments make claims that go beyond their premises, they cannot be valid and sound, the way deductive arguments are. Excellent inductive arguments that contain all true premises still leave the possibility—however slight—that their conclusions are false. So instead of *validity* and *soundness,* we'll need new terms for inductive arguments.

We'll characterize inductive arguments as *strong* or *weak,* rather than valid or invalid. When we say that an inductive argument is *strong,* we are saying nothing at all about the truth of its premises. Rather, we are saying that *if* its premises are true (*not* that they *are* true) then the premises provide strong support for the truth of the conclusion. Consider an example. Ohio State University has reduced tuition every year for the past 30 years. So there will probably be a tuition reduction at Ohio State University again next year. That's a reasonable conclusion, given the premises. That's a *strong* inductive argument. *If* the premises are true, then they provide *strong* support for the conclusion. And we can analyze the *strength* of that inductive argument without knowing anything at all about whether the premises are *actually* true (just as we can analyze the *validity* of a *deductive* argument without knowing whether its premises are *actually* true). Suppose, on the other hand, we argued that *last* year Ohio State University reduced its tuition, so probably it will do so again next year. That's a *weak* inductive argument. Basing the conclusion on only 1 year makes this a *weak* argument, and it remains a *weak* inductive argument whether the premise is true or false. Consider an inductive argument based on a survey. "We surveyed 3 U.S. citizens (selected randomly) and 2 of the 3 favor universal health care. So most U.S. citizens favor universal health care." That's a weak inductive argument. Suppose our sample were 30, and 20 favored universal health care, and we conclude that most U.S. citizens favor universal health care. That argument is stronger than the first, but still not very strong. If the sample were 1,200, and 800 favored universal health care, the argument would be fairly strong. A sample of 30,000 with 20,000 in favor would be very strong.

You recall that *valid* deductive arguments can be dead wrong (*unsound*) because their *premises* are *false.* For example, if the moon is made of green cheese, then there are mice on the moon. The moon is made of green cheese. Therefore, there are mice on the moon. That's a *valid* argument; but it's still a *lousy* argument, because its premises are *false.* The argument is *valid,* but *unsound.* Something similar applies to the argument about tuition at Ohio State: Ohio State University has reduced tuition every year for the past 30 years. So there will probably be a tuition reduction at Ohio State University again next year. That's a *strong* inductive argument; but students at Ohio State should not look forward to a tuition reduction next year, because the *premises* of that inductive argument are *false.* Ohio State certainly has not reduced tuition every year for the past 30 years; to the contrary, like most universities, it has steadily increased its tuition. Just as the deductive argument about the mice on the moon is *valid* but *unsound,* this tuition argument is *strong* but *not cogent.* For a deductive argument to be *sound,* it must meet two conditions: it must be *valid,* and all its premises must actually be true. Along similar lines, for an *inductive* argument to be *cogent*, it must be *strong*, and all its premises must actually be true. If a deductive argument is either invalid or has a false premise (or both), then we say it is *unsound*. If an inductive argument is either *weak* or has a false premise (or both), then we say it is *uncogent*.

One last point. When we are dealing with deductive arguments, they are either valid or invalid, sound or unsound. There's no in-between. It's sort of like baseball: you either win or you lose, there are no draws and no middle ground (okay, there could be a game called off on account of rain, but you get the idea). But inductive arguments are very different. There are surely some *strong* inductive arguments (there has been at least one tornado in Oklahoma every year for the past 100 years, so Oklahoma will probably have at least one tornado this year), and there are also some *weak* inductive arguments (I hit the lottery number yesterday, so I'll probably win again today). But in-between, there's a large area of gray. For example, the United States has had a flu outbreak every year for the last 5 years, so we'll probably have one this year. Is that a strong inductive argument? Well, it's not all that strong. Certainly it would be stronger if the premise stated that the United States has had a flu outbreak every year for the past 100 years; it would be weaker if it cited only the past 2 years. Exactly when does it pass from weak to strong? There's no bright line. That doesn't mean that we can never distinguish between strong and weak inductive arguments, but it does make things a bit tricky. Sorry about that.

Exercise 2-4

Some of the following arguments are deductive, and some are inductive. For each of the arguments, choose which *one* of the following alternatives applies. (a) valid, but unsound; (b) invalid; (c) sound; (d) strong, but uncogent; (e) weak; (f) cogent.

1. All stars produce energy. The Sun is a star. Therefore, the Sun produces energy.
2. The University of Michigan has reduced tuition every year for the past 20 years. So probably there will be a reduction of tuition at the University of Michigan next year.
3. Rover is a dog. No dogs can play bridge. So Rover cannot play bridge.
4. All dogs are animals. All cats are animals. Therefore, all dogs are cats.
5. If Miami is in Wyoming, then Miami is the largest city in Wyoming. Miami is in Wyoming. Therefore, Miami is the largest city in Wyoming.
6. If the Steelers score 20 touchdowns in their next game, then the Steelers will win. But the Steelers will not score 20 touchdowns in their next game. So the Steelers will not win.
7. Last year there was snow in Cleveland during February, and Cleveland also had snow in February the previous year. So Cleveland will probably get snow this year during February.
8. All undergraduates at Ohio State, Oregon State, North Carolina State, Florida State, Penn State, Arizona State, and Oklahoma State are celibate; so probably all of the undergraduates at Michigan State are also celibate.
9. Either Jupiter is the largest planet in our solar system, or all professional astronomers are totally mistaken. But it is certainly not the case that all professional astronomers are totally mistaken. So Jupiter is the largest planet in our solar system.
10. All dogs can fly. All animals that can fly have teeth. Therefore all dogs have teeth.
11. All basketballs are round, and all billiard balls are round. Therefore, all billiard balls are basketballs.
12. The United States has had a trade deficit every year for the last two decades, so the United States will probably continue to have a trade deficit for at least the next few years.
13. Either penguins can fly, or the Empire State Building is in New York City. Penguins cannot fly. Therefore, the Empire State Building is in New York City.
14. There has been a major snow storm in Los Angeles on July 4 every year for the past 50 years; so probably Los Angeles will have a major snow storm on July 4 next year.
15. All penguins are great mathematicians. George Bush is a penguin. Therefore, George Bush is a great mathematician.

16. There was a tornado in Oklahoma last year, so there will probably be a tornado in Oklahoma this year.

17. In St. Paul-Minneapolis there has been at least one day of subfreezing temperature every winter for the past 50 years; so St. Paul-Minneapolis will probably have at least one day of subfreezing temperature next winter.

18. The last 27 summer Olympic games have been held in Las Vegas, so very likely the next summer Olympics will also be held in Las Vegas.

Exercise 2-5

The following multiple-choice questions are about valid, invalid, sound, unsound, strong, weak, cogent, and uncogent arguments. In each case, select the one best answer.

1. In a *valid deductive* argument, if all the premises *are true* then the conclusion:
   a. is probably true.
   b. must be true.
   c. may or may not be true.

2. In a *strong inductive* argument, if all the premises *are true* then:
   a. the conclusion is probably true.
   b. the conclusion must be true.

3. If a deductive argument has a false premise, then:
   a. the conclusion cannot be true.
   b. the argument cannot be valid.
   c. the argument cannot be sound.

4. If a deductive argument is valid, then:
   a. all of its premises must be true.
   b. at least some of its premises must be true.
   c. any or all of its premises may be either true or false.

5. If a deductive argument is invalid, then:
   a. it must have at least one false premise.
   b. it must have a false conclusion.
   c. it may or may not have false premises and/or a false conclusion.

6. If a deductive argument has a *false* conclusion, then:
   a. the argument is valid.
   b. the argument is invalid.
   c. you can't tell from the information given whether or not the argument is valid.

7. If a deductive argument has a *true* conclusion, then:
   a. the argument is valid.
   b. the argument is invalid.
   c. you can't tell from the information given whether or not the argument is valid.

8. If a deductive argument is valid and has a false conclusion, then:
   a. all its premises must be false.
   b. at least one of its premises must be false.
   c. it may or may not have a false premise.

9. If an argument has a false conclusion but all its premises are true, then the argument *cannot* be:
   a. a valid deductive argument.
   b. a cogent inductive argument.
   c. either valid or cogent.

10. In a sound deductive argument:
    a. the conclusion is always true.

    b. the conclusion is probably true.

    c. it's impossible to tell from the information given whether the conclusion is always or probably true.

11. If all the premises of a deductive argument are false, then that argument is:

    a. valid.

    b. invalid.

    c. impossible to tell from the information given.

12. If an inductive argument contains a false premise, then it *cannot* be:

    a. strong

    b. cogent

13. If an inductive argument has a true conclusion, then the argument must be:

    a. strong

    b. cogent

    c. none of the above

14. If a strong inductive argument is uncogent, then:

    a. it must have at least one false premise.

    b. it must have a false conclusion.

    c. none of the above.

✓●┤**Study** and **Review** on **mythinkinglab.com**

REVIEW QUESTIONS

1. What is a statement? How does a statement differ from a sentence?
2. What is an argument? What is a premise?
3. What is the difference between deductive and inductive arguments?
4. What is a *valid* argument?
5. What is a *sound* argument?
6. What is a *strong* argument?
7. What is a *cogent* argument?

NOTE

[1] Wheaties is a registered trademark of General Mills, Inc., Minneapolis, Minnesota.

INTERNET RESOURCES

The Internet Encyclopedia of Philosophy has a nice brief article on inductive and deductive reasoning; go to *http://www.iep.utm.edu/ded-ind/*

    San Jose State University's Critical Thinking web page is engaging, and the material presented is clear and well organized; you can find it at *www.sjsu.edu/depts/itl/graphics/main.html.*

ADDITIONAL READING

For a much more detailed look at deductive and inductive arguments, you might examine Davis Baird, *Inductive Logic: Probability and Statistics* (Englewood Cliffs, NJ: Prentice Hall, 1992).

📖●┤**Read** the **Document** on **mythinkinglab.com**

Bruce N. Waller, "Deductive and Inductive Arguments," *Consider Philosophy.* The important but difficult distinction between deductive and inductive arguments is discussed in this passage.

3

❖ ❖ ❖

Ad Hominem Arguments

((•—⌐**Listen** to the **Chapter Audio** on **mythinkinglab.com**

We have talked about inductive and deductive arguments, valid and invalid arguments, strong and weak arguments. But little has been said about the sources of arguments. The reason is that in analyses of whether an argument is valid or invalid, strong or weak, the source of the argument is irrelevant. Criticizing the *source* of an argument rather than the argument itself commits the *ad hominem fallacy*.

THE AD HOMINEM FALLACY

Ad hominem arguments are, literally, arguments "to the person." There are many dangers, confusions, and temptations associated with ad hominem arguments. But if you faithfully follow one commandment, you can avoid most of the pitfalls and snares of the ad hominem fallacy. That commandment is

> When considering the quality of an argument, thou shalt *not* consider the *source* of the argument.

It does not matter whether the *argument* was given by Richard Nixon or Mother Teresa or Al Capone or St. Francis or God Herself: If it's an *argument*, it must stand or fall on its own merits. The argument may come from the mouth of a babe or of a sage, it may be sung in the rich resonant tones of Pavarotti or screeched in the grating cry of the Jabberwocky, it may be carved on gold tablets or scribbled on a scrap of paper—it doesn't matter. You cannot judge an argument by its source. If we should discover that an argument long attributed to Socrates was in fact given by Socrates' favorite sandalmaker, then that would be important for scholars studying ancient Greek philosophy, but it would have no bearing on the strength of the argument.

Productive *argument*—whether the argument process is adversarial or cooperative—requires an atmosphere of respect for the participants in the argument. The attacks on character and motives that have become standard practice on talk radio and on many blogs and message boards destroy the mutual respect that is the essential starting point of intelligent critical argumentative exchange; and when the conditions for fruitful argument are damaged, democracy itself is threatened. There are still blogs and forums where intelligent civil debate flourishes; but sadly, in many forums name-calling and personal invective have become so common and ugly that room for critical argument is crowded out. The following remarks—lifted from message boards that are supposedly devoted to *argument* about important issues—are typical:

> It is clear that Keyboardtek is a Kool-aid drinker and should have been in Jonestown. Keyboardtek is just another Anti-American Al Quaida collaborator who wants to destroy this country.
> And this:
> All you talk about is how evil the government is, you sound like a confederate. I bet you wish there was still slavery. Yes, the government is out to get you, the moon landing was a hoax, JFK was a conspiracy, and the government was responsible for 9/11. You are just a crazy, superstitious bastard.

Such ad hominem attacks have no place in serious critical argument: first, because they poison the atmosphere and make serious argument impossible (name-calling is not argument); and second, because they are clearly *fallacious*. The *source* of an argument is irrelevant to the *quality* of that argument: whether I am drunk or sober, conservative or liberal, a patriot or a traitor, my *argument* stands or falls on its own merits, and the character of the person giving the argument doesn't matter. You may admire Barack Obama and loathe Sarah Palin, or despise Nancy Pelosi and love Rush Limbaugh; but when they give *arguments*, you must consider those arguments on their own merits and flaws—and the virtues and vices of the *source* of the argument are irrelevant. If you read an argument that you thought was given by George Washington, and now you learn it was an argument by Benedict Arnold, that should have no effect whatsoever on your judgment about the quality of the argument.

NONFALLACIOUS AD HOMINEM ARGUMENTS

The ad hominem *fallacy* is committed when one attempts to discredit an argument by attacking the source of the argument. But not all ad hominem arguments involve the ad hominem *fallacy;* in fact, most ad hominem arguments do not commit the ad hominem fallacy. (Many people regard all ad hominem arguments as automatically fallacious. That has the advantage of being easy; it has the disadvantage of being wrong.) An ad hominem argument commits the ad hominem *fallacy* only if it attacks the *source* of an argument and claims that because of some flaw in the source of the argument the *argument itself* is flawed. If former President Richard Nixon *argues* that we should improve our trade relations with China, then we must evaluate Nixon's arguments on their own merits; to claim that the flaws in Richard Nixon's *character* weaken his *argument* is to commit the ad hominem fallacy. If Tiger Woods gives an *argument* in favor of marital fidelity, then we must evaluate Tiger's argument on its merits. Tiger himself would be a hypocrite, but his arguments may still be good arguments.

But imagine a very different situation. We are not discussing arguments at all; instead, we are simply having a discussion of famous (and infamous) Americans of the 1960s and 1970s. During our discussion, someone asserts that Richard Nixon was a terrible man ("He misused the power of the presidency, he surrounded himself with corrupt and dishonest men, he lied to the American people, he was vindictive toward those who opposed his views"). That is certainly an ad hominem *argument*, but it is not an ad hominem *fallacy*. And one may object to such an attack on Nixon: you might think it ethically wrong ("You shouldn't hit a man when he's down"), in poor taste ("If you can't say something nice, don't say anything at all"), or factually mistaken ("Nixon didn't really do all those nasty things; he was hounded out of office by the liberal press"). But whatever faults that ad hominem attack on Nixon contains, it does *not* commit the ad hominem *fallacy* because it does not attempt to refute one of Nixon's *arguments* by attacking the source of the *argument* (it simply attacks Nixon, not Nixon-as-source-of-argument).

So ad hominem arguments may be legitimate and effective. Let's say that I am running for the Senate and my opponent argues that I am unfit to be senator because I have three convictions for perjury, four for mail fraud, and five for forgery. That information may well be important to voters, who would legitimately wish to consider it in judging my fitness to serve as their senator. If, on the other hand, my opponent attacks me because I'm bald and my ears look funny, that ad hominem attack seems irrelevant to my ability to be an effective senator. It is not an *ad hominem fallacy* (it does not suggest that my *arguments* are no good because I'm bald and have funny-looking ears); but it is an *irrelevant* ad hominem argument, even if the ad hominem attacks are true. Consider another example. If Lionel Lizardliver is a candidate for a position as first-grade teacher, it will certainly be a relevant—and nonfallacious—ad hominem argument to say: Lionel should not be hired to teach first grade because he is only marginally literate, he has an extremely violent temper, and he hates small children. (To argue that Lionel is unfit because he is bow-legged and wears ugly socks would be an *irrelevant* ad hominem attack; it would not be an ad hominem *fallacy*.)

Notice that it is not the truth or falsity of the claims made in the ad hominem argument that determines whether or not the argument commits the ad hominem *fallacy*. If the claims made in the above ad hominem argument against Nixon are false, then the argument certainly will be unsound, but it will still not commit the ad hominem fallacy (though it may contain some *other* fallacy). It does not commit the ad hominem fallacy because it does not attack an *argument source.* And if Nixon gives an *argument* in favor of more trade with China, then an attempt to discredit his argument by attacking him *does* commit the ad hominem fallacy, even if everything said in the ad hominem attack is perfectly true. When ad hominem arguments are fallacious, they are fallacious not because the attack on the arguer is false; they are fallacious because the attack on the arguer is *irrelevant* to the quality of the arguer's *argument.* *Arguments* must be judged on their own merits; their origins don't matter.

Nose Size and Argument Quality

Shortly after the U.S. destruction of the Iraqi army in 2003, the Bush administration awarded an enormous contract to the Halliburton Corporation. The contract was for work on the Iraqi oil fields and a few other projects—it was difficult to know exactly what it covered, since the details were not released—and was worth at least $600 million (exactly how much the contract was worth was also left unclear; some estimates were that it would be worth closer to $6 billion). This was a no-bid contract for an enormous amount of money, the details were kept hidden, and the contract was awarded to a company that was once run by Vice President Richard Cheney (a company where many of Cheney's friends still worked, and a company that had made large campaign contributions to the Republicans). This contract raised some legitimate questions (questions that the U.S. media largely ignored); and Senator Henry Waxman from Oregon criticized the contract, arguing that it was awarded secretively and was not open to other bidders. One talk radio show host rejected Waxman's argument, on the grounds that Waxman has a large nose with flaring nostrils, and thus looks funny. You probably didn't need a course in critical thinking to know that such talk radio ad hominem attacks, common as they are, commit the ad hominem fallacy. But suppose that Senator Waxman had been giving *testimony* rather than argument. In that case, the talk radio attack on Senator Waxman would *not* have committed the ad hominem *fallacy.* (The ad hominem fallacy is committed *only* when one rejects an *argument* based on the argument *source.*) But even though it would not be an ad hominem *fallacy,* it would still be a lousy ad hominem argument; if Senator Waxman had been giving testimony, the ad hominem attack on his appearance would commit the fallacy of irrelevant reason: The size and shape of the testifier's nose obviously is *irrelevant* to the reliability and integrity of the person giving testimony.

Ad Hominem and Testimony

So not all ad hominem arguments are fallacious. To the contrary, in one situation ad hominem arguments are quite valuable. When a claim is based on *testimony*—rather than *argument*—then ad hominem arguments are an appropriate and important means of challenging the claim. *Testimony* takes its strength entirely from its source. If I argue that the defendant must be the murderer (because his fingerprints were found on the murder weapon, the victim's wallet was found in his possession, reliable eyewitnesses saw him running from the scene of the crime, etc.), then you must focus on the argument (and *not* the arguer): Is the argument valid, and are the premises true? But if I *testify* that the defendant is the murderer (because "I *saw* him do the foul deed"), then the *strength* of the testimony depends entirely on the *source* of the testimony, and you can effectively evaluate my testimony only to the degree that you have knowledge of my character, my truthfulness, my reliability.

Consider this fictional case of a jailhouse informant (Jones) who *testifies* against the defendant on trial for murder (Smith). Jones is in jail, awaiting sentencing on drug charges. Jones claims that one day while they were eating lunch at the prison cafeteria, Smith began talking about how he had committed the murder: how he had strangled the victim in the course of a nighttime burglary, when the defendant awakened and confronted him. After Jones gives his testimony about the confession by Smith, the defense attorney begins her cross-examination.

"Mr. Jones, have you ever committed perjury? Have you ever lied under oath? Have you ever taken an oath to tell the truth, the whole truth, and nothing but the truth, so help you God, and then lied?"

"I don't remember ever doing that, no."

The defense attorney looks at some papers on her desk, and then walks toward the witness. "You say you don't remember ever lying under oath? Let me refresh your memory, Mr. Jones. Two years ago, in this very courtroom, you were on trial for selling cocaine, is that right?"

"Yes, but those charges were later reduced."

"Well, we'll get to that. My question is, were you on trial for sale of cocaine?"

"Yes."

"When you testified during your trial, you swore under oath that you had never sold cocaine, that the charges against you were a mistake, is that right?"

"Yes."

"The trial was stopped, and you were allowed to plead guilty to possession. But during your sentencing hearing on the reduced charges, you explicitly admitted that you had sold cocaine, didn't you? The judge specifically asked if you had sold cocaine, and you answered that you had done so."

"Yeah, but what I said was I hadn't sold much; that I had sold some cocaine, but I was not a big cocaine dealer, or anything like that."

"So when you testified—under oath—that you had never sold cocaine, that was a lie, wasn't it? You swore that you had never sold cocaine, when in fact you had. Is that right?"

"I didn't sell much."

"Mr. Jones, listen carefully to the question. You testified under oath that you had *never* sold *any* cocaine; that was a lie, wasn't it?"

"Yes, I guess it was."

"So you lied under oath, didn't you?"

At this point the district attorney intervenes: "Objection, Your Honor. That question has been asked and answered."

"Sustained. Counselor, move on to your next question."

"Thank you, Your Honor." The defense attorney turns back to the witness. "My next question, Mr. Jones, is this. You just told this jury, under oath, that you could not remember ever lying under oath. That was a lie, wasn't it? Because you certainly did remember lying under oath, just two years ago, in this very courtroom. So when you testified that you didn't remember, that was another lie, wasn't it?"

"Well, my memory was a little vague."

"Lying just comes natural and easy to you, doesn't it, Mr. Jones? You lie whenever it's convenient."

"Your Honor," the district attorney rises to object, but the judge interrupts and addresses the defense attorney: "Counselor, that is argumentative; save your arguments for your closing. The jury will disregard the last statement from the defense counsel."

"Mr. Jones," the defense attorney resumes her questions, "when you lied under oath about never selling cocaine, did that keep you awake at night? Did your conscience trouble you? Were you troubled by telling a lie under oath?"

"Your Honor," the district attorney again rises, "I object to this question."

"No, I will allow the question. The defendant will answer the question."

Jones gives a small half-smile, then answers. "No, it didn't really bother me, I guess."

The defense attorney walks back to her desk, looks at a paper, then returns to questioning the witness.

"Mr. Jones, you said that in your trial for selling cocaine, the trial was stopped, and you were allowed to plead guilty to a lesser charge, the charge of simple possession, is that right?"

"That's right."

"Well, that was very fortunate for you, wasn't it. Here you've got this very serious charge of selling cocaine, and in fact it was an even more serious charge of selling cocaine near a school—conviction on that charge would have put you in prison for several years—and the charges get reduced to simple possession; and you were then released for time served, with no additional prison time, is that right?"

"That's right."

"Mr. Jones, you are presently in custody, aren't you? You were brought here to testify from your jail cell, and when you are done testifying you will go back to jail, is that right?"

"Yes, I've been in jail."

"Why are you being held in jail, Mr. Jones? What are the charges against you?"

"I'm charged with possession of cocaine."

"You're charged with possession. Was that the crime you were originally charged with?"

"No."

"What were the original charges?"

"I was charged with selling cocaine, but those charges were dropped."

"Actually, Mr. Jones, you were charged with selling cocaine on school property, isn't that right?"

"Yes, but I'm not charged with that now."

"No, you're not. You got lucky *again*. Charges were dropped down to simple possession. What happened before those charges were reduced? Did you have a meeting with the district attorney's office?"

"I might have."

"I'm not asking what you might have done. *Did* you meet with someone from the district attorney's office?"

"Yes."

"What happened at that meeting? What did you tell them?"

"I told them about my conversation with Sam Smith."

"With the defendant in this case, Sam Smith?"

"Yes."

"Did you tell them that you were willing to testify against Mr. Smith?"

"Yes."

"Were there any conditions on your testifying?"

"Not really conditions. I told them I was worried about the charges against me, that I was hoping for a lesser charge."

"And your hopes were answered, weren't they? Twice you've been charged with selling drugs, selling drugs in the vicinity of schools—apparently your favorite market for drug dealing—and twice the charges have been dramatically reduced, after you agreed to testify against someone else. You've gotten a very good return on your testimony, haven't you? No further questions, Your Honor."

This cross-examination brings out a number of relevant facts about the witness: facts that the jury would certainly wish to consider in weighing the credibility of the witness.

An Unassailable Witness

Not every ad hominem attack on a witness's credibility is quite as successful as the attack on Jones. The following cross-examination occurred during a 1952 murder trial at London's Central Criminal Court. Mrs. Fish—a friendly and spirited Irishwoman—had just testified that she heard screams coming from an upstairs room, and when she forced her way into the room she found the defendant's wife "naked and streaming wet and lying on the floor and clinging to the foot of the bath for dear life, and he [the defendant] with his sleeves rolled up to his armpits"; and (Mrs. Fish continued) the wife said: "He tried to drown me. He wants to kill me. Don't leave me alone with him." The defense attorney begins his cross-examination of Mrs. Fish with the following question:

"I put it to you that you are not a very reliable witness?"

"And for why should you say that, Sorr?"

"Weren't you convicted of keeping a brothel at Liverpool in 1947?"

"Sure," agrees Mrs. Fish as though brothel-keeping was the worthiest of occupations.

"And again in 1949?"

"Sure," replies Mrs. Fish, much puzzled. "But what's that got to do with drowning a poor Christian woman in her bath?"

"And then in 1949 weren't you sent to prison for procuring an abortion?"

"I was indeed," agrees Mrs. Fish fervently. "And it's you that would have done it yourself if you'd seen that poor girl all by herself as she was."[1]

The defense barrister's attack on Mrs. Fish's character and veracity is certainly relevant (it does not commit the ad hominem fallacy); however, it is doubtful that questions about this woman's "bad character" convinced the jury that she was "not a very reliable witness."

The witness is a drug dealer, who apparently specializes in selling to students; the witness is quite willing to lie under oath; and the witness is getting substantial benefits in return for his testimony (some might even say that he is being paid off for his testimony), and thus he has a motive to lie. (Of course a witness with a special interest may still tell the truth, but if the witness admits to lying whenever it is convenient, and admits that he also has a special interest that might tempt him to lie in this case, then the jury might be justified in being skeptical about that witness's testimony.)

If I am a notorious liar, severely paranoid and delusional, known to take bribes, and convicted several times of perjury, then that will severely weaken my *testimony,* but it will have no bearing at all on the validity of my *argument.* (Of course you will want to check carefully on the truth of the premises in my argument; and if any of the premises are based on my *testimony,* then my problems and flaws will be good grounds for doubting the truth of that testimony.) If I am a trained observer with a strong reputation for honesty and no special stake in this case, that will give my *testimony* substantial credibility, but any *argument* I give will have to make it on its own, without any help from my character.

DISTINGUISHING ARGUMENT FROM TESTIMONY

How do you distinguish argument from testimony? It's not always easy. Testimony often occurs in court, given by sworn witnesses; but sometimes those witnesses—especially expert witnesses—actually give arguments rather than testimony. And, of course, testimony occurs more frequently *outside* the courtroom than inside it. "Come on, lend me $10; really, you can trust me, I will certainly pay you back." "I saw your lover last night, dancing cheek-to-cheek with an attractive stranger at the Backdoor Lounge." Neither of those is sworn courtroom testimony; but both are testimony, nonetheless. Both depend for their plausibility on the trustworthiness of the testifiers.

Suppose that one of your friends meets you at the coffee shop and immediately tells you the following:

I saw them! They're here! Just now, as I was walking down Church Street on my way to the coffee shop, I heard this high-pitched hum, and I looked up just in time to see a small, bright silver sphere, about the size of a basketball, descending into the vacant lot just across from me. Six tiny purple creatures, with bright orange eyes, leaped out of their spacecraft, ran three times around the lot, picked up some bottle caps, and then jumped back into the sphere, blasted off, and swiftly ascended through the clouds and out of sight. The extraterrestrials have arrived! I saw them with my own eyes!

Doubtful Witnesses

David Eddleman was charged with being the gunman in a drive-by shooting, and in 1999 was convicted of second-degree murder and a firearm offense in a Michigan state court. The Sixth Circuit U.S. Court of Appeals reviewed his case and overturned his conviction; and in the course of that review the Court examined the key witnesses against Eddleman.

> Brian Babbitt received significant benefits from the police in exchange for his testimony. On January 3, 1997, Babbitt was arrested for the killing of Georgescu. On January 7, 1997, he was arrested again, this time for the murder of Freddy Sanchez. The Wayne County prosecutor's office granted him immunity from prosecution for both murders on January 22, 1997, in exchange for his testimony against Eddleman. . . . At the time, Babbitt also faced charges of felony assault, using a firearm in the commission of a felony, and violating probation. After negotiating the immunity agreement, the prosecutor allowed Babbitt to plead guilty to a reduced charge of aiming without malice, with a sentence of time served. . . . . The next witness, jailhouse informant Ricky O'Neal, testified . . . pursuant to a plea agreement in which the state agreed to reduce a pending charge of assault with intent to rob, which carried a possible life sentence, to two counts of felony assault, for which he received concurrent sentences of one to four years. He had an extensive prior criminal record, including convictions for breaking and entering, larceny, and unarmed robbery. The next two witnesses, Brian Weaver and Thomas Valastek, both testified that they heard Eddleman admit to the shooting. . . . Weaver may have avoided punishment for numerous probation violations by testifying against Eddleman. . . . Three other pieces of information call into question Valastek's credibility. First, he too cooperated with police only after he was arrested in connection with Georgescu's murder. Second, he admitted on cross-examination that his initial statement to police contained "a lot of lying." Third, he admitted that he chose to cooperate fully with police a day after he saw that Babbitt was receiving special perks in jail—such as family visits, outside food, and television privileges—and figured "he must have told them something really good to give him all of that."

Jury members must decide whether witnesses are trustworthy; and the extensive criminal records of these witnesses, together with the substantial benefits they received as payment for their testimony (including reducing possible life sentences to a sentence of one to four years, and in another case dropping murder charges and substituting a charge of "aiming without malice" with a sentence of time served) are certainly factors that jurors should carefully consider.

Paid Testimony

Recently, several celebrities have appeared on television talk shows, and talked about their illnesses and the successful treatments for them. Kathleen Turner, on *Good Morning America,* discussed her arthritis, and then mentioned "extraordinarily effective" new arthritis medications that viewers could learn about at a website sponsored by Amgen and Wyeth. Olympic figure skater Peggy Fleming discussed her cholesterol problem on an ABC show, and heaped praise on the prescription drug Lipitor, made by Pfizer. Lauren Bacall appeared on the *Today* show to talk about the terrible, blinding disease macular degeneration, and also to mention the eye drug Visudyne. This is a very effective promotion for the drug companies: it's not an advertisement, but an apparently heartfelt endorsement from people the viewers know and trust. In all those cases, however, the drug manufacturers paid the celebrities for their endorsements, although no one mentioned that on the shows. It might have been information that viewers would have considered valuable: Kathleen Turner, Peggy Fleming, and Lauren Bacall weren't just praising these drugs out of their altruistic desire to help viewers improve their health, but out of a desire to put money in their own pockets.[2]

Do you believe any of this story? Well, first you want to know whether your friend has a drug or alcohol problem, is he taking some sort of medication, has he been under a lot of strain lately (if 2 weeks ago he burst into the coffee shop and told you that he had just seen a herd of miniature purple and orange elephants doing tricks in the same vacant lot, that will certainly count against believing his story). In other words, your friend's claims about extraterrestrials are based entirely on his own testimony, and that testimony depends on his character, his truthfulness, his stability. (Of course you might not believe him in any case; but if he is sober, reliable, and a pillar of stability, you will give his testimony considerably more weight—and might even decide that he probably did see something strange—than you would if you knew he was a notorious trickster or drug addict.)

In contrast to the above, imagine that your friend earnestly argues that we are even now being visited by extraterrestrials:

> Look, there probably are some extraterrestrials observing our planet, perhaps even visiting our planet. Think for a minute. How many planets are there in our solar system, orbiting our little star we call the Sun? Eight, right? Now consider how many stars there are—just counting our own Milky Way galaxy, leave aside all the other galaxies, some that are vastly larger. As Carl Sagan would say, there are billions and billions of stars, OK? And it seems likely that most of those stars also have planets; in fact, astronomers have already observed planets orbiting a number of relatively nearby stars. So those billions and billions of stars probably have tens and perhaps hundreds of billions of planets, not to mention several times that many moons. Out of all those planets orbiting all those stars, does it seem likely that our little backwater planet is the only one suitable for life? Of course not. No doubt the conditions that made life possible are rather special, and quite rare; but with tens of billions of opportunities, the right conditions probably existed at least a few thousand—more likely a few million—times. That being the case, doesn't it seem likely that life developed, and began to evolve, somewhat earlier on some other planets? And if that's so, isn't it also likely that some—probably many—species on other planets circling other stars would have discovered scientific method just a few thousand years ahead of us? And imagine what our science will be like in a few thousand years! In less than a century, we have gone from uncertain flights of a few hundred feet to spacecraft that are exploring the outer reaches of our solar system. In another hundred years, where will we reach? In another thousand, we may have explored what seems almost inconceivable now: the far reaches of our entire galaxy. So it seems likely that even now, some extraterrestrial species, just a few thousand years ahead of us scientifically and technologically, is exploring our galaxy, and probably is sending scouting parties (the way we send explorers and anthropologists) to examine other civilizations and other cultures. So we must conclude that it is likely that even now we are being observed and perhaps visited by extraterrestrials.

Are you convinced? Probably not. The argument does a good deal of hand-waving and builds quickly into wild speculations from a rather thin foundation of facts. But *notice this:* You do not have to know *anything* about your friend to evaluate that argument. Whether your friend is drunk or sober, reliable or untrustworthy, stable or unbalanced, wise or foolish does not matter. Your friend has offered an *argument* for the likelihood of extraterrestrials in our midst, and the arguer's character, motives, and state of mind are irrelevant to the quality of that argument. *Unlike testimony,* the argument stands or falls on its own merits. If the argument had been given by Carl Sagan, it would not be a better argument. If it had been given by a long-term resident of a facility for the criminally insane, it would not be a weaker argument.

It is important to distinguish between argument and testimony; unfortunately, that distinction is not always easy to make. In everyday life we frequently combine testimony with argument: My *argument* may contain premises that I *testify* are true. Suppose there is a disagreement about whether Joe went to a tavern last night. Mary offers the following argument:

> Joe certainly did not go to the tavern last night. We all agree that Joe stayed in town the entire evening; and we all know that there are only two taverns in the town. The Red Lion Tavern was closed—the health department closed them down last week and they still haven't

reopened. So Joe obviously wasn't at the Red Lion. The only other tavern in town is the Student Prince, and I was there from the time it opened until closing, and Joe never set foot in the place. So Joe could not have been at a tavern last night.

Okay, that's an *argument*. But one of the key premises of Mary's argument—Joe was not at the Student Prince Tavern—is based on Mary's *testimony*. So testimony and argument get intertwined here, and that makes things difficult. But if Mary is giving testimony (and in this case she is) then she is a legitimate target of ad hominem attack. If you decide that a key premise of her argument is doubtful because it is based on her unreliable *testimony,* that would give you good reason to suspect that her argument is *unsound.*

In ordinary life, argument and testimony are often mixed together. But while argument and testimony are not always separated in day-to-day life, they are—or at least are *supposed* to be—in court. Witnesses give testimony, the attorneys give arguments, and the attorneys are *not* supposed to give *testimony.* The distinction is usually drawn quite carefully. Paul Bergman, in his instructional book *Trial Advocacy,* gives the following helpful guidance to practicing attorneys:

> When no expert has testified, the law tries to steer a course between allowing you [the attorney] to make the factfinder [judge or jury] aware of pertinent scientific knowledge, and forbidding you to insert in argument facts that are not part of the record. The general rule is that you may read from a scientific authority if it presents matters of common knowledge and illustrations drawn from common experience. But you may be forbidden to read the author's conclusion set forth in the study, or from presenting scientific experiments or theories to the factfinder if they are not matters of common knowledge.
>
> To focus the dichotomy [between argument and testimony], assume you are questioning the validity [accuracy] of an eyewitness identification. Clearly you may argue the common experience of thinking you recognize a friend, only to find out later that you were mistaken. Just as clearly, you may read from books and newspapers examples of convictions that resulted from mistaken identification. You may also read from a book describing the factors that lead to faulty identification, and then argue the presence or absence of those factors in the evidence. In many jurisdictions, you could also refer to a scientific study showing the likelihood of misidentification. These matters appear to grow out of the common knowledge and wisdom of the community. But you could probably not read the conclusion of a scientific study showing that in a case pretty much like yours, there is a great likelihood of misidentification. That would be viewed as placing expert testimony before the factfinder in the guise of argument.[3]

Thus if you wish to place expert *testimony* before the fact finder, you must produce the expert to actually *testify;* then the opposing side can (legitimately) raise questions about the qualifications and integrity of the expert witness, and the fact finder can then judge whether the witness's testimony is reliable. (That is why "hearsay" testimony—"I heard George claim that Ralph robbed the bank"—is generally *not* allowed. There is no opportunity to cross-examine George, test his truthfulness, and inquire about his character and biases and reliability.)

This distinction between *advocacy* (argument) and *testimony* is especially important in court, and judges rightfully insist on it. The lawyer is *not* testifying; the lawyers are giving *arguments,* and those arguments must be evaluated on their own merits—*not* on the merits of the arguer, and not on the basis of whether the arguer does or does not believe her own arguments. Defense lawyers often try to convey to the jury their own belief in the innocence of their clients, and prosecutors frequently try to impress upon the jury the prosecutor's own belief in the defendant's guilt. But such tactics are not legitimate. If the lawyers were *witnesses,* then it would certainly be important that they *believe* in what they testify (otherwise they are lying); but when you are evaluating an advocate's *arguments,* you must judge the arguments themselves and not the sincerity (or any other characteristic) of the advocate—whether the *advocate* is or is not convinced by the argument is irrelevant. When advocates begin to offer their own *testimony* rather than confining themselves to argument ("I sincerely believe that this defendant is innocent"), judges *should* point out the irrelevance of the advocate's own beliefs—as in the following examples from British courts:

> Serjeant Shee, while defending the poisoner Palmer, [said] to the jury: "I begin Palmer's defence and say in all sincerity that I have an entire conviction of his innocence." The Lord Chief Justice who was trying the case, Lord Campbell, told the jury: "I most strongly recommend to you that you should attend to everything that Serjeant Shee said to you with the exception of his own private opinion. It is my duty to tell you that opinion ought not to be any ingredient of your verdict. It is the duty of the advocate to press his argument on the jury, but not his opinion."
>
> Even Erskine [an outstanding barrister], carried away in defence of Tom Paine, said: "I will now lay aside the role of the advocate and address you as a man," to earn the rebuke [from the presiding judge]: "You will do nothing of the sort. The only right and license you have to appear in this court is as an advocate."[4]

Ideally, attorneys should be giving *arguments,* not testimony. They are advocates, not witnesses. But of course attorneys often *do* insert their own testimony, and judges are not always scrupulous in preventing it. This example is from the career of Jake Ehrlich, a famous San Francisco lawyer from the 1920s through the 1950s. In 1936, Ehrlich was defending a policeman—Lieutenant Henry Ludolph—accused of accepting bribes. Ehrlich's summation to the jury was passionate:

> I don't defend Ludolph as a client, not as a policeman—but as an old and dear friend. I know before God that Henry Ludolph never committed a dishonest act or took a cent of dirty money in his life.[5]

Ehrlich's *testimony* on behalf of Ludolph may or may not be true; in any case, it is out of place. The jury should decide the case on the basis of the *testimony* of the sworn *witnesses* and the *arguments* of the attorneys. But an attorney's *testimony* should be given little weight. In the first place, the attorney obviously has a strong special interest in the case and so is *not* giving unbiased testimony. Even more important, there is no opportunity for the opposing side to *challenge* the attorney's *testimony.* When a witness testifies, the witness is placed under oath and is liable to perjury charges if he or she lies. Furthermore, the witness can be challenged and cross-examined by the opposing attorney, and information about the witness's character and truthfulness and motives can be brought out by the opposing attorney. But when an *attorney* testifies, the attorney is not under oath and is not liable to perjury charges; the opposing attorney has no opportunity to cross-examine; and the other side has no chance to bring in evidence about the attorney's dishonesty, biases, tendency to exaggerate, drug addiction, general unreliability, or whatever. When you evaluate *testimony,* it is essential to know the character of the *testifier:* Is this person honest, unbiased, accurate, careful in stating only what he or she actually knows? When one of the lawyers in the case testifies, the jury cannot learn such things about the testifier. Thus "advocate testimony" ("I know my client is innocent," or—from the prosecuting attorney— "I am absolutely sure this person is guilty") should carry little or no weight. In sum: Listen carefully to the advocates' *arguments;* their *testimony* should not be part of the trial, and if it is, it should be disregarded.

In court, the distinction between advocacy and testimony is *relatively* clear; so it is obvious enough that if an attempt is made to discredit an advocate's *argument* by attacking the character of the advocate, then that attack commits the ad hominem fallacy. And attacks on witnesses who are giving testimony—attacks on their honesty, their sanity, their special interests, their mental stability—will be *relevant* to the strength of the witness's *testimony* (and thus—whether true or false—they do not commit the ad hominem *fallacy*). Outside the courtroom, the distinction between advocacy and testimony is not always so easily drawn. In any case, the point to remember is that when a claim is based on *testimony*, the claim is only as strong as the person giving the testimony (and thus questions about the character and reliability of the testifier are legitimate and important); but when an *arguer* is attempting to draw out the implications of given facts, the *argument* must be evaluated *independently* of the arguer (and questions about the character and reliability of the arguer are irrelevant, and *attacks* on the arguer commit the ad hominem fallacy).

A closely related point will perhaps help sort out these issues. Suppose the chairman of the board of a major U.S. auto manufacturer presents an *argument* for the conclusion that imports of foreign cars should be drastically restricted. The chairman argues that the importing of such autos should be restricted because they pose a health and safety hazard to U.S. consumers: The imported cars are made of inferior steel, the steel is weaker than that used in U.S.-made cars, and under the stress of high-speed driving the cars are more likely to wobble and go out of control. In this hypothetical case, the chairman is giving an *argument* for restrictions on imported autos. (He is *not* merely giving his own *testimony* against imported cars; he is *not* saying, "Look, we would all be better off if there were restrictions on imported automobiles; I know about these things, trust me.") He is instead *arguing* that inferior materials will result in obvious dangers under common driving conditions and that U.S. citizens should be protected from such dangers. Now suppose someone responds, "Don't listen to the chairman's argument! He has a strong reason for opposing imports. If there are fewer imports then he can charge a higher price for his company's cars and make more money! He's not really interested in the safety of U.S. drivers; that greedy money-grubber is just interested in making more money." That would commit the ad hominem fallacy. Even if the chairman's motivation is greed rather than concern for consumer safety, that is irrelevant: The chairman has given an *argument*, and you must examine the *argument* (not the arguer). *However,* it may still be *useful* to know that the

---

How Do You Rule?

bikenderlondon / Shutterstock

In her closing arguments to the jury in the O. J. Simpson murder trial, prosecutor Marcia Clark made the following remarks:

> I started on that side of counsel table [referring to the lawyers for the defense]. I was a defense attorney. I know what the ethical obligations are of a prosecutor. I took a cut in pay to join this office, because I believe in this job. I believe in doing it fairly and doing it right and I like the luxury of being a prosecutor. Because I have the luxury on any case of going to the judge and saying, "Guess what, Your Honor, dismiss it, it's not here."
>
> Ladies and Gentlemen, I can come to you and I can say, "Don't convict, it's not here."

> I have that right. I have that luxury. This job gives me that luxury. It doesn't give me a lot of money but it gives me that luxury. I can get up in the morning and look at myself in the mirror and say I tell you the truth, I will never ask for a conviction unless I should, unless the law says I must, unless he is proven guilty beyond a reasonable doubt on credible evidence.

At that point in her closing argument, the defense intervened with an objection. The defense claimed that Marcia Clark's remarks were improper, and that she should be forced to retract them, because she was improperly giving *testimony* about her own convictions concerning Simpson's guilt rather than presenting argument based on the evidence. Marcia Clark asserted that there was nothing improper in her closing argument. She denied that she was giving any testimony concerning her own beliefs; instead, she claimed, she was simply giving arguments based on well-known principles governing legal ethics and the ethics of prosecutors.

Was Marcia Clark improperly putting her own testimony before the jury? Or was she, quite properly, simply giving an argument? How do you rule?

Arguing for Profit

When argument is given, we must consider the argument: We cannot reject an argument based on the *source* of that argument. So when Dr. Robert Kehoe argued that lead in leaded gasoline is *not* a health hazard, it would be an ad hominem *fallacy* to reject his arguments on the basis that he is heavily funded by the lead industry. However, that does not mean that we should *ignore* the fact that he has a special interest in denying the health hazards of leaded gasoline: it should warn us to give careful scrutiny to his arguments and his research, since he does have a special bias. And in the case of Dr. Kehoe's research, that careful scrutiny pays off. One of the things Dr. Kehoe attempted to prove through his research was that the lead burned in leaded gasoline (7 million tons in the United States during the twentieth century) does not accumulate in humans, and so cannot cause lead poisoning; and that high levels of blood–lead are common and natural. As proof, he compared a group of people living in remote rural Mexico—not exposed to leaded gasoline—with people living in U.S. urban environments. Sure enough, the blood-lead content of the rural Mexicans was approximately the same level as the lead-blood level of U.S. city dwellers. Unfortunately, in his zeal to defend the lead industry, Dr. Kehoe had not randomly chosen a rural population; instead, the Mexican village he chose for comparison was heavily exposed to lead through the lead glazes it used in making its local pottery, and also from consuming food prepared and served in lead-glazed pottery. When later studies compared other rural peoples against U.S. citizens exposed to leaded gasoline, they found that the U.S. blood-lead contamination was much higher. So although we cannot reject Dr. Kehoe's argument on the basis of his payoffs from the lead industry, those payoffs should alert us to look more closely at the research that forms the basis of his argument. When that research is shown to be shoddy and biased, it is perfectly legitimate to point out the serious flaws in Dr. Kehoe's research, and the flaws in Dr. Kehoe's arguments. Such criticisms of *arguments* are not ad hominem at all, and so obviously do not commit the ad hominem fallacy. (If Dr. Kehoe *testified* that his research was accurate and unbiased— "trust me, my comparison groups were not specially selected"—then of course it *would* be legitimate to make ad hominem attacks on his *testimony*.) Finally, it is also legitimate to make an ad hominem attack against Dr. Kehoe: "Dr. Kehoe is a disgrace to the scientific community, who distorts his studies in order to cover up a major health hazard." You might make that legitimate ad hominem attack in pushing to have Dr. Kehoe fired by his university. But whatever Dr. Kehoe's flaws, you cannot reject his *arguments* because of flaws in *him*— though of course you can reject his arguments because of flaws in the arguments themselves.[6]

---

fellow giving the argument *is* chairman of the board of a U.S. auto manufacturer and *does* have a special financial interest in the issue. It will be useful, but *not* because that knowledge will be good grounds for dismissing the chairman's *argument*. Rather, it will be useful because it will prompt us to look *very carefully* at the *premises* of the chairman's argument: Are the premises in the argument really true? *Is* the steel used by foreign manufacturers inferior? We cannot reject a person's *argument* on the basis of the character or special interest of the arguer; however, *knowing* that the arguer is dishonest or greedy or has a financial interest in the issue *will* be good reason to double-check the factual claims (the premises). If the premises are false, then the argument will be unsound. If the premises are true and the argument is valid, then the argument is a sound argument no matter how selfish, despicable, biased, or untrustworthy the arguer may be. (Of course if the support for one of the *premises* is simply the *testimony* of the person giving the argument—"They really do use inferior steel; I know, because I saw them do it!"—then the character of the person giving that testimony *is* directly relevant to the value and reliability of the testimony.)

Exercise 3-1

The following examples involve ad hominem arguments; tell which ones do—and which ones do *not*—commit the ad hominem *fallacy*, and explain why.

1. Ralph claims that pornography ought to be banned because it exploits and degrades those who are involved in its production and because it provides too many opportunities for organized crime. However, I happen to know that Ralph frequently rents hard-core pornographic videotapes. Well, so much for Ralph's arguments to ban pornography!

2. Bert maintains that there was indeed a conspiracy to assassinate President John Kennedy. He says that he knows there was such a conspiracy, because he is now confessing to being part of the conspiracy, along with Oswald. However, I don't put much faith in Bert's conspiracy theory; after all, he also has confessed to being involved in the conspiracy to assassinate Abraham Lincoln.

3. Joan favors developing a system of radio receivers that would monitor the heavens for radio signals from intelligent extraterrestrials. Joan argues that there are millions of stars similar to our Sun, and so there are probably also millions of planets orbiting those stars, and thus it is likely that life evolved on at least some of those other planets. And if there is life on other planets, then it seems reasonable, so Joan argues, that at least some of those planets began their evolutionary process earlier than did Earth, and thus might well contain intelligent life that has advanced far beyond the intelligent life on Earth. If so, we might be able to learn a great deal from intercepting their radio signals. In any case, Joan thinks it is worth the investment required to try. Joan's argument sounds pretty good, and I was almost convinced that her proposed radio receivers were a good idea until I learned that she also wants to place television cameras deep in the forests so we can record the dances of the woodland elves! I'm afraid Joan's elevator doesn't go to the top floor.

4. Bill claims that Professor Paula Pithy gave him a D in eighteenth-century British history when he really deserved at least a B. Bill says that Professor Pithy didn't like him, because several times during class he noted errors in her lectures and corrected her mistakes. He says he knows more about British history than Professor Pithy does—and that she resented it, and thus gave him a much lower grade than he really deserves, and that's the only thing that kept him from making the dean's list. Well, maybe so. But Bill also claims that he was an all-state football player in high school, and I went to high school with Bill so I happen to know that Bill never even made the football team.

5. Senator Scam is running for reelection, and now he claims that he is really concerned about improving the quality of life for all of our citizens. He says he is an independent senator, and that his only goal is to promote the good of the people. But don't you believe it. Senator Scam has been raking in money from every lobbyist in Washington; in fact, he received more money from the insurance, tobacco, and health-care industry than any other senator! And those lobbyists got what they paid for: a senator who has spent the last 6 years blocking every major effort at health-care reform and blocking investigations into the activities of the major tobacco companies. And now he claims that he is only interested in the good of the people! His only real interest is in getting your vote, so he can keep raking in the money. Don't vote for that sleazy hypocrite.

6. Many physicians claim that active euthanasia is wrong and should be prohibited. They argue that active euthanasia would undermine trust in the medical profession's commitment to healing, that active euthanasia would be subject to abuse by those who simply want to get rid of older people who are viewed as burdensome, and that proper and aggressive use of pain-control medications can alleviate suffering and thus eliminate any need for euthanasia as an escape from suffering. But you shouldn't trust the arguments of those doctors. For if active euthanasia is not allowed, then those who are terminally ill will have a longer period of illness leading to their deaths, and they will require expensive long-term medical treatment, and so those very same doctors will make more money. It's not really surprising that physicians argue against active euthanasia: Blocking active euthanasia means money in their pockets and payments on their Porsches.

7. William H. Webster was named by the Securities and Exchange Commission to head a new board overseeing the accounting industry, and to clean up wrongdoing in the industry. But it turns out that when Webster was a director of U.S. Technologies, he was chairman of the audit committee for the company. While holding that position he was warned by BDO Seidman, a large accounting firm that was auditing U.S. Technologies, about serious financial problems in the company. Webster, rather than cleaning up the problems, fired the auditor. And this is the man who President Bush wanted to clean up the accounting industry. He is obviously not qualified for the job!

8. Don't take a course from Bruce! He is the most boring professor I've ever had: He sits at the desk and reads passages straight from the book, and then he reads from these old yellowed notes that he hasn't changed in 20 years—I think maybe they are notes he took when he was an undergraduate—and he mumbles, so you can't even tell what he's saying. And he gets really angry if you ask him to repeat anything or explain something. But worst of all is his exams! They are absolutely impossible: They usually ask about things the class isn't even covering, and they are so long no one has time to finish more than half the exam, and then he counts off for all the questions you didn't have time to answer. Out of 40 students in his class last semester, 32 made Fs and the rest made Ds. So when you are considering who to take for your philosophy courses, avoid Bruce like the plague.

TRICKY TYPES OF AD HOMINEM

Ad hominem attacks against arguments are fallacious. And if an ad hominem attack charges an *arguer* with stupidity or corruption, you will instantly recognize that as a *fallacious* attack on the argument. Unfortunately, some instances of ad hominem fallacy are more subtle. Instead of making obvious frontal assaults on the arguer ("Don't listen to his argument: He is a swindler and a drunkard, and he hates kittens"), the ad hominem may be more insidious. Even those more subtle forms of ad hominem fallacy will not deceive you if you always remember that the *source* of the *argument* is *irrelevant* to the strength of argument (although the source of testimony *is* relevant when judging the strength of testimony).

Bias Ad Hominem

Not all forms of ad hominem fallacy are as obvious as calling the arguer nasty names. Consider the *bias* form of the ad hominem fallacy. This fallacy occurs when an argument is disparaged on the grounds that the arguer has some special interest or bias in the question at issue. For example, the American Tobacco Institute has been running advertisements that contain *arguments against* tighter restrictions on smoking in public. The American Tobacco Institute is by no means a disinterested, neutral party. It is the public relations–lobbying branch of the tobacco industry, and it is funded by cigarette-manufacturing companies. So obviously the American Tobacco Institute and the companies it represents have a special interest in opposing restrictions on smoking: More restrictions mean less smoking, fewer cigarettes sold, and smaller profits. Thus someone might argue:

> Pay no attention to those American Tobacco Institute arguments against restrictions on smoking. You shouldn't take their arguments seriously; after all, those arguments are bought and paid for by the tobacco industry.

This sounds like an effective and forceful critique of the arguments by the American Tobacco Institute, but in fact it is an instance of the ad hominem *fallacy*. For if the American Tobacco Institute has given an argument, then their argument stands or falls on its own merits or its own faults. And it is irrelevant whether that argument was paid for by the tobacco industry or was developed by some pure, innocent, and absolutely unbiased philosopher, or whether it dropped from the heavens like manna. Remember: The source of the argument—whether good, bad, or indifferent—is *irrelevant* to the quality of the argument.

Don't misunderstand: If an argument is offered against restrictions on public smoking, it may be *useful* to know the special interests of the arguer; for if we know that the argument is being given by someone with a special interest, that may be a helpful reminder to check very carefully the premises of that argument (to be sure that any "facts" cited are genuine, that any data given are accurate, that the "truths" stated are not half-truths). But while it may be helpful to have a reminder to check carefully the soundness of the argument, it is *not* helpful—in fact it is wrong—to reject an argument because the source of the argument has a special interest or bias.

If it were true that any argument presented by a paid advocate is unsound, then a sound argument would be a rare event in the courtroom. Certainly many American attorneys and British barristers are genuinely committed to fair and just trials. But they are also involved in an adversarial system of justice that functions by having the prosecution present as strong a case as possible while the defense works to show that the defendant has not been proved guilty. And in almost all cases the prosecution and defense attorneys are paid to argue for their respective sides. So if being paid to present arguments or having a special interest made one's arguments unsound (fallacious), then a sound argument would hardly ever occur in court. But having a special interest in a position does not make one's *arguments* for that position unsound, and to *claim* that an argument is unsound merely because the person giving the argument has a special interest in the case is to commit the ad hominem *fallacy.*

But remember that the situation is completely different when ad hominem arguments are directed against *testimony.* If a witness is testifying—not presenting an argument—then the claim that he or she has a special interest in the case (and thus that one should weigh the possible effects of that special interest when evaluating the truthfulness and reliability of the witness's testimony) is certainly *relevant,* and does *not* commit the ad hominem fallacy. If the witness is the defendant's best friend, then the witness has a special interest that may influence his or her testimony. If the prosecution witness is a police officer who has worked for months to build a case against a suspected drug dealer, then convicting the defendant will be a feather in the officer's cap and the officer has a special interest in the case: The defense attorney will be justified in reminding the jury of the witness's special interest. If Hatfield and McCoy have been mortal enemies for decades, then Hatfield has a special interest in McCoy's case; and after Hatfield has testified that he saw McCoy (the defendant) running from the scene of the robbery, it is legitimate for the defense attorney to launch an ad hominem attack against Hatfield's *testimony* by charging Hatfield with a strong bias against the defendant. That is an ad hominem attack, but not an ad hominem *fallacy.* (The defense attorney's ad hominem attack on Hatfield—which reveals Hatfield's hatred of McCoy—provides important information for you as a jury member even if you do *not* decide that Hatfield is *lying.* For while Hatfield's hatred of McCoy might not lead Hatfield to lie under oath, it might influence Hatfield's perception of events. Eyewitness testimony is notoriously unreliable; if Hatfield's eyewitness perceptions are colored by his hatred of McCoy, that may make Hatfield's *honest* belief about what he observed more open to doubt. For if Hatfield already believes that McCoy is just the sort of scoundrel who would commit a robbery, then Hatfield may be more likely to "see" McCoy fleeing the scene of a robbery. If Hatfield *expects* to see McCoy running from the robbed liquor store, then the man he sees running is likely to look like McCoy.)

So it is important that you know the bias or special interest of anyone whose testimony you must evaluate. And it is quite reasonable for attorneys to make the jurors aware of any special interests or biases the witnesses may have. But of course you must still exercise caution in drawing your conclusions about the reliability of the testimony. The police officer does have a special interest in the case, but it certainly doesn't follow that the police officer will lie in order to get a conviction. The defendant's best friend strongly desires that the defendant be acquitted, but that doesn't mean that the friend is willing to commit perjury in order to bring about that acquittal. Hatfield's hatred of McCoy may not be as strong as Hatfield's love of the truth. And the defendant—who certainly has a special interest in the results of the trial—may nonetheless be testifying honestly. Sometimes people overcome their own personal interests and testify truthfully, and sometimes they do not. In order for you to decide whether the witness is testifying accurately and truthfully—and that is one of your major responsibilities as a jury member—you must weigh all the information you have about the past behavior, character, and special interests of the witness, and then make the best decision you can about the quality of the testimony. For that task, information about the character of the witness is certainly relevant, and ad hominem arguments by the opposition are one legitimate means of providing the jury with information about the person testifying. (Ad hominem attacks on *testifiers* do not commit the ad hominem fallacy; however, not every ad hominem attack on a testifier is relevant. An ad hominem argument against a testifier may make points that do not have force against the person testifying. If the defense attorney attacks the witness Hatfield because Hatfield's ears are ugly, that ad hominem attack certainly should not count for much against Hatfield's testimony.)

You might get the impression that in the courtroom all ad hominem arguments are against testimony, and thus that the ad hominem *fallacy* never occurs during trials. Not so. An example of ad hominem *fallacy* can be found in F. Lee Bailey's closing argument for the defense in the trial of George Edgerly (accused of murdering his wife). In *The Defense Never Rests*, F. Lee Bailey describes one of the most dramatic moments in his closing argument:

> At one point, I walked over to the D.A. [district attorney, the prosecution lawyer] and shouted: "Here's a man so callous as to try to put a man in the electric chair for something he didn't do just in order to get reelected."[7]

But the district attorney's motives and interests (whether they are as commendable as trying to protect society from vicious criminals or as despicable as trying to promote his own reputation for selfish political purposes) are *irrelevant;* the district attorney was giving *arguments,* not testimony, and thus an attack on the district attorney's motives is an example of ad hominem fallacy.

But the ad hominem fallacy is a two-edged sword, and in courtrooms it cuts both ways. In the famous Loeb–Leopold murder case (in which Loeb and Leopold, teenage boys from very wealthy Chicago families, stood trial for the brutal murder of a younger boy), the great criminal defense lawyer Clarence Darrow was accused by State's Attorney Crowe of defending the boys only because he received a huge fee. (This was not true; although it was rumored that Darrow received a $1 million fee, he in fact received only $40,000, and most if not all of that money went to pay for court costs and office expenses.)

The Scandal of "Jailhouse Informants"

One of the most obvious and troublesome sources for *biased* witnesses is the use of "jailhouse informants." These witnesses are convicted criminals whom authorities plant in the same cell with a suspect who has been arrested and is awaiting trial. The authorities tell the informant to befriend the suspect, and to listen carefully to everything the suspect says, in hopes that the suspect will confess his or her crime to the informant. Since the informant and suspect are together day and night, it is hoped that the suspect will eventually say something incriminating to the informant "friend." The problems with this process are obvious and profound. In the first place, the informant is a convicted criminal, and therefore not the most reliable witness in the world. But second, and even more troubling, the informant is offered a deal by the authorities: if you testify that the suspect told you something that will contribute to the suspect's conviction, then you will receive a reduced sentence or early parole (and if you cannot provide testimony helpful to the prosecution, you get nothing). So the informant is being paid for his testimony, and paid in precious coin: reduced prison time. It is easy to see how such incentives could lead to false testimony, and in fact there have been many cases of innocent people being wrongly convicted by the perjured testimony of jailhouse informants (and while there have been many cases of obviously perjurious testimony by such informants, I know of only two cases in which a jailhouse

informant was prosecuted for perjury: one was a case in which the jailhouse informant embarrassed the district attorney's office by going on television and bragging about the special deals he had gotten from the district attorney's office in exchange for his false testimony against other defendants). With these problems in mind, the Alberta Department of Justice recently issued these guidelines for use of such testimony:

1. All testimony from in-custody informants must first be reviewed by the Crown prosecutor's office and then by a Ministry of Justice official outside the prosecutor's office.
2. Jailhouse informant testimony can only be used when there is a compelling public interest.
3. Defense counsel will receive full disclosure concerning the informant's past and all details of the deal offered to the informant.
4. Jailhouse informants who lie will be criminally prosecuted.

These guidelines may not go far enough—some feel that jailhouse informants have no place in a system of justice that is supposed to protect the defendant's rights and discourage perjured testimony—but at least the problem is acknowledged, which is more than has happened in the United States.

How Do You Rule?

bikeriderlondon / Shutterstock

You are the presiding judge in a robbery trial. A witness for the prosecution (Mr. Candor) has testified that he saw the defendant running through an alley shortly after a bank robbery was committed and that the defendant had a large money bag in his left hand and a pistol in his right hand. The defendant's attorney is now cross-examining Mr. Candor:

DEFENSE ATTORNEY: Now Mr. Candor, you say you observed the defendant running through an alley.

MR. CANDOR: Yes, sir.

DEFENSE: What were you doing in the alley?

MR. CANDOR: I was talking with friends.

DEFENSE: Mr. Candor, do you spend a good deal of your time in such alleys?

MR. CANDOR: Yes, sir.

DEFENSE: You are dressed very fashionably today, Mr. Candor; is that the way you were dressed when you were chatting with your friends in the alley? Do you and your friends normally dress like that?

DISTRICT ATTORNEY: Your Honor, I must object to this line of questioning. What Mr. Candor was wearing when he observed the defendant certainly did not affect his vision; and what Mr. Candor is wearing today in court is equally irrelevant. I beg you to instruct counsel for the defense to stop these ridiculous questions and confine himself to relevant issues.

DEFENSE ATTORNEY: Your Honor, the prosecution knows full well that these are relevant and important questions. The jury has a right to know that being a prosecution witness has been very profitable for Mr. Candor: the prosecution has bought new clothes for the witness, has provided him much more comfortable accommodations—a great improvement over drafty alleyways—for the duration of the trial, given him food and money and comforts far beyond his usual experience.

DISTRICT ATTORNEY: Your Honor, where the witness sleeps, what he eats, and what he wears has no bearing on this case. The defense is simply trying to obscure the real issue: Mr. Candor's positive identification of the defendant running from the scene of the crime with a gun and the loot.

How do you rule? Do you sustain the district attorney's objection and require the defense attorney to drop this line of questioning as irrelevant? Or, do you overrule the objection and allow the defense attorney to continue asking about the witness's new suit?

But even if Crowe's claim were true, it would still be irrelevant, since Darrow's motives—whether selfish or altruistic—were irrelevant to the soundness of his arguments. Darrow returned the favor, accusing prosecutor Crowe of being a "hanging" state's attorney who "would laugh at the hanging of these boys."[8] Now if Darrow's claim were true, it would certainly indicate a severe lack of basic human sympathy in Crowe's character, and that might be good grounds for not wishing to spend your summer holidays with prosecutor Crowe. But true or not, it is irrelevant to Crowe's *arguments*. Both Darrow and Crowe are indulging in ad hominem *fallacies*. (Darrow and Crowe apparently did not take offense over this exchange of fallacious ad hominem attacks, since they remained close friends after the trial.)

Inconsistency and Ad Hominem

The charge of bias is not the only tricky form of ad hominem fallacy. Another subtle use of ad hominem fallacy is to claim that the arguer's words are inconsistent with his or her deeds. If Sandra Smith *argues* that abortions are wrong, then we must evaluate her argument

A Special Case

A nineteenth-century New York murder trial contains a striking example of an *arguer*'s special interest. In the 1857 trial of Mrs. Emma Augusta Cunningham for the premeditated murder of Dr. Harvey Burdell, the public prosecutor who argued for the conviction of Mrs. Cunningham (and thus for her execution) was also the lawyer for the blood relatives of Dr. Burdell and represented them in their efforts to claim the property of Dr. Burdell. Since one of the claims of Mrs. Cunningham (disputed by the prosecution) was that she was secretly married to Dr. Burdell, that meant that if her claims were upheld she would receive the bulk of Dr. Burdell's considerable estate. The public prosecutor—in his role as counsel for Dr. Burdell's family—thus had a special interest in having Mrs. Cunningham convicted and executed: that would get her out of the way and leave Dr Burdell's estate for the clients of the prosecutor. The defense attorney for Mrs. Cunningham made quite sure that this peculiar situation was emphasized for the jury:

> I ask again, gentlemen, why was it that such a savage attack was made upon this defenceless woman? There is only one principle upon which I can understand it. The moment the lifeless remains of Harvey Burdell are consigned to the cold and silent tomb, and even before, commences the scramble for his property. We know with what avidity his heirs, his blood relatives, have sought to snatch, and divide up among them, whatever property he left. We know how they have hunted this unfortunate woman; and I know, also, that the very Counsel of the members of that family who has appeared in the Surrogate's Court, in order, if possible, to make null and void her marriage with the deceased, so that they might get the property—that very Counsel, although a worthy man and an able lawyer, appears here to prosecute this woman to the death. Gentlemen, you all recollect, upon the Coroner's inquest, with what unmingled feelings of disgust was viewed the conduct of a certain lawyer who appeared there as Counsel for the blood relatives of the deceased, and took part in the inquest. As you mingled with your acquaintances and the people in this city, and read the newspapers, you heard the universal condemnation of the course pursued by that man; you heard denounced the indelicacy, and indecency even, of his appearing as public prosecutor, and, at the same time, as Counsel for those peculiarly interested in the death of my client.[9]

Certainly the defense counsel is correct that the actions of the prosecutor—in serving as counsel for the relatives of Burdell and also prosecuting Mrs. Cunningham—were "indelicate," and perhaps even indecent. It does appear that the prosecutor operates from a position of very special interest in this case. But distasteful as that may be—even if we regard the prosecutor with "unmingled feelings of disgust" because of such conduct—that has no bearing on his *arguments*. The prosecutor, after all, is *not* giving *testimony;* rather, he is presenting *arguments* for the guilt of the defendant. And those arguments must be evaluated on their own merits and demerits, independently of the character, interests, or flaws of the person who presents them.

on its own merits. An argument that we should "Pay no attention to Sandra's arguments against abortion, for I happen to know that Sandra herself has had *three* abortions!" would commit the ad hominem fallacy. If Joe Jones gives an impassioned *argument* in favor of vegetarianism (raising and killing animals is cruel to the animals, feeding grain to beef animals is wasteful in a world where there are many hungry people, and eating meat causes high cholesterol levels), then Joe's *argument* is not weakened by the fact that you see him wolfing down burgers later that evening. (In evaluating Joe's argument for vegetarianism, it doesn't matter whether he was eating veggie burgers or Big Macs; it would change our opinion of *Joe* if we learn that his is a hypocrite, but it should not affect our evaluation of Joe's *argument*.) Suppose that the district attorney *argues* that although the penalties for drunken driving may seem harsh, we must enforce them, for it is essential that we get drunk drivers off our highways; if later that evening you observe the district attorney stagger out of a bar and into the driver's seat of her car, that is irrelevant to the strength of the district attorney's *argument*. If you point out an inconsistency between an arguer's *argument* and her *actions,* and conclude that the inconsistency refutes her argument, then you have committed the ad hominem fallacy.

Don't get me wrong: I'm not *approving* of people who say one thing and do another. The television evangelists who preach spiritual values and the rejection of worldly wealth and then drive their limousines back to their mansions are a sleazy hypocritical lot.

Politicians who proclaim their commitment to civil rights while belonging to segregated country clubs are despicable. But being a hypocrite has nothing to do with the quality of one's arguments. *Arguments* stand or fall on their own, and the character of the arguer is irrelevant to the strength of the argument. An *argument* that smoking is extremely hazardous to health and that no one should smoke may be perfectly sound, despite the fact that the arguer smokes three packs a day.

If, on the other hand, someone is giving *testimony* (not argument), then inconsistency between words and deeds does weaken the testimony. Suppose a guru *testifies* (rather than argues) that a simple ascetic life is the way to true happiness: "*Trust* me; as you can see my own serenity, so you too can find true peace and inner joy through giving away all your possessions and eating only brown rice." If you should discover that the guru in fact owns a fleet of Cadillacs, a mansion with a Jacuzzi in Pasadena, and lives on white wine and croissants, then you are quite justified in doubting the guru's *testimony*. (But if the guru has given *arguments* to prove that a simple ascetic life is a happier life, then the guru's own luxurious—and hypocritical—lifestyle is irrelevant to the guru's arguments. In the earlier example of Joe, the hypocritical meat-eater who argues for a vegetarian diet, Joe is *not* giving testimony; thus Joe's hypocrisy is completely irrelevant to the quality of his argument.) Suppose the defendant is *testifying* in court that he is a gentle, peaceful man who would never hurt anyone and would certainly never have committed the assault and battery of which he is accused; then if the witness has a pair of brass knuckles in his shirt pocket and threatens to punch the bailiff's lights out for mispronouncing his name, you certainly may count such inconsistent behavior against his *testimony*.

Another possible confusion must be avoided. If someone gives an *argument,* then inconsistency between the argument and actions does not count against the argument. But, inconsistency *within* the argument itself is fatal. For if an argument contains inconsistent premises—premises that contradict each other—then at least one of the premises must be *false*. And if an argument contains a false premise, then the argument is *unsound*. Thus, while inconsistency between words and actions is irrelevant to the soundness of the argument, inconsistency *within* an argument is lethal for the argument.

Ad hominem arguments are tricky stuff, and dealing with inconsistency claims is one of the trickiest parts. Suppose that you and I are arguing about whether it is wrong to slaughter pigs so that we can enjoy bacon, ham, and pork chops, and you are trying to convince me that it's wrong. "Look," you say, "you oppose killing animals for fur coats, right? You say that it's not right to kill animals for the luxury of a fur coat, when we have other materials that keep you just as warm and that don't involve killing animals. Well, we have other foods that keep you just as well nourished—better, in fact— that do not require the killing of animals. So since you believe it's wrong to kill animals for the luxury of a fur coat, you should also agree that it's wrong to kill animals for the luxury of a pork chop."[10] That is a legitimate and important element of serious argument: consider what beliefs you hold, and then examine whether the claim you are currently making is consistent or inconsistent with that stock of beliefs. When you assert that my current position is inconsistent with other views that I hold, then I have several options. First, you may convince me to change my current claim: "Yes, you are right; I do think it's wrong to kill animals for the luxury of wearing their fur, and so now as I think about it, I have to also conclude that it's wrong to kill animals for the luxury of eating their flesh." Second, I may decide to revise some of my other views, and bring them into line with the claim I'm currently making: "Well, I still think it's OK to kill pigs for the luxury of pork chops; so I guess I'll have to change my stance on fur coats, and now I see nothing wrong with killing mink, fox, and seals so that humans can wear luxurious furs." Or third, I can attempt to show that my views are not really inconsistent: "No, fur coats are a luxury; but steaks and chops are a necessity." "No, the cases are really different: seals, foxes, and mink suffer when they are trapped and killed for their fur; but cows, chickens, and pigs live happy lives and die peaceful deaths at the factory farms and slaughterhouses."

Pointing out that my current position is inconsistent with my other beliefs is not an ad hominem fallacy; in fact, it's not really ad hominem at all. It's not an attack on me, but an attack on my *argument:* my position has implications that I had not thought through, implications that are inconsistent with the beliefs I hold. But notice: that is very different from saying that my *argument* is inconsistent with my *actions*. If I argue against killing animals for food while wearing a full-length mink coat, then you may think that my behavior is somewhat bizarre, and that I am a hypocrite; but no matter how weird and hypocritical the source of the argument, the argument itself must still be judged on its own merits, and not by its source. If I am giving *testimony,* however, then pointing out the inconsistency between my words and actions *is* relevant, and is a *legitimate* ad hominem argument. "Take my word for it, I know; that bridge is perfectly safe." If I now refuse to drive across the bridge, instead taking a long and inconvenient detour, then you have good reason to doubt the reliability of my *testimony* concerning the safety of the bridge. If the owner of a company insists that he absolutely is not a racist, yet there are no African Americans among his 200 employees, then his actions are evidence against his words. And if a politician asserts that she strongly supports efforts to protect our environment, but consistently votes against legislation to prevent pollution, then we are justified in doubting the truthfulness of her pro-environment testimony.

Psychological Ad Hominem

We have examined several subtle varieties of ad hominem fallacy; the last one is perhaps the most deceptive of all. Call it the psychological form of ad hominem fallacy. This form occurs in attempts to discredit an *argument* by questioning the mental state of the *arguer*. It is an insidiously effective form of ad hominem fallacy, for it often masquerades as special *sympathy* for the arguer. Consider an example: Jane Jackson gives an *argument* against abortion. Instead of answering her *argument,* someone says, "Poor Jane, it's such a tragic thing: She has always desperately wanted to have children, but she has never been able to. It's not surprising that she opposes abortions. It must break her heart when people who do not want a child have an abortion, while she wants a child so much and cannot become pregnant." Notice what such a comment does: It "explains away" Jane's argument, by implying that since we now know the unfortunate psychological source of the argument we need pay no attention to the argument itself. But whether or not that is the correct psychological account of Jane's feelings about abortion, it is *irrelevant* to the validity or invalidity of her argument. And to focus attention on the arguer instead of the argument is to commit the ad hominem fallacy.

Bertrand argues that we should immediately ban all killing of whales: Such killing threatens the survival of several species of these majestic creatures; the killing methods are cruel and painful to these sensitive mammals; and all the products we obtain from the killing of whales can be efficiently produced by other means. Someone responds, in a deeply sympathetic and pitying tone:

> Bertrand is such a sad case. You see, his mother abandoned him when he was only 4 years old; and now he subconsciously identifies whales—those huge, gentle, and powerful mammals—with the mother he lost. It's a very sad thing, and we should all be gentle with him.

Bertrand may indeed be a sad case, and his subconscious may be completely screwy; but neither Bert's subconscious nor anything else about him is at issue. The question is the soundness of his *argument*. And that argument stands or falls independently of the arguer. The argument may be *sound* even if Bertrand is a looney tune.

One more example of the psychological ad hominem fallacy is noteworthy. In 1979, during the Iranian Revolution, Iranian students stormed the U.S. embassy in Tehran, and held a number of U.S. diplomats hostage for a period of several months. When the U.S. hostages were released from the Iranian embassy, some of them *argued* that there should be an investigation of U.S. interference in the internal affairs of Iran, and they cited several strong reasons for believing that the United States had used embassy personnel for covert activities against the Iranian government. But those arguments were quickly dismissed on the grounds that these unfortunate hostages were suffering from the "Stockholm syndrome": a psychological disorder that sometimes causes long-term captives to identify with their captors. Now I'm not sure that this supposed psychological disorder of Stockholm syndrome is genuine; but I am sure that it is *irrelevant* to the *arguments* given by the returning hostages. If they are suffering from psychological problems, then certainly we should feel sympathy for them and for their ordeal as hostages. But if they give *arguments*, their arguments stand or fall independently of any characteristics—psychological or otherwise—of the arguers.

Of course if one is giving *testimony,* then evidence of psychological imbalance—evidence of paranoia, hallucinations, or delusions, for example—will indeed undermine the credibility of the testimony. (The testimony of Mehmet Ali Agca is the most dramatic example I know. Agca attempted to kill Pope John Paul II and later became the key prosecution witness against several defendants accused of plotting to kill the pope. However, some of his pronouncements during the trial—for example, that he is Jesus Christ reincarnated and that he has had visions of how the world will end—may prompt a bit of doubt concerning his mental stability; if so, one might also have some doubts about his *testimony.*) But neither an arguer's psychological imbalance nor an arguer's well-adjusted psychological stability have any bearing on the soundness of an *argument.*

INVERSE AD HOMINEM

There is a flip side to the ad hominem fallacy. Instead of *attacking* the source of an argument and then claiming that the argument is weak (as in the ad hominem fallacy), one may *praise* the source of an argument and then claim (fallaciously) that the argument is therefore strong: We'll call that the "inverse ad hominem fallacy."[11] Inverse ad hominem is not as common as ad hominem—which is sort of depressing, when you think about it, since it suggests that people give more insults than compliments.

Just as *flaws* in an argument's source do not count *against* the argument, also *virtues* in an argument's source do not count in *favor* of the argument. For example, "It took a lot of courage for Senator Blowhard to attend the meeting of the National Organization of Women and argue *against* the Equal Rights Amendment. So there must be some substance in his arguments against the ERA, since he's so courageous in presenting them." Such courage is indeed rare and wonderful, especially in an era when politicians tend to tailor their speeches to fit the tastes of their particular audience. But while we may applaud the senator's courage, that courage scores no points for his argument, which must stand or fall independently of the arguer's virtues or vices. Of course if no arguments are at stake, then simply saying something nice about someone—"Horace is the kindest person I've ever known," "Claudia is a whiz at calculus"—is certainly *not* committing the inverse ad hominem fallacy. And if someone is giving *testimony* (rather than argument), then "inverse ad hominem" support *is* relevant: Knowing that the witness (the testifier) is highly principled, profoundly truthful, psychologically sound, and completely unbiased is certainly useful when evaluating *testimony.*

Think of inverse ad hominem as the happier twin of ad hominem: It is a fallacy when ad hominem is a fallacy (when it is directed at *arguers*); and it is legitimate when ad hominem is legitimate (when evaluating testimony, deciding who to vote for, selecting the best person for a job, choosing a dentist, and determining what professor to take for cell biology).

In sum, an ad hominem attack on the source of an *argument* commits the ad hominem fallacy. *Inverse* ad hominem *support* of the source of an argument (this argument is good because its source is good) commits the inverse ad hominem fallacy. And just as ad hominem attacks are often useful and legitimate (this witness is biased, this politician is a fraud, this advertiser is a liar, this card player is a cheat, this teacher is a bore, this guy is a pig), so likewise *inverse* ad hominem praise is often valuable and *non*fallacious (this person is a good credit risk, this student is well qualified for your graduate school, this candidate is sincere and high-principled, this witness is honest and reliable and sober, this surgeon is splendid).

Samuel Johnson used a particularly apt metaphor to capture the important difference between argument and testimony. Engrave it on your memory, and you will avoid forever the traps and snares of the ad hominem and inverse ad hominem fallacies:

> Argument is argument. You cannot help paying regard to their arguments, if they are good. If it were testimony you might disregard it. Testimony is like an arrow shot from a long bow; the force of it depends on the strength of the hand that draws it. Argument is like an arrow from a cross-bow, which has equal force though shot by a child.[12]

Attacking Arguments

One word of caution in dealing with ad hominem arguments. Suppose that I give an *argument* for capital punishment. If you attack the source of the argument in an effort to discredit my argument, you have committed the ad hominem fallacy: it doesn't matter how vile or cold-hearted or irrational or self-serving the *arguer* is, you still have to consider the quality of the *argument*. But if you attack my *argument* (and not the person giving the argument), then that is *not* ad hominem fallacy, and it is not a legitimate ad hominem argument: it is not ad hominem at all. If I give an argument, it is perfectly legitimate to train all your guns on that *argument*. You can note that my argument makes a logical error, or that its premises are false, or that its premises are irrelevant to its conclusion. *Arguments* are a fair target; *arguers* are not. The main purpose of this book is to help you recognize and construct *good* arguments, and recognize and *destroy* bad arguments. So an attack on an argument is neither fallacious nor legitimate ad hominem, simply because it is *not* an ad hominem argument. Your criticism of an *argument* may succeed or fail, but so long as you are not attacking the *source* of an argument, you are *not* committing the ad hominem fallacy. So by all means, search out and destroy bad *arguments;* but leave the *arguer* out of it. Don't attack the person giving the argument; likewise, when someone criticizes one of your *arguments*, don't take it as a personal insult: An attack on your argument is not an attack on you.

Exercise 3-2

Some of the following examples are ad hominem arguments, some are inverse ad hominem arguments, and some are *neither*. For each example, first decide whether it is ad hominem, inverse ad hominem, or neither; if it is ad hominem or inverse ad hominem, determine whether it is a *fallacy*, and explain why it is or is not fallacious.

1. Ladies and gentlemen of the jury, the district attorney has argued that you should find the defendant *guilty* of burglary. But ask yourself what evidence there is that the defendant is guilty. The prosecution's whole case rests squarely on the claims made by one witness, Jack Jefferson. Jefferson claims that he saw the defendant enter the house holding an empty bag and later leave the house with the bag filled with silver and jewelry. But what about this Jack Jefferson? He admitted that he himself has participated in burglaries to support his drug habit, that he lied under oath in his own trial just 3 months ago, and that he is now cooperating with the district attorney in hopes of getting early work release from prison. I think you must conclude that the testimony of a man like Jack Jefferson cannot be certain beyond a reasonable doubt, and therefore I believe you must return a verdict of not guilty.

2. The following is a letter to the editor of the *Greensboro Daily News*.

> To the Editor:
> I have seen a lot of ludicrous positions taken by the press, but nothing like your November 21 editorial against tobacco cultivation. I must take a moment to highlight your ridiculous position.
> Your editorial suggests that North Carolina farmers should begin to produce more diverse crops because of your belief in the inevitable decline of tobacco, the "harmful product" which they grow. In short, you argue they should get away from producing and depending on revenue that comes from products which you think are harmful.
> Your editorial staff must not read too much of your paper. On this same day, two pages over, you ran a full-page advertisement for a cigarette brand. In fact, you run many ads for cigarettes. I checked your advertising rates and you make a lot of money from these ads! If your opinions are "a matter of principle," then consider how ridiculous you appear publishing principles that your paper does not live up to.[13]

3. The district attorney argued that the defendant, Sarah Sartoris, must have been the murderer because she was seen near the victim's house on the night of the murder and she had a motive for killing him. But that's certainly a weak argument. After all, Sarah had a perfectly good reason for being near the victim's house on the night of the murder: The grocery store where she shops is on that street. And besides, the victim was quite wealthy, and many people had a motive for killing him. So you should certainly not accept the district attorney's argument.

4. Ralph Rivet argues that we should simplify the federal tax code. Ralph argues that the complicated deductions and exemptions are unfair to most Americans, since only those who can afford to hire an accountant are aware of them and can benefit from them. He also argues that they lead investors to focus on avoiding taxes, rather than on investing their capital in developing solid, worthwhile, profitable industries that would provide good jobs. And Ralph, it so happens, is a highly paid tax accountant. Obviously if the federal tax code were simplified Ralph would lose a lot of the money he now makes by preparing tax returns. Yet he still argues for tax simplification! Since he certainly is not arguing just for his own narrow self-interest, we must consider his arguments to be especially powerful and convincing.

5. If you haven't quite decided who to vote for in the school board race, let me make a suggestion: Vote for Martha Manning. Before her retirement 2 years ago, she was a public school teacher for more than 30 years, including 10 years in this community and before that 20 years in public schools in Pennsylvania. So she has long and varied experience in the public schools, and she knows what is needed for good public education. Also, she is committed to keeping our schools modern and effective: Just last year, she took three courses in computer education at a state university, so that she would better understand how to effectively bring computers into the classroom. And finally, she is profoundly dedicated to providing the best education for our children: She has no further political ambitions, and no agenda other than helping our children get the best education possible. While she was a public school teacher, she was named Teacher of the Year in Pennsylvania, and was a finalist for that award while she was teaching in Ohio. When she was teaching in this community, she often took money out of her own pocket to buy supplies for her classroom. She is dedicated, progressive, experienced, and committed to good education for our children, and I think she would make a great school board member.

6. Dr. Andrews argues that abortion should be legal and unrestricted and that each woman has the right to make such difficult and intimate decisions for herself, with the aid of her own conscience and through consideration of her own moral principles and in light of her own personal situation and beliefs. But before you are persuaded by Dr. Andrews's arguments, here is something you should know: Dr. Andrews is currently conducting a massive, heavily funded research project on medical use of fetal tissue. If abortions are restricted, then it will become impossible for him to obtain the fetal tissue for his research, and he will lose his funding! When you take into consideration Dr. Andrews's special reasons for wanting abortion to remain legal and unrestricted, his arguments do not sound nearly so strong.

7. Senator Slidell argues that we should have a national sales tax of one cent for every dollar of purchases, as a means of eliminating the budget deficit. Senator Slidell argues that such a sales tax is fair to all and would raise an enormous sum of tax money and would thus eliminate the budget deficit. But in fact a sales tax is not fair: It falls heavily on the poor, who can least afford it. And besides, it would probably slow down the economy and thus would not actually raise much, if any, additional tax revenue. So when we carefully examine Senator Slidell's argument for a sales tax, we find that it is not very convincing.

8. Look, I know some of you jurors were impressed by the closing arguments of Mary Lanier, the attorney for the defense. She argued that the prosecution case was built on speculation and that there was insufficient evidence that the defendant *knew* he was transporting illegal drugs when he was arrested for hauling a bag of marijuana in the back of his truck. I admit, her argument that the defendant was an innocent dupe of drug dealers—and that he did not know that the truck he was driving was carrying marijuana—sounded pretty plausible. But before you are persuaded by her arguments, consider this: She has made a career—a very profitable career—out of defending people accused of selling drugs, and she is being paid a *very* generous fee for her work on this case. I don't think we should be impressed by the arguments of a person like that.

9. Professor Lee argues that tuition at Home State University is too high. She says that the university is spending too much money on fountains, brick sidewalks, and flowers and faculty salaries and that, if those expenditures were reduced to a more reasonable level, tuition fees could be reduced without any sacrifice in educational quality. And there is something special you should note about that argument: Professor Lee is arguing for reduced tuition even though that would mean reduced faculty salaries, and thus a reduction in her own pay! Only a person with strong principles would argue that her own pay should be reduced! Obviously, then, we must accept her conclusion that tuition is too high.

10. On April 14, 1992, Rush Limbaugh (a radio talk show host) discussed the issue of animal rights. In the course of the discussion, Limbaugh described—and rejected—the arguments put forward by the son of a wealthy Illinois cattleman. This young man argued that raising beef animals for food imposes suffering on the animals, wastes grain, and contributes to pollution, and that since we do not require beef to live—in fact, we would be healthier without it—the factory farming of beef animals is wrong. In response, Limbaugh asserted that this was a classic case of liberal guilt: The young man had become wealthy as a result of his father's beef-farming operation, and the young man had himself done no work for this wealth; so now he must attack his father and the source of his wealth in order to assuage his guilt for enjoying wealth he did not earn and in order to establish his independence from his father.

11. The tobacco companies claim that they are genuinely committed to stopping underage smoking. They say that if they are left alone, they will voluntarily act to stop minors from getting tobacco products, and they will make sure that none of their advertising is aimed at children. But you shouldn't believe their claims. Their only motive is to put up a smoke screen so that there are no real regulations imposed that would effectively limit underage smoking. After all, they have long claimed that they do not attempt to attract underage smokers—but their actions speak louder than their words. They have purposefully used advertising images of attractive, popular, and athletic young people smoking in order to attract younger smokers; and they have heavily invested in sports events attended by younger people—the Winston Cup racing series, the Virginia Slims tennis tournaments—in order to associate sports and tobacco in the minds of youths. Furthermore, they have used cartoon images—such as Joe Camel—that obviously have great appeal for the young. Given their long history of trying to make cigarettes and "smokeless tobacco" appealing to young people, combined with their powerful motive to hook a new generation of young smokers to replace the ones who are dying (many of them from the effects of tobacco), there is absolutely no reason to believe their current claims that they are committed to stopping underage use of tobacco.

12. You say that you are opposed to guaranteed health care for every U.S. citizen. But if you think about it carefully, perhaps you will change your mind. After all, you have a deep commitment to equal opportunity: You believe that all people should have the opportunity to make the most of their lives and go as far as they can go. That's why you are such a strong defender of our public schools. Just yesterday you were telling me that there is nothing more important than good, sound public schools, and that every child should have a fair opportunity to get a good education, because without that guarantee of good educational opportunity there can be no real equality of opportunity. As a believer in fair opportunity, you should also embrace universal health care. After all, nobody has a decent opportunity to achieve success if they can't get decent health care. Inadequate health care is just as great a barrier to opportunity as is an inadequate education. So as a strong believer in equal opportunity for all our citizens, you should also be a supporter of universal health care.

13. Betty Hill claimed that in 1961 she was abducted by a UFO. Hers is perhaps the most famous UFO case on record. A best-selling book (*The Interrupted Journey*, by John G. Fuller) was written about it, and in 1975 NBC ran a movie about it (*The UFO Incident*). Mrs. Hill is now retired and spends her time giving UFO lectures and observing UFOs at a landing spot she claims to have discovered in New Hampshire. *The Skeptical Inquirer* recently gave the following account of Mrs. Hill's current activities:

> Mrs. Hill claims that the UFOs come in to land several times a week; they have become such a familiar sight that she is now calling them by name. Sometimes the aliens get out and do calisthenics before taking off again, she asserts. One UFO reportedly zapped a beam at her that was so powerful that it

"blistered the paint on my car." Mrs. Hill also reports that window-peeping flying saucers sometimes fly from house to house late at night in New England, shine lights in the windows, and then move on when the occupants wake up and turn on the lights. Recently John Oswald, of Dr. J. Allen Hynek's Center for UFO Studies, accompanied Mrs. Hill on her thrice-weekly UFO vigil. Oswald, who is certainly no UFO debunker, reported: "Obviously Mrs. Hill isn't seeing eight UFOs a night. She is seeing things that are not UFOs and calling them UFOs." Mr. Oswald reports that during the vigil of April 15, 1977, Mrs. Hill was unable to "distinguish between a landed UFO and a streetlight."[14]

14. Andrew argues that abortion should not be legal, because it weakens respect for life, and thus weakens the entire weave and structure of our system of basic values. Andrew maintains that uncompromising respect for human life is the vital center of all our ethical commitments, and weakening this center will weaken the entire structure. But then, Andrew is a man, and he never has to worry about becoming pregnant; so his arguments against abortion are irrelevant.

15. Jesse Ventura, a former professional wrestler who became governor of Minnesota, returned to the wrestling ring as a referee for a highly promoted professional wrestling show. One of Minnesota's major newspapers, the *St. Paul Pioneer Press*, criticized the governor's actions, saying that he was setting a bad example for the children of the state by participating in a professional wrestling show that promotes staged violence and sexual exploitation (scantily clad young women being a major part of the pro wrestling spectacle).

16. In response to the criticisms of the *St. Paul Pioneer Press* (noted in the previous example), Governor Ventura accused the newspaper of being hypocritical, since they run advertisements for X-rated movies and for strip clubs. Calling the newspaper the "St. Paul Pioneer Porn," Governor Ventura said that

> The *St. Paul Pioneer Press* is triple-X. They are lining their pockets with pornography. They are working together with the X-rated industry. (August 29, 1999)

17. Fellow members of the Pleasant Valley Town Council, we must decide today whether to fire our police chief, Larry Lucas. As you know, it was recently discovered that after attending a law enforcement training course in New Orleans, Chief Lucas stayed an extra day and charged the cost of his hotel room to his expense account. No one objects to the chief spending an extra day in New Orleans, but of course he must pay for it out of his own pocket, and not out of the budget of the town police department. Whether an intentional or accidental misuse of department funds, this is a serious mistake, and one that we cannot tolerate in our town's chief of police. Thus I believe we must fire Chief Lucas. Now, earlier you heard Council Member Zack Zuriff argue that Chief Lucas should not be fired. Zack argued that Chief Lucas has been a good and honest police chief for 12 years, and that this mistake in filling out his expense account was merely an accounting error and not an intentional wrong, that Chief Lucas immediately reimbursed the department for the cost of the hotel room as soon as he recognized his error, and that such a small mistake does not justify the dismissal of a person with such a long and outstanding record. But I'm afraid we can't give much weight to Zack's argument for keeping the chief. After all, Zack and Chief Lucas have been friends since their high school days, and Zack is obviously offering his argument out of loyalty to his friend. Certainly it is heartwarming to see a friend like Zack stick by his comrade through adversity. Such loyalty is rare and wonderful. However, once we recognize that Zack's argument is merely the support of a loyal friend, it is clear that we should not take it seriously.

18. Alice Wykowski argues that the United States should not impose trade restrictions on China because of human rights violations by the Chinese government. She argues that reducing trade with China will only isolate China, and lead to even more restrictions on human rights; but through trade, China's people, culture, and economy will be exposed to wider influences, including the influences of respect for basic human rights. However, you should realize that Alice owns a toy importing business, and almost all of her imports are from China! And so trade restrictions against China could take money out of her pocket, while fewer trade restrictions might mean more money for Alice's import company. Her argument for more trade with China may sound good at first, but Alice's argument loses its force when you realize that more trade with China means more money for Alice.

19. Look, I know you are planning to have open-heart bypass surgery to correct your heart problems. That's fine. But I heard your surgery is scheduled with Dr. Pangloss, and that's terrible. Dr. Pangloss has been suspended from practice by the Pennsylvania Board of Medicine for botching several operations while under the influence of alcohol: that's why he moved here to Cleveland. And the Ohio Board is currently reviewing his license because of charges that he caused the death of a surgical patient through gross recklessness. And I know two people in Cleveland who sued Dr. Pangloss for

malpractice, and they both received large settlements from his insurance company. And he has had his hospital privileges revoked by at least three area hospitals, reportedly for making his hospital rounds while intoxicated. In addition, his driver's license has been permanently suspended for driving under the influence. So if you want a clumsy, reckless surgeon with a severe drinking problem cutting on your heart, then stay with Dr. Pangloss. But I strongly recommend you to find another surgeon, and stay as far away from Dr. Pangloss as you can.

20.
  JOE: We should stop providing food stamps, welfare payments, and Medicaid to the impoverished. Such payments make those who receive them dependent, and weakens their desire to do productive work, and thus traps the recipients in a cycle of poverty. So those payments actually, in the long run, harm those people who receive them.
  MOE: That argument is just an excuse for not wanting to help those who are in poverty; such an argument is merely an attempt to excuse your own callousness and lack of concern for those who are less fortunate than you.

21. Adam Forge claims to have miraculous psychic powers. He claims that he has actually made metal objects—such as spoons—bend through psychic power, and without touching them; and he claims that he can make objects move from one place to another through his special psychic forces. But Adam Forge has actually been videotaped bending spoons with his hands, and then claiming that he never touched them. He makes a lot of money by claiming to be a psychic; but whenever he is tested scientifically, he can't do the things he claims to be able to do, and he resorts to trickery. So Adam Forge is a liar and a fraud—and I see no good reason to believe any of his claims that he has performed psychic miracles and possesses psychic powers.

22.   PEOPLE WHO LIVE IN GLASS DAY-CARE CENTERS

Agnes Love, the leading opponent of higher state standards for day-care centers, has a secret.

In numerous public hearings and committee meetings at the [North Carolina] General Assembly, Love has argued against tighter regulations because she said they would price day-care services out of the reach of many parents—and would force some day-care centers to close.

But, according to documents on file at the N.C. Office of Day Care Licensing, Love's own day-care center has trouble meeting the current state standards. Her Love and Care Nursery and Kindergarten in Charlotte was issued a "disapproved" sanitation report in February because of continued improper sterilization of dishes.

Over the past 2 years, compliance officers have found repeated violations of the state's sanitation standards at Love's center. And in December 1983, inspectors discovered only one staff member present for 27 children, rather than the required three.[15]

23. Ladies and gentlemen of the jury, as you consider this case, weigh carefully the sworn testimony of Amanda Popovich. Ms. Popovich testified, under oath, that she saw the defendant at a restaurant at the very time that he is accused of robbing a liquor store on the other side of the city. Ms. Popovich is a reliable, sober citizen, with an unblemished record of honesty. Her eyesight is perfect, she is not delusional, and she has long held a responsible position as a second-grade teacher at Western Elementary, where she was selected Teacher of the Year just last year. She has no motive for lying, since she is not a friend of the defendant. She is testifying for one purpose only: to see that justice is done and that an innocent man is not wrongfully convicted. Her sworn testimony is powerful evidence that the defendant is an innocent victim of mistaken identity, and I ask that you consider the honest testimony of this good and trustworthy woman and return a verdict of not guilty.

24. Bruce says that he is willing to sell his Beanie Baby collection for a bargain price. He says that his entire collection is made up of original, authentic Beanie Babies, and he guarantees that every one of them is authentic and genuine, bought directly from the manufacturer. He claims that he has to raise money quickly to pay for his mother's surgery, and so he is going to sell his Beanie Babies for a special low price. Well, you can buy Beanie Babies from Bruce if you want to, but there are a couple of things you might want to know. First, his mother died over a decade ago, so I have some doubts about his story that he's trying to raise money for her surgery. And second, a couple of years ago he was offering to sell his baseball card collection, and he guaranteed that every card was authentic and original, and that the ballplayer signatures were genuine. But it turned out that he had made the cards himself using a photocopying machine, and that all the signatures were forged.

That time he was convicted of fraud, and he's still on probation for that baseball-card caper. So you might want to be a bit careful before buying Bruce's Beanie Babies.

25. We should select Wanda Willis as Teacher of the Year. She has been a tireless and dedicated classroom teacher, often staying long hours after school to consult with the parents of her students. She has developed innovative teaching techniques for helping children learn mathematics quickly and easily. And her enthusiasm for teaching makes her classroom a warm and happy place for her students. So I say, Wanda Willis should be our Teacher of the Year.

26. Senator Forge recently argued that there should *not* be restrictions on the sale of guns at gun shows. He argues that those who sell guns at such shows are usually small dealers, who sell only a few guns, and that they don't have the means or resources to carry out background checks on buyers. Furthermore, since the shows only last a day or so, a waiting period is not really workable. But Senator Forge is heavily funded by the National Rifle Association, and they give massive support to his election campaigns. In fact, Senator Forge is just a puppet of the NRA, and when they fill his pockets and pull his strings, out comes the argument against gun control. So in the debate over gun control, we should pay no attention to Senator Forge's arguments: They are bought and paid for by the National Rifle Association.

27. You should certainly accept Donna as a student at Home State University Law School. Donna is a person of the highest principle, with a profound commitment to honesty. She is also a brilliant student and a very hard worker. She will be an excellent law student and a wonderful attorney.

✓●⎯ **Study** and **Review** on **mythinkinglab.com**

REVIEW QUESTIONS

1. What is the ad hominem fallacy?
2. When is an ad hominem argument not an ad hominem fallacy?
3. What is inverse ad hominem? When is it a fallacy?

NOTES

[1] *The Criminal Law* by F. T. Giles (Pelican Books, 1954; 2nd ed., 1961; 3rd ed., 1963; 4th ed., 1967), p. 51, Copyright © F. T. Giles, 1954, 1961, 1963, 1967. Reproduced by permission of Penguin Books.

[2] Information from a column by Lenore Skenazy, columnist for the *New York Daily News*, printed October 29, 2002.

[3] Paul Bergman, *Trial Advocacy* (St. Paul, MN: West, 1979), pp. 323–324.

[4] Richard Du Cann, *The Art of the Advocate* (Hammondsworth, Middlesex, UK: Penguin Books, 1964), p. 40.

[5] John Wesley Noble and Bernard Averbuch, *Never Plead Guilty* (New York: Bantam Books, 1955), p. 58.

[6] Example based on information in "The Secret History of Lead," by Jamie Lincoln Kitman, in *The Nation*, March 20, 2000, p. 34.

[7] F. Lee Bailey and Harvey Aronson, *The Defense Never Rests* (New York: The New American Library, 1971), p. 40.

[8] Irving Stone, *Clarence Darrow for the Defense* (New York: Doubleday and Company, 1941), p. 465.

[9] Henry Lauren Clinton, *Celebrated Trials* (New York: Harper and Brothers, 1897), p. 149.

[10] This kind of argument is sometimes called circumstantial ad hominem; and some textbooks treat it as fallacious. But far from being fallacious, it is a central and legitimate part of careful critical argumentation: determining what views the argument participants hold, and perhaps agree on, and then attempting to work from there to a conclusion that they both accept.

[11] In past editions, I have called this the "good intentions" form of argument; but "inverse ad hominem" makes clearer the nature of the argument. There does not seem to be a standard name for this argument form. Douglas Walton suggests it might be called a "negative ethotic argument" (*Ad Hominem Arguments*, 1998, p. 213), but "inverse ad hominem" seems easier to remember and more descriptive.

[12] Samuel Johnson, *Life*, May 19, 1784.

[13] *Greensboro Daily News*.

[14] "Psychic Vibrations," *The Skeptical Inquirer*, Vol. 3, no. 1 (Fall 1978), p. 14.

[15] *The North Carolina Independent*, March 15–28, 1985, p. 2.

INTERNET RESOURCES

The Internet Encyclopedia of Philosophy contains an excellent article by Bradley Dowden, "Fallacies," that not only discusses almost every fallacy ever imagined, but also links to additional essays on most of them. You can find a discussion of ad hominem, as well as any other argument form discussed in this book. Go to *www.iep/utm.edu/fallacy*.

ADDITIONAL READING

Testimony: A Philosophical Study, by C. A. J. Coady (Tony) (Oxford, UK: Oxford University Press, 1992), is a comprehensive examination of testimony, including but not limited to courtroom testimony. And Douglas Walton's

Ad Hominem Arguments (Tuscaloosa, AL: University of Alabama Press, 1998) is a very thorough and careful study of ad hominem arguments, both fallacious and legitimate.

▯▮─Read the Document on mythinkinglab.com

Bruce N. Waller, "Ad Hominem Arguments," *Coffee and Philosophy,* pp. 4–6. This dialogue discusses both legitimate and fallacious uses of ad hominem arguments.

Manitoba Justice, "Jailhouse Informants," *The Inquiry Regarding Thomas Sophonow.* Thomas Sophonow spent four years in prison after he was wrongfully convicted of the brutal murder of a young woman who was working in a Winnipeg doughnut shop. After it became clear that Sophonow was innocent of the crime for which he had been imprisoned, the Justice Department of the province of Manitoba carried out an extensive investigation into why this miscarriage of justice had occurred, and how such mistakes could be prevented in the future. The inquiry found that one of the key factors in this wrongful conviction was reliance on the false testimony of "jailhouse informants" (e.g., jailed inmates who offer to testify against other prisoners in exchange for such benefits as reduced charges, reduced sentences, or better treatment during their term of imprisonment). Several sections of *The Inquiry Regarding Thomas Sophonow* describe the character of some of the jailhouse informants who provided false testimony that helped convict Sophonow, and also describe in general terms the problems with relying on jailhouse informants. The ad hominem attacks on the character and reliability of such jailhouse informants

are relevant and legitimate, and do *not* commit the ad hominem *fallacy.*

Report of the Kaufman Commission on Proceedings Involving Guy Paul Morin, Chapter 3, sections A–D, "Jailhouse Informants" (Ontario Ministry of the Attorney General). Another notorious case of wrongful conviction was the case of Guy Paul Morin, who spent eight years imprisoned in Canada's only "supermax" prison for the rape and murder of an eight-year-old girl who had been his next-door neighbor. The wrongful conviction of Morin—which involved police misconduct, serious mistakes in the crime lab investigations, and perjured testimony by jailhouse informants—was profoundly disturbing to Canadian citizens, and it resulted in an extensive investigation and report by a commission headed by Fred Kaufman, a former judge of the Quebec Court of Appeal. As in the *Sophonow* case, the Kaufman Commission found that the use of jailhouse informants played a major part in this wrongful conviction. The extensive examination of the jailhouse informants and their testimony—and the deals they received in exchange for their testimony—is chilling (and it led to strong restrictions on the use of jailhouse informants in Canadian courts); as in the *Sophonow* case, the ad hominem attacks on the jailhouse informants who aided in the wrongful conviction of Paul Morin are a legitimate use of ad hominem argument.

4

❖ ❖ ❖

The Second Deadly Fallacy:
The Strawman Fallacy

((•—Listen to the Chapter Audio on mythinkinglab.com

The ad hominem fallacy poisons critical thinking: when *argument* descends to the level of personal abuse, *productive* argument ceases. If the argumentative process is supposed to proceed cooperatively, then it is obvious that personal attacks poison the cooperative atmosphere. If instead the argument is conducted along adversarial lines, the character of the adversarial advocates is irrelevant to the quality of their arguments: a lecherous scoundrel may give excellent arguments, while the arguments of a paragon of virtue may be lousy. When ad hominem attacks focus on the character of the *arguers*, they distract from careful consideration of the quality of their *arguments*; and that is why—in forums in which adversarial argument is supposed to be carried on in pursuit of *truth*, such as in philosophical and scientific and legal debate—personal ad hominem attacks are regarded with contempt, and elaborate personal courtesy is the rule.

So the ad hominem fallacy—the fallacy of attacking the *source* of an *argument*—is the fallacy that is most destructive of productive critical thinking, whether adversarial or cooperative. But there is a second fallacy that is almost as bad: the *strawman* fallacy. That is the fallacy of *distorting* or *misrepresenting* someone's position or argument in order to make it easier to attack. It is a fallacy that is very common in political argument, which is probably why political argument so often produces much more heat than light. But wherever the strawman fallacy occurs, whether in cooperative or adversarial contexts, it undermines the critical thinking process. The first step in effective critical thinking is being clear on exactly what is at issue; and the strawman fallacy cripples that essential first step by painting a false picture of what is under discussion. Suppose that we are concerned about the federal budget deficit, and arguing about the best way to reduce the deficit. You maintain that we should make careful reductions in spending, while I favor a modest increase in taxes. If you represent my view as a push for much higher taxes on the middle class, while I claim that you want to cut all health-care funding for the elderly, then both of us can score cheap shots against our strawman opponents, but we can't even begin to have an intelligent discussion or debate—neither adversarial nor cooperative—about the real issue and what policy works best.

Scoring Political Points with Strawman Fallacies

In late December 2009, Umar Farouk Abdulmutallab was arrested and charged with attempting to blow up a Northwest Airlines plane that was flying into the United States, using explosives he had concealed in his underwear. The suspect was read his rights and offered a lawyer (as required by law for anyone arrested in the United States). A few days later, former Vice-President Dick Cheney made this statement about President Obama's position on dealing with suspected terrorists:

> He [Obama] seems to think if he gives terrorists the rights of Americans, lets them lawyer up and reads them their Miranda rights, we won't be at war. He seems to think if we bring the mastermind of 9/11 to New York, give him a lawyer and a trial in a civilian court, we won't be at war. He seems to think that if he closes Guantanamo and releases the hard-core al Quaeda-trained terrorists still there, we won't be at war.

But Obama's decision to follow the law requiring that those arrested in the United States be told of their *Miranda* rights and offered a lawyer does not mean that he believes that will end all terrorist attacks. The question of whether to try terrorist suspects in military or civilian courts is a serious one, that deserves serious thoughtful debate and discussion; but such serious discussion is impossible, if one side paints a strawman picture of the other view, claiming that those who favor a civilian rather than a military court are claiming that having civilian trials would end the threat of terrorism. Should we close the Guantanamo Prison, where many suspected terrorists have been held? That's a serious question: Some people argue that it provides an especially safe place to hold those who might engage in terrorist attacks on the United States; others believe that it has become a symbol of U.S. mistreatment of terrorist suspects, and has become a rallying point for recruiting those who wish to attack the United States, and that any genuine terrorists still held there could be safely held in maximum security prisons in the United States. But *no* one proposes that we release any "hard-core al Quaeda trained terrorists," and that distortion of the issue blocks the possibility of intelligent critical examination of the real question.

In an adversarial approach, strawman arguments score cheap points, and perhaps they improve ratings on talk radio shows; but strawman arguments will not convince anyone to *change* his or her views: after all, if we are engaged in an adversarial argument, you *know* what your own position is, and I'm not likely to convince you to change your position by attributing to you a view you don't hold or an argument you didn't offer. In cooperative critical thinking, the strawman fallacy is even more destructive. If you and I are deliberating together with the goal of finding a policy or developing a program that will best meet all our interests, then if I start by distorting or misrepresenting your goals and concerns you will not find me a productive partner for cooperative deliberation. The key to effective critical thinking—whether adversarial or cooperative—is being very clear on what's at issue. Strawman fallacies cripple that essential first step.

STRAW MAN

When someone is criticizing an opponent's argument or position, it is crucial to be sure that the critic is *accurately* representing her opponent's views. And this point is especially important when *we* are the critics in question. When we are confronted by a position in conflict with our own (or an argument against a position we favor), it is sorely tempting to consider that opposing position or argument in its *weakest* possible form. That makes the argument easy to dismiss, and it saves us the effort of careful critical thinking. But tempting as that approach may be, it is obviously not the path to clear thinking. And tempting as it may be to distort your opponent's argument to try to achieve a cheap victory, it is certainly fallacious to do so.

It is much easier to win a fight with a straw man than with a real man. And it is much easier to attack a weak substitute for an argument or position than the genuine article. That's why the strawman fallacy is so seductive. The *strawman* fallacy consists of distorting, and thus weakening, an opponent's arguments or views and then attacking the weaker position rather than the real one.[1]

The Principle of Charity

Instead of attempting to find the weakest version of an argument, we should do exactly the opposite: seek the strongest possible version of whatever argument or theory is being considered. If there are alternative possible interpretations of an argument, consider the *strongest* one. If there are different versions of a position, consider the most plausible one. If the language of an argument is open to several interpretations, select the interpretation that makes the argument most reasonable. In short, follow the *principle of charity* when analyzing arguments: Interpret opposing arguments as generously, as charitably, as is possible. By always giving the benefit of the doubt to whatever arguments, theories, or positions you are considering, you will have to think a good deal harder, but you will also think more carefully and be more open to promising new ideas.

If you wish to be comfortably mired in dogma and error, then the strawman fallacy is an effective weapon for you—both against your opponents' arguments and against your own doubts and questions. But if instead you wish to expand your thoughts, critically evaluate the positions you hold, and honestly examine competing views and new proposals, then the principle of charity will be invaluable.

The Strawman Fallacy

It is important that we avoid the strawman fallacy when examining arguments, and it is also important that we not be misled when others commit the strawman fallacy in their argument critiques. When you are considering a *critique* of an argument, a position, or a theory, ask yourself the following questions: Is that an accurate statement of that argument or position? Was that actually what the arguer was arguing? Were those the reasons given for the conclusion? And in particular: Is that an accurate statement of the *conclusion* of the argument?

Many strawman arguments are heavy-handed and obvious. Television evangelist Pat Robertson mailed a fundraising letter that attacked the advocates of the Equal Rights Amendment. He asserted that supporters of the Equal Rights Amendment are not really after equal rights for women: Their actual goal is to destroy the family and encourage women to leave their husbands, kill their children, destroy capitalism, become lesbians, and practice witchcraft. Certainly it is easier to argue against killing children than against the Equal Rights Amendment, but this is such an obvious and absurd distortion that it would be amusing, were it not so vicious. Slightly more subtle is William F. Buckley's distortion of the arguments of those who favor a ban on handguns:

> Now the anti-handgun fundamentalists will tell you that the mere presence of a loaded pistol means that Mr. Finnegan is going to get drunk and shoot Mrs. Finnegan. Or that when Miss Finnegan sneaks in to pay a surprise visit to her mother and father, suddenly she will be dead, taken for an intruder. Or that the Finnegan grandchild, age 6 will one day play with the pistol, it will go off, and there will be tragedy. (July 22, 1982, Universal Press Syndicate)

But of course the "anti-handgun fundamentalists" offer no such ridiculous arguments. They claim instead that the presence of a loaded pistol does increase the *likelihood* of a domestic squabble escalating into a domestic homicide, of a contemplated suicide becoming a successful suicide, of a child being killed while playing with a loaded handgun. But those accurate and depressing facts are much more difficult to ridicule than the strawman argument that Buckley attributes to his opponents. Or again, those who oppose decriminalization of drugs sometimes suggest that the proponents of decriminalization want to make drugs easily and readily available, like candy at the supermarket checkout counter. Perhaps there is someone somewhere who advocates such open and easy availability of hard drugs, but that is not the position of most of the advocates of decriminalization. They want, instead, something like an improved and expanded system of treatment clinics, or perhaps a system in which addicts must register with the government and obtain drugs from a physician, or decriminalization (with strict regulation) of marijuana. In a speech concerning new proposals for economic recovery and federal deficit reduction, President Barack Obama included these remarks: "From some on the right, I expect we'll hear a different argument—that if we must make fewer investments in our people, extend tax cuts for wealthier Americans, eliminate more regulations, and maintain the status quo on health care, our deficits will go away." But while most Republicans do seem to favor extending tax cuts for wealthier Americans, only a small fringe group want to eliminate more regulations (many do not want *additional* regulations, but few want to eliminate those that remain); and almost no one thinks it is a good idea to "maintain the status quo on health care"; and in any case, those "on the right" do not believe that such policies will cause "our deficits to go away"—to make that happen, they would be more inclined to make dramatic cuts in social programs. Conservative columnist Cal Thomas manages to pack several strawman distortions into a single sentence: "The pursuit of the radical homosexual agenda to win acceptance and special privileges for a chosen lifestyle is not consistent with the government's legitimate interest to 'promote the general welfare.' " But homosexuals are campaigning for the same rights against discrimination enjoyed by everyone else: the right not to be denied a job or housing because of sexual orientation, the right to be protected against threats and violence, the right to marry, the right to adopt: those can hardly be classified as "special privileges" when they are the common rights of citizens—rights which are often denied to homosexuals. And of course these are not special privileges being claimed by those with a "chosen lifestyle," since homosexuals no more *choose* their sexual orientation than do heterosexuals. (If you recall your "sexual awakening," did any part of it involve *choosing* whether you would be sexually attracted to Jack rather than to Jill?)

The Equal Rights Amendment, gun control, deficit reduction, and drug legalization/decriminalization are important issues, worthy of debate in a democratic society. But they should be debated honestly, without the distortions of the strawman fallacy.

The strawman examples mentioned above are rather obvious. Unfortunately, the strawman fallacy often comes in more subtle and insidious forms. Consider Figure 4-1, an example from a Mobil Oil "Observations" column. What position is Mobil attacking? How does Mobil *portray* that position? Is it an *accurate* portrayal?

First, Mobil is attacking the view of those who favor increased use of "soft energy" (such as solar power, hydroelectric power, wind power, wood burning, and other renewable energy sources). What do people who favor increased use of soft energy actually want? As they are portrayed by this Mobil advertisement, they seem to hold some very weird views. They apparently want "to give every American family of four a 40-acre farm" (last paragraph); and they supposedly want to get *all* our energy from firewood (middle paragraph). This "back-to-nature" movement (as Mobil calls it) appears to include a bunch of crazies, and we are easily led to agree with the Mobil conclusion:

> [W]e're uneasy with people who insist it [soft energy] will do the whole job . . . and who then insist on foisting their dreams on the rest of us. Especially when their dreams can't stand up to reality.

But Mobil's argument is one long strawman fallacy. Of course it would be absurd to propose that every family live on a 40-acre farm; but the proponents of increased reliance on soft energy do *not* propose such a silly thing. To portray soft energy advocates as holding such a view is to distort their positions, and thus to commit the strawman fallacy. Again, there are people who believe that we should use more firewood—in heating homes, for example—and less nuclear power. But *no* one proposes that we rely completely and exclusively "on energy generated by firewood." (Have you *ever* heard *anyone* advocate using firewood to power cars, trucks, and buses, for example?) Mobil points out how absurd it would be to try to rely *entirely* on firewood for all our energy

Observations

American dream? For every family, a country place...a farm to grow fresh food...woodstoves to chase winter's chill...solar equipment...windmills... of course, no nukes. It's an appealing vision for <u>some</u>. But for <u>everybody</u>? No. It could bring a **nightmare** future of stripped forests, crowded wilderness, scenic pollution, and social changes few Americans are ready for. *Are you?*

Soft energy: hard facts. Solar energy—straight from the sun, indirectly from winds and water, or stored up in plants (like wood)—is the *"soft path"* that some prefer to *"hard"* technologies of oil, gas, coal, and nuclear power. We're excited about the <u>potential</u> of solar power, too, and we're working hard to make it <u>practical</u> with direct, efficient conversion of sunlight into electricity. But *"practical"* isn't *"perfect."* Matter of fact, *"the soft technologists' cure may be worse in some respects than the overcivilized disease,"* warns Roderick Nash, a University of California professor of history and environmental studies.

"It may be an environmentally sound alternative, but if the wind doesn't pick up, I'm taking the bus to Toledo."

Out of sites. Take windmills: *"Far more than a few picturesque structures surrounded by tulip beds"* would be needed to generate a meaningful amount of power, Prof. Nash says. To be effective, *"forests of the machines"* would have to be placed *"in exposed, highly visible locations such as ridge lines and the shores of oceans and lakes. If offshore oil rigs offend, can a much greater number of windmills be any better?"* What about using the sun for large-scale power generation? It would involve *"thousands of square miles of aluminum, glass, plastic, and fiberglass gleaming in the sunshine."* Wood? Prof. Nash's numbers again say no: If the eastern U.S. tried to live, *"even at a lower standard, on energy generated by firewood, (that) would mean the end within a few generations of the eastern forest."*

No nukes is bad news. Prof. Nash recalls *"the once wild and beautiful Glen Canyon"* in Utah. Now it's under a 186-mile-long lake behind Glen Canyon Dam. *"A single nuclear facility occupying less than a square mile would provide as much power,"* he notes. The nuke-dam choice is especially tough in the East, he adds, where wilderness is already dwindling.

Wrong for many. That's the <u>reality</u> of *"soft energy"*— massive, often unsightly projects. But the <u>dream</u> is appealing partly because it seems small-scale and spread out, like another fantasy of the back-to-nature movement—**do-it-yourself farming** for everybody. Yet to give every American family of four a 40-acre farm would take more land—including deserts and mountains—than there is in all of the lower 48 mainland states. And such a program would surely mean **goodbye, wilderness.** Besides, what about people who like cities, or suburbs—or isolation—rather than what Prof. Nash calls the *"constant ruralism"* in between? There may be a lot of good in *"soft energy"* to <u>supplement</u> conventional power. But we're uneasy with people who insist it will do the whole job...and who then insist on foisting their dreams on the rest of us. **Especially when their dreams can't stand up to reality.**

It's a fact: Mobil is working to develop a wide variety of energy resources for America: oil, gas, coal, uranium, synthetic fuels, and solar.

Mobil

Figure 4-1 Mobil Advertisement.

needs: "If the eastern U.S. tried to live, 'even at a lower standard, on energy generated by firewood, (that) would mean the end within a few generations of the eastern forest.' " And indeed that would be an absurd proposal. But that is *not* the proposal soft energy advocates actually make. The soft energy advocates propose that we use more solar power, more wind power, and more of other such renewable energy sources and that we make a greater effort to conserve energy (through stronger minimum mileage standards for passenger cars, for example) and thus reduce our use of nuclear power and petroleum. The views of the soft energy advocates may ultimately be implausible (or they may be workable), and certainly Mobil or anyone else should be free to criticize the soft energy position. But that position is more plausible, and more difficult to attack, than the distorted positions criticized by Mobil Oil. It's always easier to attack a straw man than the real thing.

Notice the last illustration in the Mobil argument: the scarecrow, stuffed with *straw.* I have no way of knowing, but I strongly suspect that some devious critical thinker recognized the strawman nature of the Mobil argument, and slipped that illustration into their advertisement as a prank. It would be nice if all strawman fallacies were marked by straw-filled scarecrows; unfortunately, most of the time you will have to pick out the strawman distortions for yourself. But that's the problem. How do you recognize strawman fallacies? How do you know that the position Mobil is criticizing is a distortion and exaggeration of the genuine views of soft energy advocates? Obviously it's not easy. You must know *something* about their position *before* you read the Mobil essay; otherwise, how will you know that the position being attacked is not the real position soft energy advocates take? And there's no easy way to accomplish that. It requires that you study the positions in question and that you not rely entirely on the *critics* of a position for your information. If an issue interests you, and you want to effectively evaluate the arguments on both sides, you must seek out the arguments and positions of both sides. If you want to know the pros and cons of soft energy use, do *not* rely on Mobil Oil. Look up the actual claims and arguments of those who advocate the increased use of soft energy sources. And to make things even more difficult, you must be sure you are reading the positions and arguments of those who *actually* promote alternative energy, and not the views of some industry front group that pretends to support alternative energy while actually opposing it and misrepresenting it. Such groups often pose as grassroots organizations, made up of citizens concerned about a specific issue, when in fact they are funded and run by industry groups or their public relations firms (such fake grassroots organizations have become so common that they are now known as "Astroturf" groups). For example, the Workplace Health & Safety Council sounds like a good place to get the position of those who favor improving workplace safety; it is actually a lobbying group funded by companies that wish to limit or block laws promoting workplace safety. The National Wetlands Coalition sounds like a good source for arguments in favor of protecting wetlands; but in fact it is a phony citizens group that is funded by oil and natural gas companies and developers that wish to take over wetlands for development and drilling.

Picking out strawman fallacies will be a little easier in the jury box, since you will have heard the arguments that are being criticized. For example, if the prosecution lawyer uses a strawman fallacy against the arguments of the defense lawyer (i.e., the prosecution distorts a defense argument in order to make it easier to attack), you will have *heard* that defense argument, and thus you will be in a good position to decide whether the prosecution is presenting it fairly and accurately. But that is not to say that, as a jury member, detecting strawman fallacies will be easy. Try your hand at the following case, taken from the retrial of Clarence Earl Gideon, accused of breaking and entering with the intent to commit petty larceny. Gideon had been convicted almost 2 years earlier on the same charges; during that trial Gideon—unable to afford an attorney—had asked for, and been denied, legal counsel. He appealed his conviction to the U.S. Supreme Court on the grounds that he had been denied counsel, and the Supreme Court heard his appeal and ruled that a defendant facing a felony charge has a right to counsel, and that counsel must be appointed for such a defendant if he or she cannot afford to hire a lawyer. Thus the Supreme Court overturned Gideon's conviction, and Gideon, now represented by a defense lawyer paid by the state, was retried. During that retrial the leading witness for the prosecution, who had testified to seeing Gideon inside the Bay Harbor Poolroom, was subjected to a severe cross-examination. He admitted to having been convicted of car theft and admitted other facts that cast doubt on key parts of his testimony; a possible interest he might have had in framing Gideon was brought out as well. During the cross-examination, and later in his summation to the jury, the defense attorney sketched a quite plausible scenario that involved the prosecution witness's breaking into the poolroom himself and then attempting to place the blame on Gideon. The prosecutor, in his final charge to the jury, attacked the defense argument with the assertions that "There's been no evidence that Cook [the prosecution witness] and his friends took this beer and wine [from the Bay City Poolroom],"[2] thus there is not enough evidence to prove that Cook committed the crime, and therefore Gideon should be found guilty of the crime.

But the prosecution's argument involves a subtle distortion of the defense argument. For the defense was *not* trying to prove that Cook committed the crime; instead, all the defense has to establish is that there is a *possibility* that someone other than Gideon committed the crime. (Remember, all that the *defense* has to establish is that guilt has *not* been proved; *not* that the defendant is innocent, certainly not that someone else committed the crime.) So presenting the defense case as if it were attempting to prove that Cook committed the crime (rather than attempting to establish merely the possibility that someone other than Gideon committed it) *misrepresents* the defense argument in a way that makes it easier to attack, and thus commits the strawman fallacy. (Incidentally, the jury voted to acquit Gideon.)

Supreme Court Straw Man

Even the U.S. Supreme Court is not immune to the charms of the strawman fallacy. In the 1986 case of *Bowers* (attorney general for the state of Georgia) *v. Hardwick*, Hardwick appealed his conviction under a Georgia statute that prohibited sodomy. Hardwick had been charged after a police raid discovered him engaged in homosexual conduct in the privacy of his own bedroom (apparently the police had broken into the house on a drug raid, but had somehow gotten mixed up and gone to the wrong house, and decided to charge Hardwick under the sodomy statute). Hardwick's attorney argued that Hardwick's right of privacy had been violated: that the U.S. Constitution protects the right of adults to engage in intimate, consensual, nonharmful behavior in the privacy of their own homes. Georgia's law against sodomy applied to both homosexuals and heterosexuals, and so—as Justice Blackmun noted—the defendant's claim that the Georgia law "involves an unconstitutional intrusion into his privacy and his right of intimate association does not depend in any way on his sexual orientation." The Supreme Court, by a 5 to 4 majority, upheld Hardwick's conviction on the grounds that the U.S. Constitution does not recognize a "constitutional right of homosexuals to engage in acts of sodomy": "The issue presented is whether the Federal Constitution confers a fundamental right upon homosexuals to engage in sodomy and hence invalidates the laws of the many States that still make such conduct illegal and have done so for a very long time." But as Justice Blackmun pointed out in his dissent, "the majority has distorted the question this case presents." Obviously the U.S. Constitution does not recognize a "constitutional right of homosexuals to engage in acts of sodomy"; but that's a strawman argument that misrepresents Hardwick's argument and thus makes it easier to attack. Hardwick's attorney had argued that there is a fundamental right of privacy, that includes the right of all persons to be free from government interference in their most private and intimate behavior. Or as Justice Blackmun states it: "The Court [majority] claims that its decision today merely refuses to recognize a fundamental right to engage in homosexual sodomy; what the Court really has refused to recognize is the fundamental interest all individuals have in controlling the nature of their intimate associations with others."[3] (In a striking reversal of that 1986 decision, in 2003 the Supreme Court forcefully agreed with Blackmun's 1986 dissent.)

Special Strawman Varieties

A few special varieties of the strawman fallacy deserve special note. First, one of the most effective and deceptive means of distorting a position is to find someone who holds an extreme or implausible version of that position and then treat that individual's version as if it were genuinely representative. For example, it might be possible to find *someone* who believes that every family in the United States should be given 40 acres of farmland and be required to live on that land and farm it; however, such a bizarre view is *not* favored by most advocates of increased use of soft energy, and to treat that position as if it is typical of the soft energy view is certainly a distortion. In a similar manner, there may be some supporters of capital punishment who believe that condemned prisoners should be tortured on the rack before being boiled in oil, but that is not the position of most proponents of capital punishment, who favor executions in the least painful manner. To argue against capital punishment by torture as if it were the typical view of those favoring capital punishment is to pick on a straw man rather than the genuine position.

A second special strawman technique is to criticize an early and relatively crude version of a theory, neglecting the more developed and powerful current versions. Thus, a criticism of behaviorism that deals exclusively with the work of Watson (and neglects all the behaviorist work of the past half century) would be an attack on a weak and outdated strawman version of behaviorism. And an attack on the theory of evolution that dealt entirely with Darwin's early evolutionary efforts in *Origin of Species* (and neglected the further evidence and theoretical development of the past 125 years) would commit the strawman fallacy of attacking a weaker version of the target.

One standard strawman trick is to represent everyone in a large group or movement as if they supported the views of one small element of the movement. For example, suppose there is a rally in favor of Palestinian independence: it may include Jews, Catholics, Muslims, and atheists, as well as labor unions, peace activists, women's rights advocates, and students; and among the participants might be some supporters of Stalinism. If the rally is represented as being a gathering of Stalinists, that would be a strawman distortion of the aims and character of the overall group. That would be just as unfair and illogical as suggesting that because the Republican Party contains some members of the Ku Klux Klan—David Duke, a former Klan leader, was a Republican member of the Louisiana Legislature from 1990 to 1992—the Republican party shares the views of the Ku Klux Klan.

Finally, one insidious form of strawman distortion is taking part of an argument out of context. For example, suppose a member of the opposition party stated, "We must fight any administration budget proposal that reduces aid to the elderly." A member of the administration might then argue, "How can we possibly develop a budget plan when the opposition party has resolved to fight any budget proposal the administration offers?" But of course that was *not* what the opposition stated; the speaker distorted the opposition's position by taking part of it out of its context. Or imagine that a politician claims that we should first cut military spending, close tax loopholes, and cut many federal programs, and that if all those measures fail and if the budget deficit is still not substantially reduced, then we should raise taxes. If her opponent attacks her as advocating higher taxes, then her opponent is attacking a straw man.

Limits on Critical Thinking

Critical thinking is very useful, in both adversarial and cooperative settings. But if you are dealing with someone who purposefully misrepresents your views and arguments, and has no interest in genuinely discussing the issues, then critical thinking runs into a brick wall. No matter how polished your critical thinking skills, you will not persuade a tornado to be less destructive; and if you encounter someone who refuses to reason, and who grossly distorts opposing views, then critical thinking cannot gain much traction. Critical discussion of health-care policy is vitally important: the United States now spends better than 1/6 of its entire gross national product on health care, yet we have millions of people with no access to health care; health-care costs continue to rise, and major health problems often push hard-working families into bankruptcy. There are many legitimate questions about what direction the U.S. health-care system should go, and a lot of careful honest respectful argument is needed, both adversarial and cooperative, in order to find the best policies and the most effective reforms. But if the discussion is poisoned by gross and malicious distortions, those valuable debates cannot occur. One particularly vicious and obvious distortion was that some reformers wanted to set up "death panels," which would review all older patients entering hospitals and choose which ones would live and which ones should be killed. Obviously no one ever proposed anything of the sort. Instead, a law had been passed—with bipartisan support, and signed by George W. Bush—that would require that all persons admitted to hospitals be offered the opportunity to complete a living will, in which they could specify the conditions under which they would and would not want treatment. For example, many people do *not* wish to be placed on a respirator; others, who have severe heart problems and perhaps other illnesses, prefer not to be resuscitated should they stop breathing, but instead be allowed to die peacefully; others wish to reject all artificial tube feeding. On the other hand, some patients want to specify that they *do* want to be resuscitated, placed on a respirator, and tube-fed; and they have the right to make that choice for themselves: a living will empowers them to make their own choices, rather than leaving such difficult choices to others when the patient is unconscious. And if patients did not want to fill out a living will at all—"just leave all those choices to my children"—they could choose not to do so. Of course most patients *do* want to make their own choices, and like the idea of having a living will. The problem is that many patients wanted to discuss the living will with their physicians and get further information: What does tube-feeding involve? Is it unpleasant? If I am placed on a respirator, what are my chances of ever breathing again on my own? But many insurance companies were refusing to pay physicians for the time they spent discussing these important matters with their patients. The new proposal—that some people twisted into strawman claims about death panels—was only that insurance companies compensate physicians for these consultations with patients. When Congressman Barney Frank held a townhall meeting to discuss health-care reform, one questioner showed up with a picture of Barack Obama represented as Hitler, and—based on the death panel straw man— shouted this question at Congressman Frank: "My question to you is, Why do you continue to support a Nazi policy." Barney Frank quickly recognized that this was not a case in which offering careful critical argument would be productive, instead responding: "You stand there with a picture of the president defaced to look like Hitler and compare the effort to increase health care to the Nazis. Trying to have a conversation with you would be like trying to argue with a dining room table. I have no interest in doing it." If you are faced with someone who genuinely misunderstands your perspective and arguments, be patient in helping them understand your real view: just as you should be diligent in trying to understand and appreciate their actual arguments, in their strongest possible form. But if someone is dedicated to distorting your views, and is unwilling to honestly consider your actual arguments, then arguing with them is likely to be a useless endeavor.

In sum, if you remember to seek the strongest version of the arguments or positions you are criticizing or examining (follow the principle of charity), you will not be guilty of the strawman fallacy. And if you carefully question whether the attack on a position, argument, or theory is presenting an *accurate* account of the target, then you will not be taken in by strawman arguments.

Exercise 4-1

Pick out the *distortion* in each of the following strawman arguments.

1. The movement to allow prayer in public school classrooms is a major threat to our freedom. The advocates of prayer in school want to require every school child to participate in a Christian religious program prior to every school day. It violates the rights of those who follow other religions, it violates the rights of those who do not want their children religiously indoctrinated, and it violates our basic principle of separation of church and state.

2. Those who oppose prayer in the classroom want to remove religion from American life. They want to make it impossible for children to learn anything at all about religion in school, and they want to forbid your child to privately murmur a silent prayer to herself before she eats lunch or gets on the school bus.

3. The anti-abortionists are really out not only to stop abortions, but also to stop every form of birth control except the rhythm method and abstinence.

4. Those people who push for gun control take an unreasonable position. They want to ban all firearms in the United States (with the only exception being for official military use), so that not even the police will be able to carry handguns in the line of duty, and law-abiding hunters and skeet shooters will have to give up their sports.

5. Those who oppose use of animals in biology labs have it all wrong. Students aren't cutting up animals for fun; it's a key part of their study of nervous systems, skeletal forms, and muscular systems. Students learn a lot from these studies—they aren't just fun and games.

Exercise 4-2

1. Smoking (and restrictions on smoking) is a controversial issue, and strawman arguments thrive on controversy. One dispute concerns whether we should *tighten* restrictions against smoking in public places (e.g., Should all areas of all restaurants be smoke free?). What are some of the *strawman* arguments (on both sides) you have heard concerning that issue?

2. Should there be tighter restrictions on promoting and advertising cigarettes to those under age 18? What are some of the strawman arguments on that question?

3. The reckless financial practices of U.S. banking and lending institutions caused a major financial crisis in 2008, and the debate about how best to regulate those institutions is ongoing. What are some of the strawman arguments on both sides of that issue?

✔●─⌐**Study** and **Review** on **mythinkinglab.com**

REVIEW QUESTIONS

1. What is the strawman fallacy?
2. Give an example of a strawman fallacy.
3. What is the principle of charity?

NOTES

[1] Centuries ago, people with straws sticking out of their shoes could be found in the vicinity of law courts. Wearing a straw in one shoe was the signal that the "straw shoe" was willing to go into court and swear to anything—for the right price. Thus a "straw man" would offer particularly weak or doubtful evidence. In the current meaning, a *strawman argument* is the weakest possible version (perhaps a distorted version) of an argument, position, or theory.

[2] Quoted in *Gideon's Trumpet,* by Anthony Lewis (New York: Vintage Books, 1966), p. 237.

[3] U.S. Supreme Court, *Bowers v. Hardwick,* 478 U.S. 186 [1986]

INTERNET RESOURCES

The "fallacy files" contains an interesting discussion of the strawman fallacy, with some good examples; it can be found at *http://www.fallacyfiles.org/strawman.html*. Another interesting brief discussion of strawman arguments is found in Sourcewatch, at *http://www.sourcewatch.org/index. php?title=Straw_man*.

ADDITIONAL READING

Good information on "Astroturf" organizations that are supported by PR firms while pretending to be objective citizens' groups can be found in "Public Interest Pretenders," in *Consumer Reports*, May, 1994. See also Chapter 7 of John C. Stauber and Sheldon Rampton, *Toxic Sludge is Good for You* (Monroe, ME: Common Courage Press, 1995).

Read the Document on mythinkinglab.com

Deborah Tannen, *The Argument Culture*, p. 352. As Deborah Tannen notes, the conditions of adversarial argument provide fertile ground for the growing of strawman distortions and misrepresentations.

Bruce N. Waller, "Straw-Man Fallacy," *Coffee and Philosophy*, pp. 10–12. This is a discussion, in dialogue form, of the temptations and dangers of the strawman fallacy.

Holland v. Illinois, 493 U.S. 474 (1990). In this case, Daniel Holland was convicted of several criminal offenses in Cook County, Illinois. He appealed his conviction on the grounds that— by use of peremptory challenges— blacks were unfairly excluded from the jury that convicted him. The majority of the U.S. Supreme Court upheld Holland's conviction, on the grounds that the right to be tried by a jury that represents a fair cross-section of the community does not mean that the actual jury must be a fair cross-section, but only that the group from which potential jurors are selected must be a fair cross-section; and in particular, that there is no requirement that the actual jury mirror the makeup of the community, and that the important thing is only that the jury be impartial. Writing for the minority, Justice Marshall argued that the majority had attacked a strawman position: the question is not whether an actual jury must "mirror" the makeup of the community from which it is drawn, nor whether the jury members are impartial, but whether the jury is seated in a way that is free of prejudice and discrimination.

Bowers v. Hardwick, 478 U.S. 186 (1986) was a famous case involving two Georgia men who were charged with sodomy under a Georgia law which made sodomy a crime punishable by up to 20 years imprisonment (under the Georgia law, heterosexuals engaging in consensual oral sex could also be imprisoned for 20 years; but in practice, the law seemed to be aimed only at homosexual behavior). In the majority opinion (which upheld the law), the Court ruled that the Georgia law was not unconstitutional, because the U.S. Constitution does not recognize "a fundamental right to commit homosexual sodomy." In dissenting from that majority ruling, the minority argued that the majority had attacked a strawman position: no one was claiming that the U.S. Constitution recognizes a right to commit homosexual sodomy; rather, the Constitution recognizes a fundamental right of *privacy*, and a right to be free of government control and interference in one's private life. (In 2003, in the case of *Lawrence v. Texas*, the U.S. Supreme Court reversed itself, and overturned *Bowers v. Hardwick*, on basically the same grounds that Justice Blackmun had urged in his dissent in *Bowers v. Hardwick*.)

5

❖ ❖ ❖

What's the Question?

The vital first step in critical thinking is to determine the exact *conclusion*. When participants in an argument establish exactly what they are arguing about, they often find that they have been arguing at cross-purposes. When the issue is clearly defined, there is no real dispute. If a genuine difference remains, getting very clear on what's at issue often leads to a way to resolve the differences. And if you have a tight grip on exactly what is at issue, you are much less likely to be deceived by argumentative tricks and pitfalls.

Becoming clear on the question is the first and perhaps the most important step in finding the right answer. When considering an argument, the essential question is this: What is that supposed to prove? An effective argument in support of one conclusion may be a total washout in support of some other conclusion. For example, an argument describing the number of farmers, manufacturing workers, and warehouse workers who depend heavily on tobacco for their livelihood may be very effective in establishing that tobacco provides jobs for many people; however, the same argument will be useless in proving that tobacco is not a health hazard. An argument that cites the combined testimony of a number of eyewitnesses may be a strong argument for the conclusion that Alice did indeed drive away in Bob's car. But the same argument may be quite inadequate to establish that Alice is guilty of auto theft, since that will also involve the question of whether Alice had Bob's permission to take the car. A commercial might give you good reasons for using a fluoride toothpaste but fail to establish that you should be using a particular brand of fluoride toothpaste (rather than a cheaper brand with the same ingredients). An advertisement might effectively argue that being overweight is bad for your health without giving any reason to believe that the diet pills being advertised are either safe or effective. And the district attorney may clearly establish that a brutal and horrifying crime was committed, yet fail to prove that the defendant did it.

DETERMINE THE CONCLUSION

So when you reflect on an argument, consider exactly what it is claiming to prove. That is important any time you confront an argument, and it is critically important when you serve on a jury. The conclusions being aimed at by the prosecuting and defense attorneys are frequently quite complicated. For example, *exactly* what does the defense attorney attempt to prove? Exactly what is the conclusion for which the defense attorney is arguing? Stop and think about it for a moment. You are seated on a jury, and the case involves a charge of first-degree burglary: What exactly is the goal of the defendant's attorney? What is he or she attempting to prove to you? How would you state that conclusion?

The most tempting answer is that the defense attorney is attempting to prove that the defendant is innocent. That's the most tempting answer, but it's wrong. The defendant does not have to prove innocence, and if you consider the defense arguments as if they were aimed at proving the defendant's innocence, then you will consider them badly.

What is the defense attorney trying to prove? The second tempting answer is that the defense attorney is trying to establish that the defendant is *not guilty*. That's especially tempting, since if the defense attorney is successful in convincing the jury, then that's exactly the verdict the jury will return: not guilty. Even so, that is not actually what the defense is trying to prove, and it is not the question that you—as a juror—should be considering.

What conclusion is the defense attorney trying to establish? Just this: that the defendant has *not* been *proved* guilty. That's all. But that's important. A defense argument might fail to prove that the defendant is innocent of the crime but still succeed in establishing that the defendant's guilt has not been proved. For example, if the defense can show that the prosecution's key eyewitness is unreliable, that may knock an unbridgeable gap in the prosecution's attempt to prove guilt. Thus that may be quite enough to legitimately convince you to return a verdict for the defense: a verdict of acquittal, a verdict of not guilty, a verdict that the defendant has not been proved guilty. In this case, the defense failed to establish that the defendant is innocent of the crime, and if you treat the argument of the defense as if it were *trying* to establish innocence, you will conclude that it fails (for it does fail to establish the defendant's innocence). But that would be a grievous mistake, for the argument *does* accomplish its actual goal: It establishes that the defendant has not been proved guilty.

Consider this example. Imagine that you are a member of the jury in a case in which the butler is being tried on charges of first-degree murder. You are convinced by the evidence that either the butler or the gardener did the dastardly deed; you aren't quite sure which, but you think that probably it was the butler. In those circumstances you must find the butler not guilty. Clearly you are not concluding that the butler is innocent, or even that the butler is not guilty (you think he *probably* is guilty). Rather, you are concluding that the prosecution has failed to conclusively prove that the butler is guilty.

If stating the conclusion of the defense attorney's arguments is tricky, it would seem that stating the prosecutor's conclusion is easy. The conclusion of the prosecution's argument is: The defendant is guilty. But it's not quite as simple as it sounds.

Consider the seemingly clear and straightforward crime of breaking or entering. Exactly what must the prosecution prove in order for you to reasonably conclude that the defendant is guilty of breaking or entering? The obvious answer is that you must be convinced the defendant really did break or enter. That seems plausible enough, but it's not even close. One may be guilty of breaking or entering without either breaking or entering; and one may be *not* guilty of breaking or entering when one both broke and entered.

WHAT IS THE EXACT CONCLUSION?

This sounds confusing, and it is. To avoid this confusion, you must be clear on the exact details of the prosecution's conclusion. (Roughly, the prosecution's conclusion is that the defendant is guilty of breaking or entering; but substantially more detail is required.) *Exactly* what is involved in that conclusion may vary from state to state. As a jury member, you are not expected to know the law on breaking or entering, but it is most important to listen carefully as the judge explains exactly what the prosecution must establish to prove that the defendant is guilty of breaking or entering. In North Carolina, for example, the prosecution must establish four things to prove that the defendant is guilty of breaking or entering, and this is how the judge would instruct you if you were a juror in a North Carolina breaking or entering case:

> Now I [the judge] charge that for you [the jury] to find the defendant guilty of felonious breaking or entering, the State [the prosecution] must prove four things beyond a reasonable doubt.
>
> First, that there was either a breaking (which simply means the opening or removal of anything blocking entry) or an entry (walking or reaching in would be an entry) by the defendant.
>
> Second, the State must prove that it was a building that was broken or entered.
>
> Third, that the owner or tenant did not consent to the breaking or entering.
>
> And fourth, that at the time of the breaking or entering, the defendant intended to commit some specific felony.[1]

Obviously what the prosecution is attempting to prove is rather complex. In a later chapter, we will examine that conclusion in more detail. Right now the points to note are that conclusions are very important, that they often are not at all obvious, and that one must carefully determine the exact conclusion of each argument.

Careful attention to conclusions is also essential outside the courtroom. Consider an argument that occurs in advertisements for Total®[2] cereal. Some poor sod sits down to a nice bowl of raisin bran, and the announcer spoils it by telling her or him: "Hope you're hungry, cause you'll have to eat four bowls of raisin bran to get the vitamin nutrition in one bowl of Total." We are then informed that "Total has 100% of the daily recommended allowance of all these vitamins and iron," while the disparaged raisin bran has only about 25% of the recommended daily allowance. When the cereal eater is next seen, he or she is dutifully munching Total, having concluded that it's better to eat one bowl of Total since it has four times the vitamins and iron of raisin bran. At that point the announcer chimes in with the happy ending: "That's the Total difference."

What's the conclusion? The conclusion of the argument is roughly the following: Total is more nutritious than raisin bran. And keeping that conclusion clearly in view, we can evaluate the argument: Does it establish that Total is a more nutritious cereal than raisin bran? The main *premise* of the argument (i.e., the main reason given in support of the conclusion) is that Total contains 100% of the recommended daily allowance of nine vitamins and iron, and raisin bran contains only 25%. Now, *does* that premise establish that Total is more nutritious? Obviously, not by itself. Take a moment to think about what other premises would have to be added.

In order to move from "Total has more vitamins than raisin bran" to "Total is more nutritious than raisin bran," an additional premise is necessary: A cereal that contains more vitamins is more nutritious than a cereal containing fewer vitamins. And if we add that necessary but unstated premise to the argument, then the argument is *valid* (i.e., the conclusion will follow from the premises). But now we must decide whether that additional premise is true. Is it true that the cereal with more vitamins is more nutritious? No, it's false, because clearly there is much more to good nutrition than vitamins. For example, a cereal might contain lots of vitamins yet be nutritionally abysmal—because it has little or no fiber (and fiber is one of the main things you are supposed to get from cereal) and because it is very high in sugar. (In fact, when *Consumer Reports* did a study of the comparative nutritional value of various cereals, Total ranked about average.[3]) So that necessary premise—the cereal with more vitamins is more nutritious—turns out to be false, and the argument to establish the superior nutritional value of Total is thus *unsound*. Or you could simply take the argument as given, without the added false premise. In that case the argument will be *invalid*—the conclusion doesn't follow from the premises—and thus is still unsound. Two morals can be drawn: (1) Don't be misled by deceptive advertising, and (2) whenever you are evaluating an argument—whether in a jury room or watching television or reading an editorial—first pick out the conclusion of the argument and then decide how well the argument supports that conclusion.

Recognizing the conclusion is always essential to evaluating an argument, for arguments are not good or bad in absolute terms: An argument is good only if it strongly supports its specific conclusion. A very impressive argument may give strong grounds for one conclusion and be totally useless and irrelevant for establishing some other conclusion. Imagine a prosecuting attorney who—in his or her final argument to the jury—argues quite convincingly that crime is doing terrible damage to our fair city, that criminals must be put behind bars for the protection of society, and that it is the duty of all good citizens to oppose crime. Those are impressive points. But since the *issue* is whether the defendant committed the crime (*Is the defendant guilty of the crime with which he or she is charged?*), those impressive premises are useless in establishing that conclusion. If you keep in mind the *conclusion*—the question at issue—you will not be misled by such demagoguery.

Exercise 5-1

1. Sometimes politicians who are tried on criminal charges but are found not guilty claim that this verdict proves they are innocent. What is wrong with that claim?

Exercise 5-2

What is the exact conclusion of each of the following arguments? (The conclusion may not be stated precisely; in fact, in some of the arguments it may not be stated at all, but only implied.) It is important that you state it very carefully, perhaps more carefully than it is stated in the original argument. There is not a single exact way the conclusion must be stated; different people may phrase the conclusion differently. It is, however, important to specify the key assertion being made in the conclusion. That is, exactly what does the arguer want to convince you of?

1. When we consider how splendidly the planets are arranged in their orbits, how the Earth is positioned at the right distance from the Sun, how the eye is designed to see and the hand is fashioned for grasping, we must conclude that it was all arranged by some higher, greater intelligence.

2. Small farms are probably not the most efficient way to produce agricultural products; but efficiency isn't everything. We must also consider the heartbreak of those who lose farms that their families have operated for generations, the satisfaction people receive from owning and operating their own farms, the independent lifestyles of those who run their own farms and their own lives. Efficient or not, we must find some way to sustain and support the proud tradition of small farms in the United States.

3. Capital punishment requires that a number of people participate in deliberately putting a healthy human being to death. Participating in such a process—dragging a condemned human to an execution chamber, strapping that person into an immobile position, administering the killing jolt or the lethal potion, officially witnessing the whole ghastly process—must inevitably have the effect of brutalizing those who participate, making them more callous and blunting their human sympathies. Even if capital punishment could be justified on other grounds, that is too high a price to pay.

4. We should be developing a power source that will last, that will not be depleted. We shall eventually run out of coal, natural gas, petroleum, and even uranium; but we will never run out of sunlight. Or at least, when the Sun finally does burn out, there won't be any humans left to worry about power needs.

5. There are billions of stars in our galaxy, and it seems doubtful that of all the stars in the Milky Way, only our Sun would have a planet on which intelligent life evolved. Given the strong possibility that intelligent life evolved elsewhere in our galaxy, we ought to consider the possibility of contacting intelligent life forms in other parts of our galaxy. If those other intelligent life forms are only a few million years ahead of us in evolutionary terms, then there is a strong possibility that they have solved many of the problems facing our civilization—such as how to avoid destroying ourselves through nuclear war or environmental pollution. Given what we currently spend on nuclear weapons of potential destruction, shouldn't we be willing to invest a fraction of that amount in a research program to try to find some signal from other intelligent life forms in our galaxy? Compared with the benefits we might ultimately derive, the cost is quite low.

6. Look, I don't know who robbed the First Federal Bank last September. And the district attorney doesn't know, and my client (the defendant in the bank robbery case) doesn't know, and *you*, the conscientious and careful members of the jury, don't know who robbed the bank. It would be nice to get that question cleared up. I sincerely wish I could tell you who *did* rob First Federal, and we could send the robber to jail, where robbers belong. But we don't know who committed the crime—and that is part of being mature, patient, realistic adults: Sometimes we must live with the fact that we do *not* know the answers to important questions. But there is one important thing that you and I and the judge and indeed all good citizens of these United States *do* know: Every person has the right to be presumed innocent unless he or she is proved guilty beyond a reasonable doubt. And it is that certainty, a certainty that is the bedrock of our justice system, that I know each of you jurors will keep in mind as you consider your verdict.

7. We shall never get anywhere debating the moral right or wrong of abortion. The issue is too embroiled in conflicting religious beliefs and societal traditions. And besides, there is no agreement about the best way to pursue answers to moral questions: There is no agreed-upon "ethical method" comparable to the scientific method. So we should leave the question of abortion to each person's individual conscience or faith, because certainly it would be foolish to attempt to enforce a law on an issue on which there is no moral agreement in society. For when we try to force laws upon people when there is no underlying moral consensus in support of those laws, we simply encourage lawlessness and disrespect for the law.

8. When suspected witches were tortured, they usually confessed to their crimes—and named other witches as well. That's just one of the problems with torture: it often yields information, but that information is likely to be false; and it is likely to draw in as many innocent people as guilty ones. We get better and more accurate information when suspects are treated with dignity and respect, and we gain their confidence and cooperation. But even if torture worked, it is a line we should never cross. First, we should never ask any of our citizens to become torturers: to deliberately inflict severe pain on another person. There is no doubt that torture causes severe damage, if not physical then certainly psychological, to those tortured. But those who do the torturing are also damaged: ask yourself, would you want your son or daughter to become a torturer? Would you ever again feel comfortable with yourself if you had engaged in purposefully and systematically inflicting severe—by design, intolerable—pain on a fellow human? And finally, even if torture *were* effective in gaining some information, what about its larger impact? If you, or one of your friends, or your parents or your children, were subjected to torture by another country, would you *ever* forgive that country? Would you be more likely to cooperate with and help that country in the future, or would you do everything you could to strike back at the country that subjected you or your loved ones to such cruel and degrading treatment?

Exercise 5-3

Consider the Verdict

Everett Collection / Shutterstock

The defendant, Diana Whetstone, is accused of having committed the felony of theft by deception (or false pretenses misappropriation). Whetstone had approached the Spring Hill Presbyterian Church in Spring Hill, New Virginia, and offered to supply pictorial directories for the church and its members. According to the arrangement, each member of the church who wished to have his or her picture included in the directory would pay $25 and would be photographed by Whetstone. Each person photographed would receive a set of photographs, plus a pictorial church membership directory. For every six members photographed, the church would receive a free directory. There would be no cost to the church. Whetstone agreed to deliver photographs and directories within 6–8 weeks of the scheduled photography session. On August 15, 2010, church officials signed a contract with Whetstone to that effect, and on the scheduled day more than 100 members had photographs made, paying Whetstone in excess of $2,500.

Twelve weeks after the photographs had been made, church officials attempted to contact Whetstone to inquire about the delivery of the photographs and directories. Whetstone replied that there had been some technical difficulties with printing, but the photographs and directories should be available within 4–6 weeks. After an additional 7 weeks, church officials again attempted to contact Whetstone, but with no success. After waiting an additional 3 weeks, church officials contacted police and filed criminal charges against Whetstone for theft by deception.

Whetstone testified that she had intended to fulfill her contract to have the directories printed and the photographs made, but financial difficulties had plagued her. Shortly after the photography session at Spring Hill, her car had broken down, and she had had to purchase a new one. The down payment and other living expenses had taken all her funds, including the money paid by members of Spring Hill Presbyterian. She had attempted to raise money through additional photography and directory work for churches, but had been unable to secure any additional contracts for directories. She had contacted a photo processing company—Photo Power, in New Richmond—and asked about arrangements for having photos processed and directories printed, but they had refused to do the work without substantial prepayment, and (Whetstone testified) she had no funds for that purpose. (A representative of Photo Power testified that Whetstone had asked them about having directories printed, was told the cost and the prepayment requirement, and had had no further contact with them.) Whetstone testified that she had avoided contact with Spring Hill Presbyterian because she was embarrassed and because she still hoped eventually to find the money to have the directories printed.

After the testimony (by church members, Whetstone, and the Photo Power representative), the prosecution and defense present closing arguments. The prosecution contends that this is a clear case in which an unscrupulous individual set out to deceive and defraud a trusting and thus vulnerable group of people—including elderly church members with very little money—stealing more than $2,500 from them through despicable trickery. The defense contends that the defendant is an incompetent businesswoman who is lousy at planning and organizing and who also encountered bad luck, but who never intentionally deceived anyone. After closing arguments, the judge instructs the jury in the law:

> A person is guilty of theft by deception if he purposely obtains property of another by deception. A person deceives if he creates or reinforces a false impression, including false impressions as to law, value, intention, or other state of mind.[4]

Furthermore, the judge instructs, the prosecution has the full burden of proving beyond a reasonable doubt that theft was committed. The defendant does not have to prove innocence. If you have a reasonable doubt about the defendant's guilt, you must find her not guilty.

The jury retires to deliberate its verdict. One of the jurors states,

> Just think of all those unfortunate people, who trustingly paid their money for their church directories, went to tremendous trouble having their pictures taken, waited and waited for a directory, and then had their hopes and trust cruelly destroyed.

Another juror adds,

> Look, she promised to deliver directories, she took their money; no directories. She's guilty.

And another juror says,

> We have to think about this carefully. Let's get clear on exactly what's at issue. *Precisely* what is the question that must be resolved in this case? What exactly is the prosecution claiming? What is the defense claiming? What is the key issue?

How would you answer those questions? And having answered them, how would you vote: guilty or not guilty?

Exercise 5-4

Consider the Verdict

Everett Collection / Shutterstock

Look back at the law on breaking or entering. Ed Quarry, age 35, is charged with breaking or entering into the Tau Tau Tau fraternity house. It is not disputed that last October 14, a Saturday, Ed Quarry entered the fraternity house. The house was deserted at the time, with all the fraternity brothers attending the football game on campus. When one of the fraternity brothers returned to the house, he found Ed alone in the house common room, with his hands on a stereo receiver. When asked what he was doing in the house, he said he had heard there was to be a party there, and he was checking to find what time the party would start. However, he could not name any of the people in the house, and he was not a student at the university. The fraternity brother called the police, who arrested Ed and charged him with breaking or entering. The fraternity house was not locked when Ed entered; no one is sure whether the door to the house was open or closed. The prosecution maintains that Ed intended to steal stereo equipment from the fraternity house. The defense denies that Ed was intending to steal anything; instead, the defense says, he was just waiting to find out more details about a party he had heard about. However, Ed's intentions are not the focus of the defense. The fraternity brother who found Ed in the house, Rob Sawyer, has testified as a prosecution witness. Rob testifies that he found Ed in the house, and that no one else was in the house at the time. He also testified that when he saw Ed, Ed had one hand on the stereo receiver, and the other was behind the receiver, near the wires to the speakers. Furthermore, he testified that he did not know Ed, and that Ed was unable to name anyone who lived in the house, or anyone who had lived in the house recently. The prosecution ends its questions of Rob Sawyer, and the defense attorney, Janice Carson, begins her cross-examination:

"Mr. Sawyer, was the door to the fraternity house locked when everyone left for the football game?"

"No, we didn't lock it. Some of the doors to the brothers' rooms were locked, but not the outside door."

"Tell me, Mr. Sawyer, what kind of lock is there on the front door?"

"I'm not sure. I guess it's just a regular door lock, maybe a dead bolt."

"You're not sure. Perhaps if you looked at your front door key, maybe that would help. What does it say on your front door key?"

"I don't have a front door key."

"You don't have a key to the front door, Mr. Sawyer? You live there, don't you? How do you get in?"

"Well, we never keep the front door locked."

"Never keep it locked. Um hmm. Mr. Sawyer, I'm sure you have lots of friends. When your friends come over to your fraternity house looking for you, how do they locate you? Do they knock on the front door, and then your butler informs you that you have guests?"

"No, we don't have a butler."

"Well, what happens then? They knock at the front door, and one of your fraternity brothers lets them in, tells you your friends have arrived?"

"No, they just come in and look for me, maybe walk back to my room."

"And if you're not in your room, they might look for you in the kitchen? Or just sit down and wait for you?"

"Yeah, sure."

"Mr. Sawyer, do you ever have parties at the Tau Tau Tau house?"

"We have a few."

"You're under oath, now, Mr. Sawyer. Wouldn't it be more accurate to say you have a *lot*?"

"Yeah, I guess so."

"How do you invite people to your parties? Do you send out engraved invitations?"

"No, no invitations. For most parties we just put the word out, people show up."

"So you don't stand at the door checking invitations. People just walk in, that right?"

"Yeah, that's right."

"That's very democratic of you, Mr. Sawyer. Do you ever have parties outside?"

"Yeah, we have outside parties, sometimes after football games."

"What do you serve at your outdoor parties, Mr. Sawyer? What is the usual beverage? Milk? Fruit punch?"

"Usually we get a keg, put it on ice."

"Sometimes more than one keg?"

"Sometimes."

"Mr. Sawyer, with all this beer drinking, I assume that sometimes your guests have to use the bathroom, don't they?"

"Yeah, of course."

"Well, without going into detail, I assume many of your guests use the bathroom facilities in your fraternity house, right?"

"Sure."

"And they don't get anyone's specific permission to go in your house and use your bathroom, do they? People show up at your parties, many of those being people you don't even know, right? And they are welcome to just walk on into your house when they need to use the bathroom, is that right?"

"Sure, that's right."

Defense attorney Carson asks to approach the bench in order to make a motion to the judge. "Your Honor, I move for a dismissal of these charges. One essential element of being guilty of breaking or entering is that the defendant *did not have permission* to be in the building. But from the sworn testimony of the key witness for the prosecution, Mr. Sawyer, it is perfectly clear that *everyone* had permission to be in the Tau Tau Tau house. People just walked into the house, went down the halls, looked for people in the house: that was expected, that was the customary practice. They had a party, everyone came, the house was open if anyone needed to go to the bathroom, or get some ice, or whatever, you just walked in. That was the practice, Your Honor: *everyone* was welcome at Tau Tau Tau, you didn't have to knock. They wouldn't have known what to make of it if you had knocked on their front door. Your Honor, *everyone* had permission to enter Tau Tau Tau; so obviously Ed Quarry had permission to enter the house, and he *cannot* be guilty of breaking or entering."

So, how do you rule, Your Honor? Would you dismiss the breaking or entering charges against Ed Quarry? Suppose that you were the district attorney, and you are trying to *prevent* the charges from being dismissed. How would you argue to the judge that the charges should *not* be dismissed?

✓●—**Study** and **Review** on **mythinkinglab.com**

REVIEW QUESTION

1. What is the key difference between the main conclusion of the prosecution's argument and the overall conclusion of the arguments by the defense?

NOTES

[1] North Carolina Conference of Superior Court Judges and North Carolina Bar Association Foundation, *North Carolina Pattern Instructions—Criminal: Felonious Breaking or Entering.*

[2] Total is a registered trademark of General Mills, Inc.

[3] "Breakfast Cereals," *Consumer Reports,* Vol. 51, no. 10 (October 1986), pp. 628–637.

[4] Adapted from Model Penal Code and Commentaries, by the American Law Institute.

▌●┤**Read** the **Document** on **mythinkinglab.com**

Holland v. Illinois, 493 U.S. 474 (1990). This is a challenging case, in which the *majority* opinion of the Supreme Court defines the key question in one way, and the *minority* opinion argues that the real question at issue is quite different. Take your seat on the U.S. Supreme Court, and draw your own conclusion concerning what is actually at issue.

    Castaneda v. Partida, 430 U.S. 492 (1977). This case involves the question of whether discrimination was involved in the selection of members of a grand jury that was impaneled in the state of Texas. Though the basic issues are relatively clear, it is very important to note *precisely* what is the question before the U.S. Supreme Court in this case; that is, if you were a justice hearing this case, *exactly* what is the question on which you would be ruling?

6

❖ ❖ ❖

Relevant and Irrelevant Reasons

The defendant is on trial for murder. The prosecuting attorney, in her arguments to the jury, argues that this murder was one of the most brutal, heartless, horrific crimes she has ever prosecuted. Is her argument relevant or irrelevant?

It depends. If the question is whether the defendant actually committed the foul crime—the defense is claiming that this is a case of mistaken identity—then the prosecutor's arguments are irrelevant: the question is not whether the murder was brutal (everyone agrees that it was) but whether the defendant is the person who committed the crime. Arguing that the *crime* of which the defendant is accused is particularly heinous when the *question* is whether the defendant actually committed the crime is an *irrelevant reason* argument. But if the jury members are not careful, they will find themselves agreeing that the crime really was awful, and then concluding—on the basis of that *irrelevant reason*—that the defendant must be guilty.

Suppose, however, that the defendant has already been convicted of this terrible crime, and now we are in the separate *sentencing* phase of the trial: This is a case of first-degree murder, and the crime is eligible for the death penalty; and so *following* the trial to determine whether the defendant is guilty, there will be a second trial in which the jury must decide whether this crime was so terrible that it qualifies for capital punishment. In that case, the prosecutor's arguments about the brutal nature of the crime will be *relevant*. The moral of this story is an important one: When trying to decide whether the reasons given in an argument are relevant or irrelevant, *first* you must determine carefully the exact *conclusion* of the argument, that is, what question is really at issue. An argument is considered relevant or irrelevant only relative to a *conclusion*. An argument that may be vitally important for one conclusion will be utterly irrelevant to another. Of course the fact that the murder was brutal is not *absolutely* irrelevant: a brutal murder is a horrible thing. But the brutality of the murder *is* irrelevant if the question at issue is whether the defendant committed the murder or is an innocent victim of mistaken identification.

"The U.S. demand for electrical energy will steadily increase over the next three decades." Is that claim relevant, or irrelevant, to a debate about nuclear energy?

Somebody Has to Pay

A nineteenth-century Devonshire jury found the defendant guilty of stealing hay and added the following note:

"We don't think the prisoner done it, but there's been a lot taken hereabouts by someone."[1]

That is a trick question. It is impossible to say whether a reason or a premise is *relevant* until the *exact conclusion* has been specified. Information that is of vital importance in proving one conclusion will be irrelevant to some other conclusion. In this case, what is the argument about? If the argument concerns the *safety* of nuclear power, then premises concerning increased need for power will be irrelevant. If, however, the conclusion being debated is a more general one—"the development of more nuclear power plants is (is not) a good thing"—then data concerning projected power needs will certainly be *relevant*. (Of course a premise can be *relevant* without being *conclusive*. In a debate over whether to build more nuclear power plants, it will certainly be important to know whether more power is needed: If no new power sources are required, then that will count against building power plants of *any* type, including nuclear. But you might still conclude that we should *not* build more nuclear power plants—perhaps they are simply too dangerous—even though you recognize that the increased demand for power is a relevant consideration.) If the issue is whether nuclear power plants pose a serious threat to life and health, considerations of need for electrical power are *irrelevant*. (They are not *always* irrelevant: Problems of generating sufficient power for an industrialized society are real and important. But such considerations are irrelevant to this *specific* issue of nuclear power plant *safety*.)

PREMISES ARE RELEVANT OR IRRELEVANT RELATIVE TO THE CONCLUSION

The key point to remember when considering the relevance or irrelevance of premises is this: Premises, reasons, and facts are not in themselves relevant or irrelevant; rather, a premise, fact, or reason is relevant or irrelevant *relative to a specific conclusion.* So before you can start judging the relevance or irrelevance of premises, you must first be sure of exactly what conclusion is at issue.

When examining an argument, *first* determine the precise conclusion. Then, when considering the premises of the argument—the reasons given in support of the conclusion—ask yourself the following questions: Would the truth of this premise make the conclusion more likely? Would the falsity of this premise make the conclusion less likely? If the answers to those questions are yes, then the premise is relevant and actually contributes something to the argument; if the answers are no, then the premise is irrelevant—chuck it aside, for it can only confuse the issue.

Many long and fruitless arguments result from disputants plunging into argument before determining *exactly* what the argument is about. Consider this example from a Milwaukee jury room. In Wisconsin it is a felony for a person previously convicted of a felony to knowingly possess a firearm. Under the Wisconsin law it doesn't matter what the intentions of the defendant were in buying the gun. Whether the convicted felon bought the gun for target practice or robbing banks or a wall decoration is irrelevant to whether he or she violated the law. But even in such a seemingly straightforward case, distinguishing relevant from irrelevant reasons can be very complicated. In one case,[2] the defendant, a man named Reid, was charged with the crime described above: being a convicted felon knowingly in possession of a firearm. The Wisconsin law states that a person is guilty of that crime if he or she (1) has been convicted of a felony; (2) possesses a gun; and (3) knows that he or she possesses a gun (if a convicted felon bought a sealed trunk at an auction without knowing it contained a pistol, then that person would not know that he or she possessed a gun and thus would not be in violation of the law). Reid's case was unfortunate. Reid had been convicted of a felony many years earlier. After his release from prison, he had lived a number of years without getting into any trouble. He was a man of low intelligence, a functional illiterate, apparently harmless. He had seen an advertisement for a "training program" for private investigators. Reid mailed in a few dollars and received a "private detective's badge," which he always carried. Reid desperately wanted to find work that would allow him to help people ("Like that man on television, the Equalizer," as Reid stated). In pursuing this detective fantasy, Reid bought a pistol. While in a Milwaukee courtroom (he was unemployed, and he often passed his days around the courts), a sheriff's deputy asked Reid for identification. Reid proudly showed the deputy the receipt for the pistol he had bought (the receipt had Reid's name on it). The deputy asked Reid to go home, get his pistol, and turn it in to the sheriff's office. Reid immediately did so—and was arrested and held in jail. When the case went to the jury they debated long and hard about their verdict.

The jury debate focused on Reid. Many jurors argued that Reid was harmless, hardly able to understand the charges against him, certainly not aware that he was breaking the law by purchasing a handgun (the law had been passed years after Reid was released from prison, and Reid was no longer reporting to a parole officer) and with no intention of breaking the law, carried away by the hopeless fantasy of becoming an important and respected private detective who would fight for those who needed help, a man whose goal was to help others and gain respect for himself rather than to commit a crime or cause harm. To many jurors, it seemed needlessly cruel to convict this unfortunate man of the crime. Other members of the jury saw it differently: Reid's misfortunes are sad but irrelevant. Under the law there are only three conditions for being guilty of this charge: The defendant must be a convicted felon, must possess a gun, and must know that he is in possession of a gun. That's all. Reid's intentions may be good, he is probably quite harmless, and certainly his lot has been a hard one, but all those issues are irrelevant. As the law is written, Reid is guilty.

In fact, Reid's intentions and misfortunes were *relevant* to the conclusion being argued for by one side, and they were *irrelevant* to the conclusion favored by the opposing jurors. One group of jurors was arguing that Reid's intentions were irrelevant because intentions are irrelevant to whether one is *guilty* under this particular law. The evidence presented in court showed beyond a reasonable doubt that Reid violated the law, and our task as a jury is simply to decide whether or not the state has proved that Reid violated the law; therefore, we should find Reid guilty.

The other jurors agreed that Reid had violated the letter of the law, but they were claiming that in this case the exact application of the law led to an injustice. Reid was guilty of breaking the law—but Reid is also a special case in which it would be better (more just) to make an exception. Therefore, these jurors argued, Reid should be found not guilty.

What are the different conclusions for which the two groups are arguing? One group is saying that Reid should be found guilty, and the other is saying he should be found not guilty. That's true, but it is not very helpful. The different conclusions must be stated more precisely. One group is arguing: Reid is guilty under the law, *and* our *only* role is to determine legal guilt or innocence (not to decide whether this result is fair or just or desirable). The other group is arguing: Reid is guilty under the law, *but* we as a jury have a further obligation to decide whether applying the law in this case is fair and just. Once the *conclusions* of the two groups are specified, it is possible to see the issue clearly. Both groups agree that Reid is guilty under the law. The issue is not Reid's guilt or innocence. Furthermore, both groups agree that Reid is an unfortunate and probably harmless person and that convicting him is very harsh. Exactly where is the disagreement? The disagreement is over the role of the jury. One group maintains that the function of the jury is strictly as a fact finder: If the jury is convinced that the prosecution proved the defendant meets all the necessary conditions for being guilty of breaking a specific law,

How Do You Rule?

bikeriderlondon / Shutterstock

In its 1996 session (*Jaffee* v. *Redmond*, No. 95–266), the U.S. Supreme Court considered whether a licensed clinical social worker who had provided psychotherapeutic counseling to a police officer could be compelled to reveal in court the contents of those sessions. The clinical social worker (and her client) claimed that the conversations between social worker and client were protected by a "psychotherapist privilege," similar to the lawyer–client privilege or doctor–patient privilege, under which lawyers and doctors cannot be required to reveal in court what their clients and patients have told them during professional consultations. The majority of the Supreme Court ruled in favor of this psychotherapeutic privilege, and the Court's ruling was that the social worker could not be required to give evidence against her client. Justice Scalia dissented, and argued that there should be no psychotherapeutic privilege for licensed social workers. During the course of his dissenting argument he made the following comments:

> When is it, one must wonder, that *the psychotherapist* came to play such an indispensable role in the maintenance of the citizenry's mental health? For most of history, men and women have worked out their difficulties by talking to . . . parents, siblings, best friends and bartenders—none of whom was awarded a privilege against testifying in court. Ask the average citizen: Would your mental health be more significantly impaired by preventing you from seeing a psychotherapist, or by preventing you from getting advice from your mom? I have little doubt what the answer would be. Yet there is no mother–child privilege.

What is your evaluation of Justice Scalia's argument? Is it a good one, or is it fallacious?

then the jury must return a verdict of guilty. The other group believes that the jury has a role in addition to that of fact finder: The jury must decide whether a law or its particular application is *just,* and must prevent injustices from occurring.

When the different conclusions are specified, arguments can be focused on what is actually at issue. *Should* the jury stick to fact-finding, and not question whether a particular law or application of law is just (leaving such issues to legislative bodies)? That is not an easy question. There are some strong arguments both pro and con. So becoming clear on exactly what is at issue does not mean that it will then be easy to settle the issue. However, it does mean that arguments can be directed to what is really at issue. Both sides agree that the defendant is guilty—that is no longer the point, so at *this stage* of the argument, points to show that the defendant is guilty just confuse the issue. Both sides agree that strict application of the law in this case is very harsh—but that also is now beside the point. The question is what role the jury should play in our system of justice. That is what the disagreement turns on, and that is what should be argued.

The Milwaukee jury frequently discussed whether the defendant Reid *knew* that he was breaking the law. All agreed that he probably did *not* know; some insisted that that was irrelevant, and others that it was relevant and important. Again, the relevance or irrelevance of that point depends on what is at issue. It is *irrelevant* to the question of whether or not Reid actually broke the law (the law says it is a crime for a convicted felon to knowingly possess a gun; it does *not* require that the person breaking the law know that he or she is breaking the law). However, it is *relevant* to the question of whether convicting Reid would be treating him unjustly ("It's not really fair to convict him; he had no idea he was doing anything wrong"). Again, what points are relevant and are not relevant is a function of the *conclusion.* (Incidentally, in the actual case in Milwaukee, the jury members finally decided that strict application of the law in this case was unjust, and that as a jury they should prevent unjust applications of the law, and they voted unanimously for a not guilty verdict.)

Consider the Verdict

JEFF PACHOUD/ Getty Images

Suppose that the jury in the Reid's case was *not* convinced that Reid was guilty as charged, and were instead debating *that* question (*not* the issue of whether the guilty verdict is *just*, but rather the question of whether Reid is or is not actually guilty of the crime). Which of the following reasons are relevant and which are irrelevant to the conclusion that Reid is or is not guilty?

1. Reid is not guilty because: He did not know that he was breaking the law; he obviously wasn't even aware that there was a law against a convicted felon possessing a firearm; if he had been aware of the law, he would not have shown the receipt for purchase of the gun to a sheriff's deputy. *Relevant* or *irrelevant?*

2. Reid is not guilty because: He did not really *know* that he possessed a firearm. True, he bought the gun, but his mental faculties were so limited that he couldn't distinguish a gun from a stage prop; it was like a child buying a toy—a detective has a gun, he wants to be a detective, he buys a gun—but he doesn't have sufficient understanding to really know that he has a gun, since his thought categories are just too crude. *Relevant* or *irrelevant?*

3. Reid is guilty because: He possesses a gun; he bought it, owns it, knows where to find it, is able to bring it in to the sheriff's office when he is told to do so. *Relevant* or *irrelevant?*

4. Reid is guilty because: He is clearly a threat to society. Look, maybe Reid is not terribly bright, but that is cold comfort. Here's a guy who is not very bright, and likes to buy guns. We ought to get him off the streets for the protection of society. What if he decides to act like his hero, the Equalizer, and starts assaulting people? *Relevant* or *irrelevant?*

If you were on the jury for the Reid trial, would you prefer that the deliberations proceed in a "verdict-driven" (adversarial) or "evidence-driven" (cooperative) style?

The Scent of Red Herring

In 1986, the National Coalition Against Pornography ran full-page advertisements arguing that pornography should be banned and attempting to answer the arguments of those who oppose censorship. One section of the advertisement was headed "Distortions hard-core pornographers want you to believe—and facts you need to know." The second item under that heading was the following:

DISTORTION #2: Banning any pornography, no matter how vile or degrading, amounts to censorship that is not in keeping with the American way.

FACT #2: The effort to eliminate hard-core pornography is **not** censorship. *It is enforcement of the laws passed by our elected officials and interpreted by our duly appointed Supreme Court justices.* That is the very essence of democracy in action!

Many forms of speech are forbidden by law for the good of all. You can't shout "Fire!" in a crowded theater. Revealing national secrets to foreign governments is illegal. Slander and libel are against the law, and so is false advertising.

There are also effective laws prohibiting obscenity. So when judges and juries uphold those laws, it is not censorship. It is responsible democracy![3]

Leave aside questions about whether that counts as "responsible democracy" and whether laws banning pornography are comparable to laws against libel and false advertising. Instead, focus on this question: Are the reasons given by the National Coalition *relevant* to the question at issue? (Remember: In order to decide that, you must *first* decide *exactly* what conclusion is at issue.)

The question immediately at issue is *not* whether pornography should or should not be banned; rather, the question in *this* argument is, Is the banning of pornography *censorship?* (It's not a question of whether censorship is good or bad; rather, *is* the banning of pornography censorship?) The conclusion of the National Coalition's argument is that banning pornography is *not censorship*. With that conclusion clearly in mind, now ask, What *reasons* are given for that conclusion, and are they *relevant*?

The key reason given is that laws against obscenity and pornography have been passed by our elected officials, and those officials are our duly elected representatives, and so the laws they pass are democratically approved. The process is *democratic*, it is "democracy in action," it is "responsible democracy," and *therefore* it is not censorship.

But even if we assume that the process really is *democratic*, what relevance does that have to whether banning pornography counts as *censorship*? None. After all, democracies can impose censorship just as dictatorships can. Suppose the United States had a national referendum on whether to ban all Buddhist writings from the United States, and 75% of the voters favored laws banning Buddhist literature. Then Buddhist literature might be censored in the United States. It would be *democratic* censorship, and *popular* censorship, but it would still be censorship. So even *if* it is true that laws banning pornography and obscenity are democratic, that is *irrelevant* to the question of whether it is censorship. That's how irrelevant reason arguments work: You are so distracted by important and dramatic statements (in this case, statements about responsible democracy) that you forget that the statements have no bearing on the question at issue. Democracy is certainly worth talking about. But it has nothing to do with whether banning obscenity and pornography counts as censorship.

Consider a case from outside the courtroom. Just prior to the 1984 Olympics, the Mars Candy Company ran commercials showing athletes munching chocolate and caramel bars and stating that such candy bars satisfied their hunger in the midmorning or midafternoon after a tough training session. If the *conclusion* is that a candy bar will briefly satisfy hunger, then there is fairly decent support for that (quite trivial) conclusion. If instead the conclusion is that candy bars are a wholesome part of a good diet and that it is a good thing for athletes in training to eat a couple of chocolate bars a day (as the commercials certainly implied), then the fact that eating a candy bar briefly satisfies hunger is *irrelevant* to that conclusion. The point is that in order to decide the relevance and strength of the *premises*, you must first be certain of the conclusion. And if you keep the conclusion clearly in mind, you should not have too much trouble deciding whether the premises support the conclusion or whether they are instead *irrelevant*.

IRRELEVANT REASON FALLACY

The fallacy of *irrelevant reason* is committed when the reasons given in support of a conclusion are *irrelevant* to the truth or falsity of the conclusion. The reasons given may be true, they may be important in other contexts, they may even be worthy of celebration, but they have no bearing on the question at issue, and including them in the argument confuses the issue. Certainly an ax murder is a terrible thing, and we all deplore such vicious crimes, but that is *irrelevant* if the question at issue is, Did the defendant *do* that deplorable deed? If irrelevant points—like the ghastly nature of the crime—are injected into the discussion, then attention may be distracted to the horror of the crime and away from the issue. The power of irrelevant reasons to draw people off the right trail has caused the irrelevant reason fallacy to sometimes be called by a different and rather catchy name: the red herring fallacy.

The Red Herring Fallacy

The exact source of the "red herring" name for irrelevant reason is unknown, but at least there's a good story. After a foxhunt, a cloth bag of cooked herring (herring turns reddish, is very oily, and has a strong smell when cooked) was dragged across the trail of the fox; the strong smell of the herring made the hounds lose the trail (and probably

What Was the Question?

The Pharmaceutical Manufacturers Association placed a two-page color advertisement in the August 1993 issue of *Scientific American,* featuring a picture of an attractive, smiling, appealing woman, Phyllis, with her cordial cat perched contentedly on her shoulder. The text was the following:

> Ask Phyllis her opinion of the anti-stroke drug that lets her hold onto her independence and life savings.
>
> When medicines can help people like Phyllis avoid a stroke, that's obviously a good thing. What's not so apparent is how dramatically the same drugs reduce nursing home costs.
>
> Stroke often leaves survivors so disabled they require nursing home care, which now averages over $30,000 a year per patient.
>
> But drugs that reduce the risk of strokes are helping individuals and families avoid such a huge financial blow. And helping to hold down the nation's expenditures for nursing home care, estimated at $66 billion a year.
>
> America's healthcare crisis calls for this kind of cost-saving power. And new prescription drugs are our best hope for providing it.

Well, certainly drugs that prevent strokes are wonderful, and keeping Phyllis out of a nursing home and helping her "hold onto her independence and life savings" is a great benefit. But the fact that the drug to prevent strokes costs less than the cost of nursing home residence is *irrelevant*. The question is not whether the drug costs *less* than a nursing home, but whether the drug costs *more* than it should: Are the drug companies spending too much on advertising and making excessive profits and *overcharging* for the valuable life-saving drugs they produce? The cost of nursing home care is a red herring designed to draw us away from that key issue.

their lunch) and thus the hounds could be caught easily. The red herring distracts the hounds from the proper path, and sends them off the scent. And that's exactly what a "red herring"—an irrelevant reason—does in an argument: It distracts people from what is properly at issue and sends them off on irrelevant pursuits. If the debate is over whether handguns should be banned, it is relevant to consider how many people have been killed in handgun accidents. But suppose someone then asserts, "Everybody talks about handgun accidents! But think of how many people are killed each year in auto accidents! Why don't we ban automobiles?" You must hold your breath and cover your nose and stay on the trail, for a red herring has just been dragged across the argument. The danger of auto accidents is certainly serious, and perhaps on another occasion we should discuss how to reduce that danger, but that has nothing to do with the question of banning handguns. Whether there are other unacceptable dangers in society is not the issue; the question is instead whether handguns pose an unacceptable risk. Perhaps they do, perhaps they do not, but no progress will be made on that issue if the arguers are distracted by irrelevant reasons.

Remember, the first thing to ask when considering an argument is, What is the conclusion? What is this argument supposed to be proving? What is at issue? With the conclusion firmly in mind, you will not be tempted down irrelevant sidetracks, no matter how enticing and true and important they may be. Certainly it is true and important that society should be protected from vicious ax murderers; but if you remember that the question is not the proper disposal of ax murderers but rather the guilt or innocence of the defendant, then such irrelevant reasons will not divert you.

One other point: Determining the *relevance* of a premise is not the same as determining its *truth.* A true premise certainly can be irrelevant, as noted in several examples; but also, a *false* premise may be *relevant.* For example, everyone who plays the lottery wins a million dollars; I wish to win a million dollars; therefore, I should play the lottery. The first premise is *relevant;* and its falsity does not diminish its relevance. So in determining relevance or irrelevance, don't ask whether the premise is true; instead, ask whether it *matters* (for the question at issue) if the premise is true or false. If it doesn't make any difference one way or the other, then the premise is irrelevant.

A Red Herring Under the Influence

Lou Peters is 59 years old, an agnostic, living in Toledo, Ohio. He was convicted of driving under the influence of alcohol. At his sentencing, the judge gave him a choice between 30 days in jail or attending meetings of Alcoholics Anonymous. Peters chose jail, because he objected to the religious orientation of AA: part of their treatment program requires that we "turn our will and our lives over to the care of God," meetings often end with the Lord's Prayer, and meetings are frequently held in churches. Peters objected that his treatment was not fair: an option to jail was provided to religious people but not to the nonreligious.

The *Cleveland Plain Dealer* editorialized against Peters, as follows:

> How many options should society have to contrive for people who break the law and endanger the lives of others by getting drunk, getting in a car and getting on the road? . . . Peters made a rational, informed choice. When he decided against attending the AA sessions and accepting the rehabilitation that a highly effective program could have offered him, the suspension of his jail sentence was revoked, as he knew it would be.
>
> He wasn't forced to go to AA. He was, however, forced to pay for his misdeed. His dislike of the price is immaterial. He was in no position to bargain, nor should he have been.
>
> He drank. He drove. He got caught. What does he want, a reward?[4]

The editorial writer carries on at length, but never takes up the real issue. The question is not whether those convicted of drunk driving should have an option, or how many options they should have. The question is a simple one: *if* a non-jail option is given to those who are religious, does fairness (and the U.S. commitment to not giving government favor to any religious view) require that a non-jail option *also* be available for the nonreligious?

Imagine that a non-jail treatment option were provided for those convicted of drunk driving, but this treatment option required that "we take charge of our own wills and lives and reject the existence of God," and thus only agnostics and atheists could participate in this option. Christians, Jews, and Muslims would be excluded. Would that strike you as fair? Suppose Christians, Jews, and Muslims complained that if agnostics and atheists had a non-jail option, then they should have one also. Could we legitimately accuse them—as the *Plain Dealer* accuses Peters—of wanting a reward?

Exercise 6-1

For these arguments, determine whether the premises are relevant or irrelevant. (i.e., Do any of these arguments commit the irrelevant reason fallacy?)

1. The Alaskan oil pipeline is certainly *not* a threat to the environment of the Alaskan tundra (through which the pipeline passes) or to the Alaskan coastal waters. For after all, it is essential to the economic well-being of the United States that Alaskan crude oil be shipped out of Alaska through an efficient pipeline. Alaska contains the largest oil reserves in the United States, and we must have access to those oil reserves if we are to avoid costly and risky dependence on foreign oil supplies. And the Alaskan pipeline is the most cost-efficient method of making Alaskan oil available to the rest of the United States. So quite clearly the pipeline does not threaten the ecology of the Alaskan tundra or the Alaskan coastal waters.

2. There is now before Congress a proposed amendment to the U.S. Constitution that would make it illegal to burn the American flag as an act of protest. Some people oppose this amendment on the grounds that it would, for the first time in U.S. history, place a restriction on the right of political protest and of political free speech. But that's just false. The proposed ban on flag burning would in no way restrict free speech. For, after all, the American flag is a great and glorious symbol of our country; and our soldiers have fought and bled and died for that flag for over 200 years. When it is burned in protest, it causes great pain and anguish to those who dearly love the stars and stripes. Besides, there are lots of ways one can protest without burning the flag: by giving speeches, participating in marches, signing petitions, writing letters; so there would still be plenty of opportunities for political free speech if flag burning were prohibited. So a ban on flag burning obviously would not be a restriction on free speech.

3. We should certainly vote in favor of legalizing casino gambling in Washington County. For a casino in Washington County would create new jobs, and it would also have ripple effects: Restaurants and hotels and theaters would develop in the area to serve the needs of those who come to the casino.

Furthermore, since all of the casino income is subject to taxation, it would significantly increase our tax revenue. And 25% of that additional revenue will go to our local schools, and so we will be able to improve our schools and provide better education for our children. And finally, many people in Washington County now travel to casinos in Detroit, Windsor, Niagara Falls, Atlantic City, and Las Vegas; and they spend their gambling dollars there, and the money leaves the Washington County economy; if we allow casino gambling in Washington County, much of that money will stay in Washington County and will stimulate our economy, rather than being drained away. So when you consider the advantages, clearly it is time to legalize casino gambling in Washington County.

4. I urge you to vote against legalizing casino gambling in Washington County. Sure, we will raise some additional tax money; but that money will be gobbled up by the increased costs of crime, children's services, and other social costs that come from the increase in gambling and gambling addiction. When people have easy access to casino gambling, many people are tempted to gamble a little more than they can afford—and many of those people are people who can least afford their gambling losses, but who desperately and falsely hope that luck at gambling will solve their financial worries. And rather than stimulating other entertainment enterprises in the area, legal gambling sucks money away from those competing businesses. People who come to the casino stay at the casino when they eat dinner, and so there is actually a loss for local restaurants. And many people who would have spent their entertainment dollars at the theater or the movies or a concert will now go to the casino, and so other entertainment businesses wither away, rather than prosper. And finally, the money that local folks lose at the casino does not stay in Washington County! Instead, it goes to the casino corporation, which is located several states away. We do have some economic problems in Washington County, but legalizing casino gambling will not solve those problems, only make them worse.

5. Legalizing casino gambling in Washington County would *not* increase the number of people in the county suffering from gambling addiction. Most people who gamble find it a pleasant and exciting evening of entertainment, and they keep their losses well under control. And when you consider the stimulus to the local economy, the increase in tax revenue, and the new jobs that will be available, you can see that there are tremendous benefits to legalizing casino gambling in our county. So legalized casino gambling will not increase the number of gambling addicts in Washington County.

6. Some students suggest that tuition at Home State University is too high. They claim that through more cost-efficient methods, Home State could reduce tuition without any reduction in educational quality. But tuition at Home State is *not* too high. Certainly a college education is very important: Education opens the door to literature, the arts, philosophy, world history, the sciences; it also opens opportunities for professional training and an interesting career. So when you consider the wonders of a college education, it is obvious that tuition at Home State is *not* excessive.

7. Clearly having stricter gun control laws will *not* prevent shootings in our schools. Requiring more background checks and gun locks and a longer waiting period to buy guns will cause a lot of bother and trouble for honest hunters, target shooters, and legitimate gun collectors. So stricter gun laws will *not* be effective in preventing school shootings.

8. The United States has a very fair and efficient health-care system. After all, many wealthy people from around the world come to the United States for specialized medical care; and many of the most important discoveries in medical science were made here in the United States. In addition, some of the most effective drugs now in use were developed in the United States by U.S. companies. So it is obvious that the U.S. health-care system is both fair and efficient.

9. It is sometimes claimed that under our system of capital punishment we may mistakenly execute innocent people who have been wrongly convicted. But such wrongful executions are not a real danger. After all, capital punishment was approved by a democratic process, by our elected representatives, and it represents the will of the majority in the United States. Furthermore, capital punishment seems to bring a strong sense of closure and relief to the families of those whose loved ones have been the victims of terrible crimes. Therefore, there is no genuine danger of wrongful executions in the United States.

10. Some people argue that our present "War on Drugs" policy—using severe criminal penalties to imprison thousands of people who use illegal drugs—is not an effective policy for controlling drugs. But in fact the War on Drugs policy *is* highly effective. After all, illegal drugs are a major problem, causing many ruined lives and lost work hours and widespread health hazards and numerous deaths through drug overdoses. Illegal drugs are the source of enormous problems and many heartaches in this country. Illegal drugs are a serious issue, and a major challenge for our country, our communities, and our people. Therefore, it is clear that the severe criminal penalties of the War on Drugs is an effective policy for battling our drug problems.

11. *How Do You Rule?*

Comstock / Getty Images

The following is a fictitious case, taken from a story by John Mortimer, a British barrister and creator of the splendid old curmudgeon Rumpole of the Bailey (hero of many of Mortimer's stories). In this story, an artist, Harold Brittling, is charged with fraud. Brittling is charged with having sold a painting as "a genuine Septimus Cragg" (a fictitious artist, who was supposed to be one of the greatest of the Impressionists, along with Manet and Degas, and whose paintings are very valuable), when in fact—according to the charges against him—Brittling did the painting himself. Rumpole is the barrister (attorney) for the defense; Erskine-Brown is prosecuting ("appearing for the Crown"); and Edward Gandolphini is the leading expert on the works of Septimus Cragg. At this point in the story, Erskine-Brown has just finished his examination of Gandolphini (a witness for the prosecution), and Rumpole is beginning his cross-examination:

Erskine-Brown sat, apparently satisfied, and I rose up slowly, and slowly turned the picture so the witness could see it. "You said, did you not, Mr. Gandolphini, that this is a beautiful painting." I began in a way that I was pleased to see the witness didn't expect.

"It's very fine. Yes."

"Has it not at least sixty thousand pounds' worth of beauty? [the price for which the painting had been sold at auction]" I asked and then gave the jury a look.

"I can't say."

"Can you not? Isn't part of your trade reducing beauty to mere cash!"

"I value pictures, yes." I could see that Gandolphini was consciously keeping his temper.

"And would you not agree that this is a valuable picture, no matter who painted it?"

"I have said . . . " I knew that he was going to try to avoid answering the question, and I interrupted him. "You have said it's beautiful. Were you not telling the truth, Mr. Gandolphini?"

"Yes, but . . . "

"'Beauty is truth, truth beauty,' that is all ye know on earth, and all ye need to know."

I turned and gave the jury their two bobs' worth of Keats.

"Is that really all we need to know, Mr. Rumpole?" said a voice from on high.

"In this case, yes, my Lord."

"I think I'll want to hear legal argument about that, Mr. Rumpole." Featherstone [the judge] appeared to be making some form of minor joke, but I answered him seriously. "Oh, you shall. I promise you, your Lordship." I turned to the witness. "Mr. Gandolphini, by 'beauty' I suppose you mean that this picture brings joy and delight to whoever stands before it?"

"I suppose that would be a definition."

"You suppose it would. And let us suppose it turned out to have been painted by an even more famous artist than Septimus Cragg. Let us suppose it had been done by Degas or Manet . . . . If it were painted by a more famous artist it wouldn't become more of a thing of beauty and a joy to behold, would it?"

"No . . . but . . . "

"And if it were painted by a less famous artist—Joe Bloggs, say, or my Lord the learned Judge, one wet Sunday afternoon . . . . It wouldn't become *less* beautiful, would it, Mr. Gandolphini? It would have the same colourful shadows, the same feeling of light and air and breeze from the harbour. The same warmth of the human body?"

"Exactly the same, of course, but . . . "

"I don't want to interrupt . . . " Erskine-Brown rose to his feet, wanting to interrupt.

"Then don't, Mr. Erskine-Brown!" I suggested. The suggestion had no effect. Erskine-Brown made a humble submission to his Lordship. "My Lord, in my humble submission we are not investigating the beauty of this work, but the value, and the value of this picture depends on its being a genuine Septimus Cragg. Therefore my learned friend's questions seem quite irrelevant."

At which Erskine-Brown subsided in satisfaction, and his Lordship called on Rumpole to reply.

"My learned friend regards this as a perfectly ordinary criminal case," I said. "Of course it isn't. We are discussing the value of a work of art, a thing of beauty and a joy forever. We are not debating the price of fish!"[5]

How do you rule? Are Rumpole's questions relevant? Will your lordship allow Rumpole to continue this line of questioning, or will you rule that it is irrelevant to the issue before the court?

12. In the following letter, what is the conclusion of the argument offered by Benny? What reasons does he give in support of that argument? Is the reply made by Ann Landers relevant to Benny's argument and conclusion?

> Dear Ann Landers:
>
> I'm a high school senior who is speaking for a lot of others my age (17 going on 18). We have a big complaint. First I want to make it clear that we don't go out and get smashed every night. Most of us are responsible people. The kids who make trouble get the publicity. Good behavior is not news.
>
> What we are mad about is the attempt to raise the legal drinking age all over the country from 18 to 21. If we are old enough to go to war, we should be old enough to drink.
>
> I'll be interested in whether you duck this issue or print my letter.
>
> Just Benny

> Dear Benny:
>
> The folks who want to raise the legal drinking age from 18 to 21 are not being mean. They are trying to save lives—and, I might add, they are succeeding.
>
> Every state, without exception, that has raised the drinking age from 18 to 21 has reported a decrease in alcohol-related teenage deaths and injuries on the streets and highways. I know of few laws that are such surefire lifesavers.[6]

13. There is an ongoing debate about whether the District of Columbia should be a state. Those who advocate a constitutional amendment to allow statehood for the District of Columbia argue that residents are denied the basic right to be represented by their own senators and members of the U.S. House of Representatives; thus, among other problems, residents of the District of Columbia have no voice in federal law-making and so are taxed by the federal government without having representatives to vote on those taxes. That, say the supporters of statehood for the District of Columbia, amounts to "taxation without representation," a rallying cry during the days leading up to the American Revolution. The following is an argument in *answer* to the taxation-without-representation argument:

> "Taxation without representation" can hardly be an argument in favor of this [statehood for D.C.] amendment since for every 29 cents paid in federal taxation, residents of the District receive $1.00 in return. (Letter from Linda Atkins to the *Greensboro Daily News*)

Is that a *relevant* answer to the taxation-without-representation argument?

14. John Walker Lindh, the young American who joined the Taliban and was captured in the U.S. invasion of Afghanistan, was charged with conspiracy to murder U.S. nationals. John Walker Lindh's attorneys argued that statements he made while interrogated by the U.S. military should be thrown out: they were not made freely, because the conditions under which he was held were cruel and coercive. He was confined in a freezing metal container, blindfolded, and bound with handcuffs that cut off his circulation. Any statements made in such circumstances could hardly be counted as voluntary, his lawyers noted.

The U.S. attorneys prosecuting Lindh replied that Lindh was in Afghanistan of his own choice: the United States "had not plucked John Walker Lindh out of the California suburb where he used to live and dropped him into a metal container in the middle of Afghanistan." (Reported by Larry Margasak, Associated Press, March 30, 2002)

15. *How Do You Rule?*

Claudia Klauswitz is on trial for first-degree murder. She is charged with the murder of her husband. The prosecution claims that she killed him in a lover's quarrel, after discovering his affair with the babysitter. She admits that she shot him; she claims, however, that she acted in self-defense, to protect herself against a violent husband who had abused her in the past, had threatened to kill her, and then advanced upon her while she held a gun on him.

The prosecution has called as a witness the operator of a shooting range, who testifies that he knew Claudia, and that she sometimes came to the shooting range for target practice. The prosecuting attorney continues with this question: Was the defendant a good marksman with her pistol? The defense objects to the question and asks for a meeting in the judge's chambers (out of the hearing of the jury) to discuss the issue. The judge, district attorney, and defense attorney go to the judge's chambers, and the defense attorney puts her objection:

DEFENSE ATTORNEY: Your Honor, we are asking that you not allow any further questions along these lines. The prosecutor is trying to inflame the jury with an irrelevant point. The defendant is an expert shot, whose hobby is shooting at the pistol range; she has friends there, it's like a night at the bowling alley. But the prosecutor is trying to make her look like the suburban version of Billy the Kid, blazing away with her pistol at every opportunity. Of course she's an expert shot; but that has nothing to do with this case. I didn't object to the prosecution establishing that she knows how to use a pistol; but her expertise with a pistol is irrelevant. It has been well established, by the district attorney's own witnesses, that the deceased died from a bullet fired from Claudia's pistol and that the burns on his clothing indicate that the pistol was fired from a distance of not more than 18 inches. Obviously she doesn't have to be Annie Oakley to hit someone at a distance of 18 inches, and the fact that she is a good marksman is irrelevant to the question of whether she acted in self-defense. The prosecution wants to paint a picture of a wild-eyed woman blasting away at every target in sight; and that is an unfair tactic. They have no good reason for trying to show that she is an expert with a pistol; that is irrelevant in this case, and they are pursuing this line only to inflame the jury. We're asking that you not allow any more questions concerning the defendant's expertise with a pistol or her enjoyment of target shooting: They are irrelevant and inflammatory.

DISTRICT ATTORNEY: Your Honor, these questions are certainly relevant. We want to establish that the defendant not only owned a gun, but was expert in its use and, indeed, was ready to use it: She didn't need any self-defense motive; she was angry, and she used a weapon with which she was expert to vent her anger and avenge her hurt pride.

DEFENSE ATTORNEY: Your Honor, this is ridiculous. It has already been established and we do not dispute that she owned a pistol and knew how to use it. The fact that she was an expert marksman and enjoyed target shooting no more indicates that she would be likely to murder someone with a pistol than would her skill at carving a turkey indicate that she would be likely to murder someone with a knife.

How do you rule? Will you allow the prosecution to continue this line of questioning, or rule it irrelevant?

Exercise 6-2

Consider the Verdict

Nathan Jackson is on trial, charged with forgery. As he has admitted, he forged the signature of one of his professors—Professor Winston—on a letter of reference and then sent the letter without the permission or knowledge of the professor. Jackson admits having done this; he maintains, however, that this is not a case of forgery, since he had no intention of deceiving. Professor Winston had already written a letter of reference for Jackson and had mailed it to the University of North Carolina Department of Anthropology, where Jackson was applying for admission to graduate studies. However, while Professor Winston was on a trip to Europe and could not be reached, Jackson had decided to apply for graduate study at the University of New Virginia. Jackson knew that Professor Winston's letter was on the hard disk of his computer, and Jackson—having worked as Professor Winston's laboratory assistant—had easy and legitimate access to Professor Winston's office. So Jackson turned on Professor Winston's computer, found the file containing the letter of reference, revised the inside address (but left everything else the same), and printed it out. Jackson then signed Professor Winston's name and sent the letter of reference to the University of New Virginia.

When Professor Winston returned from Europe, he found a note from the University of New Virginia, acknowledging receipt of his letter of reference for Nathan Jackson. Thinking that there must have been some mistake, Professor Winston called a friend on the anthropology faculty at the University of New Virginia. The friend faxed a copy of the letter of reference back to Professor Winston, who immediately recognized that the signature was not his own. He confronted Jackson, who admitted what he had done.

Professor Winston, though disappointed in Jackson, was willing to let the matter drop. The University of New Virginia, however, had already awarded Jackson one of a very limited and highly competitive number of slots for admission to graduate study in anthropology. They felt they had been badly deceived, and that such deceit cut at the integrity of academic programs and scholarly research. Thus, they decided to take a strong stand against this sort of practice and filed forgery charges against Nathan Jackson.

The forgery law in New Virginia (where the charges were filed and the case was tried) is as follows:

> A person is guilty of forgery if, with purpose to defraud or injure anyone, or with knowledge that he is facilitating a fraud or injury to be perpetrated by anyone, the actor:
> a. alters any writing of another without his authority; or
> b. makes, completes, executes, authenticates, issues or transfers any writing so that it purports to be the act of another who did not authorize that act.[7]

The first witness for the prosecution is Professor Winston. In answer to questions from the district attorney, Professor Winston testifies that though Jackson did have access to Winston's office and was allowed to borrow books from Professor Winston's office, Jackson was not authorized to use Winston's computer, was certainly not authorized to send any sort of letter or message on behalf of Winston, was not authorized to send a letter of reference on behalf of Winston, was not authorized to sign Winston's name, and that, specifically, Winston had not given permission for Jackson to send a letter of reference from Winston to the University of New Virginia, and Winston had not and would not have given permission to Jackson to sign Winston's name to such a letter. Then the defense cross-examines:

DEFENSE ATTORNEY:	Professor Winston, you said that Nathan Jackson was your student assistant, is that correct?
PROFESSOR WINSTON:	Yes, that's correct.
DEFENSE ATTORNEY:	You had a good deal of confidence in him, did you not?
PROFESSOR WINSTON:	Yes, I did.
DEFENSE ATTORNEY:	Gave him substantial responsibilities, is that right?
PROFESSOR WINSTON:	Yes.
DEFENSE ATTORNEY:	When you left for Europe last spring, had you already turned in your final course grades?
PROFESSOR WINSTON:	I had finished determining all the grades.
DEFENSE ATTORNEY:	That is not what I asked. Had you turned in your course grades?
PROFESSOR WINSTON:	No.
DEFENSE ATTORNEY:	Did you ask Nathan Jackson to submit those grades for you?
PROFESSOR WINSTON:	Yes, I did.
DEFENSE ATTORNEY:	What did that involve?
PROFESSOR WINSTON:	He had to take the grades from my grade book, write the final grades on the registrar's grade lists, and then take the list to the registrar.
DEFENSE ATTORNEY:	That's not quite all, is it?
PROFESSOR WINSTON:	What do you mean?
DEFENSE ATTORNEY:	Isn't there a space on the grade submission forms that calls for the professor's signature?
PROFESSOR WINSTON:	Yes.
DEFENSE ATTORNEY:	You hadn't signed those forms, had you?
PROFESSOR WINSTON:	No.
DEFENSE ATTORNEY:	And so you expected Nathan Jackson to sign those for you, didn't you?
DISTRICT ATTORNEY:	Your Honor, I object to this line of questioning. Whether or not Professor Winston allowed or even instructed the defendant to sign some other

document on his behalf has no relevance to this issue; the only question is whether the defendant fraudulently and deceptively and without permission signed Professor Winston's name on the letter of reference: that is the document that is before the court, not some set of class grades.

If you were defense attorney, how would you argue for the relevance of this testimony?

Having heard the arguments of the district attorney, and now your own arguments on behalf of the defense, place yourself in the position of judge: How do you rule? Is this line of questioning relevant or irrelevant?

Let's suppose that the judge allows the question as relevant, and the cross-examination continues:

DEFENSE ATTORNEY: So, Professor Winston, when you asked Nathan Jackson to turn in your grade sheets, you expected him to sign them for you, didn't you?

PROFESSOR WINSTON: Actually, I didn't think about it; it really didn't occur to me, in the rush of leaving for Europe, that the grade sheets had to be signed.

DEFENSE ATTORNEY: But in any case, you didn't have any objection to Nathan Jackson, your very trustworthy assistant, turning in your grades and signing the forms, is that right?

PROFESSOR WINSTON: No, I guess I had no objections.

DEFENSE ATTORNEY: So in fact Nathan Jackson *was* authorized to use your signature under some circumstances, isn't that right?

DROFESSOR WINSTON: I suppose so.

DEFENSE ATTORNEY: So when you said, in your earlier testimony, that Nathan Jackson was not authorized to sign your name, that wasn't quite accurate, was it?

PROFESSOR WINSTON: No, I had forgotten about that occasion.

DEFENSE ATTORNEY: So just before you left, Nathan Jackson was authorized to sign your name on your grades. Since he was authorized to sign your name on something as important as your final grades, it wouldn't be too surprising if he then believed that he was also authorized to sign your name to a copy of a letter you had already sent on his behalf, isn't that right?

DISTRICT ATTORNEY: Objection, Your Honor; question calls for speculation.

JUDGE: Sustained.

DEFENSE ATTORNEY: Professor Winston, I just want to be sure I am quite clear on one point. The letter that Nathan sent to the University of New Virginia, except for the address, was identical to the one you sent on his behalf as a letter of reference to another graduate department, is that right?

PROFESSOR WINSTON: That is correct.

DEFENSE ATTORNEY: And I take it that the original letter of reference that you wrote for Nathan, that was an honest letter and you believed what you said and you wrote it on behalf of Nathan because that was your true opinion of him, is that right?

PROFESSOR WINSTON: That is right.

DEFENSE ATTORNEY: Thank you, Professor Winston. No further questions.

At this point, the prosecution rests.

The defense calls the defendant, Nathan Jackson, who testifies that he believed that Professor Winston would have no objection to sending the letter of reference, that he did not think that Professor Winston would mind Nathan sending the letter himself, that he had tried to contact Professor Winston before sending the letter, and that he had had no intention of deceiving the admissions committee at the University of New Virginia. During cross-examination, the district attorney raises the following question:

DISTRICT ATTORNEY: Mr. Jackson, why didn't you sign your own name to the letter of reference you sent to the University of New Virginia?

NATHAN JACKSON: Because I couldn't write a letter of reference for myself; the letters of reference have to come from professors.

DISTRICT ATTORNEY: So in fact, you wanted the Admissions Committee at the University of New Virginia to believe that the letter came from Professor Winston, is that right?

NATHAN JACKSON: It did come from him; he wrote the letter.

DISTRICT ATTORNEY:	No, he certainly did not; he wrote a letter to the University of North Carolina; he *never* wrote the letter to the University of New Virginia.
DEFENSE ATTORNEY:	Your Honor, would you please instruct the district attorney to save her arguments for her closing speech?
DISTRICT ATTORNEY:	Your Honor, would you please instruct this witness to answer my questions?
JUDGE:	That's enough; let's get back to the questions. Mr. Jackson, please answer the questions as directly as you can.
DISTRICT ATTORNEY:	Thank you, Your Honor. Now Mr. Jackson, *did* you want the Admissions Committee at the University of New Virginia to believe that the letter came from Professor Winston?
NATHAN JACKSON:	Yes.
DISTRICT ATTORNEY:	And did you want the Admissions Committee to believe that the signature at the bottom was Professor Winston's signature?
NATHAN JACKSON:	Yes.
DISTRICT ATTORNEY:	No further questions.

OK that's the case. There seems to be little doubt that Jackson faked Professor Winston's signature and that he sent a letter over that signature that Professor Winston had not authorized. So *if* there is any doubt about Jackson's guilt, what would that doubt have to turn on? (i.e., what is the key issue in this case; define it as precisely as possible.)

What is your verdict? Do you find Nathan Jackson guilty, or not guilty, of forgery? (You might find it interesting to develop the strongest argument you can on behalf of the prosecution, in favor of finding Nathan guilty; and then develop your strongest argument for the defense, in favor of a verdict of not guilty.) Suppose that we add a few things to the case; for each of these, are they *relevant* or *irrelevant*? (i.e., would they—or better, *should* they—have *any* influence on your likelihood of finding the defendant guilty, or not guilty, of forgery.)

a. Suppose that Professor Winston testified that sending the letter over his signature was just what he would have wanted Nathan to do (even though the professor had never authorized him to do so, and of course did not know of the act when Nathan did it). *Relevant* or *irrelevant*?

b. Suppose that Professor Winston, upon his return, is horrified that such a letter was sent to the University of New Virginia, since Professor Winston had already recommended another student to that program, and as a matter of policy Professor Winston never recommended more than one student to the same graduate school in a single year. (Nathan had no knowledge of Professor Winston's special policy on recommendations.) *Relevant* or *irrelevant*?

c. Suppose that Professor Winston is horrified because he had already recommended a student to the University of New Virginia and his policy is never to recommend two; and Nathan knew of Professor Winston's policy, and knew that Professor Winston had already recommended someone, before sending the letter. *Relevant* or *irrelevant*?

d. Following Professor Winston's signature, Nathan added "nj" in parentheses, to indicate that he was signing on behalf of Professor Winston. *Relevant* or *irrelevant*?

e. Instead of this being a letter of reference in support of an application for admission to the graduate program, it is a letter in support of a joint application for admission and a fellowship worth approximately $20,000 a year. *Relevant* or *irrelevant*?

✓•─ **Study** and **Review** on **mythinkinglab.com**

REVIEW QUESTIONS

1. What is the first thing you must do before you can determine whether a premise is *relevant* or *irrelevant*?
2. How do you determine whether a premise is relevant?
3. Why is it that a statement may be relevant in one argument and irrelevant in another?
4. Why is the irrelevant reason fallacy sometimes called the "red herring" fallacy?

NOTES

[1] Marshall Brown, *Wit and Humor of Bench and Bar* (Chicago, IL: T. H. Flood, 1899), p. 513.

[2] *Frontline,* with Judy Woodruff: "Inside the Jury Room." By the Network of Public Television Stations.

[3] Advertisement in *USA TODAY,* September 26, 1986, p. 13A; advertisement placed by the National Coalition Against Pornography; emphasis included in original.

[4] *Cleveland Plain Dealer,* January 10, 2003.

[5] Excerpt from *Rumpole and the Golden Thread,* by John Mortimer. Copyright © 1983 by Advanpress Ltd. Reprinted by permission of Viking Penguin, Inc.

[6] Permission granted by Ann Landers and Creators Syndicate.

[7] Adapted from *Model Penal Code and Commentaries,* by The American Law Institute.

INTERNET RESOURCES

Michael Quinion has a website—World Wide Words—on "International English from a British Viewpoint," and he has an interesting essay on the origins of the expression "red herring." It can be found at *http://www.worldwidewords.org/articles/herring.htm.*

ADDITIONAL READING

Douglas Walton's *Relevance in Argumentation* (New York: Routledge, 2003) is probably the most detailed examination of the question of relevance in arguments, and of the fallacy of irrelevant reason.

Read the Document on mythinkinglab.com

Bruce N. Waller, "Fallacy of Irrelevant Reason," *Coffee and Philosophy,* pp. 14–18. This dialogue discusses the difference between relevant and irrelevant reasons in argument.

Report of the Kaufman Commission on Proceedings Involving Guy Paul Morin (Ontario Ministry of the Attorney General). As noted in Chapter 3, this was a case in which Morin was wrongfully convicted and imprisoned, and the Kaufman Commission studies the circumstances that led to that wrongful conviction. One of the findings was that "evidence" was allowed into the trial that might have influenced the jury, but which in fact had no relevance to the question of Morin's guilt; this passage from the Commission Report describes that irrelevant material.

7

❖ ❖ ❖

Analyzing Arguments

((•⃣ **Listen** to the **Chapter Audio** on **mythinkinglab.com**

When analyzing an argument, *start with the conclusion*. If you are trying to construct a compelling argument, first decide exactly what conclusion you want to establish. If you are evaluating someone else's argument, first determine exactly what the argument is supposed to prove.

When you have picked out the conclusion, you can examine the structure of the argument in support of that conclusion. Consider this example.

> We should not build more nuclear power plants in the United States. Nuclear power is a dangerous technology: We have already experienced several nuclear accidents, and nuclear accidents have the potential to be catastrophic; even if the operators are well trained and careful and make no errors and all safety features are incorporated into the design—which is unlikely—there is always the danger that a nuclear power plant might be the target of a terrorist strike, with terrible consequences for public safety. Furthermore, nuclear power places an unfair burden on future generations: While we gain the benefit of the electricity produced, we leave for future generations the legacy of dangerously radioactive spent nuclear fuel. It's selfish and unfair to use a technology that benefits the present at the expense of future generations. Finally, we do not really need the increased power that more nuclear power plants would generate. Through careful conservation of energy—including strict requirements for energy-efficient appliances and equipment and automobiles and houses—we could reduce our power needs, and through greater use of solar and hydroelectric and wind power, we could substantially increase our supply of energy. So we should put an immediate stop to the building of new nuclear power plants.

Don't worry right now about whether that is a good or a bad argument. Let's just look at the *structure* of the argument. First: what's the *overall conclusion?*

ARGUMENT STRUCTURE

Convergent Arguments

The overall conclusion is just this: No additional nuclear power plants should be built. (It is important to note the precise conclusion. It is *not* that there should be no use of nuclear power; this argument does *not* attempt to establish that all existing nuclear power plants should be closed.)

Next, what *reasons* are given in support of that conclusion?

Three main reasons are given for the conclusion: First, nuclear power plants are dangerous; second, use of nuclear power is unfair to future generations; third, the power from additional nuclear power plants is not essential.

The next consideration is this: What is the structure of the argument? How are the reasons related to each other, and how are the reasons related to the conclusion? In answering those questions, the first issue is, Do the reasons given hang together, or does each stand independently? If one of the reasons offered were found to be *false,* would that undermine the *other* reasons also? For example, if we should be convinced that nuclear power is *not* placing an unfair burden on future generations (the *second* reason is rejected), would that destroy the whole argument? Or would we still have to evaluate the other two reasons independently?

In this case, each of the three reasons stands or falls *independently.* Consider the first reason offered against additional nuclear power plants: Nuclear power is too dangerous. If you reject that reason (you decide that nuclear power is not excessively dangerous), what effect would that have on the other two reasons? None. You might still decide that no new nuclear power plants should be built on the grounds that (second reason) nuclear energy places an unfair burden on future generations, or on the grounds that (third reason) alternative energy sources and energy conservation are better ways of meeting our future energy needs. Or suppose you reject the second reason: You decide that spent nuclear fuel can be disposed of in such a manner that it does not unfairly burden future generations. You could not just stop at that point and reject the entire argument; instead, you would still have to decide whether the remaining reasons are sufficient to establish that additional nuclear power plants are undesirable. Don't misunderstand: If an argument gives three independent reasons in support of a conclusion and one reason fails, then certainly that argument is not as strong as it would have been had all three reasons proved true. Nonetheless, the remaining reasons may still offer substantial support—perhaps sufficient support—even if one reason is rejected. (If additional nuclear power plants are very dangerous, unfair to future generations, and unneeded, those are certainly good grounds for rejecting the construction of additional nuclear power plants. But one might reasonably be convinced that it's a bad idea to construct additional nuclear power plants strictly on the grounds that nuclear power plants are very dangerous. The first reason alone might be sufficient even if the other two were rejected. The first reason alone will not offer as much support for that conclusion as all three together, but it might suffice.)

Since there are *independent* reasons, each offering *independent* support for a conclusion on which they all converge from separate directions, this argument structure is often called a *convergent* argument type. In a convergent argument, the different reasons are independent of one another, and when one falls it does not take the others down with it. Our example convergent argument is diagrammed in Figure 7-1.

Consider another example of a convergent argument. You are a juror in the burglary trial of Priscilla Prowler. The district attorney is endeavoring to prove that Ms. Prowler was indeed the villain who burglarized the Jones' home, and he offers the following evidence in support of that conclusion: Three eyewitnesses independently identify Ms. Prowler as the person seen running from the Jones' house carrying a crowbar on the night of the burglary; Ms. Prowler's fingerprints are found inside the house; Ms. Prowler's boyfriend testifies that she bragged to him about having "done the Jones job"; and when Ms. Prowler is apprehended she is wearing a diamond bracelet that was taken in the burglary, and Jones' silver is found in the trunk of her car. That's a rather strong case against Ms. Prowler. Now suppose that during the cross-examination of Ms. Prowler's boyfriend it comes out that he and Priscilla had recently been spatting because he had discovered that Priscilla had been secretly seeing an old

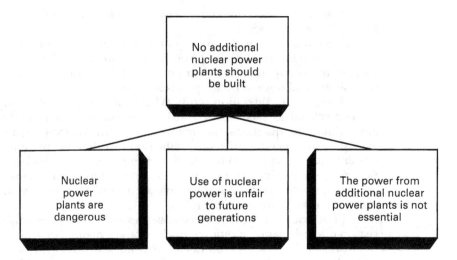

Figure 7-1   A convergent argument.

flame. As a result, you decide that the boyfriend is probably "out to get" Ms. Prowler, and you become convinced that his testimony—that Ms. Prowler bragged to him of doing the burglary—is unreliable. What effect will that have on your evaluation of the argument as a whole?

Not much, since this is a *convergent* argument offering *independent* reasons for the defendant's guilt. The boyfriend's testimony—if it is believable—would support the conclusion that Priscilla Prowler committed the burglary. The argument for her guilt is not *quite* as strong as it would be if the boyfriend's testimony were believable. But failure of that one reason does *not* undermine the entire argument, for all the other reasons for the guilty verdict remain: They are not undermined by the failure of the boyfriend's testimony. Even if we reject the boyfriend's testimony, there are still some very strong independent reasons that point to a conclusion of guilty. However, the danger is that so much attention will be drawn to the *failed* reason that the remaining reasons in support of the conclusion will be ignored.

Alibi

The famous British murder trial of Steinie Morrison (convicted in 1911 of the brutal murder of Leon Beron) offers a striking illustration of how one failed reason can overwhelm other independent reasons. Morrison's defense barrister pointed out excellent reasons for reasonable doubt of the defendant's guilt (and remember, the defense need only establish a reasonable doubt). The prosecution case rested heavily on the eyewitness identification of Morrison as the man seen with the murder victim shortly before the murder. It was established that the light was such that it would have been almost impossible to identify anyone under such conditions, and indeed the eyewitnesses admitted that they had seen newspaper photographs of the accused just prior to picking him out of a police lineup. The presiding judge's doubts are clear in his summation to the jury:

Are you satisfied beyond reasonable doubt that that is the man . . . ? Think for yourselves. With what certainty could you swear to a man whom you saw on a night like that, by the kind of light there was at those places? Can you feel certain that a man would not be mistaken? . . . Are you so sure that they [the eyewitnesses] really took notice enough, that they had opportunity enough, to be able some days afterwards to swear with certainty to the man?[1]

Unfortunately for the defendant, two girls—who apparently had become attracted to the handsome defendant—testified that they had seen him at a show the evening of the murder. However, that alibi collapsed when under cross-examination it was shown that the girls could remember nothing from the show, could not recall the price of admission, and claimed to have bought tickets at curtain time for a show that had long been sold out. That was only a small part of the defense case and obviously had no connection with the weakness of the eyewitness testimony. Apparently, however, the jurors focused on the weak—almost certainly fabricated—alibi, and gave little attention to the remaining independent points that favored reasonable doubt. They deliberated half an hour and returned a verdict of guilty.

When examining arguments, first determine the conclusion: What is this argument supposed to prove? Then consider how the argument is structured: Are there several independent reasons given for the conclusion? If so, you will have to consider each reason on its own merits and not reject the whole argument because one reason is flawed.

Linked Arguments

Convergent arguments offer independent, free-standing reasons for the conclusion. In convergent arguments, if one reason is not convincing, perhaps another will be. But not all arguments have that form. In some arguments, the premises—the reasons given in support of the conclusion—are linked together like a chain, and if one link breaks, the entire argument fails: The *linked* argument is thus only as strong as its weakest link. In short, a *linked* argument is an argument in which the reasons given depend on one another for their strength. Separately, each premise offers little or no support for the conclusion; together, they may form a powerful argument.

Consider this example. The defendant is charged with murder, and the *question* is whether the defendant is actually the person who committed the drive-by shooting of the victim (i.e., there is no question of self-defense or insanity or accidental death; the only question is the identity of the person who did the deed). One of the arguments given by the prosecution is as follows:

> White Jaguar automobiles are quite unusual in this area. The defendant owns a white Jaguar, and the car from which the fatal shots were fired has been identified by several witnesses as a white Jaguar. Therefore, there is some reason to think that the defendant is guilty of the drive-by murder.

Would that be sufficient reason to find the defendant guilty? Certainly not. Especially not when we consider that the prosecution bears the burden of proof and must do more than establish that the defendant *might* be guilty, or even that the defendant is *probably* guilty. The prosecution must prove the defendant's guilt beyond a reasonable doubt, and this argument doesn't come close. But leave that issue aside for a moment and look at the structure of the argument. We have three reasons, all supporting (though not establishing) the conclusion that the defendant is guilty. How do they support that conclusion? *Not* independently. Suppose we discover that the witnesses were lying and that the fatal shots were fired from a red van rather than from a white Jaguar. If the premise that the shots were fired from a white Jaguar falls, it brings the whole argument down with it: The other premises—the defendant owns a white Jaguar, and white Jaguars are rare—are now useless in trying to establish the guilt of the defendant. Or suppose we find that the defendant does *not* own (or have access to) a white Jaguar: Again, if that single link is broken, the entire linked argument fails. Or suppose that white Jaguars are *not* rare, but instead are the most popular car in that particular area: Again, the argument collapses. (If you have trouble seeing that, imagine that the testimony is that the fatal shots were fired from a car, and the defendant owns a car; since car ownership is hardly rare, that fact will lend no support to the claim that the defendant is the murderer.) So in this case—as in all *linked* arguments—the premises stand or fall together. If we are diagramming an

Figure 7-2 A linked argument.

argument, we need a special way of showing that. In the diagram of the *convergent* argument, the different independent lines are shown *converging* along separate paths toward the conclusion. With *linked* arguments, we want to show the premises joined as a team or unit, all of which *together* lead to the conclusion. So we might diagram the argument (as in Figure 7-2) with the premises *linked* by one line, and another line drawn from the link to the conclusion.

Subarguments

So now you know that it is essential to first pick out the conclusion, and you can distinguish the premises from the conclusion, and also distinguish among convergent and linked arguments. That's a good start at analyzing arguments and enough to handle most arguments quite effectively. But arguments can and do get more complicated, and it's important to be able to deal with that complexity; in fact, it's in dealing with the complex arguments that argument diagrams are most useful.

Look back at the first example: the argument about nuclear power. That argument was actually considerably more complex than our diagram indicated. The argument, you'll recall, goes like this:

> We should not build more nuclear power plants in the United States. Nuclear power is a dangerous technology: We have already experienced several nuclear accidents, and nuclear accidents have the potential to be catastrophic; even if the operators are well trained and careful and make no errors and all safety features are incorporated into the design—which is unlikely—there is always the danger that a nuclear power plant might be the target of a terrorist strike, with terrible consequences for public safety. Furthermore, nuclear power places an unfair burden on future generations: While we gain the benefit of the electricity produced, we leave for future generations the legacy of dangerously radioactive spent nuclear fuel. It's selfish and unfair to use a technology that benefits the present at the expense of future generations. Finally, we do not really need the increased power that more nuclear power plants would generate. Through careful conservation of energy—including strict requirements for energy-efficient appliances and equipment and automobiles and houses—we could eliminate some power requirements, and through greater use of solar and hydroelectric and wind power, we could substantially increase our supply of energy. So we should put an immediate stop to the building of new nuclear power plants.

The exact conclusion of that argument is that we should build no new nuclear power plants. In overall structure it is a convergent type of argument: Three distinct and independent reasons are given in support of that conclusion. First, nuclear power is too dangerous; second, nuclear power use is unfair to future generations; and third, additional nuclear power is not necessary. That's as far as we went in analyzing the argument, but there's still a lot further to go. The most obvious next step in analyzing that argument is to ask, Are the reasons given in support of the conclusion relevant to the conclusion? That is, do they actually support the conclusion? If they are true, do they make the conclusion more likely to be true? We have already examined relevance in an earlier chapter, so you can determine that the reasons given are relevant. But another question immediately arises: If the reasons given are true, then they *will* support the conclusion; but why should we accept the reasons given for the conclusion? That is, *are* the reasons given actually true?

In the original argument, some reasons were given *in support* of those reasons. That is, there are *sub*arguments within the larger argument, and the subarguments are arguments in favor of the premises of the overall argument. For example, look at the third reason given for the conclusion: We do not really need the increased power that additional nuclear power plants would generate. That is a key *premise* in support of the overall conclusion; but it in turn is the *conclusion* of a *sub*argument. The subargument is thus:

> We do not need the increased power that more nuclear power plants would generate. Through careful conservation of energy—including strict requirements for energy-efficient appliances and equipment and automobiles and houses—we could eliminate some power requirements, and through greater use of solar and hydroelectric and wind power, we could substantially increase our supply of energy.

The conclusion of that subargument is that the increased power that more nuclear power plants would generate is not needed. Two reasons are offered in support of *that* conclusion: First, conservation practices could reduce our demand for energy, and second, other nonnuclear power sources could supply all the power we need. There you have a subargument within the larger argument; that is, you have a sort of miniargument in support of one of the reasons that supports the overall conclusion. And notice that the *conclusion* of the subargument functions as a *premise* in the overall argument. Notice also that each of the other two reasons given in support of the overall conclusion is in turn supported by subarguments, and that each of those reasons—while functioning as a *premise* in the overall argument—is the *conclusion* for its respective subargument.

With the added detail, the diagram for the overall argument becomes a bit more complicated, but taken step by step, it should not be confusing. The basic diagram, shown in Figure 7-3, remains the same.

To that basic diagram we add diagrams of each *sub*argument. For example, the diagram of the third subargument is shown in Figure 7-4. And the second subargument is a linked argument; its diagram is shown in Figure 7-5. Now we put them together, with

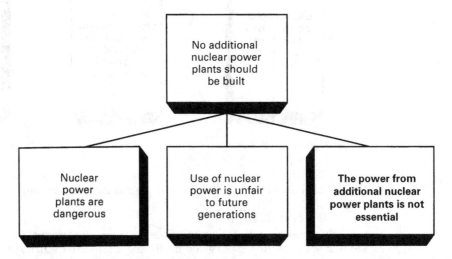

Figure 7-3   A convergent argument.

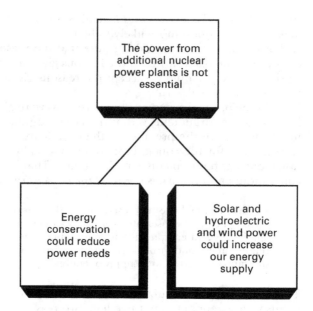

Figure 7-4 A convergent subargument.

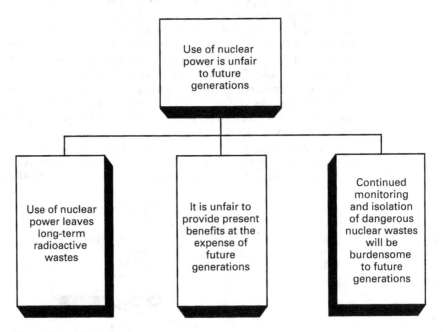

Figure 7-5 A linked subargument.

the conclusion of each subargument operating as a premise for the overall argument (Figure 7-6).

Piece of cake, right?

By examining and diagramming the above argument and subarguments, you can see that some of the *reasons* given in the argument are in turn supported by other reasons (are supported by further subarguments). But being of an inquiring and reflective

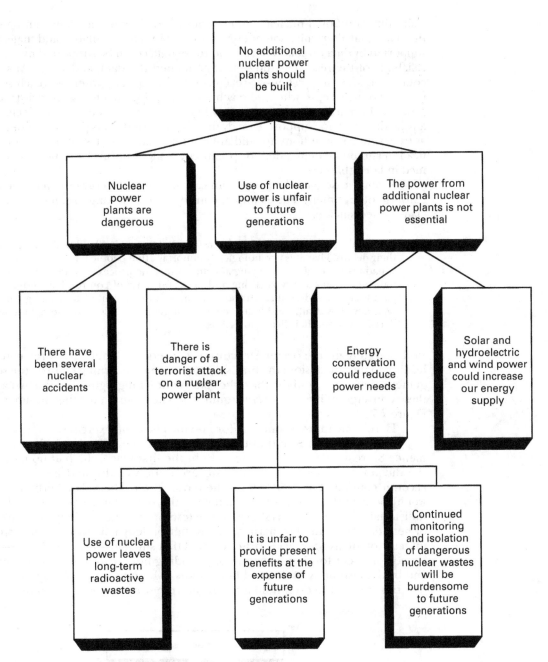

Figure 7-6   The entire argument.

nature, you no doubt asked, What about the reasons in the subargument? What supports *them?* For example, consider the claim that alternative soft energy sources are readily available: Why should I accept that? Shouldn't there be a further argument—a *sub*subargument—to support that reason?

The answer is that there *could* be such a subsubargument—and *perhaps* there *should* be. In any case, it should be noted that arguments can be pushed to many different levels: The conclusion that no new nuclear power plants should be built can be supported by the claim that additional nuclear power is not needed, and that claim can be supported by the claim that alternative soft energy sources are readily available, and that claim could be supported by data on solar energy, and those data could be supported by claims about the reliability of the research studies that generated the data, and so on. At some point, of course, we must stop: when we reach some obvious fact, when we reach some assertion that everyone accepts, when we reach an assumption that is accepted as true for the purposes of this particular argument, or when we run out of energy and decide not to press any further back for support. Exactly under what conditions premises should be accepted as true, when assumptions are and are not reasonable, and what degree and type of justification should be demanded for premises are all important questions that will be examined in later chapters.

In some cases, a linked argument can be one of the convergent elements in a larger convergent argument. For example, consider the following argument in favor of physician-assisted suicide:

> We should legalize physician-assisted suicide for terminally ill patients who wish to hasten their deaths. First, it is psychologically important that people have as much control over their situations as possible, and being able to control the process of one's death gives some terminally ill patients a very satisfying and powerful sense of control. Furthermore, excruciating pain is always undesirable, and some forms of disease cause excruciating pain that can only be relieved by death. And finally, competent people should have the right to make their own decisions about their lives and deaths.

In this argument, the overall structure is convergent. There are three convergent lines leading to the conclusion: the first is the argument concerning control, the second the argument about pain, and the third the claim concerning rights. But the first and second of these convergent lines are *linked* arguments. The diagram for that argument is shown in Figure 7-7.

Here's one more example before we turn to some exercises:

Alice should be found not guilty, because Alice did not rob the Key West Convenience Store at 10:00 P.M. on August 9. In the first place, she had no motive. Certainly she did not need money: Her parents are quite wealthy, and her personal checking account contained over $8,000 on the day of the robbery. Furthermore, such a crime would be completely out of character for the defendant. She is a gentle, nonviolent individual. Her character is shown by the testimony of her biology professor (who spoke of her adamant refusal to harm a frog in her biology laboratory), the testimony of the director of Meals-on-Wheels (who testified that she had—for over 3 years—been a dedicated volunteer for their program of providing hot meals to the elderly and disabled), and by the testimony of three of her friends (who noted that she is fiercely opposed to firearms, refused to even hold a pistol shown her by a friend, and refuses on principle

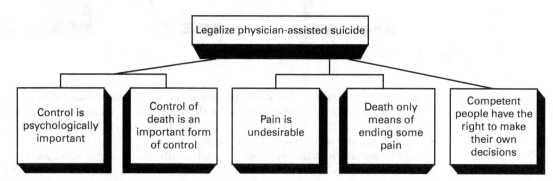

Figure 7-7 A convergent argument with linked elements.

to attend violent movies). This is not the sort of person who takes a pistol into a convenience store and robs it at gunpoint. And finally, Alice could not have been the robber because she was not in Key West when the crime was committed. She could not have been in Key West, because at 9:30 P.M. on August 9 she was in Miami, and there is no way to get from Miami to Key West in half an hour. There's no doubt she was in Miami at the time, for a professor at the University of Miami testified that he talked with Alice at 9:30 P.M. on the night of August 9 while waiting in line to get popcorn at a movie theater in Miami. And he could not have been mistaken, because he recognized her from two seminars she had taken with him at the university. Also, the usher at the theater remembered seeing her there.

The basic structure of this argument is convergent. The first strand of the argument (Figure 7-8) contains a convergent subargument to prove that Alice had no motive. The second strand of the overall convergent argument ends in the conclusion (the subconclusion) that armed robbery is out of character for Alice. That conclusion is supported by a convergent (sub)argument, as shown in Figure 7-9. The third part of the overall convergent argument is diagrammed in Figure 7-10. The third reason for the conclusion that Alice did not rob the Key West Convenience Store is the claim that Alice was not in Key West at the time of the robbery. That is in turn the conclusion of a *linked* subargument (if Miami were only 2 minutes from Key West, the sighting of Alice in Miami would carry no weight; and of course if Alice was not in Miami, it would make no difference how far Miami was from Key West). And there is another subargument (this time a convergent argument) in support of one of the linked premises: Alice was in Miami because her professor saw her in Miami *and* the usher saw her in Miami. Those two premises are *convergent* (even if the usher's testimony is mistaken, the professor's testimony would independently support the subconclusion that Alice was in Miami).

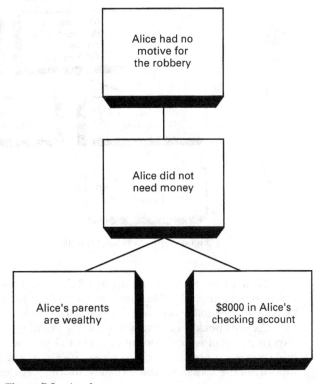

Figure 7-8   A subargument.

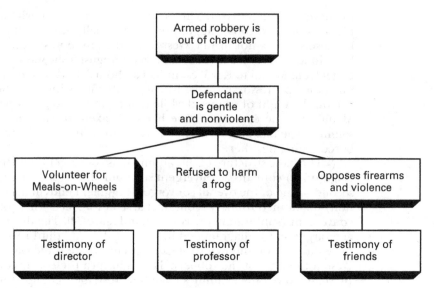

Figure 7-9   A convergent subargument.

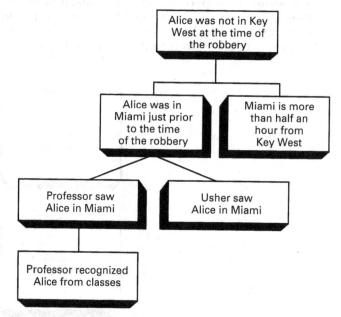

Figure 7-10   A subargument.

Now it's just a matter of putting all these arguments together. The resulting diagram is shown in Figure 7-11. The diagram might look formidable at first glance; but taken step by step, there's really nothing difficult about it.

As you check your diagram of an argument to see if the pieces are in the right place, start from the most basic premises and work your way up. At each step, ask yourself: Does this premise support the claim above it? Does it make sense to use this as a *reason* in support of the statement immediately above it? For example, check the line of argument running from "Alice's parents are wealthy" up to "Alice should be found not guilty."

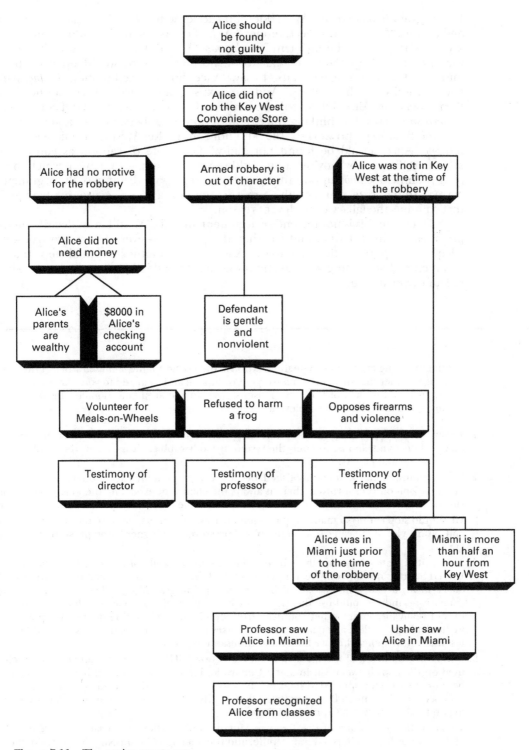

Figure 7-11   The entire argument.

Is it diagrammed correctly? Well, does it make sense to say, "Alice's parents are wealthy" and *therefore* "Alice did not need money"? Yes, of course. (And it would *not* make sense to say "Alice is gentle and nonviolent," so *therefore* "Alice did not need money"; so if you had the argument diagrammed in that form, working upward would tip you off to your mistake.) Likewise, it makes sense to say, "Alice did not need money," so *therefore* "Alice had no motive for the robbery." And the next step also works: "Alice had no motive for the robbery," so "Alice did not rob the Key West Convenience Store." (Of course that's not a *conclusive* reason for thinking Alice did not do the robbery, but certainly it's a reason.) And the final step also works: "Alice did not rob the Key West Convenience Store," and *therefore* "Alice should be found not guilty." One note of caution as you check your argument diagram by moving up the ladder: You *may* come to a point at which the underlying premise does *not* support the next step, and yet your diagram of the argument is still correct. In that case, you have the *correct* diagram for a *fallacious* argument: an argument that commits the fallacy of irrelevant reason.

Of course this is not the end of argument analysis. We still must decide whether the premises are in fact true, and whether the premises—even if they are true—provide adequate support for the conclusion. And there is another essential step in analyzing arguments: determining what assumptions are embedded in the argument. That's the task of the next section.

Exercise 7-1

For the following arguments, state the *conclusion;* then diagram the *overall structure* of the argument, showing whether that structure is convergent or linked; and then add to your diagram the subarguments (if any) for each of the main reasons given in the argument. Finally, decide whether the reasons given are relevant or irrelevant.

1. You are obviously suffering from the Wyoming Gollywobbles virus; you have green and orange spots on your knees and elbows, and only the Wyoming Gollywobbles virus causes green and orange spots on the knees and elbows.

2. Capital punishment should be abolished, because carrying out the execution has a brutalizing effect on the prison officials involved; there is always the chance of executing the wrong person; and the violence of executions teaches the wrong lesson—that the way to solve problems is through violence.

3. We should stop eating so many prepackaged microwave dinners, because they contain a lot of salt, and eating a lot of salt can cause higher blood pressure, and higher blood pressure can cause heart attacks.

4. The United States must rapidly reduce its enormous stockpile of nuclear weapons. After all, the United States is now the only real superpower, and there is no country competing with the United States in a nuclear arms race. And besides, maintaining a large nuclear arsenal is enormously expensive—and we could use the money for better purposes, such as health care. And finally, we cannot really discourage other countries from developing and testing nuclear weapons as long as we hold a huge nuclear arsenal ourselves: It makes us look like hypocrites to say that they shouldn't test nuclear weapons while we hold on to thousands of them.

5. The recent outbreak of dizziness and nausea among YSU students was caused by lawn chemicals used on the lawn between Cushwa and DeBartolo. Lawn chemicals must have been the problem, because the lawn was sprayed with herbicides very early on Tuesday morning, and all of the students who became ill attended Professor Ryle's Philosophy 697 class, which was held that Tuesday morning on the lawn between Cushwa and DeBartolo.

6. We know that it was one of the Teenage Mutant Ninja turtles who assaulted Shredder, because Shredder was karate-chopped by a reptile, and the Teenage Mutant Ninja turtles—Michelangelo, Leonardo, Donatello, and Raphael—are the only reptiles who practice karate. Shredder's assailant could not have been Michelangelo, Leonardo, or Donatello, since they were all in a newsmaker interview with April O'Neill at the time of the assault. Therefore, Raphael must have assaulted Shredder.

7. The defendant is clearly guilty of murder. After all, the murder weapon was a pistol that was bought by and registered to the defendant. And when the pistol was found, the only fingerprints on the pistol belonged to the defendant. Also, two reliable witnesses heard pistol shots, and then identified the defendant as the person running away from the scene. And finally, several people testified that on the morning of the day when the murder occurred, the defendant and the murder victim had had a bitter argument, and the defendant had threatened to kill the victim. So, obviously, the defendant is guilty as charged.

8. When O. J. Simpson was tried for the murder of Nicole Brown Simpson and Ron Goldman, some of the most important evidence was O. J. Simpson's blood found at the crime scene. The defense argued that the blood was from a blood sample Simpson had given to the police, and that the blood had been planted by the police in an effort to frame Simpson. One key part of their argument was the following:

> EDTA is a chemical that is added to blood when it is drawn as a sample (the EDTA helps to preserve the blood sample), and EDTA was added to the Simpson blood sample drawn by the police. EDTA does not occur naturally in blood at the levels that are added to blood samples. Significant levels of EDTA were found in the Simpson blood evidence from the scene of the crime. Therefore the Simpson blood evidence from the crime scene must have been from the blood sample the police collected from O. J. Simpson and then planted at the crime scene.[2]

9. We should stop spraying chemical pesticides and herbicides on the lawns at Western University. After all, there are good natural alternatives for controlling insects and weeds. Also, the chemicals used pose a hazard to students, and are especially hazardous to children when they visit the campus. Another problem is that when it rains, runoff from the chemicals runs into the sewer lines and contributes to water pollution. And finally, use of strong chemicals sets a bad example for the rest of the area: Western University should be taking the lead in reducing pollution, not contributing to pollution with the use of lawn chemicals.

10. Ladies and gentlemen of the jury, you must find the defendant, Elaine Slevert, guilty of fraud. Let's review the facts of this case. Elaine Slevert attempted to sell a painting that she claimed was "a genuine original Jackson Pollock." But, in fact, the evidence shows that the painting is a forgery, because it was painted on a canvas purchased from Empire Fine Arts. But Empire Fine Arts did not open until 1957, and Jackson Pollock died in 1956. And this obviously was not a case in which Ms. Slevert was honestly mistaken about the work being by Pollock: For when she offered the painting for sale, she claimed that she had been a friend of Pollock's and had watched Pollock create the painting. So, in sum, the defendant represented this painting as the work of Jackson Pollock, when she knew it was not. So she is guilty of fraud, and that is the verdict you should return.

11. Look, we know the burglary was committed by someone on the football team, because all three witnesses agreed that the person they saw running away with the jewel box was wearing an official warm-up suit from the North State University football team, and only North State football players have those warm-up suits. It certainly was not a defensive player, since all the defensive players were in a team meeting with the defensive coaches. And it wasn't an offensive player, since all of them are much too large to squeeze through the window where the burglar entered. The only players left are the punter and the placekicker. It wasn't the punter, since he has a broken leg and couldn't run. So the burglar must have been the placekicker.

12. Ladies and gentlemen of the jury, you must find the defendant, Morton Miller, not guilty. For it is a cornerstone of our system of justice that if there is reasonable doubt that the defendant is guilty, then the defendant must be found not guilty; and surely in this case there is at least a reasonable doubt. That doubt arises from several sources. There is doubt, first, because the main witness who claims to have seen Miller rob and shoot the victim admits that the light was bad and that she was not wearing her glasses; so how could she possibly make a positive identification? And there is doubt, second, because the defendant had absolutely no motive for committing this vile murder and robbery: He had recently won a large lottery jackpot, and thus had no need for money. And, finally, there is doubt because there is good reason to think that the defendant was not even in the city at the time of the murder. For remember, his brother testified that Morton was with him in Albany (3 hours north of Brooklyn) the very night the murder was being committed in Brooklyn; and while you might doubt a brother's alibi testimony under most circumstances, in this case the brother is a Jesuit priest, and he has a sterling reputation for honesty. Also, the waitress at Larry's Albany Diner remembers someone who looks a lot like the defendant having dinner there—where Morton said he had dinner—at the very hour when the murder was being committed in Brooklyn.

All these factors add up to a more than reasonable doubt; and that reasonable doubt requires a verdict of not guilty.

13. In criminal cases, traditionally a unanimous verdict is required to find the defendant guilty: A defendant cannot be found guilty by an 11 to 1 or 10 to 2 verdict. But recently there has been a push to change this requirement. Louisiana and Oregon now allow nonunanimous verdicts, and there have been proposals in other states to allow criminal convictions by votes of 10 to 2 or 11 to 1. But such nonunanimous verdicts are a bad idea, for several reasons. The most obvious is that before we convict someone of a crime, we want to be very, very certain that that person is really guilty. Requiring that all 12 jurors unanimously agree that the defendant is guilty is one way of protecting against convicting the innocent. But there are other reasons that are almost as important, but are perhaps less obvious, for preserving the requirement of unanimity.

    One of the things that we want the jury to do is not just vote and return a verdict, but to really deliberate together about the evidence. Requiring unanimous verdicts helps to guarantee such deliberation. Suppose you are serving on a jury, and you have some doubts about whether the defendant is really guilty. If a unanimous verdict is required for conviction, then all the other jurors have to address your reasons for doubting: Everyone has to take your reasons seriously, and try to show you why your doubts are mistaken. And at the same time, they have to consider your reasons for doubting, and perhaps they will be convinced by the reasons and arguments you offer. But if the jury can convict by an 11 to 1 vote, no one has to even listen to your reasons, if you happen to be the dissenting juror. There are already 11 votes for conviction, so no one need worry whether you are convinced or not. This is especially important in a diverse society like our own: On many juries, there may be only one or two members of important minority groups—perhaps only one African American, or one Asian, or one Latin American. If verdicts can be returned by an 11 to 1 vote, then minority members of the jury can be isolated and ignored, and their special contributions to the deliberative process may be lost.

    Finally, it is important not only that justice be done, but also that it be seen to be done. It is important that the public believe, and have reason to believe, that those who are convicted of criminal acts really are guilty beyond a reasonable doubt. But if people are convicted and imprisoned when some of the jury members who heard all the evidence are *not* convinced beyond a reasonable doubt of their guilt, then public confidence that those who are convicted are really guilty is likely to be undermined.

    In sum, it is vitally important that we insist on unanimous verdicts in criminal trials: not only for the protection of the rights of defendants, but also to preserve some vitally important social goods.[3]

14. Currently the United States has an inheritance tax, a tax on inherited estates that are valued in excess of about $2 million (i.e., there is no tax on estates until the value exceeds $2 million, considerably higher if the estate is a farm or small business). Some people want to entirely eliminate the estate tax, so that those inheriting estates of tens or even hundreds of millions of dollars would pay no tax on them. But the inheritance tax is positive and valuable. It ought to be retained, and perhaps increased. After all, those who inherit huge sums of money, for which they did nothing, are not really benefitted. To the contrary, having such a huge inheritance tends to make them lazy and less ambitious, and they tend to waste their talents. Second, the money that comes from inheritance taxes on huge estates can be used to provide those who are less fortunate—for example, those born in poverty—with access to good health care and a good education, and thus give them a genuine opportunity to achieve success. And finally, when huge estates are passed on without being taxed, then over several generations—through stock investments and other capital investment returns—our democratic system of government is put at risk, for the inherited wealth tends to accumulate and become concentrated in family dynasties, and those enormously wealthy family groups gain great power and influence over the political process, and thus our democratic principles are threatened by such concentrated power. Thus inheritance taxes are beneficial and valuable, and ought to be retained.

15. We should not ban hate speech at universities. For as ugly and hateful as racist and sexist and homophobic speech is, banning it only forces it underground, where it becomes even uglier and nastier as those whose ideas are not allowed free expression become even more bitter and resentful. Furthermore, banning such speech is not the best way to change the views of those who use such speech; instead of banning it, we must bring it out in the open and make clear how hateful and ugly and unfair such attitudes are, and openly criticize and refute those who hold such views. And finally, a ban on speech is a dangerous thing: for once we ban speech that we find hateful and offensive, that opens the door to bans on all sorts of expression of opinion, including radical ideas.

16. It must have been Gwendolyn who stole the collected works of Spinoza from the departmental library last night. After all, the only people who have a key to the library are the philosophy faculty and the religious studies faculty. And it couldn't have been one of the religious studies faculty, because they are too honest to steal anything. And all of the philosophy faculty except Gwendolyn were in Boston at the meeting of the American Philosophical Association, so they weren't around the department.

17. We should stop giving faculty special parking places closest to the classroom buildings and instead give those spaces to students. After all, students deserve the best parking places, because they pay tuition. Also, faculty need the extra exercise they would get from walking farther to class. And furthermore, students usually have to carry heavier book bags than faculty carry.

18. Every citizen of the United States should have easy access to good quality health care. After all, we believe in equal opportunity for all our citizens: that belief is demonstrated by our commitment to the right of every child to have a good publicly funded education. And decent health care is essential for genuine equal opportunity, since you certainly don't have equal opportunity if you are suffering from illnesses and can't get treatment. So obviously we should guarantee good health care for every U.S. citizen.

19. Bruce is clearly guilty of robbing the Mahoning National Bank. Consider the evidence against him. Although the robber wore a mask, the security cameras showed that the robber carried a .38 caliber revolver, and the day before the robbery Bruce purchased a .38 revolver. Also, the robber told the bank teller that "Placing all your money in this bag is a necessary condition of not getting hurt," and only Bruce would say something that stupid. And finally, the stolen money was found hidden in Bruce's garage.

20. It was Brendan Minogue who robbed the Home Savings Bank last week. It must have been Brendan: obviously the bank robber was Irish, because he was singing "Danny Boy" when he walked into the bank; and we know the robber was a philosopher, because he was carrying a copy of Aristotle's *Metaphysics*, and only a philosopher would carry Aristotle's *Metaphysics* to a bank robbery; and Brendan is the only Irish philosopher in the area.

21. The U.S. government should guarantee that every citizen of the United States has good health insurance. After all, providing health insurance for all would actually save us money overall, since it would encourage people to get early treatment rather than waiting until health problems become very severe and much more expensive to treat. Also, we claim to believe in equal opportunity for all citizens and health care is essential for equal opportunity. And finally, by providing health care for all our citizens, we would end the international embarrassment of being the only Western industrialized country without universal health care.

22. Okay, let's think about this carefully. Two hundred dollars was stolen from the special collection box in the Springfield Town Hall. Now we know that one of the Simpsons stole the money, because the money was in the box at 10:00 P.M. last night and then was missing at 8:00 this morning, and the Simpsons were locked in the Town Hall during that time, and they were the only ones there. The money was tucked away in a cabinet with a very small entrance, and so we know the thief was not Homer, since Homer is too fat to get inside the cabinet. And it wasn't Marge, because Marge is too honest to steal money; and besides, her hair is so large, she couldn't have gotten inside the small cabinet. And it wasn't Lisa, because Lisa was playing her saxophone the entire time she was in the Town Hall. And it certainly wasn't the baby: the baby was always with Marge, and the baby wouldn't be interested in the money anyway. So Bart must be the thief: He's the only one who could have stolen the money. And after all, Bart is exactly the sort of greedy kid who would do such a thing. And there's one other thing: this afternoon, Bart placed a $200 bet in the first race at Springfield Downs!

23. We should reduce the legal age for the purchase and consumption of alcoholic beverages to 18. The current law does not really prevent people who are 18 to 20 from drinking: liquor is easily available to those who really want it. Furthermore, the law is so widely violated that it causes disrespect for the law, and undermines respect for our legal system among our young people. Also, by making drinking illegal we force that age group to hide their drinking behavior rather than learning to drink responsibly and carefully with their families in public settings. And finally, there is the most basic reason of all: since we expect young people of 18 and 19 and 20 to serve as soldiers, risking and perhaps sacrificing their lives for their country, it is simply wrong to ask them to make such adult sacrifices for their country without giving them all the privileges of adulthood.

Exercise 7-2

How Do You Rule?

You are the judge in a first-degree murder case. The defendant, Bryan Beacham, is accused of murdering Arthur Attlee. The prosecution claims that Bryan and Arthur had a heated argument in a tavern over a woman named Isadora Krayzik. Following the argument, Bryan hid in the tavern parking lot until Arthur left the tavern, then Bryan ambushed Arthur, striking him in the back of the head with a heavy object, thus causing Arthur's death. (No murder weapon was recovered.)

Several prosecution witnesses testify that Bryan quarrelled with Arthur the night of the murder, and that Bryan threatened to kill Arthur. Another prosecution witness testified that Bryan was hanging around the tavern parking lot after leaving the tavern, and that he was holding an iron tire tool.

Members of an ambulance crew testified that they responded to an emergency call (the call was traced to a pay phone outside the tavern, but the caller remains unknown), and when they arrived at the tavern they found Arthur lying unconscious and with no pulse in the parking lot. They attempted to restore breathing and pulse, and continued their efforts during the drive to the emergency room, but without success.

The medical examiner testified that Arthur died as a result of a severe blow to the side of the head, which caused cardiac arrest and death. On cross-examination, however, the medical examiner admitted that it was possible that death had occurred from a heart attack, and that the blow to the head occurred after death (though he insisted it was more likely that the blow to the head occurred prior to the heart attack). Furthermore, the members of the ambulance crew testified (during cross-examination) that in their haste to get Arthur into the ambulance, one of the crew members had tripped, causing Arthur's head to bump against the edge of the rear ambulance door.

The defense called only one witness: Dr. Deborah Firestone, a specialist in forensic medicine, who testified that the cause of death was a severe heart attack, and that the blow to the head occurred several minutes after the heart attack.

Following Dr. Firestone's testimony, the defense attorney asks that you—the judge—dismiss the charges against Bryan Beacham, since there is reasonable doubt that Arthur was the victim of murder, and thus the prosecution has failed to present sufficient evidence of Bryan's guilt. The prosecution objects, claiming that whether death occurred due to a blow to the head or due to natural causes is a matter for the jury to decide, and that the evidence of Bryan's motive, his intent (as voiced in his threat), and his opportunity to kill Arthur (he was waiting in the parking lot with a potential weapon) are such strong evidence that they offset any doubts about the medical evidence. The defense responds that if there is reasonable doubt about the cause of death, then none of the other evidence matters, and the charges should be dismissed.

How do you rule? Will you dismiss the charges against Arthur, or allow the case to go to the jury?

Exercise 7-3

Try constructing your own argument, and then diagram it. Then *use* the diagrams to *improve* your argument: Are there any *gaps* in your argument? Is each step adequately supported by reasons? Are there any crucial steps that need additional support? The following are some suggestions for arguments you might construct—and then diagram—yourself.

1. For the Consider the Verdict exercise on p. 71 , write a closing argument for either the prosecution (Diana Whetstone should be found *guilty*) or the defense (Diana Whetstone should be found *not* guilty).

2. Write a closing argument for either the defense or the district attorney for the case of Nathan Jackson, in the Consider the Verdict exercise on p. 87.

3. Write a closing argument for either the defense or the district attorney for the case of Robert Ransom on p. **423**.

ASSUMPTIONS: THEIR USE AND ABUSE

We've been talking about the structure of arguments and how to get from premises to conclusions. But there's another question, of course: How do we get the premises in the first place? There are lots of sources, and we'll be examining some of them: eyewitness testimony, for example. But not all premises require further justification. Sometimes we simply agree to an assumed premise—everyone participating in the discussion accepts the premise as true, implicitly or explicitly—and then we go on from there.

Legitimate Assumptions

It is sometimes said—usually in an oracular voice, as if imparting an ageless truth—that one should never assume anything. Balderdash. We couldn't function without assumptions. When I drive through a green light I assume that the drivers for whom the light is red will stop. (If I refused to make that assumption and stopped to check, I would get rear-ended by the cars following me.) When I read a scientific report, I assume that the scientist has not deliberately faked the reported data. (If I felt I had to personally check all the results before I could profitably read a scientific report, I should certainly not read many.) When the weatherperson reports a severe blizzard in Minneapolis, I assume that he or she is honestly reporting from reliable sources, and I assume that the accompanying video of Minnesotans under the snow was not taken in Anchorage during 1979. (Sometimes, unfortunately, such trust is misplaced. Fox News has run inaccurate video reports—such as claiming that a video of a large crowd came from a Sarah Palin book signing event, when in fact it came from a McCain–Palin rally during McCain's presidential campaign. When that happens, we legitimately lose confidence in that source.) When scientists do research, they operate from many givens that are not brought into question by that particular research project. Research on lasers, for example, might make use of our knowledge of the speed of light—without *testing* what we believe to be the actual speed of light. (Of course if the research goes badly, one *might* then critically examine the underlying *assumptions*.)

Consider this argument:

> We should ban the manufacture and sale of lead-based paints. Think about what happens when you paint your house or apartment. You paint over the paint that was there, and eventually your paint is painted over, until the result is a thick coat of lead-based paint that ultimately begins to peel and flake. The small children in the house pick at the paint, then put their fingers—or even flakes of paint—into their mouths. Through these and other events, a substantial portion of the lead may ultimately end up in the children, and thus in their bloodstreams. And when that happens, the children suffer from lead poisoning, which may cause mental retardation, nervous disorders, blindness, and even death. Therefore, lead-based paints should be banned.

That seems to me a good argument. In fact, it is essentially the argument that brought about the ban of lead-based paint in most countries. But it contains a crucial assumption that is left unstated. It is a perfectly legitimate assumption, and it is so obvious and widely accepted that it is almost impossible to pick out. You may be able to find several unstated assumptions in that argument; but the most basic assumption—or at least the most basic *unstated* assumption—is quite difficult to detect. Have a go at it before you peek at the next paragraph.

The assumption is: We don't want children to suffer mental retardation, nervous disorders, blindness, or death. Now that is hardly a controversial assumption; in fact, it is because it is so universally accepted that it is both difficult to detect and unnecessary to state. (If we added to the argument "And we do not wish children to go blind or die," that would strike most people as belaboring the obvious.)

And remember the argument about Alice not being guilty? The main reason was that the crime was committed in Key West, and Alice was in Miami at the time.

> Alice could not have been the robber, since Alice was not in Key West when the crime was committed. She could not have been in Key West, because at 10:00 P.M. on August 9 she was in Miami.

But that involves an essential (unstated) assumption: It is impossible for someone to be in two different places at the same time. That is hardly an assumption that needs to be noted or supported: No further evidence or expert testimony is required to back it up. (That is not to say that it is never disputed: Some "psychics" claim to be in at least two different places—maybe more—simultaneously, through out-of-body experiences. Still, the assumption that if Alice was in Miami, then she was not in Key West at the same time seems a safe and legitimate one.) And the moral of the story is a simple one: Assumptions are sometimes perfectly legitimate.

We often make explicit assumptions—sometimes when we are in fact doubtful of their truth—in order to consider what would follow from them:

> "Assuming that the track remains very muddy, which horse do you think is more likely to win the Kentucky Derby?"
> "If we assume that the inflation rate will be low during the next year, what do you think will be the average increase in industrial wages?"

In some cases, it is useful to assume things that one believes are *false* in order to show that even if they *were* true a certain conclusion still would not follow:

> "Look, even assuming that Richard Nixon knew nothing about the Watergate break-in before it occurred, he still deserved to be impeached for helping to cover it up."
> "Even assuming that all the Sandinistas are doctrinaire Marxists, it still doesn't follow that we should support groups like the Contras who commit terrorist acts against the civilian population of Nicaragua."
> "Even if it were true that the tobacco companies really want to curb teenage smoking, it still would not be a good idea to leave efforts to reduce underage smoking to the discretion of the tobacco industry."

In short, assumptions are not the enemy. Assumptions may be wrong, of course. In the case of science, if we try to duplicate a scientist's findings and consistently find it impossible to do so, we may eventually conclude that we were mistaken in assuming that that particular scientist was reporting data honestly. If we run experiments and our results constantly conflict with our predictions, we may eventually come to believe that some of our operating assumptions were mistaken. We do occasionally find that we operated on mistaken assumptions; when that occurs we reject that assumption and try again, but we do not reject *all* assumptions.

So it is legitimate and probably essential to operate from some assumptions. The goal is not to eliminate all assumptions; rather, the point is to *recognize* the assumptions being made, especially the key ones.

Enthymemes

While we're on the subject of unstated assumptions, this may be a good time to talk about *enthymemes,* which is just a classy name for a common phenomenon. An *enthymeme* is an argument that contains a premise that is regarded as *so obvious* that it need not be stated. We've looked at a couple already: the argument about Alice not being in Key West because she was in Miami (the obvious unstated premise is that if she is in Miami, then she can't simultaneously be in Key West); and the argument about the hazards of lead-based paint, with its unstated premise that the damage and death of small children should be prevented.

My grandmother was fond of enthymemes. When I was a boy, when my grandmother thought "my eyes were bigger than my stomach," and that I had taken more food on my plate than I was likely to eat, she would rebuke me with one of her favorite sayings: "If you eat all that, then I'm the Queen of Sheba." Since it was obvious that my grandmother was not the Queen of Sheba, her conclusion was clear: "You're not going to eat all that."

Grandmothers aren't the only source of enthymemes. "Either I've got the best used-car deals in town, or my name's not Honest Bill Barton. So come on down to Honest Bill's Used Cars, 'cause Honest Bill is dealin', darlin'." Well, it doesn't take a rocket scientist to figure out that the conclusion of Honest Bill's argument is that "I've got the best used-car deals in town," and that the unstated premise in this enthymeme is, My name *is* Honest Bill Barton. (Honest Bill's argument is *valid;* whether it's *sound* is a very different question.)

Illegitimate Assumptions

In order to combat the mistaken assumption that assumptions are typically false, and should always be shunned, we have examined some legitimate and useful assumptions. But, of course, some assumptions *are* false (such as the common assumption that it is always wrong to make assumptions) or at least are controversial. Such illegitimate assumptions cause problems, and they are not infrequent.

In uninspired mystery novels, the chief inspector *assumes* that the foul murder was committed by either the duke or the cook; and in such cases, you can be confident that the villain is the duchess, or perhaps the butler, but certainly not the suspects who were assumed to be the only alternatives. And when the president of the university announces that the university must either cut classes or raise tuition, that may also be a false assumption: perhaps cutting salaries or reducing overhead should also be considered. When one of your fellow jurors announces that the defendant must be guilty, because she did not testify in her own behalf, that juror is operating from a common but false assumption: that the defendant must prove her innocence.

The problem is not with assumptions as such; assumptions are often legitimate. Nor is there a special problem with *unstated* assumptions. In the earlier examples, the assumption that Alice could not be in two places at the same time and the assumption that we do not want children to die are both left unstated, but they are so obvious and acceptable that they do not require statement. The problem is with *controversial* assumptions: assumptions that are false or at least require further support. Such controversial assumptions are particularly insidious when left unstated.

For example, many of the purveyors of pain-relief medications tout their products as *extra strength.* Anacin[4] runs a catchy little commercial in which "the Anacin difference" is strongly emphasized: The two standard aspirin tablets contain a total of 650 milligrams of aspirin; but each tablet of Anacin contains 400 milligrams of aspirin, for a total dose of 800 milligrams if two are taken. The announcer in the commercial points out this difference, and then asks the shopper which she plans to take when she next has a headache; the answer, of course, is that she plans to take Anacin and get the *extra* pain relief, the *Anacin difference* of an extra 150 milligrams of aspirin.

The Anacin commercial contains a very important unstated assumption. What is it? (Leave aside the fact that by simply taking three generic-brand aspirin tablets of 325 milligrams each, you could get more aspirin for less money than by taking two 400-milligram Anacin tablets.) In trying to detect the unstated assumption in the commercial, *first* ask, What is the *conclusion* of the commercial's argument? With the conclusion in view, it may be easier to detect the tricky unstated assumption.

The conclusion is just that two 400-milligram tablets of Anacin (aspirin) will be more effective in relieving headache than two 325-milligram tablets of aspirin. The unstated assumption is that 800 milligrams of aspirin will provide more effective headache relief than will 650 milligrams of aspirin. That *sounds* like an innocent enough assumption; but in fact it is false. Clinical studies on the effects of different dosages indicate that at 650 milligrams of aspirin, the dose–response curve levels off markedly. In other words, most people will *not* get more effective headache relief by taking 800–1,000 milligrams of aspirin than by taking 650 milligrams. A seemingly insignificant and unstated assumption turns out to be crucial for establishing the conclusion that Anacin is better: It is a crucial assumption, and it is false.[5] (Though the 800 mg dose won't relieve your headache any better than the standard 650 mg, there is one significant difference: the 800 mg dose is more likely to cause nausea.)

We typically operate under basic assumptions that shape the way we think about our world and our society. For example, our debate over national economic policies may take place within a controlling, unexamined framework of assumptions about distribution of wealth, rights to profits, and control of capital, and those invisible assumptions may tightly constrain the sorts of options and changes that can be considered. In another instance, a Senate committee might examine scrupulously the most effective method of distributing the limited supply of childhood vaccinations, but remain unaware of the structural assumptions that allow the pharmaceutical industry to control prices and limit supply; examination of those key assumptions might eliminate the problem of how to deal with vaccine shortages. The university's animal research committee may scrutinize new ways of ventilating cages and reducing the suffering of research animals, while remaining blind to their basic operating assumption that it is acceptable to use animals for research. The slaveowner may examine whether working conditions and living quarters could be improved, while being unable to see the monstrous controlling assumption of the legitimacy of slavery. And Ptolemaic astronomers may develop elaborate and elegant accounts of planetary motion, while leaving unexamined the controlling assumption that the Earth is stationary. Good critical thinking often involves reasoning from assumptions, but the best critical thinking also requires the ability to critically examine those assumptions, including the most basic social and institutional assumptions of our society.

What Does Fire Consume?

In scientific research—as in other areas of thought—it is the *unrecognized* assumptions that are most troublesome. Those assumptions are likely to be embedded in the questions posed by the scientific investigator. For example, eighteenth- and nineteenth-century biologists asked what *purpose* was served by the existence of such a variety of species. Darwin recognized that the assumption that such variety had to be explained in terms of *purposes* was questionable, and he was able to develop his mechanistic theory of natural selection by abandoning talk of purposes. Many researchers of the seventeenth and eighteenth centuries endeavored to discover what leaves the object when it is burned (What does the fire "consume" when something is "consumed by fire"?). The assumption was so natural and pervasive that it led to the development of an elaborate theory of phlogiston: Phlogiston was supposed to be the combustible material in an object, which was removed when the object burned. But by questioning that assumption, Lavoisier was able to recognize oxygen as a distinct gas and thus laid the foundation for modern chemical theory.

Assumptions can be legitimate and acceptable in the right setting, and they can be misleading and suffocating in the wrong setting. When someone tries to slip in as an assumption a point that is critical to an argument and that is also a point that might be doubted by some parties to the argument, assumptions are being used in a misleading way (more about that in Chapter 13 on begging the question). But when assumptions are used to specify some points of agreement (perhaps tentative or hypothetical or local or conditional agreement) so that attention can be focused on the key issues being contested, assumptions can do valuable work. It's impossible to argue about everything at once. If the assumptions that are operating are clearly spelled out and agreed upon, it may be possible to focus attention on the key issues. And assumptions need not be carved in stone: Today's assumption can be critically examined—and perhaps rejected—tomorrow.

Exercise 7-4

What are the important assumptions in these arguments? (Be sure to note any important *unstated* assumptions.)

1. The defense attorney argues, "Ladies and gentlemen of the jury, it is now up to you to consider a verdict in this case. When you look carefully at the evidence, I am confident you must reach a verdict of not guilty. The prosecution has simply failed to establish that my client burglarized Jones's Grocery. There is no physical evidence placing him at the site, and the only eyewitness testimony was given by a witness who has a long record of perjury, and who admits that he is giving testimony in the hope of getting a shorter sentence for himself. In short, the prosecution has not proved that the defendant is guilty. Therefore, you must return a verdict of not guilty."

2. It is wrong to raise animals for food. After all, it is wrong to inflict suffering on an animal—on any sentient creature—unnecessarily (when it is merely for the pleasure of enjoying meat, and not out of necessity).

3. We must overhaul the U.S. health-care system. The United States spends more per person—and a higher percentage of its gross national product—for health care than does any other nation. And our health-care costs continue their upward spiral. Yet while we spend more than any other country, we also have tens of millions of people with no health-care coverage and no access to medical care. And we have the highest infant mortality rate of any industrialized country. It will not be easy, but major changes are imperative.

✓●─ **Study** and **Review** on **mythinkinglab.com**

REVIEW QUESTIONS

1. What is the first step in critically analyzing an argument?
2. Define, compare, and contrast convergent arguments and linked arguments.
3. When are argument assumptions legitimate? When should they be questioned or challenged?
4. Under what circumstances might you accept an argument assumption that you believe to be false?
5. What is an enthymeme?

NOTES

[1] Mr. Justice Darling's summing-up to the jury is quoted in Edgar Lustgarten, *The Murder and the Trial* (London: Odhams Press Limited, 1960), pp. 59–60.

[2] The prosecution presented evidence that EDTA (at the levels found in Simpson's blood from the crime scene) *does* occur naturally (in blood that is *not* specially treated with EDTA). Thus, they attempted to break the middle link in the chain.

[3] This argument is adapted from Chapter 5 of Jeffrey Abramson's *We, the Jury* (New York: Basic Books, 1994).

[4] Anacin is a registered trademark of American Home Products Corporation, New York.

[5] The information on pain relievers is taken from an interesting and informative article in *Consumer Reports* 47, no. 8 (August 1982), pp. 395–399.

INTERNET RESOURCES

OpenCourseWare on Critical Thinking, Logic, and Creativity is an excellent site covering many topics in critical thinking. For good examples of (what they call) "argument mapping," go to *http://philosophy.hku.hk/think/arg/complex.php*.

ADDITIONAL READING

A number of books give excellent guidance in analyzing arguments. One of the best is Michael Scriven, *Reasoning* (New York: McGraw-Hill, 1976). Another useful approach is offered by Steven Toulmin, Richard Rieke, and Allan Janik in *An Introduction to Reasoning*, 2nd ed. (New York: Macmillan, 1984); it also contains an excellent section on appeals court reasoning.

For an approach that offers insights into the way reasoning proceeds in the most ordinary settings, see Douglas N. Walton, *Plausible Argument in Everyday Conversation* (Albany, NY: State University of New York Press, 1992).

Good discussions of the special requirements of legal reasoning can be found in Martin P. Golding, *Legal Reasoning* (New York: Alfred A. Knopf, 1984) and Kenneth J. Vandevelde, *Thinking Like a Lawyer: An Introduction to Legal Reasoning* (Boulder, CO: Westview Press, 1996). The classic text on legal reasoning is Edward H. Levi, *An Introduction to Legal Reasoning* (Chicago, IL: The University of Chicago Press, 1949), but it's not easy sledding.

The great French physical scientist of the early twentieth century Pierre Duhem was particularly clear on the role of assumptions in scientific research. See Pierre Duhem, *The Aim and Structure of Physical Theory*, translated by Philip P. Wiener (Princeton, NJ: Princeton University Press, 1954).

For another view of how science operates (and of how assumptions are used and are overthrown), see the fascinating book by Thomas Kuhn, *The Structure of Scientific Revolutions*, 2nd ed. (Chicago, IL: The University of Chicago Press, 1970).

▶ Read the Document on mythinkinglab.com

Daryl A. Bergman, "War on Drugs Fails." If you diagrammed Bergman's two arguments, would each argument be convergent or linked?

Mary Anne Warren, "On the Moral and Legal Status of Abortion," *Monist*, Vol. 57, no. 4 (1973), pp. 43–61. This is a well-known argument in favor of the right to an abortion; try drawing a diagram of that argument.

Watchtower Bible and Tract Society of New York v. *Village of Stratton*, 536 U.S. (2002). In this case, a group of Jehovah's Witnesses wished to go door-to-door in the village of Stratton, giving away literature and attempting to win converts. Stratton requires that all door-to-door canvassers register with the mayor's office and secure a permit. The group of Jehovah's Witnesses objected to securing a permit before going door-to-door, arguing that such a requirement would violate their First Amendment right of free speech. Starting with Section III of the Court opinion written by Justice Stevens, diagram the argument given by the Court in reaching its judgment, including the conclusion reached in that argument.

8

❖ ❖ ❖

The Burden of Proof

The first step in critically analyzing an argument is determining the conclusion. The second step is determining who bears the burden of proof.

I claim that extraterrestrials have built an amazing undersea city, deep in the Pacific Ocean. They are mining natural resources from below the ocean floor, and transporting these resources back to their home planet through a fleet of interstellar cargo ships. You have doubts about the existence of this ET city, and challenge me to specify its location. I can't, but I'm still sure it's there. You ask for photographs of the city; I have none. Are there unusual findings from oceanographic research that would indicate the presence of such a deep sea metropolis? I have no such data. Are there any reliable witnesses who have seen the city? None. But I am firm in my claim: Look, the Pacific Ocean is vast and deep, and most of the ocean floor is unexplored. If you are so skeptical about the undersea city, then *prove* that it does *not* exist. And if you can't prove that the ocean floor does not contain such a city, then that is strong evidence that such a city exists. At the very least, you should keep an open mind about the possibility of such a city, and put your skepticism aside.

WHO BEARS THE BURDEN OF PROOF?

You aren't likely to buy the existence of an ocean-bottom ET city as a result of this flimsy argument. There was no real proof for the claim, and anyone making a claim or an accusation bears the *burden of proof*. The person making the claim must prove it true; it is *not* up to others to prove it false. The fallacy of *appeal to ignorance* is committed when someone argues that because his or her claim cannot be proved false, it therefore should be accepted as true. But the fact that a claim cannot be proved false is no grounds for believing it true. (Certainly it does not prove that it is *not* true; it may be true, even though it is not proved so. But failure to prove a claim false is *not* proof of the claim's truth.)

Attempts to shift the burden of proof are common. In 1988, television evangelist Pat Robertson made an unsuccessful run for president of the United States; during his

Placing the Burden of Proof

The "preliminary" question of who bears the burden of proof often has great influence on which side prevails in an argument. Suppose that I am a school district superintendent, and I impose a regulation requiring that teachers beyond the fourth month of pregnancy must take an unpaid leave of absence from their teaching jobs. You claim that this rule is unfair to women teachers, because it unreasonably deprives them of the opportunity to work. (There is no reason why most pregnant teachers cannot continue to teach effectively; some individuals may be incapacitated by pregnancy, but that should be decided on a case-by-case basis.) *Does such a regulation treat women unfairly?*

Before you answer that, think about the prior question: Who bears the burden of proof? You are claiming that my rule unfairly discriminates against women; is it up to you to prove that the rule places a special hardship on women? Or should the burden of proof be on me? After all, I proposed the rule; should it be my burden to prove that the rule does *not* unfairly discriminate?

That is a difficult question. The U.S. Supreme Court attempts to resolve it this way: If you want to claim that a law or rule treats you unfairly, then you generally have the burden of proving that unfairness; however, if you are a member of a group that has traditionally suffered discrimination and unfair treatment (such as women, African Americans, members of a persecuted religion, and the physically challenged) and you claim that the law treats members of your group unfairly, then those passing the law bear the burden of proving that it is *not* discriminatory. That seems to me a legitimate way of placing the burden of proof in such cases, though it is certainly a difficult issue. In any case, we can leave further discussion of that question for your seminar in Constitutional Law. The immediate point is that placing the burden of proof can be a very difficult question, and a very important question. When a pregnancy leave case came before the U.S. Supreme Court (*Jo Carol LaFleur* v. *Cleveland Board of Education*), the Court ruled on January 21, 1974, that the school board had failed to demonstrate that their pregnancy leave rule was not discriminatory toward women (a group that had traditionally suffered discrimination), and so struck down the rule. Women might well succeed in proving that such rules are discriminatory, even if they bore the burden of that proof; but with the burden on the other side to prove that the rule is *not* unfair, women teachers certainly had an easier path to victory.[1]

campaign he claimed that there were—or at least might be—Soviet missiles in Cuba. Since all indications—from spy satellites, for example—were that there were no such missiles, the question naturally arose as to what evidence the Reverend Robertson could offer for his dramatic claim. Having none, Robertson attempted to shift the burden of proof to the other side: His claims were supported by the fact that U.S. intelligence could not conclusively prove that no such missiles existed in Cuba. And of course Robertson was partly correct: Neither the U.S. intelligence service nor anyone else could conclusively prove that there were no Soviet missiles cleverly concealed deep in some Cuban cavern or

A Burden of Proof Tragedy

Placing the burden of proof may be a life or death question. The 1986 explosion of the *Challenger* spacecraft cost the lives of seven people. The accident was traced to problems with the O-rings, which did not function properly in the freezing weather at the time of the launch, allowing fuel to leak and thus causing the deadly explosion. Morton Thiokol was the company that manufactured the O-rings, and prior to the planned *Challenger* launch, engineers from Morton Thiokol raised the possibility of danger from the frozen O-rings. In the past, if anyone raised reasonable doubts about the safety of a launch, then there had to be solid proof that the supposed danger did *not* exist before the launch could proceed: The burden of proof was always on those who claimed that it was *safe* to launch. But in this case the presumption was reversed: The spacecraft was presumed to be safe, and anyone raising doubts had to conclusively prove that there was genuine *risk* in order to stop the launch. The Morton Thiokol engineers could show reasonable grounds for concern (the O-rings had not been tested in freezing conditions); but they could not demonstrate that the O-rings actually would malfunction in the cold and thereby cause an explosion. Since the burden of proof was (wrongly) placed on the engineers to prove danger rather than on the launch team to prove safety, the launch proceeded to its disastrous end.[2]

hidden in some other unknown—and unspecified—location. But that certainly does not substantiate Robertson's claim, no more than the fact that we cannot prove that no brontosauruses live in caverns deep below New Orleans proves the existence of subterranean brontosauruses, and no more than the fact that we cannot prove that there are absolutely no extraterrestrials disguised as earthlings proves that we are in the midst of extraterrestrials. The person making the claim—of Soviet missiles, brontosauruses, or extraterrestrials—bears the burden of proof.

APPEAL TO IGNORANCE

The sensationalist tabloids have a field day with the appeal to ignorance. They publish scandalous accusations concerning the lives and loves of movie stars and politicians and then—in *support* of those stories—they point out that: "Two weeks ago we published an exclusive story about Ima Starr's torrid love affair with the Ambassador to Rutabaga; if it's not true, they should deny it, but since they haven't denied it, much less offered any proof that it is false, then it must be true." But Ima Starr and the ambassador are caught in a bind: If they ignore the story, a few people will believe it, but most will ignore it and it will soon pass, since none of the major newspapers or television networks will consider the story reliable. However, if they deny the story, then *that* is news—whenever a film star and an ambassador issue statements, the press considers it newsworthy—and those denials (along with the *charges* being denied) will receive national news coverage, and the story will not blow over quickly. So even if there is not a grain of truth to the charges, it's unlikely that a denial will be issued. And more to the point, it's not up to them to prove the charges *false* (think for a moment of how difficult it would be to *prove* that you did not have a *secret* love affair with someone); the burden of proof rests on those making the charges.

A variation on this problem occurs when a snake oil salesman—for example, someone touting the miraculous healing powers of magnets—challenges the medical community to debate: "I've proposed that a panel of distinguished medical researchers and physicians examine the wonderful benefits of my Salumagnetomed System, and I've offered to meet with them anywhere and give my evidence; I challenge them to debate me! But they keep refusing!" So why won't the AMA convene a panel to debate this wonderful new magnetic health system? For two reasons. First, such systems have already been examined carefully, and found to be useless; and if researchers took up every new variation of such quackery, they would have no time for legitimate research. And second, if a panel of "distinguished medical researchers and physicians" meet with this quack— even to roundly condemn it as fraud—he will immediately include it in his advertising, and it will greatly increase his credibility: "Try my new Salumagnetomed System, which was recently the focus of a full AMA-sponsored conference, drawing the attention of such distinguished researchers as . . . "; well, you get the picture. If legitimate scientists and physicians appear on the same platform with such quacks, it gives the quacks instant credibility: distinguished medical scientists believe it is worth taking this new magnetic therapy system seriously, and its inventor is seated on the same panel with legitimate scientists, just one top medical scientist among others.

THE BURDEN OF PROOF IN THE COURTROOM

There is a special setting in which it is vitally important to remember who bears the burden of proof, and in this setting—unfortunately—the fallacy of appeal to ignorance occurs with frightening regularity: the jury room. It is now a cornerstone of the American and British systems of criminal justice that a defendant is "innocent until proven guilty." And in fact, the principle of "presumption of innocence" was already an essential element of English law when the earliest British settlers arrived in the American colonies, and thus it can be found in the earliest rules of legal procedure formulated by the British colonists in New England. The principle that the burden of proving guilt rests on the prosecution continued to be a feature of colonial American judicial procedure, even when (as in the witchcraft trials) courts were not particularly careful concerning the quality of "evidence." This basic principle of justice is fundamental to the justice systems of many countries; for example, it is a prominent element of the Canadian Charter of Rights and Freedoms, it is a central principle of Australian Common Law (and part of the Victorian Charter of Human Rights and Responsibilities), and is one of the basic rights recognized in the 1789 French Declaration of the Rights of Man and of the Citizen.

Presumption of Innocence

Why is the "presumption of innocence" so important? First and foremost because it is simply the correct manner of reasoning. The burden of proof rightly belongs on the party that makes a claim, whether that claim is a pharmaceutical company's claim that a new drug is "safe and effective" or a tabloid's claim that extraterrestrials are hiding in Mammoth Cave or the state's claim that an individual committed a crime. If the proof can be supplied, fine; but failure to either prove or disprove the claim is just that: a failure to prove anything, which leaves the safety of the drug in doubt and the guilt of the defendant unestablished.

There is a second reason why the burden of proof lies with the one making the claim. If one were allowed to "appeal to ignorance" (appeal to the failure to disprove the claim) in order to "prove" a claim, then one would be able to "prove" the most extraordinary things. For example, it is quite impossible to prove that there is *not* a group of invisible extraterrestrials lurking in the depths of the Indian Ocean, but we should be loath to count that as proving the presence of such beings. It is not possible to prove that Rousseau never had a very secret love affair with Marie Antoinette, but lack of disproof of such an affair does not prove that such a tryst occurred. More to the point, imagine trying to *prove* that you are innocent of a murder that occurred at 11:00 P.M. 3 years ago. Unless you keep a remarkably good diary, you probably don't have an exact recollection of where you were at that time, much less a convincing alibi. (Even if you distinctly remember being in the college library with a friend all that evening, will your friend remember it? And will your friend be absolutely certain that you didn't leave—for perhaps half an hour around 11:00 P.M.—just long enough to commit the foul crime of murder?) In fact, if failure to disprove the charges were counted as proof of those charges, then we would never have an unsolved crime: Almost any crime that occurred could be "proved"—by appeal to ignorance—against some unfortunate reclusive individual who was not seen by anyone during the time of the crime. Such appeals to ignorance certainly have advantages: They have (to borrow Bertrand Russell's phrase) "all the advantages of theft over honest labor."

There is another reason for favoring a strong presumption of innocence. It has less to do with logic and more with our principles of individual freedom and justice. We believe that the rights and freedom of the individual are fundamental, and we oppose sacrificing individual rights and autonomy for the benefit of the state; therefore, the general presumption must be that the individual's rights and freedom should not be interfered with. Any *denial* of individual liberty (through criminal sanctions) requires powerful overriding reasons and the strongest and most conclusive proof. Placing the burden of proof on the defendant violates principles of liberty as well as logic. Unfortunately, jurors often reverse the burden of proof. Dr. Stanley Brodsky tells of a jury questionnaire he gave to potential jurors prior to a murder trial in Kentucky. One of the questions was, "No matter what the law says, do you agree that a defendant in a murder trial should have to prove his innocence?" Over 40% of the potential jurors marked their agreement with requiring the defendant to prove innocence—and it is likely that there were others who agreed but were reluctant to admit it.

What is involved in the "presumption of innocence" for the defendant? Most obviously, the defendant does not have to prove anything. The full burden of proof rests on the prosecution, and if the prosecution leaves a reasonable doubt after the presentation

Guilt Not Proven

In almost every country, juries in criminal trials have only two possible verdicts: guilty or not guilty. (Of course the jury may not be able to reach a verdict, resulting in a "hung jury"; and in cases when there are multiple charges, juries may find the defendant guilty of some charges and not guilty of others; and in some cases, juries may choose among different charges, such as manslaughter or second-degree murder or first-degree murder; but in each case, the question ultimately comes down to guilty or not guilty.) Scotland is different. Juries in Scotland—in a tradition that is centuries old—have the third option of a "guilt not proven" verdict. This "guilt not proven" verdict (sometimes called the "Scottish verdict") is legally equivalent to a verdict of not guilty: when a jury returns a verdict of "guilt not proven," it means that the defendant is exonerated and cannot be retried on those charges. It is sometimes suggested that other countries adopt Scotland's third verdict of "guilt not

proven." Would that be a good addition to our criminal justice system?

On one hand, the "guilt not proven" verdict seems a bit silly, since that's exactly what a "not guilty" verdict is (or at least that's what it's supposed to be). And it seems a gratuitous slap at the defendant; it's like saying, "We don't have enough evidence to determine that you are guilty, but we think you might be." However, if it reminds jurors of exactly what must be proved (and keeps them from returning a guilty verdict just because the defendant has not been able to prove his or her innocence), then it might be desirable. It would be an important reminder that the prosecution bears the entire burden of proof, and that if the prosecution fails to meet that requirement then the defendant must not be convicted. Under the presumption of innocence, if the prosecutor *fails* to prove the defendant's guilt, then the defendant is entitled to an acquittal, whether that acquittal is in the form of "not guilty" or "guilt not proven."

of its case, the defense need do nothing at all. And if the prosecution *has* managed to make a strong argument for the guilt of the defendant, the defendant need not totally shatter that argument; instead, the defense need only show that the prosecution's argument is not quite convincing. The defendant need not establish his or her innocence. Unless the prosecution can build a case that both firmly establishes the defendant's guilt and withstands all attempts by the defense to raise doubts about the case, the jury should conclude that the prosecution has not proved its case and should therefore vote not guilty.

When the Defendant Does Not Testify

The presumption of innocence is a basic principle of logic and of Anglo-American criminal law. But jurors sometimes forget the principle: They reverse the order and demand that the defendant "prove he's not guilty" or "clear herself of the charges." And there is a more subtle way in which mistakes are made about the burden of proof in criminal proceedings. When the defendant does not testify in his or her own behalf, many jurors weigh that very heavily against the defendant. But the defendant has no obligation to testify. It is not the responsibility of the defendant to prove innocence: The full burden of proof rests on the prosecution.

U.S. and Canadian courts recognize that the defendant has no obligation to testify on his or her own behalf, and judges in both countries are careful to remind jurors that the decision of a defendant not to testify in no way counts against the defendant. But all too often the defendant's decision not to testify does create a presumption against him, due to the fallacious reasoning of some jurors. Jurors are apt to think that "He didn't clear himself of the charges so he must be guilty" or "If he were not guilty he would want to take the stand and deny the charges, so he must be guilty." Or perhaps they continue to give lip service to the principle that the defendant need not testify, but in their actual deliberations they may still count the defendant's nontestimony against the defendant. But that is pure appeal to ignorance: He hasn't proved the charges *false*, so they must be true.

Until the end of the nineteenth century, defendants in British criminal cases were not allowed to testify in their own behalf. The Criminal Evidence Act of 1898 gave the defendant the right, if he or she chose, to be placed under oath and give testimony. There are many obvious benefits to such a change, and no doubt it is on the whole a

Sacco and Vanzetti

The fallacy of appeal to ignorance is at home in the supermarket tabloids and scandal sheets, but it occasionally shows up in more respectable settings. In *Sacco & Vanzetti: The Case Resolved*, Francis Russell argues that Nicolo Sacco was in fact guilty of the crime for which he was executed. (The Sacco–Vanzetti case is perhaps the most famous—or infamous—American criminal case in the twentieth century. In 1920, in South Braintree, Massachusetts, two gunmen shot and killed a paymaster and guard and stole a payroll. Nicolo Sacco and Bartolomeo Vanzetti were both active in the anarchist political movement and were thus mistrusted by the authorities. They were arrested and—largely on the basis of some rather shaky eyewitness testimony—were convicted of murder. They were electrocuted on August 27, 1927, still steadfastly asserting their innocence.) One of Russell's arguments for the guilt of Sacco is the following (it is contained in a letter Russell wrote to Dante Sacco, the son of the man who was executed):

> I cannot look on him [Nicolo Sacco] as an innocent man. I may be wrong. So much has always been indeterminate in this case. Yet in the silence of the Sacco family is, at least to outsiders, an implication of guilt. That is the only conclusion that I can draw.[3]

The fact that the son of the executed man refused to comment on the case proves nothing at all. Certainly it carries no implication that Dante Sacco agrees that his father was guilty of murder. No matter what reason Dante Sacco had for remaining silent, his silence is *not* proof that his father was guilty. To suppose that silence proves guilt (to suppose that silence proves *anything*) is to commit the fallacy of appeal to ignorance. In fact, you can no doubt think of several excellent reasons why Dante Sacco would remain silent even if he believed his father innocent.

First, Dante Sacco was only 7 years old when his father was arrested. Even if he believed his father was innocent, it is not likely that he would have any strong evidence to that effect, and he might have thus decided to keep silent.

Second, Dante Sacco was perhaps traumatized by the electrocution of his father—it's not difficult to imagine that being the effect on a 15-year-old boy—and thus could never again bear to think of the events, much less publicly speak about them.

Third, perhaps Dante Sacco wanted to get on with his own life and put the past behind him, and thus preferred not to be associated with past events. (There could be some social stigma attached to being in the family of a famous anarchist, and Dante may have wanted to avoid such social pressures.)

Fourth, Dante may have kept silent from his desire to spare his own family, including his children, from social pressure and stigma.

And finally, if Dante Sacco believed his father was innocent and had been murdered because of his political views—which is what his father claimed—then Dante might have had good reason to be fearful of speaking out against such injustices.

Perhaps those are, perhaps they are not, the real reasons why Dante Sacco remained silent concerning the execution of his father. In any case, the moral of the story is this: Silence is not proof, one way or the other.

great improvement in trial procedure and a salutary extension of the rights of the individual. However, it is by no means an unmixed blessing: Once given the *right* to give testimony on their own behalf, jurors started to *expect* defendants to take the stand and deny their guilt; and if the defendant did not testify, jurors often switched the burden of proof—"the defendant would not even deny the charges against him, so he must be guilty"—and counted the failure of the defendant to testify and to establish his innocence as proof of guilt. The right of a defendant to testify is an important right; but if jurors interpret that right as an *obligation* to testify, or as an obligation that defendants prove themselves innocent, then that right has become a terrible wrong which can and does result in wrongful convictions. And after that act there was also a danger that by not going into the witness box the defendant might lead the jury to conclude that the defendant is unable to establish innocence, and that is an equally mistaken version of misplacing the burden of proof and committing the fallacy of appeal to ignorance.

Juries and the Burden of Proof

Consider where the burden of proof lies in this fictional example of a jury debate.[5] The defendant is charged with the criminal possession of a prohibited drug. Two arresting police officers testify that they chased and caught the defendant, took him to the police

Subtle Shifts

When a juror assumes that the defendant must prove innocence, the juror obviously has misplaced the burden of proof. But there are more subtle ways of shifting the burden of proof against a defendant. Imagine that you are called for jury duty, and the case involves serious criminal charges (such as murder). You are of course committed to the principle that the prosecution bears the entire burden of proving the defendant's guilt beyond a reasonable doubt, and you start from the presumption that the defendant is innocent. Before you are seated on a jury, however, the prosecution asks the judge for a special ruling to keep the names of all potential jurors a secret and to have all potential jurors escorted from the courthouse each day by armed federal marshals. What conclusion is a juror likely to draw from such special "protection"? As William M. Kunstler has pointed out, jurors will conclude that the "defendant is so far beyond the pale that their very lives would be in danger if their identities were made public." Such a conclusion, prior to hearing any evidence, effectively torpedoes any "presumption of innocence." In an article in the *Fordham Law Review*, Abraham Abramovsky discussed the problems such policies pose for the presumption of innocence:

In effect, by his instruction with respect to anonymity, the trial judge implied that the defendants were so vicious and dangerous that anonymity was required to protect the jurors and their families from harassment, physical injury or even death. In any prior jury service, the jurors would not have been instructed to remain anonymous. Therefore the only reasonable inference that a jury could draw . . . was that protection was mandated by the character of the defendant. . . . Thus, before any evidence was introduced . . . the defendants were depicted by implication as notorious individuals. This characterization . . . eviscerated the presumption of innocence to which these defendants were entitled.

If such anonymity were really essential to protect jury members, we would be faced with a tough choice between protecting the safety of jurors and protecting the defendant's right to the presumption of innocence and to a fair and unbiased trial. But as Kunstler noted, "To my knowledge, during the more than 200 years of this Republic's existence, no juror has ever been harmed by a defendant or his or her supporters."[4]

The Right to Remain Silent

The "right to remain silent" is closely linked to the presumption of innocence: If you are charged with a crime, you have a right to remain silent (and cannot be compelled to testify), *because* the burden of proof rests entirely on the prosecution, and you are not required to say or do *anything* to establish your innocence. The right to remain silent was a cornerstone of the British judicial system, and it became firmly entrenched in the legal systems of countries—such as Canada, Australia, and the United States—that were deeply influenced by the British model of justice: the right is recognized in the Fifth Amendment to the U.S. Constitution (as one of the Bill of Rights) and is protected under sections 7 and 11 of the Canadian Charter of Rights and Freedoms. In the United States, the first words of the *Miranda* warnings are "You have a right to remain silent." That is the warning given to all who are arrested, a warning that is a staple of every episode of *Law and Order*, and a basic principle of justice. Indeed, the right to remain silent has been widely recognized as fundamental to human rights and to procedural justice: The European Court of Human rights holds that "The right to remain silent under police questioning and the privilege against self-incrimination are generally recognised

international standards which lie at the heart of the notion of a fair procedure." Sadly, that right is under attack in the place of its birth: the British justice system. The Criminal Justice and Public Order Act of 1994 permits the accused to remain silent, but also permits the judge to instruct the jury that the jurors may "draw adverse inferences" from the fact that a defendant chose not to answer questions or chose not to testify; that is, the judge can instruct the jury that they may conclude that *because* the defendant did not testify, that can be counted as some evidence of the defendant's guilt. Under this law, juries are not supposed to convict the defendant *solely* on the basis of the defendant's silence; but if there is other evidence against the defendant, then the defendant's silence can tip the scales toward conviction. There has been strong opposition to this law since its passage, and some British politicians who support the law have claimed that the law does *not* undercut the basic right to silence: you still have a right to remain silent, though if you exercise that right you will be more likely to be convicted and imprisoned. But that is absurd. It's like saying, "You have a right of free speech; but if you speak freely, you run a greater risk of being imprisoned."

station, but did not find the drug on the defendant. The police then (so they testified) returned to the scene of the arrest and found a packet of tablets of the prohibited drug, which (the police claimed) the defendant had thrown away when he was caught. The defendant denies ever having possessed the drugs and denies any knowledge of the tablets. After long discussion, the members of the jury agree (rightly or wrongly) that someone placed the drugs where they were found, and that it must have been either the defendant (who threw them there) or the police (who planted them in order to "prove" the defendant guilty). At this point an argument develops, and one member of the jury argues thus:

> Look, the question comes down to this: Do we believe the testimony of the policemen or the testimony of the defendant? It seems to me quite possible that the defendant is telling the truth, and the policemen are trying to frame him. However, it certainly seems more likely that the defendant is lying and the policemen are telling the truth. Since we have to believe one or the other, it seems only reasonable to accept the most likely story, and since the police story is the more likely to be true, we ought to accept it. And if we accept the police account, obviously we must find the defendant guilty.

What do you think of that argument? How would you explain what is wrong with it to your fellow jurors?

If it were only a question of which position is more plausible, then it might be an effective argument. That is, if it were a question of deciding whether it is more likely that the defendant discarded the drugs at the scene of the arrest or that the police planted them, then *perhaps* the police account is more likely. But that is not the question. Framing the issue that way misplaces the burden of proof. Instead of the burden of proof resting squarely on the prosecution (where it belongs), the argument places it equally on the prosecution and the defense. The proper question is not which side appears more plausible; rather, the question is whether the prosecution proved its case beyond a reasonable doubt. Even if you agree with the juror that the police story is more likely to be true, that is far from sufficient. It is not enough for the prosecution to establish that its case is more plausible; rather, the prosecution must *prove* beyond a reasonable doubt that its account of the defendant's guilt is true. The defense need not show that its version of the events is more likely to be true than the version given by the prosecution; instead, the defense need only show that there is a reasonable doubt that the prosecution's case is true. Whenever a claim is made—that an artificial sweetener is safe, that an arthritis remedy is effective, that an individual is guilty of a crime—the burden of proof rests on those making the claim. "Share and share alike" may be excellent advice in some contexts, but it is poor logic and fallacious reasoning when trying to locate the burden of proof.

Consider the Verdict

Jim Pickerell / Stock Connection Blue / Alamy

This case occurred in 2002, in Pennsylvania. Jennie Collins went to a party, where she drank what tasted like (and what she claimed she believed to be) fruit punch. She left the party and drove to the residence of a friend, Megan Neff. There she complained of a headache, then became silent. Jennie and Megan then left together to go to the home of another friend, with Jennie driving. Jennie drove past the friend's home, drove through several stop signs without stopping, and then swerved into oncoming traffic. Jennie then braked the car while Megan steered it off the road. Jennie lost consciousness, and when the police arrived she was slumped over the wheel. An ambulance was called, and Jennie screamed at and fought the ambulance workers. She was taken to the hospital, and there she tested positive for PCP.

Jennie Collins was charged with driving under the influence of a controlled substance, and a jury found her guilty. In her defense, Jennie had agreed that she was driving under the influence, but argued that her intoxication was involuntary. The judge instructed the jury that the burden of proving *involuntary* intoxication rested on the defendant, and that she had to prove by a preponderance of the evidence that her intoxication was involuntary. (She was *not* required to prove *beyond a*

reasonable doubt that her intoxication was involuntary; but the judge ruled that she still had the burden of proof: of establishing involuntary intoxication by a *preponderance* of the evidence. That is, she must convince the jury that it is *more likely than not* that her intoxication was involuntary; the prosecution must prove that she operated a vehicle while intoxicated, but does *not* have to prove that her intoxication was voluntary.)

The jury returned a verdict of guilty. Jennie Collins appealed her conviction, arguing that the trial judge erred in his instructions, that her presumption of innocence was violated, and that the burden of proving *voluntary* intoxication should rest on the prosecution.

As an appeals court judge, the case now comes to you. How do you rule?[6]

UNAPPEALING IGNORANCE

A word of caution. Appeals to ignorance do occur with depressing regularity, but be careful that you don't start seeing the fallacy when it's not really there. The fallacy of appeal to ignorance is a very specific fallacy: It occurs *only* when one argues that a claim is true because it has not been proved false. Not all ignorant statements and stupid arguments commit the fallacy of appeal to ignorance. If I claim that evil spirits cause sickness, that will reveal my profound ignorance of modern medicine; it is not, however, the fallacy of *appeal* to ignorance unless I argue that evil spirits must cause sickness because no one has been able to conclusively prove that evil spirits are not the cause of sickness. If I assert that invisible martians live in the sewers under New York City, you may well be justified in concluding that I am an ignorant—perhaps completely batty—individual, but you would be wrong to charge me with the fallacy of appeal to ignorance, for I am not *appealing* to ignorance. I may *be* ignorant, and that is unfortunate, but it is not a fallacy. In order to commit the fallacy of appeal to ignorance, I must actually make that appeal: I would have to argue that there are invisible martians in the New York sewers *because* no one has been able to prove that there are none.

So not all claims made in ignorance commit the fallacy of appeal to ignorance. On the other side of the coin, a person may commit the fallacy of appeal to ignorance without being an ignorant person. Intelligent and knowledgeable persons may easily become confused about where the burden of proof belongs on some particular issue and thus may commit the fallacy of appeal to ignorance. To avoid that fallacy, keep a careful watch on exactly what conclusion is being claimed and who is making the claim. Whoever makes the claim, brings the accusation, or asserts the theory bears the burden of proving it true.

Exercise 8-1

Each of the following cases requires you to decide *where* the burden of proof belongs. In each case, you must decide *who* is making a claim, which side is asserting something special, and who is entitled to claim that they are relying on accepted beliefs and are not asserting anything that requires special proof.

1. I am proposing to place a new mouthwash on the market. The Food and Drug Administration requires that I provide extensive tests demonstrating the safety of the mouthwash. In reply, I give the following argument:

   It's not fair to require me to prove the safety of my new Merry Mouth Mouthwash. If anyone has any doubts about the safety of Merry Mouth, then that doubter should be required to offer proof that Merry Mouth is dangerous. I haven't made any claims about the safety of Merry Mouth, so why should I be asked for any proof? You're placing the burden of proof on the wrong back. The person who makes a *claim*—namely, a claim that Merry Mouth is harmful—should have to *prove* that claim. Those who make the claim should provide the proof.

(In considering this example, think carefully about exactly what claims are made, including any implied claims.)

2. The defendant, Joe Sly, is charged with burglary. He is accused of burglarizing the home of Sam Citizen on the night of October 1, 2003, between the hours of 9:00 and 11:00 P.M., while Sam was at the movies. Sly offers as an alibi the testimony of Crandall Crook, who testifies that on the night of the burglary the two of them were playing cribbage at Crook's apartment from 8:00 P.M. straight through until after midnight. Unfortunately for Sly, on cross-examination the district attorney inquires into the history of Mr. Crook and discovers a lengthy record of burglary and perjury convictions. As you and the other members of the jury settle yourselves around the jury table, one member of the jury begins the deliberation with the following remarks:

Well, we won't be here long, will we? That's the flimsiest alibi I ever heard. I don't believe a word of what Crandall Crook said. He's lied before, and he was lying again. Since we obviously can't accept the defendant's alibi, the defense doesn't have a leg to stand on. And that's the end of it, that's enough for me: Sly must be guilty as charged.

Has your fellow juror committed a fallacy, or instead reasoned swiftly and sagaciously?

3. Suppose that an industry wishes to place a landfill on some property near a river. Some environmentalists claim that the landfill is a hazard to the river, since landfills frequently leak and the leakage from this one would be likely to seep into the nearby river. The industry claims that it will not pollute the river, that there is no danger to the environment from the landfill, and that the environmentalists are extremists who are worried about nothing. How should the burden of proof be placed? Must the environmentalists prove that the landfill is a genuine danger? Or is it up to the industry to prove that the landfill is safe?

4. When, in the sixteenth century, Copernicus proposed the heliocentric theory of the solar system (the Earth travels around the Sun, rather than the geocentric system, with the Earth being stationary and the Sun and planets orbiting the Earth), it contradicted common sense. It seemed obvious that the Earth is stationary, and obviously false that the Earth is traveling at a high rate of speed in orbit around the Sun. People felt that unless Copernicans could supply strong proof of the Copernican system, the geocentric view should be upheld. Did they place the burden of proof in the right place?

5. Ann wishes to place a small bird feeder in her yard, in the hope of attracting robins. Her neighbor, Al, doesn't like birds and doesn't want a bird feeder next door. He asserts that before Ann is allowed to place a bird feeder in her yard, she should have to show that bird feeders are not an environmental health hazard.

6. Closing argument to the jury by the district attorney in a murder trial: "Counsel for the Defense has entertained us with the ever-popular defense that lawyers call SODDI: Some Other Dude Did It. But as you consider your verdict, keep this in mind: the defense lawyer never told you who that other dude is, and never gave you any evidence that he—whoever that dude is—is the murderer."

7. Prior to the U.S.-led attack on Iraq, the United States asserted that Iraq had weapons of mass destruction (in violation of United Nations resolutions). The United States (and the weapons inspectors in Iraq) could offer no proof of such weapons, but the Bush administration insisted that the United States was not obligated to provide such proof. At a Pentagon briefing, Defense Secretary Donald Rumsfeld asserted that: "The president has repeatedly made clear, and it bears repeating, that the burden of proof is not on the United States; it's not on the United Nations or the international community to prove that Iraq has these weapons. The burden of proof is on the Iraqi regime to prove that it is disarming and to show the inspectors where the weapons are."

Exercise 8-2

Should we allow physicians to assist patients suffering with a fatal disease to commit suicide? When supporters and opponents of physician-assisted suicide debate the issue, one of the questions that invariably comes up is whether allowing physician-assisted suicide (for competent terminally ill patients who voluntarily seek it) might lead to other undesirable consequences. For example, might it weaken the commitment of medical personnel to save lives? Could it lead to the "euthanasia" of patients who have not requested it? Would it undermine patients' trust in their physicians? Supporters of physician-assisted suicide say there is no reason to think such things would happen, whereas opponents of physician-assisted suicide fear they might. But even more basic is the question of who bears the burden of proof.

Those who *favor* physician-assisted suicide say anyone who claims that allowing physician-assisted suicide would lead to these terrible consequences must give strong reasons for their claim: The opponents make the claim that the bad results are likely, and they must back up that claim with support; it is up to those who make the claims to carry the burden of proving them true, or at least possibly true. But the *opponents* of physician-assisted suicide insist that the burden of proof rests on the other side. Those who *favor* physician-assisted suicide are proposing the new policy; therefore, it is up to them to show that it has promise, and that it will not cause harm. The supporters claim we should adopt this new policy, so they must make the case for it (including the case for why it will not cause more harm than good).

So the question here is *not* whether we should or should not allow physician-assisted suicide. Instead, the question is, Who bears the burden of proof? Should *opponents* of physician-assisted suicide have to prove the likelihood of bad long-term effects on society? Or should those who *favor* physician-assisted suicide have the burden of proving that there will *not* be bad consequences from adopting their policy?

Exercise 8-3

You are a competent adult, and you make your own decisions concerning medical treatment. No matter what your physician recommends, you cannot be forced to undergo treatment against your wishes and without your informed consent. If you do not want treatment for your cancer, that's your decision. If you decide to "treat" your cancer by eating large quantities of bananas, that is also your decision. But when children are concerned, the issues become more difficult. Your hospital has diagnosed cancer in a 6-year-old child; fortunately, the cancer is treatable, and the recommended course of treatment has a success rate of approximately 80%. The child's parents refuse to allow treatment for the child. Your hospital goes to court to force the parents to allow the child to be treated. *Don't* decide how the court should rule in this case. (That will depend on all sorts of factors: How burdensome is the treatment, what is the prognosis for this particular child, what are the parents' motives in denying treatment, etc.) Instead, focus on this basic first question: Who should bear the *burden of proof* in this case? Parents are generally presumed to have the best interests of their children at heart, unless it is proved otherwise: Should we start from there, and insist that the hospital must make the case for why the parents' wishes should be overruled? On the other hand, this program of treatment is standard, nonexperimental, and lifesaving. Should the obvious interest in saving a child's life be the starting point, and the parents be required to show why such standard treatment should *not* be followed in this case?

Suppose the parents had decided to treat their child's cancer through some special megavitamin therapy, a therapy that is regarded by the medical community as useless quackery. Would this change the burden of proof? (Do the parents have to prove it is in the child's best interests? Or does the hospital have to prove that the parents' wishes should be overridden?)

Exercise 8-4

How Do You Rule?

Consider the U.S. Supreme Court ruling on the famous Nancy Cruzan case. An auto accident left Nancy Cruzan in a permanently vegetative state, with a functioning brain stem that allowed her basic life-sustaining bodily processes to continue, but with such severe brain damage that there was no hope that she would ever be able to speak, recognize anyone, or regain any level of basic cognitive functioning. After Cruzan had spent several years in those circumstances, her family—believing that it would be her wish—asked that all life-sustaining treatment, including the medical provision of nutrition and hydration, be stopped, and that Nancy thus be allowed to die. The state of Missouri opposed stopping treatment, and the case went through various appeals, finally arriving at the U.S. Supreme Court.

The majority of the Supreme Court (in a 5 to 4 decision) ruled that Missouri was within its rights in establishing an extremely high standard of proof that the incompetent individual (unable to express her own wishes) really would wish to have treatment stopped in such circumstances; and the court decided that Nancy Cruzan's family had not met that high standard of proof, and thus her treatment could not be stopped. In writing the opinion for the majority, Chief Justice William Rehnquist asserted that it is quite legitimate for a state to start from the assumption that human life must be preserved, and thus to impose a strong burden of proof on any exception (such as the exception requested by Nancy Cruzan's family on her behalf). A key passage from Rehnquist's opinion was the following:

> Whether or not Missouri's clear and convincing evidence requirement comports with the United States Constitution depends in part on what interests the state may properly seek to protect in this situation. Missouri relies on its interest in the protection and preservation of human life, and there can be no gainsaying this interest.[7]

In a review of Rehnquist's majority opinion, Ronald Dworkin vigorously disputed Rehnquist's claim that there is always—even in the case of unfortunate individuals in a permanently vegetative state—a presumption that the individuals should be kept alive (so that a heavy burden of proof would rest on the side seeking to allow the individual to die). Dworkin argued that those seeking to stop treatment should not have such a burden of proof:

> While Rehnquist concedes that Missouri's rigid rule may sometimes lead to a "mistake," he says that the Constitution does not require states to adopt procedures that work perfectly. But his arguments that the Missouri rule would even in general work to the benefit of incompetent people are question-begging; they reflect a presumption that it is normally in the best interests of permanently comatose people to live, so that they should be kept alive unless there is decisive evidence to the contrary.[8]

Dworkin regards that as an appropriate assumption when the individual is healthy or can be restored to healthy cognitive functioning, but:

> No such assumption is plausible when the life in question is only the insensate life of the permanently vegetative. That kind of life is not valuable to anyone.

Therefore, Dworkin maintains,

> Fairness argues for only one thing: the most accurate possible identification of what Nancy Cruzan's wishes were and where her interests now lie.

Therefore, since Nancy is in a permanently vegetative state, there should be no special burden of proof imposed on those who maintain that Nancy's wishes were to be allowed to die and that her interests are served in having her treatment stopped rather than continued. Instead of being required to present clear and conclusive evidence that stopping treatment fits her wishes and interests, Cruzan's family should be required only to show that the weight of evidence *tilts* to that side. The burden of proof should be *equal*, with no starting presumption that continuing to live is in Nancy Cruzan's best interest.

So take a turn on the Supreme Court. If you were ruling on this *narrow* issue of where the burden of proof should be located in the Cruzan case, where would *you* place the burden of proof? (There are at least three possibilities: You can agree with Rehnquist that the burden of proof rests on those who favor allowing her to die; you can rule that the burden of proof rests on those who want to continue life-sustaining treatment; or you can agree with Dworkin that in such cases there should be no starting presumption favoring either sustaining life or allowing death.)

Exercise 8-5

This is a controversial issue, one on which there is obviously room for intelligent disagreement. But there is also room for intelligent thought and argument, and you might enjoy thinking about it.

One of the controversies surrounding the insanity defense is, Who bears the burden of proof in cases in which the defense pleads not guilty by reason of insanity?

Those who believe that the *prosecution* should bear the burden of proving sanity argue that it is up to the prosecution to prove the defendant is *guilty*, and part of proving guilt is proving that the defendant *intended* to commit the crime (if one kills someone by accident, one cannot be guilty of first-degree murder; if one was incapable of forming a reasoned intention of killing someone, one cannot be guilty of first-degree murder); so the prosecution must bear the burden of proof of sanity. Those who think the *defense* should bear the burden of proving insanity argue that in all our dealings with one another we naturally assume that those with whom we are dealing are sane and responsible; if someone wishes to claim an *exception* to that general rule, then it is up to the person claiming the exception to provide the justification and proof.

Where should the burden of proof rest when the defendant pleads not guilty by reason of insanity?

Exercise 8-6

In some professions—such as law—one requirement for admission to the profession is supposed to be that the applicant is "of good moral character." This has always been a difficult standard to apply: trying to agree on what counts as "good moral character" is not an easy task. Leave those difficulties aside for a moment. Suppose that we decide that one condition for admission into our profession (whatever our profession is) should be that the applicant is of *good moral character.* In that case, who should bear the burden of proof? Should applicants have to *prove* they are of good moral character (perhaps through testimonials)? After all, we require that applicants for a medical license pass tests to prove that they are competent. The burden of proof is on the applicant in that case; is establishing good moral character similar to that? Or should the burden of proof be reversed? After all, we generally assume that one is of good moral character unless proven otherwise (just as we assume one is mentally competent unless proven otherwise); so perhaps the applicant should be assumed to be of good moral character unless someone can prove that she is not.

Exercise 8-7

You have every right to dress as you wish, wear your hair as you like, tattoo and pierce your body to your heart's content. You want to wear purple shorts and a day-glow orange shirt, rings through your ears and nose and tongue and navel and eyebrows, tattoos on your arms and legs and forehead, and a beard that makes you look like the Prophet Jeremiah; that's your right, enjoy yourself, it's a free country. You may have some trouble getting a job with Wall Street investment firms, and some upscale restaurants may not welcome you with open arms. Still, how you dress is your decision, your right.

Except, perhaps, in high school. As you may have experienced, some high schools—including some public high schools—have dress codes, and some of those dress codes can be rather restrictive. The courts have ruled that high school students do not lose their rights as citizens when they go to a public high school: they still have freedom of speech, freedom of religion, and freedom of the press, for example. However, the courts have also ruled that high schools do have the right to restrict dress in certain ways in order to maintain order, and to prevent disruption of the educational process. My question is a very narrow one. Assume (for the purposes of this question) that we accept the legal principle that high schools have the right to restrict dress when necessary to maintain order and prevent disruption of education. Suppose a student wishes to wear a nose ring to school, and the school objects; *who* should have the burden of proof? Should the school have to prove the piercing *is* potentially disruptive, or should the student have to prove that it is *not*?

✓●─ **Study** and **Review** on **mythinkinglab.com**

REVIEW QUESTIONS

1. Why does the burden of proof rest on the prosecution?
2. Define the fallacy of appeal to ignorance.

NOTES

[1] This case is discussed in Peter Irons, *The Courage of Their Convictions* (New York: Penguin Books, 1988).

[2] This case is discussed in Richard H. Gaskins, *Burdens of Proof in Modern Discourse* (New Haven, CT: Yale University Press, 1992), pp. 148–149.

[3] Francis Russell, *Sacco & Vanzetti: The Case Resolved* (New York: Harper & Row, 1986), p. 191. For another view of the Sacco and Vanzetti case, see Felix Frankfurter, *The Case of Sacco and Vanzetti: A Critical Analysis for Lawyers and Laymen* (Boston, MA: Little, Brown, 1969).

[4] William M. Kunstler, "The Threat of Anonymous Juries," *The Nation,* October 22, 1983.

[5] This example is inspired by Sarah McCabe's remarks on some sociological research with shadow juries ("Discussions in the Jury Room: Are They Like This?" *The British Jury System,* University of Cambridge Institute of Criminology, 1975, pp. 22–27); but it differs greatly in details and is essentially a fictional example.

[6] If you want more details, the case is reported in *Pennsylvania Discovery and Evidence Reporter,* February 3, 2003, under the headline "Sufficiency of Evidence." [It can be found in Lexis Nexis.] In the actual case, the Pennsylvania Superior Court rejected the appeal and upheld her conviction.

[7] Taken from the majority opinion, by Chief Justice William Rehnquist. *United States Supreme Court, Cruzan v. Director, Missouri Dept. of Health,* U.S. 580 SLW 4916.

[8] Ronald Dworkin, "The Right to Death," *The New York Times Review of Books,* January 31, 1991.

INTERNET RESOURCES

A good brief discussion of the burden of proof in legal proceedings can be found at *http://law.jrank.org/pages/4927/Burden-Proof.html.* For a more detailed examination, go to *http://www.worldlingo.com/ma/enwiki/en/Burden_of_proof.*

ADDITIONAL READING

A particularly good discussion of the burden of proof in legal proceedings can be found in Chapters 8 and 9 of A. A. S. Zuckerman's *The Principles of Criminal Evidence* (Oxford: Clarendon Press, 1989). The book also contains interesting material on a number of other issues, including relevance of evidence, testimony, and the role of the jury.

For an excellent, clear discussion of physician-assisted suicide and the burden of proof, read Chapter 3 of *Bioethics: A Committee Approach,* by Brendan Minogue (Sudbury, MA: Jones and Bartlett, 1996).

The definitive logical analysis of the burden of proof and the fallacy of appeal to ignorance is by Douglas N. Walton, *Arguments from Ignorance* (University Park, TX: The Pennsylvania State University Press, 1996). The writing is clear, and Walton offers a wealth of instructive examples.

Richard H. Gaskins, in *Burdens of Proof in Modern Discourse* (New Haven, CT.: Yale University Press, 1992), offers a detailed but demanding analysis of how burden of proof questions influence judicial decisions.

Read the Document on mythinkinglab.com

Bruce N. Waller, "Fallacy of Appeal to Ignorance," *Coffee and Philosophy,* pp. 6–8. In this dialogue, students discuss both the burden of proof and the fallacy of appeal to ignorance.

McMillan v. Pennsylvania, 477 U.S. 79 (1986). In this case, the U.S. Supreme Court grapples with the question of the burden of proof and the standard of proof when there are special "sentencing factors" (such as use of a firearm) that could have a substantial effect on the prison sentence of a defendant who has been found guilty.

Castaneda v. Partida, 430 U.S. 482 (1977). The question of the burden of proof—and how it shifts—is the key question in this case.

Victor v. Nebraska, 528 U.S. 225 (2000). It is a key principle of our system of criminal justice that the burden of proof rests on the prosecution, and that the prosecution must prove every element of a criminal charge "beyond a reasonable doubt." But the question of exactly what that means can be controversial. In *Victor v. Nebraska,* the U.S. Supreme Court wrestles with precisely that question.

9

❖ ❖ ❖

Language and Its Pitfalls

> "There's glory for you!"
> "I don't know what you mean by 'glory,'" Alice said.
> Humpty Dumpty smiled contemptuously. "Of course you don't—till I tell you. I meant 'There's a nice knock-down argument for you!'"
> "But 'glory' doesn't mean 'a nice knock-down argument,'" Alice objected.
> "When I use a word," Humpty Dumpty said in rather a scornful tone, "it means just what I choose it to mean—neither more nor less."
> "The question is," said Alice, "whether you can make words mean so many different things."
> "The question is," said Humpty Dumpty, "which is to be master—that's all."

Words shape the way we reason, perceive, and remember. In one study noted earlier, witnesses who were asked how fast the cars were going when they "smashed" together were likely to "remember" a violent crash, and witnesses who were asked about the speed "at contact" described a less severe crash. Careful use of language is an important tool in seeking the exact truth and the justified conclusion.

DEFINITIONS

Definitions are tricky; consider *ostensive* definitions. An ostensive definition is a common way of defining a term for those who are not familiar with it. If I have never seen a dog, you might "define" a dog for me simply by pointing to Rover: "*That's* a dog," you say, indicating the Scottish terrier running to greet us. But while ostensive definitions may be useful, they may also be very confusing. Are you indicating only this species of dog? Or perhaps only this color of dog? Or maybe you are indicating any animal with four legs; or any animal that is running; or any animal with sharp teeth; or any object moving swiftly along the ground. If you use your German shepherd in your ostensive definition of "dog," I may find it difficult to understand why the wolf we see crossing the road should not be called a dog. Philosophers, burdened with tortured imaginations, have come up with other possible confusions: Willard Van Orman Quine pointed out that when you point to an animal and say "dog," you *could* be indicating undetached animal parts. Okay, that hardly seems likely. Still, it's clear that ostensive definitions, while they can prove useful, often leave a lot unsettled.

Even clear written definitions may leave murky edges and loose ends. Suppose we define an innkeeper as one who offers rooms designed for overnight accommodation of travelers. This may be an important definition, as we may set certain legal requirements on innkeepers: for example, innkeepers may be required to provide a safe for the secure protection of the valuables of their guests. What about a steamboat taking travelers up and down the Mississippi River, and providing rooms for the travelers: Does the boat count as an inn (which would require it to provide a secure safe)? What about upper and lower berths designed for sleeping on a passenger train—are they rooms designed for overnight accommodation of travelers? What if I rent out tents to overnight travelers? What if my motel does not really cater to overnight guests, but rooms are instead rented by the hour for illicit purposes?

Definitions are often important, and legal disputes often revolve around how a word or phrase should be defined—what its boundaries are, what it covers and does not cover. Suppose I sell you my vintage 1962 Cadillac, with the original motor. It doesn't have the original spark plugs, of course, but the motor remains the original motor. But what if the carburetor has been replaced? The pistons? Is there any clear point at which it is no longer "the original motor"?

And what about the famous claim by President Bill Clinton: "I did not have sex with that woman!" Was that claim true? Depends on your definition. If "having sex" means sexual intercourse, then Bill Clinton did not have sex with Monica Lewinsky; if oral sex also qualifies as "having sex," then his statement was false.

The definition of a term—especially the *re*definition of a term—can have a major impact on important reports. In 2006, Secretary of the Interior Gale Norton released a very positive report on the state of America's wetlands. The Fish and Wildlife Service had been issuing reports on wetlands since 1954, and this was the *first* time that they had reported a net *gain* in America's wetlands. Secretary Norton used these figures to assert that the Bush program for stopping the loss of wetlands was on the right track. But in fact, the Fish and Wildlife Service reported that during the period covered, there had actually been a *loss* of over 500,000 acres of natural wetlands. What had changed was not better preservation of wetlands; instead, what changed was the *definition* of wetlands. Instead of counting only natural wetlands, the Bush administration redefined "wetlands" to include such things as reservoirs, farm ponds, and even golf course water hazards. So when all of the man-made lakes, golf course water hazards, irrigation ponds, and so forth—that had been built over the past decades—were suddenly added to the range of "wetlands," it is hardly surprising that there was an *increase* in the reported "wetlands." But that tells us nothing whatsoever about what really concerns us: that there had been a decline in natural wetlands (and in fact a severe decline in overall "wetlands," including both natural and artificial) during the reported period.

STIPULATIVE DEFINITIONS

Stipulative definitions specify the definition for a term in a particular context. "For the purposes of this law concerning breaking or entering, when any part of the body enters the building, that shall count as an entry." If I stick my little finger inside your door, normally you wouldn't say that I had *entered* your home; but under this stipulative definition, I have met the conditions for an entry. It's useful to have the term "entry" specified so precisely; otherwise we get into impossible wrangles about what counts as an entry: If I reach in through your window with only my hand, is that an entry? What about with my entire arm? What if it's only the arm up to the elbow? What if I get my arm and leg inside, but not my head? With a stipulative definition, we can avoid some—but not all—of those controversies. We are playing poker, and my three kings loses to your three aces. I wail and gnash my teeth, and complain loudly and sadly about suffering a *bad beat*. In poker parlance, a bad beat occurs whenever a very good hand loses to a better hand: when Jane's full house beats Jack's ace-high flush, Jack has suffered a bad beat. But suppose a casino poker room wishes to have a "bad beat jackpot," in which any player who suffers a severe bad beat wins a pool of money. In that case, the casino will *stipulate* their definition of a bad beat: "To qualify as a bad beat, for the purposes of winning the bad beat jackpot at the Red Diamond Casino, the losing hand must be four of a kind or better." If the bad beat is not specified in that manner, then every time a player loses a hand he or she will try to claim the bad beat jackpot.

CONTROVERSIAL DEFINITIONS

Definitions can be useful, but they can also be deceptive. In the passage quoted at the beginning of this chapter—from Lewis Carroll's marvelous *Alice in Wonderland*—Humpty Dumpty is well aware of the importance of definitions.

> "The question is," said Alice, "whether you can make words mean so many different things."
> "The question is," said Humpty Dumpty, "which is to be master—that's all."

There's a lot of wisdom in Humpty Dumpty's words: whoever controls the definitions is usually *master* of the discussion.

At what age did you become a legal *adult?* It all depends. We do not require *children* to serve in our armed forces; but once you turn 18, we can draft you and require you to risk or even sacrifice your life for whatever military ventures the government approves. So if it's a question of whether you can be drafted, or whether you can be condemned to death for your crimes, then you're an adult at age 18; but if you want to buy a beer, you're not an "adult" until you turn 21. Sounds like Humpty Dumpty was right.

"Marriage *means* a legal union between a man and a woman." If that's the definition of marriage, then same-sex marriage is ruled out; and that is one argument often offered against same-sex marriage. But even *if* that's the definition of "marriage," that definition doesn't settle much of anything; for there would remain the question of whether we should *enlarge* that definition to include marriage between gay and lesbian couples. (The debate over same-sex marriage is not a debate about the current legal definition of marriage, but a debate over whether that definition should be *changed*. The fact that the current definition of marriage excludes same-sex marriage is irrelevant to that debate.)

What counts as a *person?* The definition of that term is the epicenter of a wide range of controversies. Is a fetus a *person?* Is an embryo a person? Is someone in a permanent vegetative state still a person? Should a chimpanzee—who is capable of affection, careful planning, deception, and learning language—count as a person? Do corporations count as persons, and thus enjoy the *rights* of persons (such as the right of free speech, as the U.S. Supreme Court ruled in a very controversial 2010 decision which opened the floodgates for unlimited corporate spending to influence elections)?

Deceptive Language

There is a wide variety of ways that language can be used to deceive and mislead and misinform—and advertisers are experts at using all of them. Lawyers and politicians have also mastered many of the language tricks. So if you want to be an intelligent consumer, an effective juror, and a responsible well-informed voting citizen of a democratic country, it is important that you learn to recognize and protect yourself against these deceptive forms of language.

Using emotionally charged words to distort the picture of events is a rather obvious—but very common—way of using language to mislead. When I answered a hostile question in a political forum, I spoke firmly in favor of my principles; but when my opponent answered a hostile question, she railed against her questioner. My opponent wants to slash social security benefits; I want to place judicious restrictions on those benefits. My opponent greedily grabs all the pork-barrel money she can get for her district; I actively seek funding projects that will benefit the people who elected me. I point out important facts about my opponent's character and record, while my opponent stoops to vicious negative campaigning. My opponent goes on junkets; I go on fact-finding trips. My opponent panders to special interests; I strive to consider the concerns of every group.

But the overuse of emotionally charged words is only half of the problem—and it's not the trickiest half. Using *euphemisms*—sometimes called "doublespeak"—to hide practices and policies and events that might generate legitimate negative emotional reactions is another and even more devious way of manipulating language. Not every case of euphemism is deceptive. If we say that someone "passed on" (instead of saying he died), that may be a gentler way of breaking the sad news; certainly it sounds nicer than he "kicked the bucket," or—the British phrase—he "dropped off the twig." But many uses of euphemism (doublespeak) are not so innocent. Everyone is worried—legitimately—about the enormous number of bad loans made by financial corporations, leading to mortgage foreclosures, bank failures, and bailouts. So now companies no longer have "bad loans" on their books; those have become "nonperforming assets." And when bad financial management makes it necessary for failing companies to fire workers, the workers are no longer fired; instead, the company is "downsized" by making "workforce adjustments." Some people might worry about *sludge* (a semi-solid mixture of bacteria- and virus-laden organic matter, toxic metals, and settled solids removed from domestic and industrial waste water from sewage treatment plants) being used as fertilizer in fields in their area; but when sludge is renamed as "biosolids," it doesn't sound so scary. Bad guys torture people, but our country uses "enhanced interrogation techniques." When bombs and missiles kill innocent civilians rather than soldiers, the deaths are due to "incontinent ordinance." And when the United States invaded Iraq, that was not an unprovoked attack on another country, but an act of "preemptive defense."

The Fallacy of Ambiguity

The fallacy of ambiguity occurs when *one* meaning of a word or phrase is used in the *premises*, but a *different* meaning is used in the *conclusion*. Such fallacious arguments are probably the most difficult of all fallacies to detect. When encountering ambiguous arguments, one often has a sense that *something* is amiss, but it is very difficult to put your finger on the problem.

A politician is charged with taking bribes and is tried on those charges. After a lengthy trial with much evidence and many witnesses, the jury returns a not guilty verdict. The politician immediately calls a press conference, and asserts that after a thorough trial he has been found to be innocent: It has been proved that he never accepted bribes. What is wrong with the politician's argument?

The politician is trading on two senses, two distinct meanings, of "innocent." The *jury* decided that there was not sufficient evidence to convict the politician of accepting

Doublespeak

Doublespeak is language that pretends to communicate but really doesn't. It is language that makes the bad seem good, the negative appear positive, the unpleasant appear attractive or at least tolerable. Doublespeak is language that avoids or shifts responsibility, language that is at variance with its real or purported meaning. It is language that conceals or prevents thought; rather than extending thought, doublespeak limits it.[1]

bribes; that is, the jury decided that the politician's guilt was *not proved*. *That* sense of "innocent" merely implies that the prosecution was unable to prove the case against the politician; the jury *may* think that the politician was *probably* guilty of accepting bribes, but believe there was *reasonable doubt* that he accepted bribes. If so, the jury rightly voted for an *innocent* verdict: "innocent" only in the sense that the politician's guilt could not be conclusively proved. But on the basis of that verdict, what does the *politician conclude* in his argument to the press? He concludes that he has been proved *innocent*. "Innocent" as the politician is using the term means "in actual fact not guilty of the crime." But those are two very different meanings of "innocent." As the jury uses "innocent," it means only that the politician is not *proved* guilty (although he may in fact *be* guilty); but as the politician uses the term in his conclusion, "innocent" means in actual fact *not* guilty. When the ambiguity is removed, it is clear that the conclusion does *not* follow from the premises:

> The jury has concluded that there is a reasonable doubt that I accepted bribes. Therefore, it has been proved that I did not accept bribes.

When the ambiguity is eliminated, the invalidity of the argument is plain. But with the ambiguity in place, the argument is seductively appealing.

Ambiguity does not require a full argument to accomplish its deceptive tricks. Sometimes a single sentence will suffice. Perhaps the most notorious ambiguous statement in recent years was forcefully asserted by a U.S. president: "I did *not* have sex with that woman." In one sense that was true. Bill Clinton apparently did not have sexual intercourse with Monica Lewinsky, and that is one meaning of "having sex." But the statement was nonetheless deeply misleading, since "having sex" can also encompass other intimate sexual relations, such as oral sex. Another, though not quite so fascinating, example of ambiguity in a single sentence: "We accept all credit applications." That's a sign you sometimes see, printed in large letters, in front of automobile dealerships. Sounds good, right? I've been having a bit of trouble getting credit since I missed several payments on the mortgage, had my television set repossessed, defaulted on my cell phone bill, and the repo man got my new BMW. So I'm happy to find a car dealer that accepts all credit applications. Well, it's true they *accept* all credit applications, but "accepting" credit applications is ambiguous. It can mean they *approve* my credit application and actually give me credit (as in "We accept your offer, it's a deal"); *or* it can mean we are happy to *accept* your application, but we may turn it down after we look it over.

"Myth"

Another example of how ambiguity can cause confusion is found in the criticism made by fundamentalist-literalist Christian sects (who take the Bible "literally") against those who believe that the Bible should be interpreted as telling stories that express moral truths rather than literal facts. The nonliteralists interpret the Garden of Eden story as teaching moral and religious truths (e.g., that all humans are created equal) but not as literal biology or history. That is, they take such accounts as *myths*, as stories that teach important truths but are not themselves literally true. But the fundamentalists, when told that these stories are interpreted as myths, understand "myth" in a very different sense: as if the stories were being reduced to mere fables or fairy tales. "Myth" has those two different meanings: "story

not literally true, but teaching important truths" (as, for example, Paul Tillich uses the term); and alternatively, "a fable, a story that is untrue." Failure to distinguish the two senses has exacerbated controversy between various religious groups. The error is illustrated by this excerpt from a letter to the editor from the very irate Reverend William W. Robbins:

> I believe the first 11 chapters of Genesis are true; the liberal camp (the higher criticism, documentary hypothesis approach) has Genesis 1–11 as fable and myth.[2]

The "liberal camp" does indeed interpret Genesis 1–11 as myth, but not in the sense of fable.

Consumer Reports (September 1987) took note of a newspaper advertisement that headlined "A FULLY LOADED VINTAGE WINE CELLAR" for under $1,500. The photograph in the advertisement showed a handsome temperature-controlled cabinet, fully stocked with 440 bottles of wine. But before you run out to make your purchase, check the fine print: "Fully loaded vintage wine cellar" does *not* mean a wine cellar that is fully loaded with *wine;* rather, it means a wine cellar that is fully loaded with "free options," such as a deluxe handle and lock.

The Folger Coffee Company has a television commercial featuring famous restaurants and showing happy people enjoying splendid food at the restaurants. After they have enjoyed a sumptuous meal, the diners are served—instead of the restaurant's usual coffee—a cup of the sponsor's instant coffee. They express their delight with the coffee and then their amazement at the fact that the coffee they have just enjoyed is instant. The announcer then chimes in with the clincher: "Folgers Instant Crystals: Coffee rich enough to be served in America's finest restaurants." Impressive. After all, if these super restaurants are willing to serve this instant coffee, it must be good.

But it's not that simple. The restaurants were not open for regular business on the night the commercials were made; instead, Folgers rented the restaurants and invited people in for a free meal. Then, after they'd enjoyed this great meal—at no charge—they were served coffee and were asked, "How do you like it?" What would most people answer under those circumstances? But that's another issue. Focus on exactly what the announcer said: "Coffee rich enough to be served in America's finest restaurants." That sounds impressive, on first hearing: If America's finest restaurants will serve it, it must be rich. But the sentence is ambiguous. It can mean that the restaurant itself is willing to serve its customers that brand of instant coffee. (That would be the usual meaning, and that is what the company wants you to think.) Or it can mean something quite different. It can mean just what it literally says: The coffee is "rich enough *to be served in* America's finest restaurants"—not *by* the restaurant, just *in* the restaurant—when it is rented by the Folger Coffee Company. But just how rich does the coffee have to be for it to be served *in* the rented restaurant by the coffee company that *rented* the restaurant? (If you rent the buildings, you can serve pretty much anything you like "in America's finest restaurants.")

One more example of ambiguity: a favorite among advertisers. "Best" is an ambiguous term. In ordinary usage, when we say something is *best* we usually mean it is better than everything else in that category. "This is the *best* chocolate chip cookie I have ever tasted" means that it is better than any other chocolate chip cookie I have ever eaten. "LeBron James is the *best* player in the NBA" means there is no other NBA player as good as LeBron. "This is the *best* novel I've ever read" means I have never read a novel that can measure up to this one. But "best" has another meaning: In this use of the term "best," to say that "this is the best class I've ever taken" may just mean: All my

---

Read the Fine Print

In 1997, Millennium Sales of West Palm Beach sent out this mailing:

> This shall serve as our final notification regarding a fully detailed 1997 model car we will deliver directly to you. Failure to respond by the posted deadline date will nullify your opportunity to claim the $15,638 automobile. Failure to respond will result in forfeiture of the 1997 model car pending delivery to you.

On a separate sheet there is a list of six new 1997 model cars, including a Mustang GT and a Chevy Blazer. You select one, send in the $21.99, and they guarantee delivery. And deliver they do: a brand new 1997 model car, the one you chose. It comes in the mail, in a small box: a 1997 *model* car. And you are also entered into a drawing for the "opportunity to claim the $15,638 automobile": the full-sized 1997 model car. Good luck.[3]

classes have been rather bad, but this one is no worse than the others. "This is the best lasagna I've ever tasted" could mean that I don't much care for lasagna, and it all tastes about the same to me, and this one is as good as the rest: none of the lasagna I've had really stands out." "Mark is the best kazoo player in the world" means that—well, you get the picture. Advertisers have a field day with this ambiguity. If there is a range of products that are all equally effective—one mouthwash works as well as another in fighting bad breath, most fluoride toothpastes are equally good at fighting cavities, all detergents are equally effective in removing tough grease stains—then a mouthwash can claim that it is *proven best* against mouth odor, a detergent can advertise that tests show it is "*best* in cleaning tough stains."

Ambiguity is tricky. Examine the following argument, tell what phrase is being used *ambiguously,* and tell what meaning that phrase has in the *premises* and what (different) meaning the phrase has in the *conclusion.*

> Some Americans who hold radical political views (socialists, for example) claim that they cannot get a public hearing for their views. But that claim is absurd. Of course they can get a public hearing for their views. After all, we do have freedom of speech in America, and anyone who wants to stand on a street corner and make speeches is perfectly free to do so, and as the public walks by and perhaps stops to listen, the public will hear what the speaker says. So radicals or anyone else can indeed get a public hearing for their views.

Start by finding the *conclusion* of the argument, then line up the *premises* of the argument, and then decide what phrase is being used with *one* meaning in the premises and with a *different* meaning in the conclusion.

> What is the *conclusion?*
> Radicals can get a public hearing for their views in America.
> What are the *premises?*
> Radicals are free to speak out in public. Since radicals can speak out in public, their views can be heard by the public; that is, there is a public hearing of their radical views.
> What *key phrase* is used with two different meanings?
> "Public hearing"

What *meaning* does "public hearing" have in the conclusion? That is, when political radicals complain that they "cannot get a public hearing" for their views, *what* are they complaining about? Obviously they are not complaining that they are unable to speak on street corners. Instead, "public hearing" to the radicals means access to the public *media,* coverage of their views in newspapers, news magazines, and television newscasts. *That* is the kind of "public hearing" of which they claim to be deprived.

But what meaning does "public hearing" have in the *premises?* As used in the premises, "public hearing" means,

> heard by some (usually very small) segment of the public

Now the ambiguity should be plain. "Having access to the national news media" (one sense of "public hearing") is obviously quite different from "speaking one's views to a few people in public" (the *other* sense of "public hearing"). With the ambiguity eliminated, the argument looks like this:

> Since radicals speak to people in public, it follows that radicals have their views reported by the national news media.

Obviously that is an invalid argument.

AMPHIBOLY

Amphiboly is a special variety of ambiguity, in which a modifying word can be read as applying either narrowly or more broadly; or more generally, amphiboly is a *grammatical* form of ambiguity, in which the different possible meanings result from the grammatical structure. Amphiboly is often the stuff of rather silly jokes, though it can be used for more sinister purposes. Let's start with the jokes. My favorite amphiboly joke comes from Groucho Marx, describing his African hunting trip. "One morning I shot an elephant in my pajamas. How he got into my pajamas I'll never know." But not all uses of amphiboly are quite so innocent. "This cereal contains 100% natural fruits and grains." Sounds good, right? You would be really healthy if you started your morning eating only natural fruits and grains, with no added sugar or salt or highly processed products; and it sounds as if this cereal is made up entirely, 100%, of natural fruits and grains. That's one way of reading it. Unfortunately, that 100% may not apply to everything in the cereal; instead, it applies only to the *fruits and grains* in the cereal: *they* are 100% natural. And there actually are some 100% natural fruits and grains in this cereal—along with the sugar, salt, and all other non-natural highly processed stuff that goes in the cereal mix.

Anacin used to run an advertisement with a very clever—and very deceptive—use of amphiboly. "Anacin is the strongest pain reliever you can buy without a prescription: Stronger than aspirin." So I've got a bad headache, and I want a really strong pain reliever, something even stronger than aspirin. Anacin costs more, but it's a stronger pain reliever than aspirin, so I'm willing to shell out some extra money for that stronger pain relief. But wait a minute. Anacin just *is* aspirin, with a very small shot of caffeine thrown in. So how can Anacin be a stronger pain reliever than aspirin, when the pain reliever in Anacin *is* aspirin? No, you've got it all wrong; and Anacin is very sorry you misunderstood. The advertisement doesn't mean that Anacin is a stronger *pain reliever*, that is, it doesn't mean that Anacin is stronger *as a pain reliever*. The "*stronger*" doesn't modify "pain reliever." Rather, among all the pain relievers, Anacin is a *stronger* pain reliever than aspirin, because it contains an added drug, namely caffeine; and that makes it *stronger*, but not stronger *as* a pain reliever, just a stronger drug combination in the *class* of pain relievers (all of which are equally strong *as* pain relievers).

Exercise 9-1

Consider the Verdict

You are a juror in an auto theft case. Weldon Wheels has been charged with stealing the car of an elderly lady, wrecking it, and then abandoning it. Weldon was picked up by the police 4 days after the theft because he lived in the area of the theft and he seemed to fit the victim's description of the thief. The next day the victim identified Weldon from a police lineup as the young man she had seen speed away in her car. In court the lady appears as the chief witness for the prosecution and again identifies Weldon as the thief she saw driving away in her car as she looked out her front window. The case turns on her identification of Weldon as the thief. The defense claims that this is a case of mistaken identity, that the elderly lady glimpsed someone driving away and then in the police lineup simply picked out the person who most resembled her brief impression of the criminal and latched onto that unfortunate person—the defendant—as the car thief. Weldon insists that he was at home watching television when the theft occurred and that he knows nothing at all about the stolen car. One of the jurors offers this argument: Look, here's what this case boils down to: Was that old lady

Everett Collection / Shutterstock

telling the truth, or not? Now I don't know about the rest of you, but I am absolutely convinced of one thing: that dear old lady certainly did not go up on the witness stand, place her hand on the Bible and swear before God to tell the truth, and then coolly lie about what she saw. She has taught Sunday school for over 30 years, has lived in the same house since she was married 52 years ago, and she retired 10 years ago after teaching handicapped children for almost 40 years. She is as truthful, honest, and upright a person as there is in this country—as indeed several very respectable people testified. She could no more tell a lie under oath than she could run the high hurdles. There's certainly no doubt in my mind that she is telling the truth, and I don't see how anyone could doubt her truthfulness and honesty. So I believe she's telling the truth when she says she saw that fellow driving away in her car, and that means we must find him guilty. What do you think of this juror's argument? (Are any of the words ambiguous? If you need a hint, look back to the beginning of this chapter.)

Exercise 9-2

Identify the language deception involved in each of the following cases. In cases of ambiguity, be sure to specify exactly what word or phrase is ambiguous, what the different meanings are, and why this ambiguous use makes the argument unsound or the claim deceptive.

1. Why should anyone believe in the Darwinian account of evolution? After all, the Darwinian theory is just that—a theory, and theories are merely speculation.

2. Former President Richard Nixon is not guilty of any of the crimes connected with Watergate (perjury, breaking or entering, burglary, etc.). He certainly was not criminally involved in any of the Watergate activities. President Gerald Ford granted Nixon a complete and unconditional pardon for any crimes related to the Watergate events. And since President Ford clearly had the constitutional authority to grant such a pardon to Nixon, that makes Nixon not guilty.

3. Some complain that poor people do not receive equal justice in the U.S. courts; but that is not true, for all citizens of the United States are equal in the eyes of the law and are treated equally by the courts, no matter how rich or poor they may be.

4. SELLER: If you want the low cholesterol of corn oil, buy *Happy Heart Cooking Oil*. It contains 100% corn oil.
   CUSTOMER: No it doesn't; look, it says right there on the list of ingredients: Contains palm oil, cottonseed oil, and corn oil.
   SELLER: Well, still, it does contain 100% corn oil; it just also happens to contain some 100% palm oil and some 100% cottonseed oil.

5. We must accept some degree of repression in our society and in our political life. After all, as Freud noted and as psychiatrists generally agree, repression is the price we pay for civilization.

6. Why do prices keep increasing? Why, for example, does the cost of a new car keep going up? As we know, there are only two basic costs for all products: natural resources and labor. Natural resources are always there, and Mother Nature has not increased her prices; so all the cost increases must be coming from the labor side. The increased cost of labor—the higher wages that are paid to workers, the demands of unions for more pay and better benefits—must therefore be the real source of inflated prices. It is increased wages—the increased cost of labor—that is the sole source of inflation.[4]

7. Fortunately in the United States we live in a democracy, so all our citizens have an equal voice in our government. In our country, everyone counts equally, and no one's views or wishes get special treatment, and every citizen has an equal right to serve as mayor, governor, senator, or even president.

8. Why did you tell me that Professor Sponge is a good teacher? He's the worst teacher I've ever had; his class is boring, his lectures are incomprehensible, and he knows nothing about current developments in the field. He's certainly not a good teacher.

   No, he really is a good teacher. Of course he's lousy as an instructor, you're right about that. But he's a very good, warm-hearted, and generous person. He's genuinely good, through and through. And he happens to be a teacher, albeit a lousy one. He's a *good* teacher; not a good *teacher.*

9.   "That batter wasn't out; she beat the throw to first by a full step!

   "No, you're mistaken; she certainly was out. The umpire called her out, so she's out."

10. Ladies and gentlemen of the jury, the defendant in this case is charged with assault and theft. He is accused of a vicious, brutal, even heartless crime: knocking down an 80-year-old woman as she left the supermarket with her groceries, breaking her left arm and giving her a severe concussion, then—while she lay groaning and bleeding on the cold parking lot pavement—stealing her purse and running away. You heard the defendant's attorney, Ms. Taylor, argue that this is all a case of mistaken identity, that the defendant didn't commit this terrible crime, and that therefore the brutal nature of the crime is *irrelevant*. Well, ladies and gentlemen of the jury, you will make up your own minds about that. But I will tell you this: It will be a sad day for our fair city when our citizens and our good jury members start thinking that a brutal assault on a defenseless elderly woman is *irrelevant*. You wouldn't consider it irrelevant if it was an attack on your mother; and as far as I'm concerned, *no* attack on a frail and defenseless and vulnerable woman can ever be described as irrelevant.

Exercise 9-3

Consider the Verdict

The defendant, Ted Zurich, is a major league baseball player. He is charged with attempting to bribe a police officer. He was stopped by Officer Jones, a member of the state highway patrol, on suspicion of driving while intoxicated. Officer Jones alleges that as she approached the defendant's car, Zurich leaned out the window with his driver's license in his right hand, and a fist full of money in his left hand. When she reached the car, Zurich said (she testifies), "You can choose either hand; why don't you choose the left hand, and we'll both be a lot happier, and we can forget this whole thing."

The defense attorney, on cross-examination, asks Officer Jones if she knows any professional baseball players. She testifies that she does not. The cross-examination continues as follows:

DEFENSE ATTORNEY: "Officer Jones, do you know Seth and Louise Arthur?"
OFFICER JONES: "Yes, they lived down the street from me when I was growing up."
DEFENSE ATTORNEY: "Do you know their son, Alex Arthur?"
OFFICER JONES: "Yes, I know him; he's several years younger than I am. He was a teenager when I moved away, and I haven't seen him since."
DEFENSE ATTORNEY: "But you do know Alex Arthur, don't you? You've known him since he was a small child, isn't that right?"
OFFICER JONES: "Yes, I haven't seen him in 10 years, but I know him, and his family."
DEFENSE ATTORNEY: "Officer Jones, Alex Arthur now plays for the Louisville Sluggers. Do you know what the Louisville Sluggers are?"
OFFICER JONES: "Isn't it a baseball bat, or something like that?"
DEFENSE ATTORNEY: "There is a baseball bat by that name, but there is also a professional minor league baseball team by that name. Alex Arthur has played third base for the Louisville Sluggers for the last 2 years."
OFFICER JONES: "Well, that's nice; I had no idea what Alex was doing."
DEFENSE ATTORNEY: "But you testified that you know Alex Arthur, right? And Alex Arthur is a professional baseball player. So when you testified, under oath, that you don't know any professional baseball players, your testimony was false, wasn't it?"

1. *Was* the testimony of Officer Jones false?

2. Suppose the defense attorney claims that Officer Jones's testimony was *false*, and the prosecuting attorney claims that her testimony was *true*. What *ambiguous* word or phrase might be in dispute?

✓•⌐**Study** and **Review** on **mythinkinglab.com**

REVIEW QUESTIONS

1. What is an ostensive definition?
2. What is a stipulative definition?
3. What is "doublespeak"?
4. What is the fallacy of ambiguity?
5. Give an example of the fallacious use of ambiguity.
6. What is amphiboly?

NOTES

[1] William Lutz, *The New Doublespeak: Why No One Knows What Anyone's Saying Anymore* (New York: HarperCollins, 1996), p. 4.

[2] *Greensboro Daily News,* June 23, 1985.

[3] Reported in *Consumer Reports,* November 1997.

[4] Adapted from a letter to the editor, *Greensboro Daily News.*

INTERNET RESOURCES

Anil Gupta has an excellent and extensive discussion of definitions in the online *Stanford Encyclopedia of Philosophy.* Go to plato.stanford.edu/entries/definition. A nice brief examination of definition can be found at *www.philosophypages.com/lg/e05.htm.*

The National Council of Teachers of English gives an annual "doublespeak award" for the most misleading use of language. Some excellent examples of ambiguity and other fallacies can be found at their site. Go to *www.ncte.org,* then enter "doublespeak" in "Search NCTE."

ADDITIONAL READING

For a fascinating—and amusing, though also disturbing—look at how ambiguity, vagueness, and "doublespeak" function in advertising and politics, read *Doublespeak: From "Revenue Enhancement" to "Terminal Living"; How Government, Business, Advertisers, and Others Use Language to Deceive You,* by William Lutz (New York: HarperCollins, 1989). A more recent book by Lutz on the same subject is *The New Doublespeak: Why No One Knows What Anyone is Saying Anymore* (New York: HarperCollings, 1997).

📖•⌐**Read** the **Document** on **mythinkinglab.com**

Leonard Pitts Jr., "Can Blacks Be Racist?" This essay shows the importance of careful definitions in examining arguments.

Jack Shafer, "Weasel-Words Rip My Flesh!" "Weasel words" are among the most common language deceptions; they turn what looks like a substantive claim into a statement that actually has little or no content.

Weeks v. Angelone, 528 U.S. 225 (2000). This case deals with the question of confusing language in jury instructions, and whether a jury mistakenly understood the judge's instructions during the sentencing phase of a capital trial. When the U.S. Supreme Court heard the case, the Court split 5 to 4, with the majority ruling that the jury had correctly understood the instructions. The minority—in an argument written by Justice Stevens, and presented here—insists that there are reasons to believe that the jury was confused over ambiguities in the judge's instructions.

Report of the Kaufman Commission on Proceedings Involving Guy Paul Morin, excerpt from "Chapter II: Forensic Evidence and the Centre of Forensic Sciences," pages 83–89 (Ontario Ministry of the Attorney General). Disturbing account of how misunderstandings of how terms were being used by forensic scientists may have contributed to a wrongful conviction.

10

❖ ❖ ❖

Appeal to Authority

(((•—[**Listen** to the **Chapter Audio** on **mythinkinglab.com**

Much of what you know is based on the testimony of reliable sources. Think for a moment of your own knowledge of history, geography, physics, and biology. Some of it may have been gained firsthand: you know where Vancouver is because you've been there; you know that John McCain was the Republican presidential nominee in 2008 because you watched the election coverage; you know that acids turn litmus paper red because you have done the experiment. But almost all of your knowledge of such subjects—even if you are an expert in the field—comes from *testimony*. Through testimony of reliable authorities you may know the path of the Nile River through Africa, although you have never actually followed and charted the Nile. You accept the testimony of biologists that there are penguins in Antarctica. Your knowledge that light travels at a speed greater than 186,000 miles/second rests on reliable testimony, and it's quite reasonable to firmly believe that you know the speed of light (even though you've never measured it for yourself). And you know—by reliable testimony—that Napoleon was the French general at the Battle of Waterloo, although you did not personally observe the battle. Testimony is essential, and even in areas of expertise, experts and researchers must rely for the bulk of their knowledge on the testimony of other researchers. (That is why fraudulent research testimony—such as Sir Cyril Burt's fabricated data on identical twins—is so damaging to scientific work.)

Without the testimony of others, we would not get very far beyond our own noses in gaining knowledge of the world. (Isaac Newton generously acknowledged his own dependence on the testimony of earlier scientists: "If I have seen farther, it is by standing on the shoulders of giants.") But when we draw from testimony, it is essential that the testimony be reliable. Judging the reliability of testimony requires consideration of the *source*.

Testimony must be evaluated by two standards: Is this source of testimony trustworthy, honest? And is this source of testimony really knowledgeable about the topic in question? (The testimony of a lying expert is no more helpful than the testimony of a sincere incompetent.) If a witness identifies the defendant as the person who ran from the scene of the crime, we want to know: Is this witness *trustworthy* (does the witness have a special bias, such as a deep hatred for the defendant; does the witness have a reputation for honesty) *and* is the witness a careful observer with good eyesight (an honest witness whose eyesight is so bad that he or she could not have made an accurate identification will not provide strong testimony).

In discussing ad hominem arguments it was frequently noted that ad hominem arguments against testimony do *not* commit the ad hominem fallacy. If someone's testimony is inconsistent with his or her actions, then that inconsistency is an indication of insincerity and thus weighs against the testimony. If the person testifying has a special interest or bias, that bias should be considered when evaluating the testimony. The credibility of the testimony depends on the reliability of the source. Similar care is required in deciding whether to accept or reject a special kind of testimony: the testimony of a special *authority*, or the testimony of an *expert witness*.

AUTHORITIES AS TESTIFIERS

Suppose we disagree about which planet exerts the strongest gravitational pull. There are several ways to settle the dispute. We might visit each of the planets and take measurements. On a tighter budget, we might appeal to an *authority* on planetary astronomy. We could consult a book on the solar system written by some person whom astronomers recognize as an authority, or look it up in a standard reference book such as the *Encyclopaedia Britannica*. Appeal to such an authority is a perfectly legitimate way of gathering information and confirming beliefs, as long as we keep in mind that no source is absolute or infallible. Authorities are sometimes mistaken, authorities are sometimes dishonest, and what authorities in a field agree to be true is sometimes false. But I am sometimes mistaken about what I have seen "with my own eyes." Probably no empirically based beliefs are *absolutely* certain. If that sort of certainty were required, then we could hold no beliefs at all about the world. If we set somewhat less stringent requirements for knowledge, then appeal to genuine authorities will be one way of gaining knowledge.

CONDITIONS FOR LEGITIMATE APPEAL TO AUTHORITY

In the courtroom, expert witnesses may testify, for example, that the blood found on the defendant's shirt was the blood of the murder victim, or that the substance found in the marmalade was a lethal drug, or that the fingerprints found in the burglarized apartment were not those of the defendant. But while appeal to authorities and to expert witnesses is reasonable and useful, there are some special pitfalls: In order for an appeal to authority to be legitimate in settling an issue, the authority must be a genuine authority on that subject, and there must be *agreement* among authorities.

Consider more carefully the first requirement for legitimate appeal to authority: The person appealed to must be a genuine authority in the area in question. Thus if we are in disagreement about the gravitational force of various planets, we might reasonably be guided by the testimony of Carl Sagan. Carl Sagan was an expert on astronomy. However, if someone claims that smoking is dangerous to health because Carl Sagan said it is, then that would be a *fallacious* appeal to authority. Carl Sagan was not (and did not claim to be) an expert on the health hazards of tobacco. If there is a question concerning the behavior of chimpanzees, then Jane Goodall's testimony on the subject is authoritative, and the fact that Jane Goodall asserts a particular claim about chimp behavior is good grounds for believing it to be true. But to cite Jane Goodall's opinions about foreign policy, quasars, or toothpaste, and then to maintain that her opinions must be true because Jane Goodall asserted them, is to indulge in a *fallacious* appeal to authority.

Failed Authority

There are many famous examples of *false* claims by recognized authorities. For example, Lord Kelvin, a distinguished nineteenth-century physicist, asserted in 1895 that heavier-than-air flying machines were physically impossible; in less than a decade, the Wright brothers proved him wrong. General William C. Westmoreland, Commander of U.S. Forces in South Vietnam, thought it "inconceivable" that the Viet Cong could defeat the South Vietnamese military forces. Robert Andrews Millikan, winner of the Nobel Prize for Physics, insisted that releasing energy by splitting the atom was an absolute impossibility. Supposedly the Decca Records executive who rejected the Beatles was confident that "groups of guitars are on the way out." Ken Olson, president of Digital Equipment Corporation, was confident that "There is no reason anyone would want a computer in their home." Those cases of expert error are a useful reminder that experts are sometimes *wrong*. But don't go overboard with such cases; remember, appeal to a consensus of genuine and trustworthy authorities is often a legitimate means of gaining knowledge.

These glaring examples of mistaken expert opinion should give you a healthy dose of skepticism. But don't throw out the baby with the bathwater. Even the best authorities are not infallible, but appeal to genuine authority is often an excellent means of gaining knowledge.

Such fallacious appeals to authority seem rather obvious and would hardly deserve comment were it not for the fact that such fallacies are so often committed. You cannot turn on the television without being confronted by an expert test pilot (Chuck Yeager) giving *non*authoritative testimony concerning batteries, an expert basketball player (Michael Jordan) giving unwarranted advice about breakfast cereal, or an outstanding swimmer (Michael Phelps) giving his *non*expert views on submarine sandwiches. Perhaps the most interesting recent "celebrity" endorsement is the promotion of "BidHere"—an Internet auction site—by Jamie Jungers, a Las Vegas lingerie model who is best known for her affair with Tiger Woods. I'm not certain what Jamie Jungers might claim as an area of expertise, but I'm pretty sure it's not Internet auctions.

Fallacious appeal to authority is perhaps the most common fallacy occurring in advertisements (although advertisements are so riddled with fallacies that it may be difficult to get an accurate count on which fallacy is the leader). So the first point to check when dealing with appeals to authority is whether the individual is really an expert in that area (he or she may be an authority in some other area, with no special standing in the subject under consideration, or may be a celebrity with no real authority on *any* subject).

A Dubious Endorsement

Pfizer Pharmaceuticals has made billions of dollars from its sales of Lipitor, a cholesterol-lowering drug that is the all-time leader in sales among prescription drugs. Recently, however, a much cheaper generic version of Zocor—another cholesterol-lowering drug—has been taking market share from Lipitor. To combat this challenge, Pfizer has spent several hundred million dollars advertising Lipitor. Some of its most prominent advertisements enlisted Robert Jarvik, a leader in the development of artificial hearts, as an authoritative spokesperson. In one of those advertisements, Jarvik is seen rowing a racing shell across a beautiful mountain lake. Unfortunately, that's not actually Jarvik (who is apparently not very athletic), but instead a stunt double. But that's the least of the problems. Jarvik claims that "as a doctor" he endorses Lipitor to lower cholesterol; but Jarvik (though he has a medical degree) is not a licensed physician, has never practiced medicine, and cannot prescribe drugs. And while he claims that Lipitor has been effective for him, in fact Jarvik was not taking Lipitor at all until about a month after he started promoting the drug (for a payment from Pfizer of well over a million dollars). When the House Energy and Commerce Committee began an investigation of deceptive advertising practices by pharmaceutical companies, Pfizer decided to drop its advertising campaign.

If Tiger Woods offers you guidance on how to hit your short irons, then it is reasonable to follow his expert advice. In fact, you could hardly be blamed for mentioning Tiger's advice on every possible occasion (as in: "You can hit a 7 iron on that shot if you want, but the last time I played a round with Tiger, he advised . . . "). But Tiger's expertise in golf lends no authority to his recommendations (in television advertisements) of a particular model of car. And to believe that the car must be good because Tiger Woods recommends it is to fall prey to the *fallacious* version of appeal to authority.

If instead of *testimony* the individual were offering an *argument,* then all considerations of expertise and authority become irrelevant. If someone offers an argument (instead of expert testimony) in favor of a particular shaving cream, then that argument must be considered on its own merits, and it matters not whether the *arguer* is an ex-baseball player or a nobel laureate.

When dealing with appeals to *authority* (claims of expert *testimony*) there is a second consideration that must be noted. Not only you must be sure that the person to whom you appeal really is an *expert* in *that subject,* but you must be sure that the *subject* is one on which authorities *agree.* If the question concerns the gravitational force on some planet, then appeal to a genuine authority is legitimate, since there is consensus among authorities on that question. But if instead the issue is the safety of nuclear power plants or the long-term effects of low-level radiation or whether Secretariat was the greatest racehorse in history, then appeals to authority are *fallacious:* On those questions there is no settled agreement among the authorities in the respective areas. When that is the case—when genuine authorities disagree—we must consider the competing *arguments.* Since each side can marshal impressive and competing authorities, appeal to authority cannot be used to settle the issue.

That may not sound too difficult—and in some cases, it is not hard to distinguish legitimate from fallacious appeals to authority. But there are some notorious difficulties—problems that have troubled judges and scientists as well as philosophers. In order for an appeal to authority to be legitimate, there must be *agreement* among genuine authorities. But what counts as agreement? If every genuine expert on the subject agrees, then that is obviously sufficient. But is it necessary? Probably not. If there are 10,000 genuine experts in astronomy, and 9,999 of them agree that Jupiter is the planet with the greatest mass, then is it legitimate to appeal to authority on the question of what planet has the greatest mass? Yes, that seems like enough agreement. But what if the issue is one in which 9,000 of the astronomers hold one view, and a thousand other expert astronomers dissent? Is 90% enough to count as general agreement among authorities? Or would it be a fallacy to appeal to the authority of the majority astronomers on such a case? What if the split is 70 to 30? At 51 to 49, certainly we would say that there is no general agreement among authorities, and so appeal to authority would be fallacious. But just how close to unanimity does the agreement have to be? In *Frye* v. *United States,*[1] the 1923 U.S. Supreme Court ruled that expert testimony is legitimate if the theory or technique about which the expert is testifying is "generally accepted" as reliable in the relevant scientific community. But that leaves the question of *what counts* as "generally accepted." In answering that question, U.S. courts have generally followed the rule that if a scientific judgment has been subjected to and passed peer review through publication in an accepted scientific journal, then that is sufficient for counting it as being "generally accepted by the scientific community." That may be enough to establish that a scientific opinion is *expert,* but it obviously won't answer our question about what counts as *sufficient agreement* to make an appeal to authority legitimate: After all, scientific work by scientists who hold minority views is regularly—and rightly—published in peer-reviewed scientific journals. Recently the U.S. Supreme Court, in *Daubert* v. *Merrell Dow Pharmaceuticals, Inc.,*[2] rejected the *Frye* standard. In the *Daubert* case, the Court ruled that publication in an accepted scientific journal is not a good standard for scientific legitimacy, since some published scientific work is not reliable and some reliable scientific work has not been published.[3] Under *Daubert,* the Court ruled that in order to count as legitimate expert testimony the research *results* need not be generally accepted by the scientific community,

Dubious Authority

In a 1990 civil trial, the parents of two teenage boys sued a British heavy-metal rock band named Judas Priest. The two boys had attempted suicide (one was successful) after listening to an album by Judas Priest. The plaintiffs charged that one of Judas Priest's songs contained a subliminal phrase ("Do it") that triggered a suicidal impulse in the two boys.

Experts on cognitive psychology generally agree that subliminal messages have little if any effect on beliefs, attitudes, or behavior. The plaintiffs had an impressive expert witness, Howard Shevrin, who has published reputable research on subliminal influences. Shevrin testified that subliminal messages might induce suicidal behavior, and he insisted that "my expert judgment [is based] on a corpus of literature, on hundreds of experiments." However, when pressed to cite some of this experimental support, Shevrin could name no studies demonstrating such powerful subliminal effects on behavior.[4]

Dr. Shevrin is, of course, "entitled to his opinion"; but he is not entitled to present it as if it were based on sound scientific research and the general considered acceptance of the scientific community. In this case, Dr. Shevrin *is* an expert; but the consensus of scientific expertise goes *against* his views.

but the *methodology* used in the research must be based on scientifically sound and accepted principles. (It will still be up to the "fact finder," that is, the jury or—in trials without juries—the judge, to weigh the credibility of the expert testimony.) So directly or indirectly the Court has retained the basic but troubling standard for legitimate expertise: It must be "generally accepted" by the relevant scientific community. But what counts as "generally accepted" remains a vexed question.

Appeal to authority can be legitimate, but only when the person to whom appeal is made is genuinely an expert in that area, *and* the experts agree on the answer. If the "authority" cited is not an expert on the subject, or there is disagreement among authorities, then it is a fallacious appeal to authority.

An example of expert testimony and its evaluation may clarify the issues involved in evaluating appeals to authority. Suppose that the expert, Dr. Jones, testifies that the deceased died of a bullet wound before being submerged in water: "The bullet wound was the sole cause of death; I am absolutely certain of that as a result of my careful and expert examination of the victim, and I would stake my professional reputation on it." And Dr. Smith, equally an authority in forensic medicine, testifies that the victim was drowned and that the bullet wound alone would not have been fatal: "The victim died from drowning; the bullet wound was a serious injury, but it would not and did not cause death; death was by drowning; I am absolutely certain of that as a result of my careful and expert examination of the victim, and I would stake my professional reputation on it." In such a case, doctors Jones and Smith have *not* given *arguments* for their views; instead, they have given *expert testimony*. And since the experts disagree, it would be *fallacious* for either the prosecution or the defense to appeal to their authoritative pronouncements as establishing the truth about the cause of death.

Adrift among Authorities

One of the most difficult tasks facing a juror is the evaluation of conflicting expert testimony. The jurors at the trial of John Hinckley, Jr. (tried in the spring of 1982 for attempting to assassinate U.S. president Ronald Reagan) had the "benefit" of hearing many highly qualified experts, who were summoned by both sides to give testimony about the state of the defendant's mind at the time he committed the crime. Unfortunately, the jurors could not merely accept authority, since there certainly was no consensus among the experts: one expert testified he was clinically depressed, while another expert rejected that claim; one expert diagnosed Hinckley as schizophrenic, while an equal and opposite expert denied that diagnosis; an expert for the defense insisted that Hinckley was severely psychotic, while a prosecution expert insisted that Hinckley had never been psychotic. In such a case, the jurors must attempt to decide whether all the authorities are really experts in the field, and assuming that there are genuine authorities who give conflicting testimony, the jurors are then required to weigh the competing *arguments* of the expert witnesses (since appeal to authority is *fallacious* when authorities disagree).

But since both Jones and Smith are giving *testimony* (not argument), it is quite legitimate to direct ad hominem attacks against the two experts. An attorney might try to establish that one of the experts is not really an expert at all ("Dr. Jones, isn't it true that you bought your medical degree from a mail-order university you found in the classified section of *Soldier of Fortune?*"); or that one "expert" is not very reliable ("Dr. Smith, didn't you recently serve 3 years at Leavenworth for a perjury conviction?"); or that one expert has a strong bias or interest that is likely to slant her judgment ("Dr Jones, isn't it true that the defendant in this case is your ex-husband, with whom you are currently engaged in litigation for custody of your three children?"). If the reputation, reliability, or objectivity of one of the "experts" can be called into question, then the strength of that "expert" testimony will be weakened. In that case, counsel might argue that there is no disagreement on this issue among genuine, truthful, fair-minded experts (all the "experts" on the other side are biased, incompetent, or incapacitated) and therefore the testimony of the legitimate authority ought to be accepted.

This is tricky stuff. For if the expert is giving *arguments* for her view (rather than simply saying "take my expert word for it," she is instead saying "consider these reasons for this conclusion"), then you must consider the *arguments*, and forget the credentials and the character of the arguer. In *that* case, the witness's bias, the amount of money the witness is receiving, and the witness's credentials don't count. If the witness is giving *argument*, rather than testimony, it makes no difference whether her degree came from Harvard or the Stumpwater Institute for Delinquent Girls. Cases in which witnesses are giving *argument* (rather than eyewitness or expert *testimony*) are comparatively rare, but they do occur. If the expert "witnesses" are giving argument, rather than testimony, it is irrelevant to their arguments that they are hired guns; whether they are hired to give argument, or are giving arguments out of pure love of justice and truth, or whatever their motivations, that is *irrelevant* to proper evaluation of their *arguments*. But if they are simply *asserting* the truth of their claims on the basis of their expertise—"Take my word for it, I'm an expert"—then their status as advocates or hired guns may be weighed in the balance.

One more point concerning legitimate and fallacious appeals to authority. If there is deep disagreement among authorities about theory Z, then it is quite legitimate for the genuine authority Dr. Alice Andrews to affirm that "In my best judgment, theory Z is correct." The expert is stating her expert opinion, *not* appealing to authority. However, if Joe then says that "The respected expert Dr. Andrews says that Z is correct, so Z must be correct,"

A Tarnished Expert

My favorite example of a questionable "expert" witness occurred in a civil case in Cleveland. Claire Freeman-McCown had been fired from her job as chief executive officer of the Cuyahoga Metropolitan Housing Authority (CMHA) by the CMHA Board on grounds that she was fraudulently taking money from the agency (payments on her credit cards and on mortgages for personal property) through forging a number of documents. (It was claimed that documents supposedly signed by the CMHA Board were forgeries.) She sued CMHA for damages, claiming that the charges against her were false and malicious. Since the question of forgery was central to her case, she presented the expert testimony of F. Aurelius McKanze, who appeared as an expert forensic document examiner. He claimed that he had been a colonel in the Air Force, had done undergraduate studies at Ohio State University, and that he had a doctorate in criminal psychology from the University of Arizona. The Air Force, Ohio State, and the University of Arizona denied his claims. He also had been in prison for receiving stolen property and theft. But he did apparently have some knowledge of forgery: He had been convicted of forgery in 1973.

Freeman-McCown lost her case, and her "expert witness"—F. Aurelius McKanze—was charged with perjury. McKanze pleaded guilty, but at his sentencing he was placed on probation (rather than receiving an active prison sentence) because of letters from local physicians stating that McKanze was dying of prostate cancer that had spread throughout his body. Unfortunately for McKanze, the judge changed his mind concerning probation when it was discovered that the letters from the doctors had been forged.

Is the Authority Sincere?

Tiger Woods appears in commercials for Nike golf balls, and endorses "Nike Tour Accuracy" golf balls. Suppose that on the basis of that advertisement I assert that Nike must be the best golf balls, because Tiger Woods recommends them, and Tiger Woods is an expert golfer. Well, the fact that Tiger recommends them is certainly *relevant:* it's not like Tiger recommending a particular model of car, an area in which presumably he is no more an expert than you and I. When it comes to golf, Tiger Woods can stake a strong claim to expertise. Still, there would be some problems with this appeal to Tiger Woods as an authority on golf balls. First, there is apparently no consensus among golf experts on which golf balls are best (most touring professionals use Titleist), and thus the second condition for legitimate appeal to authority is not met. Also, Tiger Woods is getting paid—$100 million over a 5-year contract—for his recommendation of Nike golf balls. Since Tiger is giving "expert testimony" on the golf balls, it is legitimate to bring up any special interests he might have that might make him less than a perfectly objective expert witness: and receiving $100 million for his endorsement is a very special interest. Finally, the golf balls that Tiger actually uses in professional competition are not the "Nike Tour Accuracy" balls he endorses in advertisements; for his own play, Tiger uses a ball that is custom made by Nike (with a harder inner and outer core) that is not sold by Nike. Tiger's undisputed golfing greatness notwithstanding, such factors raise legitimate questions about the legitimacy of Tiger's authoritative testimony on behalf of Nike golf balls.

Does Tiger's well-publicized marital infidelity count against his expert testimony? Since it raises questions about his *truthfulness* (he promised to be faithful to his wife, and he deceived her) it does tarnish the reliability of his testimony.

---

then Joe is offering a fallacious appeal to authority. (And of course if Dr. Andrews, still testifying about the disputed theory Z, says that "In my best judgment, theory Z is correct, and since I am a recognized authority on this subject, you ought to accept theory Z as true," then in that case Dr. Andrews is fallaciously appealing to her *own* authority.)

In sum, there are several key points to remember about appeals to expert authority. When evaluating an *appeal to authority* (when the authority is offering *testimony* on the grounds of his or her status as a knowledgeable expert, and is not giving an argument), you must consider two main issues. First, is this individual really an authority in the appropriate area? (Thus ad hominem arguments aimed at undermining the claimed expertise of the authority will be relevant, and *inverse* ad hominem arguments aimed at establishing the wisdom and integrity of the expert witness will also be legitimate.) And second, is this an issue on which authorities are generally in agreement? (If not, then no appeal to authority can be legitimate.) But in many instances, unfortunately, there is a third factor that must be considered. Is this authority likely to give his or her truthful, unbiased, unslanted expert opinion? Or will the authority be tempted to slant (or even falsify) his or her expert opinion? That question will certainly be relevant (and ad hominem attacks on the honesty and objectivity of an expert authority will be relevant), since experts may be as subject to temptations of the flesh—including the cash paid by the side that hires them to testify—as anyone else. Especially in court cases, the expert authorities who appear as witnesses for both sides may not be the dedicated-only-to-truth-and-science objective independent authorities that we might wish them to be. One former president of the American Bar Association put the point quite bluntly:

> I would go into a lawsuit with an objective uncommitted independent expert about as willingly as I would occupy a foxhole with a couple of noncombatant soldiers.[5]

Often these "hired guns" cannot be trusted; thus it is important for jurors trying to weigh the value and reliability of their testimony to know something about the character of such expert testifiers, and about any special biases and influences (including cash influences) that may slant or distort their testimony.

Biased "experts" are also a problem outside of court. One of the great difficulties in dealing with claims by "authorities" is in knowing which ones are genuine experts, presenting impartial expertise, and which ones are charlatans. That problem has become even more severe in recent years, as industries and public relations firms have put together sham "foundations" that represent themselves as impartial experts, when in fact they are front groups that are bought and paid for by special industrial interests. The American Council on Science and Health claims to be an independent and objective group of research scientists. In fact, it is funded by the chemical and food-processing industries. It receives grants from Burger King, and publishes reports praising the nutritional value of fast food. It criticizes studies showing the health problems generated by tropical oils, while taking money from palm oil producers. And it asserts that "There has never been a case of ill health linked to the regulated, approved use of pesticides in this country," while receiving funds from a number of pesticide manufacturers.[6] Before you trust the reports of these "objective independent scientists," you are justified in considering the source.

Consider another example: the "Air Hygiene Foundation" sounds like a wholesome organization dedicated to improving air quality; it was in fact an industry-funded front, whose purpose was to provide cover and misinformation on behalf of industries creating silica dust, which was responsible for thousands of deaths from silicosis, a lung disease brought on by breathing silica dust, a disease that plagued workers in mining, sandblasting, pottery, and foundries, and permanently disabled many that it did not kill. Not only do such foundations carry a false air of concern for safety and the environment along with their air of disinterested objectivity, they also manage to generously sponsor "research" that conveniently "proves" the results the foundation prefers. As noted by Rampton and Stauber,

> By 1960, 63 scientific papers on the subject of asbestosis had been done, 11 of which were sponsored by the asbestos industry, the other 52 coming from hospitals and medical schools. The 11 industry studies were unanimous in denying that asbestos caused lung cancer and minimizing the seriousness of asbestosis—a position diametrically opposite to the conclusions reached by the nonindustry studies.[7]

The moral of the story: When evaluating "expert testimony," it is important to know whether the "experts" are genuine objective experts or merely paid industry hacks. And when evaluating expert testimony, it is also important to know—as with the evaluation of any testimony—whether the testifier has any special incentive that might lead him or her to testify untruthfully. For example, in the 1990s, tobacco companies paid over $150,000 to 13 scientists simply to write pro-tobacco letters to influential medical journals.[8] One might doubt the objectivity of such expert letter writers.

One last example. Latex gloves, used by nurses and doctors, cause severe allergic reactions in about 10% of the doctors and nurses who wear them. Some 200,000 nurses have developed latex allergies, and the allergies can be severely disabling, and even deadly (four nurses have died from their reactions to latex). Alternatives exist, and are now being used. But former Surgeon General C. Everett Koop testified before Congress that concern over latex gloves is a case of "borderline hysteria," and that the risks were greatly exaggerated. Dr. Koop forgot to mention in his testimony that a maker of latex gloves paid him over $600,000 to serve as a spokesman for the company. But a payment of $600,000 is something you might wish to consider in evaluating the reliability of Koop's "expert" testimony: testimony which was far outside Dr. Koop's area of expertise (his practice was in pediatric orthopedic surgery).[9]

Appeal to expert authority can be—and often is—legitimate and valuable; but before putting your trust in an appeal to authority, you must be confident that the authority really is an authority on that subject, that there is consensus among authorities on that question, and that the authority is testifying in an honest and unbiased manner. That's a lot to ask of genuine appeals to authority, but no one said that careful critical thinking would be easy.

How Do You Rule?

When O. J. Simpson was charged with murder, it was obvious that a key part of the trial evidence would be the blood stains found in Simpson's home and car, on his socks, on a glove, and at the murder scene. And central to that evidence would be DNA testing to determine whose blood it was. With that in mind, Simpson's defense team hired an expert on DNA testing: Dr. Kary B. Mullis. Dr. Mullis was not just any expert on DNA. In 1993, he had won the Nobel Prize for his breakthrough research on DNA testing. He had invented the PCR (polymerase chain-reaction) technique for identifying and reproducing DNA. Dr. Mullis believed that PCR testing was valuable in the laboratory, but that it was ill suited for criminal investigation because of the uncontrolled nature of the crime scene, and that therefore the DNA testing in criminal cases was unreliable. A major defense theme was the sloppy work of the police investigators in gathering blood evidence, transporting the evidence, and running their tests. The skeptical testimony of a Nobel Prize winner, who won the prize for his work on DNA testing, would seem to be a major triumph for the defense.

And yet the defense never called Dr. Mullis. A nobel laureate, willing to testify that the DNA testing that linked Simpson to the crime was unreliable, and yet the defense never called him. Why not?

Since Dr. Mullis was testifying as an expert, his credentials and reliability were open to attack. And Dr. Mullis was vulnerable to attack on several fronts. In the first place, since winning the Nobel Prize he had largely abandoned scientific research to devote himself to surfing, taking hallucinogenic drugs, and pursuing women. As a result, he was out of touch with recent developments in DNA research. For example, RFLP testing is a recently developed and more reliable way of making DNA identifications, and a major advance in DNA research; yet when the defense lawyers interviewed him, Dr. Mullis could not remember what RFLP testing was. Furthermore, Dr. Mullis had exhibited rather bizarre behavior and championed views that placed him well out of the mainstream of scientific research. He maintained that the HIV virus is not the cause of AIDS; and he was banned from one scientific conference after showing slides of nude women during his lecture.

When the defense was considering calling Dr. Mullis as an expert witness, they asked Judge Ito to rule that Dr. Mullis's lifestyle and character were "completely irrelevant," and that the prosecution should not be allowed to ask questions on those topics. The prosecution responded that:

> Should the defense choose to call Dr. Mullis to voice any relevant criticisms about forensic PCR applications, the prosecution is fully prepared to cross-examine Mullis on every aspect of his life which reflects on his credibility, competency, and sobriety.

If you were Judge Ito, how would you rule? Would you allow the defense to ask such questions, or would you rule that Dr. Mullis's lifestyle, drug use, and behavior are irrelevant?

POPULARITY AND TRADITION

Two special varieties of fallacious appeal to authority should be noted. Those special versions of the *fallacy* of appeal to authority are the appeal to the (false) authority of *popularity* and the appeal to the (false) authority of *tradition*. Remember that in order for appeal to authority to be legitimate and *non*fallacious, the "authority" to whom appeal is made must be genuine and must have special knowledge and expertise in the subject. But since neither the crowd (popularity) nor tradition has special knowledge, such appeals are always fallacious. These are common and distinctive fallacies, and we have special names for them: *appeal to popularity* and *appeal to traditional wisdom*.

Appeal to popularity is a common advertising ploy. Advertisements frequently suggest that a product must be good—or even the best of its type—because it is the most popular. But such an appeal to popularity would have force only if the people who buy the product were experts—and obviously they are not.

Being misled by a commercial appeal to popularity may result in wasting money on inferior products. During jury deliberation, when 12 persons are deciding whether to find the defendant guilty or not guilty, failure to recognize fallacious appeals to popularity may have more serious consequences. Suppose that after long deliberation 10 or 11 members of the jury favor one verdict, and one or two members favor another. At that point, the majority will almost certainly appeal to the weight of its numbers in an effort to persuade the dissenters to agree with them. The one or two in the minority will probably be subjected to such arguments as: "Look, everyone else on the jury agrees that the defendant is guilty; you are the only one who doubts it. Since there are so many more of us who have come to the guilty conclusion, doesn't that show you that your own conclusion must be mistaken? Be reasonable, and accept the view of the overwhelming majority. After all, 11 heads are better than one." But such an appeal to popularity is *fallacious*. The fact that a view is popular is no grounds for believing that it is correct; no more than the fact that a brand of pain reliever is the biggest seller is grounds for believing that it is the best. Neither a crowd of purchasers nor a crowd of jurors are experts. Of course, the members of the majority—and also the members of the minority—may and should offer *arguments* to convince the other side of the correctness of the conclusion favored. But appeal to popularity is not a sound argument.

Jurors are not the only ones who may be led astray by the seductive appeals of popularity. Judges have sometimes encouraged jurors to be swayed by majority opinion. In a famous (or infamous) charge to a hung jury (in *Allen* v. *United States*), the judge instructed the jury:

> that in a large proportion of cases absolute certainty could not be expected; that although the verdict must be the verdict of each individual juror, and not a mere acquiescence in the conclusion of his fellows, yet they should examine the question submitted with candor and with a proper regard and deference to the opinions of each other; that it was their duty to decide the case if they could conscientiously do so; that they should listen, with a disposition to be convinced, to each other's argument; that, if much the larger number were for conviction, a dissenting juror should consider whether his doubt was a reasonable one which made no impression upon the minds of so many men, equally honest, equally intelligent with himself. If, upon the other hand, the majority was for acquittal, the minority ought to ask themselves whether they might reasonably doubt the correctness of a judgment which was not concurred in by the majority.[10]

But the fact that a majority disagrees—or agrees—with a conclusion has no bearing on the correctness of the conclusion. The *arguments* of any group deserve careful attention, but their *numbers*—whether great or small—are irrelevant. In *rejecting* the Allen charge to the jury, the Fifth Circuit U.S. Court of Appeals cited the opinion of Judge Brown, who wrote,

> I think a mistrial from a hung jury is a safeguard to liberty. In many areas it is the sole means by which one or a few may stand out against an overwhelming public sentiment. Nothing should interfere with its exercise. In the final analysis the Allen charge itself does not make sense. All it may rightfully say is that there is a duty to consider the views of others but that a conscientious person has finally the right and duty to stand by conscience. If it says that and nothing more it is a superfluous lecture in citizenship. If it says more to declare that there is a duty to decide, it is legally incorrect as an interference with that rightful independence. The time has come, I think, to forbid this practice. Like the silver platter, this is too dear to keep. The cost in fundamental fairness is too great.[11]

And there is another cost to being convinced merely by the weight of opinion against one's position: the cost of falling into the fallacy of appeal to popularity.

A similar category of fallacious appeal is the appeal to traditional wisdom. The crowd is not expert, and neither is *tradition*. That a view or a position has been held for many years is not evidence of its *correctness*.

When in the sixteenth century Copernicus argued that the Earth is *not* stationary (but instead orbits the Sun), his opponents argued that belief in a fixed and immovable Earth had endured for centuries. But his opponents then concluded—incorrectly—that that was good reason to think the belief true. Traditional beliefs of long standing may be true, of course, but their longevity is not evidence of their truth. Neither tradition nor popularity qualifies as *expert*. Contrary to popular belief, there is no "test of time" that a long-held belief has passed. Thus the fact that abortion was for many decades believed to be wrong is irrelevant to the question of whether it is really wrong. The fact that for many years there were almost no restrictions on smoking in public places is irrelevant to the question of whether such restrictions should now be established. Conversely, while tradition carries no authority, neither does novelty. The advertiser's trumpeting of a *new* headache remedy, a *new* laundry detergent, or a *new* underarm deodorant is just as fallacious as the appeal to traditional wisdom. The newness of a product or idea counts neither for nor against it, just as the fact that a belief or idea is old gives it no special weight. Neither the soberness of age nor the fresh bloom of youth counts for or against a belief, theory, idea, or product. Appeal to tradition (like appeal to innovation) is a fallacious appeal to a source that is not genuinely authoritative, a source that has no genuine expertise.

In summary, there are real authorities in some areas, and appeal to the testimony of such authorities is legitimate. But when the "authority"—whether popularity, tradition, or an individual—is not really an expert on the subject (or when genuine authorities *do not agree*), then appeal to authority is fallacious. And since the authority is giving testimony (and the strength of the testimony depends on the integrity and expertise of the authority), ad hominem attacks *against* such appeals are legitimate: they do *not* commit the ad hominem *fallacy*.

Exercise 10-1

1. The following are appeals to authority; for each one, tell whether it is legitimate or fallacious.

   a. I've been having trouble getting my lawn to grow—the grass is not very thick, and in some spots there's really no grass at all. But yesterday while watching television I saw Don Shula, the coach of the Miami Dolphins—and he recommended this special new lawn fertilizer from Hyponex. He says it is great stuff and that it will do wonders for your lawn. Well, Don Shula is a very bright guy and is perhaps the best football coach in the National Football League. Since he thinks Hyponex is the best lawn fertilizer, I'm going to get some. It must be good stuff.

   b. You remember our argument about how to amend the U.S. Constitution? We were arguing about how many states must approve an amendment in order to pass it. Well, I have settled that question. I just talked to former U.S. Supreme Court Justice Sandra Day O'Connor and to Ronald Dworkin (Professor of Constitutional Law at New York University), and they both agreed that amendments to the Constitution must be approved by three-fourths of the states.

   c. The question of whether a computer might ever be programmed to really think—intelligently and creatively, as well as or better than the most intelligent humans—is certainly hotly debated, and top computer scientists and programmers, psychologists, and philosophers often disagree about whether such intelligent computers are really possible. Well, Hans Moravec is head of the Robotics Institute at Carnegie-Mellon University, he holds a PhD in computer science from Stanford, and he has done major research at the Stanford Artificial Intelligence Institute. In fact, he is one of the leading authorities in the world on artificial intelligence (computer intelligence) and robotics. He recently claimed that computerized robots with intelligence fully equal to that of the most intelligent human beings "will be common within 50 years." That should settle the question. If an acknowledged expert like Hans Moravec says such computer intelligence is possible, then it must really be possible.

   d. It is quite clear that high sugar soft drinks are causing health problems and contributing to obesity in elementary and middle school children. The American Medical Association, the American Heart Association, the National Institute of Health, Harvard Medical School, and the Mayo Clinic have all agreed that children's consumption of these high sugar drinks is a major cause of both obesity and health problems in school age children.

e. There is great controversy over the economic impact of opening new casinos in Ohio. Some economists claim that the new casinos would bring in thousands of new jobs, and greatly increase the tax revenue to the state. Other economists say that the casinos would not bring in more jobs, but would instead just replace some current entertainment jobs with casino jobs; and they say that tax revenue would not really increase, because the state would have to spend more money regulating and policing the casinos than we would get back in revenue. Obviously this is a controversial issue among economists. But I recently talked with the chair of the economics department at the University of Southern Ohio, Dr. Susan Corbett; and Dr. Corbett said that the casinos would definitely *not* bring more jobs or increase tax revenue! That should settle the issue: Dr. Corbett is one of the top economists in Ohio, and if she says the casinos would not bring more jobs and more tax revenue, we should accept her claim.

f. Lead poisoning is a major health hazard for children who are exposed to lead in lead-based paints and from other sources. The dangers from lead were recently confirmed by Dr. Alice Biagiotti, who is chair of the Manhattan University Medical School Department of Environmental Diseases, and has published dozens of articles on the hazards of lead: She stated that lead poisoning is one of the major causes of neurological damage to children.

g. Dr. James Solomon is one of the world leaders in nanotechnology, and he heads the Nanotechnology Research Institute at New York University for Science and Technology: Dr. Solomon's recent research led to a major breakthrough on microradiation treatments for cancer, and he shared the Nobel Prize in physics for that accomplishment. Dr. Solomon firmly believes in life after death, and he maintains that evidence from near-death experiences offers conclusive proof that life can and does continue after death. When the Nobel Prize winner in physics asserts that there is life after death, that should settle the issue for all reasonable persons.

2.

How Do You Rule?

Jacqueline Ripper is on trial for the murder of Quincy Victim. She is accused of stabbing Quincy to death after a bitter argument in a local tavern. Dr. Constance Competent, a leading authority on the identification of blood types, is appearing for the prosecution as an expert witness. She has testified that the blood on a knife identified as belonging to Ms. Ripper is the same blood type as that of the late Mr. Victim.

The prosecution continues its questioning of Dr. Competent as follows:

DISTRICT ATTORNEY: Now Dr. Competent, you have carefully examined the blood-stained knife, state's exhibit number 3?

DR. COMPETENT: Yes, I have.

DISTRICT ATTORNEY: And you have seen the defendant, Ms. Ripper, here in court?

DR. COMPETENT: Certainly.

DISTRICT ATTORNEY: In your expert judgment, would Ms. Ripper have sufficient strength to use that knife to inflict a fatal wound on a middle-aged man of average size and strength?

DEFENSE ATTORNEY: Objection, your honor. The prosecution is asking for speculation. How would Dr. Competent know how much strength is required to inflict a fatal wound, much less how much strength is in the defendant's arms? Dr. Competent is no expert in such matters.

DISTRICT ATTORNEY: Your Honor, I submit that Dr. Competent is well-qualified to answer the question. In the course of her work on identifying blood types, she has examined many fatal wounds and is thus in an excellent position to testify about such wounds. I'm sure the jury will want the benefit of the full and unfettered testimony of such an internationally renowned expert as is Dr. Competent.

Should Dr. Competent be allowed to offer expert testimony in response to the district attorney's question? That is, do you sustain the defense objection, or do you overrule and allow Dr. Competent to answer?

3. Aristotle was one of the greatest philosophers in all history. For over a thousand years, he was so widely acclaimed that he was often referred to as simply "the Philosopher": when someone spoke of "the Philosopher," everyone knew that meant Aristotle. Aristotle insisted that the path to virtuous living must be a path of moderation. In seeking to live virtuously, one should always seek the *mean*: the virtue of bravery is the mean between rashness and cowardice; the virtue of thrift is the mean between stinginess and wastefulness; and so on. This doctrine came to be called the *golden mean* account of virtue, and many people have found it useful for over 2000 years. Therefore, the life of virtue must be one of careful moderation, avoiding extremes and excesses on both sides.

How would you evaluate that argument?

4. You go to see your doctor, Dr. Joan Jones, for your annual physical checkup. After all the reports are back, she sits down with you to discuss your current state of health and how it could be improved. Dr. Jones lights up a cigarette, takes a deep puff, and starts talking:

Look, you're in pretty good health. Your blood pressure is good, and you seem to be getting enough exercise. But you really ought to stop smoking. There have now been many reliable studies—by the American Cancer Society and others—that show that smoking is the major cause of lung cancer and that it also greatly increases your chances of developing cancer of the mouth, cancer of the throat, emphysema, or having a heart attack. You want to avoid cancer and heart attacks, right? Then you should quit smoking.

What effect should Dr. Jones's smoking have on your evaluation of what she says?

5. You go to see your doctor, Dr. Sam Smith, for your annual physical checkup. After all the reports are back, he sits down with you to discuss your current state of health and how it could be improved. Dr. Smith lights up a cigarette, takes a deep puff, and starts talking:

Look, you're in pretty good health. Your blood pressure is good, and you seem to be getting enough exercise. However, you really ought to stop smoking. Listen to me: I've seen what smoking does to people, and it's not pretty. I've watched patients die in agony from lung cancer. Take it from me: Everyone ought to stop smoking.

What effect should Dr. Smith's smoking have on your evaluation of what he says?

6.

How Do You Rule?

Bob Daemmrich / Alamy

This is a civil case, in which Dr. Lawrence Logan is being sued for malpractice. Dr. Logan is an oncologist. The lawsuit against him is asking for heavy damages on behalf of Janice Joust, a 35-year-old woman whose family doctor referred her to Dr. Logan. Dr. Logan examined her briefly, ran very few tests, and concluded that she was not suffering from cancer, but instead was feeling the effects of a lingering bronchial infection; Dr. Logan assured her that the infection would soon clear up on its own. Unfortunately, Ms. Joust developed lung cancer; when she was checked by Dr. Logan it was—the plaintiff claims—at a very early and treatable stage that could have been discovered with adequate testing. During the months following, while the patient received no treatment, the cancer spread throughout her body; by the time Ms. Joust went to another oncologist, the cancer was far advanced. Ms. Joust underwent several treatments, but a few months after beginning those treatments she died from the cancer. The witness on the stand is Dr. Carl Covington, who is also an oncologist, and shares a practice with Dr. Logan and three other oncologists. Dr. Covington has testified—as an expert witness for the defense—that Dr. Logan carried out a thorough and professionally competent examination of Ms. Joust; and that—in Dr. Covington's professional opinion—Ms. Joust's cancer had not been present when she was examined, but had begun at a later date. Now, Dr. Covington is being cross-examined by the plaintiff's attorney.

"Dr. Covington, you share a practice with Dr. Logan, is that correct?"

"Yes, with Dr. Logan and three other physicians; the Brightwood Oncology Center."

"Could you tell me, Dr. Covington, how you manage your malpractice insurance? Do you buy it individually, or as a group?"

"We purchase malpractice coverage through a group policy; all of the physicians at Brightwood are on the same plan."

"Did your insurance premiums go up last year?"

"The premiums increase just about every year; you lawyers make sure of that."

"Was there a particularly big increase in your insurance costs last year?"

"There was a substantial increase, yes."

"Do you know why there was such an increase, Dr. Covington? Did your insurance agent give you any reason?"

"He said it was because of all the frivolous malpractice suits you lawyers are filing."

"Is that what he said, Dr. Covington? Or did he give you a more specific reason? Let me remind you that you are testifying under oath."

"He said that part of the increase was because of a malpractice suit that had been filed against a physician in the practice during the previous year."

"Who was that physician, Dr. Covington?"

"I was."

"I see. And what was the result of that malpractice suit that was filed against you?"

"The jury found in favor of the plaintiff."

"Yes, thank you, Dr. Covington. And what damages did the jury award?"

"One and a quarter million."

"That's one and a quarter million *dollars*?"

"Obviously."

"And the damages against you were for failing to give additional chemotherapy treatments that might well have prevented the return of a cancer that resulted in the death of a forty-year-old mother of three; is that right, Dr. Covington? Is that one of the frivolous cases you were referring to?"

"Your Honor," the defense counsel rises to object; "counselor is badgering the witness, and that question is argumentative."

"I withdraw the question. Now Dr. Covington, what would happen to your malpractice insurance if the jury reaches a verdict against Dr. Logan? Did your insurer tell you anything about that?"

"No, nothing that I remember."

"Let me refresh your memory, Doctor. This is a letter from Northern Medical Insurance, addressed to Brightwood Oncology. Is that a letter from your malpractice insurer?"

Dr. Covington looks at the letter. "It appears to be."

"Appearances can be deceiving, Dr. Covington. I'm not asking about appearances. Is that or is it not a letter from your malpractice insurance company, addressed to your medical practice?"

"Yes, it is."

"What does that letter say?"

"It says that if the company has to pay another large malpractice settlement on behalf of Brightwood, that they will double our premiums."

"They will double your premiums. Tell me, Dr. Covington, how much would your own insurance costs go up, how much more would you have to pay, if this jury decides this case in favor of the family of Ms. Joust? How much would that cost you out of pocket?"

At this point the attorney for Dr. Logan objects. "Your Honor, these questions are irrelevant. This case is about the professional work of Dr. Logan. This tiresome talk about medical malpractice insurance, which is a terrible burden on all physicians, has nothing to do with the issue at hand."

How do you rule? Will you sustain this objection, or overrule and allow the questions along this line to continue?

✓•—**Study** and **Review** on **mythinkinglab.com**

REVIEW QUESTIONS

1. What is the *fallacy* of appeal to authority?
2. Under what conditions is appeal to authority legitimate?
3. What is the *fallacy* of appeal to popularity? Why is it a fallacy?

NOTES

1 *Frye* v. *United States,* 293 F. 1010–1019.

2 *Daubert* v. *Merrell Dow Pharmaceuticals, Inc.,* 61 U.S.L.W. 4801–4812.

3 There has been much discussion of the *Daubert* case; for a clear and brief examination of some of the issues, see an article by Alexander Morgan Capron, "Facts, Values, and Expert Testimony," in *Hastings Center Report* (September–October 1993).

4 For an excellent discussion of the issues in this case, see Timothy E. Moore, "Scientific Consensus and Expert Testimony: Lessons from the Judas Priest Trial," *Skeptical Inquirer* (November–December 1996).

5 Peter W. Huber, *Galileo's Revenge* (New York: Basic Books, 1991), p. 18; quoted from "From the People Who Brought You the Twinkie Defense: The Rise of the Expert Witness Industry," *Washington Monthly* (June 1987), p. 33.

6 For more details, see Chapter 11 of *Toxic Sludge is Good for You,* by John Stauber and Sheldon Rampton (Monroe, ME: Common Courage Press, 1995); and an article by Howard Kurtz, "Dr. Whelan's Media Operation," in *Columbia Journalism Review* (March–April 1990).

7 Sheldon Rampton and John Stauber, *Trust Us, We're Experts* (New York: Tarcher/Putnam, 2001), p. 86.

8 Ibid, p. 199.

9 Ibid, p. 256.

10 164 U.S. 492 (1896).

11 297 F.2d 754, 759 (5th Cir. 1962).

INTERNET RESOURCES

Some very nice examples of appeal to authority and appeal to popularity can be found at *http://www.cbsd.org/sites/teachers/hs/NMUNROE/Student%20Documents/11-%20Basics%20of%20 Rhetoric%20Unit%20Materials/Fallacies%20pp.pdf.*

ADDITIONAL READING

A meticulous and extensive study of appeal to popularity can be found in Douglas Walton, *Appeal to Popular Opinion* (University Park, Pennsylvania: Pennsylvania State University Press, 1999). For a careful study of expert testimony and appeal to authority, see Walton's *Appeal to Expert Opinion: Arguments from Authority* (University Park, Pennsylvania: Pennsylvania State University Press, 1997)

For more on expert testimony, see *Testimony: A Philosophical Study,* by C. A. J. Coady (New York: Oxford University Press, 1992).

For a detailed discussion of the *Frye* and *Daubert* legal standards for expert testimony, see Kenneth R. Foster and Peter W. Huber, *Judging Science: Scientific Knowledge and the Federal Courts* (Cambridge, MA: The MIT Press, 1997), especially Chapter 9.

Jeff Chesen, in "Canada's Use of Expert Witnesses and Scientific Evidence Admissibility," is a very clear examination of the Canadian approach to expert testimony, and the historical development of that approach. The paper was published by the National Clearinghouse for Science, Technology, & the Law, July 2006; it can be found online at www.ncstl.org/evident/July,%202006.

An interesting and very readable case of conflict over "expert" testimony—including a helpful analysis of the standards for expert testimony—is found in Timothy E. Moore, "Scientific Consensus and Expert Testimony: Lessons from the Judas Priest Trial," *Skeptical Inquirer,* Vol. 20, no. 6, November/December 1996.

Sheldon Rampton and John Stauber, *Trust Us, We're Experts!* (New York: Tarcher/Putnam, 2001), is a fascinating and in-depth study of how "experts for hire" can be used to manipulate public opinion.

For an excellent article on how "scientific" studies can be distorted and manipulated, see "The Secret History of Lead," by Jamie Lincoln Kitman, in *The Nation* (March 20, 2000).

▭▭ ●⊢ **Read** the **Document** on **mythinkinglab.com**

Andrew Fenton, "Rwanda Is So Hot Right Now." In this essay, Fenton examines the question of inconsistency between the actions and the publicized views of celebrities; a crucial question here will be whether the celebrities are offering arguments (in which case, the character of the arguer—whether sincere or hypocritical—is irrelevant) or whether they are presenting their views as based on their own special authority (in the latter case, their inconsistency or hypocrisy would raise legitimate questions concerning their special *testimony*).

Tom Brown Jr., "An Opinion with Substance." This is an illustration of a genuine authority, whose expert opinion is worthy of careful consideration.

Daubert v. Merrell Dow Pharmaceuticals, 509 U.S. 579 (1993). This is the clearest statement of the current standard adopted by the U.S. Supreme Court for dealing with questions of expert witnesses and appeals to expert authority. It marks a significant change from the earlier standard; whether it is an improvement—and whether it ultimately offers a workable standard—remains a matter of debate (note that in his dissent, Justice Rehnquist clearly thinks the *Daubert* standard still has problems).

Cumulative Exercises One (Chapters 1 through 10)

The following are examples of the various sorts of arguments we examined in Chapters 1 to 10. Some are fallacious; some are not. For each example, *first* tell what form the argument is (such as ad hominem), *then* determine whether the argument is or is not fallacious. So for each argument, you should write something like this: fallacious appeal to authority or nonfallacious ad hominem.

As a brief guide, these are the argument forms that may be included in these exercises:

Ad hominem: sometimes a fallacy, sometimes not
Inverse ad hominem: sometimes a fallacy, sometimes not
Strawman: always a fallacy
Irrelevant reason (or red herring): always a fallacy
Appeal to ignorance: always a fallacy
Ambiguity: always a fallacy
Appeal to authority: sometimes a fallacy, sometimes not
Appeal to popularity: always a fallacy
Appeal to tradition (traditional wisdom): always a fallacy

---

1. Philosophy courses are very valuable for all college students. After all, if students do not take philosophy, then philosophy professors would lose their job. And since philosophy professors have no other marketable skills, and many are old and run down, most of them would not be able to find another job, and their children would go hungry, and they would lose their homes, and their families would be destitute. So obviously philosophy is a useful and beneficial course for all students.

2. Ever since the comets crashed into Jupiter a few years ago, some people have been afraid that a comet might strike Earth, with cataclysmic consequences. There is, of course, a very small danger of that; but the chances are very small. I have talked with Dr. Alice McGovern, professor of Astronomy at Harvard University, who assured me that given the vast distances in space and the relatively tiny size of Earth, the likelihood of a comet striking Earth any time in the next five centuries is very small indeed. When I called Dr. Seth Zarech, scientific director of NASA, he agreed with Dr. McGovern. And Dr. George Maravich, who is chair of the Astronomy Department at the University of Michigan, said exactly the same thing. So obviously there is very little risk of Earth being struck by a comet anytime in the near future.

3. During the recent intensive debate over health-care reform, Sarah Palin argued that the proposed reforms were bad, because they would involve setting up death panels that could decide to kill any elderly patients who were admitted to hospitals. Some people said her argument was not a good argument: that it committed the strawman fallacy, and distorted the position it criticized. But in fact Palin's argument *was* a good argument, because it was successful in convincing many people to oppose health-care reform, and that was Palin's goal.

4. Fifty dollars is missing from the store cash register. Laura Ring was working at that cash register for part of the day, and someone suggested that Laura might have stolen the money. Well, I don't know what happened to that money: maybe it was lost, or someone made a mistake making change, or whatever. But I do know this: Laura certainly did not steal the $50. I have known Laura for over 10 years, and she is one of the most honest, high-principled people I have ever known. George Washington would tell a lie before Laura would, and it would never even occur to her to steal money. When Laura tells you something, you can count on it. And when Laura does a job, she does it honestly and to the best of her ability. She is completely trustworthy, and honest through and through; and she certainly is no thief.

5. Some people complain about the profits being raked in by the major oil companies: Exxon made a profit of 8 billion dollars in the last quarter, and Chevron made 4 billion. They claim that the oil companies are making enormous and unfair profits, while we consumers are paying painfully high prices for gasoline. But no one should take their criticisms seriously. Apparently they believe that people in the oil industry should work for free, and that investors in Exxon and Chevron have no right to make a profit on their investment. They think that all profits are wrong, and that no company should ever make a profit for its work. They apparently want to abolish capitalism altogether, and do away with our free enterprise system.

6. There may be many opinions about music; but we can settle right now the question of what was the greatest piece of music ever written. Yesterday I heard a lecture by Fyodor Smirnoff, the music director and conductor of the Moscow Symphony Orchestra. Smirnoff is not only a great conductor, but is also a wonderful composer and an expert on musical history. In his lecture, Smirnoff asserted that Mozart's 23rd Symphony is the greatest single piece of music ever written. That should settle the issue once and for all: if Smirnoff says Mozart's 23rd Symphony is the greatest music ever written, then it must be the greatest.

7. There are some people who favor a ban on trophy hunting. That is, some want to ban the hunting of lions, bears, elephants, and tigers for trophies. But trophy hunting has been a sport enjoyed for many decades by trophy hunters. All through the nineteenth and twentieth centuries, trophy hunting has been regarded as an exciting, legitimate, and morally acceptable sport, and so trophy hunting should certainly not be banned or condemned.

8. Melba Martin has been arguing that more efforts and money should be invested in cleaning up the Mahoning River. She points out that the pollution of the river poses health hazards, and that if the river were cleaned up, it would become a valuable recreational resource, and if the river were clean then restaurants and other businesses would probably be built along the river in Youngstown, just as happened with the Flats in Cleveland, and that could lead to the revitalization of the Youngstown urban area. Her arguments sound pretty good, when you first hear them. But then I discovered that Melba owns some land along the southern Mahoning River, and if the river is cleaned up then her property will substantially increase in value. So I can't really give much weight to Melba's arguments.

9. The defense has claimed that Melissa Johnson is not guilty of murder, because she shot her husband by accident, and unintentionally. Her husband, Art Johnson, returned a day early from a business trip, arriving in the middle of the night. He didn't turn on the lights, because he apparently didn't want to awaken his wife. When Melissa heard someone enter the house, she thought it was a burglar; there had been burglaries in the neighborhood, and she was terrified. So when she saw her husband's dark figure in the hallway, she aimed her pistol at him and pulled the trigger, thinking it was an intruder who might harm or even kill her. But notice this, ladies and gentlemen of the jury: when Melissa picked up that pistol, aimed it, and pulled the trigger, she definitely *intended* to shoot the person she saw in the hallway. That person happened to be her husband; and so clearly you must conclude that she intentionally shot and killed her husband.

10. Art claims that the reason Julie made the dean's honor list is that she buys all her papers from an Internet term paper service. He said he saw her credit card bill, and it had hundreds of dollars of charges to TermPaperPro.Com. But you should keep in mind that Julie and Art used to be lovers, and last year Julie dumped Art, and Art has hated her ever since. And besides, Julie has always

made better grades than Art, and he's really jealous of her. And Art has been known to spread false rumors about other people he doesn't like. So I would be really skeptical of what Art says about Julie.

11. Some people claim that McDonald's promotes bad eating habits: they target children in their advertising and provide toys that reward children, even toddlers, for eating high-fat hamburgers and fries and high-sugar soft drinks; and those childhood eating habits tend to carry over into adulthood. But such criticisms of McDonald's are nonsense. After all, McDonald's provides clean, safe restaurants where the whole family can enjoy themselves together, local McDonald's restaurants often sponsor little league teams and youth soccer leagues, and lots of high school students get valuable experience in their first real jobs at McDonald's. So there is no basis for the claim that McDonald's promotes unhealthy eating habits.

12. Recently there has been fierce debate over the best way of preventing and controlling crime, with some experts pushing for more educational, prevention, and early-intervention programs, and less use of prison sentences. But former U.S. attorney general Edwin Meese asserts that the best way to stop juvenile crime is through a get-tough policy that treats young offenders very harshly, giving them long prison sentences in adult prisons. Attorney General Meese has dealt with issues of justice and crime for many years, and as attorney general he served as the top law enforcement officer of the United States; so Meese's program of getting tough on juvenile offenders must be the best way of handling that problem.

13. The U.S. Congress has recently passed legislation that allows people to be held in jail for longer periods when they have not been convicted of crimes, allows the government to tap into phone lines and listen in on private conversations almost without restriction, and even suspends the basic right of trial by jury for some types of crimes. Some people say that these are an assault on our basic rights and that such policies threaten our liberties. But in fact these policies do not threaten our basic rights and liberties. For these are desperate and dangerous times, and the threat of terrorism is very real. Indeed, we are now in a full *war* against terrorism. So these new policies obviously do not pose a threat to our basic rights and liberties.

14. Bill Gates, the chairman of Microsoft, argues that every U.S. citizen should have access to a computer and to the Internet. He points out that the Internet is a very important source of information, and that if some people do not have access to the Internet they will be left out of the information age, and they will not have equal opportunity for success. Access to the Internet, Gates argues, is just a matter of giving everyone fair opportunity. But you should realize that as the chairman and major owner of Microsoft, Bill Gates obviously stands to make more money as more people use computers and start using the Internet. In fact, the more people use computers and the Internet, the richer Bill Gates will become. So Gates's arguments are not really that convincing when you understand the financial stake he has in them.

15. Former President Jimmy Carter argued that we should not rush into a war with Iraq. He said that as the strongest nation in the world, we should set a good example for the rest of the world in showing how to resolve conflicts peacefully. He also noted that the Middle East is already a very unstable region, and a war there would only increase tensions and perhaps lead to a wider war. And I say we should have accepted former President Carter's argument: after all, he has enormous foreign policy experience, and his years of working with Habitat for Humanity instead of using his fame for his own selfish gains show that he is a person who has dedicated himself to making the world better.

16. Some people argue that we should stop doing medical tests on chimpanzees: they say that chimpanzees are very sensitive animals, closely related to humans; they suffer pain just as we do, and suffer severe depression when kept in isolation, and that it is wrong to inflict suffering on such sensitive animals, especially when we have other means of running medical tests that would not impose such suffering on these highly intelligent animals so closely related to ourselves. But we should pay no attention to the complaints of these anti-science zealots. They want to put an end to all scientific research, and stop all scientific progress. If they had their way, we would never make any advances in medical treatment.

17. This makes me so mad. Jeff's paper won the Philosophy Department Langston Prize for outstanding undergraduate paper, an award of $500. I should have won that prize. Jeff's paper was plagiarized! I just know it was. Okay, I couldn't find the source he copied it from, and I can't really prove he stole that paper. But it's clear that he did. After all, he couldn't prove that he wrote it himself. He said he typed it on his computer, and revised as he went, and so there's no old version of the paper. Sounds very suspicious to me! He has no proof at all that he didn't steal the paper, and so obviously that's exactly what he did.

18. Al Gore argues that we must take steps to reduce pollution: he argues that unless we significantly reduce pollution we'll face major problems of global warming, flooding, and severe food shortages. But it turns out that Al Gore often travels in a private jet, and private jet travel causes major pollution problems, and in terms of pollution it is one of the *worst* methods of travel. As long as Al Gore travels in private jets, there's no reason to take his arguments against pollution seriously.

19. Bobby Parks claims that some of the university librarians are plotting to kill him. He says that one afternoon while he was downstairs looking for a book, he overheard four librarians discussing a plan to poison him. Unfortunately, however, Bobby is addicted to amphetamines, and amphetamine addicts often become nervous and paranoid and fearful of *everyone* around them. So I certainly don't place much confidence in Bobby's claims that the librarians are trying to kill him.

20. Look, we all agree that Bruce is an honest person, who always tells the truth. So when Bruce says that he saw extraterrestrials land on Glenwood Avenue, he was telling the truth. Therefore, it must be true that there were extraterrestrials landing on Glenwood Avenue.

21. One proposal to pay for expanding health care is a special tax of 1% on all income over $250,000/year for individuals or $500,000 a year for couples. But what those people who are proposing that tax really want is to tax away all wealth whatsoever, and make everyone in America exactly equal in income. If they get their way, no one in this country will be wealthy, and no American child can ever again dream of becoming wealthy.

22. State Senator Owens recently argued that we should increase the state tobacco tax in North Carolina. He pointed out that North Carolina has the lowest tobacco tax in the country and that much-needed revenue for our schools could be gained through adding a small state tax of 3 cents a pack on cigarettes. Well, as everyone knows, the tobacco industry is *very* powerful in North Carolina, and it strongly opposes any increase in tobacco taxes. By arguing for an increase in the tobacco tax, Senator Owens bravely risked offending all the tobacco farmers and tobacco manufacturing workers in the state, as well as all the smokers. It takes a lot of courage for a senator to argue for such a controversial position, and any politician showing that much courage and conviction must be giving strong arguments.

23. Oysters are an effective aphrodisiac: Eating oysters will improve your love life and make you more passionate. That is clearly true, since there is no scientific evidence that conclusively proves that eating oysters does not improve your love life and increase passion.

24. Ladies and gentlemen of the jury, you have heard the chief prosecution witness swear that he saw the defendant running from the burglarized store the night of the burglary. But don't believe a word of it! After all, that witness has himself been convicted of burglary charges, and he is testifying against the defendant in hopes that the defendant will be convicted and he (the witness) will therefore no longer be a suspect in this burglary.

25. Some people claim that it is important that a defendant be allowed to have his lawyer present at any lineup in which the defendant participates, so that the lawyer can guard against unfair lineups. But in fact defendants do not really need lawyers present at lineups. For, in the first place, if the defendant's lawyer has to be called in before the lineup, then that will take lots of time and probably will cause delays in setting up the lineup, and it will thus increase the workload of our already overworked police forces. And besides, since many defendants cannot afford attorneys and instead have court-appointed attorneys or public defenders, that would greatly increase the cost to taxpayers, since it would be the taxpayers who would have to pay for the time the defendant's lawyer spends at the lineup. So lawyers are not really needed to guarantee that the defendant is not placed in an unfair lineup.

26. Dr. Stanley Steamer has told us that there is no reason to worry about nuclear power. He says that he has studied nuclear power carefully and is an expert on all the possible hazards as well as safety features of nuclear power plants. He also says that he can absolutely guarantee that nuclear power plants currently operated in the United States are not dangerous. But in fact it turns out that Dr. Steamer was recently fired from his teaching position at the University of Nebraska when it was discovered that he had falsified research data and lied about his graduate work (his doctorate is in American history, not, as he had claimed, in nuclear physics). Well, so much for Dr. Steamer's assurances about the safety of nuclear power!

27. Ronald Shelby has been accused of bribing a city engineer in order to get a paving contract in New York City. You heard him testify that he did not know any elected officials in New York City; but now we have evidence that Mario Tucomia, an elected city councilman for Manhattan, was one of Ronald's high school classmates, from 15 years ago, at their Queens high school: Ronald and Mario were on the same basketball team. Ronald says that he lost track of Mario over the years, and had no idea that Mario had been elected to the city council. Maybe so. But one thing is clear. Ronald definitely knows Mario Tucomia; so when Ronald testified that he didn't know any New York City elected officials, he lied under oath.

28. The gene for baldness is a recessive gene. That question was settled when we called James Watson, professor of Genetics at Harvard and winner of the Nobel Prize for his work on genetics, who stated that the gene for baldness is indeed recessive.

29. Governor Fob James of Alabama supports corporal punishment in schools, and backed state legislation allowing public schools to use spanking as punishment. Replying to critics (who cited studies showing that spanking is strongly associated with antisocial behavior in children), the governor's spokesman, Alfred Sawyer, defended corporal punishment thus: "It's a time-tested method of discipline. It's been used for thousands of years by parents and teachers" (Reported by Brenda Coleman, Associated Press, August 18, 1997).

30. Wendell Sly is the worst candidate for governor in this century. When he was a U.S. Senator he was twice censured by the Senate for misusing his office for personal financial gain; and 8 years ago he was convicted of insurance fraud for faking an automobile accident; and just last year he was disbarred (lost his license to practice law) because he used a client's money for his own investments. He is not a person who can be trusted with the public confidence and the public treasury.

31. There is concern about the current push to release patients from hospitals more rapidly. Patients undergoing heart surgery, mastectomies, and other major surgeries are sent home days earlier than they would have been a few years ago, and some people claim that such early hospital releases reduce the quality of patient care and pose a risk to patient health. But in fact the earlier releases do not pose any risk for patient health. Keeping patients in hospitals is enormously expensive, and every day in a hospital drives the cost of treatment higher and higher. And we have to find ways of getting our health-care costs under control, so that both insurance rates and government expenditures on health care can be kept to a reasonable level. And releasing hospital patients earlier is one way of reducing our high medical costs. So clearly the early release of patients does not threaten the health of patients.

32. Some people are opposed to the planned missile defense system—the "Star Wars" system—that is designed to intercept and destroy any missiles that are launched against the United States. Those opponents of the system say it has never been tested effectively, that it would be very easy to overwhelm with dummy missiles, and that the real danger is not from missiles launched from outside the United States but instead from bombs smuggled into the United States. But those people who oppose the missile defense system don't live in the real world. They believe that we should never do anything to protect ourselves from attacks. They would just watch while missiles fall on our cities, and never fight back and do nothing to prevent it. Apparently they think that the world is safe and peaceful, and the United States is not in any danger of attack from anyone.

33. Arthur Kraft has been arguing that the Olympic Games have become overcommercialized. He says that having all the manufacturers of soft drinks, cameras, sportswear, and even junk foods promote themselves as "official sponsors of the 2008 Olympics" cheapens the games, and he argues that selling the rights to carry the Olympic torch across the country was a new low in crass commercialization of the Olympics. But Arthur Kraft's arguments against overcommercialization of the Olympics are not convincing: He himself is Vice President of Marketing for Belch Brewery, which makes Spring Mountain Beer, and Spring Mountain Beer heavily advertised that it is "the favorite beer of America's Olympic athletes"!

34. There are literally millions of stars in our galaxy, and many of them must have planets similar to our own Earth. Since obviously we have not investigated all of those stars and planets, we certainly cannot conclude that none of them contains intelligent life. So there must be intelligent life elsewhere in our galaxy.

35. Ladies and gentlemen of the jury, it is now up to you to decide whether to find the defendant guilty or not guilty of the charges against him. As you consider your verdict, bear in mind the vicious nature of the crime with which the defendant is charged. He is accused of stabbing to death an elderly woman in order to rob her of her life savings. That crime was one of the most vicious murders ever committed in this state. Thus I urge you to return a verdict of guilty.

36. The chairman of the Northeast Ohio Sierra Club, Brian Ulm, has argued that we should not change the Endangered Species Act, because through the act we have been able to bring 267 species back from the brink of extinction, and the cost has not been excessive: He notes that fewer than one construction project in 200 is stopped because of enforcement of the Endangered Species Act; and he argues that that is not too great a price to pay for preserving species and environments for future generations. But Ulm's arguments shouldn't carry much weight: He is just the spokesperson for a bunch of environmental extremists who really don't care about economic progress and job creation, and who are just sounding alarms so they can recruit more members and raise more money.

37. The New York Yankees won the World Series, but they did it by cheating: they paid off the umpires to make sure all the calls went in favor of the Yankees. OK, I don't have any solid proof that the Yankees bribed the umpires; *but*, the Yankees have never offered any proof whatsoever that they did *not* bribe the umpires; in fact, they have never denied or answered my charges of cheating. So unless they can prove that they didn't pay off the umpires, it is only reasonable to conclude that they did.

38. James Cash has argued that Central Power's electric rates are too high: that Central Power's profits are excessive and that Central Power could save money through more efficient operation, and thus that Central Power ought to lower its rates to consumers. And James Cash actually owns a lot of Central Power stock, and would himself profit from *higher* electric rates; therefore, obviously James Cash is unselfishly arguing against his own financial interests, and we should accept his argument and his conclusion.

39. The United States still allows capital punishment; but we are almost alone in the world in still using capital punishment. Canada, Australia, Mexico, all countries in Europe, and all the countries in South America have abolished capital punishment; and it is obviously time for the United States to also abolish capital punishment.

40. Some people are skeptical of astrology and astrological predictions, but obviously there is at least some truth to astrology, since none of the skeptics has been able to conclusively prove that all forms of astrology are completely wrong.

41. Some people are skeptical of astrology and astrological predictions, but obviously there is at least some truth to astrology, since astrologers and astrology have been around for well over 2,000 years.

42. Recently there has been great concern about the number of concussions suffered by football players, and the long-term health effects of repeated concussions for football players. But there is really no health danger from playing football. After all, football is a wonderful sport that brings together old friends at tailgate parties, brings alumni back to campus to see their old classmates and cheer for the home team, and it is lots of fun for kids from peewee football all the way through college. So this stuff about the health dangers from playing football is just nonsense.

43. Chanelle argues that we should stop using animals as research subjects, because it involves cruelty to animals, the research is often unreliable because some chemicals cause little or no harm to laboratory animals but are very harmful to humans, and by using in vitro cellular studies and computer simulations we can effectively replace animal studies; and above all, Chanelle argues, it is simply wrong to use other living beings that are capable of pleasure and pain for our selfish purposes. But Chanelle's arguments are ridiculous; she often wears leather shoes, she always carries a beautiful leather bag, and she frequently wears a leather vest and an expensive leather jacket—not to mention the beautiful hand-tooled leather seats in her sports car! Unless the animals that provided the leather for Chanelle's jacket and shoes and bag donated their skins to Chanelle happily and voluntarily, Chanelle's argument against using animals for research is a hypocritical failure.

44. The Mayan calendar predicts the end of the world in 2012. A lot of people are skeptical: they doubt that the Mayan calendar is a reliable source. Well, before you make any plans for 2013, just remember this: No one has been able to prove that the Mayan prediction is *not* accurate. And until someone offers that proof, we should accept the Mayan calendar as an accurate prediction of the end of the world.

45. Women in the United States have always taken their husbands' family names when they married. So why shouldn't women today do so? If it was good enough for our mothers and grandmothers, it ought to be good enough for women today. So contemporary women who want to keep their own names after marriage are obviously wrong.

46. Whatever you do, don't get stuck at a dinner party with Bruce Waller as your dinner companion. He tells these incredibly long-winded and boring stories about horse racing, his table manners resemble a shark in a feeding frenzy, and he drinks too much and then becomes obnoxious and insulting.

47. Gary Aldrich wrote *Unlimited Access: An FBI Agent Inside the Clinton White House*. In the book, Aldrich claims that Bill Clinton frequently slipped out of the White House in a car driven by one of his aides. Clinton would supposedly hide in the back seat, covered by a blanket, while the car was driven to a

Marriott Hotel, where Clinton would meet a woman for late-night affairs. When Aldrich was challenged to provide proof for this story by George Will (on ABC-TV), Aldrich stuck by his story, offering the following support for his belief in the truth of the rumor that he had heard and on which he had based his account: He accepted it as true because "I was unable to knock down that possibility" that the story might be true.

48. Opponents of capital punishment sometimes claim that there is a danger that innocent people will be executed. But that is not really a danger. After all, our society is swamped with violent, vicious crimes, and we must have strong measures in response. Swift and severe punishment is essential to control crime and to properly express society's deep disgust with the most vicious and depraved criminal acts. So there is no real danger of executing the innocent.

49. I suppose there will always be disagreement about which movies are best, but the question of what is the best American movie ever made should no longer be in doubt. Carolyn Ponder teaches film at the University of Michigan—in fact, she holds the Wickliffe Chair of film studies at the University, and is a highly regarded scholar and critic—and she has written several excellent books on films, and American films are her specialty. She states in her most recent book that she considers *Days of Heaven* to be the best American film ever made. That settles it. If Professor Ponder says that *Days of Heaven* is the best American film, then it must be so.

50. Representative Henry Hyde argued that President Clinton—in having an affair and trying to cover it up—was guilty of perjury and obstruction of justice, and that his crimes undermined the dignity of and trust in the presidency, and that the only way to uphold our basic principle of equal justice for all would be to convict the president and remove him from office. But then it turns out that Henry Hyde himself had a long-term affair, and had been lying about it for years. Besides, what Hyde was really interested in was removing a popular Democratic president from office so that the Republicans (Hyde's own party) would have a better chance of winning future elections. So the arguments of this self-serving hypocrite shouldn't carry much weight with anyone.

51. The British monarchy has been under attack during recent years, with one tabloid-reported scandal followed by another. The monarchy was defended by Prince Philip, the Duke of Edinburgh, as follows:

> The British monarchy has been around for the last thousand years. If it's lasted that long, it can't be all that bad.

52. We should not allow wastewater containing mercury to be discharged near our reservoir. After all, mercury poses a very serious and long-term health hazard: Dr. Elizabeth Tarski, professor of Environmental Health at Harvard Medical School, says that mercury pollution is one of the most severe threats to public water supplies; Dr. Warren Jacobs, scientific director of the Hazardous Wastes Division of the U.S. Environmental Protection Agency, says that mercury is especially dangerous to children, and that water pollution is a main source of mercury poisoning; and Dr. Laura Systra, recent Nobel Prize winner in biochemistry, asserts that mercury and lead are the greatest environmental hazards to our water supplies.

53. Everybody seems to be all upset about how much money is being given to politicians for political campaigns, and how that money gains special influence and special favors for the contributors. But politicians collecting money in such a way is not really a bad thing: that's just how the system works. Members of Congress get money from corporations, state legislators receive money from local businesses, presidential candidates get money from everywhere. And it's not just in the United States. The same thing happens in Europe, in Latin America, in South America; and it's very common throughout Asia. In short, everywhere you find politicians, you find people and corporations giving them money and expecting favors and special consideration in return. There's nothing wrong with it: that's just the way the system works, all across the United States and around the world, from the smallest town council elections to the largest presidential campaign.

54. Naming sports teams "Indians" or "Braves" or "Redskins" cannot really be offensive and demeaning to anyone or any group. After all, spectator sports are good, wholesome family entertainment. Sports teams are sources of great school and community pride, and sports teams often enhance the sense of community of the schools or cities that they represent.

55. You remember we were arguing about who painted the beautiful frescoes in the Sistine Chapel? Joe said it was Leonardo da Vinci, and Jane said it was Michelangelo. Well, Jane was right: my art history professor, Dr. Reynolds, said it was Michelangelo; and when I looked up Michelangelo in the Encyclopaedia Britannica, the Britannica article on Michelangelo agreed with Dr. Reynolds.

56. I believe we have to find the defendant guilty as charged. Look, I'm not sure that the evidence that he committed the murder is all that strong. But there's one thing I just can't get around: If the defendant didn't murder Joe, then who did? After all, the defendant did have a motive; and the defense was not able to suggest anyone else who had a motive for killing Joe. So if you have doubts about the defendant being guilty of killing poor Joe, answer me one thing: Who did it? Someone certainly did, and since the defense couldn't suggest any better suspect—in fact, could not think of any other suspect at all—I think we have to conclude that the defendant is guilty as charged.

57. As members of the jury, we have to decide whether the defendant, Brendan O'Malley, is guilty of arson. Look at the case against Brendan: the key evidence was given by Andrew Johnston, who was Brendan's cellmate at the local jail. Andrew swore that Brendan told him about planning the arson, and about how he needed the insurance money. But can you really trust Andrew? After all, he was in jail because he was guilty of credit card fraud, passing bad checks, and receiving stolen merchandise—so his honesty and integrity are certainly open to serious doubt. And his motive for testifying against Brendan is his hope of getting a reduced sentence for his own crimes, so he obviously has a strong incentive to make up a story. Thus there are strong reasons to doubt Andrew's testimony; and if you have doubts about that testimony, then how can you possibly find Brendan guilty?

58. There is often disagreement about the details of what diet is best for your health. But there are some truths about diet that are now well established, and the most basic is this: You should eat several servings of fresh fruits and vegetables every day. That is the unanimous recommendation of the American Heart Association, the U.S. Department of Health, the Surgeon General, the Canadian Ministry for Health, and the faculty of the Harvard Institute for Public Health. So it is clear that eating a diet rich in fruits and vegetables is good for you.

59. Jim Cohan runs a business based in Los Angeles that provides organ transplants in such places as the Philippines, Mexico, Korea, and other third-world countries. The transplants are available to any one who can pay for them—but they are not covered by insurance, and are very expensive (approximately $200,000 for each operation). Some people are concerned that the organs are being transplanted from third-world peasants into very wealthy Americans, and that desperately poor people may sell a kidney to support their families, and the very wealthy then receive the purchased kidney. Cohan does not find that troubling. As he states, "That goes on everywhere. It goes on in this country, and it goes on elsewhere. That's how it is." (This example is based on a column by Joe Dirck in the June 28, 1994, *Cleveland Plain Dealer*.)

11

❖ ❖ ❖

Arguments by Analogy

((•─Listen to the Chapter Audio on mythinkinglab.com

Analogies are common, useful, and confusing. Helpful as analogies can be, they often cause problems. The problems start with the different *types* of analogies. There are at least three distinct and different uses of analogy, each serving a different purpose. The *figurative analogy* draws a picture, and is designed to provide a clearer and simpler perspective on a confusing or complicated subject. A good figurative analogy can be very valuable, but it is *not* an *argument*, and it must not be used or evaluated as if it were an argument. In contrast, a *deductive argument by analogy* certainly is an argument, and it can have powerful reasons for its conclusion. If you offer an effective *deductive argument* by analogy, then your argument carries all the strength and certainty of a sound deductive argument: given the truth of the premises of a good deductive argument by analogy, the conclusion *must* follow. Finally, it is important not to confuse figurative analogies and deductive arguments by analogy with a third type of analogy: the *inductive* argument by analogy. Inductive arguments by analogy are useful analogical arguments, and we often employ them in our day-to-day reasoning; but they do not establish their conclusions with the knockdown certainty of *deductive* arguments by analogy. That does *not* make inductive arguments by analogy *inferior* to deductive arguments by analogy: They function well in many contexts. But it does mean that inductive arguments by analogy must be carefully distinguished from *deductive* analogy arguments, and also from *figurative* analogies (which are not arguments at all).

FIGURATIVE ANALOGY

Before attempting to *evaluate* an analogy, you must first decide what *sort* of analogy it is, and what task that analogy is designed to perform. Just as there are different types of boats designed for different purposes, there are different types of analogies with very different functions. A sailboat, a fishing boat, and a ferry boat are all useful boats, but for very different tasks. Jill's sailboat is perfect for an afternoon of sailing in the bay, but if we are going fishing we'll be much happier with Kareem's fishing boat. Neither will be of much use in ferrying cars across the inlet, but both perform well when used for the right purposes.

The above paragraph contains an analogy. It draws an analogy between the functions of boats and the functions of analogies. But notice that the boat analogy is *not* an argument: It's an *illustration,* a picture. It compares analogies with boats, in hopes of elucidating the way analogies work. It does not *argue,* but it does *explain.*

A more elaborate example of a figurative (illustrative) analogy is the comparison of Freud's theory of neuroses with steam escaping from a steam boiler. Freud claimed that neuroses (such as compulsive hand washing, or a compulsion to check that all the doors are locked) result from a buildup of frustrated desires; when those desires can find no productive outlet, they are released through nonproductive neurotic behavior. The situation is somewhat like (here is the figurative analogy) the buildup of steam in a steam engine. When the steam pressure cannot be converted into productive force (to drive a piston), excessive steam builds up in the boiler. Either the boiler explodes or the steam is released unproductively through safety valves and tiny cracks in the boiler. Just as the steam escapes from the boiler to prevent the boiler from exploding, so excessive psychological pressure is released through neuroses to keep the psyche from cracking up.

This is a fairly helpful figurative analogy. It gives us a useful way of visualizing, organizing, and understanding Freud's rather complex and difficult theory of the neuroses. *But,* it does *not* provide any *reason* to accept Freud's theory; it does not offer an *argument* in favor of Freud's theory. The analogy may make Freud's theory more understandable, but it does *not* make it more plausible. So it would be a mistake to accept a theory or claim because of a particularly good figurative analogy, and it would be a mistake to *claim* that a theory or position is true on the basis of a figurative analogy. On the other hand, if someone gives a figurative analogy, it would *also* be a mistake to fault that analogy because it is not an *argument.* It may be a good figurative analogy without being an argument. (That would be like—figurative analogy—faulting Jill's sailboat because it can't ferry cars across a river.)

You will occasionally hear it said that analogies never *prove* anything. That is true, if it is said of *figurative* analogies. Figurative analogies do not prove anything because, as noted above, they do not present arguments. However, there are some types of analogy that certainly *do* present *arguments* and do *prove* things. One such type will be called *deductive* arguments by analogy.

DEDUCTIVE ARGUMENT BY ANALOGY

Consider this example of deductive *argument* by analogy:

> We would think it wrong for creatures from outer space, vastly more intelligent than humans, to inflict pain on us in raising humans for the luxury of grilled human. So analogously, it is wrong for us to inflict pain on animals (in raising and killing them for luxury food) just because we are more intelligent than they are.

That is an *argument* by analogy, and not merely an illustration. How does the argument work?

As always, the first step is to pick out the conclusion: It is wrong to inflict pain on animals in raising them for food (food that is *not* essential for life). What is the *argument* for that conclusion?

It starts by pointing out something that (it is assumed) we all accept: It would be wrong for superintelligent space invaders to cause human suffering by raising humans for slaughter. Next we ask, *Why* do we believe that would be wrong? This is the tricky part. The *principle* behind this analogy is not stated explicitly. In fact, there may be disagreement about the exact principle behind the argument. But the principle might be stated thus: Beings of superior intelligence are not justified in inflicting suffering on less intelligent species in raising them for nonessential food products. The analogy is powerful because if we believe that, then we are also compelled to conclude that it is wrong for humans to cause the suffering of less intelligent species (such as cattle) to provide the luxury of steaks for humans. That is, the *same reason* we think it would be wrong for superintelligent space invaders to raise us for their barbecues can also be applied to the case of humans raising animals of lower intelligence for our steak houses.[1] The argument claims that causing pain and death to animals is *similar* to—*analogous* to—having some intellectually superior space invaders cause pain and death to humans. We all agree that it would be wrong for these superior invaders to raise us for slaughter. Thus, in order to be *consistent* we must conclude that it is also wrong for us to inflict suffering on animals of lower intelligence by raising them for slaughter.

Let's look at exactly how that argument goes. It might be outlined in the following manner:

> It would be wrong for superintelligent space invaders to cause humans to suffer by raising humans for slaughter.
>
> The reason it would be wrong is because it is wrong for one group to inflict unnecessary suffering on another group just because the former has more intelligence than the latter.
>
> Therefore, it is wrong for humans to inflict unnecessary suffering on other, less intelligent species by raising them for slaughter.

Is that a good argument? Is that deductive argument by analogy sound? When evaluating deductive arguments by analogy, you must consider two distinct questions: First, *is* the principle behind the analogy true? Second, *is* it a good analogy (i.e., do both cases fit under the principle)? Consider first how one might *challenge* this deductive argument by analogy by challenging the *principle:*

> That's a good analogy, but I cannot agree with the principle to which you appeal. I agree that humans eating beef animals *is* like space invaders of superior intelligence eating humans, and *if* the latter is wrong, then the former is also wrong. But I don't think *either* would be wrong. If there are beings of superior intelligence, then they have a right to inflict suffering on human beings as they raise us for luxury food; by the same token, humans have the right to raise less intelligent species for luxury food. In short, it may be a good analogy, but I *reject* the principle on which it depends.

If a person is challenging the *principle* behind the deductive argument by analogy, then as soon as we say, "It would be wrong for superintelligent space invaders to raise humans for their human burgers," that challenger will respond: "Stop right there; I don't agree with that. If the invaders are more intelligent than humans, then it *would* be right for them to slaughter humans." If someone takes that line then the game is up for that analogy. There may or may not be other arguments that we could use to convince such a person that it is wrong to raise and kill animals for food, but *this* deductive argument by analogy will not help. And that brings out the *limits* of deductive arguments by analogy. Such an argument can remind people quite forcefully of principles they already hold, and use of an appropriate analogy can compel people to recognize that the principles they hold apply in ways they had not considered, such as: "I *don't* think that superior intelligence gives one the right to inflict suffering on others, so I need to rethink my attitude toward other species." But if someone rejects the *principle* behind the analogy, then the argument by deductive analogy will be a nonstarter. Deductive arguments by analogy do not argue for the *principle;* rather, they are concerned with the further implications of a principle that (it is hoped) we all share.

So the first way of rejecting a deductive argument by analogy is to reject the principle to which the analogy appeals. But there is a second way—perhaps more common—of rejecting deductive arguments by analogy. One can claim that the *analogy* is a bad analogy: The two cases are significantly different and are not really analogous. That is, one can claim that the two cases do not in fact fit under or point to the same principle. Consider again the

---

Losing an Argument with My Kids

When driving on a trip with my kids, I would often be asked, "How much farther is it, Daddy?" On one occasion I assured them it would only be a few more minutes, be patient. They watched the clock as the minutes passed: 5, 10, 15. We still had not arrived. Finally, after 30 minutes, our destination came in sight.

"I thought you said it would only be a few minutes." "Well, that was only a few minutes," I replied. My kids were not buying it. "Thirty minutes is not a few minutes. Suppose we asked if we could eat a few cookies, and you said okay, and then we ate 30 cookies, would you count that as just eating a few cookies?"

---

analogy between extraterrestrials of superior intelligence raising and slaughtering humans, and humans raising and slaughtering animals of still lower intelligence. Someone might claim it is *not* a good analogy, because even if the extraterrestrials have much more intelligence than do humans, that is still only a higher degree of intelligence; whereas the differences between human intelligence and the abilities of lower animals are differences in kind, not merely differences in degree. Thus—one would argue in *rejecting the analogy*—the relevant principle is not that it is right to raise and slaughter animals because humans have more intelligence than do other species; rather, the real principle is that it is right for *intelligent* species to raise and slaughter any species that is *not* intelligent.

In that rejection of the deductive argument by analogy the *analogy* is rejected. One claims that the two cases do *not* fit under the same principle, that the two cases are *not* sufficiently similar, that the two instances are *different* in relevant and important respects.

A Double-Barreled Attack on an Analogy

On December 16, 1996, the U.S. Supreme Court ruled in *Melissa Brooks v. Mississippi* that people cannot be prevented from appealing the termination of their parental rights just because they cannot afford to pay court costs. Writing for the majority, Justice Ruth Bader Ginsburg argued that a parent's loss of a child was of such "magnitude and permanence" that it is "barely distinguishable from criminal condemnation" and since the court's precedents had removed financial barriers to criminal appeals, analogously there should be no financial barriers to appealing the loss of one's children.

In opposition, Justice Clarence Thomas argued that loss of children was not analogous to loss of liberty, and so the precedents did not apply; furthermore, he argued that even if the cases did fall under the same precedent, the main earlier precedent (1956) was wrong and should be reversed: Persons should not have a right to criminal appeals if they do not have the money to pay for them.

In this case, the U.S. Supreme Court is using a deductive argument by analogy to decide a new case: Since we agree that criminal defendants should not be deprived of the right of appeal simply because they are not wealthy enough to pay for the appeal, we must also, by analogy, hold that parents should not be deprived of the right to appeal the loss of their children just because they cannot pay the high costs of an appeal. Justice

Thomas's response illustrates the *two* ways of attacking a deductive argument by analogy: First, he attacks the analogy (being deprived of your children is not analogous to being deprived of your liberty); and, second, he attacks the principle (those who cannot afford the high costs of appeal have no right to appeal their criminal convictions: so *neither* has a right of appeal).

It seems to me—and to the majority of Supreme Court justices—that there is a strong analogy between criminal appeals and appeals of loss of parental rights: The reasons we have for giving citizens special protection against the state depriving us of liberty would also apply to the state depriving us of our children. Concerning his attack on the *principle,* here we simply reach different convictions about what seems *fair.* Justice Thomas rejects the basic principle that those accused of crime should have full and fair access to a defense, even if they are not wealthy. For example, if during the trial the prosecutor concealed evidence that would have proved my innocence, and I was thus wrongly convicted, then—on Justice Thomas's view—unless I can afford to pay the high costs of filing and pursuing an appeal, I have no right to seek the overturning of my wrongful conviction. Thomas considers that my tough luck, but not unfair. That seems to me callous, cruel, and fundamentally unfair; but it certainly does reject the basic fairness principle on which this argument by analogy is based.

I am not saying that the above criticism of that analogy really works (in fact, I do *not* think it works). But that is one important way of criticizing deductive arguments by analogy.

Is that an *accurate* criticism of the argument by analogy? Is it a good analogy? That is a tough question. I think that the above argument by deductive analogy is an accurate analogy, and that the criticism of the analogy is faulty. I do not think that there is a difference in kind between the intelligence of humans and the intelligence of other animals. But the present purpose is only to illustrate how deductive arguments by analogy work, how they can be criticized, and what makes those criticisms strong or weak.

Are Corporations Analogous to Persons?

In *Citizens United v. Federal Elections Commission*—a case decided in 2010 by a 5 to 4 majority—the U. S. Supreme Court ruled that corporations can spend unlimited sums of money in political campaigns. That decision dismantled the McCain-Feingold Act (passed by Congress with bipartisan support in 2002 and signed into law by President George W. Bush), overturned restrictions on corporate electioneering which had been in place for over a century, and rejected key precedents established by a series of earlier Supreme Court decisions. This remarkable exercise in judicial activism was based on an analogy between corporations and *persons*. You and I, as persons, have the right to free speech; corporations are like persons; therefore, consistency requires that corporations also have the right of free speech. Therefore, corporations have the right to speak as loudly as they wish: They may spend unlimited amounts of money speaking and campaigning—through advertising—for political candidates the corporations believe will be favorable to their interests. If a multibillion dollar corporation such as Exxon-Mobil wants to overturn regulations restricting oil-drilling in environmentally sensitive coastal areas, it could spend a billion dollars electing hand-picked senators to vote for eliminating those restrictions and giving very favorable lease arrangements to the oil company; it would be money well spent, as the resulting profits would be many times that. If foreign investors have majority control of a U.S. corporation, they could spend unlimited sums influencing U.S. elections. If a multibillion dollar pharmaceutical corporation wants to invest a billion dollars electing senators who will extend the patent life on drugs and block cheaper generic substitutes while greatly enriching the pharmaceutical companies—well, you get the picture. This Supreme Court decision will have an enormous impact on the democratic process in the United States. Was the analogical argument used to justify that decision a good one? Are *corporations* really analogous to flesh and blood individual citizen persons? Ronald Dworkin, a professor of constitutional law at NYU, argues that the persons–corporations analogy given by Justice Kennedy (who wrote the majority opinion) is flawed:

> The nerve of his argument—that corporations must be treated like real people under the First Amendment—

is in my view preposterous. Corporations are legal fictions. They have no opinions of their own to contribute and no rights to participate with equal voice or vote in politics.[2]

And indeed attempting to draw an analogy between the legal fiction of corporate persons and the flesh and blood citizens of a country is preposterous. It is both legally and morally acceptable to buy or sell a corporation; it has always been morally wrong to buy or sell a person, and has been legally prohibited since the Civil War. When the executives of Enron Corporation destroyed the corporation for their own personal profit, they were guilty of a number of financial crimes; but they were not guilty of first-degree murder, as they would have been had they purposefully killed a person. It is perfectly legitimate to split a corporation into parts; we frown on that when dealing with persons.

But not only is the analogy bad, but the principle behind the analogy is very doubtful. We do believe in the personal right of free speech, but few believe that right should have no limits. My right of free speech doesn't give me the right to use my massive resources to drown out all other participants in the debate. If I am allowed to spend a billion dollars buying advertising for my political views, then I can overwhelm any opposing voices. If we are engaged in a political debate, we would agree that all of us should be able to speak our minds and give our arguments and critique the arguments given by others: that is essential for genuine democratic processes and good critical thinking. But if I use a bullhorn, and every time someone else tries to offer an argument or criticize my argument I drown them out, that does *not* enhance critical thinking or democratic deliberation. So the *principle* that all persons have a right to free speech does not imply that persons should be allowed to spend unlimited funds in promoting their own ideas and blocking consideration of opposing views. Even if we accept the strained analogy between persons and corporations, most of us will find the principle of *unlimited* spending to *amplify* the speech of the wealthy (whether corporations or real persons) a very doubtful principle. In short, this Supreme Court decision weds a faulty analogy with a questionable general principle.

Exercise 11-1

When we are confronted with a deductive argument by analogy, there are two different and distinct ways to attack the argument by analogy. First, one can argue that the analogy is a bad one: The principle behind the first case does not apply to the second. Second, one can say that even if the two cases *do* fit under the same principle, the principle is *wrong*.

The examples in the exercises below are all *deductive arguments by analogy*. For each one, describe and *illustrate* the two basic ways of *attacking* that deductive argument by analogy: First, by attacking the analogy itself; and, second, by disputing the *principle* behind the analogy. For example, consider this deductive argument by analogy: Suppose an 8-year-old child does something really awful: takes a gun and shoots one of her playmates, for example. You wouldn't execute that 8-year-old, would you? We would think it wrong to execute the child, even though she did something terrible. Well, Randall Flauss is severely retarded, and has the mental capacity of an 8-year-old. He did something terrible, it's true. But just as you think the 8-year-old child should not be executed for committing a terrible wrong, likewise you must conclude that it would be wrong to execute Randall, who has the same mental powers as an 8-year-old.

How would you attack that deductive argument by analogy? First, you might attack the *principle* behind the analogy. The principle is that we think it is wrong to execute children. To attack the *principle*, you have to attack the starting point of the analogy: No, there is nothing wrong with executing children; if an 8-year-old kills her playmate, then the child should suffer lethal injection; and so should the person with the mental capacity of an 8-year-old. Second, you could argue that the two cases don't fit under the same principle: We should spare the child, but not because she has the *mental* capacity of an 8-year-old, but because she *is* a child; but Randall is not a child, whatever his mental capacity may be. (Incidentally, I think the analogy is a good one, and that this attack on the analogy is flawed; this merely illustrates the two different *ways* of attacking deductive arguments by analogy.)

1. We should not require people to wear seatbelts when they drive or ride in their cars. After all, if you choose not to wear your seatbelt, that certainly is hazardous to your health and it may be foolish, but it doesn't harm anyone except yourself. Requiring adults to wear seatbelts is like requiring people to exercise regularly. Just like not wearing your seatbelt, it may be foolish not to exercise, but it doesn't harm anyone except you. Since we think that requiring people to get regular exercise would be wrong, we must also conclude that requiring people to wear seatbelts is wrong.

2. It is wrong to ban smoking on airplanes. It's just not fair. Maybe smoking is a disgusting habit, OK; but it shouldn't be banned on commercial flights. After all, I think chewing gum—people chomping big wads of gum and blowing big, sticky, gooey bubble gum bubbles—is disgusting; but it would be wrong to *ban* chewing gum on commercial flights. So, in the same way, since it's wrong to ban gum chewing, it is also wrong to ban smoking.

3. We should not have restrictions on what medications people can take; that is, we should not require people to get a doctor's prescription to buy drugs. Once a medicine is approved for human use, people should be able to buy whatever medications they choose. After all, we think people should be able to buy any food they want so, in like manner, we ought to let people buy whatever medication they want. You don't need a prescription to buy food; why should you need a prescription to buy drugs? People ought to be free to make their own choices. If you want to consult a nutritionist for advice on what foods are best for you, fine; but it shouldn't be required. And if you want to consult a physician about what drugs are best for you, fine; but that shouldn't be required either.

4. University students should not be required to attend class in order to pass a course. When you enroll in a class and pay your tuition, that gives you the right to attend the class. But it doesn't mean you should be *required* to attend class. It's like buying a season ticket to watch the Cleveland Indians. When you buy the ticket, that gives you the right to attend every game, if you wish to do so; but it certainly doesn't give the Cleveland Indians the right to *require* you to attend every game. Likewise, paying your tuition for a class gives you the right to attend, but it doesn't give your professor the right to *require* you to attend.

5. Look, suppose you are an American citizen who is living in England, France, Argentina, or some other foreign country. Maybe you have a job there, or you are attending a foreign university. You get picked up by the police, charged with a crime. You should have the same rights to a fair and

public trial as any citizen of that country, right? Well, if you believe that you, as a foreigner living in another country, should have the right to a fair trial just like any citizen of the country you are visiting, likewise you should agree that foreigners who are living in this country and who are charged with crimes should have exactly the same rights to a fair and public trial that any citizen of the United States has.

6. There is currently a severe shortage of organs for transplant, and many persons who need organs will not get them because of the shortage. Some maintain that given this severe shortage, we should deny liver transplants to those who need a new liver because of liver damage caused by excessive drinking. But denying liver transplants to those whose livers were damaged by excessive drinking would be unfair and unjust. It would be like denying heart transplants to those who need a new heart because they damaged their hearts through overeating or neglecting to exercise.

7. Some people object to euthanasia (or "mercy killing," that is, the killing of a suffering terminally ill person who requests a painless death) on the grounds that killing a patient is "playing God," and we should not interfere in natural processes. But that won't work. After all, when we actively intervene—through surgery, ventilators, antibiotics, and dialysis machines—to *save* the lives of those who are ill, we are certainly going against the "natural process" of disease by *preventing* death. Since we think it is alright to actively interfere in natural processes to *prevent* or *delay* death when patients request it, we should likewise approve of intervening to *cause* or *hasten* death when a sick and suffering patient requests that.

8. In the debate over capital punishment, the opponents of capital punishment always bring up the danger of mistakenly executing someone who is actually innocent; and they say that the danger of mistakenly executing the innocent is a reason to ban capital punishment. Well, it's obviously true that many people have been wrongly convicted, and so there is a strong possibility that if we continue with capital punishment we will occasionally execute someone who is innocent. But just because innocent people may sometimes be killed, that's no reason to stop our program of capital punishment. After all, think about our policy of sending fire trucks racing through the streets to put out fires. When we do that, sometimes the fire trucks accidentally collide with other cars, and innocent people are accidentally killed. But we don't think that because fighting fires sometimes results in accidental deaths we should therefore stop sending fire trucks racing to put out fires. Likewise, the fact that innocent people may sometimes be mistakenly killed is no reason to stop our policy of capital punishment.

9. Suppose you had to have surgery done on your knee. Would you want a surgeon who was favored by a majority of people who have no expertise in surgery? Would you want to have your surgeon selected by a vote of people who know nothing about surgery? Selected by taxi drivers and high school English teachers and farmers, by economics professors and electricians and store clerks? No, of course not. You would want your surgeon chosen by experts who are experts in medicine and surgery. Now think about our legislators, the people who write the laws and regulations that govern us. That's at least as important to your well-being as some minor surgery on your knee. And likewise, the best thing would be to have our legislators chosen by experts who really know something about government and legislation, not voted on by chemistry teachers and construction workers and truck drivers and police officers. That's why democracy makes no sense.

10. You believe that you should have the right to put a large Christmas nativity scene—complete with angels and star of Bethlehem—in front of your house, right? Well, likewise, you should also agree that the county has the same right to place a Christmas nativity scene in front of the county courthouse.

The Fallacy of Faulty Analogy

To get a better sense of deductive arguments by analogy, let's look at an analogy that is clearly *fallacious*. Consider the following argument by deductive analogy:

Why should the government regulate and restrict the rates charged by the utility companies? Utility companies should be free to set their rates as they wish. After all, if you open a restaurant, you are free to charge your customers whatever you wish for a hamburger; if you open a dry cleaning shop, you can charge what you wish for your cleaning services. Similarly, utility companies should also be free to charge whatever they want, without any government restrictions.

What is the conclusion of this deductive argument by analogy? The argument concludes that the rates charged by utility companies should not be subject to government regulation; the utility companies should be free to charge whatever they wish. What sort of argument is given for that conclusion? The argument uses an analogy: It argues that utility rates are similar to prices charged by restaurants and dry cleaners, and since restaurant owners and cleaners are rightly free to charge what they wish, rates charged by utility companies should also be unregulated. The argument claims that these cases are relevantly similar, and therefore if we are to consistently hold to our principles, we must treat like cases alike.

The argument might be outlined thus:

> You believe restaurants should be free to set their own prices.
>
> The reason you believe restaurants should be free to set their own prices is because you believe that all businesses should be free to set their own prices.
>
> Since utility companies are also businesses, they fit under the same principle, and therefore you should conclude that utility companies should also be free to set their own prices without government regulation.

But *are* these cases similar? Do they fit under the same principle? No.

The utility companies are *monopolies*. If you wish to open a competitive company to your local electric company and try to beat that company's prices, you are out of luck: The utility company is granted, by law, a *monopoly* on utilities in its area. No one is allowed to set up a company to compete with it. But of course that does not apply to Joe's Diner or Joline's Dry Cleaning. If you think that Joe is charging too much for a hamburger, or that Joline is overpricing her cleaning, you can buy your lunch and get your clothes cleaned somewhere else, and you are welcome to set up a competing diner or dry cleaner and underprice Joe or Joline. That makes the cases compared in the analogy very different. Why do we believe that Joe should be free to charge what he wishes? Because we can always go to a different restaurant if Joe gets a bit too pricey. But if Homestate Power raises my utility rates, what options do I have? I can either pay them or sit in the dark. I can't shop around for a lower rate, because there are no competing utility companies.

So the principle we *actually* hold is this: We believe that all *competitive* companies should be free to set their prices as they wish. Utility monopolies do *not* fit under that principle, because they are monopolies and are not competitive; therefore, the analogy fails, since the supposedly analogous cases are not really analogous. This deductive argument by analogy is a *faulty analogy* (often called the *fallacy of questionable analogy*).

Notice that there are certainly *other* differences between restaurants and electric utilities. So it is important that you pick out the *relevant* difference, the difference that actually makes this a faulty analogy. For example, another difference between dry cleaners and electric utility companies is that electricity is more important to us than dry cleaning. I would rather sit with dirty clothes in a heated, lighted house watching television than spend cold, dark evenings in my freshly starched shirt. But in this case, that is not the *relevant* difference; that is *not* why electric utility rates are regulated and restaurant prices are unregulated. After all, food is at least as important as electricity, but you can charge whatever you please at your grocery store (since you do not have a government-enforced monopoly).

Lawyers would call this an investigation of the *dispositive facts:* What are the key facts behind the belief that restaurants and dry cleaners should be able to set their own prices? Not that the services or products they offer are nonessentials; rather, the dispositive facts are their status as *competitive* businesses.

Bubble Gum Beer

A 1999 episode of the popular television series *Law and Order* offers a good example of deductive argument by analogy, and of an attack on such an argument. In this fictional case, a man had converted a semiautomatic pistol into a fully automatic (continuous fire) weapon and then used the pistol to attack a group of students in Central Park, killing 15.

After convicting the gunman, the district attorney went after the gun manufacturer. The manufacture and sale of fully automatic pistols was illegal, but semiautomatic pistols were legal. However, the "Rolf 9" (the gun used in the fictional murder) could be very easily converted from semiautomatic to fully automatic. The district attorney claimed that the manufacturer knew that, and that the manufacturer purposefully designed the gun for easy conversion in order to increase sales. Mr. Webber, the CEO of Rolf Firearms, was charged with 15 counts of second-degree murder. The district attorney's cross-examination of Mr. Webber contained the following dialogue:

DISTRICT ATTORNEY: You knew your guns were being sold illegally to criminals [by people who had converted them into automatic weapons].

DEFENDANT WEBBER: We have no control over that. If a liquor store sells beer to an adult who turns around and sells it to a minor, is the brewer responsible?

DISTRICT ATTORNEY: He is if he makes bubble gum–flavored beer.

The defendant is offering an argument by analogy: Since you think the brewer is not responsible if his beer is sold illegally to a minor without the brewer's knowledge, by analogy you must conclude that a gun manufacturer is not responsible if his product is sold illegally without his knowledge. The district attorney claims that is a faulty analogy: The reason we do not hold the brewer responsible is because the beer is not designed to be particularly attractive to minors; but if a manufacturer (or brewer) purposefully designs a product that will be particularly attractive for illegal uses (illegal sales to minors, or conversion to illegal automatic pistols), then the manufacturer is responsible.

Deductive arguments by analogy can always be restated *without* the analogy, and it is often easier to analyze them in that form. Consider the animal rights argument *without* the analogy:

It is wrong to inflict suffering on an animal by raising it and killing it for luxury food merely because the animal is of lower intelligence than whoever is killing it.
The human practice of raising and killing animals for food violates this principle.
Therefore, it is wrong for humans to raise and kill animals for food.

With the argument in this form it is somewhat clearer. Objections to the argument can be focused more precisely. One might argue that the basic principle is wrong ("It is not wrong for the more intelligent to inflict suffering on the less intelligent") or argue that it is not the relevant principle ("It is all right for humans to raise and kill animals for food because God granted us a special right to do so; it's not because humans are more intelligent"); or argue that present practices of raising and killing animals do not fit under the principle ("Farm animals live very happy and contented lives; they are not discomforted by being castrated, caged, confined in tight quarters, and herded to the abattoir").

When analyzing a deductive argument by analogy, you may find it useful to rephrase the argument by stating the principle explicitly (and eliminating the analogy); however, the argument without the analogy may not have the same impact as the original analogical argument. Use of an analogy may be a powerful means of pushing people to think more carefully about their principles and beliefs. An argument about whether more intelligent animals have the right to inflict suffering on the less intelligent may have the same logical implications as an argument about whether superintelligent extraterrestrials have the right to raise humans for human burgers; but the analogy forces us to come to grips with specific details of the issue. Deductive arguments by analogy are often difficult to analyze, but they are important arguments that prod us to serious scrutiny of our beliefs and principles.

A Faulty Analogy

In one of his columns, William F. Buckley, Jr., criticized remarks made by (former) Associate Justice Lewis Powell of the U.S. Supreme Court. In discussing why the Supreme Court had ruled that the voting age should be lowered to 18, Powell stated,

> In the simplest of terms, the Court decided that when young people were being drafted and asked to go to war and risk their lives at age 18, the time had come to extend to them the right to participate as citizens in the decisions that affected them so seriously.

Buckley responded to Powell's comments with this analogy:

> An interesting line of reasoning, which to be sure could be extended to assert that because girls can and do bear children at age 11, they should have the vote

concerning the statutory age of marriage. But never mind the logic.

But let's mind the logic. Is that a good analogy? Do the cases fit under the same principle?

Obviously not. Why does Powell think that 18-year-olds should have the right to vote? *Not* just because there are governmental policies and issues that affect them; *that* would apply at a much earlier age, as Buckley notes. Rather, Powell's principle is that the age at which one is considered old enough to be *required* to risk and possibly sacrifice one's life for one's country should also be considered an appropriate age for participation as a voting citizen in forming the policies of one's government. But that reasoning cannot be extended to cover 11-year-olds who bear children: The analogy does not hold, since the country is certainly not *requiring* 11-year-olds to bear children. Like many bad analogies, Buckley's is cute, even striking; but it's still a faulty analogy.

Exercise 11-2

For each of the following analogies, *first* tell whether it is a *figurative* analogy or a *deductive* argument by analogy; and, *second*, tell whether it is a *legitimate* analogy or a *faulty* analogy. (In some cases, you may be able to read the analogy as *either* figurative *or* deductive.)

1. Ladies and gentlemen of the jury, my client, Seth Briddle, is charged with armed robbery. His fate now rests in your hands. You will have to weigh the evidence that you have heard, including the testimony of one eyewitness who saw the robber for only a few seconds on a dark street; and the testimony of an admitted drug dealer who claims that Mr. Briddle confessed the crime to him in the prison exercise yard. You are the sole judges of that evidence, of the reliability of the eyewitness identification and the truthfulness of the claims made by this admitted drug dealer who is eager to get a reduced sentence for his crimes. And having weighed the evidence carefully, you must decide whether to find Mr. Briddle guilty or not guilty. You understand that it is a basic principle of our system of justice that an accused person must be found *not guilty* unless everyone on the jury is certain—certain *beyond a reasonable doubt*—that he is guilty.

   "Certain *beyond a reasonable doubt*": now exactly what does that mean? It does not mean that you think he *might* be guilty. And it does not mean that you think he is *probably* guilty. And it does not mean that you think he is *very likely* guilty. This is a very serious matter, members of the jury; this is a basic question of justice or injustice. This is serious business. Suppose you are driving on a trip with your family, and you come to a high bridge over a deep canyon, and that bridge looks sort of old and rusty and shaky. And there's a police officer there, and you stop and ask this police officer, "Officer, is it safe to cross that bridge?" And the police officer says, "Well, I think that bridge might be safe." You would turn around, and you wouldn't drive across that bridge with your family. Suppose the officer says, "Well, that bridge is getting old and weak, and it shakes a lot, but it's probably safe." Still, you wouldn't take a chance and drive your family on to that bridge. Or maybe the officer says, "Well, the bridge is *very likely* safe." That wouldn't be good enough, would it? You wouldn't risk the life of you and your family unless you were *certain* that bridge was safe, if there was *no reasonable doubt* of the safety of that bridge. That's what it means when you are certain beyond a reasonable doubt. If you think it is just barely *possible* that bridge is going to collapse, you would not take your family onto that bridge. And if you think it is just barely *possible* that Seth Briddle is innocent of the charges against him, then you must not find him guilty.

2. A decent education is essential in order to have genuine equal opportunity for success in our society. That's why we guarantee everyone, rich or poor, an opportunity to get a good, publicly funded education. Likewise, decent health care is also essential for equal opportunity: After all, you don't really have much of an opportunity for success if you are sick and can't get decent medical treatment. So since we insist that a decent education is a basic right of all citizens, we also ought to insist that every citizen has a basic right to decent health care.

3. In discussing whether there should be mandatory drug testing for college athletes, sports columnist Irwin Smallwood drew the following analogy:

> As one person asked me the other day in an earnest discussion of the college side of the issue, "What is the difference in saying you've got to make a passing grade in math and saying you've got to make a passing grade in physical condition? Is a random test for dangerous drugs different from a pop quiz in math?"
>
> Of course, it is not that simple. But maybe it's not so complicated, either. Is there *really* a difference in permitting authorities to test you mentally and allowing them to test you physically? I wonder.[3]

4. In Italy there are some majestic marble quarries. Huge blocks of marble are cut and then fashioned into sculptures. Artists send plaster forms, and workmen at the local studios chisel the final, usually much larger sculpture from a marble block. In a *National Geographic* article on the quarries, this process is discussed:

> This news, startling at first, made sense when I thought about it. Obviously, an artist like [Henry] Moore, who may turn out six massive works a year, doesn't take a chisel and singlehandedly carve a 12-foot-high statue.
>
> Instead, I learned, he creates a plaster mold called a maquette. Then an artisan nails a series of studs, called points, into the form and uses calipers to transfer the proportions to the larger scale.
>
> In the Henraux studio I held a maquette Moore had created. The doll-size abstract form had recently been scaled up to an 80-ton sculpture destined for a downtown Miami development. Moore would visit the studio sometime later to supervise the final stages of production.
>
> "So who is the artist," I asked Nicoli, referring to the giant thumb. "Your workmen or the sculptor?" Nicoli waved his hand impatiently. It is an old debate: "The artist is the composer of the symphony. He does not waste time trying to play all the parts. If he uses the orchestra, or workmen, he can make the most beautiful music. We are not creators. We are proud to be executors."[4]

5. In a *Newsweek* interview, singer-songwriter Country Joe McDonald made the following remarks concerning the need for change:

> Will the old line let the new take over and save the planet, or will our old thoughts and traditions lead us to annihilation? The American system is over 200 years old. It's a very old system. You wouldn't be using a 200-year-old toilet in your house and wouldn't drive on the freeways in a 200-year-old vehicle.[5]

6. A few health-care professionals object to caring for AIDS patients because they fear that providing such care may put them at risk of developing the AIDS virus. If proper precautions are taken, the risk is very small, but it remains a risk. Still, doctors and nurses and other health-care professionals have a duty to take that small risk and care for patients with AIDS. When they voluntarily decided to become health-care professionals, they knew that facing some risk from infectious diseases was part of the job. In like manner, when police officers and firefighters take their jobs, they recognize that they will sometimes be exposed to danger as part of their work. But having voluntarily taken the job, they cannot refuse to take on the risks that go with the job. Like professional firefighters, health-care professionals must not shirk the dangers that are part of their chosen work.[6]

7. Some people argue that *abstinence* is the only absolutely safe way to avoid pregnancy and sexually transmitted diseases, so we should only teach high school students that they should be sexually abstinent until marriage, and *not* teach them about contraception or about methods to reduce the risk of sexually transmitted disease. That's like saying that since the only way to completely prevent teenage auto accidents is to not use cars, teenagers should not be taught to drive safely and use seatbelts, but should instead be instructed never to ride in cars.

8. Students at Home State University are complaining because some of the classes with small enrollments have been dropped, and students now have to take a different class. But it doesn't make sense to have a class that is only a third or a quarter full, when there are other classes with plenty of seats available. Suppose we have 10 parking lots around campus, and only 2 are full, while 4 are only half full, and 4 are only a quarter full. It wouldn't make sense for us to spend money keeping all those parking lots open, right? Instead, we could close most of the lots that are only a quarter full, and the students could easily park in the other lots that are half full. In the same way, it makes no sense to pay people to teach classes that have only a few students when there are lots of other good classes that still have openings.

9. The way we fund public schools in Ohio is really unfair: Some school districts in wealthy suburban districts—like Hudson and Chagrin Falls—have lots of money, and they hire top teachers and provide all sorts of special courses and tutoring and computer facilities; while other school districts—especially those in poor rural regions—have very little money, and students have much larger classes, few or no computers, and no special courses or tutoring. It's unfair, because students from rich districts get a big educational advantage over students in poor districts. Some people claim that it *is* fair, because some students in the poor schools still outperform some of the students in the wealthy schools. But that doesn't prove that the funding is fair: Look, suppose you have a 1 mile race, and some of the runners get top quality running shoes plus a 10-second head start, while the others have to run in heavy boots and they start 10 seconds later. Some of the runners wearing heavy boots will still outrun some of the runners in running shoes; but that certainly doesn't mean that the race was *fair.*

10. The Alaskan Wilderness area is a beautiful wild area that provides essential habitat for many endangered species, and there is no other place like it anywhere in the world. Perhaps there's some oil there, and some people want to drill for oil in this fabulous wild preserve; but drilling for oil—with all the heavy equipment and roads and oil pipelines that requires—would destroy the delicate ecosystem there, and that wonderful wilderness would be lost forever, and we could save much more oil than would be produced there simply by adopting stronger fuel efficiency standards for our cars and trucks. Destroying the Alaskan Wilderness area in order to produce oil is like burning a beautiful and unique and irreplaceable painting by Van Gogh in order to roast marshmallows.

11. Some people object to euthanasia (or "mercy killing," that is, the killing of a suffering terminally ill person who requests a painless death) on the grounds that killing a patient is "playing God," and we should not interfere in natural processes. But that won't work. After all, when we actively intervene—through surgery, ventilators, antibiotics, and dialysis machines—to *save* the lives of those who are ill, we are certainly going against the "natural process" of disease by *preventing* death. Since we think it is alright to actively intervene to *prevent* or *delay* death when patients request it, we should likewise approve of intervening to *cause* or *hasten* death when a sick patient requests it.

12. Imagine that you are watching an enormous fireworks display, perhaps a mile away; flying through all those bursts of brilliant light, there is a tiny firefly. Now, imagine trying to pick out that firefly as it flies through the exploding fireworks. That's what it is like for astronomers trying to discover a planet the size of Earth in orbit around another star.

Analyzing a Deductive Argument by Analogy

Deductive arguments by analogy are challenging, and working through them requires careful thought. For practice, consider Judith Jarvis Thomson's forceful argument by analogy on the question of abortion. Thomson begins by granting (for the sake of argument) a claim she does not in fact believe: that the fetus is a person from the moment of conception. She is *arguing* that even if it were true the fetus is a person, there would *still* be cases in which a woman would have a right to an abortion. (The main part of the argument—and the deductive argument by analogy—begins in the third paragraph, when Thomson asks you "to imagine this.")

I think that the fetus is not a person from the moment of conception. A newly fertilized ovum, a newly implanted clump of cells, is no more a person than an acorn is an oak tree. But I shall not discuss any of this. For it seems to me to be of great interest to ask what happens if, for the sake of argument, we allow the premise [we assume that the fetus is a person from the moment of conception]. How, precisely, are we supposed to get from there to the conclusion that abortion is morally impermissible? Opponents of abortion commonly spend most of their time establishing that the fetus is a person, and hardly any time explaining the step from there to the impermissibility of abortion. I suggest that the step they take is neither easy nor obvious, that it calls for closer examination than it is commonly given, and that when we do give it this closer examination we shall feel inclined to reject it.

I propose, then, that we grant that the fetus is a person from the moment of conception. How does the argument go from here? Something like this, I take it. Every person has a right to life. So the fetus has a right to life. No doubt the mother has a right to decide what shall happen in and to her body; everyone would grant that. But surely a person's right to life is stronger and more stringent than the mother's right to decide what happens in and to her body, and so outweighs it. So the fetus may not be killed; an abortion may not be performed.

It sounds plausible. But now let me ask you to imagine this. You wake up in the morning and find yourself back to back in bed with an unconscious violinist. A famous unconscious violinist. He has been found to have a fatal kidney ailment, and the Society of Music Lovers has canvassed all the available medical records and found that you alone have the right blood to help. They have therefore kidnapped you, and last night the violinist's circulatory system was plugged into yours, so that your kidneys can be used to extract poisons from his blood as well as your own. The director of the hospital now tells you, "Look, we're sorry the Society of Music Lovers did this to you—we would never have permitted it if we had known. But still, they did it, and the violinist now is plugged into you. To unplug you would be to kill him. But never mind, it's only for nine months. By then he will have recovered from his ailment, and can be safely unplugged from you." Is it morally incumbent on you to accede to this situation? No doubt it would be very nice of you if you did, a great kindness. But do you *have* to accede to it? What if it were not nine months, but nine years? Or longer still? What if the director of the hospital says, "Tough luck, I agree, but you've now got to stay in bed, with the violinist plugged into you for the rest of your life. Because remember this. All persons have a right to life, and violinists are persons. Granted you have a right to decide what happens in and to your body, but a person's right to life outweighs your right to decide what happens in and to your body. So you cannot ever be unplugged from him." I imagine you would regard this as outrageous, which suggests that something really is wrong with that plausible-sounding argument I mentioned a moment ago.[7]

In analyzing Thomson's argument, try to answer the following seven questions:

1. State as precisely as possible the exact conclusion for which Thomson is arguing. (Note that it is a very *narrow* conclusion.)
2. Exactly what is the analogy *between?* (i.e., What two objects or situations are being *compared?*)
3. What special *similarities* does Thomson think there are between the two situations?
4. What principle (implied, but not stated) is Thomson's analogy pointing toward?
5. Do you agree with the principle?
6. *Is* this a good analogy? That is, do both cases fit under the same principle? (Does the reason for thinking one has a right to detach from the violinist also apply to detaching from a fetus?)
7. How would you rephrase this argument without using an analogy?

Try your own answers to those questions *before* you read mine. After all, critical thinking is like chess: It's more fun to play than to watch (figurative analogy).

1. The conclusion of the argument is as follows: A woman who is pregnant as the result of rape has a right to terminate the pregnancy. (The conclusion is *not* that a woman has a right to an abortion under any and all circumstances; that would not immediately follow from *this* analogy. Thomson argues later in her essay that a woman's right to an abortion is *not limited* to cases of rape; but that goes beyond our present concerns.)
2. The analogy is between a woman who is carrying (supporting) a fetus that is the result of a rape and an individual who is supporting the life of a violinist as a result of kidnap.
3. The special *similarity* in the two cases is that in both situations an individual has been *forced* into a position in which she is supporting the life of another, and in both cases the only way of escaping this situation involves allowing another person to die.
4. What is the principle behind the analogy? (i.e., Why do we believe—assuming that we do—that a person has the right to unplug herself from the violinist?) That is the tough part. Perhaps it is something like this: No one has an obligation to sustain the life of another when

one has done nothing to take on that obligation. And if that is roughly the principle we share, then we must agree that both the kidnap victim and the rape victim have the right to detach themselves. But that probably doesn't fully capture the principle. In any case, if it *were* the principle, it would be open to this analogical counterattack (as developed by J. M. Fischer):

> Suppose you have planned for many years to take a trip to a very remote place in the Himalaya mountains. You have secured a cabin in an extremely remote and inaccessible place in the mountains. You wish to be alone; you have enough supplies for yourself, and also some extras in case of an emergency. Unfortunately, a very evil man has kidnapped an innocent person and brought him to die in the desolate mountain country near your cabin. The innocent person wanders for hours and finally happens upon your cabin.
>
> You have the following problem. You can radio for help, but because of the remoteness and inaccessibility of your cabin and the relatively primitive technology of the country in which it is located, the rescue party will require nine months to reach your cabin. Thus, you are faced with a choice. You can let the innocent stranger into your cabin and provide food and shelter until the rescue party arrives in nine months, or you can forcibly prevent him from entering your cabin (or staying there) and thus cause his death (or perhaps allow him to die). (It is evident that he will die unless you allow him to stay in the cabin.)
>
> It seems to me that it would be morally impermissible for you to prevent the innocent stranger from coming into (or staying in) your cabin. Even though it is *your* cabin and allowing the stranger in would cause considerable inconvenience, you may not let him die on your doorstep.[8]

So *if* the principle behind Thomson's violinist analogy is just that one has no obligation to save a life if one has done nothing special to take on that obligation, then it is probably a principle we would reject, since (as Fischer's analogy shows) most of us would say that we *do* have an obligation to save the life of the kidnapped stranger, though we have done nothing special to take on that obligation. (Notice that if we believe that we *do* have an obligation to take in the innocent stranger—and I think that Fischer is correct that most of us would agree that we do—then that is no small obligation. It would imply, for example, that we have strong obligations to save the lives of those innocent victims of war, flood, and drought whom we find on our world doorstep and whom we could save at considerably less trouble to ourselves than is being asked of the Himalaya cabin dweller; for whatever the basic principle behind Fischer's argument, it would almost certainly apply to saving those other innocent victims as well.)

But it seems to me that the principle involved in the violinist example is narrower than the one in Fischer's mountain-cabin analogy. Thus Thomson's violinist example is not really analogous to Fischer's cabin example. The more specific principle pointed to by Thomson's analogy is something like this: Assuming that one has done nothing to take on some special obligation, one has no special obligation to allow his or her *body* to be used for someone else's benefit. That seems to capture the essence of Thomson's analogy much more effectively. After all, it is one thing to suppose that we have an obligation to provide help to save the lives of innocent strangers; it is quite another to suppose that each of us has a special obligation to allow our *bodies* to be used—without our consent—to provide such help. Thus the principle that Thomson's analogy powerfully emphasizes is our basic right to decide what is done to and within our own bodies.

5. Do you agree with that principle? Some will, and some will not. Some will think that Thomson's principle is correct and that no one who has been kidnapped or raped is obligated to stay hooked up to a violinist or a fetus. Others will disagree: They will say that one *does* have an obligation to others (or at least an obligation to sustain another's life) in any circumstances whatever. They will believe that it doesn't matter whether I volunteered to let the violinist use my kidneys, or was kidnapped, or whatever; if I *can* sustain a life, then I am always obligated to do so (even if it means spending the rest of my own life in a hospital bed).

Fischer offers a counteranalogy to this statement of Thomson's principle. His example goes like this:

> Suppose you are in a hospital room recovering from major surgery. Because of the nature of the surgery, you must stay in the hospital room in bed for nine more months. Now the story goes just as in Thomson's violinist case: A great violinist has been brought into your room and attached to your kidneys.[9]

Figure 11-1   Calvin offers an analogy. *From* There's Treasure Everywhere, *by Bill Watterson. (Kansas City, Missouri: Andrews and McMeel, 1996).*

Fischer asserts that in this case "it would be impermissible for you to detach yourself from the violinist and thereby cause his death." But that hardly seems obvious. Certainly it would be nice of you to agree to stay hooked up to the violinist in this case; but would it be *impermissible* to refuse? It seems to me that it would *not* be impermissible to refuse to allow one's body to be used in this way; to the contrary, one *does* have a right to decide what will be done to and what uses will be made of one's own body. (*If* you agree with Fischer that one can *not* refuse to allow one's body to be used by the violinist, then that would seem to imply a whole host of *very* strong obligations: an obligation to donate organs after death, as well as an obligation—that *cannot* be refused—to donate blood or bone marrow or even your single superfluous kidney to anyone who has a special need for them. While I think all such donations are morally commendable, I do not think they can legitimately be *required* of anyone.)

So do we accept Thomson's principle? That is a complicated and controversial ethical issue, and we shall certainly not resolve it here. But remember: If an individual *rejects* that principle—as Fischer appears to do—then this argument by analogy will be of no use in trying to convince that individual.

6. Is it a good analogy? I think it is. The two cases *do* fit under the same principle: *If* one thinks the kidnapped person has a right to unhook herself from the violinist, then one must also—in order to be consistent—conclude that a woman who has been raped has a right to an abortion.
7. How could we rephrase the argument without using the analogy? Roughly, like this:

> Assuming that one has done nothing to voluntarily place one's self under a special obligation, then one has no special obligation to allow his or her body to be used for someone else's benefit or even to save or sustain someone's life. A woman who has been raped has done nothing to take on an obligation to allow the fetus the use of her body. Therefore, a woman who is pregnant as the result of rape is not obligated to sustain the life of the fetus and has a right to an abortion.

What does this deductive argument by analogy prove? Simply this: that if you think that you have a right to unhook yourself from the violinist (if you think that you cannot be coerced into such use of your own body), then you must also believe that a woman who is pregnant as a result of rape has a right to an abortion. That is an important analogical argument, and it proves something important; but it proves it only for those who agree with the underlying principle.

Thomson's deductive argument by analogy illustrates what arguments by analogy can accomplish. The argument makes us think about a difficult and controversial issue in a new light, from a new perspective; and it forces us to consider more carefully the exact implications of the principles we hold. If we *agree* with the principle behind Thomson's argument, then we must also agree that a woman who has been raped has the right to an abortion. If we *reject* that principle, then we have much stronger and more burdensome obligations to other people than we might have realized.

Deductive Arguments by Analogy and Cooperative Critical Thinking

Deductive analogical arguments are often found in adversarial settings. If you listen to the oral arguments concerning a case before the U.S. Supreme Court, the advocates for both sides often deploy deductive arguments by analogy to support their respective positions. One advocate argues that the case currently under consideration is analogous to a case (a precedent) previously decided by the Court; the opposing advocate argues that the case is a better fit with a different precedent, and so that second precedent should be followed. But while deductive arguments by analogy are effective in adversarial contests, they are perhaps even more important in *cooperative* critical thinking, when those involved in the discussion are working together to find an answer satisfactory to everyone. Deductive arguments by analogy *start* by seeking common ground: We *all* agree on this starting point, right? We *all* accept this principle, don't we?

Suppose we are arguing about guaranteeing good health care for *all* the children of the United States. "Look," you might say,

> [W]e believe that every child in the United States should have the opportunity to get a good education, agreed? Well, *why* do we believe in universal education? Why do we agree that all children, regardless of the wealth or poverty of their families, should have access to a good education? The answer is this: We believe that every citizen should have a fair *opportunity* to make the most of themselves, to use their talents and abilities and energies effectively; we believe that *everyone* should have a fair chance, should not be deprived of a fair chance to get ahead. And we recognize that an opportunity for a decent education is essential for fair opportunity. Well, likewise, you can't really have a fair opportunity in life if you don't have decent health care to treat your illnesses: just as being deprived of an education undercuts your opportunity for success, in the same way being subject to untreated illness also deprives you of genuine opportunity.

That deductive argument by analogy starts by looking for basic areas of *agreement* between us, and then tries to build on that common foundation to develop new areas of cooperative agreement. Rather than emphasizing what divides us, the key step is finding what beliefs we share, or what values we hold in common. From that common cooperative base, we push out to find other areas of agreement—perhaps areas of agreement that we had not hitherto recognized. Using this deductive argument by analogy, you might well convince me to think further about the implications of values we hold in common, and how to extend those values into new questions. Or maybe it won't be that easy. Perhaps we both believe in equal opportunity, and I agree that educational opportunities are essential for equal opportunity, but I don't think health care is so important. Because we have already established a common base of agreement, now we can focus our discussion more precisely and productively on the implications of lacking health care, and on what that means for lack of genuine opportunity. Our further discussion along those lines won't necessarily convince me that all children should have access to decent health care; but there is probably no method of argument that has a better *chance* of convincing me.

Or perhaps I won't even agree with your starting point. "Wait a minute," I say; "I don't agree that every child should have an opportunity to succeed. Maybe education *is* essential for genuine opportunity; maybe access to health care is also essential; but I don't see why anyone should believe that every child should have a decent opportunity. If some kids lack access to education and health care, and so they have no real chance in life, that's tough; but the world *is* tough; so what? If kids from poor families have no opportunity for an education and no access to health care, then they have no real chance of success; but I don't see anything wrong with that." If that is my response to your effort to find a common foundation of shared values, then your deductive argument by analogy is not likely to get very far in convincing me that all children should have decent health care. Still, you have learned something valuable: you have learned not to waste your time arguing with me about this issue. We have such fundamentally different views that it is unlikely that any argument you could give would make a dent in my beliefs. Critical thinking and critical argument are very valuable, but they aren't superpowers; and learning when they are, and are not, likely to be effective is one part of becoming a good critical thinker. Perhaps good arguments could have reshaped Hitler during his formative years, but it is very doubtful that any arguments could have impacted the adult Hitler's vile views. Critical thinking will also be of little help in stopping the charge of an enraged bull elephant, or convincing a crocodile that you are a bad choice for lunch. But in the right contexts, critical thinking can be very helpful in enlarging agreements, settling disputes, finding solutions, and reaching reasonable conclusions. That's not bad.

The Fallacy of Analogical Literalism

Good analogies can be powerful arguments and striking illustrations, but they must be distinguished from fallacious uses of *faulty* analogy.

A special fallacy related to analogies might be called "the fallacy of analogical literalism." That is the fallacy of treating an analogy too literally. After all, an analogy is just that: an *analogy*. When you offer an analogy, you are claiming that there are some *relevant similarities* between cases that are admittedly quite *different*. That is the whole point of using an analogy: If the cases were *exactly* the same, then there would not be an analogy at all. The usefulness of the analogy lies in comparing things that are different in order to see the issue in a new light. If one attacks an *analogy* on the grounds that the cases being compared are not *exactly* alike, then one is committing the *fallacy* of analogical literalism.

Plea Bargaining

"Plea bargaining" is a very common practice in the United States. In fact, the vast majority of criminal charges are settled not by trials, but instead by plea bargains between the defendant (usually represented by an attorney) and the prosecutor (someone from the district attorney's office). In plea bargaining, the defendant agrees to plead guilty, in exchange for some concession from the prosecutor: reduced charges, or perhaps the recommendation of a minimum sentence. Suppose I'm charged with two serious crimes. If I go to trial and am convicted, I will probably be sentenced to 15 years in prison. You're

the prosecutor. Your office is overloaded with cases, and you want to avoid another trial. Besides, the court calendar is jammed. So you offer me (and my attorney) a deal. If I will plead guilty to just one of the crimes, you will drop the other charge, and I'll get a 5-year prison sentence. Of course I can take my chances and go to trial. But my chances aren't very good: I can't afford a high-priced defense lawyer, and the public defender assigned to my case doesn't seem all that energetic. So, do I take the definite 5 years, or roll the dice and maybe get acquitted, but more likely have to serve a 15-year sentence? (Of course if I'm innocent, I don't like the idea of a 5-year sentence for something I didn't do. But I know that the innocent often get wrongfully convicted, and the odds don't look good for me.) So I go along with the plea bargain. Everyone is satisfied: I have to serve 5 years, but I avoid the risk of 15. The prosecutor eliminates a case from her overloaded schedule, the judge avoids a lengthy jury trial that would force the court schedule even further behind. But has justice been done?

Kenneth Kipnis ("Criminal Justice and the Negotiated Plea," *Ethics*, vol. 86 [1976]) argues that plea bargaining should be eliminated from the criminal justice system, and that it is fundamentally opposed to the practices of genuine justice and fairness. Kipnis asks us to imagine the following scenario. You turn in a term paper to your professor, who is known to be a tough grader. You would like to get an A on the paper, but you *really* want to avoid a D or F. Your tough professor looks over the first page of the paper, glances at the rest, and

offers a deal. "If I go ahead and grade this paper, I would probably give it a grade of D. Of course there's a chance that it's better than it looks at first glance, so it might be an A, but that's not likely. But I'm sort of pressed for time right now. Tell you what I'll do. If you will pass up your right to have your paper graded carefully and conscientiously, I'll give you a B. What do you say?"

Certainly this might be convenient for both the professor and student. In fact, if we adopted it generally, we could save ourselves a lot of time: professors could eliminate the burden of grading, and students could spend less effort on their papers. But convenient as this might be, we would hardly consider it fair and just. After all, your grade is supposed to be based on what you did, on what your paper justly deserves, not on the best bargain you can strike. Likewise, convenient as plea bargaining might be, it fails to meet the standards of fairness and justice that our criminal justice system is supposed to be guided by.

Consider the figurative analogy between a steam engine and neuroses. Neuroses are not *exactly* like steam escaping from a steam boiler. The analogy is designed to *illustrate* Freud's theory of neuroses, to describe something that is like Freud's theory in *some* respects. Imagine the following attack on that figurative analogy:

How Do You Rule?

bikeriderlondon / Shutterstock

Imagine that you are a U.S. Supreme Court justice. You are considering a case—*Rosenberger v. University of Virginia*—in which a student organization was denied funding to publish a Christian magazine (*Wide Awake: A Christian Perspective at the University of Virginia*). The students asked for $5,800 to cover printing costs for the magazine. The money was requested from the Student Activities Fund, which provides funding to recognized student groups for various activities, including publications. The funds come from a mandatory student activity fee, paid by all university students. The guidelines for the Student Activities Fund specify that funds cannot be used to promote religious belief, including specifically belief "in

or about a deity or an ultimate reality." The *Rosenberger* suit alleges that the denial of funds on this basis is an illegitimate restriction of the students' free speech; in opposition, the university contends that allowing the funds to be used to promote a specific religious belief would be in conflict with the Establishment Clause of the U.S. Constitution, which forbids the state (and thus a state-supported university) from promoting any religious perspective.

The goals of this Christian publication are not in doubt: it is the publication of an avowedly Christian evangelical group of students, the purpose of which is to promote efforts to convert students to a particular set of Christian beliefs (their publication is designed to encourage evangelical activities by members of the group, and also to publish material that will influence other students to accept a specific set of religious doctrines). The question is whether such a specifically religious publication should be supported by money from the University of Virginia Student Activities Fund.

As the Supreme Court examined this issue, one question concerned a *precedent* established by an earlier case: the *Lamb's Chapel v. Center Moriches Union Free School District*, which the court had decided in 1993 (just two years prior to the present case). In that case, the school district allowed the after-hours use of its facilities

(continued)

by community groups, but prohibited the use of facilities for the purposes of promoting religious beliefs. The Lamb's Chapel group wished to use school facilities to show films that promoted Christianity, and the school district rejected their request. The Lamb's Chapel group sued, claiming that their rights of free speech were violated by this restriction. The Supreme Court ruled in the *Lamb's Chapel* case that because public school facilities were being offered for after-hours use to other community groups, the school district could not prevent religious groups from using the facilities for religious programs. The justices who *favored* the Wide Awake organization claimed that the Lamb's Chapel precedent applied to the new case: by *analogy* with the *Lamb's Chapel* case, since the Court has ruled that public schools must make public facilities equally available to secular and religious programs, by the same principle a public university must make student funds equally available to secular and religious organizations and

publications. The justices who *opposed* the Wide Awake demand claimed that the *Lamb's Chapel* case was *not* analogous: that the two cases do *not* fit under the same principle, that there are important differences between the two cases such that the precedent in the *Lamb's Chapel* case does not apply to the Wide Awake case.

Leave aside the larger question of how you (as a Supreme Court justice) would rule in this case; instead, concentrate only on the question of whether the *Lamb's Chapel* case is a good precedent, a good *analogy*. If you were an attorney arguing the case on behalf of the University of Virginia, how would you argue that it is *not* a good analogy?

Having considered the analogy carefully, how would you rule on that *specific question*: Is the *Lamb's Chapel* case a good analogy to the Wide Awake case? (On the larger issue, the Supreme Court ruled in favor of Wide Awake, but the ruling was by only a 5 to 4 majority, and the Court was deeply divided on the issue.)

That is a ridiculous analogy. You can't compare human neuroses to steam escaping from a boiler. A steam boiler is made of metal, and humans aren't made of metal. And although human bodies do contain a lot of water, the water certainly never gets anywhere close to the boiling point. If the water in your body reached the boiling point, you wouldn't be neurotic, you'd be dead. So the analogy between human neuroses and escaping steam is a stupid one.

Such an attack commits the fallacy of analogical literalism. It misses the point of the figurative analogy. The analogy does not claim that neuroses are *exactly* like steam escaping from a boiler; rather, it says that they are similar in some instructive ways. The attack on the analogy picks out some *irrelevant* differences. It misses the point of the illustration and thus commits the fallacy of analogical literalism.

Suppose that someone makes this attack on Thomson's deductive argument by analogy:

Thomson's comparison of a fetus and a violinist is absurd. Certainly no fetus can play the violin; and besides, a fetus doesn't have a problem with kidney failure, since its mother's kidneys function for the fetus.

That criticism commits the fallacy of analogical literalism. Whether the individual to whom the kidnap victim is attached is a violinist or a baseball player or a ski bum is *irrelevant;* all that is required is that that individual be a human being. And whether the individual is suffering from kidney failure or whatever is also irrelevant; all that is required is that if the kidnap victim is detached, that individual will die. The differences are irrelevant, because they do not prevent the two cases from fitting under the same *principle.* Picking on irrelevant points in the analogy commits the fallacy of analogical literalism: it treats the analogy too literally.

Caution! Watch for Analogies That Look Like Slippery Slopes!

It is sometimes difficult to tell whether an argument is an analogy or a slippery slope argument. Slippery slope arguments will be discussed in more detail in the following chapter: They claim that a proposed policy or act is wrong because it is the first step down a slippery slope that will lead to some horrible result. "If you let this robbery defendant go free, more robberies will occur and there will be a breakdown of law and order and we will have anarchy in the streets!" But arguments by analogy sometimes look like slippery slope fallacies. "If you think it is alright to ban books that contain ideas or materials that you consider offensive, then you must also think it would be alright to ban books like the Bible, because some groups find it offensive." That looks a bit like a slippery slope argument, but it is not. It is instead an argument by analogy, which claims that what you are doing is essentially similar to (analogous to) something else. Banning a novel is like banning the Bible, and since you do not believe that the Bible should be banned, you should not favor banning of *any* books. (That may or may not be a good argument by analogy, but it does not commit the slippery slope fallacy.) If it *were* a slippery slope fallacy, the argument would go like *this*: "If you start by banning a few novels, the next thing you know all sorts of books, including the Bible, will be banned." But that *isn't* what the original argument says.

In some cases, however, it is difficult to determine whether an argument is using an analogy or is instead a slippery slope argument. A few years ago some people, especially high school principals, became upset when a number of students stopped wearing bras. One case involved a junior high school student in Portage, Michigan, who was twice suspended from Portage Central Junior High School for attending class braless. The principal of the high school defended his policy with this argument: "If I say okay to a girl who feels more comfortable coming to school without a bra, what do I say to another student who wants to come in his pajamas or bathing suit?" Is that argument a slippery slope fallacy ("If I allow her to attend classes braless, tomorrow students will show up in pajamas and by the end of the school year they will be wearing bikinis to class!") or is it an argument by analogy ("Attending class braless is like attending class in your pajamas; it's certainly wrong to allow students to attend class in their pajamas, so it is also wrong to allow students to attend class braless")? It's hard to tell; you could call it either way. (Perhaps it doesn't much matter: It will be either a slippery slope fallacy or a faulty deductive argument by analogy. In either case it's a lousy argument.)

The moral of the story is this: Don't be too hasty in accusing someone of the slippery slope fallacy; consider whether the argument might instead be a deductive argument by analogy.

The U.S. Supreme Court and a Questionable Analogy

One of the most significant cases involving capital punishment was the *McCleskey* case (*McCleskey v. Kemp*, 481 U.S.), ruled on by the Supreme Court in 1987. The majority of the Supreme Court offered an argument by analogy that resembles a slippery slope argument.

Warren McCleskey, an African American man, had been sentenced to death for the murder of a white man. The crime had occurred in Georgia, and on appeal McCleskey's lawyers argued that the death penalty was being unfairly applied, because in similar cases in which the victim was black, the death penalty was much less frequent: That is, in Georgia those who murdered whites were much more likely to receive the death penalty than were those who murdered blacks.[10]

The Supreme Court rejected McCleskey's argument, saying that just because statistics showed that a much higher percentage of murderers of white victims received the death penalty, that was not adequate proof of discrimination against blacks. The majority of the

Court offered this analogy: We must not accept claims of death penalty discrimination on the basis of statistics showing that murderers of white victims are more likely to receive the death penalty; that would be analogous to (and would open the door for) claiming that because some study shows that murderers of physically attractive victims are more likely to receive the death penalty, that therefore there is discrimination on the basis of the physical attractiveness of the victims. Since we would not accept such statistically supported discrimination claims in the case of the physical attractiveness of the victims, neither should we accept such claims concerning the race of the victim.

Jeffrey Abramson offers a scorching critique of the Court's *McCleskey* argument by analogy:

The Court makes the fatuous claim that, if it were to accept mere statistical correlations between race and the death penalty as evidence of invidious

(continued)

discrimination, then it would also have to accept, as adequate proof of discrimination, bald statistics showing a correlation between capital punishment and a victim's physical attractiveness. But there is a huge difference between the two demonstrations. In the case of race, history gives meaning to the statistics. Throughout the antebellum period, Georgia openly ran a dual death penalty system, differentiating between crimes committed by and against blacks and those committed by and against whites. For instance, the death penalty was automatic for murders committed by blacks, whereas juries might recommend life for anyone else convicted of murder. The state penal code specified that the rape of a free white female by a black "shall be" punishable by death. Rape by others of a free white female triggered a prison term of two to twenty years. Most telling is that if the rape was of a black woman, the law provided punishment "by fine or imprisonment, at the discretion of the court."

Precisely because the historical connection between race and the death penalty runs so deeply and is so ugly, the *McCleskey* Court erred in characterizing racial disparities in Georgia death sentencing as "unexplained" but not "necessarily invidious."

On the other hand, such an agnostic reaction might well be appropriate to some new social science study showing a correlation between defendants' facial characteristics and death penalty rates. In the absence of a history of legal discrimination against certain facial types, the numbers are not as important as those involved when the issue is race. In short, the Court's reasoning does not do justice to the special scourge— the special burden—that race and the death penalty place upon the land.[11]

INDUCTIVE ARGUMENTS BY ANALOGY

We have discussed figurative analogies (which are not arguments at all) and deductive *arguments* by analogy (which *require* the truth of the conclusion if one accepts both the truth of the premises and the correctness of the analogy). There is another use of analogies that should be mentioned: *inductive* arguments by analogy.

Inductive arguments by analogy are quite common. For example:

> Allison Affluent lives in suburban Richmond, she has three children in private schools, she belongs to two country clubs, she drives a Cadillac, and she wears large diamonds on four fingers—and she is a member of the Republican Party. So it seems likely that Penelope Prosperous—who lives in the same suburban neighborhood, also has three children in private schools, belongs to the same country clubs, drives a Caddie, and wears lots of diamonds—will also be a Republican.

That's a decent inductive argument by analogy. If two people have that many characteristics in common, it's a fairly good bet that they also share some other characteristic. But *notice* that even though it's a reasonable argument, the conclusion may still be false. It is possible that Penelope is a Democrat. Although we would expect Allison and Penelope, given their similar features, to have many other similarities, it is quite possible that Allison and Penelope have absolutely nothing else in common: They may be opposites in every other respect. Thus *inductive* arguments by analogy may be quite useful, and may give us *probable* conclusions, but the conclusions of inductive arguments are at best highly probable.

Inductive arguments by analogy are helpful, and we often rely on them. If last year I bought a pair of shoes of a particular brand, price, style, and they were durable and comfortable, then I reasonably expect that if I buy another pair of similar brand, price, and style the new pair should also be durable and comfortable. That is a reasonable expectation, a reasonable use of inductive argument by analogy; my conclusions, however, might still be mistaken, and the new shoes may be awful.

Here is one more example of inductive argument by analogy:

> Last week the race horse Luscious Lips won a one-mile race on this track under muddy conditions with jockey Jones against horses similar to the ones she is racing against today. So Luscious Lips will be a good bet to win today, since she is racing at the same distance with the same jockey under similar conditions.

Indeed Luscious Lips will be a good bet; that's a fairly strong inductive argument by analogy. And—an important but tricky consideration—the points of analogy are *relevant:* Same jockey, same distance, similar competition (if the points of similarity were that both races are on Wednesday, both under a new moon, both on a day when the stock market is up, and in both races the same bugler played the call to the colors and the same track announcer called the race, these points of inductive analogy would *not* carry much weight). So this is a reasonably strong inductive argument by analogy. But don't bet the rent money, for that inductive argument by analogy does *not* make Luscious Lips a sure winner.

When is an inductive analogy a good analogy? Keep in mind we are discussing *inductive* arguments by analogy, so the line will not be quite so clear as the line between good and bad *deductive* arguments. There are two basic requirements for a good inductive analogy. First, they must share some characteristics; that is, they must be alike in various ways. And second, the ways in which they are alike must be *relevant* to the conclusion drawn by the inductive analogy. The more *relevant* are the points of analogy, the stronger is the inductive argument by analogy.

Suppose we are discussing movies, and I recommend *Days of Heaven* to you: I liked that movie, so I think you will also. Why do I think that? Well, because we are *alike,* we are *analogous,* in many relevant respects: We like the same novels, the same poems, and the same music; so chances are we'll also like the same movies. Those are relevant characteristics on which to draw an inductive analogy. But what if I said, We'll probably like the same movies, because we have the same blood type, we're the same height, we're both mammals, and we were both born in the twentieth century? Those shared characteristics wouldn't give us much reason to think we'll like the same movies. What if we like the same food? Or we vote for the same political candidates? Are those relevant similarities for movie tastes? I'm not sure; that's an empirical question that we could only answer by doing research on what characteristics generally go together. They're probably better than height and blood type, but they don't strike me as particularly important similarities for drawing a conclusion about favorite films. And finally, characteristics that might be strongly relevant for one inductive analogy will be useless for another: If we have the same blood pressure, cholesterol level, and smoking habits, those may be very relevant for an inductive analogy between your state of health and mine; but they won't be very useful if we are drawing a conclusion about similar tastes in novels.

The distinction between inductive and deductive analogical arguments is important; fortunately, it is not a difficult distinction to draw. A deductive argument by analogy uses an analogy to point toward a principle that it is assumed we all accept and then claims that in order to be *consistent* you *must* accept an analogous case that also fits under that principle. In contrast, an inductive analogy draws a comparison between cases and then suggests that since the analogy holds in some respects, it is *likely* to hold in other respects as well (but it does not suggest that there would be some *inconsistency* if the analogy did not hold). For example, a *deductive* argument about vegetarianism might go like this:

> You believe that it would be wrong for superintelligent extraterrestrials to kill and eat us just because they are more intelligent than we are; therefore, you must also conclude that it is wrong for us to kill and eat less intelligent animals.

An *inductive* analogical argument might look like this:

> You are disgusted by fur coats, and so is Brenda; you buy cruelty-free cosmetics (that avoid animal-testing), and so does Brenda; you prefer organic foods, and so does Brenda. Furthermore, you also believe that it is wrong for us to kill and eat other animals; so probably [by inductive analogy] Brenda also believes it is wrong to kill and eat other animals.

But Brenda may be a dedicated carnivore; the suggestion in the inductive argument (as opposed to the *deductive* use of analogy) is that it's *likely* that Brenda, like you, is a vegetarian; but there is no claim in the inductive argument that she *must* be vegetarian in order to be consistent.

In conclusion, inductive arguments by analogy are quite different from figurative analogies and from deductive arguments by analogy. Each use of analogy is helpful in its own way, but each is a very *different* use of analogy and must be evaluated on its own terms. Distinguishing inductive analogies from figurative and deductive analogies is relatively easy. Distinguishing figurative analogies from deductive arguments by analogy is sometimes tougher. Thomson's violinist analogy is clearly a deductive argument, and the analogy between steam engines and Freud's theory of neuroses is definitely figurative. But sometimes the line is not so clear—and in some cases it is possible to interpret an analogy *either* deductively or figuratively.

Exercise 11-4

This section of exercises includes questions concerning *types* of analogy (figurative, deductive, and inductive); questions about the *analysis* of both legitimate and fallacious analogies; and questions that cover the various fallacies associated with analogies (faulty analogy and the fallacy of analogical literalism). Read the specific instructions for each exercise.

1. Marijuana is a lot like alcohol. Since the production, sale, and use of alcohol is legal, we ought to make the production, sale, and use of marijuana also legal.

   What *type* of analogy is that? What is the principle implied by the analogy? Is it a good analogy? Describe two different ways one might argue *against* that argument by analogy.

2. Alcohol is a lot like marijuana. Since the production, sale, and use of marijuana is illegal, we ought to make the production, sale, and use of alcohol also illegal.

   Compare argument 2 with argument 1. On what points would a person giving argument 1 *agree* with a person giving argument 2? On what crucial point would they *disagree*?

3. PAULA: Drinking alcohol is like looking through rose-colored glasses: It distorts our view of reality and makes us less capable of dealing with our real problems.

   PAUL: That's not true. Drinking alcohol is nothing like wearing glasses. After all, you drink with your mouth, not with your eyes.

   Is that criticism of the analogy legitimate or fallacious?

4. It is not right to expect Senator Foghorn to tell us whether she cast her Senate vote for or against cutting the Medicare budget. That would be like requiring you or me or some other citizen to tell how he or she voted in the last election. I have a right to vote in private, and so does Senator Foghorn.

   What type of analogy is that? Is it a legitimate or a faulty analogy?

5. Judith Jarvis Thomson denies that the fetus is a person from the moment of conception. She states that "a newly fertilized ovum, a newly implanted clump of cells, is no more a person than an acorn is an oak tree." But Thomson's comparison of a fetus to an acorn and a person to an oak tree is quite ridiculous. They are not at all alike: For one thing, an oak tree is a plant, and a person is an animal.

   What use of analogy is Thomson offering here? Is the criticism legitimate or fallacious?

6. Consider an analogy from the world of sports (or at least from the *business* of sports). This example is drawn from 1982, when the National Football League was in the midst of a player strike. The National Football League Players Association was proposing that the NFLPA receive 55% of the gross revenues of the 28 NFL teams, and from that money they would pay all players' salaries, insurance, severance pay, and play-off and Super Bowl money. One player who opposed the strike argued against the proposal with this analogy:

I don't believe that is very fair. I have my own business (a sporting goods store), and if an employee told me he wanted 55% of the gross without risking any capital investment, I'd have a hard time taking him seriously.[12]

Is that a good analogy? (Note carefully exactly what the analogy is comparing.)

7. Look, you're going to do fine on the final exam. Last year I had a student just like you: She attended class regularly, worked hard, studied hard, just like you do. And she flunked the first exam, then did a little better on the second exam, just like you did. And then she aced the final exam, so there's a good chance you'll also ace the final. What type of analogy is that?

8. In her closing statement in the O. J. Simpson case, prosecutor Marcia Clark noted that jurors must be convinced "beyond a reasonable doubt" in order to find Simpson guilty, and she suggested that jurors should think of putting together a jigsaw puzzle when trying to understand proof beyond a reasonable doubt. In a jigsaw puzzle, all the pieces don't have to be perfectly in place to see the whole picture: "If you're missing a couple of pieces of the sky, you still have the picture."

   What type of analogy is that? Is it a good analogy?

9. Suppose that we are discussing the question of how much information physicians should tell their patients. For example, if a patient has terminal cancer, should the physician inform the patient? As we discuss this question, one physician makes the following assertion:

   > Doctors should give unpleasant information to their patients very carefully and cautiously, and in small doses, just like medicine. When we give strong medicines to patients, we often "titrate" the dose, giving small doses over a long period of time in order to reduce any bad side effects of the powerful and potentially harmful medication. In the same way, when we have unpleasant news to give to patients, we should "titrate" the information, providing it in small bits and pieces over an extended period, so the patient will not be harmed by receiving too much bad news all at once.

   The physician is here using an analogy. What type of analogy is it? Is it a good use of analogy, or a questionable analogy?

10. Dr. John Turjanovich is a psychologist. He is in practice by himself, and is ably assisted by his office manager, Valerie Todd. Dr. Turjanovich has only one complaint about Ms. Todd's work: She refuses to run personal errands for him, like picking up his lunch or taking his car to be repaired. When asked, Ms. Todd firmly declines, "I run your office, and I do it well; but I'm not your personal servant." Dr. Turjanovich considers her stance stubborn and unreasonable: "Look, I'm not asking you to work extra. All I'm asking is that during your working hours, you run a few personal errands for me. I pay you for every hour you work. As long as the work isn't immoral or illegal, you should do whatever task I assign you."

    One day Ms. Todd informs Dr. Turjanovich that the next client, Mr. Winston, had just called to say that he couldn't make it for his scheduled 1-hour appointment: He was tied up in a very important meeting. "I hope you told him that I will have to charge him for the one-hour session," Dr. Turjanovich replies. "All my clients know I have a strict policy: Clients must give at least a 48-hour notice prior to cancelling an appointment, or they are charged for the appointment."

    "Yes, I told him," Ms. Todd answers. "He said that was fine. But he also asked if you could do a couple of things for him. He's very busy this afternoon, and he wants you to pick up his airline tickets at the travel agency on South Madison, and his dry cleaning at the shop on Church Street, and drop them off at his office. He said that since he was paying for an hour of your time, you shouldn't mind spending the time helping him out."

    "No way! The nerve of that guy! I'm his psychologist, not his valet. He can run his own errands."

    "I'm glad you feel that way," Ms. Todd replied. "I agree with you completely. If anyone wants personal errands run, they should hire an errand person, or do it themselves—not ask their psychologist or office manager to do it for them."

    Ms. Todd seized an opportunity to offer Dr. Turjanovich an analogy. What type of analogy is it? Is it a good analogy, or a faulty analogy?

11. The U.S. Department of Justice filed an antitrust suit against Microsoft, claiming that Microsoft engaged in unfair and monopolistic trade practices that took advantage of the dominance of the Microsoft Windows computer program as an operating system. One of the government claims was that Microsoft forced computer manufacturers to bundle its MSIE browser with Windows 98, and would not allow Netscape browser (a Microsoft competitor) to be bundled with the Windows operating system, thus gaining an unfair advantage over Netscape. Bill Gates, CEO of Microsoft, claimed

that no one should expect Microsoft to include Netscape in its Windows operating system; and to support his claim he offered the following analogy:

> Forcing Microsoft to include Netscape's competing software in our operating system is like requiring Coca Cola to include three cans of Pepsi in every six-pack it sells.

How would you evaluate Gates's analogy? Is it legitimate, or a faulty analogy?

Exercise 11-5

For each of the analogies in the exercises below, first identify what *type* of analogy it is (deductive, figurative, or inductive); second, tell whether it is a *legitimate* or *faulty* analogy; and third, identify any *other* fallacies that occur (particularly the fallacy of analogical literalism).

1. Dr. Henry Lee, an expert on the science of criminal investigation, testified for the defense in the O. J. Simpson murder trial. After noting some mistakes that the Los Angeles Police Department made in their collection of evidence, Dr. Lee compared it to finding cockroaches in spaghetti: You find one or two cockroaches in a bowl of spaghetti, you don't have to go through the whole bowl to see if there are more cockroaches present or absent.

2. There is now a law making it illegal for health maintenance organizations (HMOs) to restrict what member physicians can tell their patients. For example, if there were a treatment that the physician thought would benefit her patient, but the physician's HMO would not provide the treatment, then some HMOs would not allow the physician to mention that treatment to her patient. Some spokespersons for the HMOs argued that there was nothing wrong in such restrictions: after all, if you go to a car dealer to buy a new car, the dealership may legitimately have a rule that its salespersons are not allowed to tell customers about some other manufacturer's car that might be better for them. Such restrictions on what employees are allowed to tell customers are very common, and doctors employed by HMOs should follow the same rules.

3. Bruce Waller argues that since we think it would be wrong for extraterrestrial invaders—who are more intelligent and powerful than humans—to raise humans for slaughter just because they enjoy the taste of humans, then, in a like manner, we must also conclude that it is wrong for humans to kill and eat cows and pigs just because we are more intelligent and more powerful and because we happen to like the taste of beef and pork. But Bruce's argument is lousy. You can't compare raising humans for slaughter with raising cattle or swine for slaughter. After all, humans grow much more slowly than do cows and pigs, and human flesh contains too much gristle to be really tasty.

4. While Enid Waldholtz was a member of Congress, representing Utah, evidence showed that her husband and campaign manager, Joe Waldholtz, had illegally conned some $4 million from other people, and that much of that stolen money had been illegally invested in Enid Waldholtz's election campaign (in violation of federal election laws). The huge illegal investment of advertising money had boosted her failing campaign, and led to her victory. Since her congressional seat was won with stolen money through illegal funding, the question was raised whether she would resign. Someone posed the question thus:

> If Joe Waldholtz had used the stolen money to buy a car for Enid, it would be right for Enid to give up ownership of the car after discovering it was bought with stolen money. Similarly, since her congressional seat was bought with stolen money, she ought to resign from Congress.

5. (Overheard in a bar, in a conversation between an older man and a young woman he has just met): "Look, I know I'm older than you, but that shouldn't keep you from going out with me. Haven't you ever heard, the older the violin, the sweeter the music?"

6. JOE: I never wear my seatbelt in the car. I once heard of a guy whose car flipped upside down, and he was knocked unconscious. Well, he was wearing his seatbelt, and as he was hanging there from the shoulder harness, he slipped a bit and the belt got up against his neck. If the rescue people hadn't arrived quickly, he would have choked to death! I think it's a bad idea to wear seatbelts.

JOAN: Come on, Joe, that's just crazy. Of course there might be some fluke accident in which a seatbelt causes injury, but they certainly prevent lots more injuries than they cause. Saying that people shouldn't wear seatbelts because there might be some very unusual circumstances when they cause injury is like telling your children to play in the street instead of their front yard, because once a child was injured by a car that went out of control and slid into the yard where the child was playing.

7. Columnist Irwin Smallwood used the following analogy to counter "the criticism of those young men who choose to forgo their senior [college athletic] seasons in order to sign lucrative professional contracts":

    Imagine, if you will, a brilliant young acting student at the North Carolina School of the Arts. He's a junior, but he's accepted as one of the best in the country. Francis Ford Coppola comes to town and offers him the lead in the new movie he's about to produce, with a signing bonus of, say, $500,000, and a guarantee of $1 million upon completion of the movie.

    Out charges the chancellor, baton in hand, and chases Coppola from the campus, screaming something like, "You can't sign that boy. His class hasn't graduated yet."

    An impossible scenario, you say?

    Of course it is. But isn't that exactly what is happening in college athletics these days?[13]

8. The Levenger Company sells pens, lamps, office furniture, and various other articles. In one of their catalogs they offer the Aeron Chair, which they claim is the "the world's most comfortable task chair." It's a bit pricey, as they admit: $979, plus shipping and handling. But they claim that that should not deter you from buying the chair:

    The Aeron Chair isn't cheap. But how much time do you spend in your chair—probably more than you spend in your car—and what did you pay for that?

9. Last year, I had a patient a lot like you. She is a nonsmoker, a light drinker, a regular jogger, eats lots of fruit, watches her weight, and she's only 2 years older than you. She's also a college student, and single; and she has strong family support, just like you do. We caught her cancer at almost exactly the same stage as yours, and she went through precisely the same treatment program that you will be on. She made a complete recovery, so there's good reason to believe that you also have an excellent chance of recovery.

10. Robert Eckardt, who deals with health grants for the Cleveland Foundation, claims that the U.S. health-care system is too concerned with treating short-term acute illness, while neglecting the preventive measures and early intervention that could prevent severe illnesses. Eckardt compared the U.S. medical system to treating the injuries from a flood of cars crashing off the edge of a cliff, without worrying about why so many cars are running over the cliff in the first place.[14]

11. Suppose that a car dealer is selling cars that he claims are brand new and in excellent condition, and then it turns out that the cars he is selling as new are really used cars that had been driven 50,000 miles and have had the odometers rolled back and have serious flaws, and the car dealer made millions of dollars from this deception. Well, that dealer would be guilty of fraud, and he ought to be put in jail. Kenneth Lay, the chief executive officer of Enron, made millions of dollars selling Enron stock—stock that was grossly misrepresented: it was supposed to be stock in a company that was making a profit and had very little debt, but in fact the company had large hidden debts in offshore accounts and was actually losing lots of money, and Ken Lay knew it. So Ken Lay made a lot of money misrepresenting Enron stock. Since the car dealer who lied about his cars is guilty of fraud, you ought to agree that Ken Lay is likewise guilty of fraud.

12. In the Pacific Northwest, there has been considerable controversy over logging and its effects on the environment. Some people who want to restrict logging have pointed out that logging destroys the habitat of an endangered species, the spotted owl, and that logging should be restricted in order to save the spotted owl. Rush Limbaugh, in one of his radio discussions, wondered what the problem was. Suppose the loggers cut down the trees where the spotted owls nest; well, they can just move. After all, what do you do if a construction project—a highway, for example—destroys your home? You move to a new community. The spotted owls can do the same: When their forest is logged, they can move to a new one.

13. If Professor Jones knows that one of her colleagues is incompetent, and no longer capable of effective teaching (whether because of drug abuse, laziness, or whatever), then Professor Jones has an

obligation to report the incompetent professor and to have that professor removed from the class-room. After all, it is obvious that if Doctor Smith knows that one of her fellow physicians is incompetent, then Doctor Smith certainly has an obligation to see to it that her incompetent colleague is not allowed to continue practicing medicine: Doctor Smith is obligated to try to keep the incompetent physician out of the operating room. Thus, in the same way, if Professor Jones knows that one of her fellow professors is incompetent, then Professor Jones is obligated to take steps to keep that incompetent professor out of the classroom.

14. Some wealthy school districts spend more than three times as much on the education of each child in their districts as is spent in educating children from poorer districts. Some people complain that that is unfair: They say it's like having a race in which some of the runners get to wear expensive running shoes, while the others must plod along in clunky old boots. But that's a silly comparison: School is nothing like a race; after all, you race with your feet, but school concentrates on your mind, not your feet.

15. In 1997, the U.S. Forest Service auctioned off timber sales in Washington's Okanogan National Forest. The top bid for the Thunder Mountain timber parcel was $15,000. The bid was submitted by environmentalists who wanted to pay the money to the Forest Service, then leave the huge, centuries-old trees uncut and the area undisturbed. Their bid was rejected, however, in favor of AA Logging, who planned to cut the trees and sell them. Environmentalists protested that the tract should have gone to the highest bidder, and that it didn't matter whether the bidder wanted to cut the trees or preserve them. Chris West, vice president of the Northwest Forestry Association (representing logging interests in Oregon and Washington), maintains that the forestry service was correct in refusing to accept the environmentalists' bid, and he offered the following analogy:

> Bidding on a government contract is the same whether it is harvesting a timber sale or building a plane or painting a building. If you don't intend to do the work, the contract should not be awarded to you.

16. Some states have proposed that the pay of public school teachers be based on quality of teaching, and the teaching quality would be determined by the standardized test scores of their students: teachers whose students make the highest scores would get the largest raises, while teachers with low-scoring students would get smaller raises or nothing, and the teachers of low-scoring students would also be first in line for dismissal. But that is a terrible way of determining teacher quality. It's like trying to decide who is the best jockey by looking only at the outcome of the race. But if Jorge is riding Secretariat, and Manuel is on a much weaker horse that rarely finishes higher than last, then Manuel might be a much better jockey though he loses by 20 lengths to Jorge. Likewise, if Jill has students who are already excellent readers and have enjoyed every educational advantage, and Joan is teaching students from much weaker educational backgrounds, then Joan may be the superior teacher though her students' test scores fall well below the scores achieved by Jill's students.

17. A woman needs a man like a fish needs a bicycle.

18. Some Home State University students want more student participation in the administration of HSU, including more student members on the board of trustees and more student involvement in the academic senate. But it would be absurd to give students a major role in governing HSU; that would be like giving inmates a stronger voice in how the prison is run.

19. "A newly fertilized ovum, a newly implanted clump of cells, is no more a person than an acorn is an oak tree" (Judith Jarvis Thomson).

20. Voters in Cincinnati passed a referendum that denied gays and lesbians the same protection from discrimination in jobs and housing that the law gives other minorities, and that barred the city council from ever granting such protection. The law was challenged by advocates of gay rights, and the case was heard by the Sixth Circuit U.S. Court of Appeals. That court upheld the law barring protection for gays and lesbians; and one of the central arguments given by the court was that homosexuals were not entitled to civil rights protection because it was possible for them to hide their homosexual identity. The court claimed that: "Those persons having a homosexual 'orientation' simply do not, as such, comprise an identifiable class. Many homosexuals successfully conceal their orientation. Homosexuals generally are not identifiable 'on sight' unless they elect to be so identifiable by conduct (such as public displays of homosexual affection or self-proclamation of homosexual tendencies)."

Columnist Tom Teepen, national correspondent of Cox Newspapers, criticized the court's ruling with the following argument (taken from his column of May 23, 1995):

> Imagine a court ruling that civil rights protection is due only those Hispanic Americans who, having duly changed their names to something like Reginald Rutherford-Wiggleroom, still look Hispanic. Or that even the new Rutherford-Wiggleroom cedes any claim to protection if he slips and blurts out a little Spanish.
> Do Hasidic Jews take themselves beyond the pale of the Constitution because who'd know the difference if they'd just cut their curls, shave their beards, and stop wearing those boring black clothes? (Reprinted by permission of Tom Teepen and Cox Newspapers)

21. In U.S. college and university athletic programs, football typically receives the lion's share of the athletic budget: the most scholarships, the most coaches, the largest expenditures for fields, stadiums, and equipment. There have been proposals to reduce the amount of money spent on college football; one such proposal is that the NCAA reduce the number of football scholarships allowed each of its member schools from 95 to 85. Beano Cook, a sports commentator, opposed that reduction in a radio interview. His argument was roughly as follows:

> There are about 30 college sports recognized by the NCAA, including football, rowing, gymnastics, swimming, and many others. For many colleges, football is the only one of those sports that is actually a money maker. If I had a business that had 30 divisions, and 29 of those divisions were losing money and one division was making money, and I had an accountant who came in to advise me and he recommended cuts in the division that was *making* money, then I'd fire that accountant.

22. From the syndicated column of Tim Giago, in *Indian Country Today*, on the subject of having college and professional sports teams use "mascots" and team names that depict Native Americans:

> On a recent talk show, I spoke with a young lady who had been a cheerleader for a team called the "Indians." She said, "When I put on my feathers and war paint, donned my buckskin and beads, I felt I was honoring Indians." I asked her, "If your team was called the African-Americans, and you painted your face black, put on an Afro wig and donned a dashiki and danced around singing songs and making noises you thought to be African, would you be honoring blacks?" Her answer was "No! Of course not. That would be insulting to them." End of discussion.[15]

23. Richard Aquinas is on trial for kidnapping. Evidence shows that his daughter, Elizabeth, a college graduate, age 23, had joined an Eastern religion of which Richard disapproved. He hired a group of deprogrammers to try to convert her away from her new religion. Richard invited Elizabeth to meet him at a suburban restaurant for dinner; when she arrived outside the restaurant, the deprogrammers forced her into their car and drove her to a remote farmhouse, where she was kept against her wishes for 1 week, while they made various efforts to turn her against her new religious beliefs. Richard was at the farmhouse at various times during the week, and Elizabeth frequently begged to be released and allowed to leave. Richard testified that he refused her requests, because he thought the religion she had joined was a false one. He was deeply concerned for his daughter's physical and spiritual well-being, and he was committed to converting her back to her old beliefs. The deprogramming efforts failed, and at the end of a week she was released. She went to the police, and kidnapping charges were filed.

When the case goes to the jury, there is heated discussion. Everyone agrees that Richard did participate in the kidnapping; but there is a split over whether he really did wrong. One person argues that Richard could not really be doing wrong, because he really and sincerely believed that what he was doing was right. Another juror offers the following argument in response:

> Look, just because someone believes in what they are doing, that doesn't make it right. The notorious Nazi, Heinrich Himmler, was head of the SS and commanded the Nazi death camps. It seems obvious from his writings and from what is known about him that he sincerely believed in the Nazi goals, and believed that his dedicated effort to kill all Jews was right. But though he believed in what he was doing, that certainly did not make what he was doing right. If anything, what he did was made more vile: He didn't perform murder out of passion or sudden anger, but instead carried out a reflective and deliberate policy of mass murder. His deep and genuine dedication to that purpose—and his belief in its rightness—makes him even more evil, not less.

Now I'm not saying that Richard Aquinas is anything like Himmler, or that his kidnapping was even remotely as bad as Himmler's atrocities. But the point is, Himmler's sincere belief that he was doing the right thing was no justification for his acts; and Richard Aquinas's sincere belief that he was doing right is no justification for the kidnapping of his daughter.

24. The next example is from Lon L. Fuller's hypothetical "Case of the Speluncean Explorers." (The setting is "the Supreme Court of Newgarth," in the year 4300.) The case is an appeal of the murder conviction of four men. The four are cave explorers who, with one other companion, were trapped in a cave for 32 days without provisions. The five cast lots, and the loser, a man named Whetmore, was killed and eaten by the other four. Without this desperate procedure, all five would have died. One of the fictional appeals court judges gives this opinion:

> The usual conditions of human existence incline us to think of human life as an absolute value, not to be sacrificed under any circumstances. There is much that is fictitious about this conception even when it is applied to the ordinary relations of society. We have an illustration of this truth in the very case before us. Ten workmen were killed in the process of removing the rocks from the opening to the cave. Did not the engineers and government officials who directed the rescue effort know that the operations they were undertaking were dangerous and involved a serious risk to the lives of the workmen executing them? If it was proper that these ten lives should be sacrificed to save the lives of five imprisoned explorers, why then are we told it was wrong for these explorers to carry out an arrangement which would save four lives at the cost of one?
>
> Every highway, every tunnel, every building project involves a risk to human life. Taking these projects in the aggregate, we can calculate with some precision how many deaths the construction of them will require; statisticians can tell you the average cost in human lives of a thousand miles of a four-lane concrete highway. Yet we deliberately and knowingly incur and pay this cost on the assumption that the values obtained for those who survive outweigh the loss. If these things can be said of a society functioning above ground in a normal and ordinary manner, what shall we say of the supposed absolute value of a human life in the desperate situation in which these defendants and their companion Whetmore found themselves?[16]

25. When politicians deceive the public, it's not really so bad; it's just part of the game. After all, when you watch a football game, often the quarterback will pretend to hand the ball to a running back, and then actually throw a pass. And at a basketball game, sometimes the player with the ball will fake a shot, and then pass the ball. And in volleyball, a player at the net will act like she is going to pound the ball straight down, and then she'll make a little tap over the frontline. Likewise, politicians often pretend to be in favor of protecting the environment and guaranteeing patients' rights to health care while they are campaigning, but those are just tricks, and they shouldn't be blamed when they don't actually live up to their campaign promises. If you approve of fakes and tricks in football, basketball, and volleyball, then you shouldn't object to tricks in politics, either.

26. Students who pay tuition for taking a course should be able to take whatever parts of the course they wish, and skip any parts they don't enjoy. It's like buying a meal at a restaurant: If you buy spaghetti and meatballs and you eat the spaghetti but don't like the meatballs and you don't eat them, the restaurant certainly doesn't require you to eat the meatballs.

27. BILL: I don't think it's fair that a woman golfer gets to play on the men's tour, but men can't play on the women's tour. If Annika Sorenstam is allowed to play on the men's tour, then male golfers should be allowed to play on the women's professional golf circuit.

    WALTER: Look, remember when you played summer league baseball? Remember the year you were 10, there was a 10 and under division, but you were a really good player, so they let you "play up" in the 12 and under division, so you would be playing against better competition? Well, it was good for you, right? You had fun, and you improved your skills, and you certainly didn't dominate the league. And it wasn't unfair to the other kids. But what if some of the 12-year-olds had said, well, if Bill gets to play in our division, we should get to play in the 10 and under division. But that wouldn't work: 12-year-olds are generally bigger and stronger than 10-year-olds, and allowing 12-year-olds to play in the 10-year-old division would wreck it; but letting an occasional outstanding 10-year-old play against better competition in the 12-year-old division obviously doesn't put the 12-year-olds at a special disadvantage. Likewise, men are generally bigger and stronger than women. So letting men play in the women's division would wreck it; but allowing an occasional outstanding woman to play in the men's division allows an outstanding woman golfer to hone her skills against tough competition, causes no harm, and puts no one at a special disadvantage.

28. Mathematician John Allen Paulos, when interviewed on The Motley Fool Radio Show, discussing whether high school students should be allowed to use calculators: Yes, they should, he said, because once they've learned basic calculations, the important thing is to teach them the concepts of mathematics, not how to calculate. "People often confuse computation with mathematics, in ways that they don't confuse other subjects. No one says, 'You're a great typist; you ought to write a novel.' "

29. Members of the jury, you have heard the evidence, and now it is up to you to decide on a verdict. My client, Melissa Rhodes, is accused of robbery. As the judge will tell you, the prosecution bears the burden of *proving* that accusation. The defense does *not* have to prove that she is *innocent;* rather, the prosecution must *prove* that she is guilty. And they have to prove that charge *beyond a reasonable doubt.* Now, what does that mean: "beyond a reasonable doubt"? Sometimes it's described like this: to be certain beyond a reasonable doubt means that you have the kind of certainty that you would be willing to act upon in matters of serious consequence. Think of it this way: Suppose you are taking your family to grandmother's house for Sunday dinner, and on the way you have to cross a bridge over a deep ravine. Before you take your family over that bridge, you want to be *certain beyond a reasonable doubt* that the bridge is safe. That doesn't mean that you have to be sure that the bridge would hold up if somebody dropped an aircraft carrier on top of it: that goes *beyond* the confidence you need. But on the other hand, it means that you have to be a lot more confident than just *probably.* If you were thinking of driving your family across that bridge, and the county engineer told you to go ahead, the bridge is *probably* safe, well, you wouldn't drive across, would you? Now suppose that you were 90% confident that the bridge was safe: don't worry, there's just 1 chance in 10 that the bridge will collapse as you drive across; you wouldn't take that chance, right? What if it were 95% safe? There's only 1 chance in 20 that you and your family will go plunging down that ravine when the bridge collapses: that's *not* being certain; you wouldn't act on that sort of probability; you wouldn't drive across that bridge. If you are 95% certain that the bridge is safe, then *don't* drive across it, it wouldn't be *reasonable* to drive across it; and if you're 95% certain that the defendant is guilty, that is *not* certainty beyond a *reasonable* doubt, and you should *not convict,* you should find Melissa Rhodes *not guilty.* Don't drive across that bridge to conviction unless you are genuinely *certain beyond a reasonable doubt.* If the prosecution's case won't hold up that much weight, then Melissa Rhodes is entitled to a verdict of *not* guilty.

30. It's not surprising that many of the people of Iraq oppose the U.S. troops in Iraq. After all, people tend to get angry at troops that are occupying their country, even if they believe that the intentions of the occupying troops are good. I mean, I may not like the president, and maybe I think he has done terrible things as President of the United States. But if the Canadians sent an invading army into the United States to get rid of the president, and Canadian troops were occupying the United States, I would still be really angry at those Canadian troops, even if I believed they were trying to help us. Likewise, we shouldn't be surprised that the Iraqis are angry at the U.S. troops in their country.

31. Cleveland State University and Youngstown State University are both urban universities, both are located in Northeast Ohio, both are state universities that receive most of their funding from the state and from student tuition, neither has a large endowment, both are primarily undergraduate institutions, and both Cleveland State and YSU have had modest enrollment increases over the past several years. I just learned that Cleveland State will have a tuition increase next fall, so it seems likely that YSU will also increase tuition in the fall.

Exercise 11-6

When judges make rulings in new cases, they are supposed to be guided by *precedents:* judicial rulings in earlier cases that govern the way later cases are decided. But of course no two cases are exactly the same, so the question often arises: Exactly how does the old precedent apply in this new case? And since there are many precedents from many old cases, there is also the question of which precedents apply (and which do not). In civil cases, lawyers for the plaintiff and the defendant often argue about which precedents are relevant, and exactly how the relevant precedents should be applied. That involves trying to determine exactly what the precedents establish; that is, exactly what is the *principle* behind the precedent.

Consider an example. Wicker attended a garden party at the home of Young. While strolling in Young's backyard, Wicker wandered over to a small pasture where Young's horse was grazing. When Wicker leaned against the fence and extended his hand toward the horse, the horse turned and severely bit Wicker. The injury was quite painful, and required several stitches at a hospital emergency room. Wicker is suing Young for damages. Suppose that one of the guiding precedents in the case is *Andrews v. Millstone*, in which the court ruled that Millstone was liable for damages inflicted to Andrews (a carpenter whom Millstone had hired to build a backyard gazebo) by Millstone's dog, which had bitten Andrews when Andrews walked over to the dog's pen and extended his hand.

The attorney for the *defendant* will argue that that precedent should be interpreted *narrowly*, and that it does not apply to the present case: for example, the ruling in the precedent applies only to dogs, not horses; or it applies only to hired workers, not to invited guests. The attorney for the *plaintiff* will argue that the precedent should be interpreted more *broadly*, so that it covers not only a carpenter bitten by a dog but also a guest bitten by a horse. But the plaintiff's attorney must be careful not to interpret the precedent *too* broadly: That would make it possible for the defense attorney to argue that the plaintiff's interpretation leads to absurd results. For example, if the plaintiff's attorney claims that the precedent shows that the owner of the property is liable for any harm that befalls anyone who is on the property with the owner's permission, then, the defense attorney could easily argue, that would make the property owner liable for damages if a meteorite should strike one of his or her guests, and since that is absurd, that interpretation of the precedent is obviously mistaken.

In trying to determine how to interpret a precedent, what we are doing is trying to formulate the *principle* behind the precedent. Wicker's attorney might say that the cases are *analogous* (the two cases fit under the same *principle*) because the principle behind the precedent is that the owner of property has an obligation to warn those he or she invites onto the property of any known hazard. Young's attorney replies that the precedent is actually based on a much narrower principle: The owner of property has an obligation to warn those whom he or she *hires* of any dangerous *dogs*. (What is the *true* precedent? That is a thorny question, one that logicians, legal scholars, and judges vigorously debate. Some claim that there is really no hidden *true* principle behind the precedent; instead, it is a matter of working out the details of the precedent with further and additional rulings. Those are questions you can save for your legal philosophy course.)

In the following exercise, you will be given a case, and then a governing precedent (sometimes more than one). Your job is to interpret the precedent (or precedents) and the new case, *first* as the plaintiff's attorney (interpreting the *principle* behind the precedent in such a way that it applies also to the new case), and, *second*, as the defendant's attorney (interpreting the *principle* behind the precedent so that it does *not* apply to the new case). That is, as attorney for the plaintiff you will argue that the cases make a *legitimate* deductive argument by analogy; and then as defense attorney you will argue that the principle does *not* apply to the two cases, and that it is a *fallacious* deductive argument by analogy. (Depending on whether the precedent is cited by the defense attorney or by the attorney for the plaintiff, the roles may be reversed.) So, for the case considered above, your answer would look like this:

PLAINTIFF: The owner of property has an obligation to warn those he or she invites onto the property of any known (and less than obvious) hazard.
DEFENDANT: The owner of property has an obligation to warn those whom he or she *hires* to come onto the property of any dangerous *dogs*.

And last but not least, you should gather your robes about you and make a judicial ruling: Who is right, counsel for the plaintiff or counsel for the defendant? (i.e., for each case, is this a legitimate deductive argument by analogy, or is it fallacious?)

(All of these cases are fictional, as are the precedents cited.)

1. Lawrence Ruggles is suing Alexis Levine for damages suffered at an afternoon barbecue at her farm. Both sides agree on the basic facts of the case: Lawrence was at Alexis's farm by her invitation, attending a party; Alexis owns a large, mixed-breed dog, Prince, that becomes nervous around strangers and tends to bite; Alexis warned all her guests—she gave a general verbal warning to the assembled group not to go near Prince, because (as she said): "He is very excitable, and he can be vicious." Lawrence was present, and heard the warning. Prince was chained to his dog house by a 14-foot chain. Lawrence was walking around the farm after eating lunch, talking with another guest, when (without realizing it) he walked to within about 12 feet of Prince. Prince suddenly rushed at Lawrence, biting him severely in the leg, causing a deep gash that required emergency medical treatment.

The attorney for defendant Levine claims that there is a key precedent for the case: *Whittle v. Cox*. In that case, Whittle was a guest at an outdoor party at Cox's house. Cox's dog was in a fenced dog yard, with a fence about 4 feet high; there was a sign posted on the fence, saying, "Danger: Bad Dog." (Cox gave no verbal warning to his guests.) Whittle, while engaged in conversation, casually leaned against a corner of the dog yard fence, his hand at his side. When his fingers passed through the fence, the dog lunged and bit Whittle's hand, leaving a deep, ragged laceration that required emergency room treatment. The appeals court had ruled that Cox was not liable for the damages suffered by Whittle.

First, how will counsel for the defense interpret the principle behind the precedent (so that it *also* applies to *Ruggles v. Levine*)? Second, how could counsel for the plaintiff interpret the precedent so that it does *not* apply to the present case? And third, Your Honor, how would you rule? Does the precedent cover this case, or does it not?

2. Annette Bowers is the plaintiff in *Bowers v. West Athens*. Ms. Bowers is suing West Athens to compel the city to allow her to operate a small sewing business out of her home. Bowers designs and sews custom-made clothing for about a dozen women. She consults with her customers at her home about the design they want. She then designs and sews the clothing they order, and she also does the final fitting at her home. The section of West Athens in which Bowers lives is zoned noncommercial, and the city has ruled that her sewing business is in violation of the zoning ordinance. The attorney for Bowers argues that there is a precedent in the case: The city has allowed Joan Girard to teach piano lessons in her home to about 15 students, and Girard's home is on the same block as Bowers's house, and the same zoning regulations apply to both houses. How would the plaintiff's attorney argue that the precedent established for Girard's business applies to Bowers's sewing business (that the two cases are analogous)? How might the city attorney for West Athens argue that the *Bowers* case does *not* fit under the *Girard* precedent? And finally, how would you rule on the case?

3. This is the same case as no. 2, above, but with one addition: Bowers's attorney cites the *Girard* case, as well as the additional case of Anthony Torelli, another person living in the same zoning district with Bowers and Girard. Torelli is a craftsman, who carves wooden figures in a shop in his basement, and sells the figures on weekends at craft shows throughout the region. Torelli also has approval from the city to operate his craft business out of his home. With this additional precedent, Bowers's case now seems stronger, and the challenge for the city attorney is more difficult: How would the city attorney interpret the cases so that the precedent established by the *Girard* and *Torelli* cases does *not* apply to *Bowers*? How would the plaintiff's attorney interpret the precedents? (*Possibly* this will require no change in the plaintiff's interpretation, but there may be a way of making it stronger.) And again, as the judge, how would you rule?

4. In the village of Breezewood there is a city ordinance prohibiting advertising signs that are larger than 3 feet by 3 feet. John Albers owns a furniture store in Breezewood, and he has been cited by the city for violating the sign ordinance. Albers has parked a large truck trailer in front of his store, near the highway. Painted on the side of the trailer is a sign in bright red letters, with a background in sky blue; the sign reads, "Albers Furniture: Some Sell Cheaper, but None Sell Better." The trailer has been parked in the same place, without moving, for over 3 months.

Albers's attorney argues that there is a binding precedent in the case. She claims that in the case of *Winston v. West Athens*, the city of West Athens filed charges against a candidate for the city council (Winston) who had a pickup truck in which he had placed a large (12 feet by 15 feet) sign, saying, "Elect Winston for a Better West Athens." Every day Winston would drive the truck to his restaurant in downtown West Athens and park it in a prominent place on Main Street. In that case, the court had ruled in favor of Winston: that Winston was not in violation of the ordinance, and could continue to park his truck in front of his restaurant.

How would Albers's attorney argue that both cases fit under the same principle? How would the West Athens city attorney argue that the *Winston* case is *not* analogous, that the precedent does *not* apply, and that the cases do *not* fit under the same principle? And finally, how would you rule?

5. Johnny, age 8, is scheduled for a trip to the dentist—and he is not too thrilled about the idea. However, he does see an opportunity for gain. "Mom, can I have a special present for going to the

dentist without complaining? I think the whole thing is pretty awful, and I hate it when they poke around on my gums. But if I could get a present, it wouldn't seem so bad."

"No, Honey, you can't get a present just because you go to the dentist."

"That's not fair. Yesterday when Julie (Johnny's sister, age 6) had to get a vaccination shot, you promised her she could get a special present if she was brave and didn't complain. So if she gets a present for going to the doctor, I should get a present for going to the dentist."

The precedent here is Julie's present as a reward for being brave while getting a shot. How can the plaintiff (Johnny) interpret that precedent so that going to the dentist fits under the same principle? How can mom (appearing for the defense) interpret the Julie-present precedent so that the two cases are not analogous?

6. This is a case before the student judicial board at Home State University: Teresa Villanti was a student in Professor Cedric Seisner's course on Greek mythology. Professor Seisner assigned a paper, due Friday, November 1. Teresa turned in her paper a day late, and was penalized a letter grade. She is appealing the grade, on the grounds that the reason she turned her paper in late was that she drove with friends to a football game that Home State University was playing against a distant rival, and that she had to leave before class in order to make the drive. Furthermore, another student in her class, Arthur Wallace, plays in the Home State University band, and missed class to take the band bus to the same football game; he also turned his paper in a day late, and his grade was not penalized. Since Arthur's grade was not penalized, Teresa argues that it is unfair that her grade be penalized.

Taking the case of Arthur Wallace as a precedent, how would you (as student attorney for Teresa) formulate the principle behind the precedent? How might Professor Seisner formulate the governing principle in order to claim that the two cases are *not* analogous? How would you rule on this grade appeal?

7. The hearings of the student judicial board continue with a new case. Professor Sarah Black assigned a paper to her ancient philosophy seminar, due in class on November 1, with a letter grade penalty for late papers. Class met from 10:00 to 11:30 A.M. on Fridays. Andrew Wythe delivered his paper to Professor Black on Friday afternoon (at about 1:00 P.M.) at her office, and was penalized a letter grade. Laura Strope brought her paper to the classroom at 11:35 A.M.; class was over, but Professor Black was continuing the discussion of the morning seminar with two students, while she gathered her notes. Laura's grade was not penalized.

Using the case of Laura Strope as a precedent, how could Andrew (the plaintiff) present the principle behind the precedent to argue that (by analogy) his grade also should not have been penalized? How could Professor Black formulate the principle to justify penalizing Andrew but not Laura? How would you rule?

8. This case is a modification of no. 7, above. In addition to the case of Laura Strope, Andrew has found another precedent: Bryan Nash, another student in Professor Black's seminar (with an unfortunate tendency to oversleep), was rushing to class with his paper at 11:45 A.M. As he approached the classroom building, he saw Professor Black walking across campus with Laura Strope and another student from the class; they were discussing Home State University's upcoming football game. Bryan handed his paper to Professor Black, and his grade was not penalized. How would the two sides interpret the precedents, and how would you rule?

9. Travis Carter has been convicted of breaking or entering. To be guilty of breaking or entering, four things must be established: first, that the defendant either broke into or entered the building; second, that what he broke into or entered was indeed a building; third, that the defendant did not have permission to enter the building; and fourth, that the defendant broke into or entered with the intention of committing a felony. In his trial, there was evidence that Carter had slipped into a building site late at night, with the intention of stealing plumbing materials. The jury found that he had intended to steal building materials, that he did not have the permission of the owner to be on the property, and that he was indeed inside the building that was under construction. The judge advised the jury that although the building Carter entered was still under construction, it nonetheless counted as a building. (The framing of the building was complete, and the walls were up along with the overhead beams, but there was no roof on the building at the time Carter entered; instead, the site was protected from the elements by heavy plastic sheeting.) However, Carter's attorney is appealing the breaking or entering conviction on the grounds that the judge's instruction was mistaken, and that what Carter entered was not in fact a building, but only a building site; and so one of the necessary conditions for breaking or entering was not met, and that Carter's conviction must therefore be overturned. (Carter could then be tried for illegal trespass, and perhaps theft; but not for breaking or entering.)

When Carter's case comes before the court of appeals, Carter's attorney argues that there is a strong precedent for not counting the area Carter entered as a building. The appeals court had ruled, in the previous year, on a case in which Howard Alston had been convicted of breaking or entering into a camp house (used during hunting season by a group of hunters) that had a floor and four rough walls, but was covered by a heavy tarpaulin rather than a permanent roof. In the *Alston* case, the appeals court reversed Alston's conviction, ruling that the camp house was really a glorified tent, rather than a real building.

How could Carter's attorney interpret the precedent to make the governing principle also apply to Carter's case? The district attorney, who is the prosecuting attorney in the *Carter* case, argues that the *Alston* precedent does *not* apply to the *Carter* case. How would that argument go? And again, how would you rule?

10. In a variation on case no. 9, above, suppose that, in *addition* to the defense's citation of the *Alston* case, the district attorney (who is trying to *uphold* the conviction) offers another precedent: the case of Patricia Plummer. Two years earlier, the court of appeals upheld the conviction of Patricia Plummer, who had been convicted of breaking or entering after she was apprehended in a building that was under repair. The building had lost its roof in a tornado, and was covered by a heavy tarpaulin while repairs were made to the rest of the house. The court had ruled that the house was indeed a building, and remained so while repairs were being made.

How would the district attorney interpret the *two* precedents so that the *Plummer* case is analogous to Carter's case, but the *Alston* case is not? How could the defense attorney formulate the principle behind the *Alston* precedent so that the court's ruling in the *Plummer* case is not in conflict with it? Does this additional precedent change your ruling?

Exercise 11-7

How Do You Rule?

You are a member of the Supreme Court of the State of New Virginia; the case before you is an appeal from Arnold Avery. Avery was convicted of second-degree burglary for having broken into a station wagon that was serving as the home of Elizabeth Watson and stealing jewelry, valued at $600, from the front seat. Several facts are not in dispute: Avery admits to having broken into the station wagon during the night with the intention of stealing the jewelry; he admits stealing the jewelry; and it is established that the break-in occurred at night. It is also established that the victim, Watson, was living in the station wagon—it was her sole place of residence—which was parked on a vacant lot, and that she had been living in the vehicle for 6 weeks prior to the crime. She had covered the back three windows of the station wagon with brown paper attached with tape; she kept a container of water and some bread and peanut butter in the back seat, and she slept in a sleeping bag in the back of the station wagon. Avery was tried on charges of second-degree burglary. He was found guilty.

The law of New Virginia regarding burglary is as follows:

> A person is guilty of burglary if he enters a building or occupied structure with purpose to commit a crime therein, unless the premises are at the time open to the public or the actor is licensed or privileged to enter.
>
> Burglary is a felony of the second degree if it is perpetrated in the dwelling of another at night.
>
> "Occupied structure" means any structure, vehicle or place adapted for overnight accommodation of persons, or for carrying on business therein.[17]

The defendant appeals his conviction on the grounds that the station wagon was not an "occupied structure" as defined by the law, and therefore burglary, as defined by New Virginia law, could not have been committed, and his conviction should be overturned. (Since it is agreed that no weapons were employed or threats uttered, and it is also agreed that the defendant did unlawfully take the jewelry from the station wagon, the defendant is willing to offer a plea of guilty to the lesser charge of third-degree felony theft.)

Your Supreme Court colleagues present opposing arguments. Justice Burdette argues,

Two years ago we heard a case quite similar to this. A man—with no permanent address—had pulled his station wagon into a rest area and was sleeping in the back in a sleeping bag. Another man—the defendant, Molina—entered the front door of the station wagon while the victim slept and stole the victim's wallet (containing $600). He was convicted of second-degree burglary; but on appeal, we reversed that verdict, finding that the victim's station wagon did not qualify under New Virginia law as an "occupied structure." It is obvious that the same thing applies here, and we must follow the precedent that we set in the Molina case.

Justice Spahn disagrees,

No, Justice Burdette, this case is only superficially similar to that one; the only similarity is in the station wagons, but there the similarity ends and relevant differences appear. This case is in fact much closer to the precedent we set last year in the Lowery case. As you recall, Lowery had been convicted of burglary for entering the camper of the victim and stealing a television and stereo system while the victim slept in the bunk of the camper. The victim was in the habit of spending six months out of each year parked in the camper at a campsite near the ocean. We ruled in that case that the camper certainly was a "vehicle or place adapted for overnight accommodation of persons," and thus was an "occupied structure" under New Virginia burglary law, and thus was protected by the laws pertaining to burglary. So we upheld the conviction of the defendant, Lowery, for second-degree burglary.

Justice Burdette:

But surely you are not comparing that camper—with its fold-down bunk and its sink and refrigerator and television set—to the station wagon in which this unfortunate woman was sleeping! She was merely sleeping in her car; it happens that she had been sleeping in her car for a longer time than had the victim in the Molina case; but that doesn't change anything. That doesn't transform her station wagon into a "structure, vehicle or place adapted for overnight accommodation of persons." It may have been used for that, but it was not adapted to that purpose, and thus is not an "occupied structure" under the law.

Justice Spahn:

Justice Burdette, that is unfair. It is not just that the victim was sleeping in the station wagon; rather, it was certainly an occupied structure, that had indeed been adapted for overnight accommodation of persons. Not very elegantly adapted, that's true; the victim could not afford a fold-down bunk and a television set. But she had made the most of what she had. She taped up window coverings, she supplied herself with a water bottle, and she made her home as comfortable as possible for overnight accommodation. The fact that she couldn't afford lace curtains and a television set and a refrigerator should not deprive her of her right of protection of her home under the New Virginia burglary laws.

Which is the appropriate precedent for this case? That is, which analogy is correct? In short, Your Honor, do you vote with Justice Burdette to overturn the burglary conviction, or do you side with Justice Spahn in upholding the conviction?

Exercise 11-8

In 1992, the Supreme Court of the United States ruled on the case of *Hudson v. McMillian* (No. 90-6531, decided February 25, 1992). The facts of the case were not in dispute, and Justice O'Connor (writing for the majority) described the situation in this way:

At the time of the incident that is the subject of this suit, petitioner Keith Hudson was an inmate at the state penitentiary in Angola, Louisiana. Respondents Jack McMillian, Marvin Woods, and Arthur Mezo served as corrections security officers at the Angola facility. During the early morning hours of October 30, 1983, Husdon and McMillian argued. Assisted by Woods, McMillian then placed Hudson in handcuffs and shackles, took the prisoner out of his cell, and walked him toward the penitentiary's "administrative lockdown" area. Hudson testified that, on the way there, McMillian punched Hudson in the mouth, eyes, chest, and stomach while Woods held the inmate in place and kicked and punched him from behind. He further testified that Mezo, the supervisor on duty, watched the beating but merely told the officers "not to have too much fun." As a result of this episode, Hudson suffered minor bruises and swelling of his face, mouth, and lip. The blows also loosened Hudson's teeth and cracked his partial dental plate, rendering it unusable for several months.

Justice O'Connor (writing for the majority of the Court) argued that this was clearly a case in which force was not being applied to maintain order, but was instead a case of "maliciously and sadistically" causing harm: "an unnecessary and wanton infliction of pain" that is in violation of the Eighth Amendment forbidding cruel and unusual punishment. The beating suffered by the prisoner Hudson caused no major or permanent injury, but was nonetheless a violation of the right of all U.S. citizens (guaranteed by the Eighth Amendment to the Constitution) to be free from cruel and unusual punishment.

In support of the majority opinion, Justice Blackmun stated the principle quite forcefully:

> The Court today appropriately puts to rest a seriously misguided view that pain inflicted by an excessive use of force is actionable under the Eighth Amendment only when coupled with "significant injury," *e.g.*, injury that requires medical attention or leaves permanent marks. Indeed, were we to hold to the contrary, we might place various kinds of state-sponsored torture and abuse—of the kind ingeniously designed to cause pain but without a telltale "significant injury"—entirely beyond the pale of the Constitution. In other words, the constitutional prohibition of "cruel and unusual punishments" then might not constrain prison officials from lashing prisoners with leather straps, whipping them with rubber hoses, beating them with naked fists, shocking them with electric currents, asphyxiating them short of death, intentionally exposing them to undue heat or cold, or forcibly injecting them with psychosis-inducing drugs. These techniques, commonly thought to be practiced only outside this Nation's borders, are hardly unknown within this Nation's prisons.

Justices Thomas and Scalia dissented from this judgment, claiming that such beatings were not in violation of the Eighth Amendment against cruel and unusual punishment. They argued that since this was a case in which the prisoner suffered no permanent injury, the case was analogous to earlier cases in which the Supreme Court had ruled that prisoners' rights were *not* violated: specifically, cases in which prisoners argued (unsuccessfully) that since they were being given unappetizing food, they were being subjected to cruel and unusual punishment. Thomas and Scalia argue that the beating of Hudson (since it involves no permanent injury, but is merely unpleasant) should be regarded as analogous to being served unappetizing food. And since the Court had in the past ruled that giving prisoners unappetizing food is not cruel and unusual punishment, therefore beating them (without inflicting permanent injury) is likewise not cruel and unusual punishment.

How would you evaluate the analogy given by Thomas and Scalia? Is it legitimate, or is it fallacious?

Exercise 11-9

How Do You Rule?

Anderson Jack and George Louie Charlie are members of the Tsartlip Band of Coast Salish Indians of British Columbia. They shot and killed a deer for use in a religious ceremony (the ceremony involved burning the type of food eaten by one of their ancestors, to satisfy the ancestor's spirit). Since the deer was killed out of season (in violation of the Wildlife Act) they were arrested and tried. During their trial they admitted killing the deer, but argued that they should not be prosecuted since that would be an interference with their right to the free practice of their religion. They were convicted, and they appealed their conviction to the British Columbia Court of Appeal ([1982] 5 W.W.R. 193). The court of appeal upheld the conviction, and the opinion was written by Mr. Justice Craig, who argued as follows, using an analogy:

> In this case, I am concerned entirely with a religious practice. Much argument was directed to the question of "freedom of religion," which phrase I think would be better expressed as "liberty of conscience." There can be no question as to the existence of that liberty; but when it comes to the practices which flow from a religious belief, that is, conduct, the State has a legitimate interest in restricting them, should it be necessary to do so, in the interest of public order and decency. To take an extreme example, an old-fashioned Aztec in this country could believe as he wished, but when he practiced his rite of human

sacrifice he would have to answer for it at the Assizes [courts]. It is safe to say, I think, that generally speaking a practice arising from a sincerely held religious belief may be restrained if it is a breach of the peace, or interferes with public or private rights or otherwise amounts to an illegal act.

Do you agree with Mr. Justice Craig's analogy? And do you dismiss the appeal, and let the conviction stand, or would you grant the appeal and overturn the conviction?

Mr. Justice Hutcheon dissented, and voted in favor of allowing the appeal and reversing the conviction. He argued,

> The ritual [for which the defendants killed the deer] is not harmful to society, is not opposed to the common good and is not in violation of the rights of any other individual. I have concluded that they were not guilty of an offence and that this appeal should be allowed. The law is aimed at wildlife conservation. There is no suggestion that the loss of one deer for the purpose of the ritual would impair the legislative purpose.

Mr. Justice Hutcheon is attempting to counter the argument of Mr. Justice Craig. Is this an effective counterargument? That is, consider Mr. Justice Hutcheon's argument as an attack on Mr. Justice Craig's *analogy* between forbidding the Coast Salish Indians from hunting deer out of season and forbidding the Aztec ritual of human sacrifice: Mr. Justice Hutcheon claims the two cases are not really analogous. Fill in the details of Mr. Justice Hutcheson's argument (in particular, describe how Mr. Justice Hutcheon interprets the *principle* behind Mr. Justice Craig's Aztec analogy, and explain how he would argue that the principle does *not* apply to the case of Jack and Charlie).

The case was appealed to the Supreme Court of Canada ([1985] 2 S.C.R. 332). The Supreme Court rejected the appeal, ruling that the killing of the deer was not part of the ritual (the ritual involved burning the meat, not killing the deer), thus freedom of religious practice was not an issue. Suppose that the Supreme Court had offered this analogy:

> The defendants were not convicted because of their practice of a religious ritual. The ritual involved burning meat, and there is no law against that. Instead, the defendants were convicted for killing a deer out of season. It happens they wanted the deer for purposes of a religious ritual, but that is irrelevant. After all, suppose my religion involves a ritual of putting money in a collection plate, and I lack the money for the ritual. If I steal the money, and then use the money in the ritual, I can't claim that my theft should not be punished because it is part of a religious ritual. Putting the money in the plate is part of the ritual, but obtaining the money (by theft or otherwise) is not. Likewise, the defendants have every right to practice their ritual of burning meat; but they do not have a right to violate the Conservation Act to get the meat. Getting the meat is no part of the ritual, just as getting the money to put in the plate is no part of my ritual, and neither of us can maintain that our illegal acts are protected as religious practices. Would that be a good argument by analogy? Why or why not?

Suppose that the ritual were more elaborate: It requires not only burning the meat, but also hunting and killing the sacrificial deer on a specific day (a day that is not within the hunting season). Would that affect your ruling? Under those circumstances, would you uphold or overturn the conviction?

Exercise 11-10

How Do You Rule?

Frank Dallas and Walt Murphy are admitted drug smugglers who use a small freighter, the *Seasprite*, to haul marijuana from South America to drop off points in international waters off the coast of Alaska. They travel up the coast of Canada, but they make it a point to stay in international waters so they cannot be stopped by the Canadian authorities. On one of their trips, they encounter problems off the Canadian coast: the engine is overheating, their navigation devices are not working, and the weather is going from bad to worse. As the storm worsens, they fear that the ship will be sunk and all hands lost, so they head for a small bay along the British

Columbia coast. They make it into the bay, but the storm is severe and their depthfinder is broken, and so they run aground near the shore. As the tide goes out, the grounded ship begins to list badly to one side. The captain, fearing that the ship will capsize, orders the crew to unload all the cargo onto the shore. They do so, and soon about 30 tons of marijuana are sitting on the shore, covered with tarps. At that point, police officers enter the bay in a police boat, and apprehend Dallas and Murphy and their crew. Dallas and Murphy are charged with importing marijuana into Canada, and with possession of marijuana with the intent of trafficking.

Dallas and Murphy go to trial, and are convicted. They appeal their case, arguing that they had no intent of smuggling marijuana into Canada or of selling marijuana in Canada. Instead, they came into Canada because their lives were in danger on the high sea, and the storm compelled them to seek safety.

Justice Carpenter argues that the conviction should be upheld: Dallas and Murphy may have been forced ashore by the storm, but they still smuggled an illegal substance into Canada, and they possessed the drugs with intent to sell them, since they were obviously not holding 30 tons of marijuana for their own personal use.

Justice Miller disagrees. She argues that the convictions should be overturned. They may have intended to traffic in marijuana, but they intended to do so on the open seas, not in Canada; and it is not a violation of Canadian law to traffic in marijuana on the open seas, any more than it violates Canadian law to traffic in marijuana in Sweden. And they certainly were not smuggling drugs into Canada. Look, suppose they had been hauling a load of tractors, which they had planned to unload in Alaska. And suppose they were forced ashore by the storm, and forced to unload their cargo on the Canadian coast. Surely no one would accuse these shipwrecked sailors of smuggling tractors into Canada. In this case, the cargo was marijuana rather than tractors, but the principle remains the same. Don't misunderstand: I think Dallas and Murphy are vile and despicable, but vile and despicable as they are, they did not violate Canadian law.

So how do you rule? Would you vote with Miller to overturn the convictions, or with Carpenter to uphold the convictions? Do you agree with Justice Miller's analogy? Why or why not?[18]

✔●⌐**Study** and **Review** on **mythinkinglab.com**

REVIEW QUESTIONS

1. What is a figurative analogy?
2. What does a good deductive argument by analogy prove?
3. There are basically two different ways of opposing a deductive argument by analogy; describe both.
4. What is the fallacy of analogical literalism?
5. Give an example of an inductive argument by analogy.

NOTES

[1]   F. Lee Bailey and Harvey Aronson, *The Defense Never Rests* (New York: Stein and Day, 1971), p. 90.

[2]   "The 'Devastating' Decision," *New York Review of Books*, February 25, 2010.

[3]   Irwin Smallwood column, *Greensboro News & Record*, Sunday, July 20, 1986.

[4]   *National Geographic*, July 1982.

[5]   Interview of Country Joe McDonald, *Newsweek*, November 28, 1983, p. 76.

[6]   This example was adapted from Brendan Minogue, *Bioethics: A Committee Approach* (Sudbury, MA: Jones and Bartlett, 1996), pp. 335–336.

[7]   Judith Jarvis Thomson, "A Defense of Abortion," *Philosophy and Public Affairs*, Vol. 1, no. 1 (Fall 1971). Copyright ©1971, by Princeton University Press. Excerpt, pp. 48–49, reprinted with permission of Princeton University Press.

[8]   John Martin Fischer, "Abortion and Self-Determination," *Social Philosophy*, Vol. 22, no. 2 (Fall 1991), p. 6.

[9]   Ibid, p. 7.

[10]   McCleskey's lawyers relied on an important and extensive study that was reported in David C. Baldus, George Woodworth, and Charles A. Pulaski, Jr., *Equal Justice and the Death Penalty: A Legal and Empirical Analysis* (Boston, MA: Northeastern University Press, 1990).

[11] Jeffrey Abramson, *We, the Jury* (New York: Basic Books, 1994), pp. 233–235. Copyright ©1994 by Basic Books. Epilogue to the paperback edition Copyright ©1995 by Basic Books. Reprinted by permission of Jeffrey Abramson, a division of HarperCollins Publishers, Inc.

[12] *Greensboro Daily News,* July 18, 1982.

[13] Irwin Smallwood, *Greensboro Daily News & Record,* September 6, 1987.

[14] Reported by Brian E. Albrecht, *Cleveland Plain Dealer,* December 1996.

[15] Reprinted by permission of Tim Giago and *Indian Country Today.*

[16] Lon L. Fuller, "The Case of the Speluncean Explorers," *Harvard Law Review,* Vol. 62, no. 4 (1949), pp. 616–623.

[17] The "Law of New Virginia" is adapted from the 1985 *Model Penal Code and Commentaries,* by The American Law Institute.

[18] This case was inspired by the case of *Perka v. Regina,* which was examined by the Supreme Court of Canada in 1984 (2 S.C.R. 232). I discovered the case in an excellent book by Jerome E. Beckenback: *Canadian Cases in the Philosophy of Law,* 3rd ed. Though inspired by an actual case, I have made substantial changes in the case (including the invention of a fictional precedent and fictional arguments by fictional justices), so the resulting example is pure fiction.

INTERNET RESOURCES

An article by Grant LaMond, "Precedent and Analogy in Legal Reasoning," can be found online in the excellent *Stanford Encyclopedia of Philosophy* (an invaluable resource for almost any topic in philosophy); go to *Plato.stanford.edu.*

ADDITIONAL READING

For an excellent discussion of analogies, especially analogical reasoning in the courts, see Martin P. Golding, *Legal Reasoning* (New York: Alfred A. Knopf, 1984), especially Chapter 3.

Thinking Like a Lawyer, by Kenneth J. Vandevelde (Boulder, CO: Westview Press, 1996), is a very entertaining and readable discussion of analogy in law. It's not easy reading, but it is very clear, uses a minimum of jargon, and offers wonderful examples.

The classic and still fascinating study of analogy in legal reasoning is by Eugene. H. Levy: *An Introduction to Legal Reasoning* (Chicago, IL: University of Chicago Press, 1948).

An article by Thomas J. McKay, "Analogy and Argument," in *Teaching Philosophy,* Vol. 20, no. 1. (March 1997), pp. 49–60, presents an interesting analysis of analogies that is somewhat different from the model presented here. McKay analyzes arguments by analogy in a way that is very similar to the analysis of deductive arguments by analogy presented in this chapter; however, he attempts to treat all uses of analogy as fitting under that analysis, and makes no distinction among deductive, inductive, and figurative analogies. You might find it interesting to read McKay's article, and then make your own critical decision about what model works best: McKay's account, the model presented in this chapter, or some new model of your own contrivance.

Bruce N. Waller, "Classifying and Analyzing Analogies," *Informal Logic,* Vol. 21, no. 3 (2001), pp. 199–218, develops the distinctions among types of analogies in more depth.

There are two interesting articles in *Reasoning in Ethics and Law: The Role of Theory, Principles and Facts,* edited by Albert W. Musschenga and Wim J. van der Steen (Aldershot, Hampshire, UK: Ashgate, 1999): "The Reconstruction of Legal Analogy-Argumentation," by Harm Kloosterhuis, pp. 89–106; and "Set a Sprat to Catch a Whale: The Structure, Strength and Function of Analogical Inferences," by Henri Wijsbek, pp. 63–88.

Cass R. Sunstein, *Legal Reasoning and Political Conflict* (Oxford: Oxford University Press, 1996), is an excellent study of legal reasoning, with special emphasis on the use of reasoning from precedents and reasoning by analogy.

▨●▭ Read the Document on mythinkinglab.com

David Abel, "Peek Performance." This argument by analogy deals with a case of student cheating: Is the analogy a good one, or is it misleading?

Denis Diderot, *Conversation with Maréchale de.* This dialogue by an eighteenth-century French philosopher and essayist, Diderot, is an elaborate argument by analogy, dealing with the question of whether a just God would punish those who do not believe in God.

U.S. Supreme Court, *Griffin v. Illinois,* 351 U.S. 12, 19 (1956). In order for a convicted criminal to obtain an appeals court review of his or her case, that person must provide a transcript of the original trial. The transcript is often rather expensive, and thus poor people often have no means of obtaining a transcript, and so are effectively excluded from appealing their convictions. In this case, Griffin—who was convicted of armed robbery—wished to appeal his case on grounds of error, but could not afford a transcript; he claimed that this was a violation of the Due Process and Equal Protections clauses of the Fourteenth Amendment (because it deprived poor people of a right to appeal that wealthier people enjoyed). The Court ruled in favor of Griffin, requiring that Illinois provide a trial transcript for persons wishing to appeal who could not pay for a transcript. In the argument for that conclusion, an argument by analogy plays a key part.

Jack and Charlie v. The Queen [1985] 2 S.C.R. 332. An interesting Canadian case in which the defendants acknowledge killing a deer out of season, but argue that it is required for a religious ritual of the Coast Salish people. The Court examines and critiques several analogies in the course of its arguments.

M. L. B., Petitioner, v. S. L. J., 519 U.S. 102 (1996). In this case, a Mississippi Chancery Court declared M.L.B. an unfit mother for her two children, terminated all her parental rights toward the two children, and granted full custody of the two children to their biological father and his new wife. M.L.B. wished to appeal this ruling, but lacked the necessary funds (approximately $2,500) for the appeal. She argued that the state of Mississippi should provide funds for the appeal, just as it would fund a criminal appeal for someone without the means to pay. The state of Mississippi refused to fund the appeal, arguing that it had no obligation to fund such an appeal (since this was not a criminal case). The Supreme Court ruled in favor of M.L.B., stating that the state was required to pay the necessary costs to make it possible for M.L.B. to appeal; Justice Ginsburg's argument for that conclusion relied heavily on an interesting analogical argument.

12

❖ ❖ ❖

Some Distinctive Arguments and Potential Pitfalls: Slippery Slope, Dilemma, and Golden Mean Arguments

((•─Listen to the Chapter Audio on mythinkinglab.com

This chapter deals with several types of argument that pose special dangers of deception. They are not always fallacious—slippery slope and dilemma arguments can be quite legitimate—but they all have insidiously fallacious forms, present special challenges, and require special attention.

SLIPPERY SLOPE

You encounter slippery slope arguments everywhere: in the courtroom, in political debate, in bioethics, in questions of social policy. Sometimes they are legitimate arguments; often they are not.

As noted in the previous chapter, a *slippery slope* argument basically claims that an innocent-looking step should not be taken (or an innocent-looking policy should not be adopted) because it will lead to a bad result. The first step down the slope may be tempting; but do not take it, because once you start down that slope, it will be difficult or impossible to stop, and disaster awaits at the bottom. The argument goes by several common names. It is sometimes called the *wedge* argument: Once the thin entering wedge slips under the bark and into the wood, it can be driven ever deeper into the solid log, until what had seemed a small break finally results in splitting the log into pieces. Occasionally people speak of the *domino* argument: Push down one domino and it starts a long sequence. Lawyers often call it the "parade of horribles" argument. Politicians seem to favor "the camel's nose is in the tent" argument; I'm not quite sure how that name started, but the idea seems to be that once the camel gets its nose in the tent, it is difficult to keep the rest of the camel outside.

If good and substantial reasons are given for supposing that the innocent first step really will lead to bad consequences, then the slippery slope argument is *legitimate*. The reasons given need not be conclusive; so long as some substantive reasons are given, no slippery slope *fallacy* is involved. The slippery slope *fallacy* is committed when one claims that an innocent-looking first step will lead to bad consequences, *without* giving *reasons*. If we honor the requests by competent adults suffering from a fatal disease and intervene to give them the requested quick and painless death, then it will lead to the forced involuntary killing of the elderly and the disabled and ultimately anyone deemed "undesirable" or burdensome. If you try a puff of marijuana, you will move on to cocaine and will wind up a hopeless, homeless, and hardened heroin addict. Notice that a *legitimate* slippery slope argument requires more than just a series of steps leading to a disastrous conclusion; there must be *reasons* for why those steps are likely to occur.

You may hear such arguments in court. For example, the prosecuting attorney may encourage you (the jury) to be stern, severe, and courageous and not to shrink from your duty of demanding severe punishment for this guilty defendant; otherwise, this crime will be unpunished, criminals will run amok, and the social fabric of society will be threatened. Or as the great hero of John Mortimer's novels—the defending barrister, Rumpole of the Bailey—once described the opening speech of the prosecution:

> I sat containing myself as best I could whilst that aristocratic voice opened the case to the jury as though, if Dobbs were not convicted, there would be a total breakdown of law and order, rioting in the streets and human sacrifices in the crypt of St. Paul's Cathedral.[1]

Separating Slippery Slopes from Straw Men

In the previous chapter, it was noted that deductive arguments by analogy often sound like slippery slopes: If we ban burning the American flag in protest, then must we also ban cursing the American flag in protest? Would we then ban burning copies of the U.S. Constitution or the Declaration of Independence in protest? Where would this ban on political protest lead? That sounds like a slippery slope argument: If you start with a ban on burning the American flag, ultimately you will wind up with a ban on all political protest. But rather than a slippery slope argument, it is probably more plausible to interpret this as an *analogy*. Banning protestors from burning the American flag is like banning protestors from other forms of political protest; we think it would be wrong to limit political protest in those ways, so consistency requires that we allow flag burning as well, even if most people are deeply disturbed by it.

Slippery slope arguments are also easily confused with *strawman* arguments. Suppose I say that we should *ban* physician-assisted suicide (euthanasia) because it would involve having doctors choose who will live and who will die, and would give doctors the right to kill any patient the doctor judges *unfit* or as having a "poor quality of life." That is a *strawman* argument. Those who favor physician-assisted suicide want very tight restrictions on when it would be allowed, and they would absolutely require that *only* those who have *freely chosen* to end their own lives (because they are suffering from a debilitating disease) would be candidates for physician-assisted suicide. But if I argue instead that while the initial plan is to allow physician-assisted suicide only for those who freely and competently choose it, but that once that is in place it will gradually *lead* to the killing of unconscious patients, and then to all patients with terminal diseases (whether they request it or not) and *ultimately* to the killing of anyone society judges unfit, then *that* is a slippery slope argument. In the slippery slope argument, I am *not* attributing that extreme position to those who favor physician-assisted suicide (indeed, I may believe that they would deplore an outcome in which the "unfit" are involuntarily killed). Rather, I am claiming that the policy they are advocating would *lead* to this result, *not* (as in straw man) that this eventual result is one they favor. If I claim that gun control advocates want to ban all private ownership of firearms, that is a strawman argument; if I claim instead that a ban on the private ownership of automatic rifles and machine guns would *lead* to a total ban on the private ownership of firearms, that is a slippery slope argument.

The Slippery Slope Fallacy

Like many argument tricks, slippery slope fallacies are easy to spot once you know what to look for. Slippery slope fallacies focus attention on some gruesome end result and fail to show that such a horrible result will actually follow. We are mesmerized by the terrors at the bottom of the slope and forget to ask whether the slope is in fact that slippery.

Examples are legion. When fluoride was added to the public water supply, the writer David Reuben argued that this could lead to nutritional supplements in our water, and then tranquilizers to keep citizens from raising disturbances, and ultimately to birth-control chemicals directed toward neighborhoods with large populations of "undesirables."

Now certainly the thought of placing massive doses of tranquilizers in the public water supply to control the population and birth-control chemicals to reduce the birth rate of ethnic groups is morally repulsive. It would be a horrible violation of our autonomy, our dignity, and our basic rights as citizens—indeed, a violation of our basic rights as autonomous persons. But before we become obsessed with the genuine horror of such programs, we should stop and notice that there is not the ghost of a reason for supposing that such dreadful results would follow from placing fluoride in the public water system. There is no reason given for supposing that adding fluoride will lead to adding vitamins, much less that adding fluoride will lead all the way down to adding tranquilizers and birth-control chemicals. The slide from fluoride to tranquilizers and birth-control chemicals descends down an implausible and fallacious slippery slope.

Notice that the above slippery slope fallacy *does* give *steps*. It's still a *fallacy*, because it gives no *reasons* why one step leads to another. And providing reasons for *some* steps is not enough; there must be a reason for *each* step down the slope (though, of course, to further complicate things, the reasons for some of the steps *might* be considered so obvious that they need not be stated).

Genuine Slippery Slopes

Not all slippery slope arguments commit the slippery slope *fallacy*. There *are* some dangerous slippery slopes, and it is well to avoid them. Current acts often *do* have further

---

A Steep, Slippery Slope

A dramatic example of a slippery slope fallacy occurred in an 1847 murder trial in New York. The climax of the prosecutor's final speech to the jury was as follows:

> If mawkish sympathy enters the jurybox—if ever mawkish sympathy takes control of the jurybox, if men surrender their feelings as men, then there is but one other step to take. Mawkish sympathy has then but to ascend to the judiciary, which, thank God, it has not yet reached! Then strike the scales away from the hands of Justice, pull the bandage away from one eye and place it on both, and let the community know that while it is true that juries

> "When human life is in debate
> Can ne'er too long deliberate"
> yet, that if they deliberate to such an extent as to give immunity to crime, by acquittal, when circumstances are damning, there will come into the world, and be inaugurated, that millennial triumph of the powers of darkness of which we all have read in Holy Writ.[2]

Now *that* is really sliding down the slope: If the jury fails to convict, then they will usher in the "millennial triumph of the powers of darkness"; in other words, failure to convict will result in a millennium of Satanic rule.

effects that warrant examination. Suppose we are considering whether to allow a manufacturer of hydraulic fluid to dump millions of gallons of PCB-contaminated wastes into a small stream. Someone who opposes such dumping might argue that (*because* of the direction of water flow and the cumulative effects of contaminants on animals higher in the food chain) the PCBs will run from that stream into a downstream river, will accumulate in fish, will pollute our drinking water with a known cancer-causing agent, and will eventually result in pollution of rivers, the killing of wildlife, and a severe hazard to humans who use the water downstream. That argument points out further undesirable effects that will result from allowing the proposed PCB dumping, but certainly the argument does *not* commit the slippery slope fallacy. The arguer has given good *reasons* to believe that undesirable results will follow from this action; thus that argument is not a slippery slope fallacy. Some actions *do* have bad effects, and we should be wary of them. And if one gives *reasons* for why and how a particular action will lead to bad effects, then that is not a slippery slope fallacy. The slippery slope fallacy occurs when one claims that an action will have bad consequences, but fails to give grounds for the claim that such bad consequences will follow. If I assert that you should not smoke marijuana because it will result in heroin addiction, then I have committed the slippery slope fallacy. *But,* if I argue that you should not try heroin (because it is strongly addictive, and small initial amounts can easily lead to an addictive desire for regular and increasing doses, and thus a likely result is the misery of drug addiction), that *slippery slope argument* is *not* a slippery slope *fallacy.*

Someone might argue that initial marijuana use should be avoided, because doing a little marijuana makes it psychologically easier to do more, and once you have crossed the line into *any* sort of illegal drug use, access to harder drugs is likely to be easier; and once you have experimented with mild drugs, the temptation to try other, more powerful drugs becomes stronger. Therefore, in order to avoid the increased likelihood of using harder drugs, you should avoid even the lightest use of marijuana. That may not be a very strong slippery slope argument: The reasons given for thinking that the first innocent step may lead to disaster are hardly conclusive. Still, reasons are given, and those reasons must be considered: It cannot simply be dismissed as a slippery slope *fallacy,* even if one ultimately judges the argument inadequate.

Distinguishing slippery slope *fallacies* from legitimate slippery slope arguments can be tough, and sometimes judgments will differ. When we are evaluating a slippery slope argument, you may decide that the reasons given for some of the steps are so flimsy that they don't really count as reasons (and thus the argument is a slippery slope *fallacy*); whereas I may think those *weak* reasons are still reasons, and so not regard the argument as a slippery slope fallacy (but instead just a very *weak* argument). Or again, the *reasons* for one step may strike you as so *obvious* that they need not be stated, whereas I may think the missing reasons not at all obvious (and thus I count the argument as a slippery slope *fallacy*). So there's often room for disagreement: No one promised critical thinking would be easy or obvious. But the main thing in considering slippery slope arguments *is* clear: Are there good *reasons* to think the slope really is slippery?

By focusing attention on some dreadful eventuality, slippery slope fallacies distract us from what is actually at issue. Certainly it is important to consider all the consequences of our acts and policies, but it is also important to think carefully about what those consequences will be. Do not be stampeded into opposing some act or policy by someone's unsupported assertion of the dire consequences that will follow. Remember: If someone makes a claim, it is up to that individual to give reasons in support of that claim. The burden of proving that terrible consequences will follow rests with the person making that claim. To simply assert that dreadful results will follow, without giving any reasons for that assertion, is to commit the slippery slope fallacy. But don't jump to the other extreme of supposing that all slippery slope arguments are fallacies. There are some genuinely treacherous slippery slopes, and legitimate slippery slope arguments perform the important function of warning us of them. As is generally the case in intelligent critical thinking, there is no cookbook formula for deciding whether a slippery slope argument is or is not fallacious. You must consider whether real reasons are given for thinking that the first step will actually lead down a dangerous slope (*if* there are none, then it is obviously a slippery slope fallacy), and you must evaluate the strength of those reasons.

Exercise 12-1

Look over the following examples and decide which ones are instances of the slippery slope *fallacy* and which ones give well-founded warnings of genuine slippery slope dangers.

1. "[The environmentalists'] real thrust is not clean air, or clean water, or parks, or wildlife but the form of government under which America will live. Look what happened to Germany in the 1930s. The dignity of man was subordinated to the powers of Nazism. The dignity of man was subordinated in Russia. Those are the forces that this thing can evolve into."[3]

2. It is very frustrating when our manufacturers fail to win a share of a foreign market; and when that happens, we are tempted to respond by imposing tariffs on goods from the country where we failed to achieve a decent market share, in an effort to force the other country to open their markets to our goods. In extreme cases, perhaps such punitive tariffs are necessary, but they should be used very rarely, and avoided if at all possible. For what happens if we can't sell our paint in Tangistan, and so decide to slap a punitive tariff on radios imported from Tangistan? That makes the radio manufacturers in Tangistan angry, and they pressure their government to respond with a punitive tariff—and so Tangistan places high tariffs on all the cameras we export to that country. And then our camera manufacturers get angry, and they call for high tariffs against all fruits and vegetables imported from Tangistan. And soon you have the makings of an all-out trade war between the two countries, with all the problems for both manufacturers and consumers that such a trade war causes.

3. We must stop this movement for a moment of silence in public schools. Because once you allow a moment of silence it soon becomes a moment of teachers leading prayers, and before long the schools and the government are supporting a specific religion, and that can soon lead to a government-sponsored religion and to the ban of all religions other than the one favored by the government.

4. Mike Huckabee, the former governor of Arkansas, claimed in his recent book (*A Simple Government*) that research on the comparative effectiveness of various medical treatments (studies to determine which medical treatments are actually effective, which are ineffective, and the degrees and conditions of treatment effectiveness) are "the seeds from which the poisonous tree of death panels will grow."

5. Attorney General Edwin Meese III made the following remarks in a prayer breakfast at the Christian Legal Society, September 29, 1985:

By gradually removing from public education and public discourse all references to traditional religion . . . and by substituting instead the jargon and the ritual and the morality of cult and of self, we run the risk of subordinating all other religions to a new secular religion. . . . In its application, the principle of neutrality towards all religions has often been transformed by some into a hostility toward anything religious. The danger is that religion, which has been such an important force in our country, could lose its social and historical, indeed, its public character.

There are nations, we should remind ourselves, where religion has just this status, where the cause of religion, and its expression, has been reduced to something that people can only do behind locked doors.[4]

6. The following is an argument by a district attorney to an assistant district attorney:

I know you are tempted to tell your witness to lie in order to make his identification of the defendant stronger. None of us doubts that the defendant in this case is really guilty, and we want him to be convicted. But you must not encourage your key witness to perjure himself in order to obtain a conviction. For there is always the chance that the witness's lies will be discovered; and then that witness—in order to avoid perjury charges—will confess that he was coached to lie by the district attorney's office. And if that sort of thing were made public, then juries would stop believing prosecution witnesses, and we would find it almost impossible to convict anyone.

7. *Jury nullification* is the decision by jury members not to convict a defendant who is guilty under the law, because the jury members believe the law is unjust or because the application of the law in this particular case would be wrong. Jury nullification is a very dangerous thing. If jury members can ignore the law in their deliberations, then next they may decide to ignore the law when they are no longer jurors: They may ignore laws against filing fraudulent income tax returns, and they may decide to ignore laws regulating how they dispose of hazardous wastes, and they may even ignore laws forbidding theft and violent assault. And once some people start ignoring laws, others are likely to follow their lead. Then before you know it, we are living in an anarchistic and lawless society, where all laws are ignored and no one is safe in either property or person. So we must stop this jury nullification movement, and avoid the terrible harms to which it may lead.

8. In truth, a few cigarettes are not likely to do you any real harm. But the problem is, after you smoke a few cigarettes, it becomes very appealing to smoke a few more. And before long, you have started smoking as part of a social habit, and then you want cigarettes a bit more often—with your morning coffee, after lunch, while you're driving, a couple in the evening. Soon smoking becomes a deeply ingrained habit, and then it swiftly becomes an addiction: Nicotine, after all, is a powerfully addictive drug. So you wind up with a very expensive smoking habit that makes you smell awful, leaves you more vulnerable to colds and other infections, significantly increases your risk for cancer and strokes and respiratory problems, and eventually puts your children at risk from secondhand smoke. Then you will probably want to quit smoking, and you will find that it's a difficult or impossible job to break the smoking habit and the nicotine addiction. So the best way to avoid those problems is to avoid smoking those first innocent-looking cigarettes.

9. In the following argument, St. John of Chrysostom warns believers of the dangers of laughter:

> To laugh, to speak jocosely, does not seem an acknowledged sin, but it leads to acknowledged sin. Thus laughter often gives birth to foul discourse, and foul discourse to actions still more foul. Often from words and laughter proceed railing and insult; and from railing and insult, blows and wounds, and from blows and wounds, slaughter and murder. If then, thou wouldst take good counsel for thyself, avoid not merely foul words, and foul deeds, or blows, and wounds, and murders, but unseasonable laughter itself.[5]

10. In 1989, the U.S. Supreme Court struck down as unconstitutional state laws that make it a crime to burn the U.S. flag as part of a protest or demonstration. The court ruled that since burning the flag is an expression of political protest, it is protected under the First Amendment guarantees of freedom of speech. Justice William Brennan wrote the majority opinion, and one of his key arguments was the following:

> To conclude that the Government may permit designated symbols [such as the flag] to be used to communicate only a limited set of messages would be to enter territory having no discernible or defensible boundaries. Could the Government, on this theory, prohibit the burning of state flags? Of copies of the Presidential seal? Of the Constitution? In evaluating these choices under the First Amendment, how would we decide which symbols were sufficiently special to warrant this unique status? To do so, we would be forced to consult our own political preferences, and impose them on the citizenry, in the very way that the First Amendment forbids us to do.[6]

11. J. Gay-Williams offers the following slippery slope argument against active euthanasia (against active intervention to purposefully hasten the death of one who is suffering during the course of a terminal disease and voluntarily requests a speedier death). (This is the toughest of the examples, and there is probably room for legitimate disagreement in analyzing it.)

> Finally, euthanasia as a policy is a slippery slope. A person apparently hopelessly ill may be allowed to take his own life. Then he may be permitted to deputize others to do it for him should he no longer be able to act. The judgment of others then becomes the ruling factor. Already at this point euthanasia is not personal and voluntary, for others are acting "on behalf of" the patients as they see fit. This may well incline them to act on behalf of other patients who have not authorized them to exercise their judgment. It is only a short step, then, from voluntary euthanasia (self-inflicted or authorized), to directed euthanasia administered to a patient who has given no authorization, to involuntary

euthanasia conducted as part of a social policy. . . . Embedded in a social policy, it would give society or its representatives the authority to eliminate all those who might be considered too "ill" to function normally any longer. The dangers of euthanasia are too great to all to run the risk of approving it in any form. The first slippery step may well lead to a serious and harmful fall.[7]

12. Critical thinking courses should be banned from universities. For when students take critical thinking, they begin to think more carefully and precisely, and are less easily swayed by emotional appeals. Pretty soon they begin to be less moved by emotions and feelings generally, whether they are dealing with arguments or not. Gradually they become colder and more callous, and all feelings of warmth, kindness, and sympathy begin to dry up, until eventually they turn into cold, calculating, heartless automatons. So unless we want our students turned into callous, pitiless, and loveless machines, we must forbid students to take critical thinking.

13. Childhood obesity is a major health problem in the United States, with the number of obese children increasing, along with increases in childhood diabetes and childhood heart problems. If we really want to tackle the problem of childhood obesity, the best way is to deal with it early, because once children become overweight, then it is easy to get a progression into health-threatening obesity. The overweight child tends to tire more quickly and run slower, and so is not as good at sports; and so the child is often embarrassed when trying to play sports or participate in exercise, and so avoids them; and by avoiding exercise and sports, the child gains more weight and becomes even less likely to be active. And when the child gains weight, he or she may be ridiculed by other children, and become isolated and depressed; and then the child tends to take comfort in food, and the weight continues to increase. Sitting alone in front of the television with a bag of potato chips or a box of cookies—rather than running and playing with friends—is the path to serious weight and health problems. So if we want to deal effectively with the problem of childhood obesity, we should make serious efforts to prevent the earliest stages of excessive weight gain in children.

14. Some people want to be allowed to go to Canada and buy prescription drugs from Canadian pharmacies, at significantly lower prices than are charged for the same drugs in the United States. That doesn't sound so bad, really; but the problem is, where would it stop? If we allow people to buy drugs from Canada, then next they'll want to buy drugs from other countries, as well. And then they'll want to buy drugs from anyone they like, without any regulations at all: people will be mixing up batches of drugs in their basements, and selling them on street corners. But that would be a tragedy, resulting in many deaths and injuries from drugs that are dangerous and useless. If we don't want that kind of terrible abuse, we have to stop those people who are wanting to buy drugs from Canadian pharmacies.

Exercise 12-2

Slippery slope arguments and strawman arguments often sound very similar. The slippery slope argument claims that an initial first step is not so bad, but that it will *lead* to eventual disaster—a disastrous outcome which no one really wants. *Strawman* arguments claim that a policy or position *is* terrible, and that the policy *is* what someone wants (when in fact no one actually favors that policy: the strawman fallacy *distorts* or *misrepresents* the opposing view). For the following arguments, tell which ones are *slippery slopes* and which ones are *straw men*.

1. Animal rights advocates think that all life is equal, and that all life is equally sacred, so we shouldn't experiment on animals or kill animals for furs. But their position is ridiculous: Potatoes are alive, and the animal rights advocates dig them up and eat them; and alfalfa sprouts are living things, but the animal rights people kill and eat them; and bacteria are alive, but the animal rights supporters take medicine to kill bacteria, and use disinfectants to kill disease-spreading bacteria. So obviously, on closer examination, the animal rights view falls apart.

2. Advocates of animal rights oppose killing animals for food, and for fur coats; and they push for alternatives to animal testing in experiments. Okay, it may not seem so bad to ban fur coats, and there are some good alternatives to animal testing for drugs, and I can even imagine becoming a vegetarian. The problem is that once you let these animal rights folks get their foot in the door, they won't stop there. The next thing you know they will forbid the killing of insects, and so we won't be able to control mosquitoes and flies and fleas; and then they will forbid the killing of bacteria, and

so if you get a bacterial infection, you won't be allowed to take an antibiotic. And finally, they will declare that all plant life has to be protected, and so you won't be able to eat any crop that requires killing the plant—such as potatoes or carrots or peanuts. Pretty soon we'll all be living on apples and peaches—if we're lucky, and the insects don't destroy the peach and apple trees.

3. It's not that regulation of the oil companies is so bad in itself: they are making enormous profits right now, and just placing some restrictions on their profits might be okay. But what would follow? Once the oil company profits are regulated, the government will start regulating the profits of other companies: and before you know it, you'll have a federal inspector capping the profit you can make on your hot dog stand, and some government bureaucrat capping the profit you can make on your soybean crop or in your jewelry store. And once profits are regulated, more regulation will follow—restrictions on what you can sell, and when, and to whom; and you start down that road, you wind up doing away with our free enterprise system.

4. Some people complain about the profits being raked in by the major oil companies: Exxon made a profit of 10 billion dollars in the last quarter, and Chevron made 4 billion. They claim that the oil companies are making enormous and unfair profits, while we consumers are paying painfully high prices for gasoline. But no one should take their criticisms seriously. Apparently they believe that people in the oil industry should work for free, and that investors in Exxon and Chevron have no right to make a profit on their investment. They think that all profits are wrong, and that no company should ever make a profit for its work. They apparently want to abolish capitalism altogether, and do away with our free enterprise system.

5. "Medical use of marijuana." Doesn't sound so bad, does it? Folks who are having cancer treatments, maybe marijuana could relieve some of the pain and the nausea: Who would want to deny such comforts to cancer patients? But let me tell you about the *real* agenda of the medical marijuana advocates. They want to make marijuana freely available to anyone who wants it, sick or not, without restriction: to sick people, sure; but also to healthy people, and even to children, without any regulation. And marijuana is just part of it. They favor a policy of "anything goes" on drugs: they want not only marijuana, but also cocaine and heroin and meth to be easily available to *anyone* who wants to buy it, with no age restrictions. If you think it's a good idea to have cocaine and heroin pushers selling drugs to elementary school children, then you will embrace the position of those people who are in favor of medical marijuana.

6. There are those who want to allow the medicinal use of marijuana, especially for the relief of pain for those undergoing cancer treatments. It sounds like a good idea at first, but consider the longer view: If a cancer patient is allowed to use marijuana, then that patient's legal marijuana will be readily available to the family members and friends of the patient; and then cancer patients, in order to raise some extra money for their expensive treatments, will begin to sell the marijuana to nonpatients. And once they start to sell marijuana, it's a very easy step to selling other drugs like cocaine and heroin. So if we want to avoid a major expansion of the market in illegal drugs, we must not allow the medicinal use of marijuana.

DILEMMAS, FALSE AND TRUE

After all the witnesses have been called, and all the evidence has been presented, and the district attorney and the defense attorney have made their closing arguments—and just before the jury retires to consider its verdict—the judge will give instructions to the jury. Among those instructions might be something like the following:

> Ladies and Gentlemen of the Jury, in order to return a verdict of guilty, you must be certain beyond a reasonable doubt that the defendant really is guilty. Each of you must decide that question: Every individual jury member must examine the evidence, consider the testimony, and each of you must conclude—beyond a reasonable doubt—that the defendant is guilty; or you must vote not guilty. Either you are certain beyond a reasonable doubt that the defendant is guilty, or you must return a verdict of not guilty.

The judge has posed a *dilemma* for the jury: You must choose among these limited alternatives; these are the *only* alternatives available. Is it a true dilemma or a false dilemma?

Genuine Dilemmas

That depends. *Are* those the only real alternatives? If so, that is a *genuine* dilemma. If other alternatives are available, then it is a *false* dilemma. And in this case, there really are no other possibilities: You must be certain beyond a reasonable doubt that the defendant is guilty, or you must find the defendant not guilty. That is, there are no other possibilities *if* you are honoring the principle of the defendant's presumed innocence, and *if* you are a conscientious juror. And, of course, the judge's instructions are given in that context, with those assumptions. Obviously it is possible for a juror to vote guilty when he is not convinced beyond a reasonable doubt of the defendant's guilt: A juror might vote guilty out of prejudice, or out of contrariness, or arbitrarily (without really considering the evidence and arguments at all). But *if* you are living up to the responsibilities you accepted as a jury member, then you must choose between the alternatives posed by the judge: guilty beyond a reasonable doubt, or not guilty. (Of course there is the possibility that the jury as a whole will not be able to reach a unanimous verdict, and so will return no verdict at all. But that is not really a third alternative, for the dilemma posed by the judge was not to the jury as a whole, but to each individual juror: *Each one* must decide between guilty beyond a reasonable doubt and not guilty.)

False Dilemmas

So there are *genuine* dilemmas; but there are also false dilemmas. A *false* dilemma involves a failure of imagination, a failure to consider one or more genuine possibilities. The defendant is accused of having murdered Lord Rutabaga, and the butler has testified that as he stepped onto the terrace to serve tea, he looked over to the croquet course and saw the defendant shoot Lord Rutabaga and then run away. The barrister for the crown (the prosecuting attorney) argues,

> Either the butler actually saw the defendant kill Lord Rutabaga (as he testified), or the but-ler is telling a particularly vicious lie. But the butler is well-known for his truthfulness: He has been in service for many years without the slightest stain on his integrity, and many witnesses have testified to his deep commitment to truthfulness. Furthermore, the butler has no reason to lie about what he saw: He has no grudge against the defendant, nor does he have anything to hide. So we must accept the butler's truthfulness. It is not reasonable to believe that the butler is lying. And it follows that we must agree that the defendant killed Lord Rutabaga, as charged.

Consider the Verdict

Jim Pickerell / Stock Connection Blue / Alamy

Suppose that one of your fellow jurors is disturbed by this stark choice between guilty beyond a reasonable doubt and not guilty, and he offers the following objection:

> Look, I can't be forced to decide between definitely guilty and not guilty; it's just not that simple. I'm not quite convinced that the defendant is guilty. The evidence presented by the prosecution left a few holes, and I think that the defendant's alibi witness was fairly believable. But still, I think the defendant probably is really guilty as charged; so I don't feel comfortable voting not guilty, either. There's got to be another alternative.

How would you respond?

Pared down to its essentials, the argument goes like this:

> Either the butler saw the defendant kill Lord Rutabaga, or the butler is lying. The butler is not lying. Therefore, the butler saw the defendant kill Lord Rutabaga.

That is certainly a *valid* argument. Either *A* or *B;* not *B;* therefore, *A.* If the premises are true, the conclusion will also be true.

But is it a *sound* argument? That is, *are* the premises all true? Is it true that the only genuine possibilities are that either the butler is lying or the butler actually saw the defendant kill Lord Rutabaga? What other reasonable possibilities come to mind?

Given the notorious unreliability of eyewitnesses, one possibility is that the butler is honestly testifying to what he believes he observed, but his observations were mistaken. Perhaps he saw a man who looked a lot like the defendant kill Lord Rutabaga, but his identification of the defendant as the murderer is an honest misidentification. Maybe there are other possibilities. But if there is just one additional genuine possibility that the argument neglects, then the argument commits the fallacy of false dilemma.

Why Arguments Based on False Dilemmas Sound Plausible.   False dilemma arguments often *sound* very convincing. In the first place, false dilemma arguments are almost always *valid* arguments. In the case above, the conclusion does follow from the premises; the problem is that one of the premises is false: It is not true that either the butler is lying or the butler observed the defendant murder Lord Rutabaga, since there is *another* possibility. And the second reason why false dilemma arguments sound so compelling is that one's attention is usually drawn away to a premise that *is* true. In the argument above, what point does the prosecuting barrister emphasize? *Not* the false dilemma, but instead the second premise: the premise that states that the butler is *not* lying. Very strong reasons are given in support of that premise, and if we are not careful, we shall forget that no reasons have been given why we should believe the crucial dilemma premise.

Figure 12-1   Hagar the Horrible Cartoon
Reprinted with special permission of King Features Syndicate.

Consider the Verdict

Jim Pickerell / Stock Connection Blue / Alamy

The defendant is charged with murder. A shot from a high-powered rifle, which he admits he was holding, passed through two victims, killing both. The defendant admits holding the rifle, but claims he was just showing the gun to his two friends. The prosecuting attorney is cross-examining the defendant:

Q: Who pulled the trigger?
A: Who pulled the trigger? Well . . . I don't know. It went off.

Q: You don't know who pulled the trigger?
A: Well, I don't know how—
Q: Did Marlene pull the trigger?
A: No, sir.
Q: Did Marty pull the trigger?
A: No, sir.
Q: Anyone else in the room?
A: No, sir.
Q: I will ask you again, Mr. Cartwright. It's a very simple question. Please listen to the question: Who pulled the trigger?
A: I presume my hand must have done it.[8]

Has the prosecuting attorney posed a genuine dilemma for the defendant? (Marlene, Marty, or the defendant pulled the trigger; and it wasn't either Marlene or Marty.) Or is this a false dilemma?

Consider another example from outside the courtroom. Money is tight, the university budget has been slashed by the governor, and the president of the university comes before the assembled students with this argument:

> My friends, we are in a terrible situation. Our funds from the state have been severely cut, and we are faced with a terrible choice: We must either close the university library or raise tuition. Now we all agree that the library cannot be closed. The library is the heart and soul of a university, the vital center of our educational and research activities, the link between our university community and the thoughts, ideas, and discoveries of all peoples and all ages. Furthermore, closing the library would mean that we would lose our accreditation, and our professional schools would have to close. So the library must be kept open at all costs. Thus we have no choice: It is with profound regret that I inform you that tuition payments will have to increase.

This argument pulls all the false dilemma tricks. It poses an either–or situation (close the library or raise tuition) and then rejects one of the alternatives, leaving only one possibility. And the result is a *valid* argument. Combined with that validity is a premise that is true and well-supported: Almost the entire argument is devoted to a powerful and convincing case in support of keeping the library open. So between the validity of the argument and the ringing truth of one premise, it is easy to overlook the crucial false dilemma lurking in the first premise: We must either close the library or raise tuition. That, of course, is a *false* dilemma. It requires little imagination to think of some other possibilities, such as cutting the athletic budget, doing an emergency alumni fundraising drive, cutting some administrative positions, or (God forbid) cutting faculty salaries. So this argument is valid, and one important premise is true: But the argument is *unsound* because the dilemma premise is *false*.

False dilemmas sometimes come in the form of false trilemmas, false quadrilemmas, false pentalemmas, and so on. That is, sometimes a false dilemma mentions more

Consider the Verdict

Jim Pickerell / Stock Connection Blue / Alamy

In a breaking or entering case, one juror offers the following argument in favor of a guilty verdict:

> Our deliberations have been going in circles for the last hour. Some jurors have said that they believe the defendant really did go into the vacant house just to get out of the rain, as he claims. Other jurors think his motives were not so innocent, and that he was in fact planning to steal the appliances and light fixtures, as the prosecution asserts. Well, I think this is a simple case: Was the guy in the house rightfully, or was he there illegally? He certainly wasn't there rightfully: He didn't own the house, he wasn't a tenant, and he did not have the owner's permission. Since he wasn't there rightfully, he must have been there illegally. It's simple when you think about it logically: He was there illegally, and that means he is guilty of illegal breaking or entering.

Is the juror right? Is the case that simple?

---

than two options—perhaps it considers a great many options—but still fails to consider *all* the possible options. "Sally must love or hate me or be completely indifferent to me. She doesn't hate me, since she seems to enjoy spending time with me, and she is not completely indifferent to me, since she once sent me flowers. So she must love me." Unfortunately for this lover's argument, Sally has some other possibilities: She may be mildly attracted to me, she may find me pleasant company but think of me only as a friend, she may find me rather distasteful but still regard me as the least distasteful of the people she currently knows, and so on. The fact that three options are considered does not prove that all the possibilities have been exhausted.

Dilemmas in Conditional Form.   Dilemma arguments are typically in either–or form, as in the following example: We must either raise tuition or close the library. But sometimes dilemmas dress up as conditionals, just to keep life interesting: If we don't raise tuition, then we must close the library. That's still the same old false dilemma (if we do not take the alternative of raising tuition, then the only other possibility is closing the library), and changing it to a conditional doesn't make it any less a dilemma or any less false.

Legitimate dilemmas can also be cast as conditionals. Consider this standard either–or dilemma: "Either we must be certain beyond a reasonable doubt that the defendant is guilty, or we should return a verdict of not guilty." That's a legitimate dilemma, and it remains a legitimate dilemma when phrased in conditional form: "If we are not certain beyond a reasonable doubt that the defendant is guilty, then we should return a verdict of not guilty." Those statements are logically equivalent. It's not hard to see that they make the same claim. Suppose I say, "Either you pass the final or you will flunk the course." That means the same as: "If you don't pass the final, you'll flunk the course." The dilemma claims that at least one of the alternatives *must* be true; so *if* the first alternative is *not* the case, then the second *must* be. When the judge tells you "either pay your fine or go to jail," that means that if you do *not* pay your fine (the first alternative is not the case) then the second alternative *must* be so (you must go to jail).

So you should watch for dilemmas—both false and true—in conditional form. "If you don't support this tax levy, then you don't care about better education for our children" (i.e., either you support this tax levy or you don't care about education). "If you support this tax levy, then you don't care about the tax burden on retired homeowners."

"If secondhand smoking does not cause lung cancer, then secondhand smoking is not harmful" (which is equivalent to "either secondhand smoking causes lung cancer or it is not harmful"). "If you don't believe my claim that I saw the Loch Ness Monster, then you must think I'm a liar." "If you don't believe in the Biblical account of Creation, then you are an atheist." It might be easier if dilemmas always came in plain vanilla either–or form, but variety keeps life interesting and critical thinking a challenge.

False Dilemma Combined with StrawMan

One particularly nasty form of the fallacy of false dilemma requires special note. This fallacy is the foul issue of the marriage of false dilemma to strawman. Here is an example:

JACK: I think building the MX missiles is a great idea.
JILL: I really don't think we should build the MX missiles; they are tremendously expensive, and our nuclear arsenal is already massive.
JACK: Oh, I guess you are one of those people who want to do away with all our weapons and not have any military defenses at all.

Well, no; that's not what Jill wants, and it is not what she suggested. Jack has first set up a *false dilemma* (either we build additional MX missiles or we do away with our military completely) and then *distorted* Jill's position (set up a straw man) by suggesting that her view is the *extreme* position that he falsely presents as the only option to the view he favors.
 Consider another example:

> We must not ban the sale of cigarettes in vending machines. Of course some people want to banish all tobacco products, and forbid competent adults from making their own choices about whether or not to smoke. But we should not consent to such government-imposed paternalistic restrictions on our right to choose—which includes, of course, our right as free adults to make choices that others regard as bad for us. So we should not ban cigarette vending machines.

But the proposal to ban cigarette vending machines (so that children don't have easy access to cigarettes) is *not* the same as proposing a total ban on cigarettes. This argument sets up a *false* dilemma (either allow cigarette vending machines or ban cigarettes altogether) and attributes the *strawman* alternative (totally ban cigarettes) to those who are actually proposing only a ban on cigarette vending machines.
 As the above examples indicate, it is important to avoid the temptation to suppose that everything can be lumped easily into extreme categories. In the old Westerns—and perhaps in some soap operas—the good guys are absolutely pure of heart and the villains have no redeeming virtues, but many items in the world do not fit so easily into extreme categories. A chocolate-covered granola bar hardly qualifies as health food, but on the other hand, it's probably not a severe hazard to your health. Is Jones brilliant or stupid? Some people are brilliant, and unfortunately some are stupid, but most of us fall somewhere in between. Not everything nor everyone fits into extreme categories.

Consider the Possibilities

When reasoning, it is important to be sure you have considered the possibilities thoroughly. One of the great hazards to effective thought is getting stuck in ruts, the failure to explore alternatives. It is not enough to judge rationally among the alternatives if the most promising or most plausible alternatives have been forgotten.

Consider the Verdict

Jim Pickerell / Stock Connection Blue / Alamy

During jury deliberations, one juror argues in favor of a guilty verdict:

> We've got to come to a decision. Is the defendant guilty or innocent? Well, it is certainly doubtful that the guy is innocent. After all, several witnesses saw him near the scene of the crime, and everyone agrees that he had a strong motive for killing the guy. So which will it be? I say guilty!

How would you respond?

But don't get carried away. There are possibilities and then there are possibilities. For instance, if we are weighing the butler's testimony, it is important that we consider all the reasonable possibilities: Was the butler describing events exactly as they actually happened? Was the butler lying? Was the butler honestly mistaken? Was the butler a demented paranoid with a vivid imagination? Was the butler covering up for the chambermaid? But we should not accuse someone of the fallacy of false dilemma because that person has neglected some far-fetched logical possibility. For example, it is *conceivable* that an invisible spirit intercepted the bullet from the defendant's gun before it struck Lord Rutabaga, and then this invisible being fired its own invisible gun at Lord Rutabaga, killing Lord Rutabaga with a bullet identical to the one fired by the defendant. Thus, it is possible that an invisible spirit killed Lord Rutabaga, and the defendant is innocent (or is at most guilty of *attempted* murder). If the prosecuting barrister fails to consider *that* possibility in her efforts to prove the defendant guilty, we shall hardly be justified in charging the prosecuting barrister with false dilemma.

Exactly where do we draw the line between reasonable and unreasonable possibilities? That question has no easy answer. What is today regarded as the most far-fetched possibility may tomorrow be accepted as scientific truth. The notion that additional hydrogen atoms could come into being out of nothing strikes me as preposterous, but some brilliant astrophysicists propose it as a genuine possibility. Most Americans regarded the early Watergate charges brought against the Nixon administration as too incredible to be seriously considered, but they turned out to be true. Most intelligent people of the sixteenth century regarded the Copernican theory as ridiculous. You should try to stay open and flexible when considering possibilities, but without becoming so bogged down in absurdly far-fetched speculations that critical reasoning is stifled.

Exercise 12-3

In the following arguments, decide whether each is or is not a false dilemma; if it is a false dilemma, state the false dilemma clearly and describe at least one possibility that has been ignored.

1. New Sweet Lips Sweetener has been proved safe! We have carried out very extensive tests on many species of laboratory animals, as well as long-term tests on volunteers who have been using Sweet Lips in food and in beverages, and we have shown conclusively that Sweet Lips is not carcinogenic. So you and your family can be safe and sweet with Sweet Lips!

2. Jesus of Nazareth was either a lunatic or he is truly God. After all, anyone who goes around claiming that he is God—as the New Testament shows that Jesus did—must be either batty or telling the truth. Now certainly Jesus was no lunatic: Jesus's Sermon on the Mount is clearly not the ravings of a lunatic. So it follows that Jesus must indeed be God.

3. Either we must continue to have strict criminal laws prohibiting possession and sale of such drugs as marijuana, cocaine, opium, and heroin or we must do away with all restrictions on the use and sale of such drugs. But eliminating such restrictions is absurd and unthinkable. It would mean that companies could openly promote and advertise cocaine, opium, and heroin and distribute free samples to everyone. Obviously we do not want free samples of such drugs handed out at the malls and stuffed into mailboxes. And we cannot allow anyone to encourage the use of such dangerous and addictive drugs through slick advertising and promotional campaigns. Therefore, we must continue to have and enforce strict criminal laws prohibiting the possession and sale of marijuana, cocaine, opium, and heroin.

4. Here are the facts: Ralph Rambunctious was found lying dead on his kitchen floor; he had suffered 11 deep stab wounds in his chest and back, any one of which would have caused his death. Now clearly knives don't just jump off kitchen counters and stab people, so obviously either Ralph must have committed suicide or someone must have killed him. Certainly Ralph did not commit suicide. He might have stabbed himself once, but he certainly could not have stabbed himself 11 times, and he could not have stabbed himself in the back. The conclusion is inescapable: Someone killed Ralph.

5. Either studying logic will make me an infallible reasoner or it is useless.

6. You don't think that every American college student should be required to take a minimum of six courses in American history? Well, I guess you think it's not important for students to know anything about American history.

7. Either there truly is a Loch Ness Monster or a lot of good upright Scots with no motive for lying are telling outrageous lies.

8. Either the Bible is the literal and absolutely true word of God or it is just a book of silly fables.

9. It's a simple question: Do you believe in God, or are you an atheist?

10. Either there is truly a strange sea creature in Loch Ness (the "Loch Ness Monster") or there is not. If there is some such creature, then obviously it would be worthwhile to find and study it. If there is not such a creature, then it would be worthwhile to prove once and for all that no such creature exists. Either way, a serious scientific search for the Loch Ness Monster is worth doing.

11. ROMEO: Let's go to the big Fourth of July celebration! There will be lots of patriotic speeches, and we'll celebrate all the great American military victories, and we'll sing patriotic songs, and we'll honor America as the greatest nation on Earth!

    JULIET: No, I don't think so; I don't like nationalistic celebrations; I think we ought to concentrate more on international harmony than on patriotism and nationalism.

    ROMEO: Well don't go, then; you must be one of those America-haters.

12. ANTONY: I don't think we should have censorship laws that ban movies, books, or magazines as obscene.

    CLEOPATRA: Oh, I guess you think it's good for children to attend pornographic movies and for obscene materials to be presented on public billboards.

13. Imagine a rape case in which a secretary accuses her employer of raping her one night when they were working late at the office. The defense attorney cross-examines the secretary—following her testimony for the prosecution:

    DEFENSE ATTORNEY: "Ms. Smith, did you hate your boss?"
    WITNESS: "No, certainly not."
    DEFENSE ATTORNEY: "Then you were in fact in love with him, weren't you?"

14. Ladies and gentlemen of the jury, the evidence points conclusively to a verdict of guilty. The prosecution has established that on the night Richard Wiley was brutally murdered, there were only three people at Richard Wiley's home: Richard Wiley, the unfortunate victim; the defendant, Amos Steward; and Richard Wiley's brother, Albert Wiley. Richard Wiley did not commit suicide: He was stabbed 14 times in the back, and those were not self-inflicted wounds. So obviously he was murdered either by his brother, Albert, or by the defendant, Amos Steward. But his brother is paralyzed from the neck down, and cannot move his arms. So you must conclude that the defendant, Amos Steward, is indeed the murderer.

15. Either secondhand smoking (breathing the smoke from cigarettes smoked by others) causes lung cancer or it is not harmful. Many careful, well-designed studies have conclusively established that secondhand smoking does not cause lung cancer. In fact, study after study has established that there is no link between secondhand smoking and lung cancer. Therefore, secondhand smoking is not harmful.

16. Fellow members of the jury, this is an easy case. Barbara Brent is charged with murdering her husband. Now either she didn't kill him or she murdered him in cold blood. But obviously she did kill him: She admitted that she shot him, as he approached her. She pulled the trigger herself, the gun was in her hand. So there's really only one possible conclusion: Barbara Brent murdered her husband, and we should find her guilty of murder.

17. In 2003, the U.S. Supreme Court ruled that a Maryland death-row inmate, Kevin Wiggins, was entitled to a new sentencing hearing, on the grounds that his lawyers had acted incompetently at his original trial. During the sentencing phase of his original trial (after Wiggins had already been convicted of murder), Wiggins's lawyers had an opportunity to present any mitigating circumstances that might persuade a jury to sentence the defendant to life in prison rather than capital punishment. Wiggins had suffered terrible abuse as a child—repeated sexual abuse, left alone for days at a time without food, forced to eat garbage to survive, severely and purposefully burned by his mother. There was some question about whether Wiggins's lawyers knew his terrible childhood history (one of Wiggins's lawyers testified he was aware of Wiggins's brutal childhood). But whether the lawyer knew or not doesn't really matter. If the lawyer did *not* know, then he did an incompetent investigation into his defendant's background. On the other hand, if the lawyer *did* know and did not use this information as mitigating evidence in his appeal to the jury, then the lawyer is incompetent in preparing his defense. Either the lawyer knew about the childhood abuse or he didn't; either way, the lawyer was incompetent, and the defendant is entitled to a new sentencing hearing.

18. California is running these massive budget deficits, not taking in enough tax money to cover the costs of schools and prisons and highway construction and all the other programs the state must run. These deficits are causing major economic problems for the state, and placing the state on the very edge of bankruptcy and economic crisis. If we don't want big state deficits and bankruptcy, then we are going to have to make major cuts in spending on education. And certainly we don't want deficits and bankruptcy: that would cause economic chaos, and everyone in the state would suffer, and businesses would leave the state. So California must make major spending cuts in education.

19. Look, in the United States we have a choice between continuing to run huge budget deficits or making severe cuts in federal health-care spending. Now we certainly don't want the United States to continue running enormous budget deficits: that would eventually wreck our whole economy. Therefore, the only legitimate economic policy is to make severe cuts in federal spending on health care.

20. Under the Patriot Act, passed by Congress shortly after the 9-11 terrorist attacks, anyone suspected of being a terrorist or being connected with terrorists can be picked up and held in prison indefinitely, without having access to a lawyer, without being charged with any crime, and without anyone even knowing that he or she has been imprisoned. Some people object to such secret arrests and imprisonments that can be carried out without any right to a hearing in court or access to a lawyer or opportunity to call friends or family. And true, these do seem like harsh measures. But the fact is, we are faced with a terrible choice: either we ignore the danger of terrorist attacks, and just wait passively for the next terrorist strike; or we must suspend the basic rights of our citizens and allow secret arrest and imprisonment of anyone who is a suspect. Obviously we can't just ignore the threat of terrorism: we know how terrible terrorist attacks can be. And so we must take the other alternative of secret arrests and indefinite secret imprisonment.

21. There are those who argue that we should close the Guantanamo Prison facility, because of the accounts of prisoner abuse that occurred there. But the problem is, if we close the Guantanamo Bay Prison, then we'll have to release the prisoners who are held there. Maybe some of those prisoners were falsely accused, and some of them probably had nothing to do with terrorism. But still, *some* of those prisoners probably are terrorists, and pose a severe threat to the security of the United States. We can't just turn them loose to carry out terrorist plots. So we must keep the Guantanamo Bay Prison open.

GOLDEN MEAN

In the fourth century B.C.E., the Greek philosopher Aristotle taught that we should seek "the mean":

> [I]t is in the nature of things for the virtues to be destroyed by excess and deficiency. . . . Excessive or insufficient training destroys strength, just as too much or too little food and drink ruins health. The right amount, however, brings health and preserves it. So this applies to moderation, bravery, and the other virtues. . . . Moderation and bravery are destroyed by excess and deficiency, but are kept flourishing by the mean.[9]

The Golden Mean Fallacy

This ethical doctrine has come to be known as "the golden mean." It may—or may not—be good moral guidance. But whatever its usefulness in ethics, it is certainly a fallacy when appealed to in argument. The fact that a position is the *mean* between two extremes (i.e., the "middle-of-the-road" position, the "moderate" or "compromise" view) does not make it correct. The moderate view may be the correct one, but it may just as easily be wrong.

Suppose we are considering whether it should be legal for 18-year-olds to purchase alcoholic beverages. Some people want to deny 18-year-olds the right to buy alcohol; others favor a legal drinking age of 18. Someone then argues,

> Look, allowing 18-year-olds to drink any and all sorts of alcoholic beverages is excessive; but prohibiting *all* drinking by 18-year-olds goes too far in the other direction. Obviously, then, we should allow 18-year-olds to buy beer, but make 21 the legal age for hard liquor.

That is a common type of argument, and many people find it persuasive, but it is completely fallacious. The fallacy committed is the *fallacy of the golden mean*. The position proposed may be *moderate*, but it does not follow that it is *correct*.

There are two clear reasons why golden mean arguments are fallacious. First, the moderate position may be (and often is) simply false: An extreme position is frequently the correct one. When Copernicus proposed that Earth travels around the Sun, that was an extreme claim, but nonetheless true. (The more *moderate* position was proposed by Tycho Brahe, who suggested that the Sun travels around Earth, but all the *planets* revolve around the Sun rather than around Earth. It was a brilliant compromise, but a mistaken one.) In the mid-nineteenth century, the abolitionists (who wanted to completely *abolish* slavery) held an extreme position: those who wanted to continue slavery in the states where it already existed but not allow slavery in the new Western territories were taking a moderate position. Certainly the extremist abolitionist view was the right one. In the late nineteenth century, there was much controversy concerning the age of Earth. Archbishop Ussher held the extreme view that Earth is only a few thousand years old; Charles Darwin took the other extreme, maintaining it must be hundreds of millions of years old; and Lord Kelvin was the moderate, placing Earth's age at several million years. In fact, the correct view (about 4.6 billion years) turned out to be much more extreme than even Darwin had thought. So the first reason that golden mean arguments are fallacious is that the extreme position has been and often is correct.

Constructing Golden Mean Fallacies

There is another clear indication of the fallaciousness of the golden mean argument: It is possible to use golden mean arguments to argue for almost any position, even contradictory ones. (And any argument form that can yield contradictory conclusions is obviously doing something wrong.) Consider an issue currently debated: handgun control. Someone favoring the *banning* of handguns might argue:

> We should not go to the extreme of banning all guns; people should be free to own rifles and shotguns. But neither should we go to the other extreme, and allow people to own particularly dangerous and criminally well-suited weapons like handguns. So obviously the right position is to ban handguns, but allow rifles and shotguns.

The *opponent* of bans on handguns might argue:

> I don't believe that people should be allowed to own howitzers, mortars, and antiaircraft weapons, but we should not go to the other extreme and ban smaller firearms like rifles, pistols, and shotguns. So obviously we should take the moderate path, and allow handguns.

So here we have contradictory conclusions, each supported equally well—or rather, equally *badly* and fallaciously—by the golden mean fallacy.

It is easy to contrive a golden mean argument for almost any issue. Consider the question of whether the use of seatbelts should be mandatory. The proponent of mandatory use of seatbelts might argue:

> It would be wrong to require that every possible safety device be used by all automobile riders. Riders should not have to wear crash helmets and fire-resistant suits. But it would also be wrong to allow automobile riders to unnecessarily risk death and injury by neglecting the simple, easy, and effective safety device of seatbelts. Therefore, seatbelt use should be mandatory.

The opponent constructs an equal and opposite (and equally fallacious) golden mean argument *against* mandatory use of seatbelts:

> It would be wrong to go to the extreme of *requiring* automobile riders to wear seatbelts. On the other hand, we should not *forbid* people to wear seatbelts if they choose to do so, and perhaps we should even require that all cars be equipped with seatbelts. The solution, then, is to have seatbelts available for those who wish to wear them, but not require anyone to wear seatbelts.

These golden mean arguments lead with equal implausibility to contradictory conclusions. Simply showing that something can be cast as the "moderate" position does nothing to establish the desirability or plausibility of that position.

The golden mean fallacy occurs in many contexts, but it is especially common—and especially egregious—in the jury room. In 1967, Dr. Carl Coppolino was tried in Florida for allegedly poisoning his wife with succinylcholine chloride. After approximately 6 hours of deliberation, the jury returned a verdict of guilty of murder in the *second degree*. Not premeditated first-degree murder, but *un*premeditated second-degree murder. But the prosecution claimed that Coppolino had planned the murder, bought the drug, and purposefully injected his wife with a lethal dose of that dangerous drug. *If* Dr. Coppolino carried out this murder, it was certainly a carefully planned and premeditated murder, *not*

Sacred Middle Ground

Often those who commit the golden mean fallacy suppose that merely affirming a position as the "middle of the road" is sufficient reason to adopt it. For example, Lynn Wilhoite, president of the Hudson (Ohio) PTA, announced support for a moment of silence during graduation ceremonies: "The Hudson PTA endorses the tradition of a moment of silence, seeing that stance as a middle ground between official prayer [and no prayer]."[10]

(as in second-degree murder) a spontaneous unplanned murder, such as might be committed in the heat of passion. So how could the jury reach a verdict of guilty of *second* degree unpremeditated murder?

It is not difficult to imagine how the jury arrived at its verdict. The evidence presented by the prosecution was all circumstantial, and the testimony of the state's expert witnesses concerning traces of the poison left in the system was technical and difficult and was opposed by testimony from defense experts. The jury apparently believed that the prosecution had made a fairly strong but not completely convincing case that Coppolino had poisoned his wife. But (forgetting about the proper placement of the burden of proof *and* succumbing to the golden mean fallacy) they *probably* reasoned,

> We aren't quite convinced that Coppolino poisoned his wife, so a verdict of guilty of first-degree murder would be too strong; but there is some evidence of his guilt, so we don't want to go to the other extreme and find him not guilty; obviously we should take the compromise route and find him guilty of the lesser charge of second-degree murder.

I don't know which of the two extremes—not guilty, guilty of first-degree murder—was the correct conclusion, but clearly the "middle-of-the-road" position was wrong.

This is not to say that the middle-of-the-road position is *always* wrong. Jim Hightower, former Texas State Commissioner of Agriculture, eloquently expresses his disdain for moderate views: "There's nothing in the middle-of-the-road except white lines and dead armadillos." But that's overstating it. Sometimes the truth does fall in the middle. But it can also be found in the extremes. Pointing out that a position or view is the middle position is *not* a good argument in its favor; to claim that a conclusion is *right* because it is "moderate" is to commit the golden mean fallacy. So mark carefully what the golden mean fallacy is *not*—It is *not* the fallacy of taking the middle-of-the-road position, for there is no such fallacy. And contrast that with what the golden mean

---

A Jury Compromise

The golden mean verdict in the trial of Dr. Carl Coppolino is a particularly striking case, but it is not an isolated one. Juries have long been tempted by such fallacious compromises. The noted nineteenth-century New York trial lawyer H. L. Clinton mentions the case of Dr. E. M. Brown, which Clinton calls "an extraordinary case, full of thrilling and tragic incidents." According to Clinton (who acted as defense attorney for Dr. Brown), one of the tragic incidents was that Dr. Brown was initially indicted for first-degree murder. Clinton maintains that that indictment was a serious mistake by the presiding judge: Dr. Brown should have been indicted on charges of, at worst, manslaughter. As Clinton describes the problem:

> The disadvantages of a trial under that indictment [for murder instead of manslaughter] were great. As the District Attorney would ask for a conviction of a capital offense, and the defendant's Counsel would strive for an acquittal, there would be great danger that the jury would compromise on a verdict for a minor offense. Had there been a trial on the former indictment for manslaughter, the effect of the evidence in favor of the defendant would probably have been to secure an acquittal.

But the charge was murder, rather than manslaughter; and Clinton describes the result:

> [If the defendant had been tried on an indictment for manslaughter, then] the result would undoubtedly have been an acquittal. The disadvantages of going to trial on an indictment for murder were very great. The jury would be very apt to think that if they refused to sustain the contention of the prosecution, that the case was one of murder either in the first or second degree, . . . they were very liberal to the defense; and that a conviction for manslaughter in the fourth degree, the lowest grade of homicide known to the law, would be a substantial victory for Dr. Brown. Although the evidence entitled him to a verdict of acquittal, it was not strange, under the circumstances, that the jury rendered a verdict against him of manslaughter in the fourth degree.[11]

If the prosecution is asking for a first-degree murder conviction, then a verdict of not guilty is certainly the opposite extreme from what the prosecution is demanding; but *if* "the evidence entitled him to a verdict of acquittal," then that *extreme* verdict was the correct one—and the moderate tendency ("let's convict him of the mildest possible charge") was mistaken.

The Charms of the Golden Mean

The temptation to see a compromise as reasonable is very powerful, perhaps especially so after long deliberation in a jury room. Suppose that you are a juror, and the defendant has been charged with breaking or entering and arson. The prosecution claims that the defendant broke into an empty house with the intention of stealing whatever was left there; but finding nothing worth stealing, he started a fire that caused significant damage to the house. The defense insists that this is a case of mistaken identity. You and your fellow jurors have been deliberating for a long time, everyone is rather tired and tempers are getting a bit short. Half of the jurors believe there is sufficient evidence to convict the defendant on both charges; the other jurors agree that there is some evidence of guilt, but insist that the evidence is too weak to establish that the defendant is guilty beyond a reasonable doubt. Finally, someone says, "Look, let's be reasonable. You people don't think there's enough evidence to convict the guy for arson and breaking or entering. We think there is enough evidence. Let's put our heads together and meet halfway. We'll agree to find him not guilty of the arson charge, if you will agree to a guilty verdict on the breaking or entering." That will be tempting, and it may seem like a reasonable solution to the problem. It is tempting, but it's not reasonable. It's convenient, and it avoids the hard work of thinking long and carefully about but what verdict is actually right; but it commits the golden mean fallacy, and there is no reason whatsoever to suppose that the compromise verdict is correct.

fallacy actually *is:* The golden mean fallacy *is* the fallacy of supposing that *if* something is the compromise, moderate, or middle-of-the-road position that is in itself a reason for thinking that the position is right. It's *not* a fallacy to take the moderate position; it *is* a fallacy to claim that the moderate position is right simply *because* it is moderate.

Compromise is sometimes desirable. If we are making plans to have dinner together and I want to grab a burger and fries at Joe's Greasy Spoon and you want a leisurely dinner at Antoine's, then perhaps we can find some compromise that would please us both. But finding the truth, as opposed to working out agreeable social occasions, is not so easy. If Darwin (who placed the age of Earth at several million years) and Ussher (who insisted it was not more than a few thousand years old) had met in a spirit of friendship and compromise and agreed to work out their differences, they might have come up with a compromise position that would set Earth's age at half a million years. But such a compromise would have yielded a mistaken conclusion. And the same applies to jury deliberations. If the jury disagrees about where to go for lunch, by all means try to work out an amicable compromise. But jurors should *never* compromise on a criminal verdict. If half the jurors favor a not guilty verdict and the other half favor a verdict of guilty of first-degree murder, it will *not* be acceptable to compromise on a verdict of guilty of second-degree murder.

The wrongfulness of compromising on a criminal jury verdict is worth repeating, so I'll repeat it: *Do not* reach your verdict by trying to work out a compromise. There will be a tremendous amount of pressure to do so. After several hours of deliberation, with the members of the jury still unable to agree on a verdict, pressure will build to come up with some sort of agreement. But it is much better to agree to disagree—and thus wind up with a hung jury and no decision—than to reach a decision fallaciously by means of the golden mean fallacy.

Exercise 12-4

Develop golden mean arguments for *each* of the following claims. (Make sure that the arguments you develop are really *golden mean* fallacies. For an example, look back at the two golden mean fallacies *for* and *against* handgun control.)

1. a. Smoking in public restaurants should be banned.

   b. Smoking in public restaurants should not be banned.

2. a. Passive euthanasia should be permitted.

   b. Passive euthanasia should be prohibited.

(Euthanasia is the killing or allowing to die of an individual who is suffering from an incurable disease, in order to prevent the person from further suffering. *Passive* euthanasia is *allowing* someone to die by withholding medical treatment that would prolong life. For example, *not* using an artificial respirator to prolong life would count as passive euthanasia. Passive euthanasia is contrasted with *active* euthanasia, in which something, such as the injection of a drug, is done to hasten death.)

3. a. Marijuana should be legalized.

 b. Marijuana should not be legalized.

4. a. Capital punishment should be employed.

 b. Capital punishment should be banned.

5. a. We should eliminate the inheritance tax.

 b. We should keep the inheritance tax.

6. a. There should be mandatory drug testing for all college students.

 b. There should not be mandatory drug testing for all college students.

7. a. We should raise the speed limit to 70 mph.

 b. We should keep the speed limit at 55 mph.

✓●─ **Study** and **Review** on **mythinkinglab.com**

REVIEW QUESTIONS

1. What is the slippery slope *fallacy*?
2. Under what conditions are slippery slope arguments *not* fallacious?
3. Define the fallacy of false dilemma.
4. How can a false dilemma argument be fallacious when it is a *valid* argument?
5. What is the golden mean fallacy?
6. What is the *difference* between a golden mean fallacy and a nonfallacious argument for some moderate position?

NOTES

[1] John Mortimer, *Rumpole for the Defense* (Hammondsworth, Middlesex: Penguin Books), p. 112.

[2] The speech of District Attorney A. Oakley Hall in the trial of Cunningham-Burdell, quoted in Henry Lauren Clinton, *Celebrated Trials* (New York: Harper & Brothers, 1897), p. 189.

[3] James G. Watt, U.S. Secretary of the Interior, January 24, 1983. Taken from Christopher Cerf and Victor Navasky, *The Experts Speak: The Definitive Compendium of Authoritative Misinformation* (New York: Pantheon Books, 1984), p. 39.

[4] Quotation of Edwin Meese from a news report by the *L.A. Times–Washington Post* News Service.

[5] *Post-Nicene Fathers*, V.ix.442. I found this example in Douglas Walton's *Slippery Slope Arguments* (see "Additional Reading"); he credits J. F. Little, L. A. Groarke, and C. W. Tindale, *Good Reasoning Matters!* (Toronto, ON: McClelland & Stewart, 1989).

[6] *Texas* v. *Johnson* 1989:10; Douglas Walton includes a particularly interesting discussion of this case in his *Slippery Slope Arguments*, pp. 267–277 (see "Additional Reading").

[7] J. Gay-Williams, "The Wrongfulness of Euthanasia," in *Intervention and Reflection*, 4th ed., edited by Ronald Munson (Belmont, CA: Wadsworth 1992), p. 158.

[8] From *You're the Jury* by Judge Norbert Ehrenfreund and Lawrence Treat, Copyright © 1992 by Judge Norbert Ehrenfreund and Lawrence Treat. Reprinted by permission of Henry Holt & Co., Inc.

[9] Aristotle, *Nicomachean Ethics,* Book II.

[10] From the *Cleveland Plain Dealer*, May 14, 1996.

[11] Henry Lauren Clinton, *Celebrated Trials* (New York: Harper & Brothers 1897), pp. 302, 315.

INTERNET RESOURCES

For a remarkably detailed, extensive, and insightful examination of slippery slope arguments in the law, see an article by Eugene Volokh, "The Mechanisms of the Slippery Slope," which was published in *Harvard Law Review* and is available online at *http://www2.law.ucla.edu/volokh/slippery.htm*. Dahlia Lithwick published a very clear analysis of some often used slippery slope arguments; it is in *Slate*, at *http://www.slate.com/id/2100824/*. There are some nice examples of false dilemma arguments at *http://www.drury.edu/ess/Logic/Informal/Bifurcation.html*.

ADDITIONAL READING

For a particularly good study of slippery slope arguments, see Frederick Schauer, "Slippery Slopes," *Harvard Law Review*, Vol. 99, no. 2 (December 1985), pp. 361–383.

Discussion of slippery slope arguments is a standard feature in most books on critical thinking, and many helpful discussions and marvelous examples of slippery slope thinking can be found in such sources. An interesting perspective on slippery slope arguments is offered in Chapter 7 of Garrett Hardin's *Filters against Folly* (New York: Viking Penquin, 1985).

An excellent, insightful, and thorough study of slippery slope arguments can be found in Douglas Walton's *Slippery Slope Arguments* (Oxford: Clarendon Press, 1992). Walton's book is rich in examples and perceptive in analysis, and its special strength is its emphasis on the legitimate use of slippery slope arguments.

Bernard Williams has an excellent paper on slippery slope arguments: "Which Slopes are Slippery?" It can be found in Bernard Williams, *Making Sense of Humanity* (Cambridge, UK: Cambridge University Press, 1995).

Eugene Volokh offers a remarkably deep and interesting study of slippery slope arguments—in law and politics—complete with wonderful examples, and even a neat cartoon illustration of the slippery slope argument. Entitled "The Mechanisms of the Slippery Slope," it was published in *Harvard Law Review*, Vol. 116 (2003); it can be found online at www.law.ucla.edu/volokh/slippery.htm.

A good example of a jury reaching a verdict through golden mean reasoning is found in the case of *State* v. *Schaeffer*, in *You're the Jury*, by Judge Norbert Ehrenfreund and Lawrence Treat (New York: Henry Holt, 1992). (If you would like some realistic practice at jury deliberation, the book by Ehrenfreund and Treat presents a variety of very interesting cases.)

Read the Document on mythinkinglab.com

Barbara Defoe Whitehead, "What We Owe." An insightful rejection of a false dilemma.

Carol Ezzell, "Why? The Neuroscience of Suicide." An example of the dangers of false dilemmas in considering causal factors.

Holland v. Illinois, 493 U.S. 474 (1990). This is a case concerning the use of peremptory challenges to exclude blacks from a jury. The majority in this case (in a 5 to 4 decision) ruled that the use of peremptory challenges to exclude blacks from the jury was not a reason to overturn the guilty verdict. Justice Marshall, writing for the minority, argued that the verdict should be overturned because the exclusion violated the Sixth Amendment to the Constitution. In Justice Marshall's argument (reproduced here), he states that the argument of the majority contains a false dilemma (a "false dichotomy") as well as a fallacious slippery slope argument (the majority claims that "acceptance of Holland's argument would be the first step down a slippery slope").

Matrixx Initiatives v. James Siracusano, U.S. Supreme Court (2011). In this case—dealing with a claim that Matrixx Initiatives concealed unfavorable information from investors—the Court examines a dilemma argument proposed in defense of Matrixx Initiatives, to the effect that if data regarding risk factors for one of its medications is not "statistically significant," then it is of little or no importance.

13

❖ ❖ ❖

Begging the Question

When a magician draws a rabbit out of her hat, she simply removes what she had managed to hide there earlier. It's a great trick, and it is often done very convincingly—but it doesn't create any new rabbits. The same applies to question-begging arguments. It is easy to pull a conclusion out of an argument if I have previously hidden the conclusion in the premises. And it often looks impressive, but it doesn't really prove anything new.

The problem with begging the question is that it spins its wheels, it goes nowhere: It does not take up the burden of proof and go forward with it. Instead, a question-begging argument simply assumes as a premise what it purports to be *proving*.

Arguments are supposed to give us reasons for believing the conclusion. But you cannot support the conclusion by using the conclusion. If we are trying to build a bridge across a river, we must first find a solid foundation, then sink the pilings into that foundation, and finally conclude by placing the trestle onto the pilings. If our civil engineer proposed using the trestle to support itself, we would look for another civil engineer. And if someone proposes to support a conclusion by appeal to that same conclusion, then we should look for another argument.

THE PROBLEM WITH QUESTION-BEGGING ARGUMENTS

Notice that question-begging arguments are certainly *valid*. A valid argument is one in which the conclusion follows from the premises; or more exactly, *if* its premises are true then its conclusion *must* be true. If the conclusion is contained in the premises, then the conclusion must follow from the premises. If the premises are all true, and the conclusion is contained among the premises, then the conclusion certainly will have to be true. So the problem with question-begging arguments is not invalidity. Rather, the problem with question-begging arguments is that they turn in a circle: They don't give us any real *reasons* for believing the conclusion to be true. An argument cannot pull itself up by its own bootstraps.

When the magician pulls a rabbit out of her hat, we all know that it was done by sleight of hand, but it's not always easy to tell how the magician managed to get the rabbit into the hat. That's also true of question-begging arguments: It's not always easy to recognize the question-begging premises. But take the simplest cases first. If our magician—in plain view of the audience—sticks a rabbit in her hat and then pulls it out, we aren't likely to be very impressed by the trick. And some question-begging arguments are almost that obvious. They seem to rely on the hope that if the conclusion is repeated often enough—in a loud and confident voice—then people will believe the conclusion to be true (despite the fact that no evidence has been given in support of the conclusion). For example, "Socialism will not work as an economic system, because it is perfectly obvious that socialism is not workable as an economic system." Such an "argument" is rather like the bellman's "argument" in Lewis Carroll's "The Hunting of the Snark":

> "Just the place for a Snark!" the Bellman cried,
> As he landed his crew with care;
> Supporting each man on the top of the tide
> By a finger entwined in his hair.
> "Just the place for a Snark!
> I have said it twice:
> That alone should encourage the crew.
> Just the place for a Snark!
> I have said it thrice:
> What I tell you three times is true."[1]

Strange as it may seem, many people seem to think that merely repeating the conclusion is a convincing argument. Thus the district attorney in her closing "argument" to the jury argues, "The defendant is guilty as charged! He knows it, I know it, and, members of the jury, you also know it! He is guilty of mugging that poor old lady to steal her grocery money! He is guilty, and thus justice demands that you speedily return with a verdict of guilty!" Such "arguments" offer no reason to believe in the defendant's guilt or the snark's proximity. And I trust that neither you nor the bellman's crew will be deceived by such brazen uses of question begging.

A New and Confusing Use of "Begs the Question"

Unfortunately, the phrase "begs the question" has recently taken on a new use, a use that is very different from naming the fallacy described in this chapter. This new use is often directed at suspected half-truths, as in the following: "Professor Snodgrass told us that some students do very well in this class; that begs the question of what happens to the other students." Or as in this: "The label says that this pesticide does not cause cancer; that begs the question of what other health problems it might cause, such as nerve damage." Obviously there's no way to ban the use of "begs the question" in this context, but be careful not to confuse the two very different uses.

SUBTLE FORMS OF QUESTION BEGGING

No one should be misled by the blatant begging the question practiced by the bellman. Unfortunately, begging-the-question fallacies also occur in much trickier forms. One is through use of synonyms.

Synonymous Begging the Question

Consider the following brief argument:

> Socialism is not a workable economic system, because an economic system in which the means of production are collectively owned cannot work.

But socialism *is* an economic system in which the means of production are collectively owned. So the premise merely repeats the conclusion, albeit in a slightly disguised (synonymous) form. The premise gives us no independent grounds for believing the conclusion to be true, and the argument commits the fallacy of begging the question (the synonymous form of that fallacy).

The synonymous form of begging the question may sometimes appear in more elaborate disguises:

> Abortion is wrong; for it is always wrong to voluntarily and purposefully destroy a living and growing and developing human fetus.

But that is precisely what abortion is. Merely restating a synonymous form of the conclusion is not giving an *argument* for that conclusion.

Generalization Begging the Question

In some cases of begging the question, the premise is a *generalization* that contains the conclusion as an instance of that generalization. For example,

> John Hinckley should not be excused on grounds of insanity; for no one should escape punishment for an assassination attempt on the grounds that he or she is insane.

Certainly if *no one* should escape punishment on grounds of insanity then it follows that Hinckley should not. But the question at issue—the claim that the "argument" is supposed to be *proving*—is whether Hinckley should be excused on grounds of insanity; merely stating a general principle that contains the conclusion as an instance is to beg the question.

Suppose we are discussing what courses should be general requirements for students at Home State University, and someone offers the following argument:

> A critical thinking course should be required of all students at Home State University, because obviously every university student should have to take at least one course in critical thinking.

True, if *all* university students should be required to take critical thinking, then that *includes* the students at Home State. But the premise is just a more inclusive, general claim that *begs* the question at issue.

Consider another example of the generalization form of begging the question. In 1983, a Korean airliner (Flight KAL 007) was shot down by a Soviet war plane over sensitive Soviet airspace. Why was Flight KAL 007 flying over a major Soviet naval center during a scheduled Soviet training exercise?

Was it a strange sequence of tragic errors? Or was it the deliberate use of a commercial airliner for spying? Or what? It is an important question, and there have been interesting arguments for a variety of views. Suppose someone offers the following argument:

> South Korean Flight KAL 007 was *not* on a spy mission because the United States and its allies never use commercial passenger flights for spying.

Such an argument begs the question. The question at issue is whether this particular flight was used for spying. To assume—as a premise, and without further argument—that *no* such flights are used for spying is to assume the very point in question, and thus to beg the question.

Of course not all uses of general principles involve begging the question. Suppose that some mercury is dropped on the floor and forms into small balls. If someone inquires why the mercury is in small balls, it may be helpful to explain that mercury always forms into small spheres in such circumstances. (i.e., no one shaped the mercury into spheres; it is a natural property of mercury to arrange itself in that manner.) One may then want *further* explanation of mercury and its properties and why it behaves so differently from water; but while the explanation already given may be rather superficial, it is *not* a question-begging explanation. Explaining some specific event by subsuming it under a general principle is a legitimate and common explanatory device, both in science and elsewhere. It is a legitimate explanatory practice when there is *agreement* concerning the specific event and we simply want explanation of why it happened. But if the event or case is a controversial one, and there is *disagreement* about the particular event (Was Flight KAL 007 spying or was it careless? Should students at Home State University be required to take a critical thinking course? Is Hinckley's behavior excusable on grounds of insanity, or is it not?), then trying to settle the controversy by appeal to a general principle that includes the controversial case commits the fallacy of begging the question.

Circular Begging the Question

Begging the question can be even more indirect, and even more insidious. Sometimes *circular* arguments travel such a convoluted circular path that it is difficult to detect exactly where the question begging occurs. Consider a standard, and relatively easy, example:

> God exists. We know that to be true, since the Bible plainly tells us that God exists. And we know that what the Bible tells us is true, since the Bible is the word of God.

In this argument an essential *premise* (the Bible is the word of God) *assumes* the truth of the *conclusion* (for the Bible to be the word of God, then God must first *exist*).

But circular begging the question can be more subtle. There has long been controversy concerning whether the U.S. Constitution should be amended to allow residents of the District of Columbia representation in the Congress and Senate. One person (in a letter to the editor of the *Greensboro Daily News*) gave this argument against such a constitutional amendment:

> This past August the U.S. Senate and House of Representatives voted on and approved the District of Columbia representation amendment [to the U.S. Constitution]. The amendment is now before the states and must obtain ratification by three-quarters of them by 1985 or it will die.
>
> Basically this amendment would give the 700,000 citizens of the District of Columbia voting delegates in either house of Congress. In the words of the amendment, the District should have representation "as though it were a state."
>
> Article I of the Constitution directs the members of the House shall be chosen from the "several states," and that two senators shall be chosen from "each state." That should settle the issue once and for all. The District of Columbia is not a state and giving it representation as such is an outright and flagrant violation of the Constitution.

In order to see the question-begging trick, the first step—as always in critically examining arguments—is to determine exactly what the *conclusion* is. (Without knowing what the conclusion is, we can't tell whether it is being slipped in among the premises; we won't even know what to look for.) The conclusion here is clear enough: The amendment to the Constitution giving D.C. representation should *not* be passed. But why not? Because the Constitution clearly specifies that members of the House and Senate should be chosen from the *states,* and the District of Columbia is *not* a state; therefore, giving D.C. representation in the House and Senate "is an outright and flagrant violation of the Constitution." That's true: Giving the District of Columbia representation in the House and Senate *would* be a violation of the Constitution as it stands, and so would require an *amendment* to the

Constitution. But the *question at issue* is whether there *should* be such an amendment to change the Constitution. By assuming that "violating" (changing) the Constitution must be wrong, the argument moves in a circle and begs the question. Obviously if "violating"/changing the Constitution is wrong, then it is wrong to change the Constitution, and the D.C. representation amendment must be wrong; but the question is whether this *amendment* is a good one, whether it is *right* in this instance to *amend* the Constitution.

The circular form of the begging-the-question fallacy can be found in recent discussions of child abuse testimony. Any case that depends heavily on the testimony of children poses serious difficulties. There are dangers that children may have trouble distinguishing fantasy from reality, but there are also dangers that children may be confused and frightened—or even intentionally intimidated—during their testimony. Such problems are exacerbated in child abuse cases; there is a danger that the child abuser may have threatened or physically abused the child in such a way that the child is afraid to testify against the abuser, particularly when the child abuser is present in the courtroom. On the other hand, one of our most important safeguards against false accusations is that the accused has the right to face his or her accuser. If you were accused of a crime you would certainly want to know who was accusing you and hear your accuser's testimony and face that person in court. So there is a genuine problem here, and it is not at all obvious how it should be resolved. But *one question-begging* argument is sometimes given in favor of allowing children in child abuse cases to give their testimony without the defendant being present. That argument goes something like this:

> It is doubly wrong to allow defendants in child abuse cases to be present when the abused children give their testimony. These child abusers often use terrible threats to keep the abused children from telling anyone about the abuse. To allow such vicious people to continue their intimidation of the children by being present when the children testify—and thus to perhaps avoid conviction—compounds their abuse of the children and extends that abuse into the courtroom.

There may or may not be good arguments against allowing the defendant to be present during all testimony, but certainly the *above* argument is fallacious. To *assume* that the defendant's presence would terrify the testifying children because of the threats the defendant has made against the children is to beg the essential question: *Did* the defendant make such threats? *Is* the defendant guilty as charged? While it is important to make the

---

Damned If You Do, Damned If You Don't

The trial of Carlyle W. Harris, charged with murdering his wife by administering morphine to her, was a famous trial of several decades ago. In his closing address to the jury, the prosecuting attorney included these remarks:

> It is pretended by Mr. Taylor [defense attorney], in solemn mockery of your intelligence and manhood, that you should acquit his client because throughout all the nine months that Harris has been in prison and throughout this long trial he has always maintained his self-respect, and could look into the eyes of each juryman with a confidence and assurance which, in Mr. Taylor's judgment, could only arise from a sustaining knowledge of innocence in his heart . . . . Is he innocent because he can look a jury in the face? Why, could any man whose conscience wasn't fairly choked in his breast look any honest man in the face after there had been proved against him what has been proven in this case against Harris? This is not innocence, to my mind; it shows an utter lack of conscience and of feeling.[2]

Let us grant the weakness of the defense's claim that Harris's ability to look the jurors in the face is evidence of his innocence. However, when the prosecution maintains that Harris's ability to look the jurors in the face proves that the defendant is utterly without conscience and feeling—how else could a guilty man look jurors squarely in the face—that is a case of arguing in a circle, of begging the question at issue: *Is* Harris guilty?

situation as comfortable and secure as possible for children giving testimony, it should also be remembered that the testimony of children can be terribly and tragically wrong. The Salem witchcraft trials, in which several unfortunate and innocent women were condemned to death on the basis of the testimony of a group of children, should suffice to remind us that we must also safeguard the rights of defendants. And in particular, we must safeguard the presumption of innocence—an essential condition for both fair trials and accurate thinking.

FALSE CHARGES OF BEGGING THE QUESTION

Begging the question is always a fallacy; but *not every case* in which the conclusion is *repeated* is a case of fallacious begging the question. In a lengthy argument, it may be helpful to have the conclusion repeated several times—otherwise, those listening to the argument may forget exactly what the argument is supposed to be proving. It is often useful to *start* an argument by stating what you intend to prove, then giving your premises in support of your conclusion, and finally *repeating* the conclusion that your argument proves. That is *not* begging the question. Begging the question occurs when the conclusion is *used* as a *premise*. Simply repeating the conclusion is not *using* it as a premise. (Of course if there is nothing to the "argument" other than repetitions of the conclusion, that would indeed be begging the question, but don't make false accusations of begging the question merely because the conclusion is stated more than once.)

In sum, watch out for the fallacy of begging the question, in all its treacherous guises. But don't start seeing the question-begging fallacies when they aren't really there. It's a fallacy to *beg* the question; it is *not* a fallacy to *restate* the conclusion.

Self-Sealing Arguments

There are two important close relations of the begging-the-question fallacy, and they go by special names: self-sealing arguments and complex questions. Self-sealing arguments are perhaps the most subtle and misleading of the question-begging arguments. The self-sealing fallacy might also be called the no-true-Scotsman fallacy, in honor of the following delightful example of that fallacy (developed by Antony Flew[3]): A particularly proud Scotsman picks up the morning paper and reads that an Englishman has committed a horrendous sex crime. "No *Scot* would do such a thing!" our Scotsman exclaims. But the very next day he reads an account of the even more vicious and scandalous sex crime committed by Mr. Angus MacSporran of Aberdeen, Scotland. Confronted with such a clear counterexample to his claim that no Scot would commit such a crime, our proud Scotsman ought to withdraw his claim, or at least retreat to the milder claim that *very few* Scotsmen would commit such a crime. But instead he "saves" his original claim: "No *true* Scotsman would do such a thing."

That manner of "saving" a claim turns it into a self-sealing fallacy. What begins as a substantive empirical claim is turned into an empty formula that is "true by definition." The original claim was a strong, although doubtful, one: No individual of Scottish descent would ever commit a vicious sex crime. But when the claim is modified in order to preserve it, what sort of claim is it? What is a "true Scotsman"? Merely a person of Scottish descent who would never commit a vicious sex crime. So the claim ends up as: No person of Scottish descent who would never commit a vicious sex crime will ever commit a vicious sex crime. That's true, but it doesn't tell us much. In fact, it doesn't tell us anything at all. Instead, it merely proposes a very peculiar and not very useful definition for "true Scotsman." The *truth* of the claim is "sealed in" by making the claim empty, vacuous, a mere truth-by-arbitrary-definition.

The self-sealing fallacy is frequently used to make claims that sound important but are in fact vacuous. You have perhaps found yourself caught in the recurring late-night dorm discussion of whether people are selfish or generous. Some provocative individual asserts that everyone acts always and only for *selfish* purposes. And immediately that claim is contested. "My mother," you say, "certainly is not always motivated by selfishness. I well remember the nights she sacrificed her own rest, staying by my bedside holding a cool cloth to my fevered brow for hours on end. And even as we speak, she is sending me all her extra money in order to pay for my college books." But your opponent refuses to budge: "She is still motivated by selfishness; it's just that she takes more pleasure in buying you books than in buying for herself, and more comfort in mopping your fevered brow than in sleeping. She is selfishly doing what she wants to do." Unless we look closely, this will appear a strong argument. How can we answer? No matter what examples we propose—a self-sacrificing mother, a loyal and selfless friend—our opponent can handle them: The individual is pursuing his or her own interests, is doing what brings the most pleasure. But what appears a strong position is actually an empty one. This person is using a peculiar—and self-sealing—definition of "selfishness." In the ordinary meaning of "selfish," we do *not* count an individual as selfish who does good for someone simply out of a generous desire to help that person. That is precisely what we regard as *un*selfish behavior. If "selfish" behavior is redefined as "all behavior done from any motive whatso-ever," then certainly all behavior will be "selfish" behavior, in an empty sense. Indeed, under such a definition of "selfish" it would be *impossible* by *definition* to do any act that was not selfish. But that shows the emptiness of the new definition. The claim that all human behavior is selfishly motivated is supposed to be a real claim about humans and their behavior. But under the self-sealing definition of "selfish," the claim has no empirical content, it tells us nothing about humans or about human motivation; instead, "All people are 'selfish'" expresses an empty verbal formula that is true by definition.

This last point shows the way to *answer* self-sealing arguments. You cannot answer such an argument by attempting to find a counterexample, as you could if the claim being made were a genuine empirical claim about the world. After all, the tricky thing about self-sealing arguments is that they prevent anything from *counting* as a counterex-ample. Instead, when refuting a self-sealing argument you must make its actual structure clear; that is, you must show that its conclusion has been transformed from a factual assertion to a mere verbal formula. And the best way of showing that is to challenge the person offering a self-sealing argument to state what he or she would be willing to *count* as a genuine counterexample to the claim. If nothing can possibly count against it, then it is true by definition rather than being a claim about the observable, testable, empirical world we live in.

In fact, that is a good way to test some of your own beliefs: Possibly some beliefs you thought were about the real world have degenerated into comforting verbal vacuities. That can happen quite easily to our particularly cherished beliefs. I strongly believe that anyone who commits a murder must be psychologically unbalanced, and that therefore we should think more about how to reform or cure such murderers (while protecting society against such criminally sick individuals), and reject notions of vengeance against murderers. I can cite plenty of examples of mentally ill murderers: Loeb and Leopold, the wealthy Chicago youths who killed a playmate as a sort of bizarre experiment; David Berkowitz, the "son of Sam" murderer, who received messages from his dog; John Hinckley, who lived in a fantasy world inhabited by teenage movie stars; Albert DeSalvo, "the Boston Strangler," who was driven mad by a sequence of events (including his daughter's crippling illnesses). But suppose my claim is challenged: Here is a murderer whom all competent psychiatrists and psychologists believe to be sane, whose psychological test results show up normal, who does not exhibit any bizarre behavior patterns, who is not delusional, who has no neurological damage to his brain, has no history of mental illness; this murderer robs a bank and coolly kills a witness to prevent identification (and thus improve his chances of not being captured). Is that murderer a counterexample to my claim? If I admit that he is a sane murderer, then I must give up my claim that *all* murder-ers are insane ("Very well; I should say instead that *most,* but perhaps not all, murderers are insane") but at least the claim will remain a significant factual claim about the mental condition of murderers. But suppose that instead I say (as I am very tempted to say): "No, I still believe he is insane; for anyone who murders another human being must be insane." Then my claim is no longer about the mental condition of murderers; rather, it is an arbitrary verbal stipulation: As I am now using the terms, to murder someone is by *definition* to be insane. But then to say that a murderer is insane is no longer to say something significant: It is merely to say that someone who is insane is insane, because my special self-sealing meaning of "murderer" includes insanity as part of its meaning. If I cannot state what I would *count* as a sane murderer, then that is a sign that what was originally a significant empirical claim has become an empty verbalism.

Self-sealing arguments are also a means of concealing our prejudices and stereotypes from the light of critical examination. Bill is driving Jill to the airport, when a car pulls in front of them and forces Bill to slam on his brakes. The careless driver is a woman, and Bill exclaims vehemently: "*Damn* woman drivers. All women are awful drivers and shouldn't be allowed on the road." As they drive on, Bill enlarges on the subject: "See that guy driving ahead of us? Now he's a good driver. He stays in his lane, keeps a steady speed, doesn't talk on his cell phone or send text messages, signals when he's about to change lanes. He's a good driver, not like those lousy woman drivers." At the next traffic light, however, Bill catches up to the car ahead, and as he pulls alongside, the good driver turns out to be a woman! Jill is delighted: "You see, women aren't all bad drivers; you're just prejudiced. That woman is certainly a good driver, as you yourself pointed out." However, Bill can hang on to his prejudices, by swift use of a self-sealing argument: "Well, she's not really a woman driver; she drives like a man." "Woman driver" is now being used by Bill in a self-sealing manner: It means a driver who is a woman and is a lousy driver. So of course any "woman driver" must be, by self-sealing definition, a lousy driver. The problem is that once this challenge to his prejudices is past, Bill is likely to switch back to the larger original claim that all *women* are bad drivers. Thus he can maintain his prejudice in the face of almost any contrary evidence.

Complex Questions

> "How am I to get in?" asked Alice again, in a louder tone.
> "*Are* you to get in at all?" said the Footman. "That's the first question, you know."
> It was, no doubt; only Alice did not like to be told so. "It's really dreadful," she muttered to herself, "the way all the creatures argue. It's enough to drive one crazy!"[4]

Another fallacy from the begging-the-question family is *complex question*. "Are you still drinking too heavily?" Whether you answer yes or no, you seem to be admitting that at one time you *did* drink excessively. And that is how complex questions *beg* the question: They embed an assumption within a question. By answering the question, you seem to grant the embedded assumption.

Complex questions are standard stuff for Hollywood depictions of trials. The shrewd district attorney asks the villainous defendant: "Why did you leave the diamond necklace behind when you robbed Lady Bigbucks's country estate?" "I didn't see a diamond necklace," replies the hapless defendant, thereby admitting that he indeed is the thief. But such loaded questions are not very likely in actual courtrooms. The defense attorney would certainly, and rightly, object before the witness had a chance to answer, and the judge would not only uphold the objection but would probably rebuke the district attorney for asking such a question. If complex questions occur at all in the courtroom, they are likely to be confined to the summation speeches made by the prosecution and defense just before the case goes to the jury, for lawyers are generally granted a good deal of latitude in their summations. At that point the defense attorney may rhetorically ask, "Do you really want to convict this person on such a flimsy patchwork of evidence?" And the prosecuting attorney may ask, "Do you want to have it on your conscience that you returned a dangerous criminal to the streets?"

Incidentally, complex questions are not the same as *leading* questions. A leading question *leads* in a specific direction, but allows the witness to decline going in the suggested direction: "You hate the defendant, don't you?" That is a leading question, but the witness can simply answer: "No, I don't." A *complex* question commits the witness to an underlying assumption no matter how the question is answered: "Was it the investment you lost in the defendant's business that caused you to hate him?" Whether the witness answers yes or no, the assumption remains that the witness hates the defendant; the only question left is *why* the witness hates him (was it because of a failed investment or is there some other reason?).

Complex questions may be unusual in court, but they are common in everyday life. When they escape detection, they insidiously control thought. For example, "What type of therapy is most effective in treating homosexuality?" "How do we gain our knowledge of right and wrong?" "What is the purpose of human existence?"

All of the above questions contain at least one unstated but controversial assumption. Failure to recognize those assumptions will fix the framework of discussion in a way that begs important questions. The most important issues may be settled before you even realize the discussion has started. "What is the most effective treatment for homosexuality?" If we accept that statement of the question, then the whole discussion will presuppose some very dubious assumptions: First, that homosexuality is a disease that should be *treated*, and second, that homosexuality is bad (like disease) and should be eliminated. Revealing those concealed assumptions may make the question irrelevant (we shall not ask how to *treat* homosexuality if it is neither a disease nor undesirable).

So be wary of complex (and loaded) questions: They may control discussion and constrict the range of possibilities considered. Don't be in such haste to get to the answer that you overlook dangerous assumptions concealed in the question. In biased surveys, complex questions are often called *loaded* questions. They are a common trick in fake or manipulated "surveys" that are designed to give whatever result the surveyor desires, and which can then be publicized as "genuine public opinion." For example, "Do you support government 'make-work' programs that will provide temporary jobs while greatly increasing the budget deficit?" is likely to yield a very different survey result than "Do you favor job programs that will put unemployed American workers to work on projects that will make our highways and bridges safer and better?" And, "Do you believe that every child in America should have good health care?" will get a different result from "Do you want the federal government interfering in your child's health care?"

On the other hand, not all assumptions—and not all questions that contain assumptions—are question begging. A complex question is being used by the automobile salesperson who smoothly slides into the question of how you intend to pay for the car—"Shall we put this on our special 60-month super-low payment plan, or would you prefer to pay it off in only 3 years?"—when you have not quite decided whether you want

By permission of Johnny Hart and Creators Syndicate.

Figure 13-1   Beware of complex questions!

to buy the car at all. But if it has *already* been settled that you are buying the car, then the same question may *not* beg the question. In a breaking or entering case, the defendant denies ever having been in the building he is accused of entering; the prosecuting attorney then asks him: "What were you doing inside the building?" That is a complex question that includes the assumption that the defendant *was* inside the building—and whether the defendant was inside the building is a disputed question that should not be *begged* by embedding it in a complex question. But suppose that in a different breaking or entering case, the defendant *admits* that she was inside the building (but claims she had the owner's permission). In *that* case, if the prosecuting attorney asks the same question ("What were you doing inside the building?"), it will *not* be a complex question; for in this case, whether the defendant was in the building is *not* in dispute. The moral of the story is this: A question that contains an assumption is not always question begging. If the assumption is not controversial—but is instead an assumption that all the parties to the discussion recognize and accept—then no questions are begged by *making* the assumption. (Of course the assumption may be *false*, but the assumption does not beg the question.) The complex question *fallacy* occurs *only* when the assumption being made is a controversial one.

Complex Cross-Examination

Subtle complex questions sometimes do occur during cross-examination. (They must be so subtle that the opposing attorney does not catch them.) The following is a particularly good—at least a particularly tricky—example. Seymour Wishman was the defense attorney for Johnny Sayres, charged with murdering a man named Leander. The defense would claim that Johnny acted in self-defense. Wishman describes what happened:

> The first witness the D.A. called was a fat lady who said she had seen Johnny and the victim arguing. When their words had gotten "really angry," she testified, she had sensed danger and jumped over the bar.
>
> "I saw him take out a gun," she said, pointing at Johnny, who was sitting next to me at counsel table, "and I ducked down behind the bar. Then I heard these shots, four or five of them. Some people screamed, 'He shot Leander! He done shot Leander!' When I looked up, three people was standing over him. And the man was gone." . . .
>
> I began my cross-examination by asking this woman how much she weighed. When she said "two hundred pounds, more or less," I had her step down from the witness stand and walk to the edge of the jury box. I stood next to her, in front of the waist-high wooden wall separating us from the jury. . . .
>
> "How high was the bar you say you jumped over? Hold up your hand to show the height of the bar in comparison to the jury box."
>
> The woman looked at me suspiciously, and then held up her hand.
>
> "Let the record reflect," I said, "that the witness is indicating a height of approximately four feet. Now how much do you really weigh? Something closer to two hundred fifty than to two hundred pounds, wouldn't you say?" Actually, she looked closer to a thousand pounds to me and probably to the jury.
>
> "Well, maybe that's a fact."
>
> "And you're telling us you jumped over this bar?"
>
> "That's a fact."
>
> "You must have been mighty scared."
>
> "Ain't that the truth."
>
> "They must have been arguing pretty bad, the two of them, for you to have been that scared."
>
> "And how! I ain't ordinarily what you'd call no high *jumper.*"
>
> The jury and I laughed.
>
> "So I guess being so scared, you didn't see, with your jumping over this bar and hiding behind it and all, whether Leander reached for his gun before Johnny reached for his?"
>
> "That's right."

Before reading on, examine the above cross-examination and try to pick out exactly where the complex question occurs, and what important assumption is hidden in that complex question. (That is not an easy task, and it is not surprising that the district attorney failed to notice the use of the complex question.)

The defense attorney continues the story:

> I ended my questioning there, leaving the woman standing in front of the jury. There hadn't been any evidence that Leander had a gun, and the witness's answer let stand the existence of the gun assumed in my question. The prosecutor should have objected, but he didn't.[5]

Exercise 13-1

The following examples include begging the question, self-sealing, and complex question fallacies, *and* some arguments that are *not* question begging. (Remember: Simply repeating the conclusion does not count as begging the question; the conclusion must be *used* as a premise.) For each argument, tell whether it is question begging, self-sealing, complex question, or *not* question begging at all.

1. Some skeptics claim that people who report seeing flying saucers are not really careful observers and probably were mistaken about what they thought they saw. But, in fact, people who report seeing flying saucers *are* careful observers—for if they weren't careful observers they wouldn't have seen the flying saucers at all, would they?

2. We must place some limit on the amount of money a candidate can be allowed to spend in a political campaign, since unlimited spending by political candidates must be stopped.

3. REUBEN: When people who are in love get married, the marriage never ends in divorce.
   RACHEL: I think you're wrong about that. After all, Richard Burton and Elizabeth Taylor were deeply and passionately in love, but their marriage ended in divorce.
   REUBEN: Well, Richard Burton and Elizabeth Taylor must not have really been in love.

4. How is it that psychics are able to accurately predict details about the distant future? Are they in touch with some divine force, or is it perhaps a gift from demonic forces? Or does their power come from some other source?

5. We should find the defendant not guilty. There is certainly reasonable doubt about his identity as the robber: He was identified by only one person; she admitted under cross-examination that she wasn't really certain of the identification; and the faulty lineup from which she originally identified the defendant was not a fair one. So those are reasons for reasonable doubt, and given that reasonable doubt, we should return a verdict of not guilty. Besides, the defendant had an excellent and believable alibi, and that alone is enough to convince me that it is doubtful that this defendant is the person who robbed the jewelry store, and thus that we should vote not guilty. Those points put together add up to a verdict of not guilty.

6. The North Carolina Tar Heels are the best college basketball team in the country this year, and they never lose a game. It's true that they lost three games to Duke, and two to Maryland; but those games really don't count, because Duke and Maryland just caught the Tar Heels on bad days, and they got a lot of lucky bounces. So the Tar Heels didn't really lose, even though Duke and Maryland might have scored a few more points in those games.

7. Atheists should not be allowed to speak on state college campuses, since people who deny the existence of God should be banned from speaking at state colleges.

8. Smoking is not actually addictive: Smokers can stop smoking if they wish to do so. Some people seem to try very hard to quit smoking without success, and sometimes they claim that they really want to stop smoking but just cannot do so. But obviously those people (who say they are trying to stop smoking but cannot stop) do not really want to stop smoking, for anyone who truly wants to stop smoking can stop.

9. Some people question whether our government is sufficiently concerned about the safety of nuclear power plants. Obviously our government *does* take great care about the safety of nuclear power plants, for our government allows many nuclear power plants to operate, and our government certainly would not allow nuclear power plants to operate if they were not safe.

10. We should not pass a capital gains (income from stocks, bonds, and other investments) tax cut. Almost every dollar of a capital gains tax cut would go to the wealthiest 5% of our citizens, and they are already the people whose income is increasing most rapidly, and they are obviously the people least in need of tax savings. Furthermore, such a tax cut would run the danger of overstimulating the economy, driving up inflation, and thus pose a danger to our economic prosperity. So clearly there should not be a reduction of capital gains taxes.

11. Alcoholism cannot be considered a disease. Alcoholism is a serious social problem, and no social problem should be classified as a disease.

12. From September 1972 through January 1973, the California trial of Juan Corona, accused of the murder of 25 men, was a national news story. The crimes with which Corona was charged were

particularly gruesome. The bodies of 25 old men were found buried in shallow graves; the victims had been hacked to death, and the prosecution claimed that Corona was the mass murderer.

During the trial, and during the jury's week-long deliberation, Corona's wife and four young daughters were always nearby. The jury carried on long, intense, and often bitter deliberations, requiring a full week before reaching a verdict. A number of the jurors doubted that Corona had committed the murders through several days of deliberation. One of the key arguments for conviction—that was particularly convincing to two of the jurors who originally were most doubtful of Corona's guilt—was, briefly, this: "What if we let Corona go and he not only returns to killing more old men but he harms his own children? . . . What if Corona is indeed guilty but [we] don't convict him and so he goes back to not only hurting poor old men but his own family?"[6]

13. Why is it that Home State University professors are such warm, caring, generous people? Is it because they love teaching, and it makes them happy and warm? Or because spending so much time on our beautiful university campus puts them in a warm and generous mood?

14. Home State students are wonderful, and their honesty, honor, and integrity are truly amazing. No Home State student would ever do anything dishonest, and certainly would never cheat on an exam or plagiarize a paper. OK, I know that Wendell Wicclair was recently suspended from Home State for buying three of his term papers online and claiming that he wrote them himself, cheating on his final exam, and stealing someone's wallet and a book bag from a computer lab. But Wendell doesn't count: he was never a genuine Home State student, because he never really had the true Home State spirit of honesty and integrity.

15. The United States should have guaranteed health care for *every* U.S. citizen. We are a democracy, and we claim to believe that every citizen is equal, and entitled to life, liberty, and pursuit of happiness. Well, if some of our citizens can't get medical treatment for their illnesses, and die prematurely from diseases that could be cured, then we are not living up to our principles of equality and opportunity for our citizens. So if we really take our democratic principles seriously, we must have health care for every citizen. Furthermore, not having universal health care actually costs us a lot of money. For when people don't have access to health care, they put off checkups and delay treatments, and instead of being treated at less cost for a minor problem, they wind up in an emergency room requiring very expensive treatment for an advanced illness. Not only that, but we lose a lot of money because people without health care miss more work, and they contribute less to the economy. So for sound economic reasons, we should have universal health care. And finally, universal health care is simply the right thing to do: It should be obvious to anyone that in a wealthy country in which many people live in mansions and drive limousines and have yachts and beach cottages and ski chalets, it is just wrong for some people to be denied basic health care while other citizens are living lives of wasteful luxury. So universal health care is a policy that should be adopted and implemented in the United States.

Exercise 13-2

For each of the following questions, tell what *assumption* (or assumptions) is embedded in the question. (In some cases, there may be several assumptions—be sure you note *all* the important assumptions contained in each question.)

1. Why do women think less analytically than men?
2. What programs must be cut in order to balance the federal budget?
3. Why have baseballs become so much livelier?
4. Who designed the U.S. plan for dealing with an extraterrestrial invasion?
5. What is the best way to gain knowledge of right and wrong?
6. What makes humans different-in-kind from animals?
7. How does my mind cause my body to do things?
8. What is the purpose of human life?
9. When did you become a witch?
10. When did Columbus discover America?
11. What valuable insights have you gained from reading this chapter?

✓•⌐**Study** and **Review** on **mythinkinglab.com**

REVIEW QUESTIONS

1. What is a question-begging argument?
2. Give an example of synonymous begging the question.
3. Give an example of circular begging the question.
4. How should a self-sealing argument be answered?
5. What is a complex question?
6. Under what circumstances are assumptions in arguments legitimate? When are they not legitimate?

NOTES

[1] Lewis Carroll, "The Hunting of the Snark," in *The Collected Verse of Lewis Carroll* (London: Macmillan, 1932), p. 271.

[2] Reprinted with permission of Macmillan Publishing Company from *Gentlemen of the Jury*, by Francis L. Wellman, Copyright © 1924 by Macmillan Publishing Company, renewed 1952 by Ethel Wellman, pp. 132–133.

[3] Antony Flew, *Thinking Straight* (Buffalo, NY: Prometheus Books, 1977), p. 47.

[4] Lewis Carroll, *Alice in Wonderland*, Chapter 6.

[5] Seymour Wishman, *Confessions of a Criminal Lawyer* (Hammondsworth, Middlesex: Penguin Books, 1981), pp. 171–173. First published in the United States by Times Books, 1981. © Seymour Wishman, 1981.

[6] Victor Villasenor, *Jury* (Boston, MA: Little, Brown, 1977), p. 140.

INTERNET RESOURCES

Some good examples of begging the question and complex question (which the site calls "Fallacies of Inappropriate Presumption") can be found at the Critical Thinking Web, at *http://philosophy.hku.hk/think/arg/complex.php*.

ADDITIONAL READING

Douglas N. Walton, *Begging the Question: Circular Reasoning as a Tactic of Argumentation* (Westport, CT: Greenwood Press, 1991), is a very detailed study of question-begging arguments, with a wealth of examples.

▭•⌐**Read** the **Document** on **mythinkinglab.com**

Bruce N. Waller, "Fallacy of Begging the Question," *Coffee and Philosophy*, pp. 13–14. Discusses ways in which claims are made without any genuine support.

Cumulative Exercises Two (Chapters 1 through 13)

This second set of cumulative exercises is similar to the first (some are fallacious, some are not); but in addition to the argument types covered in the first set of exercises, this set also contains examples of argument forms (fallacious and nonfallacious) covered in Chapters 11, 12, and 13. For each example, *first* tell what form the argument is (such as slippery slope), *then* determine whether the argument is or is not fallacious.

The argument forms included are as follows:

Ad hominem: sometimes a fallacy, sometimes not
Inverse ad hominem: sometimes a fallacy, sometimes not
Strawman: always a fallacy
Irrelevant reason (or red herring): always a fallacy
Appeal to ignorance: always a fallacy
Ambiguity: always a fallacy
Appeal to authority: sometimes a fallacy, sometimes not
Appeal to popularity: always a fallacy
Appeal to tradition (traditional wisdom): always a fallacy
Analogies (deductive, inductive, figurative): Sometimes fallacious, sometimes legitimate
Analogical literalism: always a fallacy
Slippery slope: sometimes a fallacy, sometimes not
Dilemma arguments: sometimes the fallacy of false dilemma, sometimes a genuine dilemma
Golden mean: always a fallacy (though it is *not* inherently fallacious to advocate a moderate position)
Begging the question: always a fallacy
Self-sealing argument: always a fallacy
Complex question: always a fallacy (though embedded *non*controversial assumptions do not commit this fallacy)

1. There have been some people who want to raise questions about the safety of our new BUGMURDER insecticide. They say that there is evidence that BUGMURDER causes cancer, heart problems, and nervous disorders. But in fact new BUGMURDER is the most effective insecticide ever introduced! It absolutely kills all the bugs that damage lawns and gardens, and destroys the insects that damage agricultural crops; so with BUGMURDER you can have greener lawns, bigger tomatoes, and larger wheat harvests. So obviously these claims about the health risks of wonderful new BUGMURDER are just a lot of nonsense.

2. The American Cancer Society wants to run advertisements and programs to discourage young people from starting to smoke and encourage smokers to stop. But what they really want is a ban on all tobacco products: a ban that would make it illegal for anyone, of any age, to use tobacco in any form. They want to make tobacco use a criminal offense, and give people long prison terms just for possessing a pack of cigarettes or taking a chew of tobacco. If they had their way, the prisons would be full of tobacco-chewing baseball players and cigar-smoking executives and cigarette-smoking adults. But that would place terrible restrictions on our freedoms: after all, we believe that adults should be able to choose even harmful activities if they wish. So we must stop this American Cancer Society campaign.

3. There is of course enormous controversy over the Israeli–Palestinian conflict in the Middle East, and experts have proposed many different and divergent approaches to resolving the conflict. But Professor Edward Chandler is a political scientist at Harvard University, and is a world-renowned expert on Middle East politics; and his view is that the best solution is to set up a United Nations force that will guard the Palestine–Israel border and keep the peace. Professor Chandler has spent his entire career studying this region, and so his position should be accepted as the most promising.

4. Ohio is now running a large budget deficit: current projections indicate that the state is short well over a billion dollars. So we are faced with a very tough choice: either close the prisons or make huge cuts in higher-education spending. But obviously we cannot close the prisons. That would mean releasing thousands of dangerous criminals onto our streets, and that would overwhelm our police forces, and might well result in a crime wave. So hard as it is, we are forced to make huge cuts in higher education.

5. Bruce Waller argues that every college student should be required to take a course in critical thinking. He says that it is useful for students to learn basic principles of evaluating arguments no matter what their major: whether they are mathematicians or English majors, engineers or historians, sociologists or chemists, they can all benefit from the basic reasoning techniques learned in critical thinking. And Bruce also says that all students should have to take critical thinking because all students are citizens in a democracy, and they must be competent critical thinkers when they decide how to vote, when they serve on school boards or juries, and generally to be effective, thoughtful, self-governing citizens participating in our democratic society. But you should keep one thing in mind as you listen to Bruce's argument: he wrote a critical thinking textbook, and every time a new copy of that text is sold, Bruce picks up a buck or two. If every student took critical thinking and bought Bruce's textbook, Bruce would pocket several thousand dollars. So it's not hard to guess why that greedy sleaze wants all students to take critical thinking! And when you keep that in mind, it's hard to take seriously Bruce's argument for requiring critical thinking.

6. There is currently controversy over whether we should include "under God" in the U.S. Pledge of Allegiance. But obviously we *should* include "under God" in the pledge. After all, we've had "under God" in our pledge for half a century. Our parents and even our grandparents said "under God" in the pledge. So certainly we should not change it now.

7. You remember we were talking about who was the Union Commanding General at the Battle of Gettysburg? Well, I called Shelby Foote, the author of an outstanding history of the Civil War, and I also called Professor Bunting, who teaches Civil War history at the University of Michigan, and both said that it was General Meade. So Meade must have been the Union Commanding General at the Battle of Gettysburg.

8. It is very important that you vote. Voting is one of your responsibilities as a citizen. And if you neglect that responsibility, then soon you may neglect other responsibilities. You start with neglecting to vote, and next you neglect to obey the traffic laws, and then you neglect your responsibility to pay your taxes, and you begin to ignore your job responsibilities, and eventually you begin to neglect your responsibilities to your family. So if you don't want to end up a useless parasite who takes no responsibility and makes no contributions to the good of society, then be sure to honor your responsibility to vote.

9. Suppose the quarterback fakes a handoff to the halfback and then throws a long pass. There's nothing wrong with that, right? In the same way, suppose I'm selling a used car, and I fake the number of miles on the car—it actually has 150,00 miles, but I turn the odometer back to only 50,000. Since you agree that it's okay to run a fake in football, you should also approve of me running a fake when I sell a car.

10. Remember the Total cereal advertisement? The one that argued that Total cereal is more nutritious than raisin bran, because it contains more vitamins than raisin bran? Some people say that the

argument is not a good argument, because the conclusion doesn't follow from the premises. But in fact it's a very good argument, since it significantly increased sales of Total cereal.

11. Travis Traylor is one of the candidates for Dean of the College of Arts and Sciences at our university. But he is *not* the person we should select for that important position. He was fired from his last position as chair of the philosophy department at North State University when he got in an argument with another professor and took a swing at him. The year before, he had a medical leave to deal with his alcohol problems. And recently his PhD was revoked, because evidence proved that he had plagiarized his dissertation. Traylor cheats on his research, he has a nasty temper, and he has a serious drinking problem: He is not the sort of person we want to hire as our dean.

12. We can either keep all marijuana use illegal, or we can legalize marijuana and eliminate all restrictions on the sale and use of marijuana. But it would be absurd to eliminate all restrictions on marijuana: that would mean that school children could buy marijuana out of vending machines, and people could smoke marijuana as they drive, and marijuana could be advertised to children during Saturday morning cartoons. Clearly, then, we must keep all uses of marijuana strictly illegal.

13. Legalizing marijuana for recreational use would be going too far. On the other hand, a total and absolute ban on any use of marijuana seems too severe. What we should do is make marijuana available for medicinal use, only with a doctor's prescription. That is a good, reasonable solution.

14. If you want a great bioethics class, take Brendan Minogue. He is a superb teacher, who presents material in a way that is both clear and entertaining. And he stays very current with the rapidly changing field of bioethics through his reading, writing, and hospital consulting work. Finally, he's a very nice guy, who is generous and fair to his students. If you're looking for a fascinating class taught by a wonderful teacher, take Brendan's bioethics.

15. John McCain recently proposed dropping the 14 cents a gallon federal gasoline tax during the summer months. But that's just silly, and it's not going to really help us with the basic problem of super high gas prices. It would be like your university tripling the tuition price, and then dropping a five dollar lab fee for your chemistry course. It doesn't really deal with the basic problem of higher costs.

16. Professor Webble should be fired from the university! Last year, he accepted bribes from several students to pass them in his courses, an article he recently published as his own work was in fact plagiarized from someone else's writings, he has made racist remarks during his lectures, and over the past two years at least seven of his students have made complaints of sexual harassment against him. The man should be fired, and quickly.

17. The United States has thousands of nuclear bombs. Since we are the only superpower in the world, obviously we should not build more nuclear bombs. On the other hand, we need not start destroying any of our nuclear weapons. The more moderate course of simply maintaining our present nuclear arsenal is obviously the best policy.

18. Philosophy is central and essential for a good university education. All of the really good universities require students to take several philosophy courses before they graduate, because the best universities are those that recognize the vital importance of philosophy for a good education.

19. Senator Shepherd argues that the new combination airplane–helicopter that is being built for the U.S. military—the Osprey—should be scrapped. He points out that it has been involved in several crashes already, and thus poses a danger to our troops; that the cost of the project is enormous, and the funds could be better spent on other projects; and that the aircraft is not fast enough to serve as an airplane, nor stable enough to really work as a helicopter, and thus will never be an effective military aircraft. And before you pass judgment on Senator Shepherd's argument, you should know that the Osprey is actually being built in his home state, and that stopping the project will cost jobs in his state, and will be enormously unpopular with the voters of his state, and may ultimately cost Senator Shepherd his Senate seat! If he is willing to put his political career on the line for what he believes, then his reasons must be strong ones, and we should accept Senator Shepherd's argument for scrapping the Osprey.

20. There is currently controversy over whether we should include "under God" in the U.S. Pledge of Allegiance. But we should pay no attention to those people who want to remove "under God" from the pledge. What they want is to change the pledge to "one nation, with no God." They want to ban all public worship and public prayer, and board up all the churches, temples, and mosques. If they have their way, you could only pray and worship in secret!

21. The French ambassador to the United Nations argued that Saddam Hussein was not a threat, because arms inspection keeps him from building dangerous weapons. And the ambassador also argued that Saddam's weapons were being destroyed, that inspections were working, and that war against Iraq would result in thousands of civilian casualties, and might destabilize the Middle East, and so we should not go to war against Saddam. But there's something you should keep in mind: France got a significant amount of its oil from Saddam, and so France obviously had an interest in preventing a war against Saddam. That being the case, we shouldn't be fooled by these self-serving French arguments against war with Saddam.

22. Some critics have charged that the United States has tortured and mistreated prisoners captured in Afghanistan and Iraq, soaking them with water and leaving them chained in extremely cold, dark rooms for many days, keeping them bound and blindfolded for long periods, depriving them of sleep for days on end, and on one occasion packing prisoners tightly into steel drums that were exposed to bright sunshine until many died from the heat or from suffocation. But these charges are clearly false, for the United States never engages in torture or mistreatment of prisoners.

23. New York has recently passed a ban on the use of trans fat (which causes high cholesterol and heart disease, and is found in many cooking oils) in restaurants. One of the people who campaigned in favor of the ban on trans fat said that banning trans fat in restaurant foods is like banning lead from house paint (lead in house paint has been banned in the United States for several years because of its health risks), since both cause severe health problems. But that's a bad comparison: paint comes in many different bright colors, while the cooking oils that contain trans fat are all a dull yellowish color, and they would look really ugly on the walls of your house.

24. Almost all the Iraqi citizens are delighted that the U.S. military forces are in Iraq, and the Iraqis fervently hope that the U.S. forces will remain there for many years to run the country and keep order. True, there have been some massive demonstrations by thousands of Iraqis demanding that the U.S. military leave Iraq. But those Iraqi demonstrators are just agitators, and not real citizens of Iraq, because all the real Iraqis are happy to have the U.S. military in their country.

25. The CIA developed the SARS virus, and spread it into China in order to weaken the Chinese military and undermine the Chinese economy. Some people might have doubts about whether the CIA would do such a thing. But keep this in mind: The CIA has offered absolutely no proof that they did not spread SARS, and they have not even denied doing so! So SARS must be a CIA conspiracy.

26. William Bennett is the best-selling author of *The Book of Virtues*. Bennett constantly argues in favor of the traditional virtues, such as honesty, thrift, patriotism, traditional family roles, and self-reliance: the values that Bennett and other social conservatives call "family values." But now comes news that Bill Bennett is a high-stakes gambler, who has lost hundreds of thousands of dollars during gambling sprees at a number of Atlantic City casinos. Well, blowing hundreds of thousands of dollars in sleazy casinos is not exactly practicing thrift, nor is it a great way to spend quality time with your family. So nobody should be fooled by "Blackjack Bill Bennett" and his arguments for "family values."

27. It has been suggested that I plagiarized my term paper. But certainly I did not, because plagiarism is dishonest, and I am a completely honest person.

28. In the fall of 2000, a study—performed by a consultant who often works for the U.S. Environmental Protection Agency, and called "state of the art" by a spokesperson for the American Lung Association—reported that air pollution for electric power plants in the United States kills more than 30,000 Americans every year. Ralph DiNicola, a spokesperson for FirstEnergy Corporation, had this response to the report.

> "It is one thing to stand on the sidelines and bark about what the problem is, and a totally different responsibility to produce reliable, affordable electricity in an environmentally responsible manner. While these people would like to grow food in their back yards, and pedal bicycles to power medical diagnostic equipment, that is not what the rest of the world wants to do." (Reported in *The Cleveland Plain Dealer*, October 17, 2000)

29. Senator Lodge claims to be deeply concerned about the problems of the small farmer, and he pledges that if he is reelected he will devote strong and sincere efforts to helping small farmers and preventing small farmers from being forced into bankruptcy. But his record speaks louder than his words. During his last term in the Senate, he consistently voted against all proposals to provide debt relief for deeply indebted small farmers, he opposed every farm-aid bill, he voted to cut funding for a low-cost federal loan program for farmers; and furthermore, Senator Lodge supported proposals

to place heavier taxes on farm machinery and on chemical fertilizer, thus making the cost of operating small farms even more expensive. When you look at Senator Lodge's actual record, I think you must conclude that he is lying about his dedication to helping the small farmer. Today he says he is concerned about the small farmer, but only because he wants the votes of small farmers. Senator Lodge is not trustworthy.

30. The views of those who favor the mandatory use of seatbelts are absurd. They claim that if everyone is required by law to wear seatbelts when riding in a car, then there will be no more automobile fatalities, and that serious automobile injuries will be almost entirely eliminated. But that is an absurd view. Clearly some automobile accidents are so bad that even the best seatbelts would not prevent serious injury or death. (After all, there are still serious injuries and deaths in stock car racing, and stock car drivers all wear elaborate seatbelts.) And besides, seatbelts could not prevent all traffic fatalities, since some of the victims of auto accidents are pedestrians—and certainly seatbelts would not save *their* lives. So the claims of the advocates of mandatory use of seatbelts are really ridiculous.

31. It is wrong to place limits on smoking in public places. Tobacco smoking started in North America, and down through the centuries Americans have always smoked in public. In restaurants, in buses, in streetcars, in stores—even in stagecoaches—Americans have smoked in public. And now some people want to restrict smoking in public places. We've never had restrictions on smoking in public places, and we shouldn't start now.

32. Some people argue that capital punishment is unfair because the poor are much more likely to be executed than are rich murderers, who practically never face the death penalty. But what about the murder *victims?* Certainly *they* were not treated fairly. So those arguments about the unfairness of capital punishment don't really work.

33. During the last 3 years, the tuition at YSU has steadily increased while the number of courses offered for students has decreased. Some students complain that it's like being charged more and more for a cheeseburger while the cheeseburger gets smaller and smaller. But that's a bad comparison: after all, eating cheeseburgers causes high cholesterol, but whatever its problems, a university education does not increase your cholesterol level.

34. We obviously cannot stop killing and eating farm animals; we cannot become vegetarians as some people recommend. If we don't kill and eat farm animals, what are we supposed to do with them? We would have to turn the cows and pigs loose to roam over the countryside and wreck people's yards and cause danger on the highways. Obviously it's better to kill the animals for food than to have them running loose and causing havoc.

35. It was a sad day for Corn Valley College when it started its MBA program. Once a college starts one master's degree program, it soon develops other graduate programs. And then doctoral programs are developed, and soon a law school and a medical school are added, and more graduate and professional students enroll, and the undergraduate enrollment becomes massive. Thus starting from the MBA program, Corn Valley College will be transformed from a small, friendly, personal college into a huge, impersonal university.

36. Clearly we should not go overboard with this Star Wars satellite antimissile system and invest hundreds of billions of dollars in the total system. But at the other extreme, it would be foolish to ignore the possible military advantages of the Star Wars system. Obviously, then, what we should do is invest some money in developing a limited Star Wars system, but hold off on developing the total system.

37. This world is the best that could possibly exist. That follows from the fact that it was created by an infinite and perfect God, and anything created by a perfect God must necessarily be perfect. And we know that God is perfect, because we can see God's perfection reflected in the perfection of this best of all possible worlds that God created.

38. Phyllis Schlafly claims that we should return to the "traditional" family structure, with the husband as the head of the household and the woman taking care of the home and family. She argues that the arrangement will make for more stable marriages and more secure children and stronger families. But then Phyllis Schlafly leaves her own home to go on lecture tours and to work with her "Eagle Forum" organization. Well, as far as Phyllis Schlafly is concerned, her actions speak so loudly against her arguments that I can't hear a word she says!

39. BILL: In all groups, some individual steps out as a leader and guides the group's behavior.
    PHIL: That often happens, but not always. What about our discussion group last night? No one emerged as a leader; instead, we all participated equally in the discussion.
    BILL: In that case there is still a leader; it's just that the group as a whole shares the individual leader role.

40. Ladies and gentlemen of the jury, consider the evidence that the prosecution has offered against my client, the defendant. The key prosecution evidence is the testimony of Robert Sly, who claims he saw the defendant stab Albert Oakes to death. But consider carefully: Can you really believe the unsubstantiated claims of Robert Sly? He has been previously convicted of second-degree murder, armed robbery, and credit card fraud; and he is testifying in this case in hopes of getting a reduced sentence. Indeed, he himself might well be suspected of murdering Albert Oakes, and so it would be very convenient for Robert to have someone else convicted for that crime! The prosecution case rests on the reliability of convicted murderer and swindler Robert Sly—who obviously has a motive for lying! No reasonable juror could fail to have a reasonable doubt about the testimony of a scoundrel like Sly; and so I ask for a verdict of not guilty.

41. This stuff about equal rights for women is nonsense. Those equal rights people want to make wives the heads of households, they want to require that all major U.S. corporations have a woman president, that no man ever be paid more than the lowest-paid woman, and they want at least half the players in the National Football League to be women.

42. Okay, it's true that our factory does pose some accident risks to our workers: perhaps severe risks of injury, even death. But people take risks every day: they smoke, they drive too fast, they play dangerous sports, they drink too much. Some even drive race cars and go skydiving and hang gliding, all of which are very dangerous. We think it's okay for people to take risks in other areas of life, right? So likewise we must conclude that there is nothing wrong with workers also facing risks when they come to work in our factory.

43. It would be going too far to allow doctors to administer lethal drugs to terminally ill patients who want to die. But then neither does it seem right to force terminally ill patients to continue to receive life-lengthening treatment. The solution, then, is to allow terminally ill patients to refuse life-sustaining treatment, but not allow the giving of drugs that would actually cause death.

44. People who advocate animal rights claim that dogs, cats, monkeys, cows, and deer have rights—such as the rights not to be abused, not to have pain inflicted upon them, not to be used in experiments. But obviously the animal rights position is wrong, because only humans have rights.

45. OK, fellow jurors, this is a tough case. But let's start with some of the facts. First, the blood found on the defendant's jacket was not the same type as the murder victim's blood. That was established by the expert testimony of Dr. Cone, of Harvard Medical School; Dr. Jones, clinical director of the Blood Research Division of the National Institutes of Health; and Dr. Morton, who won the Nobel Prize for her research on blood transfusions. They all asserted that the blood was not that of the murder victim, and no testimony was offered that disputed their assertions.

46. Why is it that philosophy majors make so much money? Is it because of their high intelligence? Their perseverance? Or is it some other factor?

47. It is a mistake to raise the legal drinking age to 21. If this year we raise the drinking age to 21, next year it will be raised to 25, and then to 30; and before you know it, you'll be able to draw social security before you're old enough to legally drink a beer.

48. It is quite clear that some individuals have actually lived previous lives in past ages, because after all, no one has been able to prove that such claims of previous lives are false.

49. Bruce argues that we should abolish capital punishment. Bruce argues that it is clearly a cruel punishment and thus violates our constitutional prohibition against cruel and unusual punishment. He also argues that it focuses too much attention and energy on individuals who commit terrible crimes, instead of seeking out and changing the social and psychological conditions that cause crime. And finally, Bruce argues that because of the major problems with eyewitness identification, it is quite possible—even likely—that we will wind up executing innocent people; and in support of that last point, he notes the many cases of people in prison and on death row who have been proved innocent of the charges for which they were convicted, mainly through use of new DNA evidence that proved their innocence. But look, Bruce is really just an aging hippie, and you know how those people are: they walk around in a daze from all the drugs they did in their youth, they wear worn-out jeans and flash the peace sign and say, "Whatever turns you on, Man." Bruce's brain was permanently addled during his younger days. His thinking was never very clear, and every day as he gets older his hair gets greyer and his mind gets more confused. So you needn't pay much attention to Bruce's arguments against capital punishment; Bruce hasn't lived in the real world since before Woodstock.

50. If General Motors closes this plant and replaces it with a manufacturing plant in a foreign country paying lower wages, that is likely to have a terrible effect on this community. Of course only 300 jobs would be lost, which may not sound like much in a town of 50,000; but the bad effects tend to multiply. Not only are 300 workers unemployed; in addition, those workers and their families will have their incomes severely cut, and thus they will spend significantly less. They will buy less furniture, fewer appliances, delay putting a new roof on the house, cancel the plans they made with a local travel agent for a summer vacation, give up their plans to take their children to the orthodontist, cancel contracts to have houses painted and decks added, eat out less often at local restaurants. Thus the ripple effect on the economy is likely to be substantial, affecting not just 300 laid-off workers and their families, but also appliance and furniture stores, painting and building contractors, travel agents: All are likely to lay off workers to cover the loss of income. Some businesses will probably close. And between closed businesses and unemployed workers, the tax base for the city and county begins to shrink. And this reduction in tax revenue happens at precisely the time when more people are unemployed and thus in need of government services. Thus tax money that would have gone to repair roads and improve education is lost, and more workers, in local schools and in local government, lose their jobs. So while a company may claim that its decision to close a manufacturing plant will have little negative impact on the local community, it is not true: The long-term, overall effects to the local economy and to the local quality of life are likely to be substantial and painful.

51. Perhaps 18 is too young for strong liquor like whiskey and vodka. But on the other hand, we shouldn't completely prohibit 18-year-olds from drinking alcoholic beverages. We should therefore set 18 as the legal age for beer and 21 as the legal age for hard liquor.

52. It is sometimes said that boxing is an excessively dangerous sport that often results in brain and eye injuries. But such claims are false. Boxing is a fast and exciting sport that requires hard training, quick reflexes, and tremendous endurance. And if you want to talk about injuries, what about football? Every week some poor quarterback gets carried off the field, and usually some other players as well.

53. Capital punishment is wrong, because it is wrong to take the life of a human being, no matter what crime that human being has committed.

54. Whatever you do, don't peek at anyone else's paper during the exam! If you cheat on an exam, then tomorrow you will be tempted to cheat on your income tax. And cheating on your taxes may lead to other sorts of theft, such as shoplifting. And of course it doesn't take much to go from shoplifting to armed robbery. So don't cheat on your exam—it can easily lead to terrible, violent crimes!

55. Katherine Bonds argues that we must drastically reduce the federal budget deficit, and that the only fair, reasonable, and effective means of making such a reduction is by placing heavier taxes on the wealthiest people. She argues that those people made the most money from the policies that caused the deficit, and that they are the ones who can afford to pay more taxes without suffering hardship, and that if we really want to reduce the deficit we have to take the money from those who have it: and the rich are obviously the people with money. Katherine's argument has special cogency, since she is a very wealthy woman with an income of well over $1 million a year, and she herself would be among the most heavily taxed if we adopted the policies for which she argues.

56. English has been the standard language used in the United States since the birth of the nation. Our Declaration of Independence and our Constitution were written in English, and all our official business has been conducted in English for well over 200 years. It has always been expected that immigrants to the United States would learn English. Through the last two centuries, people have come to the United States from every corner of the globe, speaking every language; and they and their children have learned to speak English. Of course it is fine for people to speak another language as well, and use that language with their family and friends if they wish; but English has been *the* common language for all U.S. citizens for our entire history, and it must remain so.

57. We must stop those people who favor censorship of television. They want to eliminate all programs that have anything to do with sex, ban any programs that have any violence at all, and forbid shows that contain even the mildest profanities. If they have their way, the only programs that will be allowed on television will be *Lassie* and *Little House on the Prairie*.

58. This guy, Merlin Magellan, claims that he can bend spoons without touching them. He claims that simply by concentrating his psychic powers on them, he causes them to bend. Now either he's a real psychic, or he is severely self-deluded and delusional, or he is a fraud. He is not delusional, for he has been thoroughly tested by competent psychologists who all agree that he does not suffer from delusions. And it does not seem likely that he really has psychic powers, for he has never been able to successfully demonstrate those powers under controlled observation, and there are several

magicians who can duplicate his "psychic" feats and without any use of "psychic powers." So we have to conclude that Merlin Magellan is a fraud.

59. Our power company is not overcharging for electricity. When you think of all the wonderful things electricity powers that our ancestors did not have—electric lights, refrigerators, air conditioners, fans, electric blankets, microwave ovens, radios, televisions, computers—it is obvious that electricity has greatly enriched our lives and made our homes more convenient, interesting, and comfortable. So when we consider all the great benefits of electricity, it is obvious that the price we pay for electricity is a bargain.

60. Alice Autry argues that children should be in school year round, rather than having a 3-month summer vacation. She argues that the long vacation period causes kids to forget much of what they have learned during the year, and so much of the following fall is spent reteaching material students have forgotten over the summer. Also, with an extra 3 months of school, students would have more time to study valuable additional materials—such as foreign languages—that are too often neglected. And there's something you should know about Alice: she is the owner of a major water park, and if kids are in school all summer, then they will not be able to go to her water park as often, and she will suffer serious financial losses. Since she believes in year-round schooling so much that she's willing to lose money to support it, that obviously gives special strength to her arguments in favor of year-round schooling.

61. Some people object to the logo of the Cleveland Indians, claiming that "Chief Wahoo" is offensive to Native Americans, that it is probably racist, and that at the very least it is in very bad taste. But, in fact, there is absolutely nothing wrong with the Indians' logo; after all, lots of Indians fans from throughout Ohio love the logo, and clothing and caps with Chief Wahoo on them are among the top sellers of baseball merchandise. That many fans certainly can't be wrong.

62. Obviously we don't want to impose tests for illegal drugs on *everyone* in society. On the other hand, we certainly should not eliminate all tests for illegal drugs. The best program, then, must be to steer a middle course: Do random drug testing on *some* groups (such as all people between ages 15 and 25, a prime group for use of illegal drugs) but not on everyone.

63. Giordano Bruno was an early follower of Copernicus. The Copernican theory (which has the Sun at the center of the solar system and the planets orbiting the Sun) replaced the older Ptolemaic theory (according to which Earth is stationary at the center, and the Sun and planets circle Earth). Bruno believed that one implication of the Copernican theory was that the Sun was only one of many suns, and that there must therefore be many other worlds with intelligent life, and that each such world must have its own god or at least its own special manifestation of god. This view was condemned as heretical by the Catholic Church, and in 1600 Bruno was burned at the stake after refusing to renounce his views. Bruno's theory about there being many worlds and thus many gods may sound a bit strange, but there must be something to it, since Bruno believed it so strongly that he was willing to die for it.

64. Logic should be banned from our colleges. When people take logic, they begin to think carefully and logically. Then they are less swayed by emotions. Soon they completely eliminate emotions and feelings from their lives. Before you know it, they are cold and uncaring, and they become incapable of loving.

65. Everything that happens has a purpose. We know that to be true, since nothing happens without a purpose.

66. Elizabeth F. Loftus, an authority on the psychology of perception and on eyewitnesses, has argued that experts on the reliability of eyewitnesses ought to be allowed to testify in court as expert witnesses. She claims that most lay persons (including, of course, most jury members) fail to understand how easily an eyewitness can be mistaken about what the witness sincerely believes he or she remembers observing. But since Elizabeth Loftus is an expert on eyewitness testimony, if such expert witnesses were permitted to testify for the defense, then she would be much in demand as an expert witness—and she would make substantial amounts of money for appearing as an expert witness. When we see her potential profits if experts on eyewitnesses are allowed to testify, we also see where her arguments are coming from and exactly what *her* arguments are worth: not much.

67. There is now a version of the U.S. National Anthem that is sung in Spanish! That's just *wrong*! Our National Anthem has been sung in English ever since it was written, almost 200 years ago; our grandparents sang it in English, and it was sung in English during World War I and World War II, and our school children have sung it in English for decade after decade. So it is obviously wrong to have a Spanish language version of the U.S. National Anthem.

68. In the United States, everyone participates in politics. Some people may believe that they do not participate: those people who do not follow political issues are not registered to vote and do not vote, are not affiliated with any political party, and never discuss politics. But those people still participate, since they participate in politics by abstaining. Their refusal to participate is a type of participation, so actually everyone participates.

69. Laetrile (the drug made from apricot pits, which some people claim cures cancer) should not be banned in this country. After all, we're not suggesting that cancer patients should be *required* to have laetrile treatments. But on the other extreme, the drug should not be *banned*. The solution obviously is to let it be freely available to those who want it.

70. When you are buying a new car battery, it's hard to know which car battery you should choose. But remember one thing: Chuck Yeager says that AC Delco batteries are the best you can buy—and Chuck Yeager is one of the greatest test pilots of all time. So AC Delco batteries must really be the best.

71. All of the controversy about regulating insecticides is nonsense. In fact, we have to decide whether to ban all insecticides in the United States or to let farmers use any insecticides they desire. Now clearly we can't completely eliminate the use of insecticides, for that would mean that farmers would have almost no way of keeping insects from their crops, and the result would be tremendous crop losses, and perhaps even severe food shortages. So we must allow farmers to use any insecticides they desire, without restrictions.

72. We must not legalize marijuana. The legalization of marijuana would mean that it would not be a criminal act to possess marijuana. But certainly it is, and must remain, a criminal act to possess an illegal drug like marijuana. Therefore, we must oppose legalizing marijuana.

73. We should not attempt to cultivate marginal land that has thin topsoil. When it is plowed, the light, poor, sandy soil is subject to the effects of wind and water erosion, and as the soil becomes even worse through erosion it can hold less water, causing the water to run off faster and hasten erosion. Furthermore, as the water runs off faster, it cuts gullies and ditches, causing the water to run even faster and erode the soil still more severely, and, as the soil is blown, the force of the dust particles blown by the wind also increases the speed of erosion. The result is not just the destruction and erosion of the plowed area; as the erosion and washing spread, they may undermine surrounding vegetation, destroy windbreaks, and further hasten and exacerbate the effects of wind and water erosion. Like many things that we do to our environment, small, innocent-looking acts can cause long-term devastation.

74. There are people who want to raise doubts about the reliability of eyewitness testimony. They note that eyewitness identifications are often erroneous, and that juries tend to give eyewitness testimony and identifications much more weight than they should, since jurors are often unaware of all the ways eyewitness testimony can go wrong. But it is wrong to cast doubts on the use of eyewitness testimony in court. Our courts and our juries have relied on eyewitness testimony for literally hundreds of years, and eyewitness testimony has been a central part of our justice system during all that time.

75. You've got trouble, right here in River City. Some people are planning to open a pool hall. And once a pool hall opens in town, the next step is gambling. And then pornography. And then prostitutes and organized crime. You have to stop that trend before it gets started.

76. Ladies and gentlemen of the jury, the defendant has been accused of stealing social security checks from sick, disabled, and elderly people. He testified that he did not steal the social security checks, that this is all a case of mistaken identification. But as you consider his testimony, ask yourself carefully and seriously: Can you really believe the testimony of a man who steals money from the sick, disabled, and aged?

77. Ladies and gentlemen of the jury, you heard Mrs. Smith testify that she saw the defendant standing on the front porch of the burglarized house on the afternoon of the burglary. She testified that she had known the defendant since he was a boy and that she talked with him for about 10 minutes that afternoon on the porch. Now there are really only three possibilities here: that Mrs. Smith actually did see the defendant on the front porch on that afternoon; or that Mrs. Smith is lying about what she has sworn to; or that Mrs. Smith was mistaken. Now certainly Mrs. Smith was not mistaken: After all, she is of sound mind and good eyesight, she has known the defendant for many years, she stood within 10 feet of him and talked with him, and she remembers the exact date because she had just returned from an important meeting. And obviously Mrs. Smith was not lying: Her honesty is beyond reproach, and she would never lie to the court after she has sworn to tell the truth.

Therefore, you must conclude that Mrs. Smith actually did see the defendant standing on the front porch of the burglarized house, as she testified.

78. Vegetarians give arguments against eating meat: they say that it causes suffering for animals, that it is a very inefficient way of producing food, that it causes health problems, and that raising cattle and other animals for food causes great environmental damage. But these are people who just can't face up to the harsh realities of our brutal world, in which predators kill their prey, and often the predators are in their turn eaten by animals higher on the food chain. These vegetarians just can't stand to acknowledge that the world involves killing, whether the killers are army ants or Bengal tigers or human butchers. Who knows why these vegetarians refuse to face this reality: maybe they saw *Bambi* at a tender age, or maybe they are just too weak and cowardly for our harsh world. But whatever the cause of their problems, it is clear that these weak and unrealistic vegetarians are not saying anything that deserves our attention.

79. The position of those who support active euthanasia is not just absurd; in fact, it is profoundly dangerous. They favor allowing doctors to administer lethal drugs to bring a swift death to those who are suffering, but they want to allow the doctors to make the decision and administer the lethal drugs, without even requiring the consent of the person to be killed. So the doctors could make all the decisions. If you go into the hospital with a stomachache, the doctor could decide to put you out of your misery by swiftly ending your life. This would pose a terrible risk to all of us, and would severely undermine not only our respect for life but also our rights of self-determination. So obviously we must oppose and defeat efforts to legalize active euthanasia.

80. What is the best way of reducing the federal deficit? That question is no longer in doubt. Milton Friedman, professor of Economics at the University of Chicago and a Nobel Prize winner in economics, asserts that the best means of reducing the deficit is by cutting federal taxes. So if Professor Friedman recommends it, that is certainly the best policy.

81. Either it is always wrong to tell a lie or there is nothing wrong with lying. Now certainly there are some times when lying is not wrong. For example, when the members of the German resistance (who worked against the Nazis) were captured, they lied about their membership in the resistance—but surely telling such lies was not wrong. And those who worked on the Underground Railroad (to smuggle escaped slaves out of the South and up to Canada) frequently had to lie to cover up their operations. And again, such lies were not wrong. So certainly it is not always wrong to tell a lie. And thus it follows that there is nothing wrong with lying.

82. No scientist believes in creationism. I know that Marshall Murdock—who has a PhD in biochemistry from Stanford, is currently head of a pharmacological research project at the University of Chicago, and who has published dozens of major scientific articles in reputable scientific journals—is a believer in creationism. But he is not a real scientist, since no genuine scientist could believe in creationism.

83. Some people suggest that those who lose their jobs will easily be able to secure another. It's not that easy. In fact, it often becomes tougher and tougher to get another job after being out of work. Your work skills may become rusty, and, with rapidly changing technology, they may even become outdated; there's a gap in your resume, and the longer you are out of work the larger the gap grows; your contacts with people in your type of work begin to dry up; sooner or later you have less money, and perhaps can't afford a classy suit or stylish haircut; you lose employee health insurance benefits, so perhaps your health declines; eventually you lose your confidence and find it tougher to get to job interviews; as you get more desperate, it shows in interviews, and you get more rejections, which makes you still more desperate and depressed, and depression breeds lethargy. So we should recognize that often for those who have lost jobs and have been out of work for a time, it gets harder and harder to find work, more and more difficult to climb back up the increasingly steep hill toward productive employment, and thus they may need special programs to help them back into the workplace.

84. Don't vote for Gene Grenling for mayor. He has no interest in making our city a better place for all our citizens; instead, he just wants to enrich himself and some of his friends by using the mayor's office to increase the value of his real-estate holdings. Also, he is not a friend of the environment: He has no interest in protecting our air and water quality, and has been a long-time opponent of even the most modest recycling programs. Don't vote for this narrow-minded, selfish, egotistical man.

85. Your children will love delicious, new wild tropical fruit poppers! They're made with real fruit, so you know they're good, and good for you.

86. One of your fellow jurors offers this argument:

> Look, I'm not sure that there is really overwhelming evidence that the defendant is guilty; but there's one thing that bothers me: If the defendant didn't murder Kelly, then who did? After all, the defendant did have a motive, and the defense was not able to suggest anyone else who had a motive for killing Kelly. So if you think the defendant didn't kill Kelly, answer me one thing: Who did it? Someone certainly did, and since the defendant couldn't suggest any better suspect—in fact, couldn't even think of any other suspect at all—I think we have to conclude that the defendant is guilty.

87. Okay, it's true that I took ten dollars from Laura's purse when we were all at her house for our review session on critical thinking. But it wasn't really stealing. After all, Laura served pizza and beer during the study session, and Brenda ate four pieces of pizza and drank three beers, and she took them without paying for them. And pizza and beer are expensive: what Brenda ate and drank was probably worth at least 10 dollars. So if there is nothing wrong with Brenda taking ten dollars worth of pizza and beer at Laura's house without paying for it, then obviously there's nothing wrong with me taking ten dollars out of Laura's purse.

88. Lisa claims that she saw Anita's boyfriend, Angelo, at a tavern on the west side of town. Lisa says that Angelo was sitting with his old high school girlfriend, in a back booth, and they were being *very* friendly. But frankly, I don't believe a word of what Lisa says. After all, she hates Angelo, and would do anything to break up Angelo and Anita; and besides, Lisa loves to spread rumors, and she's not always very careful about whether the rumors she spreads are actually true.

89. It is sometimes claimed that if funding for school lunch programs is cut, then many poor children will lose the one nutritious meal that they consistently receive, and many children will go hungry and suffer from malnutrition. But those claims are false and unfounded. After all, we must make cuts in federal spending in order to balance the budget, and it is essential that we balance the budget and stop running up this enormous deficit and debt. So cutting funds for school lunch programs will not deprive children of food, and will not result in malnutrition among poor children.

90. It would be a mistake to stop using team names such as the Washington Redskins, Cleveland Indians, and Atlanta Braves. After all, U.S. sports teams have used such names for many decades; indeed, the use of such team nicknames is almost as old as the games themselves.

91. For several years there has been a profound controversy—involving medical professionals, patients, politicians, and ethicists—about active *euthanasia* ("mercy killing") and physician-assisted suicide. But Dr. Willard Gaylin, a distinguished psychiatrist who is a former director of the Hastings Center for Applied Ethics, is widely recognized as an expert in the field of bioethics. And Doctor Gaylin clearly and decisively asserts that active euthanasia is wrong, and no medical personnel can legitimately participate in such practices. That should settle the issue. When such an outstanding bioethicist as Dr. Gaylin, who has devoted much of his career to studying, teaching, and writing about bioethics, says that active euthanasia is wrong, it must really be wrong.

92. Avoid these computer simulation games like the plague! Oh, I know they seem fine the first time or two you play them: just good innocent fun. But what happens is that the computer-simulated reality becomes very tempting: Your computer is always ready to play, it never complains when you win a game, it doesn't even mind if you cheat a bit. So computer simulations soon become more appealing than real life, and before you know it you're spending all your time with your computer-simulation friends, and then you stop going out with your flesh-and-blood friends. You become more and more isolated and stranger and stranger, until you wind up a total computer hermit, cut off from all real, personal human contact. The best way to avoid the computer-simulation trap is simple: don't start!

93. It would be a terrible mistake to destroy all of our forests and wilderness areas, leaving only a vast, concrete jungle. But that doesn't mean we must go to the other extreme, and preserve all our forests and wilderness areas. Obviously, a reasonable solution, then, is to preserve some of the most important and beautiful wilderness areas, but to allow the rest to be logged and developed for housing and commercial projects.

94. There is now before Congress a proposed amendment to the U.S. Constitution. This amendment would prohibit the burning of the U.S. flag as an act of protest or dissent. Some people try to make the issue seem complicated. It is actually a simple matter, and it comes down to this: Do you favor protecting and celebrating the American flag as a special honored symbol of our country and our heritage? Or do you think it's fine when protestors burn the American flag?

95. Lyndon Johnson was definitely involved in the plot to assassinate President John Kennedy. After all, Johnson had a motive to kill Kennedy: Johnson wanted to be president. And the most compelling evidence of Johnson's involvement is just this: He never, during his entire lifetime, offered conclusive evidence that he was *not* involved in an assassination conspiracy against Kennedy! Obviously, then, Johnson must have been involved—perhaps even the ring leader!

96. Opponents of capital punishment sometimes claim that there is a danger that innocent people will be executed. But that is not a real danger. After all, no one is really innocent. As Jesus said, "Let him who is innocent cast the first stone." We are all guilty of something. And since no one is genuinely innocent, there cannot be a danger of executing an innocent person.

97. No genuine patriot, who really loves his country, ever criticizes his country during time of war. I know that Abraham Lincoln, while he was a senator, argued that the United States was in the wrong during the U.S. war against Mexico; and many decorated U.S. war heroes from World War II opposed U.S. involvement in the Vietnam War. But those people couldn't really be patriots, for no genuine patriot would question his own country's acts during wartime.

98. Professor Lisa Lawrence argues that all university students should be required to take a minimum of 16 hours of a foreign language. Lisa notes that the rapid expansion of the world economy makes it vital for students to be able to communicate with other cultures if they are to be successful in business, and she also argues that it is a vital part of a broad education for students to study another culture, in order to gain more perspective on their own culture. And, Lisa argues, in order to genuinely understand another culture, it is necessary that students be able to read the literature of that culture and to communicate with its members in their own language. Perhaps the most important thing you should note about Lisa's argument is this: She is not a member of the foreign language faculty; she teaches in the philosophy department, and, in fact, if all students were required to take 16 hours of foreign language, then fewer students would have the time to take philosophy courses. That means that Lisa's own department would be threatened by a loss of students—and Lisa's own job might be jeopardized by a declining enrollment in philosophy courses! And yet Lisa's commitment to the study of foreign languages is so strong, she is willing to put her own job at risk by arguing for the importance of foreign language study. Since Lisa's convictions are so strong and sincere, we obviously ought to accept her arguments.

99. The health-care system of the United States is the fairest and most efficient in the world. After all, we have a tremendous number of dedicated doctors, nurses, and medical specialists, and we have a large number of hospitals. We lead the world in performing transplant surgery, and much of the most important medical research takes place in the United States.

100. Members of the jury, this is not a difficult case. The defendant, Sandra Banks, shot and killed her husband. Now either that shooting was an accident, or she is guilty of cold-blooded and calculated first-degree murder. But certainly it was not an accident. As she herself testified, she intended to shoot him. So it follows that she must be guilty of murder in the first degree.

101. So now researchers in England have actually cloned a sheep! This is an exciting scientific breakthrough, but it also carries risks of abuse. We should not place a total ban on this important area of scientific research; but, of course, neither should we allow it to move too swiftly into areas that may cause problems and for which we are not adequately prepared. The best policy, therefore, is to continue to allow cloning and research on cloning, but place a strict ban on the cloning of humans.

102. Former President Bill Clinton argues that it is very important that we raise the minimum wage. He points out that the minimum wage has not been raised for years, and that those who work for a minimum wage work full time for wages that leave them deep in poverty. He also notes that the salaries of CEOs are the highest in history, and he argues that it is fundamentally unfair for them to receive millions of dollars while some of their workers receive wages that leave them in poverty. And Clinton also points out that if the minimum wage is increased, then workers will have more money to spend, and their spending will provide a needed boost for the economy. But you should keep in mind that Bill Clinton is a man who lied under oath about a sexual affair, and who also lied to his wife and to the American people about his affair. It's clear that the man is a liar, and his argument for raising the minimum wage is worthless.

103. Bruce Waller says that there are bald eagles nesting in Mill Creek Park. He claims to have seen several bald eagles there, and says that he saw one bald eagle sitting on a nest containing eggs. Well, Bruce probably does believe that he saw bald eagles in Mill Creek Park. But Bruce knows absolutely nothing about birds: He couldn't distinguish a bald eagle from a Canada goose, much less tell an eagle from a hawk. Plus his eyes are so bad, even if he knew what a bald eagle looked like, he still couldn't see an eagle well enough to identify it if the eagle were more than 10 feet away from him.

And while Bruce certainly wouldn't lie about what he thought he saw, he does have a vivid imagination: Last year he was walking through Mill Creek Park and reported seeing a grizzly bear. It turned out to be just a large raccoon! So we should be very skeptical about Bruce's reports of seeing bald eagles in Mill Creek Park.

104. Look, half of us think the defendant was driving recklessly when he struck and killed a jogger, and so he should be convicted of aggravated vehicular homicide. The others on our jury maintain that he was not driving recklessly, that the accident was unavoidable and was the result of the jogger's recklessness. Well, we're never going to settle that. So let's meet in the middle: Let's find him guilty of the lesser charge of vehicular homicide, which merely requires driver negligence, not recklessness. That should satisfy everyone.

105. Those who want to increase the speed with which capital punishment sentences are carried out hold a completely unreasonable and unworkable position. They want to string people up without any review of the charges against them, and without any opportunity for them to appeal their convictions to higher courts, and for the worst crimes without having any trial at all. They want to bring back vigilante justice, in which gangs of citizens swiftly execute anyone they happen to think is guilty. And they want capital punishment not just for murder and treason, but also for any crimes of theft, including shoplifting and passing bad checks. Thus their position is vicious, unreasonable, and totally unacceptable.

106. If I am suffering from a painful and fatal disease, it is my right to decide whether I want to end my life more swiftly by taking (or by having a physician give me) a lethal drug. To deny me the right of determining when my life will be ended is to deny my right to self-determination concerning how I will live and how I will end my life. Once we start down that path, it is just a short step from deciding that I cannot decide to end my life to deciding that I cannot decide to reject medical treatment. And from there, if we can require people to get medical treatment, then we can require people to exercise, to eat fruits and vegetables, and to floss their teeth after every meal. Indeed, that path leads to total control of every individual's life, and total denial of all individual freedom. So we should not start down that path toward loss of freedom by denying individuals the freedom to choose to end their own lives through active euthanasia or physician-assisted suicide.

107. Students complain that the Home State University tuition increase is too much; but in fact, the tuition increase is very modest and reasonable. By law, the maximum amount that HSU could have raised tuition was 8%; and certainly that would have been too much. On the other hand, it would hardly be reasonable to have no tuition increase at all. So the tuition increase, of a modest 4%, is actually a good, moderate solution to a difficult issue.

108. Premarital sex is wicked and evil. The best evidence for this is that those who engage in premarital sex often feel guilty about it. There are, of course, some people who engage in premarital sex and do not feel guilty, but they are obviously people who are so depraved that they have reached the point that they can do wicked things without even feeling guilty.

109. Betsy Hart is a commentator on CNN and the Fox News Channel. In a newspaper column on June 12, 1998, she discussed a resolution passed by the Southern Baptist Convention: a resolution that affirms as a Biblical principle the doctrine that "wives must submit to their husbands." The resolution drew widespread criticism, but Betsy Hart defended it, claiming that its critics are "elites" who look down on the Southern Baptists; she then offered this answer to all the criticism:

> So, back to the Southern Baptist Convention and the specifics of what's causing all the fuss. I can't imagine elites really would say, for starters, that contrary to this Scripture, women should always demand their own way. Is that a healthy model for anyone?

110. We have to make a basic choice in our society. Either we allow continued development, construction, expansion, industrial buildup, and accept the fact that sometimes that development must involve destruction of natural environments, increases in pollution, and even the extinction of some species; or we must take the other alternative, and stop all construction projects, halt any further development, and slowly bring our industrial society to a painful, grinding stop. Since we obviously cannot afford to call a halt to all construction and development, it follows that we must continue development and stop worrying about destruction of the natural environment and the extinction of species.

111. Some folks complain that the United States has a larger percentage of its population in prison than any other Western country; well, that's true. But then they say that we ought to try to reduce the U.S. prison population, that the United States is imprisoning far too many people. But that's just nonsense. Apparently these people think that murderers, bank robbers, and rapists should be free to commit

their crimes without any prison time. When people do the crime, they should do the time—and those people who think we should reduce the U.S. prison population haven't really thought enough about how terrible it would really be to turn these vicious criminals loose with little or no punishment.

112. Many people have a very strong desire to smoke cigarettes. Since many people genuinely do have such a desire to smoke, it is obvious that smoking is desirable. Furthermore, anything that is truly desirable cannot really be a bad thing. Therefore, smoking cannot really be bad.

113. There are many people who believe that the United States should sign the international treaty agreeing to a ban on the use of land mines. But in fact, the United States certainly should *not* sign the test ban treaty, and then get rid of all our land mines. If today we eliminate land mines from our arsenal, then tomorrow someone will want to do away with tanks, and the next day there will be a push for eliminating bombers—after all, bombers kill civilians too. And then there will be a ban on machine guns, hand grenades, and rifles; and before you know it, the United States will be totally disarmed, and at the mercy of any hostile nation that wishes to attack us. So we must not agree to this proposed ban of land mines.

114. Some people argue that we must place limits on the amount of medical care and medical resources that people can consume. They claim that without some limits on the amount of health care that can be demanded by individuals, it will be impossible to provide health care for all citizens. But we obviously should *not* place limits on the health-care resources consumed by individuals, for there must be no restrictions on the amount of health-care resources available to individuals who want them and can afford them.

115. Suppose you own a restaurant, and a customer comes in and orders a steak with a baked potato. In your restaurant, the steak is served with a nice green salad and some hot bread; but your customer says, "No, no bread or salad for me; I'll just have the steak and potato." You wouldn't say, "No, sorry, you *must* eat the salad before you can have your steak." That would be ridiculous. Well, in the same way, when a student comes to Home State University and wants to take courses in biology or sociology or English literature, HSU also offers to teach them courses in math and in composition. And if a student says, "No, thank you, I just want to take the biology courses, or the sociology courses; no math or composition for me," then it's also ridiculous for HSU to say, "No, sorry, you *must* take the math and the composition before you can have the courses in biology and sociology." Just like the diner who is free to choose what he does and doesn't want to eat, students at HSU should be free to choose what courses they do and do not want to take.

116. You can certainly trust us, because we are men of integrity.

117. Some people have criticized my closing argument for the prosecution, claiming that it was not a good argument because it played on the emotions of the jury, inflaming them over the gruesome nature of the crime, and blinding the jurors to the lack of solid evidence against the defendant. But in fact it was a very good argument: It convinced all 12 jurors to vote for conviction; and that's what I call a damned good argument.

118. George J. Annas, a bioethicist, favors a ban on the cloning of humans. (Cloning is a technique of producing a genetically identical organism through the use of genetic material from the original organism.) He has claimed that a cloned human would be the first human genetically identical to its one parent. His claim was challenged by R. C. Lewontin, a biologist and population geneticist, who argued that:

> A child by cloning has a full set of chromosomes like anyone else, half of which were derived from a mother and half from a father. It happens that these chromosomes were passed through another individual, the cloning donor, on the way to the child. That donor is certainly not the child's "parent" in any biological sense, but simply an earlier offspring of the original parents. (R. C. Lewontin, "Confusion over Cloning," *New York Review of Books* [October 23, 1997], pp. 20–23)

Annas responds to Lewontin's challenge as follows:

> Lewontin takes genetic reductionism to perhaps its logical extreme. People become no more than containers of their parents' genes, and their parents have the right to treat them not as individual human beings, but rather as human embryos—entities that can be split and replicated at their whim without any consideration of the child's choice or welfare. Children (even adult children), according to Lewontin's view, have no say in whether they are replicated or not, because it is their parents, not they, who are reproducing. (George J. Annas, "Why We Should Ban Human Cloning," *The New England Journal of Medicine*, Vol. 339, no. 2 (July 9, 1998), pp. 122–125)

14

❖ ❖ ❖

Necessary and Sufficient Conditions

(((•─[Listen to the **Chapter Audio** on **mythinkinglab.com**

Whether you are reading an editorial, watching a commercial, or serving on a jury, detecting the exact conclusion is of the first importance. But that is often a complex task. If you are serving on the jury during a breaking or entering case, it is easy enough to state the conclusion that the prosecution is attempting to prove: The defendant is guilty of breaking or entering. That's right as far as it goes, but it doesn't go very far.

NECESSARY CONDITIONS

The judge's instructions to the jury will describe *exactly* what must be proved in order to convict of breaking or entering. If you don't know exactly what *counts* as breaking or entering, then your careful attention to the evidence and your finely honed logical capacities will be useless. This is true for every argument you examine: If you aren't clear about the conclusion of the argument, it will be impossible to effectively evaluate the argument.

If you are serving as a jury member (in North Carolina) in a breaking and entering trial, the judge's instructions will probably include the following:

> Now I [the judge] charge that for you [the jury] to find the defendant guilty of felonious breaking or entering, the State [the prosecution] must prove four things beyond a reasonable doubt.
>
> First, that there was either a breaking (which simply means the opening or removal of anything blocking entry) or an entry (walking or reaching in would be an entry) by the defendant.
>
> Second, the State must prove that it was a building that was broken or entered.
>
> Third, that the owner or tenant did not consent to the breaking or entering.
>
> And fourth, that at the time of the breaking or entering, the defendant intended to commit some specific felony.[1]

So the judge instructs, along with some other points. And the jury retires to consider its verdict. Now we come down to brass tacks, and probably to rampant confusion. For Chauncey (one of your fellow jurors) the verdict is perfectly clear: The defendant was *caught in the house*, so obviously the defendant is guilty as charged. Now suppose that you agree with Chauncey that the evidence shows the defendant was caught in the house; does that prove the defendant guilty of breaking or entering?

No, of course it doesn't. Chauncey is so fixed on the fact that two of the conditions for breaking or entering have been met (the defendant *did* enter, and entered a *building*) that he has neglected the other two conditions. That is, Chauncey has confused *necessary* conditions with *sufficient* conditions. One necessary condition for finding the defendant guilty of breaking or entering is that you be convinced that the defendant either broke or entered. (Thus if you think that perhaps the defendant neither broke nor entered, you would have to vote not guilty.) But while that is a necessary condition for guilt, it is not *sufficient*.

In many cases in which the defendant is charged with breaking or entering, there is no doubt that the defendant entered the building. In such a case the defendant may admit that she entered the building, but claim that the owner had given permission. Or perhaps the defendant will admit entering, but claim that he had no intention of committing any felony. ("I lost the key to my apartment," he claims, "and when I went around to the back to crawl in a window, I got confused and crawled in the window to the neighboring apartment thinking it was my own; they all look alike, there are 12 identical apartments running along the back of the building, the light was bad, and I didn't realize my mistake until I was in the apartment and heard someone yelling for the police. It was an innocent mistake: certainly I wasn't intending to steal anything.") This is a case in which the defense admits that the first three conditions for breaking or entering are met; but the defense case rests on its claim that the fourth necessary condition (that at the time of the entering the defendant intended to commit a felony such as larceny) was *not* met. And if you—as a juror—decide that there is a reasonable doubt that the defendant intended to commit a felony, then you must vote not guilty.

Each of the four conditions is a necessary condition for finding the defendant guilty of breaking or entering. Taken altogether, they are *sufficient* for finding the defendant guilty of breaking or entering. That is, if you are certain that all four conditions are met (one, the defendant did either break or enter; two, it was a *building* into which the defendant either broke or entered; three, the owner or tenant had not given permission; and four, the defendant did intend to commit a specific felony), then you should conclude that the defendant did violate the law.

We have been considering the charge of breaking or entering: It has four conditions, each of which is necessary and jointly they are sufficient. But for other charges the necessary and sufficient conditions may be quite different. Consider a case in which a defendant in North Carolina (the law and conditions will obviously

Argue Your Case

Everett Collection / Shutterstock

You are defense counsel for Corena, a teenager charged with breaking or entering. Corena was picked up by the police in a high school late at night: There's no question that she was there, and that she had broken into the locked building (she has admitted prying a window open in order to get inside). What questions would you now ask Corena—this is your first interview with her—in order to decide what sort of defense to present (or perhaps whether to plead guilty and ask for mercy)? In other words, what sort of defense could you make against the breaking or entering charges?

differ from state to state) is charged with illegal gambling. The judge instructs the jury as follows:

Now I charge that for you to find the defendant guilty of gambling, the state must prove one of two things beyond a reasonable doubt:

> First, that the defendant bet money on a game of chance.
> Or second, that the defendant played at a game of chance because money was being bet on it.
> So I charge that if you find from the evidence beyond a reasonable doubt that on or about August 15, 2010, the defendant either bet money on a game of chance or played at a game of chance because money was being bet on it, it would be your duty to return a verdict of guilty as charged. However, if you do not so find or have a reasonable doubt as to both these things, it would be your duty to return a verdict of not guilty.[2]

Having heard all the evidence, the closing arguments, and the judge's charge to the jury, you retire to the jury room to begin deliberation. Beatrice (one of the jurors) argues that the verdict must be *not guilty:* "I'm convinced that the defendant was in the alley where the dice game was taking place, and he was betting money on it. But the game was broken up by the police before he ever had his turn at rolling the dice. There's really no evidence that he ever held the dice in his hand, and certainly no evidence that he ever rolled them. So it has not been proved that he ever played the game at all. And since there is at least a reasonable doubt about whether he played the game, we can't find him guilty of gambling." What is wrong with Beatrice's argument for acquittal?

Distinguishing Necessary from Sufficient Conditions

Beatrice has confused sufficient conditions with necessary conditions. If the defendant *either* played at a game of chance because money was being bet on it *or* bet money on a game of chance, then the defendant is guilty of gambling. Each of those conditions is sufficient; *neither* of those conditions is *necessary*. If the law were that in order to be guilty of gambling one must both bet money on and play a game of chance, then Beatrice's point would strongly support a verdict of not guilty; but since to be guilty of gambling (in contrast to felonious breaking or entering) *each* condition is sufficient, Beatrice's argument does not offer grounds for acquittal.

Argue Your Case

You are a defense attorney, and your client has been charged with felonious gambling. Apparently there is no evidence that the defendant himself placed any bets. However, there are several eyewitnesses who are willing to testify that he was a major participant in a darts match at the Dew Drop Inn, in which other people bet large sums of money. Thus the prosecution is arguing that the defendant meets a sufficient condition for being guilty of felonious gambling: He played at a game of chance because money was being bet on it. What line would your defense take? On what grounds might you argue that the defendant is *not* guilty (or at least that there is reasonable doubt of the defendant's guilt) of felonious gambling?

SUFFICIENT CONDITIONS

In sum, when considering exactly what conclusions the prosecution and the defense are trying to prove, it is crucial to understand the necessary and sufficient conditions for verdicts of guilty and of not guilty. In order to be quite certain that you are comfortable with this, try thinking about the breaking or entering case from another angle. We considered what the prosecution was trying to prove in order to prove the defendant guilty of breaking or entering, and certainly that is the best way to think about it, since the prosecution bears the burden of proof, and the defense does *not* have to prove innocence. However, as an exercise think about what would be sufficient for a verdict of not guilty in a case of felonious breaking or entering. That is, when the defense presents its case (in answer to the prosecution's arguments), exactly what is the defense trying to prove? Exactly what would be sufficient to support a verdict of not guilty? Or in other words, give one *sufficient* condition for a verdict of *not* guilty.

If you answered that a *sufficient* condition for a not guilty verdict is that the defendant neither broke nor entered, then you are correct: That is sufficient for a verdict of not guilty. But in fact it is more than sufficient. Is there a weaker claim that would still be a sufficient condition for a verdict of not guilty? (Remember: The burden of proof is on the prosecution.)

A weaker claim that would still be a sufficient condition for a not guilty verdict is: There is a reasonable doubt that the defendant either broke or entered. That is, it is a sufficient condition for a not guilty verdict if one can show that there is a reasonable doubt about any one of the *necessary* conditions for a guilty verdict. If one of the necessary conditions is not *proved* beyond a reasonable doubt, that is *sufficient* for a verdict of not guilty. Of course, if the defense can prove that one of the necessary conditions for guilt is not met (not that it is merely doubtful, but that it actually is false), that would be *more* than sufficient for a verdict of not guilty.

NECESSARY AND SUFFICIENT CONDITIONS IN ORDINARY LANGUAGE

When we talk about the judge's instructions to the jury, then necessary and sufficient conditions can sound rather formidable. Actually, you think in terms of necessary and sufficient conditions all the time—though you may not use those terms. Sitting in the coffee shop this morning, one of your friends asserted: "The Maple Leafs *have* to have a good goalkeeper to win the Stanley Cup." That is, a good goalkeeper is a *necessary* (not a sufficient) condition of the Maple Leafs winning the Stanley Cup. And before your history class, you told a friend: "If I make a B on this exam, then I'll pass the course." Which is to say, making a B is a *sufficient* condition for passing the course. Consider a few more examples. If the Cardinals had one more good starting pitcher, they would win the pennant; if I finish my term paper tonight, I'll go to the beach this weekend; if you hit the ball to Sarah's backhand, you will beat her; if the inflation rate drops, the Democrats will win the election. All those cases make claims about *sufficient* conditions. One additional good starting pitcher is a *sufficient* condition for the Cards to win the pennant; finishing your term paper is a *sufficient* condition for going to the beach; and so on. You have also made many statements about *necessary* conditions, although again you probably did not use that phrase. You said, for example, that the Celtics would win the title only if they had a healthy point guard, that you would have another drink only if someone would drive you home, that you would shop at Walmart only if it were unionized, that you would go out with Ralph only if he were magically turned into a handsome prince. In those cases, you are claiming that a healthy point guard is a *necessary* condition for winning the title, that having someone drive you home is a *necessary* condition for taking another drink. So don't let all this talk about necessary and sufficient conditions intimidate you: You have been thinking in terms of necessary and sufficient conditions for years.

One more illustration. Suppose we are driving rather aimlessly around North America. After a few days of wandering, we find ourselves facing an enormous body of water. We're uncertain of our location, but we know (somehow) that this is either Lake Ontario or the Pacific Ocean, but we don't know which. Suddenly, off in the distance, you spot a whale surging up through the waves. "Hark," you say, "this must be the Pacific Ocean!" So, how did you reach that conclusion?

There are two possibilities. Probably you thought that since there are whales, this must be an ocean. That is, whales are a *sufficient* condition for determining that the water is an ocean. But you might also have reasoned from the other direction: An ocean is a *necessary* condition for whales. Both ways of thinking are equally correct: Whales are a *sufficient* condition for the existence of an ocean, and an ocean is a *necessary* condition for whales. In sum, when *A* is a *sufficient* condition for *B*, then *B* is a *necessary* condition for *A*.

Here are some rather pedestrian examples. Drinking a quart of gin is a sufficient condition for drunkenness. So if you know that Alisdair drank a quart of gin, you can safely conclude that Alisdair is drunk; and if Alisdair is not drunk, you are justified in concluding that Alisdair did not drink a quart of gin. But you are not justified in concluding, from the fact that Alisdair is snookered, that Alisdair drank a quart of gin (he might have drunk a quart of vodka, which also suffices for drunkenness). And from the fact that Alisdair has sworn off quarts of gin, you cannot conclude that Alisdair is not drunk; he may have substituted a quart of bourbon. In short, a quart of gin is *sufficient* for drunkenness, but not *necessary*.

Having four legs is a necessary condition for winning the Kentucky Derby. Thus if we know that Secretariat won the Kentucky Derby, we are justified in concluding that Secretariat has four legs. And if we know that Raunchy Runner has only three legs, we know that Raunchy Runner cannot win the Kentucky Derby. But from the fact that Run Dusty Run did not win the Kentucky Derby, we certainly cannot conclude that Run Dusty Run does not have four legs. That is, four legs is a *necessary*—but not a sufficient—condition for winning the Kentucky Derby.

Exercise 14-1

For these cases, look back at the conditions for breaking or entering, and tell whether the following testimony would count *for* or *against* conviction on charges of *breaking* or *entering* (the testimony might also count in favor of or against conviction on some *other* charge—don't worry about that).

1. George is charged with breaking or entering into Mary's apartment and stealing her television set. Mary is testifying: "Sure, I told George he could come in and watch the football game on my television while I was at work—in fact, I told him to have a beer and make himself at home. But I certainly didn't tell him he could steal my television set and sell it!"

2. Jim is charged with breaking or entering and theft of Joe's lawnmower. Joe is testifying: "Look, I saw the guy with my own eyes. I was sitting in the den watching Monday Night Football. The outside light was on, and I happened to glance out the window as Jim came sneaking into the yard. He broke the lock on the back gate of the fence and then uncovered the lawnmower (I store it under a tarpaulin in the backyard) and rolled it away."

3. Mary is charged with breaking or entering a store with the intention of stealing a television set. Mary is testifying: "OK, so I did crawl in through the window. But I didn't break the window. That window has been broken for over a month. I just stuck my hand in and moved the latch and raised the window. I never broke anything."

Exercise 14-2

For each statement, select the statement that expresses the same idea as the original.

1. If we score three touchdowns, we'll beat State.
   a. Scoring three touchdowns is a *sufficient* condition for beating State.
   b. Scoring three touchdowns is a *necessary* condition for beating State.
2. We must have dreams in order to change the world.
   a. Dreams are a *sufficient* condition for changing the world.
   b. Dreams are a *necessary* condition for changing the world.
3. Confidence is essential for being a good athlete.
   a. Confidence is a *sufficient* condition for being a good athlete.
   b. Confidence is a *necessary* condition for being a good athlete.
4. If the hurricane turns north, then Galveston will be evacuated.
   a. The hurricane turning north is a *sufficient* condition for Galveston being evacuated.
   b. The hurricane turning north is a *necessary* condition for Galveston being evacuated.

Exercise 14-3

Sutliff is caught in an empty apartment in an area known for heavy drug dealing. He testifies that he is addicted to cocaine and that he was attempting to find an apartment where he had previously purchased drugs for the purpose of buying cocaine. In order to avoid suspicion, the drug dealer required that those wishing to purchase drugs had to climb in a side window that opened onto an alley. Sutliff claims that he had been under the influence of drugs and in the dark he had mistakenly climbed into the wrong window. He thought he was going into the apartment of the drug dealer, which he certainly had permission to enter. Unfortunately, in his confusion, he entered a vacant apartment in the same building, where he was apprehended by the police and charged with breaking and entering. Since he also was carrying a very small amount of cocaine, he was also charged with drug possession, and he pleaded guilty to that charge.
Sutliff's defense attorney argues:

> This is all a terrible mistake. Poor Sutliff is an addict, true enough; and he has already entered a plea of guilty of drug possession. But he's not guilty of breaking or entering. He did of course enter the building, but it was an accident: He intended to go somewhere else. This is like you having a bit too much to drink, and then coming home and walking into the wrong apartment by mistake. It's an accident, not a crime, and whatever else you may be guilty of, neither you nor Sutliff is guilty of breaking or entering.

The prosecuting attorney argues:

> Think carefully, Ladies and Gentlemen of the Jury, and you must conclude that Sutliff is guilty. Even if you believe that Sutliff entered the apartment by accident, certainly he did *not* enter it with the permission of the owner. And he *did* enter the building, as he admits. And as he further admits, he entered with the *intention* of committing a felony, namely, purchasing illegal drugs. That's all that is required in order to be guilty of breaking or entering, and since there is certainty on each and every point, you must return a verdict of guilty of breaking or entering.

What's your verdict? Guilty or not guilty?

CONDITIONAL STATEMENTS

A few terms will make it easier to discuss necessary and sufficient conditions. An "if-then" statement—such as "If the sun shines, we'll go on a picnic"—is called a *conditional* statement. The first part of the statement ("the sun shines") is called the *antecedent*. (That's easy to remember: "ante" means prior to.) The antecedent is the first, or prior, part of the conditional statement. When you play poker, each player makes an *ante* prior to dealing the cards; *ante*bellum mansions are mansions built *before* the "bellum," or before the war; *ante*diluvian means that something is so old and outdated that it existed *before* the Biblical flood. (Of course, that model doesn't always fit: An antelope is not an animal that precedes a lope.) The last half of the conditional statement ("we'll go on a picnic") is called the *consequent*. (Please notice that that's consequ*ent*, and *not* consequ*ence*.) So a *conditional* statement is simply one in which the antecedent is a *condition* of the consequent. The consequent is true on the *condition* that the antecedent is true; in other words, the consequent is asserted to be *conditionally* true.

It is sometimes useful to write conditional statements in shortened symbolic form. To do so, we need a symbol for "if-then." There are two standard ones: → and ⊃. (Not very imaginatively, logicians call the first symbol an arrow, and the second a horseshoe.) You can use either symbol you prefer; I'll use the arrow. So if we use *S* to stand for "the sun shines" and *P* to stand for "we'll go on a picnic," then "If the sun shines, we'll go on a picnic" would be symbolized as:

$$S \rightarrow P$$

What this states is that *S* is a sufficient condition for *P*. It claims that if *S* is true, then *P* must also be true.

In actual fact, the antecedent is rarely a completely sufficient condition for the consequent. What the conditional statement should be understood to say is that if the antecedent is true (*and* there are no weird extraordinary circumstances), then the consequent will also be true. If the sun shines, we'll go on a picnic; the sun shining is a *sufficient* condition for going on a picnic. But there are a lot of other conditions that are assumed and that are so numerous and so obvious that it would be useless to try to specify them. If I tell you that "If the sun shines, we'll go on a picnic," you take for granted that that means something like "If everything remains normal and the sun shines, then we'll go on a picnic." Obviously, the sun shining by itself is not entirely sufficient, for if the sun shines but I am severely injured by a meteorite or there is a major earthquake or there is a meltdown at a nearby nuclear power plant, then we certainly cannot go on a picnic. I can't state all *those* conditions in my conditional statement ("If the sun shines and there is no nuclear meltdown and no meteorite falls on me and there is no earthquake and the air continues to contain sufficient oxygen to sustain life and I am not arrested for conspiracy and the car does not turn into a pumpkin, then we'll go on a picnic"). When I say that "If the Cardinals get another good starting pitcher, they will win the pennant," I obviously mean if all conditions remain the same, then the additional pitcher will be sufficient for the Cards to win the pennant. (I am not claiming that the Cards would win with an additional pitcher even if all the other players suddenly decided to become Buddhist monks and quit the game of baseball; but since that would be a great change from current conditions, it is not necessary to add that qualification.) Even in court it is rightfully assumed that jurors will understand that a statement of sufficient conditions does not state *every* condition, but instead assumes that the situation is normal. For example, betting money on a game of chance is a *sufficient* condition for being guilty of violating the North Carolina gaming statutes. But of course there are other conditions that are assumed: No one is holding a gun to the head of the bettor, the bettor is not working as an undercover agent for the police, and so on.

ALTERNATIVE WAYS OF STATING NECESSARY AND SUFFICIENT CONDITIONS

Consider this statement: "If the defendant's fingerprints are on the pistol, then the defendant is guilty." (Don't worry for the moment whether that conditional statement is *true;* just focus on exactly what it *means*.) How would you express that statement in terms of necessary conditions? In terms of sufficient conditions?

"The defendant's fingerprints are a sufficient condition for the defendant's guilt." Or alternatively, and a little less naturally—but still correctly—it could be stated: "The defendant's guilt is a necessary condition of the defendant's fingerprints being on the pistol."

The sentence—"If the defendant's fingerprints are on the pistol, then the defendant is guilty"—might be phrased differently without changing the meaning: "The defendant is guilty if the defendant's fingerprints are on the pistol." (The sentence still *means* the same: "The defendant's fingerprints are a sufficient condition for the defendant's guilt.") In this case, the *antecedent* ("the defendant's fingerprints are on the pistol") occurs last in the sentence, while the *consequent* ("the defendant is guilty") occurs first. The moral is this: Don't assume that the first part of every conditional statement is the antecedent; you must read the sentence carefully and determine what it actually means. You must determine what is being presented as the *condition*, the *if*, the *antecedent*, and what is said to follow from that condition (the *consequent*).

Suppose that instead the sentence is this: "The defendant is guilty *only* if the defendant's fingerprints are on the pistol." That "only" seems an innocent addition, but it changes the claim entirely. How would you express *that* sentence in terms of necessary and sufficient conditions? (Think carefully about it. *If* you can answer that question, then you have a good grasp of necessary and sufficient conditions. Of course if you cannot answer it, that does *not* imply that you do *not* have a good grasp of necessary and sufficient conditions. It is a sufficient—rather than *necessary*—condition of understanding.)

How can "The defendant is guilty *only* if the defendant's fingerprints are on the pistol" be stated in terms of necessary and sufficient conditions? That sentence asserts that the defendant's fingerprints are a *necessary* condition for the defendant's guilt. (If there are no fingerprints, the defendant is not guilty.) Or another way of putting it: The defendant's guilt is a *sufficient* condition for finding the defendant's fingerprints. (That is, if the defendant is guilty, you will find the defendant's fingerprints on the pistol.) This is a common and useful way of focusing on necessary conditions. For example, a defense attorney who wants to focus the attention of the jury on the essential role played by a rather weak prosecution witness might say in her summation to the jury, "You can find the defendant guilty *only if* you believe the testimony of the prosecution's key witness—that scurrilous character who has been convicted three times for perjury and twice for fraud. The prosecution's entire case rests on that sleazy foundation."

Necessary and sufficient conditions can be a trifle tricky. Here's a hint that might help you keep track of them. Consider a statement like this: If the economy improves, then the Democrats will win the election. We could represent that as a conditional statement, thusly:

$$E(economy\ improves) \rightarrow W(Democrats\ win)$$

That is,

$$E \rightarrow W$$

Once we have it in the form of a conditional statement, it's easy to read off statements of sufficient and necessary conditions. Just remember this golden rule of conditional statements: The *antecedent* is a *sufficient* condition for the *consequent*, and the *consequent* is a *necessary* condition for the *antecedent*. Thus, the economy improving is a sufficient condition for the Democrats' winning; and the Democrats' winning is a necessary condition of the economy improving. So, of course, once you know necessary conditions you can easily state sufficient conditions (and vice versa), just by plugging in that handy formula. When you know, for example, that oxygen is a necessary condition of life, then you also know that life is a sufficient condition for oxygen (i.e., where you find life you know there must be oxygen); and that could also be written as:

$$Life \rightarrow Oxygen$$

BOTH NECESSARY AND SUFFICIENT

One more thing. Occasionally we want to assert a particularly strong relation. For example, some television evangelists claim that "You will go to Heaven if and only if you follow my religion." That is, you will go to Heaven *if* you follow my religion, *and* you will go to Heaven *only* if you follow my religion. Or in other words, following my religion is *both* a necessary *and* a sufficient condition for going to Heaven. Another example: If the only way you can develop collywobbles disease is by being bitten by the collywobble bug, and if the bite of the collywobble bug always causes collywobbles disease, then the bite of the collywobble bug is a necessary and sufficient condition for collywobble disease; one develops collywobble disease *if and only if* one is bitten by the collywobble bug. But note that that claim is stronger than—and quite different from—the claim that if one is bitten by the collywobble bug, one will develop collywobble disease. And the "if and only if" claim is also stronger than the claim that if one develops collywobble disease, then one was bitten by the collywobble bug. The statement that "One develops collywobble disease if *and* only if one is bitten by the collywobble bug" is stronger than either of those claims because it *combines* both of them. (If you know that it's true that "If one is bitten by the collywobble bug, one develops collywobble disease," then from the fact that you have collywobble disease, what can you conclude about what bit you? Nothing. Perhaps you were bitten by the collywobble bug, or perhaps you were bitten by some other bug that carries collywobble disease; perhaps you developed collywobble disease from some other source. *But,* if you know that it's true that "One develops collywobble disease *if and only if* one is bitten by the collywobble bug," then from the fact that you have collywobble disease you *could* rightfully conclude that you must have been bitten by the dreaded collywobble bug.)

Suppose the judge instructs you that "A person is not criminally responsible if and only if his unlawful act was the product of mental disease or mental defect." In that case, if you determine that the defendant's assault was the product of mental disease, then you know that the person is not criminally responsible. *And,* if you determine that the assault was *not* the product of mental disease or mental defect, then you know that the defendant *is* criminally responsible (according to the judge's instructions).

Exercise 14-4

For each statement, select the best description of the necessary and sufficient conditions claims.

1. "Lots of teams with great quarterbacks never win the Super Bowl; but no team can win the Super Bowl without a great quarterback."

    A great quarterback is _____ condition for winning the Super Bowl.

    a. a necessary

    b. a sufficient

    c. a necessary and sufficient

    d. neither a necessary nor a sufficient

2. "People who smoke are much more likely to develop lung cancer than are people who don't; of course, some people who do not smoke also develop lung cancer, and many smokers never develop lung cancer."

    That statement claims that smoking is what sort of condition for lung cancer?

    a. necessary

    b. sufficient

    c. necessary and sufficient

    d. neither necessary nor sufficient

3. "You must pass the final exam in order to pass logic."

   Passing the final exam is _____ condition for passing logic.

   a. a necessary
   b. a sufficient
   c. a necessary and sufficient
   d. neither a necessary nor a sufficient

4. "If you drink lots of lime juice, then you'll never suffer from scurvy."

   Drinking lots of lime juice is _____ condition for avoiding scurvy.

   a. a necessary
   b. a sufficient
   c. a necessary and sufficient
   d. neither a necessary nor a sufficient

5. "If we are going to have a real democracy, then we must place limits on how much money the wealthy can spend to control elections."

   Limits on money spent to control elections is _____ condition for a real democracy.

   a. a necessary
   b. a sufficient
   c. a necessary and sufficient
   d. neither a necessary nor a sufficient

6. "If you think positively, then you'll be a success; if you don't think positively, then you'll never amount to anything."

   Positive thinking is _____ condition for success.

   a. a necessary
   b. a sufficient
   c. a necessary and sufficient
   d. neither a necessary nor a sufficient

7. "If the track is muddy, then Muddy Mother will win the race."

   A muddy track is _____ condition for Muddy Mother's winning the race.

   a. a necessary
   b. a sufficient
   c. a necessary and sufficient
   d. neither a necessary nor a sufficient

8. "Muddy Mother will not win unless the track is muddy."

   A muddy track is _____ condition for Muddy Mother's winning the race.

   a. a necessary
   b. a sufficient
   c. a necessary and sufficient
   d. neither a necessary nor a sufficient

9. "A heavy rain within the next 3 days is our only hope for saving the wheat crop."

   A heavy rain within the next 3 days is _____ condition for saving the wheat crop.

   a. a necessary
   b. a sufficient
   c. a necessary and sufficient
   d. neither a necessary nor a sufficient

10. "I'm not going on a picnic in the rain."

    Rain is _____ condition for my *not* going on a picnic.

    a. a necessary
    b. a sufficient
    c. a necessary and sufficient
    d. neither a necessary nor a sufficient

11. "I'm not going on a picnic in the rain."

   The *absence* of rain is _____ condition for my going on a picnic.

   a. a necessary
   b. a sufficient
   c. a necessary and sufficient
   d. neither a necessary nor a sufficient

12. "If you exercise regularly, then you will reduce your chances of a heart attack—though of course regular exercisers sometimes have heart attacks. And if you do not exercise regularly, then you are more likely to suffer a heart attack—though some who never exercise do manage to avoid heart attacks."

   Regular exercise is _____ condition for avoiding heart attacks.

   a. a necessary
   b. a sufficient
   c. a necessary and sufficient
   d. neither a necessary nor a sufficient

13. "Wages will increase only if the budget is balanced."

   A balanced budget is _____ condition for increased wages.

   a. a necessary
   b. a sufficient
   c. a necessary and sufficient
   d. neither a necessary nor a sufficient

14. "The Giants will win if their quarterback is healthy, but the Giants cannot win if their quarterback is not healthy."

   A healthy quarterback is _____ condition for the Giants to win.

   a. a necessary
   b. a sufficient
   c. a necessary and sufficient
   d. neither a necessary nor a sufficient

15. "You will pass the exam if you studied all weekend."

   Studying all weekend is _____ condition for passing the exam.

   a. a necessary
   b. a sufficient
   c. a necessary and sufficient
   d. neither a necessary nor a sufficient

16. "You will pass the exam only if you studied all weekend."

   Studying all weekend is _____ condition for passing the exam.

   a. a necessary
   b. a sufficient
   c. a necessary and sufficient
   d. neither a necessary nor a sufficient

17. "Enrollment will increase if the tuition is reduced; but there are many other things that could also increase enrollment, without reducing tuition." That statement means that:

   a. Reduced tuition is a necessary condition for increasing enrollment.
   b. Reduced tuition is a sufficient condition for increasing enrollment.
   c. Reduced tuition is both a necessary and a sufficient condition for increasing enrollment.
   d. Reduced tuition is neither a necessary nor a sufficient condition for increasing enrollment.

18. "I would go on a date with Bruce only if he owned a bright red Porsche." That statement means that:

   a. Bruce owning a bright red Porsche is a necessary condition for my going on a date with Bruce.
   b. Bruce owning a bright red Porsche is a sufficient condition for my going on a date with Bruce.

    c. Bruce owning a bright red Porsche is both a necessary and a sufficient condition for my going on a date with Bruce.

    d. Bruce owning a bright red Porsche is neither a necessary nor a sufficient condition for my going on a date with Bruce.

19. "If the Ohio legislature appropriates more funds for YSU, then there will not be a tuition increase at YSU; unfortunately, however, more funds from the Ohio legislature is the only way YSU can avoid increasing tuition."

        That statement implies that:

    a. More funds from the legislature is a necessary condition for not increasing tuition.

    b. More funds from the legislature is a sufficient condition for not increasing tuition.

    c. More funds from the legislature is both a necessary and a sufficient condition for not increasing tuition.

    d. More funds from the legislature is neither a necessary nor a sufficient condition for not increasing tuition.

20. "Doing well on the first exam is nice, but you don't have to do well on the first exam to make a good grade in the course; on the other hand, it's also possible to do well on the first exam and still get a lousy grade in the course." That statement implies that:

    a. Doing well on the first exam is a necessary condition for getting a good grade in the course.

    b. Doing well on the first exam is a sufficient condition for getting a good grade in the course.

    c. Doing well on the first exam is both necessary and sufficient for getting a good grade in the course.

    d. Doing well on the first exam is neither necessary nor sufficient for getting a good grade in the course.

21. "If the Pirates have strong pitching, then they will be contenders for the pennant; but without strong pitching, they can't be contenders for the pennant."

    a. Strong pitching is a necessary condition for the Pirates to be contenders for the pennant.

    b. Strong pitching is a sufficient condition for the Pirates to be contenders for the pennant.

    c. Strong pitching is both a necessary and a sufficient condition for the Pirates to be contenders for the pennant.

    d. Strong pitching is neither a necessary nor a sufficient condition for the Pirates to be contenders for the pennant.

22. "If you have good friends, then you will be happy; but without good friends, happiness is impossible."

        Good friends are _____ condition for happiness.

    a. a necessary

    b. a sufficient

    c. a necessary and sufficient

    d. neither a necessary nor a sufficient

23. "Without good friends, happiness is impossible; but even good friends cannot guarantee happiness."

        Good friends are _____ condition for happiness.

    a. a necessary

    b. a sufficient

    c. a necessary and sufficient

    d. neither a necessary nor a sufficient

24. "I'll take critical thinking only if it is required for graduation." Being required for graduation is what kind of requirement for my taking critical thinking?

    a. necessary

    b. sufficient

    c. necessary and sufficient

    d. neither necessary nor sufficient

25. "If you are good at critical thinking, then you will become wealthy; and in fact, no one can become wealthy without being good at critical thinking." Being good at critical thinking is what kind of condition for becoming wealthy?

    a. necessary

    b. sufficient

c. both necessary and sufficient

d. neither necessary nor sufficient

26. "The conflict between India and Pakistan can be resolved only if the United Nations intervenes." According to that statement, United Nations intervention is what kind of condition for resolving the conflict between India and Pakistan?

    a. necessary

    b. sufficient

    c. both necessary and sufficient

    d. neither necessary nor sufficient

27. "If the Palestinians have an independent homeland, then there will be peace in the Middle East, and having an independent Palestinian homeland is the only way to have peace in the Middle East" means that an independent Palestinian homeland is:

    a. a necessary condition for peace

    b. a sufficient condition for peace

    c. both a necessary and sufficient condition for peace

    d. neither a necessary nor a sufficient condition for peace

28. "If the United States signs the treaty banning land mines, then the use of land mines will be greatly reduced around the world." The United States signing the treaty is what kind of condition for a great reduction in use of land mines?

    a. necessary

    b. sufficient

    c. necessary and sufficient

    d. neither necessary nor sufficient

29. "If the university is struck by a massive meteorite, then the exam will be cancelled; but that is the only way the exam will be cancelled." The university being struck by a massive meteorite is what kind of condition for cancelling the exam?

    a. necessary

    b. sufficient

    c. both necessary and sufficient

    d. neither necessary nor sufficient

30. "If you use special insider information when you buy or sell stock, then you are guilty of a criminal act." That statement implies that using special insider information is what kind of condition for being guilty of a criminal act?

    a. a necessary condition.

    b. a sufficient condition.

    c. both a necessary and a sufficient condition.

    d. neither a necessary nor a sufficient condition.

31. "If there are bloodstains on the knife, then the butler is guilty of murder."

    Bloodstains on the knife are _____ condition of the butler's being guilty.

    a. a necessary

    b. a sufficient

    c. a necessary and sufficient

    d. neither a necessary nor a sufficient

32. "The butler is guilty of murder if there are bloodstains on the knife."

    Bloodstains on the knife are _____ condition of the butler's being guilty.

    a. a necessary

    b. a sufficient

    c. a necessary and sufficient

    d. neither a necessary nor a sufficient

33. "The butler is guilty of murder only if there are bloodstains on the knife."

     Bloodstains on the knife are _____ condition of the butler's being guilty.

   a. a necessary
   b. a sufficient
   c. a necessary and sufficient
   d. neither a necessary nor a sufficient

34. "Only if there are bloodstains on the knife is the butler guilty of murder."

     Bloodstains on the knife are _____ condition of the butler's being guilty.

   a. a necessary
   b. a sufficient
   c. a necessary and sufficient
   d. neither a necessary nor a sufficient

35. "If there are bloodstains on the knife, then the butler is guilty of murder."

     The butler's being guilty of murder is _____ condition of there being bloodstains on the knife.

   a. a necessary
   b. a sufficient
   c. a necessary and sufficient
   d. neither a necessary nor a sufficient

36. "The butler is guilty of murder only if there are bloodstains on the knife."

     The butler's being guilty of murder is _____ condition of there being bloodstains on the knife.

   a. a necessary
   b. a sufficient
   c. a necessary and sufficient
   d. neither a necessary nor a sufficient

Exercise 14-5

For the following, rephrase each sentence into two statements: one of necessary conditions and the other of sufficient conditions. (In some cases, it may seem more natural to speak of sufficient conditions, and in other cases it may seem more natural to speak of necessary conditions; remember, all if-then sentences *can* be correctly recast both ways, even though one way may sound better.) Third, diagram each sentence using an arrow.

Example: If Tiger Woods putts well, he will beat me at golf.
Sufficient: Putting well is a sufficient condition for Tiger beating me at golf.
Necessary: Beating me at golf is a necessary condition of Tiger putting well.
(Note that it would be *wrong* to say that Tiger putting well is a *necessary* condition for beating me at golf; in fact, Tiger could putt atrociously and still destroy me.)

     Diagram: T → B

1. If Joe is guilty of breaking or entering into Jack's apartment, then Joe did not have Jack's permission to enter the apartment.
2. If the defendant drove the getaway car, then she is guilty of armed robbery.
3. The Red Sox will win the pennant only if their hitting improves.
4. There is no joy in Mudville if Mighty Casey struck out.
5. If it doesn't fit, you must acquit.
6. We will stop the killing in our schools only if we have stronger gun control.
7. You have to play to win. (Advertising slogan for one of the state lotteries.)
8. We should find the defendant guilty only if we are certain beyond a reasonable doubt that he committed the crime.
9. You will pass the course if you answer this question correctly.

10. You will pass the course only if you answer this question correctly.
11. If the groundhog does not see his shadow, then we will have an early spring.
12. You've got to see it to believe it.
13. If I see it then I'll believe it.
14. If there is snow, then the tomato crop will be ruined.
15. Having this surgery is your only chance of survival.

VALID INFERENCES FROM NECESSARY AND SUFFICIENT CONDITIONS

Suppose we are deliberating our verdict in a case of first-degree burglary. A witness for the defense has claimed that she was with the defendant during the entire night on which the burglary occurred and that the defendant never left her house. This testimony, if believed, establishes a strong alibi for the defendant. One juror comments, "If the alibi witness was telling the truth, then the defendant is not guilty. And certainly she was telling the truth: I believed every word she said. Therefore, the defendant is not guilty." That juror's argument might be presented thus:

> The truthfulness of the alibi witness's testimony is a sufficient condition for finding the defendant not guilty. The alibi witness was truthful. Therefore, the defendant is not guilty.

The argument might be presented in symbolic form as follows. (*A* stands for "the alibi witness is telling the truth"; *D* stands for "the defendant is not guilty"; the three dots in a triangle shape mean "it follows that"—they mark the conclusion; and, as you remember, the arrow stands for "if-then.")

$A \rightarrow D$

A **Modus Ponens—Valid**

$\therefore D$

Modus Ponens

That is a deductively valid argument. I don't know whether the premises are true or are not true (perhaps the alibi witness was in fact lying), but certainly the conclusion *follows* from the premises. *If* the premises are true, then the conclusion *must* be true. *A* is a sufficient condition for *D*; *A* is the case; therefore, *D* must follow. This form of argument is so common that it has been christened with a special name: *modus ponens*. Sometimes it is also called *affirming the antecedent*. That's a good name for this argument form, since that's exactly what it does. It makes a conditional statement, and then *affirms the antecedent* of that conditional statement, and draws as a conclusion the *consequent* of that conditional statement.

So far in this chapter we have talked mainly about sufficient conditions, but conditional statements also make claims about *necessary* conditions. Back to the jury room. One juror says, "If the alibi witness was telling the truth, then the defendant is innocent." Another juror replies, "Well, the defendant must be innocent, because certainly that angelic alibi witness was telling the truth." In this case, the juror is focusing on the innocence of the defendant as a *necessary* condition of the truthfulness of the witness. The point to note is that any conditional statement can be expressed *either* in terms of *necessary* conditions *or* in terms of *sufficient* conditions. Thus, a conditional statement such as "If the witness is telling the truth, then the defendant is innocent" can be correctly expressed in terms of *sufficient* conditions ("The truthfulness of the witness is a sufficient condition for the innocence of the defendant"), and it can also be correctly expressed in terms of *necessary* conditions ("The innocence of the defendant is a necessary condition for the truthfulness of the witness"). Sometimes it will seem more natural to express a conditional statement in terms of sufficient conditions; at other times it will seem more natural to express a conditional statement in terms of necessary conditions (which way seems more natural probably depends on what our particular interest is). For example, the statement "If there are whales, then that is saltwater" could be stated as "Whales are a sufficient condition for saltwater" (we would find that the natural way of stating it if we were trying to decide whether a body of water was saltwater or freshwater, and we saw a whale cavorting in it); or it could be stated as "Saltwater is a necessary condition for whales" (that would be the natural way of stating it if we were interested in knowing where to look for whales or what sort of conditions we would have to maintain in order to keep whales in our fishbowl).

With the whale–saltwater example in hand, it is easy to see why it is essential to keep the antecedent and consequent in the proper order. It is one thing to say: "If there are whales, then there is saltwater." It is something quite different to say: "If there is saltwater, then there are whales." The former statement is true; the latter statement is false (there was saltwater for millions of years before whales evolved). If whales are a sufficient condition for saltwater, then saltwater is a necessary condition for whales; but whales being sufficient for saltwater does *not* make saltwater sufficient for whales, and saltwater being necessary for whales does not make saltwater sufficient for whales. If I make a perfect score on every exam, then I'll pass logic; that is *not* the same as saying that if I pass logic, then I'll make a perfect score on every exam. It is *true* that if tuition, room, and board are provided free at State U., then many students will attend State U.; it is *false* that if many students attend State U., then tuition, room, and board will be free.

Now go back to the juror who focused on *necessary* conditions: "The defendant must be innocent, because certainly the alibi witness was telling the truth." That is, the innocence of the defendant is a *necessary* condition of the truthfulness of the alibi witness. In this case, the juror is again reasoning by *modus ponens:* If the witness is telling the truth, then the defendant is innocent; the witness *is* telling the truth; therefore, the defendant is innocent. But imagine another juror, who is absolutely convinced that the defendant is *not* innocent, but is instead guilty as charged. (We need not worry here about *why* the juror is so certain of that—perhaps because the juror believes, as many jurors do, that anyone charged with a crime must be guilty, or perhaps because the juror took one look at the defendant and decided that the defendant looked like the "criminal type." This juror accepts the truth of the *conditional* statement ("If the witness is telling the truth, then the defendant is innocent") but *also* believes that the defendant is *not* innocent. What conclusion must that juror draw concerning the truthfulness of the alibi witness?

That juror would have to conclude that the alibi witness is *not* telling the truth. Since the innocence of the defendant is a *necessary* condition of the veracity of the witness, if the juror believes that the defendant is *not* innocent then the juror believes that a *necessary* condition of the witness being truthful is *not* met; therefore, the witness cannot be telling the truth. The same symbols will be used: *A* stands for "the alibi witness is telling the truth"; *D* stands for "the defendant is innocent"; → is the symbol for "if-then"; and ~ will be used as a negation sign, simply meaning "it is *not* the case that." Using those symbols, the juror's deduction can be symbolized as follows:

$A \rightarrow D$

$\sim D$ ***Modus Tollens*—Valid**

$\therefore \sim A$

This form of argument is very common. You use it all the time. Your friend Joe is a notorious procrastinator who never works on anything until the very last moment.

Thus you know that "If Joe is in the library, then Joe must have a term paper due tomorrow morning." But you also know that "Joe does not have a term paper due tomorrow morning." Thus you conclude—as the conclusion of a valid deductive argument—that Joe is *not* in the library. Or take another example: "If Louise drank that entire fifth of gin last night, then Louise will have a terrible hangover this morning. But Louise obviously does not have a hangover. Therefore, Louise did not drink the entire fifth of gin."

Modus Tollens

This is such a common form of *valid* deductive argument that it has been given a special name: *modus tollens.* You might prefer to call it *denying the consequent,* since that is exactly what it does: One premise is a conditional, another premise *denies* the *consequent* of that conditional, and the conclusion is the denial of the antecedent of the conditional. (Another way of thinking of it is that a *modus tollens* argument *denies a necessary* condition of *X,* and on the basis of that denial concludes that *X* is not the case.)

FALLACIES BASED ON CONFUSION BETWEEN NECESSARY AND SUFFICIENT CONDITIONS

We have looked at two very common *valid* argument forms that use conditional statements: *modus ponens* and *modus tollens.* Unfortunately, there are also some common *invalid, fallacious* argument forms that look and sound a lot like the valid ones. It is important to reason correctly from necessary and sufficient conditions, but it is equally important to detect and avoid some very common *errors.* Back again to the burglary case and the alibi witness. All the jurors agree that "If the alibi witness is telling the truth, then the defendant is innocent." Suppose a juror now says, "It's true that *if* the alibi witness is telling the truth, then the defendant is innocent, but I just did not believe that alibi witness—her story didn't ring true to me. Therefore, the defendant is *not* innocent: The defendant is guilty as charged." That sounds like a good argument; it sounds a lot like the *valid* argument form *modus tollens.* But it is not. It is an *invalid* argument. Think carefully about that argument, and try to state exactly how it differs from *modus tollens.* Also, try to state, in terms of necessary and sufficient conditions, exactly what *error* that argument commits.

The *valid* argument form *modus tollens* goes like this:

$A \rightarrow D$

$\sim D$ **Modus Tollens—Valid**

$\therefore \sim A$

The Fallacy of Denying the Antecedent

In *modus tollens,* the second premise *denies the consequent.* But in the *invalid* argument under consideration ("If the alibi witness is telling the truth, then the defendant is innocent; the alibi witness is not telling the truth; therefore, the defendant is not innocent"), the second premise does not deny the *consequent;* instead, the premise denies the *antecedent:*

$A \rightarrow D$

$\sim A$ **Denying the Antecedent—Invalid**

$\therefore \sim D$

That may appear to be an insignificant difference, but in fact it makes all the difference in the world: *Modus tollens* is a *valid* argument, but this argument—which denies the *antecedent*—is an *invalid*, fallacious argument. (That's exactly what this *invalid* argument form is called: the *fallacy of denying the antecedent*.) The *difference* is that in *modus tollens* the premise denies a *necessary* condition for *A* and then deduces—correctly—that *A* is not the case. In the fallacious argument the premise denies a *sufficient* (not a necessary) condition for *D*, and from that, one *cannot* conclude that *D* is not the case. Perhaps that sounds a bit tricky. It's not. Think of it this way: If LeBron James and Kevin Durant play basketball for Western High School, then Western High will have a winning season. (That's true, right? I mean, no matter *who* the other players are, if LeBron and Kevin play for Western High, then Western High is going to win more than its share of basketball games.) But LeBron James and Kevin Durant will *not* play for Western High (that's also true; both LeBron and Kevin have other plans for the basketball season). Does it follow that Western High will *not* have a winning season? Certainly not. LeBron and Kevin are a *sufficient* condition for a winning season, but they are *not* a *necessary* condition. To conclude that because LeBron and Kevin will not play for Western, therefore Western will not have a winning season is to mistake a *sufficient* condition for a *necessary* condition. Take another example, one that is perhaps more immediately relevant. If you study logic 8 hours *every day* for the rest of the semester, then you will pass logic (I personally guarantee it). But, you say, I can't possibly study logic 8 hours every day—it would take all my time from my other courses, not to mention cutting into my social life. So what follows? That you will not pass logic? Of course not. Studying logic 8 hours every day is a *sufficient* condition for passing logic, but it is by no means a *necessary* condition.

> If I study logic 8 hours every day, then I'll pass logic.
> I shall not study logic 8 hours every day.
> Therefore, I shall not pass logic.

That argument commits the *fallacy* of *denying the antecedent*. It is an *invalid* argument. It mistakenly treats a *sufficient* condition as if it were a *necessary* condition.

The Fallacy of Affirming the Consequent

There is another *fallacious* argument form that sounds and looks a lot like a *valid* argument form but is *invalid*. Once again to the jury room. The jurors agree that if the alibi witness is telling the truth, then the defendant is innocent. Now suppose that there is a dispute about the truthfulness of the alibi witness: Some jurors think she is telling the truth, others insist she is lying. In the middle of this dispute, word comes from the judge that the jurors can go home! Another person has just confessed to committing the burglary, and all charges against the defendant have now been dropped. The trial is over; the defendant is innocent. At that point one of the jurors who had been insisting on the truthfulness of the alibi witness turns to one of the doubters and says, "There, now you see, she *was* telling the truth, just as I claimed." Is the truthfulness of the witness in fact proved by the innocence of the defendant?

The juror has made a mistake: The fact that the defendant is innocent (together with the conditional that if the witness is telling the truth, then the defendant is innocent) does *not* prove that the witness is telling the truth. The juror has confused a *sufficient* condition with a *necessary* condition. The truthfulness of the witness is a *sufficient* condition—but is *not necessary*—for the innocence of the defendant. If Sabrina makes a perfect score on every exam, then she'll pass the course. So suppose that Sabrina passes the course. Can we conclude that Sabrina made a perfect score on every exam? Of course not. Making a perfect score on every exam is *sufficient* for passing the course: a perfect score on every exam would guarantee a passing grade. But that is not *necessary* for passing the course. Or if you prefer, we can look at this from another angle. Passing the course is a *necessary* result of perfect scores on every exam; passing the course is a *necessary condition* of making perfect scores on all exams. But a passing grade in the course is not a *sufficient* condition of making perfect scores on every exam. Thus Sabrina may pass the course even though she did not achieve perfection on every exam. In the same way, the innocence of the defendant is a *necessary* condition of the truthfulness of the alibi witness, but it is not a *sufficient* condition. The defendant may be innocent even though the alibi witness is not telling the truth.

Look closely at the form of the argument. The form of the juror's argument is as follows:

$A \rightarrow D$

D **Affirming the Consequent—Invalid**

$\therefore A$

That looks and sounds a lot like a valid *modus ponens* type of argument. But there is a very important difference. In the *valid* argument form *modus ponens*, the second premise *affirms* the *antecedent* of the conditional statement, and then draws the *consequent* as a conclusion. But in the *invalid* argument above, the juror *affirms* the *consequent* (*not* the antecedent) in the second premise, and then draws the antecedent as a conclusion. And that *invalid, fallacious* argument form is called by exactly that name: the *fallacy* of *affirming the consequent.*

Like denying the antecedent, affirming the consequent is a very common fallacy. It sounds like a perfectly good argument—and usually both the person giving the argument and the persons hearing the argument are deceived by it. For example, a senator supporting a tax decrease argues, "If taxes are too high, then the economy slows down; and the economy certainly has slowed down; obviously, then, taxes must be too high." And it does sound obvious, until one examines the argument closely and recognizes the fallacy of affirming the consequent. "If grading becomes easier at Home State U., then the grade point averages of students will increase. And indeed students are getting higher grade point averages. So grading at Home State U. must be getting easier." Sounds plausible and maybe the conclusion is true, but certainly that argument does not *prove* that the conclusion is true, since it is invalid: It commits the fallacy of affirming the consequent.

DETECTING ARGUMENT FORMS

Recognizing valid *modus ponens* and *modus tollens* arguments (and distinguishing them from the look-alike fallacies of affirming the consequent and denying the antecedent) requires careful attention to the *forms* of the arguments. But those forms can be tricky to detect. For one thing, the premises can be switched around (the conditional premise isn't always first), and the conclusion isn't always stated last. For example:

> If Jill drove the getaway car, then Jill is guilty.
> Jill drove the getaway car. Therefore, Jill is guilty.

That's the valid argument form *modus ponens*. But suppose the argument is stated like this:

> Jill is guilty, because Jill drove the getaway car.
> And if Jill drove the getaway car, then Jill is guilty.

That's exactly the same argument, with exactly the same argument form: *modus ponens*. The premises and conclusion are in a different order, but that doesn't change the *form* of the argument.

Another source of potential confusion is *negation*. Look again at the *modus ponens* argument just considered:

> If Jill drove the getaway car, then Jill is guilty.
> Jill drove the getaway car. Therefore, Jill is guilty.

That argument could be diagrammed like this:

$D \rightarrow G$
D
$\therefore G$

Like all *modus ponens* arguments, one premise *affirms* the *antecedent* of the other premise. But what about this argument:

> If Joe did not intend to steal the jacket, then Joe is not guilty of shoplifting. Joe did not intend to steal the jacket. Therefore, Joe is not guilty of shoplifting.

That argument could be represented in symbols like this:

$\sim I \rightarrow \sim G$
$\sim I$
$\therefore \sim G$

At first glance the *form* of that argument may look very different from the *modus ponens* argument of the previous example. But in fact the form is the same: The argument is just dressed up with a few negations. The antecedent of the conditional is this: Joe did *not* intend to steal. The other premise *affirms* that antecedent. Since the antecedent is a negation, the affirmation of that antecedent is also a negation. If I say "Nixon was *not* a good president," you *affirm* what I say by *also* stating a negation: "True, Nixon was not a good president." To *deny* my negative statement, you would say: "Nixon *was* a good president." Or you *could* say: "It is *not* the case that Nixon was *not* a good president," which—through double negation—is the equivalent of saying simply "Nixon was a good president."

The same points apply to argument forms like the fallacy of denying the antecedent. The standard form of that fallacy is this:

> If the Maple Leafs score five goals, then the Maple Leafs will win. But the Maple Leafs will not score five goals. Therefore, the Maple Leafs will not win.

In symbolic form, this is stated as:

$S \rightarrow W$
$\sim S$
$\therefore \sim W$

Compare that with this argument:

> If Joe did not know the car was stolen, then Joe is not guilty. But Joe did know the car was stolen. Therefore, Joe is guilty.

In symbolic form, that's:

$\sim K \rightarrow \sim G$
K
$\therefore G$

Again, that may look rather different from the prior example of denying the antecedent; but it's exactly the same form. The antecedent of the conditional is a negation: Joe did *not* know. The negative antecedent is *denied* by saying: Joe *did* know.

If that seems confusing, think more about negations and denials of negations. It's a snowy, overcast day. Since I love the snow, I greet you cheerily: "It's a beautiful day!" Your taste in weather runs to balmier temperatures, and you *deny* my statement with a *negation:* "It is *not* a beautiful day." If I am in the mood to argue, I may *deny* your negation, in either of two ways: "It *is* a beautiful day" or alternatively (by negating your negation), "It is *not* the case that it is *not* a beautiful day." So don't let negations obscure things: Just look at the *forms* of the arguments.

When we add negations to our arguments, and then try to figure out what *form* the argument is, sometimes it looks a bit scary. For example,

$$L \rightarrow G$$
$$\frac{\sim G}{\therefore \sim L}$$

You immediately (or almost immediately) recognize that as *modus tollens*, right? But suppose it looks like this:

$$\sim L \rightarrow \sim G$$
$$\frac{G}{\therefore L}$$

That's just the same thing: the second premise denies the consequent of the first premise (the consequent is *not G,* and the second premise denies that by asserting *G*). When we put it in that form, it may look a bit intimidating. But it's not. You use that argument form all the time, and you immediately understand it when you hear it. There's a great old blues song, and the main line of the song goes like this: "If I don't love you, baby, then grits ain't groceries, eggs ain't poultry, and Mona Lisa was a man." If someone says that to you—"If I don't love you, baby, then grits ain't groceries"—you *immediately* know that he or she is saying that "I *do* love you, baby." Right? But how did you reach that conclusion? By *modus tollens*. The argument goes like this:

> If I do not love you, then grits are not groceries.
> Grits are groceries.
> Therefore, I love you.

Four Argument Forms

These are the four argument forms discussed in this chapter. *Modus ponens* and *modus tollens* are legitimate, nonfallacious arguments; denying the antecedent and affirming the consequent are fallacious.

$$P \rightarrow Q$$
$$\frac{P}{\therefore Q}$$

This is *modus ponens;* it's a valid argument form.

$$P \rightarrow Q$$
$$\frac{\sim Q}{\therefore \sim P}$$

This is *modus tollens;* it's a valid argument form.

$$P \rightarrow Q$$
$$\frac{\sim P}{\therefore \sim Q}$$

This is denying the antecedent; it's an invalid argument form.

$$P \rightarrow Q$$
$$\frac{Q}{\therefore P}$$

This is affirming the consequent; it's an invalid argument form.

Loses something in translation, doesn't it? Still, it's just the *modus tollens* form of argument; symbolized, it looks like this:

$$\sim L \rightarrow \sim G$$
$$\underline{G}$$
$$\therefore L$$

Actually, as originally stated, the argument is an *enthymeme*. One premise ("Grits *are* groceries") is regarded as so obvious that it need not be stated. But you have to fill it in to get the whole argument.

Now, that's as hard as these get; and if you don't get frightened by all the squiggles and arrows, that's really not so hard, right? One last point, but an important one: when diagramming arguments, you will find it much easier if you *start with the conclusion.*

Exercise 14-6

For the following arguments, identify the *form* of each argument (*modus ponens*, *modus tollens*, denying the antecedent, or affirming the consequent).

1. $A \rightarrow B$
   B
   $\therefore A$

2. $A \rightarrow B$
   A
   $\therefore B$

3. $A \rightarrow B$
   $\sim A$
   $\therefore \sim B$

4. $\sim A \rightarrow \sim B$
   $\sim A$
   $\therefore \sim B$

5. $\sim A \rightarrow B$
   $\sim A$
   $\therefore B$

6. $A \rightarrow \sim B$
   B
   $\therefore \sim A$

7. $\sim A \rightarrow B$
   A
   $\therefore \sim B$

8. $\sim A \rightarrow \sim B$
   A
   $\therefore B$

Exercise 14-7

For the following arguments, identify the *form* of each argument (*modus ponens*, *modus tollens*, denying the antecedent, or affirming the consequent), and state whether the argument is valid or invalid.

1. If OPQ Enterprises stock is a good investment, then OPQ must have strong management. But the management of OPQ is not strong. So OPQ stock is not a good investment.

2. If Dusty Dancer can get the early lead, then Dusty Dancer will win the race. But Dusty Dancer cannot get the early lead (since he starts from the outside post position), so Dusty Dancer won't win the race.

3. If Susan knew that the diamond necklace was stolen, then she is guilty of receiving stolen merchandise. And she certainly did know that the necklace was stolen, so Susan is guilty.

4. If critical thinking is hazardous to your health, then several critical thinking students would suffer from colds this semester. And several critical thinking students *have* suffered from colds this semester. Therefore, critical thinking must be a health hazard.

5. If Julie had Jim's permission to be in his (Jim's) apartment, then Julie is not guilty of breaking or entering. But Jim never gave Julie permission to enter his apartment, so Julie must be guilty of breaking or entering.

6. If you don't get nervous, then you'll do fine on the exam. And you are not going to get nervous, so you'll do fine on the exam.

7. If the doctor did not check the level of dosage for the prescribed medication, then she is guilty of medical negligence. But it is well established that she *did* carefully check the level of dosage; and so clearly she is not guilty of medical negligence.

8. If Ron had Rachel's permission to stay in her mountain cabin for the weekend, then Ron is not guilty of burglary. And Rachel did give Ron permission to stay in her cabin, so Ron is not guilty of burglary.

9. When I bought this car, you warned me that if I failed to keep the car properly serviced, then there would be no guarantee on the car. Well, I *have* kept the car properly serviced—I have it completely serviced every 3,000 miles. Now the car has broken down, and I expect you to fix it—I kept the car properly serviced, so the car must still be guaranteed.

10. Wow, Jill must have won the lottery! Yesterday she said that if she won the lottery, then she wouldn't be in class today. And sure enough, Jill is not in class today.

11. If there were no process of appeals and review, then there would be a danger of imprisoning innocent people. But we do have an extensive appeals and review system, so there is no danger of imprisoning the innocent.

12. If studying logic improves your sex life, then there will be a great demand for logic. And there is a great demand for logic: The logic courses are all filled. Therefore, the study of logic must improve your sex life.

13. The defendant is guilty of breaking or entering only if she intended to commit a felony when she entered the house. Now certainly she had no intention of committing a felony when she opened the door and walked in: She saw the "For Sale" sign in the yard and was simply looking the house over with the idea that she might like to buy it. Therefore, the defendant is not guilty of breaking or entering.

14. I shall pass tomorrow's history exam if I study all night. Well, I guess I won't pass my history exam, since I have to work at the restaurant late tonight and so I obviously can't study all night.

15. I shall pass tomorrow's history exam only if I study all night. I certainly shall pass that history exam: I've never flunked a history exam, and I'm not about to start now. I guess that means I'll have to study all night.

16. If capital punishment is to be morally acceptable, then there must be *no* possibility of mistakenly executing the innocent. But obviously there *is* a possibility of executing innocent people (after all, there have been dozens of convictions overturned by newly discovered DNA evidence, cases in which people were wrongly convicted and imprisoned). So capital punishment is *not* morally acceptable.

17. The United States is a very wealthy country and spends about 16% of its gross national product on health care. If the United States had a well-organized and efficient health-care system, then no one in the United States would be denied decent health care. But in fact many people—millions of people—in the United States are denied decent health care. So obviously the United States does not have a well-organized and efficient health-care system.

18. If the defendant drove the getaway car, then she is guilty. So she is obviously not guilty, because it is well established that she did not drive the getaway car.

19. The defendant is guilty of breaking or entering only if she intended to steal something. But she certainly never intended to steal anything. Therefore, the defendant is not guilty.

20. If the defendant is guilty, then the alibi witness did not tell the truth. It is obvious that the alibi witness did not tell the truth: She lied from beginning to end. So the defendant is certainly guilty.

21. If the defendant is guilty, then the alibi witness did not tell the truth. The defendant is certainly guilty: You can tell by her weak chin and beady eyes. So the alibi witness lied.

22. If the defendant is guilty, then the alibi witness did not tell the truth. So the defendant is not guilty, since the alibi witness certainly told the truth.

23. If the defendant had carried a pistol, then she would be guilty. But she is obviously not guilty, since she did not carry a pistol.

24. If we did not have effective means of controlling and alleviating severe pain, then active euthanasia (mercy killing) would be morally acceptable. But through medical advances we now have very effective methods of controlling and alleviating even the most severe pain. So, obviously, active euthanasia is not morally acceptable.

25. If this exam is too hard, then critical thinking students will look tired and miserable. So obviously this exam is indeed too hard, since critical thinking students look extremely tired and miserable.

26. If the defendant was in California on the morning of July 1, then she could not have robbed the Mahoning National Bank that afternoon. So the defendant must not have robbed the Mahoning National Bank the afternoon of July 1, since it is certainly well established that she was indeed in California on the morning of July 1.

27. If the murder weapon did not belong to Jones, then we might conclude that Jones is not guilty. But in fact it has been conclusively proved that the murder weapon did belong to Jones. So we must conclude that Jones really is guilty.

28. The only way to ban pornography from the Internet is to have some powerful police group control all Internet traffic. But we don't want police control of the Internet: It should be free and open. So we should not attempt to ban pornography from the Internet.

29. Robert is guilty of negligent homicide only if he did not exercise due caution. But Robert is a careful driver, and he was exercising due caution. So we must find Robert not guilty of negligent homicide.

30. If Rachel is guilty of first-degree murder, then she intended to kill Ralph. And, indeed, she did intend to kill him, as she admitted in her own testimony. Therefore, Rachel is guilty of first-degree murder.

31. Certainly Jones is not guilty of breaking into West Building. After all, as a registered student at the university, Jones had permission to be in West Building. And if Jones had permission to be in West Building, then he cannot be guilty of breaking or entering into West Building.

32. If no one passed the critical thinking exam, then it was too difficult. But some people *did* pass the critical thinking exam, so clearly the exam was not too difficult.

33. Bruce is guilty of check fraud only if he knew there was no money in his account. But Bruce certainly did not know that there was no money in his account: He is a complete idiot about everything related to finances. So Bruce is not guilty of check fraud.

34. If you do not make any mistakes on this exam, then obviously you are sober. So clearly you are not sober, since you did make a mistake.

35. MORTON: "Barbara just said she would go out with me!"
    ALLEN: "You're kidding! I thought she said she hated your guts, and that she would never go out with you under any circumstances."
    MORTON: "Well, she must have changed her mind. I just called her and asked her to go out, and she said she wouldn't go out with me if I were the last man on Earth. So, since I'm certainly not the last man on Earth, that must mean that she's willing to go out with me."

Exercise 14-8

In the case depicted in Figure 14-1, Larsen E. Pettyfogger *originally intends* to draw the conclusion that, I can beat your rap and have you out on the streets in 3 days. The first premise of his argument is, if I can't beat your rap and have you out on the streets in 3 days, my name isn't Larsen E. Pettyfogger. That argument has a second premise, which is so obvious that he does not bother to state it (thus the argument is an *enthymeme*). What is that premise? Is that argument (that he originally intends to make) deductively valid? Is it sound?

Things do not turn out as Larsen E. had expected. He winds up concluding that his name is not Larsen E. Pettyfogger (thus his letterheads are useless). The first premise remains the same. What is the second premise—again, it is left unstated—in the new argument? Is that argument deductively valid? Is it sound?

By permission of Johnny Hart and Creators Syndicate.

Figure 14-1

✓●─│**Study** and **Review** on **mythinkinglab.com**

REVIEW QUESTIONS

1. What is a conditional statement?
2. Diagram the valid argument form *modus ponens*.
3. Diagram the invalid argument form denying the antecedent.
4. Explain, in terms of necessary and sufficient conditions, the error that is made in the fallacy of affirming the consequent.

NOTES

[1] North Carolina Conference of Superior Court Judges and North Carolina Bar Association Foundation, *North Carolina Pattern Instructions—Criminal: Felonious Breaking or Entering.*

[2] North Carolina Conference of Superior Court Judges and North Carolina Bar Association Foundation, *North Carolina Pattern Instructions—Criminal: Gambling.*

INTERNET RESOURCES

The BBC has a nice page for Valid and Invalid Argument, which covers all the argument forms examined in this chapter; it is at *http://www.bbc.co.uk/dna/h2g2/A821107*

ADDITIONAL READING

Almost any introductory logic text will provide more extensive coverage of all of these argument forms; one excellent source is the text by Virginia Klenk, *Understanding Symbolic Logic*, 5th Edition (Upper Saddle River, NJ: Prentice Hall, 2007).

📖●─│**Read** the **Document** on **mythinkinglab.com**

Mary Anne Warren, "On the Moral and Legal Status of Abortion," *Monist*, Vol. 57, no. 4 (1973): 43–61. In the section of the essay included here, Mary Anne Warren examines the necessary and sufficient conditions for being a "person."

Weeks v. Angelone, 528 U.S. 225 (2000). This involves the sentencing phase of a capital murder case that occurred in Virginia. After Weeks was found guilty of capital murder, the question became one of whether the defendant should be sentenced to life imprisonment or to death. The dissenting opinion by Justice Stevens (included here) argues that there was indeed confusion on the jury concerning the necessary and sufficient conditions for the death sentence.

State of North Carolina v. Rich, 351 NC 386. This is a case that came before the Supreme Court of North Carolina, involving the necessary conditions for second-degree murder.

15

❖ ❖ ❖

Scientific and Causal Reasoning

((•⊣**Listen** to the **Chapter Audio** on **mythinkinglab.com**

You flipped a switch and caused the light to turn on. You turned the key and caused the engine to start. Hatfield shot McCoy through the heart and caused McCoy's death. The drought caused the failure of the corn crop. Those are perfectly reasonable and legitimate causal claims. But determining causes is not always easy. In fact, causal reasoning is subject to a variety of pitfalls and problems. Consider a case:

> Lawyers sometimes hire "jury selection specialists" to help them in seating a jury. These specialists use social science research techniques in an effort to select favorable jurors for their side, or, at the very least, to weed out any *un*favorable potential jurors. The practice has been a controversial issue in recent years. Most of the debate has been over whether such methods are fair. However, there has also been debate about whether the methods really *work*.

There have been strong claims in support of the effectiveness of social science methods in jury selection. For example, Litigation Sciences, a company that provides such services, claims in its promotional literature that: "To date, where our advice and recommendations have been employed, our clients have achieved successful results in over 95 percent of the cases in which we have been involved."[1] Certainly when the defense has used jury selection experts in criminal cases the acquittal rate has been much better than average.

What does that show? It seems to indicate that "scientific jury selection techniques" are effective, that such techniques can result in a favorable verdict. But is that the correct conclusion? It's true that legal teams using scientific jury selection techniques have a high success rate. But does it follow that the scientific jury selection techniques are the *cause* of the success?

Before going further, try to think of at least one reason for *doubting* that scientific jury selection *causes* successful trial results.

(If you need a hint, consider this: Hiring social scientists to do the research necessary for effective scientific jury selection is quite expensive.)

Okay, why are defense teams that use scientific jury selection techniques successful? *Perhaps* because the scientific jury selection techniques are so effective that they cause the

Who Is Guilty?

Thinking about causality can be perplexing, but also entertaining. Here's a favorite law school puzzler. Arthur, Bert, and Carl are all members of the French Foreign Legion, stationed far out in the desert. Both Bert and Carl hate Arthur, and separately they plot his murder. When Arthur is ordered to go alone on a long mission across the hot, dry desert, both men see their opportunity. Shortly before Arthur leaves, Bert puts a deadly poison in his canteen. A few minutes later, Carl, not knowing about the poison, pours all the (poisoned) water out of Arthur's canteen, and replaces the water with sand. Arthur goes on his journey, and dies of thirst. Now obviously both Bert and Carl are evil men who plotted murder and *attempted* to murder Arthur. But the question is this: Who was the actual *murderer*? That is, who *caused* Arthur's murder?

side using them to win. But perhaps not. Perhaps the scientific jury selection techniques are ineffectual and other factors are the cause of success. One such factor might be that the hiring of teams of social scientists is costly; defendants who can afford such teams must have large sums of money to spend on their defense teams (which means that they not only hire social scientists but also hire a number of high-powered defense lawyers, private investigators to seek out evidence in their favor, and experts to testify for the defense). In short, it may not be the scientific jury selection techniques that are the cause of success; it may instead be that defendants who can afford those techniques can also afford all the other trial advantages that money can buy. Perhaps the actual cause of success is the advantage of having a team of highly qualified lawyers who are working full time on the case (rather than the public defender who, for most criminal defendants, squeezes a few minutes out of an overloaded schedule).[2]

DISTINGUISHING CAUSATION FROM CORRELATION

So the first problem in determining causes is distinguishing genuine causal factors from the various incidental associations. If two sets of phenomena are strongly correlated (when one occurs the second usually follows), that indicates there *may* be a causal relation between the two, and further inquiry along those lines would certainly be justified; but that would *not* be sufficient to prove a causal link. There are several possible reasons for such correlations among events. One, the first *may* indeed be the cause of the second. Two, the causal relation may go in the opposite direction. A striking example of that sort of confusion is the case of the New Hebrides Islanders. The islanders believed that lice caused good health. They based this belief on the fact that healthy islanders were all infested with lice (lice lived in abundance on the tropical islands and it was all but impossible to avoid infestation), while sick islanders had no lice on them. A natural conclusion was that lice caused good health, and loss of lice caused sickness. But in fact the causal relation was exactly the reverse: Lice prefer a narrow range of body temperatures in their hosts, and when the islanders became sick their body temperatures rose above the louse comfort level and the lice sought other lodgings. Being healthy caused the presence of lice and being sick—with a fever—caused the absence of lice. Loss of lice was the result of sickness, not the cause.[3]

A third way in which two positively correlated phenomena may be related is that both may be causally linked to some third set of events. Consider again the use of scientific jury selection techniques. Defendants who have used such techniques have enjoyed an unusually high acquittal rate. But it may be that the *cause* of the acquittals was not the use of scientific jury selection techniques; rather, the cause may have been another factor that caused *both* the use of scientific jury selection techniques *and* the acquittals—namely, the financial resources that employed *both* the scientific jury selectors *and* the time and undivided efforts of the best defense lawyers. Even if scientific jury selection techniques are totally useless, one would still expect to find a high positive correlation between the defense's use of scientific jury selection techniques and acquittals—at least, one would expect to find such a correlation so long as the most expensive defense lawyers believe that such jury selection techniques are useful. (This is *not* to suggest that scientific jury selection techniques are ineffective. But the mere fact that there is a positive correlation between acquittals and defendants' use of such techniques does not *prove* a *causal* relation between the two.)

Suppose that a study discovers that parents who drink bottled water have healthier children. Obviously the people who sell bottled water would be delighted, and probably feature it in their advertising. But would it actually indicate that drinking bottled water *causes* parents to have healthier children? No, by no means. After all, parents who drink bottled water are probably more affluent, and thus can afford better health care for their children, and are less likely to live in hazardous surroundings and thus their children are less likely to be exposed to environmental hazards. Furthermore, parents who drink bottled water may be more health *conscious* than most, and thus are more careful about their children's diets, exercise, vaccinations, and checkups. Those are more likely to be the significant causal factors affecting the health of their children. All of those are *confounding* factors that make it difficult to determine whether the parents' drinking of bottled water is actually the cause of better health in children.[4] A study of heavy coffee drinkers—those drinking eight or more cups of coffee a day—found that they were more likely have heart attacks. One *possibility*, of course, is that drinking lots of coffee is a causal factor for heart attacks. But consider for a moment some of the *other* characteristics that heavy coffee drinkers are likely to have. First, they are more likely to smoke (of course many heavy coffee drinkers do not smoke; but heavy coffee drinkers are more *likely* to smoke than are those who drink little or no coffee, and thus it might be the greater likelihood of smoking that is the actual causal factor for the increased number of heart attacks). And as a heavy coffee drinker, where do I get my afternoon fix of coffee? At the coffee shop, where there is always a tempting array of pastries; or maybe at the drive-thru window of the donut shop. So perhaps it's not the coffee, but the fact that heavy coffee drinkers are more likely to be eating fattening pastries. Also, heavy coffee drinkers are probably less likely to be getting a lot of exercise; and maybe they are not getting enough sleep; and perhaps they are more likely to be under considerable stress at work. So if people who drink lots of coffee are more likely to have heart attacks, it may be all those associated/correlated factors that are the real causal culprits; in fact, it *could* be that if these smoking non-exercising pastry-eaters were *not* drinking coffee they would be having heart attacks at an even higher rate.

Figure 15-1   The Middletons Cartoon

What A Lucky Person

Coincidence can be very persuasive. Here's an example favored by both statisticians and philosophers. We hold a quarter-flipping contest. The quarters used are perfectly balanced, the contest is not rigged, and there is no way to cheat (a machine flips the quarters): the quarters are just as likely to land heads as tails. Approximately a million people enter the contest, and they are paired off, with the winners at each stage meeting in the next stage

of the contest. After about 20 rounds, we finally have a winner. The way the contest was set up, *someone* had to win. But after winning 20 rounds, the winner would very likely conclude that he or she was a "lucky person," that he or she had the special *property* of being *lucky*. That is, there's a strong temptation to attribute a specific cause, impose a causal pattern, on events that are merely *coincidence.*

There is a fourth possibility for why there is positive correlation between two sets of phenomena: It's possible that the correlation is accidental, that there is no causal relation at all. If I rub my rabbit's foot just prior to the drawing of the daily lottery number and then my number is drawn, I may conclude that rubbing the lucky rabbit foot caused my good fortune; if next week I repeat the procedure and win again, I may become firmly convinced of the positive causal efficacy of rabbit-foot rubbing. There is a positive correlation between the two. But what I am forgetting, of course, is the number of times that I crossed my fingers, wore my lucky cap, gripped a horseshoe, and kissed a four-leaf clover without success. If I, and thousands of other lottery players, try a multitude of "lucky charms," then some of them, by chance, will be positively correlated with good luck in the lottery. (And, of course, the positive correlation of the lucky charm with lottery luck may be exaggerated: The times I rubbed the rabbit's foot and won tend to be quite memorable; the many times I rubbed the rabbit's foot and lost are easily forgotten.)

A nice example of coincidence masquerading as a special cause is discussed by Michael Shermer.[5] Michael Drosnin recently wrote a couple of best-selling books called *Bible Code* and *Bible Code II*. The *Bible Code* game is easy to play. Start with the first few books of the Old Testament. Then have your computer generate a printout of every 7th letter (or 3rd, or 13th, or whatever you wish), filling page after page with your printout. Then start looking through the dozens of pages. Look hard: right to left, left to right, diagonally, up and down, in circles or squares, whatever you like. Lo and behold, you will find all sorts of wonders! When Drosnin did this, he found "predictions" or "prophecies" of all sorts of amazing things: the Oklahoma City bombing, the September 11 attack on the World Trade Center, the collision between Jupiter and comet Shoemaker-Levy 9, the notorious affair between President Bill Clinton and Monica Lewinsky, and the assassination of Israeli prime minister Yitzhak Rabin. When skeptics scoffed that these were not genuine predictions, but merely after-the-fact concoctions, Drosnin offered a challenge: "When my critics find a message about the assassination of a prime minister encrypted in *Moby Dick*, I'll believe them." Australian mathematician Brenda McKay took the challenge, and soon generated *nine* "encrypted predictions" of political assassinations in *Moby Dick*. The moral of this story is a simple one: If you look hard enough for a pattern, you can almost always find one (whether you are looking for a pattern in the numbers worn by the winning Super Bowl quarterbacks or a pattern generated by choosing the seventh letter from a book); and when you find a patterned *correlation* between events, that correlation may be the result of *coincidence,* and *not* the result of any causal link.

Suppose we do a study at your old high school. We randomly select 20 students who drink beer, and 20 students who do not drink, and we track them for a year. At the end of the year the students who do not drink had a GPA of 3.1, while the beer-drinking students had a GPA of 2.9. And so we conclude: drinking beer causes high school students to make lower grades.

Chain Letter Causation

Trust the Lord and He will light your way. This prayer has been sent to you for good luck. The luck has been brought to you. You are to receive good luck within 4 days of receiving this letter. Send copies of this to people you think need good luck. Do not keep this letter. It must leave you within 96 hours after you receive it.

While in the Philippines, General Walker lost his life 6 days after he received this letter. He failed to circulate the prayer; however, before his death he received $775,000. Take note of the following: C. S. Dias received the chain in 1953. He made 20 copies and sent them; a few days later he won $2 million. Carlice Grant received the chain letter and forgot it, and a few days later he lost his job. He found the letter and sent it, 5 days later he got a better job. Darin Fairchild received the chain and not believing it, threw it away. Nine days later he died. For no reason whatsoever should this chain be broken.

Well, maybe. Certainly that's possible. But even if our results are *accurate* (and none of our subjects are lying about their drinking habits), that would *not* establish that drinking beer causes lower grades. Not even close. We can think of *three other possibilities* (other than drinking beer causes lower grades) to account for our results. First (and perhaps most likely), there is some other factor *associated* with both beer drinking and lower grades that is the actual cause: For example, it might well be that students who do not drink beer have more parental supervision and parental involvement, and not only do their parents *discourage* them from drinking beer, but they also *encourage* them to get their homework done, make sure they get any needed tutoring, take them to the library, and praise them for good grades. The involvement of parents would be a *confounder,* a factor that *confounds* and confuses the relation between the factors studied. So perhaps it is not the beer drinking that causes lower grades, but instead the lack of parental involvement and encouragement.

Or second, maybe the causal relationship runs in reverse. Rather than beer drinking causing lower grades, making lower grades drives students to drink.

Or third—and a distinct possibility in a study this small—maybe the results were mere coincidence. We happened to get one nondrinker who is a brilliant student with a 4.0 average, and one occasional beer drinker who is a lousy student (with a 0.1 average). In a study this small, that would be enough to skew the results.

What can we conclude from our study? *Maybe* beer drinking causes lower grades; but just as likely, *maybe* there is a third factor (a confounder) that is the actual cause, or maybe the causal relationship runs in reverse, or maybe the results were simply coincidence. In short, causal claims are important, but it is also important to consider them critically, and to be skeptical of causal claims drawn on insufficient evidence.

Exercise 15-1

In discussing the difference between causation and correlation, we discussed four different possibilities when two events are correlated. One is that the first may be the cause of the second; what are the other three, and how would they apply to the cases below?

1. We recently did a study, and found that elderly people who had pets were significantly healthier than elderly people without pets. One possibility is that having a pet causes better health among elderly persons. But there are three other possibilities for explaining that correlation, OTHER THAN that having a pet causes better health; what are the other three possibilities?

2. Mary Spio, editor of the singles lifestyle magazine *One2One Living,* cautions singles against living together before marriage, because studies have shown that living together leads to less relationship stability, lower chances of the couple getting married, and greater likelihood of divorce if they do marry. Perhaps living together before marriage does have those effects, but this data certainly does not establish that; what are the other possibilities?

3. When high school band and orchestra directors are trying to convince parents to invest the money and time required to have their children participate, they often tell the parents—what is true—that high school students who learn to play a musical instrument and participate in musical groups consistently make (on average) higher grades and score higher on SAT and ACT exams than do students who are not involved in instrumental performance. The directors conclude that participating in band or orchestra *causes* high school students to improve their academic performance. I'm not questioning the value of band and orchestra for high school students: I think they're great. But the fact that student musicians perform better academically does *not* show that playing an instrument caused the students to have greater academic success. What are the other possibilities?

4. A recent study found that elderly people who gamble at casinos are generally in better health than those of similar age who do *not* engage in casino gambling. So if you want to keep her healthy take grandma to the casino! Well, maybe: perhaps there's something about the lights and sounds and excitement that gets the blood moving and the energy flowing, and maybe casino gambling really does promote good health in the elderly. But I doubt it. What are the other possibilities?

5. We recently checked the data, and found that Western State University students who take critical thinking have a higher graduation rate than Western State students who do not take critical thinking. One possibility is that taking critical thinking causes students to be more successful students and more likely to graduate. But there are three other possibilities for explaining that correlation, OTHER THAN that taking critical thinking causes higher graduation rates; what are the other three possibilities?

THE QUESTIONABLE CAUSE FALLACY

An unjustified causal claim commits the *questionable cause fallacy*. (In polite company the fallacy of questionable cause sometimes goes by a classier name: *post hoc, ergo propter hoc*. Its close friends sometimes call it by its first name: the *post hoc* fallacy. *Post hoc, ergo propter hoc* is a Latin phrase meaning "After this, therefore because of this.")

To see the difficulties in ascertaining genuine causal relations, consider the problem of placebos. You've seen the pain-reliever commercials: A woman is struggling to control three energetic children and prepare dinner—and then the dog knocks over a table, breaking a vase and scattering water and flowers all over the living room. The woman, not surprisingly, yells at the kids, kicks the dog, and develops a bit of a headache. The concerned announcer suggests that she try two tablets of this wonderful, new, super-strength, fast-acting miracle pain reliever: new Happy-Head. We see her 10 minutes later, wearing a warm smile and playing tag with the kids and giving the dog a doggy treat. "What happened to your headache?" inquires the good Samaritan announcer. "It's gone, and I feel great," she replies, "that Happy-Head really works."

Well, perhaps it does. But even assuming that this is an accurate story, and the woman *does* feel much better after taking the medication, it does not follow that it was the medication that caused her to feel better. It may well have been the *placebo* effect of *taking* the medication. (A *placebo* is a pill that looks like medication and passes for medicine, but in fact contains no medication: a "sugar pill.") Studies have shown that in many instances subjects who are given a placebo will be relieved of their pain, especially if the placebo is given with dramatic flourish, as a wonderful new product. So it will be easy enough for purveyors of a new headache remedy to obtain glowing testimonials for the effectiveness of their product, simply as a result of the placebo effect—even if the product itself is totally useless. (The notorious *Head-On* headache remedy—with the loud obnoxious commercials—made a lot of money with the placebo effect. The only drugs in *Head-On* have no proven effect on headaches; but even if they did, it wouldn't matter, because the *Head-On* that is sold over the counter is *diluted* to less than one part per billion of active ingredient. By the time it goes in the package, it is basically just water: water at a very steep price. But apparently rubbing water on your head—*if* you believe it's a powerful medication—can be a very effective headache placebo for many people.)

How, then, can we tell the real cause? Is it the medication itself? Or is it the placebo effect? That is, if we wanted to test the effectiveness of a new pain-relief medication, how would we do it? By testing *two* groups: an *experimental* group, who get the actual medication, and a *control* group that is as closely matched as possible with the experimental group and is given placebos (the pills are the same size and color, so that both groups think they are receiving identical medication). Then we test to see whether the group taking the medication has a higher rate of pain relief than does the group taking the placebo. If the group receiving the actual medication (the experimental group) has a higher rate of pain relief than the placebo group (the control group), *and* the two groups are evenly matched, then it is reasonable to conclude that the medication *does* contribute to the relief of pain, that it is causally effective in relieving pain.

Returning to the question of the causal efficacy of scientific jury selection techniques in gaining favorable verdicts, we can see another possible complication in sorting out the causes: the placebo effect. Perhaps the *use* of elaborate jury selection procedures has the side effect of *encouraging* the lawyers who employ the techniques and *daunting* the opposing lawyers. For example, if the defense has used such techniques, then the defense lawyers may believe—rightly or wrongly—that the jurors are sympathetic to their side, and thus the defense lawyers will be more confident and probably more effective. The opposite will be true for the opposing lawyers: They are likely to feel—again, rightly or wrongly—that the jurors are regarding them unfavorably, and thus may be less cordial to the jury as well as less effective in their arguments. In short, use of scientific jury selection techniques may operate as a sort of placebo; thus the *use* of the techniques might cause success even if the techniques in themselves are of no value.[6]

Exercise 15-2

The following exercises make causal claims. It is possible that the causal claims are true; but for most of the cases, it is more likely that the causal claims are false.

A. For each claim, explain why you might have doubts about the claimed causal relation. (What relevant factors have been omitted from consideration? What other factors might account for the result?)

B. We noted that when there is a correlation, a causal claim based on that correlation may be *false* because of these other possibilities: (1) the causal relation might run in reverse (good health causes lice infestation); (2) there may be some other factor that causes both series of events (defendants who use jury consultants are successful in their defense *and* they also have enough money to afford jury consultants *and* top lawyers, expert witnesses, and detectives); and (3) the correlation may be accidental. For each of the following cases, tell which of those three other possibilities might account for the correlation.

1. Last year, the Lake Wobegon Whippets won only 2 games and lost 18. This year they actually had a winning season, winning 11 games and losing 8. The team is made up of the same players as last year, except that one additional player was added: a substitute outfielder, Walter "Molasses" Inqvist. He didn't seem like that great a player, but the facts speak for themselves: Walter is the only new player, so he must be the cause of the Whippets' great improvement.[7]

2. We have done a careful study, and we have found that the alumni of Old Ivy College, an exclusive and outrageously expensive private college, had an average income last year of over $300,000. It is expensive to attend Old Ivy College, but the facts speak for themselves: it's clearly worth it. Attending Old Ivy obviously results in much higher income.

3. We ought to look into the new reading program that was developed last year at the Frog Junction High School. Frog Junction High is a small school—2 years ago its graduating class was four, and the same number graduated last year—but it is clear that their new reading program works. After all, the SAT scores of their graduating seniors jumped an average of almost 100 points the year they started the reading program.

4. When people who have smoked regularly for a number of years *stop* smoking, their mortality rate (roughly, the rate at which they die) is actually *higher* during the first year after they stop than is the mortality rate for those who continue to smoke. Obviously there is something about *stopping* smoking that is hazardous to your health. (Hint: Consider under what circumstances many people finally stop smoking. [Incidentally, the study results cited in this example are accurate: The mortality rate for those who stop smoking *is* higher during the first year than for those who continue; in subsequent years the mortality rate for the continuing smokers is substantially greater than for those who stopped.])

5. I had been feeling sort of tired and run down the last few months. A friend suggested I try taking a special tonic: Professor Wonderful's High-Potency Maximum-Strength Power Booster. He said it worked wonders for him. Well, the stuff tastes vile, and it's expensive, but it works great! I've got my old vim and vigor back. Dr. Wonderful makes a wonderful—and genuinely effective—tonic!

6. We had a cookout last night, and I got a terrible case of indigestion later that evening. We had basically the same stuff we always have: hot dogs, potato salad, coleslaw, and beer. I ate and drank about the same amount I usually do, and everything we had was our usual brand—except the hot dogs, which were a new brand we hadn't tried before. Believe me, I won't try them again. I never get indigestion, but I did last night. Must have been those new hot dogs.

7. In 1996 in the United States, states which had the death penalty had a murder rate that was almost twice as high as the murder rate for states without the death penalty: states with the death penalty had a murder rate of 7.1 for every 100,000 residents, while states without the death penalty had a murder rate of 3.6 for every 100,000. Year after year, states that practice capital punishment have a higher murder rate than states that have abolished capital punishment. The evidence is clear: the death penalty actually causes a higher murder rate.

8. Since the 1950s, rock music has become increasingly popular in our society, and during the same period, the crime rate has risen and the use of illegal drugs has also increased. The evidence is clear: Rock music causes crime and drug abuse.

9. Yesterday I went to the track and discovered something that is going to make me rich. In the first race, the jockey on the winning horse was wearing green colors—and he was the only jockey in the race wearing green. The second race had 10 horses, and only two of the jockeys wore green silks: Sure enough, one of the jockeys wearing green won. In the third race only one jockey was wearing green, and his horse finished out of the money. But in the fourth race three jockeys wore green, and one of them won and another finished third! In the next five races, there were at least eight horses in each race, and in each race there was only one jockey in green silks—and in those five races, the jockeys wearing green won twice, finished second twice, and finished out of the money only once. I don't know what it is, but obviously there is something about having its jockey wear green silks that makes a horse run faster.

10. Some years ago, there were people who claimed that when babies hear recordings of the music of Mozart, that experience enhances and strengthens their intelligence. Some people were skeptical, but now the results have proven that claim is true! We have followed the development of 50 children whose mothers played the music of Mozart for them when they were infants, and those children are now 19 years old; and they had a higher than average rate of graduation from high school, their SAT scores were substantially above the national average, and a significant number of them—much greater than chance—have been admitted to very prestigious colleges and universities. So clearly when babies listen to the music of Mozart, it makes them smarter.

11. University Hospital has a very high mortality rate; that is, a higher percentage of patients admitted to University Hospital die during their stay than at some of the other hospitals around the state. So University Hospital must be a lousy hospital that is placing the lives of its patients in great jeopardy.

12. You may have heard that Arizona is a great place for people suffering from respiratory diseases: warm, very dry, and its desert environment produces relatively few plants that provoke allergic reactions. But don't you believe it! In fact, Arizona is a particularly hazardous state for people with respiratory diseases: It has one of the highest death rates from respiratory diseases of any state in the United States.

13. I finally figured out why good old Home State University loses. It's because they get nervous when they have to play in front of very large crowds! Just look at the record. Last year we lost only two games, to Michigan and Florida, and those games had the biggest crowds of any games Home State played. The year before, Home State again lost only two games, to Penn State and Florida State,

again, these games drew the biggest crowds of the year. And the year before, Home State's only losses were to Notre Dame and Nebraska, and those games also drew the largest crowds that year. So if we want Home State to have an undefeated season, we have to figure out some way to reduce the crowd size in their big games.

14. We recently did a study, and found that teenage boys who play violent video games (such as Grand Theft Auto) are significantly more likely to commit crimes. Clearly these violent video games are causing an increase in crime among our young people.

THE METHOD OF SCIENCE

The method described above for testing pain-relief medication makes use of a randomized controlled experiment; in medical research, it would be called a randomized clinical trial. We take two cases that are as close to identical as possible, with the exception of one key difference. Then we see if the results in one case are different from the results in the other case. If there is a difference in results, then the factor that was present in the one case but not in the other must be the *cause* of that difference. Thus if we are testing the causal efficacy of a proposed pain-relief nostrum, we need two groups that are as similar as possible. (Obviously we would not want the control group—which takes the placebo—to be college students and the experimental group—which takes the medication—to be members of a retirement community; in such a case, we would not know whether the *cause* of any difference was age, differences in health, or the powers of the medication.) Furthermore, it is essential that the *only* difference in the test situation is that one group gets the medication and the other does not. That's why the control group receives a placebo: We don't want one group taking a pill and the other group doing nothing. It is also important that the placebo and the medication are identical in size, weight, color, and taste. And it is essential that the two groups be treated the same by the people administering the medication and the placebo (the placebo should be dosed out with the same care as the actual medication); thus, we may use what is called a "double-blind" procedure, in which those giving the pills do not know whether they are giving placebos or medication (it's *double*-blind because there is a double layer of "blindness" as to who is getting placebos—both the test subjects and those who deal directly with those subjects are ignorant of which pills are medication and which are placebos).

It is a difficult task to isolate a *single* difference between groups that are otherwise essentially similar. For example, some of the earliest studies of the effects of smoking on development of lung cancer were almost useless because the smokers included a higher percentage of city dwellers than did the nonsmokers, and people who live in cities are somewhat more likely to develop cancer than are those who live in rural areas. Only when studies matched smokers and nonsmokers for *every* relevant characteristic (diet, work environment, age, gender, residence) could it be reliably determined that the significant *difference* in lung cancer rates between smokers and nonsmokers was *caused* by smoking.

The case of the causal relation between smoking and cancer offers an opportunity to repeat an oft-repeated but never stale maxim of logical thinking: Be careful to note the *exact conclusion*. In the above case, the conclusion of the lung cancer–smoking researchers was *not* that smoking is *the* cause (or the only cause) of lung cancer. Rather, the conclusion is that smoking is *a* cause of lung cancer, that if one smokes one is more likely to develop lung cancer than if one does not, that if everyone smokes there will be more cases of lung cancer than if no one smokes. It's important that the exact conclusion be noted; otherwise, one might think that the causal conclusion could be *refuted* by an argument like this: "Well, Uncle Joe smoked two packs a day for 60 years, and he died last year at age 79 when a tree fell on him. He certainly never had lung cancer. So don't tell me that smoking causes lung cancer." That argument would work *if* the smoking studies concluded that smoking *always* causes lung cancer; but that is not the claim. Rather, the claim is that smoking is the cause of some cases of lung cancer: that there are people who develop lung cancer because of their smoking, people who would not have developed lung cancer had they not smoked. So pointing out one individual who smoked but did not develop lung cancer will not refute that argument.

Randomized Studies and Prospective Studies

In 1846, Ignaz Semmelweis was a physician at Vienna General Hospital. He noticed that between 1844 and 1846, in the First Maternity Division (where the mothers were attended by physicians), 10% of the women giving birth died from childbed fever. During the same period, the mortality rate from childbed fever in the Second Maternity Division (in which midwives attended the mothers) was only 2%.

Semmelweis wondered why there was such a large difference. He realized that the physicians attending women in the First Maternity Division were also working in the autopsy room, studying cadavers, just prior to assisting in deliveries. The midwives, of course, had not been in the autopsy room. Semmelweis hypothesized that there might be some source of infection being spread by the hands of the doctors from the cadavers to the mothers. Semmelweis tested his hypothesis by requiring that all physicians entering the maternity ward first wash their hands in a solution of chlorinated lime to remove whatever it was that was causing childbed fever, and then comparing the number of cases of childbed fever now occurring with the previous rate.

In Semmelweis's experiment, the *control* group are the women who gave birth earlier while under the care of physicians who had *not* washed their hands. The *experimental* group are the women who are now giving birth under the care of physicians who *had* washed their hands. This was one of the great experiments in medical history, but it had some problems. It might have been better if he had randomly selected a group of doctors to use lime solution, and others to wash with something much weaker, or not wash at all; but if he reasonably thought that washing might save lives, then it might be unethical to use that sort of control group. However, there might have been some important differences between the earlier circumstances when doctors were *not* washing their hands and the later situation when doctors were. For example, suppose that during the earlier period there had been an epidemic of fever, but it had subsided by the time Semmelweis tried his experiment. Or there might have been a large turnover among the doctors, and some very bad doctors had retired and been replaced by newer, more effective doctors. Or some new delivery technique had been developed that was now widely in use. Or maybe the doctors were simply older and more experienced. We wouldn't know if the reduction in childbed fever was the result of washing hands or from some other cause. That's why the *best* way to run the experiment would be by randomly dividing the doctors into wash and not-wash groups, and then recording the difference in childbed fever rates. (It might be even better if each doctor alternated washing and not washing, and then the results were compared.) That way any differences are *controlled* for through randomization, and any factors that might have influenced the number of childbed fever cases would be cancelled out, with the single exception of washing and not washing. Suppose that in the past year many women of childbearing age had begun to eat a new food, perhaps a new type of vegetable, that (unknown to anyone) gave limited immunity from childbed fever to those who ate it. In that case, Semmelweis would have gotten a lower rate of childbed fever, but the cause might not have been the washing. If the nonwashing and washing doctors had been divided randomly, then the patients of both the control and the experimental groups would be equally likely to eat the new diet, and any differences in rate of childbed fever could safely be attributed to the new routine of hand washing.

So *randomized* experimental design is the scientific ideal. But it's not always possible to use that design. For example, suppose we want to know the effects of smoking two packs of cigarettes a day, starting at age 16, over a period of 10 years. The best method for determining that would be by taking a group of several thousand 16-year-olds, dividing them randomly into two groups, and having the experimental group smoke two packs a day for 10 years and keep the control group from smoking at all. But that would be a morally appalling experiment. After all, several years ago we suspected that cigarette smoking was profoundly harmful to health; and so we certainly can't run an experiment in which we have people do something that we strongly suspect will cause them great harm. Instead, we might run a *prospective* (sometimes called an *epidemiological*) test: We will search out a thousand kids who started smoking two packs a day at age 16, and then find a thousand nonsmoking kids (for our *control* group) who we can *match* with the smokers in our experimental group. The problem is, what features should we match for? It won't be enough just to match a 16-year-old male smoker with a 16-year-old male nonsmoker. Smokers and nonsmokers may differ in many other ways that are very important to health. For example, it may be that the smokers generally don't get as much exercise, or perhaps they drink more on average, or maybe they don't get as much sleep, or maybe they tend to eat more junk food, or perhaps they are more likely to work around pesticides or industrial chemicals, or maybe they tend to live in urban areas and are more likely to breathe polluted air. And even if we can find a match on all those characteristics, there might still be some characteristic that we hadn't considered. It turns out that prolonged exposure to asbestos increases one's risk for developing cancer. But we didn't know that until recently, and so we would not have thought to control for asbestos exposure. That's not to say that *prospective* studies are useless. If they are carefully conducted, they can reveal very important causal results. But they are difficult to run, and it is *very* difficult to be sure that we have controlled for all the potential causal factors.

Making Predictions

Semmelweis used a controlled experiment to test his theory. The test turned out as he had hoped, and indicated that washing hands with chlorinated lime reduces the spread of childbed fever. But in this case the test was also designed to prove a larger hypothesis: roughly, the hypothesis that disease is spread by something (germs, though Semmelweis didn't call it that) that is transmitted from others with the disease. That is, many diseases, including childbed fever, are caused by infection from an external source, rather than by some internal process (such as an excess of "black bile"). Semmelweis used a controlled experiment as part of his scientific work, but important as controlled experiments are, they are not the whole of the scientific process. Exactly how does the "scientific method" work?

A popular but *false* notion of scientific method is that scientists gather lots of data, collect many observations, and finally devise a hypothesis to account for all their observations. It's a pleasant image, the scientist working in her lab or looking through her telescope or rambling around the rain forest gathering more and more samples and data and information, then finally squeezing it all together into a true scientific theory. But it's not really the way the scientific method works. One problem with that popular image is that there is just too much to look for. A scientist might make an enormous number of observations, but they would be a terrible jumble, and it would be all but impossible to winnow out the important and relevant data from the distractions. Instead, in applying the *scientific method*, scientists devise a *hypothesis;* then they make a *prediction* based on that hypothesis; and the success of that prediction *confirms* the truth of their theory. That's a bit oversimplified, but it's at least a rough outline of what scientific method involves.

None of this is to deny the importance of scientific observation and data collection, of course. After all, if Semmelweis hadn't noticed that the mortality rate was much higher in the First Maternity Division than in the Second Division, he would not have formulated his hypothesis. But in order to test and prove his hypothesis, Semmelweis could not just go on collecting data. Instead, he had to follow the basic three steps of scientific method. First, devise a theory or hypothesis that would account for the phenomena (in the popular model, that is the *final* step; in the actual scientific method, it is the *first* step). Second, make a *prediction* based on that theory (Semmelweis predicted a dramatic drop in childbed fever). Third, *test* to see if that prediction is accurate.

Consider one of the most famous of scientific theories: Newton's laws of motion. In 1687, Isaac Newton proposed that everything—balls that are hit in Fenway Park, spacecraft that orbit the Earth, the planets that orbit the Sun—is subject to a set of simple laws: In the absence of any force, the momentum of a body remains constant; if there is a force acting on a body, that body will accelerate by an amount directly proportional to the strength of the force and inversely proportional to the mass of the body; if a body exerts a force on a second body, then the second exerts an equal and opposite force on the first; and finally, any two bodies exert forces on each other that are proportional to the product of their masses divided by the square of the distance between them. This is an exciting and extraordinary theory, building on the work of Copernicus, Kepler, and Galileo, and bringing together both celestial and terrestrial motions under one set of simple and precise laws. But was it true? Some scientists remained skeptical: After all, these gravitational forces Newton was talking about, forces acting over enormous distances and requiring no physical contact, sounded a bit mysterious. But in 1705, Edmond Halley published a remarkable prediction, based on Newton's theory and on astronomical reports of earlier comets. Halley predicted that a comet would reappear on Christmas, in 1758. Now *that* is a prediction! It's not like predicting that Bruce will drink coffee tomorrow morning, or that undergraduates will show up in Florida in the spring, or that Buffalo will have a blizzard in February. Comets were strange and mysterious: they seemed to follow no set pattern, they showed up out of nowhere, and they were often seen as divine warnings of doom and disaster. Halley's prediction was not only dramatic, it was also remarkably accurate, with the comet appearing right on schedule. Newtonian theory had already established its worth by 1758, but the success of Halley's prediction was the crowning proof.

When Predictions Go Wrong

But not every prediction is so successful. In the sixteenth century, Copernicus proposed the Copernican theory, in opposition to the reigning Ptolemaic theory. According to the Ptolemaic theory, the Earth is stationary and unmoving, and the Sun, the planets, and the realm of fixed stars (the sphere on which all the stars are fixed) all circle around the stationary Earth. Copernicus proposed that the Sun was the center, and the Earth and the other planets were all in orbit around the Sun, while the Earth revolved daily on its axis. According to Copernicus, it took 1 day for the Earth to turn and 1 year for the Earth to travel around the Sun (rather than, as in the Ptolemaic theory, it took 1 day for the Sun to orbit the Earth). Which theory was right, the Copernican or the Ptolemaic? How would you test them? (Remember, it's the sixteenth century: there are no telescopes, no space shuttles, no space stations.)

Think about what each theory predicts. According to the Ptolemaic theory, the Earth is stationary, fixed. But the Copernican theory claims that the Earth travels all the way around the Sun, every year. Suppose today is October 1. The Ptolemaic theory says that 6 months from now, on April 1, the Earth will be exactly where it is today; it will not have moved an inch. But the Copernican theory asserts that on April 1 the Earth will be an enormous distance from here, way over on the other side of the Sun. So if the Copernican theory is true, then when we take a sighting on the stars today, and calculate the angles between them, and then take another sighting from our new position on April 1, we should get a different result because of the differences in our locations (just as when you look from a distance at two skyscrapers and measure the angle between them, and then move a few hundred yards and take another measurement, you should get a different measurement). That observed difference is called the *stellar parallax*. The Copernican theory predicts you will observe the stellar parallax; the Ptolemaic theory predicts you will not.

A very ingenious experiment. So they ran the test, and the result: No stellar parallax. So what do we conclude? The Copernican theory is false. We have to give it up. The prediction failed.

Well, no, not exactly. Some people rejected the Copernican theory; but many who believed the Copernican theory were disappointed, but they did *not* reject the theory. Instead, they questioned some of the *background assumptions* that had been made in testing the theory. In particular, they questioned one crucial assumption: that the stars are close enough that moving from one side of the Sun to the other should make a measurable difference in the angles of the stars. Instead of rejecting the Copernican theory, they rejected that assumption, and concluded the stars are so far away from us (compared to the distance the Earth travels around the Sun) that we are unable to detect any difference in angle (like if you moved only an inch and looked again at the skyscrapers).

It turns out, of course, that the Copernicans were right: The stars are *much* farther away than the people of the sixteenth century had imagined (in fact, at distances so enormous that most of us have difficulty getting any sense of it). The Copernican prediction, incidentally, *was* finally confirmed: The stellar parallax was observed, but not until centuries later with much better observational instruments.

The moral of the story is this: The scientific method involves making predictions, and the success of those predictions supports the truth of the theory. But the falsification of a theory is not quite as simple and straightforward as it might first appear. If our prediction proves false, it may mean that the theory is just wrong, and should be rejected. Or it may mean that we need to reexamine some of the background assumptions that the theory makes, or question some of the data involved in our prediction.

Suppose you run an experiment: Dip a piece of litmus paper in acid. Your chemistry professor tells you about acids and bases, and your prediction is that the litmus paper will turn red when you dip it in the acid. You grasp the paper, dip it in the liquid, and it turns *green,* not red. Don't get your hopes up. You didn't just make a great scientific breakthrough, and refute the entire theory of acids and bases. You probably dipped it in your coffee. Or perhaps your acid solution got contaminated when you spilled your beer in it. Or maybe you got the wrong paper: your chemistry professor said litmus paper, and you thought she said Christmas paper, so you used bright green Christmas wrapping paper. Before we count your litmus experiment as a refutation of our theories of acids and bases, we will check very carefully for any errors you made in procedures and calculations. And you would have to duplicate your experiment, while we observe closely.

So confirming and refuting hypotheses is a complicated process, involving drawing predictions and testing them; and failure of the predictions does not always entail rejection of the hypothesis. We may instead question the background assumptions (Are the stars really so close?) or the specific data (Was that really litmus paper that you dipped in the acid?) Still, there are some important points to note concerning the legitimate testing of hypotheses. First, there must be a *prediction.* Merely finding a hypothesis that will account for the data is not enough. After all, there are always plenty of hypotheses that would account for any phenomena. How do we account for the spectacular "northern lights," the aurora borealis that spreads curtains of shimmering color across northern skies? They are caused by Jill Frost: She is the magical sister of Jack Frost, who paints all the trees in their autumn colors. Jack paints leaves, Jill paints skies. It "explains" the existence of the northern lights; but unfortunately for my Jill Frost hypothesis, it makes no predictions and gives us no guidance for our further investigations into the aurora borealis phenomenon. In contrast, consider the hypothesis that the northern lights are caused by electrically charged particles from the Sun that are trapped by the Earth's magnetic field. That hypothesis allows us to *predict* that solar eruptions will be followed by displays of the northern lights, that as the Sun moves toward a period of sun spot maximum there will be more displays of the northern lights, and as the sun spot cycle approaches sun spot minimum there will be fewer.

Faulty "Scientific" Claims

So it is not enough that our hypothesis "account for" the phenomena. That's the easy part. Consider Erich von Daniken's "ancient astronauts" hypothesis in *Chariots of the Gods*. Why did ancient peoples build a set of gigantic lines on the plain of Nazca? They were, according to von Daniken, aircraft runways built according to instructions from ancient astronauts who visited Earth from other stars. (Why did these extraordinary visitors, whose super-advanced technology had mastered the ability to travel the almost unimaginable distances between stars, need the help of ancient peoples to construct a set of runways? That's not altogether clear, but let that pass.) Well, that would explain it. But so would many other hypotheses: An ancient earthly civilization learned to fly, and built the runways themselves; or an ancient civilization built the lines as astronomical calendars, or perhaps for religious ceremonies, or maybe just for esthetic enjoyment; or Jill Frost built the lines as a break from painting the northern lights. Coming up with a hypothesis to explain the phenomena is not the hard part; the challenge is to develop a hypothesis that is *testable* (that makes testable predictions) *and* that passes the test.

Second, it is not enough that the hypothesis involve predictions. The predictions must be of a special sort: They must be predictions that could not be made without the hypothesis, and they must be predictions that are sufficiently detailed and specific that they could be *wrong*. Suppose you *predict*, based on my astrological sign or the lines in my palm, that I will suffer disappointments. That prediction will surely be accurate, but the success of that prediction won't provide any support for the hypothesis that astrological forces shape my destiny. After all, the prediction is hardly surprising: It's a prediction anyone could have made, and without any use of astrological theory. Also, the predictions must be specific enough that they could possibly be *wrong*. In the summer of 1993, Washington, D.C., was the scene of a great experiment in the powers of transcendental meditation. More than 5,000 trained meditators from around the world converged on the capital. Their purpose was to meditate together, thus producing a "coherent consciousness field" that would have a calming effect on the entire city. They predicted that the intense meditation would reduce crime in the city by 20%. Unfortunately, the summer of 1993 was the most violent in the history of the district, with the murder rate reaching record highs—records that still remain. One might imagine that this would refute the hypothesis that group transcendental meditation can reduce violence. No, not at all. It turns out, according to the organizers of the meditation "experiment," that violent crime in the district had been *reduced* by 18%! But how could that be? The murder rate had hit record highs, hadn't it? True; but the violent crime rate had been reduced 18% from what it *would* have been without the transcendental meditation. How did they arrive at that figure? By a rigorous analysis that included considerations of fluctuations in the Earth's magnetic field. But of course a prediction that there will be a decrease from the unknowable data of what the murder rate "would have been" is the sort of prediction that can *not* be wrong.[9]

Another way to make "safe" predictions is by making them vague, or ambiguous, so that lots of things can be said to fit them. The "prophecies" of Nostradamus are a good example. You can also make your predictions safe from falsification by using a scattergun approach: Make lots of predictions, and surely at least one will be a hit (and most people will forget the failures). This is a favorite technique of "psychics" who see into the future. Jeane Dixon was one of the most famous. She successfully predicted that John F. Kennedy would die in office (since he would likely spend 8 years in office, that was not too amazing, but still, not bad). She also predicted (shortly before his unpredicted death) that Elvis Presley would give several benefit performances, she predicted that Princess Diana would have a daughter, that during the 1970s the two-party system would vanish, Richard M. Nixon has "good vibrations" and will serve the country well, Vice President Agnew will rise in stature (he was convicted of accepting bribes and resigned in disgrace), the pollution problem will be solved in 1971, and Fidel Castro will be removed from office in 1970. But she did get some right: She predicted that there would be earthquakes "in the eastern part of the world."

How to Be a Successful Psychic

Tamara Rand is a "psychic to the stars" who provides (for a generous fee) psychic advice to Hollywood stars. She offered a videotape (shown on the *Today* show, *Good Morning America*, and CNN) of a local television show from January 6, 1981. On the videotape of a local television show, Tamara Rand predicted that President Reagan would be shot in the chest by a sandy-haired young man with the initials J. H. The young man would be from a wealthy family, and the assassination attempt would occur during the last week of March or the first week of April. Sure enough, on March 29, 1981, John Hinckley—the sandy-haired son of a wealthy family— shot Reagan in the chest. That's indeed an amazing and specific prediction. However, it turned out that the supposed local television show had never actually aired, and the tape was made by the show's host with Tamara Rand on March 31, two days *after* the assassination attempt.[10]

As noted before, if a prediction fails, it may yet be possible to salvage the hypothesis: perhaps a background assumption was wrong, or the experiment wasn't carried out correctly, or the observations were in error. But there is a limit to this "ad hoc rescue" of favored hypotheses. Consider the famous "Shroud of Turin" (the shroud kept in the cathedral of Turin, which shows an image of a man and which some claimed to have been the burial shroud of Jesus). In the late 1980s, small samples of the shroud were, with the permission of the Roman Catholic Church, tested by radiocarbon dating. The test was quite elaborate: samples were given to independent labs in Oxford, Zurich, and Tucson. In addition to the samples from the shroud, each lab was given control substances for which the age was already known: threads from an 800-year-old garment, linen from a 900-year-old tomb, and linen from a second-century mummy of Cleopatra. None of the samples were identified for any of the labs. All the control samples were correctly dated by all three labs, and the three labs also agreed in dating the material from the shroud at approximately 1350. Does that disprove the claim that the Shroud of Turin was the burial shroud of Jesus? By no means, suggests one defender of the shroud: The reason the carbon-dating gave the origin of the shroud as fourteenth century is because a burst of neutrons from the body of Christ as He arose from the dead created additional carbon-14 nuclei, making the cloth appear centuries younger than it actually is. But that is merely the ad hoc rescue of a cherished hypothesis: there is no reason whatsoever to believe that such a burst occurred (it was not mentioned in Scripture), except to save the theory.[11] In short, when a prediction does not work out, it is possible that some of the background assumptions or procedures were flawed; but then the burden of proof rests on those who claim such errors, and ad hoc rescues cannot carry that burden.

Occam's Razor.   Legitimate scientific claims must be subject to test, and in particular they must be subject to tests that expose them to the possibility of falsification. There is a second standard for scientific reasoning, and it has a catchy name: the principle of parsimony, which is better known as *Occam's Razor*. The principle was formulated by William of Occam, a fourteenth-century philosopher and theologian. Occam (sometimes spelled "Ockham") formulated the principle as "What can be done with fewer assumptions is done in vain with more." It is sometimes stated thus: "Entities are not to be multiplied without necessity." Or in other words, be *parsimonious*, be *thrifty*, in formulating scientific explanations. That may sound strange, but it's an idea you will likely recognize as one of your own.

"'Tis a blessing to be simple," says the opening line of the famous folk song, and scientists agree. If we favored more complicated explanations over simpler ones, then we could "explain" anything; but the explanations would be rather weird, and they wouldn't offer much help. My watch has stopped. "Must need a new battery," you say. "No," I reply, "it's not the battery; the problem is that my little watch elf is taking a nap, and so he's stopped moving the gears." "There's no watch elf! It's just an old battery." "No, I'll show you." I bang the watch briskly on a table, and the hands start to move again. "You see, I awakened the elf, and he started moving the gears again." When the watch soon stops, it's because the elf returned to slumber. You open the watch, and find no elf. "You see, there's no elf there." "He's there alright," I reply. "But he's very shy, and he hides. Besides, he can make himself invisible." You place a new battery in the watch, and now it runs fine, without stopping. "You see, it's the battery that drives the watch; there's no elf." "There is too an elf," I insist; "but he's a battery-powered elf, and he was getting really run down. That's why he was sleeping so much. Now that he has a new battery, he's back on the job driving the gears and running the watch."

This is a silly dialogue, of course. But it's silly only because of our commitment to the principle of parsimony, our commitment to Occam's Razor. When giving explanations, don't make assumptions that are not required. Or another way of stating it: When there are competing explanations, both of which give adequate accounts of what is to be explained, the *simpler* or more *parsimonious* explanation is better. I can "explain" the workings of my watch quite effectively by means of my elf hypothesis: when the watch stops, the elf is asleep; when the watch slows down, the elf is tired; when the watch keeps accurate time, the elf is on top of his game; when the watch is inaccurate, the elf has been drinking. The problem is that this explanation is not as *parsimonious* as the competing explanation: it adds to the explanatory story a very special additional entity, an elf (and not just any elf: an elf that can make itself invisible). If you let me add elves, ghosts, and miracles to my explanatory scheme, then I can "explain" anything; but the explanations violate the principle of Occam's Razor, and are not as efficient and effective as the simpler explanations in terms of rundown batteries and rust.

Think back to Von Daniken's "explanation" of the lines on the plain of Nazca. The hypothesis that they were constructed as landing strips for ancient astronauts would certainly account for them; but as already noted, that hypothesis is not open to falsifiability. As it turns out, it also violates Occam's Razor: it is hardly the *simplest* hypothesis that would account for the phenomena. After all, many ancient peoples constructed elaborate astronomical devices (Stonehenge was apparently one), since they spent many nights observing the skies, and keeping track of seasons would be valuable to them (berries ripen in different areas at different times, game migrates at specific times of the year, crops must be planted within a relatively narrow opportunity range in order to avoid the last frost and be harvested before the first). Such an explanation not only involves predictions (some arrangement of the lines should mark the vernal equinox, for example), but is also simpler: it appeals to practices we already recognize, and does *not* require the positing of very special extraterrestrials who could somehow swiftly travel billions of miles between stars and yet had not learned to land without long runways, and who disappeared with little trace and have never returned.

It often happens that the extra entities that violate Occam's Razor also make theories unfalsifiable. The watch elf, for example, is not only a superfluous complication, but also a complication that makes the watch elf theory unfalsifiable: no matter what my watch does, an invisible watch elf is always a ready explanation. Ancient astronauts are blessed with similar powers.

Confirmation Bias

There is one more problem with the elf hypothesis. The "predictions" it makes are so general and vague that the hypothesis is subject to "confirmation bias." This is a problem that plagues attempts to determine causation, and that provides false support for dubious scientific hypotheses. Suppose I have devised a new treatment for the common cold: light-intensive therapeutic energy, or LITE. My treatment procedure consists in giving patients very brief sessions under a sun lamp, at regular intervals, for 2 days. Following the sun lamp sessions, I check on my patients: sure enough, many are showing significant improvement. LITE therapy is a success!

Well, maybe; but that certainly is not proved by my tests. First, as we noted earlier, this "test" is useless because there is no *control* group for comparison. It may be that patients would start to feel better after a couple of days with or without LITE therapy (their cold symptoms eventually go away with or without treatment). Or it may be that the patients benefit from a placebo effect: They expect that this wonderful new treatment will cure them, so they start to feel better. Or maybe it's not LITE therapy that helps, but just the fact that these patients spend more time lying down and resting during "LITE therapy," and it is the additional rest that causes improvement. Or maybe patients who come in for special treatment for their colds also drink more orange juice and get more exercise, and so they would recover more swiftly anyway. Without a control group, this "test" is useless. But there's another problem if I am running the tests and reporting the results. I have great confidence in and high hopes for my new LITE therapy. So I fully expect to see significant improvements in my LITE therapy patients; and sure enough, I see what I expected. After all, what will count as "improvement"? The standards are vague: fewer sniffles, less coughing, maybe fewer aches and pains, or just a little more energy. Any of those might count as improvements, and if I expect to see such improvements, then it is likely that I'll find what I'm looking for. Not because I'm being deceitful, but because "confirmation bias" is influencing what I notice (and what I fail to notice: this patient's sniffles and coughs have increased, but she *seems* to have a bit more energy; looks like therapeutic improvement to me). Confirmation bias comes into play in lots of situations: the vague predictions of your horoscope seem accurate, because you are inclined to look for ways they are confirmed and ignore the ways they are wrong.

Eliminating confirmation bias is not easy, but it is hardly impossible. Before we run the test of LITE therapy, we agree on the standards for improvement in patient condition. Then we have *someone else* (who does not know whether the patient being examined is in the control or the experimental group) evaluate the patient's condition. That is, the experiment must be *double*-blind: The patient does not know if she is in the control or the experimental group, and the *evaluator* does not know what group the patient is in. If any confirmation bias remains (and by having an independent evaluator, it should be minimized), then it will apply to both the control and the experimental groups, and thus the effects of the bias will be canceled out.

So if you're taking a new "natural delight herbal energy boost and serenity enhancer," and sure enough you notice that you have more energy and you are becoming more serene and less bothered by everyday annoyances; well, maybe this new natural herbal remedy really works. Or maybe it's the placebo effect. Or maybe you are subject to confirmation bias: You are simply more attuned to the times when you have greater energy and greater serenity, and pay less heed to periods of exhaustion and anxiety.

The moral of this story is a simple one: Determining causality is a *very* difficult process. There are many ways that careful, honest experimenters can go wrong, and there are lots more ways that frauds and charlatans can fabricate what appear to be plausible causal claims. Merely observing that one event followed another, or that there is a correlation between two sets of phenomena, indicates that there is a possible causal link; but such observations fall far short of establishing causality.

Scientific Integrity, Scientific Cooperation, and Research Manipulation

The flourishing of science requires trust, trustworthiness, freedom, and openness. When science is at its best, the scientific enterprise is a special combination of both cooperative and adversarial critical thinking. Good scientific inquiry builds on a foundation of trust and openness. Jane's research—whether in sociology, psychology, biology, physics, or pharmacology—builds upon and draws from the research of many others. Isaac Newton, one of the greatest scientists of all time, expressed this idea modestly and accurately: "If I have seen farther than others, it is because I stood on the shoulders of giants." Without the work of Copernicus, Kepler, and Galileo, Newton could never have made his great discoveries. If their work had not been made public, or if their research had been falsified, then Newton could not have developed his famous laws of motion. And what is true of Newton's work in physics is true for all scientists in all disciplines

Effective scientific research is a cooperative process that requires trust and openness. Research typically builds on the work of other researchers: when those research findings are hidden (because, for example, someone believes that the research results can be turned to a profit-making enterprise, and thus keeps the results secret in order to gain an economic advantage) scientific research is slowed; when the research results are flawed, or even purposefully distorted (as when a pharmaceutical company manipulates a study to make a drug seem more effective than it actually is), other researchers who rely on the honesty and accuracy of that research are led in the wrong direction. When published research indicates that a new type of drug may be a significant improvement in the treatment of a disease, not only are those who use the drug deceived, but the researchers who rely on that research to push their own research in this new and promising direction will have been led badly astray. Thus, effective scientific research requires a basic level of trust and cooperation.

Though cooperation is basic to successful scientific research, there is also a vital role for adversarial argument. In the sciences, all ideas and theories and hypotheses are open to challenge. If you start from the principle that humans were created by God (and that humans did not evolve through natural processes), and you hold that principle as an article of faith and refuse to consider challenges to that principle, then you may *call* your position "creation science," but it is faith rather than science. The best scientific theories make bold claims and original testable predictions; and open themselves to strong challenge and possible refutation. A theory that makes very safe "predictions"—and which makes such careful or uncertain claims that it is protected from challenge—is not a useful scientific hypothesis; in fact, it may not be a *scientific* hypothesis at all. Science grows and develops through bold theories that invite challenge and criticism. A vital element of good science is the adversarial attempt to *refute* theories. Sometimes that effort succeeds, and a theory is rejected; indeed, most scientific theories are ultimately challenged and rejected and replaced, but we learn a great deal through the process of developing the theory and testing its implications (the phlogiston theory of combustion—a burning fire consumes phlogiston; paper is rich in phlogiston, and iron has little—was a valuable framework for the research leading to the discovery of oxygen and ultimately to our theory of gasses). Often the effort to refute a theory leads to major discoveries and theoretical improvements: For example, when the failure to detect a stellar parallax challenged the Copernican theory, astronomers began to take seriously the idea that the distance between the Earth and the stars is much greater than we had imagined. Only when a theory deals successfully with the most rigorous challenges scientists can devise do we accept the theory as true. Ideally, this essential adversarial process should remain cordial and cooperative; in fact, some of the most rigorous challenges to the theory may be devised by those who hope the theory can meet the challenges. Above all, it must remain open: when theories are treated as immune to challenge—as the Catholic Church treated Aristotelian physics and Ptolemaic astronomy theory from the Medieval period until well into the seventeenth century—scientific inquiry is stifled and scientific development is slowed or stopped. Sadly, the blocking—rather than welcoming—of challenges to scientific claims can still happen, and the results are still damaging. When a pharmaceutical company wins FDA approval for a drug, it must offer scientific evidence that the drug is reasonably safe and effective; and when the profits from sale of that drug may amount to billions of dollars, the pharmaceutical company may not be eager to consider scientific challenges to the efficacy or the safety of its major moneymaker. Vioxx—a drug developed by Merck to reduce pain, especially for arthritis sufferers, which had annual sales in excess of $2 billion—has been withdrawn from the market because it was found to increase the danger of hypertension, blood-clotting, strokes, and heart attacks. Evidence of the danger from Vioxx became available soon after the drug was released (one study found that patients on Vioxx were five times as likely to suffer heart attacks than were patients taking an alternative painkiller). But rather than encourage scientific inquiry that might threaten its profits, Merck exerted pressure to silence its critics: Dr. Gurkipal Singh, a Stanford University researcher, was told by Merck representatives that his career would be ruined if he continued challenging the safety of Vioxx. When an in-house study of aprotinin—a drug marketed by Bayer to control bleeding in surgical patients—indicated that the drug could cause kidney failure and congestive heart failure, the company suppressed the study. Eli Lilly hid a study showing that Prozac could cause suicide; GlaxoSmithKline did the same with its study showing that its antidepressant best-seller, Paxil, might increase the risk of suicide among children and adolescents. A Glaxo-SmithKline drug, Avandia, is used in the treatment of diabetes; in 2006 its sales exceeded $3 billion. When research indicated that the drug increased the danger of heart attacks (in comparison with a competing drug that produced the same positive results without the increased risk), GlaxoSmithKline responded by attacking its scientific critics. Dr. John Buse, Professor of Medicine at the University of North Carolina, was threatened with lawsuits if he continued to raise questions about the safety of Avandia (and a threat of legal action by a multibillion dollar corporation with unlimited legal resources is a frightening threat indeed). A report by a bipartisan Senate committee—chaired by Montana Democrat Max Baucus and Iowa Republican Charles Grassley—found that in response to the research challenging the safety of Avandia, executives at GlaxoSmithKline:

> Attempted to intimidate independent physicians, focused on strategies to minimize or misrepresent findings that Avandia may increase cardiovascular risk, and sought ways to downplay findings that a competing drug might reduce cardiovascular risk.

Perhaps the most notorious contemporary case of attacking—rather than welcoming—scientific criticism is the case of Dr. Nancy Olivieri, a researcher at the University of Toronto who did research on a drug produced by Apotex (used to treat a rare blood disorder). Dr. Olivieri discovered that the drug was not very effective, and that the study indicated the drug might have lethal side effects. Though warned by Apotex not to publish her results, Dr. Olivieri went ahead with publication. She was fired by the university (it was later revealed that Apotex was discussing with the university president a 12.7 million dollar donation to the university) amidst charges of wrongdoing; later she was cleared of all charges, and returned to her university position. Whatever the motive—whether protecting religious doctrine or protecting profits—the suppression of scientific challenges has a chilling effect on scientific inquiry.

Exercise 15-3

1. A few years ago, a study was done that showed that hospital patients in rooms with windows recovered faster (i.e., they were released from the hospital earlier) than patients in rooms with no windows, and patients in rooms with windows also had a lower mortality rate. It may have been a reliable, carefully controlled study. But suppose there is a causal study that simply compares patients in rooms with windows with patients in windowless rooms, and concludes on the basis of that study that patients in rooms with windows recover faster and are less likely to die in the hospital. Can you think of some factors that might invalidate that causal claim? That is, it turns out to be true that patients in rooms with windows recover faster, but it may be that having a window is not the cause of their swifter recovery. What would be some of the potential causal factors that you would have to *control* for in order to do a reliable study on this issue? What are some of the possible causes for swifter recovery that might be *associated* with having a room with a window, even if having a window is not itself a cause of the improved recovery rate?

2. Think back to the example at the beginning of the chapter: Does the use of scientific jury selection techniques cause success for the side employing them? You will recall that *one* of the problems with answering that causal question is the fact that the side using jury selection techniques probably also has the funds to secure other advantages (such as a team of outstanding lawyers). Another problem in determining whether the jury selection techniques are causally effective is the problem of the placebo effect: Perhaps it is not the jury selection techniques themselves that are causally effective, but the fact that *use* of such techniques increases the confidence of the side that uses them. Suppose that you are a social scientist—with substantial funding—and you want to *find out* whether the jury selection techniques are genuinely effective, whether they are a real cause of success for the side using them. Describe in detail *how* you would develop a *test* or *experiment* to answer that causal question. (Obviously you cannot use real cases with real juries; instead, you will have to set up mock cases with mock juries that simulate as closely as possible the real thing. That, incidentally, is how much of the jury research is carried out by social scientists.)

3. You are a state public health investigator. A small community, Riverboro, in your state has experienced an unusually high number of thyroid cancers. For a community its size, three to five cases of thyroid cancer in a 5-year period would be normal; during the past 5 years, Riverboro residents have suffered 20 cases of thyroid cancer. Your task is to find the *cause* of this high incidence of thyroid cancer. Develop in detail a *plan* for discovering the cause.

✓● **Study** and **Review** on **mythinkinglab.com**

REVIEW QUESTIONS

1. There can be a strong correlation between phenomena when there is no causal relation between them; describe several ways that might occur.
2. What is the placebo effect?
3. What is a double-blind experiment, and why are double-blind experiments used?
4. What is a randomized controlled experiment?
5. What is a prospective experiment?
6. What is the principle of Occam's Razor?

NOTES

[1]   Quoted in Valerie P. Hans and Neil Vidmar, *Judging the Jury* (New York: Plenum Press, 1986), p. 90.

[2]   For a powerful and disturbing discussion of the inequities in our judicial system—and the difference in treatment received by the wealthy and the impoverished—see Lois G. Forer, *Money and Justice: Who Owns the Courts* (New York: W. W. Norton, 1984).

[3]   This example is taken from Darrell Huff, *How to Lie with Statistics* (New York: W. W. Norton, 1954), pp. 98–99.

[4]   This example is adapted from John Allen Paulos, *A Mathematician Reads the Newspaper* (New York: Anchor Books, 1995), p. 137.

[5]   Michael Shermer, "Codified Claptrap," *Scientific American* (June 2003), p. 35.

[6]   This point was suggested in Valerie P. Hans and Neil Vidmar, *Judging the Jury* (New York: Plenum Press, 1986), p. 91.

[7]   Fans of Garrison Keillor's "Prairie Home Companion" program on Public Radio International will have no trouble recognizing the inspiration for this example.

[8]   Letter to the Editor, *Greensboro Daily News*.

[9]   For more on this example, see Robert L. Park, *Voodoo Science* (Oxford: Oxford University Press, 2000), pp. 28–30.

[10]   This story is told in Kendrick Frazier and James Randi, "Predictions after the Fact: Lessons of the Tamara Rand Hoax," *Skeptical Inquirer* (Fall 1981), pp. 4–7.

[11]   This case is discussed by Chet Raymo, in *Skeptics and True Believers* (New York: Walker and Company, 1998), pp. 14–17.

INTERNET RESOURCES

Sheldon Krimsky, the author of *Science in the Private Interest: Has the Lure of Profits Corrupted Biomedical Research?*, has an excellent website on "corrupted science"; go to *www.Tufts.edu/~skrimsky/corrupted-science.htm.*

ADDITIONAL READING

Among the classic philosophical works on causality is David Hume's *Inquiry Concerning the Human Understanding*, Edited by L. A. Shelby-Bigge (Oxford: Open Court Publishing Company, 1946).

An excellent, more recent study by a philosopher who is an authority on Hume is John Leslie, *The Cement of the Universe* (Oxford, UK: Oxford University Press, 1974).

John Stuart Mill's influential work on causality is *A System of Logic Ratiocinative and Inductive*, 8th ed. (London: Trubner and Co., 1886).

For more on the relation of legal issues to questions of causation, see the powerful study by H. L. A. Hart and Tony Honoré, *Causation in the Law*, 2nd ed. (Oxford: Clarendon Press, 1985).

An excellent introduction to causal reasoning in science is Ronald N. Giere, *Understanding Scientific Reasoning*, 4th ed. (New York: Holt, Rinehart & Winston, 1997).

Cynthia Crossen, *Tainted Truth: The Manipulation of Fact in America* (New York: Simon & Schuster, 1994), is a very readable account of how "scientific" research is sometimes manipulated for the benefit of advertisers and pharmaceutical companies; the chapter on use of scientific experts and scientific evidence in the courtroom is especially interesting. Sheldon Krimsky, *Science in the Private Interest: Has the Lure of Profits Corrupted Biomedical Research?* (Lanham, MD: Rowman and Littlefield, 2003), is a powerful account of the problems that have developed as scientific research has become entangled with the goals of corporate profit.

Marcia Angell—a physician who is the former editor of *The New England Journal of Medicine*—has written an incisive critique of flawed research in the pharmaceutical industry: *The Truth About the Drug Companies: How They Deceive Us and What to Do About It* (New York: Random House, 2004).

Thomas O. McGarity and Wendy E. Wagner, *Bending Science: How Special Interests Corrupt Public Health Research* (Cambridge, MA: Harvard University Press, 2008), is a detailed examination of the misuse and distortion of scientific evidence and scientific studies, especially in the court system but elsewhere as well.

Read the Document on mythinkinglab.com

Anthony Schmitz, "Food News Blues." An interesting essay on the limits and problems of popular press reporting on science.

Jerome Groopman, "How Doctors Think." Discusses some of the problems physicians encounter in drawing conclusions about diagnoses.

Matrixx Initiatives v. James Siracusano, U.S. Supreme Court (2011). This case involved serious questions of possible side effects of a drug, and the related causal questions.

Report of the Kaufman Commission on Proceedings Involving Guy Paul Morin, Executive Summary, pp. 4–9, "Chapter II" (Ontario Ministry of the Attorney General). This passage outlines some serious errors of forensic science that contributed to the wrongful conviction of Guy Paul Morin.

16

❖ ❖ ❖

The Truth, the Whole Truth, and Nothing but the Truth

Our main concern has been with what follows from premises: *If* the premises of this argument are true, do they give us good and sufficient reason to believe the conclusion? But obviously that is not all there is to evaluating arguments. It is equally important to ask: *Are* those premises really true?

How do we decide whether the premises are true? As noted in the discussion of assumptions, we don't always decide. Sometimes—and sometimes legitimately—we simply start from premises we all accept: premises that we all assume to be true, at least for the moment. But sometimes we require stronger support for our premises. One common source of support was discussed in Chapter 10: Appeal to the testimony of an appropriate authority is one way of attempting to establish the truth of premises. But authorities and experts aren't the only ones who testify to the truth of premises. There is another sort of testimony that deserves special attention: eyewitness testimony.

Figure 16-1   Drawing of seven human heads

299

EYEWITNESS TESTIMONY

In Chapter 10, there was extensive discussion of expert testimony: psychiatrists who testify about the sanity or insanity of the defendant, ballistics experts who testify concerning what gun fired the fatal bullet, and so on. But what about eyewitness testimony: the person who claims to have observed the defendant running from the scene of the crime, the witness who testifies that she saw the defendant holding a gun on the bank teller, the individual who swears that he heard the defendant planning the crime? How do we evaluate such eyewitness testimony?

Cautiously. Very cautiously.

Is the witness telling the truth? That's an *ambiguous* question: It can mean two very different things. In one meaning the question is this: "Is the witness telling the truth as she remembers it (is she lying or telling the truth)?" But the question can also mean something very different: "Is this witness—who is trying his best to be honest—really describing the events accurately, or are his honest efforts mistaken?" In one sense, "truth" means honesty, and telling the truth is contrasted with lying. In the other sense, "truth" means an accurate statement, and it is contrasted with error. Thus a witness may be telling the "truth" (in the sense of testifying honestly to what she remembers) and still be giving false (erroneous) testimony. This point is made quite elegantly by Hugo Munsterburg in *On the Witness Stand:*

> We are too easily inclined to confuse the idea of truth in a subjective and in an objective sense. A German proverb says, "Children and fools speak the truth," and with it goes the old "In vino veritas." Of course, no one can suppose that children, fools, and tipsy men have a deeper insight into true relations than the sober and grown-up remainder of mankind. What is meant is only that all the motives are lacking, which, in our social turmoil, may lead others to the intentional hiding of the truth. Children do not suppress the truth, because they are naive; the fools do not suppress it, because they are reckless; and the mind under the influence of wine does not suppress it, because the suppressing mechanism of inhibition is temporarily paralyzed by alcohol. The subjective truth may thus be secured, and yet the idle talk of the drunkard and the child and the fool may be objectively untrue from beginning to end.[1]

Potential Sources of Eyewitness Error

At least four things must be considered when evaluating eyewitness testimony: First, was the witness in a position to make accurate observations; second, how were the witness's observations influenced by the witness's state of mind, her prior beliefs and expectations,

---

Mistaken Identity

One of the most famous cases of mistaken identity involved a Roman Catholic priest, Father Bernard Pagano. In 1979, Father Pagano was on trial, charged with six armed robberies that had occurred in the Philadelphia area. Seven eyewitnesses confidently identified Father Pagano as the well-dressed, soft-spoken, and unfailingly courteous "Gentleman Bandit" who had robbed them at gunpoint. The eyewitness evidence seemed quite convincing, and Father Pagano was well on his way to conviction for armed robbery, when another man—Ronald Clouser, who at age 39 was 14 years younger than the taller balding accused priest—confessed to the robberies. Clouser turned himself in, stating that he could not live with himself if he allowed the priest to be wrongly convicted. Clouser knew details of the robberies that only the robber could have known, and he was ultimately convicted of the robberies. The trial of Father Pagano was halted, and the court apologized to the wrongly identified priest.

perhaps even by mental disorder; third, in what ways have the witness's recollection of the events been influenced during the time between making the observations and giving testimony; and finally, is the witness testifying to the truth as she remembers it, or is the witness lying?

Notice that of the four key questions concerning testimony, only one focuses on the honesty of the witness; *three* of the conditions are concerned with whether an honest witness is testifying *accurately*. Let's start with those. First, was the witness in a position to accurately observe the events in question? (Was the light good? Was the car moving too fast for the witness to get a clear view of the driver? Was the distance too great for the witness to make an accurate identification? Was the witness wearing his glasses?) It is not uncommon for people to be so eager to help—they sincerely want to help solve a crime or make sure that the right person is blamed for an auto accident or perhaps they just like the importance of being a witness—that they convince themselves they clearly observed events they could not have seen. Thus it is important for attorneys to ask about—and for jurors to consider—the situation in which the observations were made: Is it plausible to believe that the witness could observe what he or she claims to have observed? Consider this example:

> In a very celebrated capital trial . . . the prosecution encountered difficulty in identifying the prisoner. She was charged with murder and with robbing the home in which the murder was committed. It was claimed that she left the house and crossed from Brooklyn to New York in a ferryboat before daylight. A woman was called as a witness for the prosecution who testified that she saw the prisoner on board, that she knew her, and she seemed to think she could not be mistaken. Upon being asked on cross-examination why she was so positive as to the identity, she said that she had not seen her since she (the prisoner) was a little girl about four or five years old (she was then about forty); but she identified her by her nose. She was asked if she saw the prisoner's nose. She said: "Oh no, I could not see her nose; she had on a thick veil, and, besides, it was dark. But I saw the impression the tip end of her nose made on her veil, so that I recognized it as the nose peculiar to her family."[2]

Even if the witness was physically in a position to make accurate observations, there is another question that must be answered: Was the witness's state of mind such that she could make accurate observations? Was the witness so frightened that he saw only the pistol and could not possibly identify the robber? Did the witness's belief that Jones is an aggressive bully influence her perception of who actually threw a punch? Was the witness so prejudiced that he merely assumed—rather than actually observed—that the person who pulled the knife was the black man rather than the white man?

Observations of criminal activity are stressful—particularly if the observer is the *victim* of a violent crime. It is commonly supposed that people observe and remember more accurately under stress, but experiments indicate that instead of stress improving perception, it is more likely to weaken it. As Elizabeth Loftus (an authority on the psychology of eyewitness observation) states,

> People are characteristically upset when they see a crime or an accident, the time when the information that makes up the memory is acquired. Many people think that their memory becomes more precise at these times. "I was so frightened by him that I'll never forget that face" is a common remark of victims of serious crimes. In fact, people who witness fearful events remember the details of them less accurately than they recall ordinary happenings. Stress or fear disrupts perception and, therefore, memory.[3]

Preconceptions.   Stress is not the only influence that can distort perceptions. One of the most important influences on our perceptions—and our memories, and thus our testimony—is our expectations. A dramatic example of how expectations can influence perceptions is afforded by the famous study done by Jerome Bruner and Leo Postman.[4]

Figure 16-2 Drawing of seven animals

They showed subjects cards that were very similar to ordinary playing cards but were changed in a clear way. For example, they flashed pictures of normal playing cards and of cards in which the colors were reversed (including a black ace of diamonds and a red two of spades). Subjects found it very difficult to correctly describe the trick cards; because of their strong expectations, they frequently "saw" the black ace of diamonds as red, or saw the red two of spades as a heart rather than a spade, or saw the card as "black and red mixed" or as "grayish red."

Look at Figure 16-2. What do you see when you look at these drawings? You see some clever drawings of ordinary animals, right? A goose, a fish, a rooster, a rabbit, a dog, a cat, a rat. Now think back to the drawings in Figure 16-1: the sketches of seven human heads. Do you see any similarities between the bald-headed man—the second drawing in the second row—and the drawing of the rat? In the first case, the other drawings influenced you to expect a human head, and that is what you probably saw, but when the same drawing is placed with animal drawings, you see a rat.[5]

Preconceptions influence not only the way we see objects, but also the way we see events. Albert Hastorf and Hadley Cantril[6] studied observers' memories of a Dartmouth-Princeton football game that had become quite nasty. They found—perhaps not surprisingly—that Princeton fans perceived that the Dartmouth team was responsible for most of the dirty play, while the Dartmouth fans had seen more dirty play by the Princeton players. In watching identical films of the game, Princeton fans "saw" Dartmouth players commit twice as many infractions as were observed by Dartmouth fans, and the Princeton fans were much more likely to see the Dartmouth infractions as "flagrant," while the Dartmouth fans tended to classify the Dartmouth infractions as "mild." Along the same lines, it is a quite common occurrence in civil trials concerning the collision of ships that the crews of the ships testify without exception in support of their own ship and place the blame on the movements of the other ship. Some of that result may be attributable to pressure from shipmates, but it is likely that much of the conflicting testimony is simply the result of people "seeing" what they want and expect: their own ship being navigated correctly, and some other ship committing the violation. In short, expectations can and do strongly influence what is observed—and thus they can have terribly distorting effects upon testimony. A person who has strong expectations concerning some event—and particularly someone who is prejudiced against some of the participants—may sincerely believe that she is testifying truthfully. But there is a strong possibility that the witness's preconceptions are causing false perceptions, false memories, and false testimony.

Veterinarian Says Flying Objects, Cattle Mutilations May Be Related

(Headline in *Sioux City Journal,* September 1974)

The 1974 reports of "cattle mutilation" in Nebraska and South Dakota offer an example of how changed expectations can lead people to see ordinary events as bizarre and sinister. During the late summer of 1974, there were widespread reports of UFO sightings (and scattered reports of a "monster thing") in Nebraska and South Dakota. Around the same time, there was a report of a "cattle mutilation": someone or something had supposedly carried out a bizarre mutilation of some beef animals in northeastern Nebraska. It did not seem to be the work of thieves, since the carcasses had not been stripped of high-quality meat. Since the authorities paid little attention to the question of what had caused the "mutilations," speculation quickly took over and the mutilations were linked with the UFOs and the monster. Soon reports of cattle mutilations were rampant: nearly one hundred cases were reported between mid-August and the end of October.

Who were the cattle mutilators? Extraterrestrials who had arrived on the UFOs? The "monster thing," as some suggested? Or was it members of a Satan-worshipping cult, as others believed? None of the above. When the state veterinary-diagnostic laboratories of Nebraska and South Dakota examined the "mutilated" carcasses, they found that every one of them had died of natural causes, and that the supposed mutilations were caused by predators tearing away soft parts of the dead animals.

Obviously cattle which had been partially eaten by predators had been seen prior to the mutilation hysteria; but under the strong influence of belief that mutilations were occurring (the newspapers were filled with headlines about "mutilations," and law enforcement officials warned people to watch out for strange incidents) people expected to see mutilations when they found dead cattle—and that expectation caused many people to see purposeful mutilations where before they would have seen merely a partially eaten carcass.[7]

Observing a UFO

In 1968, the breakup of a Soviet launch rocket provided an excellent example of how honest witnesses can "see" remarkable things that are not really there. When the rocket reentered the atmosphere, it began to break up into bright, glowing fragments that scattered across several states. Many people saw the fragments pass high over head, and filed a number of detailed reports: A group of observers in Indiana all agreed that they saw cigar-shaped aircraft with bright windows moving in silence at an altitude of 1,000 feet; and other observers saw craft in the shape of inverted saucers, flying in a low formation. In earlier centuries it might have been a band of angels, or perhaps sky serpents. But with UFO preconceptions, it is easy to see flaming fragments as remarkably detailed spaceships. And rather than a group observation being more accurate, the group members may feed off each other's excited reports to become increasingly confident and unified in their erroneous perceptions.[8]

When judging the reliability of eyewitness testimony, you must consider whether the witness was in a position to accurately observe, and you must also consider whether the witness's observations may have been distorted by expectations or prejudices. But even if the witness observes events correctly, the testimony may still be unreliable. The third thing to consider when evaluating the "probative value" of testimony (lawyer talk for the reliability or trustworthiness of the evidence) is this: Does the witness accurately recall what he or she observed?

Filling-in Memories.   The accuracy of a person's memories is a difficult thing to gauge. Memory is a complicated process, and as all of us are painfully aware, our memories can play tricks on us. Elizabeth Loftus describes the problem:

> Human memory does not work like a videotape recorder or a movie camera. When a person wants to remember something, he or she does not simply pluck a whole memory intact out of a "memory store." The memory is constructed from stored and available bits of information; any gaps in the information are filled in unconsciously by inferences. When these fragments are integrated and make sense, they form what we call "memory."[9]

Thus some of our memories of events are there because that is exactly what we observed, but some of our memories are parts that we *created*—from our assumptions, expectations, beliefs, imaginations—to fill in the gaps. The problem is, we can't tell which is which, so we may *honestly* testify to something we distinctly remember observing, but which is in fact a part of our "memory" we filled in (but did not actually observe).

Loftus offers this example of how honest people can confidently fill memory gaps with elaborate illusions.

> Some years ago during a course on cognitive psychology I gave my students the following assignment: I told them to go out and create in someone's mind a "memory" for something that did not exist. . . . One group of students conducted their study as follows: Two female students entered a train station, one of them leaving her large bag on a bench while both walked away to check the train schedules. While they were gone, a male student lurked over to the bag, reached in, and pretended to pull out an object and stuff it under his coat. He then walked away quickly. When the women returned, the older one noticed that her bag had been tampered with, and began to cry, "Oh my God, my tape recorder is missing!" She went on to lament that her boss had loaned it to her for a special reason, that it was very expensive, and so on. The two women began to talk to the real eyewitnesses who were in the vicinity. Most were extremely cooperative in offering sympathy and whatever details could be recalled. The older woman asked these witnesses for their telephone numbers "in case I need it for insurance purposes." Most gladly gave their number.
>
> One week later an "insurance agent" called the eyewitnesses as part of a routine investigation of the theft. All were asked for whatever details they could remember, and finally, they were asked, "Did you see the tape recorder?" Although there was in fact no tape recorder, over half of the eyewitnesses "remembered" seeing it, and nearly all of these could describe it in reasonably good detail. Their descriptions were quite different from one another: some said it was gray and others said black; some said it was in a case, others said it was not; some said it had an antenna, others claimed it did not. Their descriptions indicated a rather vivid "memory" for a tape recorder that was never seen.[10]

The Power of Suggestion. Unconscious filling in can play havoc with memory, causing an honest and sincere person to affirm as true what may be objectively false. There are many subtle factors that may influence the way memories are filled in, including the way questions about the events are asked. Elizabeth Loftus describes an experiment she conducted with some other researchers that revealed how the way questions are asked can affect memories:

> People viewed films of automobile accidents and then answered questions about what they saw. The question "About how fast were the cars going when they smashed into each other?" elicited a higher estimate of speed than questions using the verbs *collided, bumped, contacted,* or *hit* in place of *smashed.*
>
> Smashed had other implications as well. A week later, the same people were asked, "Did you see any broken glass?" In spite of the fact there was no glass involved, those who had been asked the question with the verb *smash* were more likely to answer yes than the others.[11]

For a more mundane example of how the wording of questions can affect memories, consider this case. A number of people were interviewed during market research about headaches and commercial headache remedies. Half were asked, "In terms of the total number of products, how many other products have you tried? 1? 2? 3?" Those asked that question reported trying an average of 3.3 other products. The other half of the interview subjects were asked, "In terms of the total number of products, how many other products have you tried? 1? 5? 10?" Those asked the question in that form remembered using an average of 5.2 other products. In the same survey, half of those interviewed were asked, "Do you get headaches frequently and, if so, how often?" They answered that they had an average of 2.2 headaches per week. The others were asked, "Do you get headaches occasionally and, if so, how often?" The question is almost identical; but the subjects asked the question in that form reported an average of only 0.7 headaches per week.[12]

Asking the Right Question

The way a question is framed can influence the answer, as illustrated by this story by Leo Katz:

> . . . two monks, Theophilus and Gottlieb, . . . are quarreling over whether one may engage in smoking and praying at the same time. Theophilus, an unbending ascetic, says no. Gottlieb, an easy-going smoker, says why not. They meet again some weeks later.

Theophilus triumphantly reports, "I took the issue to the pope. I asked him point-blank 'Is it permissible to smoke during prayer?' and he said 'Absolutely not.' " Gottlieb protests: "That's not what he said when I asked him." He smiles sheepishly. "Of course I did phrase the question a little differently. I asked him 'Is it permissible to pray while I smoke?' and he said 'Of course.' "[13]

Nowhere is the danger of suggestion more severe than in eyewitness identifications. Again, Elizabeth Loftus offers the best account of the problem:

> Keep the obliging nature of witnesses in mind, and also the circumstances surrounding a criminal identification. Usually the police show witnesses several photographs or a lineup. In both cases the witnesses look at a set of faces to see if anyone appears familiar. Witnesses know that the culprit may not be in the set, but many believe that the police would not conduct the test unless they had a good suspect. Although witnesses try hard to identify the true criminal, when they are uncertain—or when no one exactly matching their memory appears in the lineup—they will often identify the person who best matches their recollection of the criminal.[14]

Even the most carefully conducted procedures of suspect identification may therefore yield false—but sincere—identifications. Unfortunately, not all lineup procedures are scrupulously conducted (see Figure 16-3). As Loftus notes,

This illustration is taken from G. R. Loftus and E. F. Loftus, *Human Memory: The Processing of Information* (Hillsdale, N.J.: Erlbaum Press, 1976). Used by permission.

Figure 16-3   Cartoon—four people in a lineup

But many lineups used in actual criminal cases are grossly suggestive, and the identifications they produce should be considered worthless. In a lineup conducted in Minnesota, a black suspect stood next to five white men; in another case, a six-foot-three-inch suspect was placed in a lineup with nonsuspects who were all under five feet ten inches tall; in a case where the offender was known to be in his teens, an eighteen-year-old suspect was placed in a lineup with five nonsuspects, all over the age of forty. In a case I worked on from 1986 to 1988, a man was accused of murdering eight people on a fishing boat in Alaska. Eyewitnesses had provided police with a general physical description of the man they saw at the murder scene, including one very specific detail—the man they saw wore a baseball cap. In the photo lineup, the suspect was the only person wearing a baseball cap.[15]

Other problems can arise with identifications on the basis of witness memories. "Photo-bias" can play tricks on a sincere person's memory, as indicated by this experiment at the University of Nebraska:

> An hour or so after "witnesses" watched some "criminals" committing a "crime," they looked through mugshots that included some of the "criminals" they had seen. A week later, lineups were staged and the "witnesses" were asked to indicate those who had taken part in the original "crime." Eight percent of the people in the lineup were identified as criminals; yet they had neither taken part in the "crime" nor been among the mugshots. A full 20 percent of the innocent people whose photographs had been included among the mugshots were falsely identified also. Despite the fact that none of these people had committed a crime, nor had they ever before been seen in person, they were recognized from photographs and identified as criminals.[16]

Thus seeing photographs can cause an "unconscious transference" in which someone seen in one situation is confused in memory with persons from a different situation. Photo-bias is a special problem in eyewitness identification: After being assaulted and robbed, I go to the police station to look through photographs. I see a mug shot that

---

Improving Lineups

Lineups are a common means of having eyewitnesses pick out the person who committed the crime. But even at their best, eyewitness identifications from lineups are notoriously subject to error (and as already noted, the actual lineups are often far from being at their best). There is probably no way to make lineup identifications really reliable; but are there ways to significantly improve the procedure?

As an obvious starting point, we should occasionally use "control" lineups, in which no suspect appears in the lineup. If I walk into the observation room, fully expecting that *someone* in the lineup *must* be the person who robbed me, then I am likely to pick out the person most resembling my memory of the robber (and then fill in that memory with the more exact image I now have of the person in the lineup). If instead I know that sometimes lineups are set up with no suspects included, as a *check* on the accuracy of identifications, then I will be less likely to latch onto someone in the lineup who has some superficial resemblance to the robber.

Another major improvement would involve "blinding" the lineup: that is, make sure that the person who observes the lineup with the eyewitness does not know

which person in the lineup is the suspect. Even if the police officer with the eyewitness is *not* trying to coach the eyewitness to pick the "right person" from the lineup—and sadly, that sometimes happens—the most conscientious officer may still give the eyewitness subtle and unintended cues to help in identifying the suspect. It doesn't have to be something as gross as "Did you take a close look at number two?" It could be only that the officer looks more at the suspect, or speaks differently to the suspect than to the other persons in the lineup: when the eyewitness asks person number three in the lineup to turn sideways, the police officer—who relays the order to the lineup—might speak more courteously than when giving the order to number two, the suspect. Or perhaps when the eyewitness indicates it *might* be number three (not the suspect) the police officer frowns and urges her to take her time; but when the eyewitness indicates it *might* be number two, the officer smiles and says thanks for your help.

Finally, all lineup procedures should be taped, so that any irregularities in the lineup—that could lead to mistaken identifications—can be challenged by the defendant's counsel.

I think *might* resemble my assailant. Later the person from the photograph shows up in a lineup. Now I am *certain* that he is the man who assaulted me (and by the time I see him again in court, my confidence in that identification is even stronger). Perhaps I'm right. But there is also the possibility that my identification is the result of *photo-bias:* I remember the person in the photograph, and use that memory to fill in the forgotten face of my assailant. At that point, my complete confidence in my (mistaken) eyewitness identification may well persuade the jury to convict an innocent defendant.

Similar memory tricks can occur without photographs. After being held up at gunpoint, a railway ticket agent observed a police lineup and confidently identified a sailor as the armed robber. However, further evidence proved that the sailor could not have been the robber. It turned out that the sailor had purchased tickets from the railway agent on three occasions prior to the robbery, and thus when the agent saw the sailor in the lineup, the sailor looked familiar. The agent apparently made an unconscious transference of the memory of the ticket-buying sailor to the event of the robbery.[17]

In short, there are many ways that a sincere witness's memory may make mistakes: It may be influenced by subsequent events (such as seeing a photograph); it may fill in with other beliefs and assumptions (including prejudices); it may be colored by the way questions are asked; it may latch onto a current image and substitute that image for a fading and fuzzy memory (as when a witness replaces his vague memory of the actual criminal with the vivid image of the person standing before him in a lineup). In spite of all this, eyewitnesses may testify accurately—but it is important to be aware of the pitfalls and dangers of even the most honest and sincere eyewitness testimony, and to realize that when an attorney is questioning the way lineups were carried out or the way identifications were handled she may be raising very significant questions.

Judging the Honesty of a Witness

There is probably a greater problem with sincerely mistaken witnesses than with witnesses who consciously and purposefully mislead—that is, who lie. Still, the fourth factor to consider when evaluating witnesses is whether the witness is *honest.* If we assume that the witness really could see what happened, that no presuppositions or prejudices clouded

---

Filling-in Memories

One of the most interesting and ironic cases of mistaken eyewitness identification—based on memories "filled-in" from other experiences and observations—involved an experimental psychologist and memory researcher who found himself charged with a brutal assault and rape:

Donald M. Thomson, an Australian psychologist and lawyer, undoubtedly will never forget the day 15 years ago when he walked into a Sydney police station on routine court-related business and was arrested for assault and rape in a weird turn of events worthy of an Alfred Hitchcock movie.

The evening before his arrest, Thomson appeared on a local television program, where he discussed psychological research on eyewitness testimony and how people might best remember the faces of criminals observed during a robbery. As he spoke, a Sydney woman watching the show was attacked, raped, and left unconscious in her apartment. When she awoke several hours later, she called the police and named Thomson as her assailant.

The following day, after Thomson's arrest, the woman confidently selected him as the perpetrator from a lineup of possible rapists at the police station.

Thomson, of course, professed his innocence. "The police didn't believe me at first," he recalls, "but I had appeared on a live television show when the crime occurred, so I had a good alibi."

Officials quickly dropped the charges when they realized the woman had unwittingly substituted Thomson's televised face for that of the attacker. "She had apparently watched my television appearance very closely, but it's not clear if she ever saw her assailant's face," says Thomson.[18]

the witness's perception, that the witness's memory has not filled in inaccurate details, and that no suggestions have distorted the witness's memories, then there is still a final question: Is the witness telling the truth as he or she remembers it?

We may have difficulty with the sincere but mistaken witness: the witness who is testifying falsely but honestly *believes* he is telling the truth. The *lying* witness is another matter—surely we can distinguish a liar from an honest person.

Or so we imagine. But like many of our cherished beliefs, that one is probably false. When we think carefully about it, we realize that distinguishing truthful witnesses from dishonest ones is a very difficult task. Honest witnesses may—due to nervousness or shyness or insecurity—give an appearance of uncertainty or even dishonesty. For many people, speaking in a public courtroom (before a judge, attorneys, a dozen jurors, and possibly a number of spectators) is a frightening experience. The courtroom and judicial procedures may be quite familiar to the judge and the attorneys, but they are often strange and alien to witnesses. When a hostile attorney is subjecting the witness to harsh cross-examination, in a strange setting, before a crowd of strangers, the situation may be terrifying. It is hardly surprising that in those conditions an honest witness may become so nervous that he or she gives the impression of not being quite certain about testimony, or the impression that he or she is being evasive and dishonest. Furthermore, those with less education or who have less self-confidence may be more hesitant in answering questions, and less assertive and forthright in their answers. Jury members might easily conclude that such a witness is less certain of the testimony being given, while the testimony of a more confident or "higher status" witness may appear more believable. Whether a witness is well-educated and self-confident has nothing to do with whether that witness is honest, but it may have a great deal to do with whether jurors *believe* the witness is honest.

Several studies have been made of whether it is ordinarily possible to distinguish lies from honest reports. All indications are that—despite the confidence most people feel in being able to detect liars—generally we are not able to distinguish liars from the truthful. In fact, research findings show that people's ability to distinguish honest witnesses from liars is no better than chance; that is, if one is attempting to determine whether or not a person is lying by simply observing that person's behavior while talking, then flipping a coin is likely to work as well as watching the person carefully.[19]

That does not mean that it is always impossible to tell when a witness is telling the truth and when a witness is lying. It simply means that trying to distinguish a liar from a truth-teller by watching whether the witness is nervous, squints, answers slowly, smiles uncomfortably, or has a weak chin is not going to work. The best way of going about that is by judging carefully the *content* of what the witness says: Does it conflict with known facts? Does it contain inconsistencies? Is it inherently implausible? Does it hold together as a whole? Also, keep in mind that when judging the reliability of *testimony* it is legitimate and useful to consider the *source* of the testimony: Does the witness have a strong reputation for honesty, or does his past behavior reveal evidence of disregard for truthfulness? Does the witness have ulterior motives or prejudices?

A "jailhouse informant" is promised a substantial reduction in prison time if he hears—and testifies to—incriminating statements made while the defendant is in jail awaiting trial. That strong motive for lying is a much more important factor in judging the truthfulness of the witness than is a weak chin, beady eyes, or nervous twitch. Listening carefully to testimony and evaluating it for consistency, coherency, and plausibility is harder work than merely looking for easy (but inaccurate) "tip-offs" to lying or truth-telling. But as already noted, discovering the truth is often hard work.

Four possible sources for the inaccuracy of eyewitness testimony have been noted: the witness may not have been in a position to observe accurately; the witness's preconceptions, prejudices, or some other influence may have distorted the witness's observations; even if the witness's original observations were accurate, subsequent events and the passage of time and the filling in of details may have resulted in inaccurate memories of the events; and finally, the witness may be consciously lying.

Eyewitness testimony is often important, and it should be examined closely. But the point is, it should be *examined,* and all the ways it could be misleading and false should be kept in mind. Even the most sincere eyewitness report can be mistaken, and unfortunately not every eyewitness is trying to give an accurate report.

In sum, listen carefully and cautiously to eyewitness testimony. It may be accurate and useful, but there are also ways it can go wrong. True premises are essential for legitimate arguments; if we mistakenly take false premises for true, it will not be too surprising if we reach false conclusions. And false conclusions can have unfortunate consequences: They may lead us to eat the wrong breakfast cereal, buy the wrong car, vote for the wrong candidate, or convict an innocent person.

Exercise 16-1

1. For each of the following, tell *why* it would be important to know *who* is making the statement.

   a. I was at the Republican campaign rally for the Republican candidate for governor, and it was quite successful. There was a huge crowd, at least a thousand people.

   b. I was in Chile last week, and while I was there I talked to a great many people. Almost all of them are very supportive of the present government and think things are getting better in Chile.

   c. I think Old State University's football team is getting better. I was at their game last week, and, although they lost, they worked hard and played well the entire game.

   d. The Chevrolet Cavalier must be an excellent car. I talked with a number of people who own them, and they are really pleased.

   e. I really don't think there is any sexual harassment at this college. I have never talked to anyone connected with the college who has complained of sexual harassment.

   f. The president of our university is very popular with the faculty. In fact, every faculty member I have ever talked with about President Logan speaks very highly of him.

   g. I am certain that the person I saw running out of the convenience store with the gun in his hand was the defendant.

2. Imagine that you are an absolutely unscrupulous district attorney, willing to do anything—including convicting an innocent person—in order to get a conviction in a particularly notorious criminal case. (i.e., you don't much care *who* is convicted—guilty or innocent—so long as you get a conviction of someone.) You have two witnesses to the crime—a murder during the robbery of an all-night diner—but neither is very confident of being able to identify the killer. What could you do to *influence* those witnesses so that they will not only identify someone as the killer, but also testify *confidently* (you aren't concerned about whether they testify *accurately*) that that person *is* the killer *and* that the murder was a particularly brutal one. (Describe the steps you would take, from the first steps of "identification" to the day of the trial.)

THE WHOLE TRUTH

It's important that arguments contain *true* premises, that witnesses tell the *truth.* It is also important that arguments and witnesses tell the *whole* truth. A particularly deceptive style of argument involves using true premises but *omitting* or *suppressing* some points that would lead to a very different conclusion.

A clear case of *omission* of important information is an old Shell Oil commercial. You might remember it. The commercial starts with two identical cars lined up on a track. An equal measure of gasoline is placed in each car; the gasoline in the two cars is identical, except that the gasoline in car A contains *platformate* (the wonder additive that goes in all Shell gasoline) and the gasoline in car B does *not* contain *platformate.* The cars start down the track. Car B soon sputters to a halt, while car A whizzes along, tears through a huge banner, and looks as if it could continue forever! The moral of the story: If *you* want great gas mileage, then buy New Shell with *platformate.*

Sounds good, right? Shell gasoline has platformate, gasoline with platformate gives better mileage—so, since I want better mileage, I think I'll buy Shell.

It does sound good, and it sold a lot of gasoline. But the commercial left something out. The commercial did not tell a lie; it just did not tell the whole truth. What important information was omitted?

Platformate really does increase gasoline mileage. It truly is a valuable gasoline additive. The Shell commercial neglected to mention one thing: Practically *all* the standard brands of gasoline sold in the United States at that time contained platformate. So the fact that Shell *also* contained platformate was *not* a good reason to buy Shell rather than some other brand. That's an example of *suppressed evidence.* By failing to mention that almost all gasolines contain platformate, Shell *implied* that Shell gasoline was unique—which it was not. The evidence suppressed was certainly relevant and important. Once the suppressed evidence is included, it is clear that the conclusion—Shell gasoline gives better gas mileage than other gasolines—does not follow.

Shell is not the only company to advertise a "special feature" of its product while suppressing the fact that its competitors also have that feature. Since people have become concerned about having artificial preservatives in their foods, some jam and jelly producers have begun to put "NO ARTIFICIAL PRESERVATIVES" in bold letters on their labels. The label is true, but misleading: *No* jams or jellies contain artificial preservatives, because sugar is the only preservative agent used in jams and jellies. Since people are now concerned—legitimately—about cholesterol, one company now advertises that its canned pineapple contains "no cholesterol." Certainly the advertisement is true: Cholesterol is found only in animal products, so there is no cholesterol in that brand of canned pineapple. But if consumers are led to believe that that particular brand of canned pineapple is therefore *different* from other brands, then the advertisement is misleading (by *suppressing* the fact that no canned pineapple contains cholesterol).

Zest soap used a dramatic television commercial showing a woman holding two photographs in front of two transparent containers of soapy water. She dipped one of the photographs into (what the announcer called) "her favorite soap," the other into the container with Zest. After rinsing the pictures in clear water, she held them up to the camera. The photograph from the Zest container had rinsed clear and bright; but the soap from the other container had left a film on the photograph. The woman then hammered home the point: "I don't like the fact that the soap is staying on our skin like that!" We at home, lounging through another commercial, began to feel a sticky soap film clogging our pores, and we resolved to buy a few bars of that clear-rinsing Zest. And

---

Maybe Not the Whole Truth

When the Enron financial scandal became public (Enron filed the largest bankruptcy in U.S. history in late 2001, destroying the investments of many stockholders and the pension funds of employees), the close friendship between Enron CEO Kenneth Lay and President George W. Bush threatened to become embarrassing. Enron executives had been deeply involved in the Bush administration development of an energy plan, and some of the provisions in that plan resulted in large benefits for Enron; and Enron executives, particularly Kenneth Lay, had been major contributors to Bush's political campaigns. When news broke that Lay had sought help from high-ranking administration officials shortly before declaring bankruptcy, reporters questioned Bush about his close relationship with Lay, and how long it had lasted. "He was a supporter of Ann Richards [Bush's Democratic opponent in the campaign for governor of Texas] in my run in 1994," Bush answered. And that was true. But what Bush neglected to mention was that in that 1994 race Ken Lay and Enron donated $12,500 to Richards and $146,500 to Bush. (Information from Texans for Public Justice)

it's true: Zest does rinse off, it doesn't leave a sticky film. When a consumer reviewer (writing for the *Atlanta Constitution*) tested Zest, Zest did indeed rinse clean, leaving no sticky film on a photograph. However, the reviewer tested five other standard brands of soap (Ivory, Palmolive, Dial, Camay, and Coast) and *none* of them left a sticky film. Zest does not leave a sticky film, true enough; but neither do any of its major competitors.

Anacin has used a variety of advertising pitches that trade on the same basic ploy: "Four out of five doctors recommend the pain reliever in Anacin!" "Anacin has the pain reliever DOCTORS recommend MOST!" True, true; or rather, half true. The "pain reliever in Anacin" *is* "the pain reliever doctors recommend most," since doctors most often recommend aspirin (as in, "Take two aspirin and call me in the morning"), and the pain reliever in Anacin is just aspirin. It's the same aspirin you can buy for a fraction of the price of Anacin's slickly advertised version.

Advertising for *Triumph*—a brand of low-tar cigarette produced by Lorillard—attempted to win points against a major low-tar competitor, *Merit*. The advertising claimed (correctly) that in a taste test of Triumph against Merit "an amazing 60% said Triumph tastes as good or better than Merit." Sounds like Triumph won the taste test by a wide margin, right? Well, not quite. Turns out that 40% preferred Merit, 36% chose Triumph, and 24% said they couldn't tell the difference.

Advertisers are not the only ones using half-truths. Not long before Enron's falsification of financial records became public and Enron stock crashed, CEO Kenneth Lay assured Enron employees that Enron stock was a good buy, and told them that he himself had recently purchased Enron stock. That was true: He had exercised a stock option to buy Enron stock. What he failed to report to the Enron employees was that he had recently sold far more Enron stock than he had purchased.

Important social debates can also trade on half-truths and suppressed evidence. In 2009 and 2010, there was a huge struggle over health-care reform in the United States. One reform package, supported by President Obama and most Democrats, called for expanding medical care to cover most of the millions of uninsured, preventing insurance companies from refusing to cover those with pre-existing conditions or dropping from coverage those who develop major health problems, and placing limits on the increases in premiums that insurance companies could charge—with the goal of making affordable health insurance more widely available, and preventing citizens from being excluded from coverage. In criticizing that plan, Republican Senator Lamar Alexander stated that if the health reform issue passes, then "for millions of Americans, insurance premiums will go up." Economist Paul Krugman had this response to Senator Alexander's half-truth:

> Wow, I guess you could say that he wasn't technically lying, since the Congressional Budget Office analysis of the Senate Democrats' plan does say that average payments for insurance would go up. But it also makes it clear that this would buy more and better coverage. The "price of a given amount of insurance coverage" would fall, not rise—and the actual cost to many Americans would fall sharply thanks to federal aid.

In 2009, the United States spent more than 17% of its gross national product on health care—far more than any other country in the world—yet millions of U.S. citizens have no health care, and many others have health-care coverage only periodically or have severely substandard health care. And the United States—while spending more money per person on health care than any other country—has one of the highest infant mortality rates of any industrialized nation. So what should the United States do? The question of what sort of health-care reforms would work best is an issue of vital importance that deserves complete and open and honest debate. When the whole truth is obscured by half-truths, such debate is impossible. And that observation applies whether the issue is health care, the innocence or guilt of a defendant, or the quality of a breakfast cereal. But how do we find the whole truth when an important part of it is hidden from view?

ARE THE PREMISES TRUE?

Getting the *truth*—and the *whole* truth—is an essential part of deciding the soundness of arguments. It is important to question the truth of premises, whether they occur in commercials, editorials, or courtrooms. But there's the rub. How do you discover whether the premises are true? How do you know whether the advertiser is lying to you? How can you tell whether the editorial writer is omitting important facts? How do you determine whether the witness is telling the truth? Certainly it's important to know whether the premises are actually true and that no relevant information is concealed; but *how* can you know?

Digging for Truth

Unfortunately, there's no easy way. You can lounge in your hammock and analyze arguments for *validity* to your heart's content. Does the conclusion follow from the premises? That's a question we can answer without research, observations, experiments,

---

An Innocent Man on Death Row

In 1976, a Dallas policeman was brutally gunned down as he approached a car he had stopped. In 1977, Randall Adams was convicted of the murder. Sentenced to death, he spent the next 12 years on death row. He was finally released when evidence that had been hidden during the trial was uncovered and a key prosecution witness admitted that he (and not Adams) had killed the policeman, that Adams had not been present, and that he had testified against Adams to avoid being blamed himself and also to receive lesser sentences for other criminal charges.

During the trial a star witness for the prosecution was Emily Miller, who testified that she drove slowly past the stopped car as the policeman approached it. She identified Randall Adams as the man she had seen in the car that was stopped by the policeman, shortly before the policeman was murdered. She testified that she had picked Adams out of a lineup, which was true. What was left out of her testimony, however, was much more important than what was included: She came forward only after she learned that there was a large reward for evidence in the case; she initially reported that the man she had seen in the car was African American (Adams is white); and when she looked at the lineup, she first identified someone other than Adams—finally identifying Adams only after she was told that she had picked the wrong man, and after Adams was pointed out to her as the primary suspect.[20]

Urban Myths

Starting in 1997, dire warnings began to circulate by way of e-mail, faxes, and even a business traveler warning posted by travel agents: Highly efficient medical crime rings were operating in major American cities. Targeting business travelers who stop by hotel or airport lounges for a drink, a gang member offers to buy the traveler a drink, and then slips a drug into the drink. When the drugged traveler awakens, he is sitting in a hotel room bathtub, submerged in ice, with a note instructing the traveler to call 911. The traveler discovers a neat incision in his back, and learns that a criminal gang of medical experts have carefully removed one of his kidneys, which has been used for a very profitable kidney transplant. So beware!

That is, beware of this and other "urban legends" that make the rounds and gather momentum as they spread. They take on a life of their own, backed up by testimony from an elusive "friend of a friend" or "cousin of a friend of one of my coworkers" or a "reliable source that told my brother-in-law" (or other impossible-to-check hearsay evidence). The implausibility of this story—Why would wealthy surgeons participate in such a scheme? How would such purloined organs be checked for tissue matches? Why has there never been a documented case of such kidney theft reported in the United States?—does not prevent it from spreading and gaining wide acceptance?[21]

or expert authorities. But when we ask about the *truth* of the premises—and whether some relevant information has been omitted—we must go out into the cold world and try to find the facts. That's hard work.

Suppose you are examining arguments about the desirability of using landfills for the disposal of solid hazardous wastes, and in an argument in *favor* of using landfills, this premise occurs: "The new landfill technology makes it possible to design hazardous waste landfills in such a manner that there is absolutely no danger of wastes from the landfill contaminating groundwater." It's not difficult to see that that premise is relevant to the question of whether we should use landfills. In fact, when that premise is combined with the premise that landfills are one of the least expensive ways of dealing with hazardous wastes, the result is strong support of the conclusion that we should use landfills for disposing of hazardous wastes. But is the premise *true?* We *cannot* answer that question by looking more carefully at the argument; instead, we must go out and get *reliable* information about landfill technology—and since that is a controversial topic, it will not be easy to find reliable information that will tell us whether that premise is true.

There's no simple menu for determining the truth or falsity of premises. Determining the truth of premises means determining the way things are in the world, and that is what physicists, detectives, historians, economists, meteorologists, sociologists, physicians, astronomers, microbiologists, consumers, and jurors—indeed all of us at various times—spend their lives trying to ascertain. There is no easy answer to the question of how to tell whether the premises are true and complete. I'm sorry about it; that's just the way it is; it's not my fault.

However, a couple of suggestions may help. First, try to get information from a *variety* of sources, especially on controversial topics. If you read only one newspaper, you will get only the news—and the perspectives on the news—that the paper selects. The same applies even more strongly to watching only one network newscast, in which time constraints make the selection of news even more important. (Some of the journals of news analysis do an excellent job of providing detailed reports on topics that newspapers cover superficially or not at all.) And there are a number of excellent online news resources that can give you access to news perspectives from around the world. One of the toughest problems in considering arguments is discovering what has been *omitted;* to find what is left out of one source you must examine the same issue as discussed by *other* sources. If two sources *differ* in their premises (one source asserts as a premise that landfills are safe, while another source asserts that all landfills will ultimately leak hazardous wastes), then you may still have a difficult time knowing which to believe, but at least you will know which premises must be questioned and examined.

Consider the Source

A second suggestion for dealing with the problem of detecting false premises and important omissions is this: Consider the source. If the source of the argument has a special interest in the issue or a special bias, then you should be on guard against false premises and important omissions. Obviously when you watch a television commercial you should keep in mind that the commercial is designed to sell you something: The commercial is not a neutral, unbiased source of information, and you should be alert for false claims and significant omissions. When the American Tobacco Institute—the public relations group for the tobacco industry, paid for by the tobacco industry—offers an argument against restrictions on smoking in public, it is well to bear in mind that the American Tobacco Institute has a special ax to grind, and you should therefore scrutinize its premises closely. However, while it is good practice to use special care in considering whether a biased arguer's premises are true and whether they omit important facts, it would be *wrong* to *reject* an argument simply because the person giving the argument has a special interest. *Knowing* that the arguer has a special interest should make us more cautious in examining the truth of the premises, but it is *not* a reason to *reject* an argument. If the American Tobacco Institute gives an argument against restrictions on public smoking, then that argument must stand or fall on *its own merits*. If the premises are false, or if the argument is invalid, then those are good reasons to reject an argument. If the source of the argument is biased, that is good reason to give the argument and its premises special scrutiny—but that is *not in itself* a reason to *reject* the argument. To reject an argument solely on the grounds that the source of the argument is biased or has a special interest is to commit the ad hominem *fallacy*. Arguments from interested sources are sometimes sound arguments, just as arguments from neutral sources are sometimes unsound. However, if rather than *arguments* you are examining reports or testimony (when, for example, a pharmaceutical company assures us that they have tested this new drug and it is quite safe) then consideration of the special interests and motives and truthfulness of the source is essential.

Exercise 16-2

Below are several claims (the sorts of claims that might serve as key premises in arguments). Obviously you *cannot* know, merely by reading the claims, whether they are true or whether they involve significant *omissions*. But you can decide what further *checks* you would want to run, what further information you would want to obtain, before accepting those claims at face value. (In particular, think about what is *implied* by each of these claims and whether they might be "half-truths," where what is left out changes the significance of what is included.) For each claim, state what further information would be helpful in evaluating the claim.

1. An apple juice label proclaims in bright letters: "Contains no added sugar!"
2. A brand of toothpaste advertises: "Contains fluoride, proven effective in combatting cavities."
3. A candy company advertises that one of its candy bars is an "official snack food of the 1992 Olympics."
4. A power company that operates nuclear power generators claims that its containment procedures make it all but impossible for dangerous levels of radiation to escape into the atmosphere.
5. The producer of a powerful commercial herbicide claims that there is no evidence that that herbicide causes cancer in humans.
6. A politician asserts that during his term as governor, cocaine use among teenagers dropped significantly.
7. A politician claims that under her proposed tax cut, most of the people receiving tax cuts will be middle-class families.
8. In 1999, a battery-powered Sanyo cheese grater was advertised with the assurance that "this product is Y2K compliant."[22]
9. Some people are concerned that widespread exposure to toxic chemicals (from insecticides, pesticides, and pollution) pose a significant and increasing health threat. David Shaw of the *Los Angeles Times* wrote an article challenging such claims. In the article he quoted Paul Portney (of "Resources for the Future"): "If everything is as harmful as we're told, how come we're healthier and living longer than ever before?" To back up this point, Shaw quoted data from the National Cancer Institute: "The age-adjusted mortality rate for all cancers combined except lung cancer has been declining since 1950, except for those 85 and over."

   Taken by themselves, these points would seem to suggest that our environment is getting healthier, not more hazardous; but is anything of importance left out?[23]

✓● **Study** and **Review** on **mythinkinglab.com**

REVIEW QUESTIONS

1. What are the major sources of error in eyewitness testimony?
2. What is photo-bias?
3. What are the dangers of eyewitness identifications from lineups?

NOTES

1.   Hugo Munsterburg, *On the Witness Stand* (Garden City, NY: Doubleday, Page, 1913), p. 47.

2.   Henry Lauren Clinton, *Celebrated Trials* (New York: Harper & Brothers, 1897), pp. 347–348.

3.   Elizabeth F. Loftus, "The Eyewitness on Trial," *Trial* (October 1980), p. 32.

4.   Jerome S. Bruner and Leo Postman, "On the Perception of Incongruity: A Paradigm," *Journal of Personality,* 18 (1949), pp. 206–223.

5.   The drawings were originally developed by B. Richard Bugelski and D. A. Alampay for an experiment described in "The Role of Frequency in Developing Perceptual Sets," *Canadian Journal of Psychology,* 15 (1961), pp. 205–211. Used by permission.

6.   Albert H. Hastorf and Hadley Cantril, "They Saw a Game: A Case Study," *Journal of Abnormal and Social Psychology,* 49 (1954), pp. 129–134.

7.   The story of the cattle mutilations is told in detail in "Cattle Mutilations: An Episode of Collective Delusion," by James R. Stewart, in *Paranormal Borderlands of Science,* edited by Kendrick Frazier (Buffalo, NY: Prometheus Books, 1981), pp. 288–299; the information in this example is from that essay.

8.   For details on this episode, see Philip J. Klass, *UFO's Explained* (New York: Random House, 1974); and an article by Klass, "UFOs," In *Science and the Paranormal* (New York: Charles Scribner's Sons, 1981).

9.   Elizabeth F. Loftus, "The Eyewitness on Trial," *Trial* (October 1980), p. 31.

10.   Reprinted by permission of the publishers from *Eyewitness Testimony* by Elizabeth F. Loftus (Cambridge, MA: Harvard University Press). Copyright ©1979 by the President and Fellows of Harvard College, pp. 61–62.

11.   Elizabeth F. Loftus, "The Eyewitness on Trial," *Trial* (October 1980), p. 32.

12.   Reprinted by permission of the publishers from *Eyewitness Testimony,* by Elizabeth F. Loftus (Cambridge, MA: Harvard University Press). Copyright ©1979 by the President and Fellows of Harvard College, pp. 94–95.

13.   From Leo Katz, *Bad Acts and Guilty Minds: Conundrums of the Criminal Law* (Chicago, IL: The University of Chicago Press, 1987, p. 197)

14.   Elizabeth F. Loftus, "The Eyewitness on Trial," *Trial* (October 1980), p. 33.

15.   Elizabeth Loftus and Katherine Ketcham, *Witness for the Defense* (New York: St. Martin's Press, 1991), p. 24.

16.   Elizabeth F. Loftus, "The Eyewitness on Trial," *Trial* (October 1980), p. 33.

17.   This example is taken from Patrick M. Wall, *Eyewitness Identification of Criminal Cases* (Springfield, IL: Charles C. Thomas, 1965).

18.   From G. Bower, "Awareness, the Unconscious, and Repression: An Experimental Psychologist's Perspective." In J. L. Singer, ed., *Repression and Dissociation* (Chicago, IL: University of Chicago Press, 1990).

19.   John E. Hocking, Gerald R. Miller, and Norman E. Fontes, "Videotape in the Courtroom: Witness Deception," *Trial* (April 1978), pp. 53–54.

20.   For details of the *Randall Adams* case, see *Adams* v. *Texas,* by Randall Adams, William Hoffer, and Marilyn Mona Hoffer (New York: St. Martin's Press, 1991).

21.   For an amusing but instructive study of this and many more "urban legends" or "urban myths," see Jan Harold Brunvand's *Too Good to Be True: The Colossal Book of Urban Legends* (New York: W. W. Norton, 1999).

22.   I discovered this example in the section of *Consumer Reports* dedicated to reporting on misleading advertisements.

23.   This example was drawn from John Stauber and Sheldon Rampton, *Toxic Sludge Is Good for You* (Monroe, ME: Common Courage Press, 1995), p. 191.

INTERNET RESOURCES

One of the best websites I've ever visited is at *www.pbs.org/wgbh/pages/frontline/shows/dna.* The site is based around a superb *Frontline* documentary, "What Jennifer Saw." This is the best site I know of concerning eyewitness identification. Be sure to check out the section "The Photos," where you can try your hand at making a composite picture of a suspect, and see exactly how confusing photo spreads and lineups can be. (There are connections at this site to other documentary-based sites done by *Frontline;* all are worth a visit.)

     Elizabeth Loftus, an expert on the psychology of eyewitness testimony, has a home page at *www.faculty.washington.edu/eloftus.* It contains many of her articles on eyewitness identification, psychology of memory, problems with claims of "repressed memories," and a variety of related topics.

Gary Wells, Distinguished Professor of Psychology at Iowa State University and an expert on eyewitness testimony, has a wonderful and very accessible website investigating many aspects of eyewitness testimony, ways it can go wrong, and suggestions for improving it. Go to *www.psychology.iastate.edu/faculty/gwells*.

www.caught.net/cases/eyewit.htm is an interesting site, focusing on cases of mistaken eyewitness testimony and mistaken identifications.

The Innocence Project has been a major force in increasing awareness of the number of innocent people who have been wrongly convicted, and they have done remarkable work in helping to overturn the unjust convictions of many prisoners and freeing inmates who served many years in prison for crimes they did not commit. Their website—*www.innocenceproject.org*—is very good, with many links as well as excellent articles and studies. If you go to their site and then go to "Understand the Causes," you will find their very informative material on eyewitness misidentification: one of the major factors leading to wrongful convictions.

The site of the James Randi Educational Foundation is *www.randi.org*. James Randi, a magician, is a dedicated and outstanding debunker of pseudoscience and psychic frauds. (Read about Randi's "$1 Million Paranormal Challenge!")

The address for the Committee for the Scientific Investigation of Claims of the Paranormal is *www.csicop.org*. They publish *Skeptical Inquirer* (a delightful journal), and their site features examination of "paranormal" and psychic claims, and also includes an excellent annotated bibliography.

Factcheck.org (a project of the Annenberg Public Policy Center of the University of Pennsylvania) is a wonderful site for uncovering half-truths in politics and advertising. It attacks deceptive claims without fear or favor, revealing false and misleading claims from across the political spectrum. It is far and away the best source for finding and analyzing half-truths.

ADDITIONAL READING

For an excellent account of research on eyewitness testimony, see "The Reliability of Eyewitness Testimony: A Psychological Perspective," by Steven Penrod, Elizabeth Loftus, and John Winkler, in *The Psychology of the Courtroom*, edited by Norman L. Kerr and Robert M. Bray (New York: Academic Press, 1982), pp. 119–168.

The classic work on eyewitnesses and eyewitness reliability is Hugo Munsterberg, *On the Witness Stand* (Garden City, NY: Doubleday, Page, 1913).

A particularly good work is Elizabeth F. Loftus, *Eyewitness Testimony* (Cambridge, MA: Harvard University Press, 1979).

A very readable book, describing cases in which Loftus has testified, is Elizabeth Loftus and Katherine Ketcham, *Witness for the Defense* (New York: St. Martin's Press, 1991).

A disturbing account of mistaken convictions, many based on eyewitness testimony, can be found in Edwin M. Borchard, *Convicting the Innocent* (Garden City, NY: Garden City, 1932). Borchard, a law professor at Yale University, wrote the book in response to a district attorney's statement that "Innocent men are never convicted. Don't worry about it, it never happens in the world. It is a physical impossibility" (From the Preface).

A contemporary study of wrongful convictions can be found in *Actual Innocence: Five Days to Execution, and Other Dispatches from the Wrongly Convicted*, by Barry Scheck, Peter Neufeld, and Jim Dwyer (New York: Doubleday, 2000). Focusing on false convictions discovered by the use of DNA evidence, the book documents a number of mistaken convictions and examines the major factors contributing to such miscarriages of justice.

Who Will Tell the People: The Betrayal of American Democracy, by William Greider (New York: Simon & Schuster, 1992), is a profound yet very readable book that details and documents how democracy in the United States has been corrupted by the vast and concentrated power of special economic interests, and describes the deceptions and half-truths that are used to cover the process. Greider's book is disturbing, but he also includes some positive suggestions for reclaiming democratic processes.

A book that is very entertaining while also highly informative is *Toxic Sludge Is Good for You!: Lies, Damn Lies and the Public Relations Industry*, by John Stauber and Sheldon Rampton (Monroe, ME: Common Courage Press, 1995). It is particularly good on the deceptions spun by many of the corporations portraying themselves as "environmentally friendly," and anyone concerned with environmental issues will find the book of special value.

An incisive study of how public opinion is manipulated by half-truths (and sometimes whole lies) is *PR!: A Social History of Spin*, by Stuart Ewen (New York: Basic Books, 1996).

How to Think About Weird Things, 6th ed., by Theodore Schick, Jr., and Lewis Vaughn (New York: McGraw-Hill, 2011), contains excellent material (especially Chapter 5) on faulty eyewitness observation and the development of false (particularly pseudoscientific) beliefs.

The back inside cover of *Consumer Reports* is devoted to misleading advertisements, often involving half-truths and ambiguities.

Read the Document on mythinkinglab.com

Clive Thompson, "There's a Sucker Born in Every Medial Prefrontal Cortex." A report on how "image" can affect our sensory and taste perceptions.

Report of the Kaufman Commission on Proceedings Involving Guy Paul Morin, Chapter 3, sections A–D, "Jailhouse Informants" (Ontario Ministry of the Attorney General). Describes the severe problems associated with reliance on the testimony of "jailhouse informants."

Manitoba Justice, "Jailhouse Informants," *The Inquiry Regarding Thomas Sophonow.*" Gives accounts of some of the less than reliable testimony offered by jailhouse informants that led to the wrongful conviction of Thomas Sophonow.

Manitoba Justice, "Jailhouse Informants," *The Inquiry Regarding Thomas Sophonow.* "Eyewitness Identification." Describes in detail some of the problems that can arise in eyewitness identification, especially when photo lineups are involved.

Cumulative Exercises Three

The following examples cover all the various sorts of arguments examined in this book, with the exception of statistical fallacies. As always, some are fallacious and some are not. For each example, *first* tell what form the argument is (such as questionable cause); *then* determine whether the argument is or is not fallacious.

The argument forms we have examined are as follows:

Ad hominem: sometimes a fallacy, sometimes not
Inverse ad hominem: sometimes a fallacy, sometimes not
Strawman: always a fallacy
Irrelevant reason (or red herring): always a fallacy
Appeal to ignorance: always a fallacy
Ambiguity: always a fallacy
Appeal to authority: sometimes a fallacy, sometimes not
Appeal to popularity: always a fallacy
Appeal to tradition (traditional wisdom): always a fallacy
Analogies (deductive, inductive, figurative): sometimes fallacious, sometimes legitimate
Analogical literalism: always a fallacy
Slippery slope: sometimes a fallacy, sometimes not
Dilemma arguments: sometimes the fallacy of false dilemma, sometimes a genuine dilemma
Golden mean: always a fallacy (though it is *not* inherently fallacious to advocate a moderate position)
Begging the question: always a fallacy
Self-sealing argument: always a fallacy
Complex question: always a fallacy (though embedded *non*controversial assumptions do not commit this fallacy)
Modus ponens: not a fallacy, a valid argument form
Modus tollens: not a fallacy, a valid argument form
Denying the antecedent: always a fallacy
Affirming the consequent: always a fallacy
Causal arguments: some are legitimate, some commit the fallacy of questionable cause

---

1. Felicia Staunton argues that we should lower the legal age for buying tobacco products to 16. She points out that teenagers who really want to smoke are usually able to obtain cigarettes, and making that illegal encourages them to make a habit of breaking the law. Also, she argues that making

tobacco legal only for those age 18 and older leads younger teenagers to regard smoking as something adult, and thus makes it more appealing. But before you accept her arguments for lowering the legal age for tobacco, you should be aware that Ms. Staunton is a major investor in Philip Morris, the world's leading cigarette manufacturer, so the more teenagers who are hooked on cigarettes, the more money she makes. Ms. Staunton's arguments are designed to increase her wealth rather than arrive at the truth.

2. Guaranteeing health-care coverage for every citizen of the United States would be too expensive; on the other hand, as a wealthy country, it is wrong for the United States to have almost 40 million people without health coverage. A good solution is to guarantee health care for all citizens under age 18, but not provide guaranteed health care for all adults.

3. Obviously we should find the defendant guilty of burglary. He claims that he was nowhere near the scene of the burglary. On the night of April 19, when a burglar broke into two homes on Glenwood Avenue, the defendant claims he was home alone watching television, and that he went to bed early and never even left the house that night. But that's about the weakest alibi I've ever heard! No one saw him at home, as he admits; he didn't receive any phone calls that he can remember. And so in fact he has absolutely no proof that he was at home anytime that night, much less that he was home for the entire night. Based on that, we must find the defendant guilty as charged.

4. Downloading copies of songs off the Internet is stealing music that belongs to the performers and publishers. It's just like taking a gun and robbing a bank, stealing money that belongs to others: just because the money is there and you can take it, that doesn't make it right. Likewise, just because you have a modem, and the music is there, that doesn't make it right. Both cases are simply theft. If you think bank robbery is wrong, then you should also condemn the unpaid downloading of music from the Internet.

5. Ladies and gentlemen of the jury, it is now up to you to decide whether Wayne Winston is guilty of arson. As you consider the evidence in this case, keep in mind the testimony given by Laura Hammond. She testified that on the night of the fire, just one hour before the fire that burned down the Winston Shoe Store, she saw Wayne Winston walking into the store carrying a can of gasoline. And Laura knows Wayne Winston well, and her eyes are very good, and so she was unlikely to be mistaken. Furthermore, Laura has no motive whatsoever for lying about what she saw: she is not getting any reward or benefit for her testimony; in fact, she had to give up part of her vacation to come here and testify. And she has a strong reputation for honesty, and is well known in the community for being a reliable and trustworthy person.

6. There are those who want to restrict the amount of money that private citizens can give to political campaigns. It may sound like a good idea to have politics less dominated by money. But watch out! Once there are laws limiting how much money you can give to politicians, next will come limits on how you spend the rest of your money: there will soon be limits on how much you can spend on medical care, and how much you can spend to send your kids to college. And before you know it, you'll need government permission to buy your kid a birthday present, and a government permit to buy a cup of coffee at the local diner. If you don't want the government controlling every dime you spend, then don't let them get a foot in the door: vote against this dangerous proposal to limit private contributions to political campaigns.

7. Art Sinn has been recommending that people buy vacation condominiums in the new Mahoning River Woods development. He says that the Mahoning River will soon become a major vacation spot, and the condominiums will quickly increase in value, and are thus an excellent investment. Well, maybe. But before you rush out and drop a hundred grand on a Mahoning River Woods condo, you ought to know that Art Sinn is making a hefty commission on every condo sold; and the last condo development he pushed, Green Lake Leisure Condos, turned out to be a real bust, and the buyers wound up losing a lot of money.

8. Look, don't worry about it, riding with Bill is perfectly safe. Of course if Bill were not sober, then it would not be safe to ride with him. But he is sober: he hasn't had a drink all day. So it is safe to ride with Bill.

9. Some people complain that the U.S. drug companies charge excessive prices for the drugs they sell, and that the excessive prices and excessive profits of the pharmaceutical industry cause hardships for many people who need the drugs. But those people who complain about the high costs of drugs apparently believe that the researchers, salespeople, managers, and workers in the drug industry should just work for free, and that stockholders and investors in the drug companies should not be allowed to make any return on their investments, and that the drug companies should just manufacture and then give away for free any prescription drug that anyone needs or wants. Obviously if

they got their way, the entire pharmaceutical industry would quickly go bankrupt, and then no one would produce the drugs that are so vital for our health and well-being.

10. For several years, there has been controversy about allowing snowmobiles in Yellowstone National Park. One argument given by those who oppose snowmobiles is that in the winter, Yellowstone is beautiful and quiet, and in the wonderful stillness one can experience a sense of the sublime, and can quietly commune with nature in its pure essence; they say that allowing noisy snowmobiles into the park would be like allowing loud noise in a symphony hall: it disrupts the whole experience, it makes it impossible for those who want to enjoy the sublime sounds of music to really have that experience. But that comparison is absurd. When you are listening to an orchestra concert, you are listening to beautiful sounds; when you are at Yellowstone in winter, you are experiencing *silence*, rather than trying to listen to music.

11. There has been a proposal that the university holiday decoration include a large Christmas nativity scene on the lawn between Kilcawley and Cushwa Halls, complete with angels and music and a large star of Bethlehem. Some people object that the university should not have a nativity scene on campus, because that would be an endorsement of Christianity and would violate the requirement that state schools not endorse religions. But a nativity scene would *not* be an endorsement of Christianity. After all, nativity scenes are very beautiful, and many people enjoy them, and a beautiful nativity scene would probably encourage many area residents to visit the university campus over the holidays. So a nativity scene would not violate the rule that state schools cannot endorse religions.

12. If everyone fails this final exam, then it is too hard. But certainly not everyone will fail this final exam, so clearly the exam is not too hard.

13. I went online and bought a term paper on colonial history—I paid $25 for it!—and turned it in to Dr. Meredith for my early American history seminar term paper; and she had the nerve to give me an F on the paper, and claim that I cheated! That's just totally unfair. I bought the paper with my own money, it belonged to me, and so I had the right to use the paper any way I wished. Suppose you buy a car, and pay for it with your own money. You didn't *make* the car, but when you pay for it, the car belongs to you and you can do whatever you wish with it: you can drive it, or sell it, or give it to a friend. Likewise, when I bought the term paper with my own money it was mine, even though I didn't actually make it; and therefore I should be free to do whatever I wish with the term paper: read it, give it to a friend, or turn it in for my class.

14. Why does President Obama want to destroy our health-care system? Is it some sort of hatred for doctors and nurses? Or is it because he is young and healthy, and so he doesn't see the importance of health care?

15. If there was no effective communications in New Orleans after Hurricane Katrina, then the Federal Emergency Management Administration (FEMA) did a lousy planning job. So obviously FEMA did do a lousy job, because New Orleans did not have effective communications after Hurricane Katrina.

16. On the campus of the University of North Carolina at Chapel Hill, in the main entrance quad-rangle, there is a large statue of a Confederate soldier, in honor of the Confederate soldiers who fought during the Civil War. Some people are now complaining about the statue: they say that it is wrong for the university to have a statue honoring those who fought to preserve slavery. But in fact the statue has been there for more than a century, and for almost that entire time there were no complaints; to the contrary, for many decades the statue was a special beloved part of the university—the students nicknamed the soldier in the monument "Silent Sam." Silent Sam has been a part of the University of North Carolina for over a century, and so it would be wrong to remove him now.

17. In the main quadrangle of the University of North Carolina at Chapel Hill, there is a large statue of a Confederate soldier, as part of a memorial honoring those soldiers who fought for the Confederacy. The statue has become controversial, because many students believe that it is wrong for the university to have a monument honoring those who fought to preserve slavery. Some suggest that if we place a statue honoring some abolitionist—such as Sojourner Truth—nearby, that will solve the problem. Now a statue honoring Sojourner Truth would be a fine thing, but it won't solve the problem. Look, suppose someone had erected a statue honoring Adolph Hitler or Nazi prison guards; if we now placed a monument nearby honoring the brave Jewish resistance fighters in the Warsaw Ghetto, that would not make everything fine: we still shouldn't have a statue honoring the Nazis. Likewise, we shouldn't have a monument honoring those who fought to preserve slavery, whether we have some monument in honor of the abolitionists or not.

18. Recently there has been controversy over whether the parking deck between Cushwa and DeBartolo is safe. Well, I happened to be walking through that parking deck with Terbucky, who is a professor in the psychology department, and a brilliant researcher whose work has been published in the top psychology journals in the world. Professor Terbucky looked carefully at the parking deck, and she said it was structurally sound and perfectly safe. That should settle the issue: when Professor Terbucky says the deck is safe, you know it's really safe.

19. If we did not have effective means of controlling and alleviating severe pain, then active euthanasia (mercy killing) would be morally acceptable. But through medical advances we now have very effective methods of controlling and alleviating even the most severe pain. So obviously active euthanasia is not morally acceptable.

20. Several studies have shown that Scotch drinkers have an average income that is almost twice as high as the income of people who do not drink Scotch. So clearly if you want to make money, you should drink Scotch: I don't know what it is, but there must be something about drinking Scotch that causes people to make more money.

21. Some people are concerned about the effects of the enormous amount of violent and hardcore pornography on the Internet, and the easy access that children have to such sites. But such Internet pornography sites are not really a danger to our children. The Internet is in fact one of the greatest educational resources in the world: students, even including very young children, can easily explore a vast range of topics, finding material for their papers and just browsing to explore anything from dinosaurs to space travel. It is like having a vast library at your fingertips, a wonderful and constantly updated world encyclopedia, an opportunity to meet people and explore cultures all around the world. When we put the whole thing in perspective, it is clear that there is no danger to children from Internet hardcore pornography.

22. Ladies and gentlemen of the jury, we have presented you with solid, substantial evidence to show that Happy Nose cold remedy is in fact a dangerous and hazardous drug that has caused a number of cases of kidney damage and even complete kidney failure in the unfortunate people who took this drug. As you recall, the defense called Dr. Jones, an "expert on drugs and pharmaceuticals," who testified that in his expert opinion the kidney damage was merely coincidental, and that there was nothing in Happy Nose cold remedy that could have caused kidney damage. But as you weigh Dr. Jones's testimony, keep in mind that he makes his living—and a very handsome living—by being a hired gun who testifies for drug companies that are being sued. He has appeared in 14 different cases over the last 6 months, testifying about drugs that patients had claimed to be harmful, and in every one of those cases he testified that the drug in question was not harmful. And in every one of those cases, he received a consulting fee of $50,000, plus an additional fee of $1,000 for every hour of testimony! Dr. Jones claims to be an "impartial expert" on drugs; but when he is being paid over $50,000 for his testimony, do you really think he is just an impartial expert?

23. You remember our discussion of whether jurors were allowed to discuss a case during the trial, before the case goes to the jury? I said that they were not permitted to discuss the case during the trial, and I was right! I talked to F. Lee Bailey, Marcia Clark, Cardozo Law School Professor Barry Scheck, and Supreme Court Justice Alan Souter; all agreed that jurors are not allowed to discuss cases while the trial is still in progress.

24. Darling, you shouldn't be angry at me; I've never been unfaithful to you. OK, I admit that I did spend that weekend with Tony, and then there was that time I had a little fling with Robert, and last year I did slip off to Abe's apartment a few times during lunch, and maybe there were one or two others. But I wasn't really cheating on you, because I was always faithful to you in my heart, even if my body occasionally strayed. So I've never really been unfaithful.

25. When you download music off the Internet, you are basically stealing that music from the artists and composers and producers who own the rights to that music. And maybe you think taking a song or two or three is not such a big deal. But if you think it's okay to steal music, then maybe next you will think it's okay to shoplift a few items when you're visiting the mall, and soon you'll be embezzling money from your employer, and from there it's not far to holding up convenience stores and robbing banks. So to avoid a life of violent crime, don't start with stealing music through the Internet.

26. The United States has recently passed legislation suspending some of our basic liberties, such as the right not to be held in prison without being charged, and the right of private conversation between attorneys and their clients, and the right of an accused person to know who his or her accusers are. There is some opposition to this suspension of our liberties, but in fact the suspension is perfectly

justified. After all, the United States is at war, and we have always suspended liberties in war time: During the Vietnam War, we limited the freedom of the press; during World War II, we placed severe restrictions on freedom of speech and also held many Japanese people in prison without bringing charges against them; and similar things happened in the Civil War. So there's nothing wrong with suspending liberties during the war on terrorism; it's what we have always done in times of war.

27. We are now embroiled in controversy over whether to drill for oil in the Alaskan wilderness area. The Bush administration wants to open the entire area to oil exploration, while environmentalists want the area preserved in its natural wilderness state with no oil drilling. But there's no reason this controversy cannot be resolved reasonably: obviously the right solution is to keep half the wilderness area wild and not allow drilling there, but open the other half for oil wells.

28. Ladies and gentlemen of the jury, you have listened carefully to all the evidence and all the testimony in this case. As district attorney, I ask that you find the defendant *guilty* of the charge of bank robbery. And as you deliberate your verdict, I want you to especially remember the testimony of Lisa Falcone, the bank teller who was robbed. She testified, under oath, that the defendant was the man she saw rob the bank. Now clearly Lisa Falcone has no motive for lying or deceiving, and I think you must conclude that she is a truthful witness, who went into the witness box and swore to tell the truth and *did* tell the truth. And she testified that the *defendant* was the man who robbed the bank. If you believe that she was testifying truthfully, then you must conclude that what she told you was the truth: that the defendant really was the man who robbed the bank.

29. We are now spending millions of dollars on increased airport and air travel security. But it's a total waste of time and money. Either the new security measures must make air travel absolutely safe, or they are totally useless. But there's no way airport security measures can make air travel perfectly safe; after all, there is always the possibility of pilot error or mechanical failure. So clearly we must conclude that the airport security measures are useless.

30. We recently did a study of graduating seniors, and we found that students who made a grade of A in critical thinking were significantly more likely to graduate with honors than were students who had never taken critical thinking. So clearly doing well in the critical thinking class causes students to make higher grades in all their classes.

31. If the United States had adequate banking and financial market regulation, then we would not have had massive bank failures and the bankruptcy of major insurance and investment companies. But we certainly *did* have those bank failures and bankruptcies. So clearly the banking and financial market regulation in the United States is not adequate.

32. Our economy is going through a rough patch right now; but that should not lead people to worry about the basic health of the U.S. economy. In fact, the U.S. economy is still basically in good shape, because the U.S. economy is fundamentally sound and healthy.

33. The United States tortured some of the prisoners now being held in Guantanamo Bay Military Prison—they were waterboarded, beaten, deprived of sleep for long periods, exposed to long periods of cold, and spent many hours chained into stressful positions from which they could not move. Some people say that the confessions that these prisoners gave after being tortured should not be used against them in court. But that's silly. Look, think of medical experiments. Sometimes people who volunteer for those experiments suffer harm; but we don't conclude that because someone suffered harm during the experiment, we should throw out all the information we gained from the experiment. So likewise, just because the prisoners suffered harm from being tortured, that doesn't mean that we should throw out the information—the confessions—we gained from the torture.

34. Jimmy Carter is a warm, generous man, who since serving as president has devoted his life to working with Habitat for Humanity to provide homes for the homeless, and who has worked tirelessly to promote democracy and stop conflicts around the world. Carter argues that the United States should negotiate with the Hamas movement, because Hamas is a major force in the Middle East and the elected government in Gaza, and that therefore we cannot have real peace in the Middle East without serious talks and negotiations with Hamas. There are those who say that Hamas is a terrorist group, and that we should never talk with Hamas. But if someone as self-sacrificing, sincere, and dedicated to peace as Jimmy Carter argues in favor of negotiating with Hamas, then clearly his argument should carry special force, and so negotiating with Hamas must be a good idea.

35. There were many great artists of the Renaissance period—Michelangelo, Da Vinci, Raphael, and many others. Some art experts say Da Vinci was the best, some say Michelangelo was greatest,

some favor Raphael, and others have their own favorites. But my art history professor—Alice Krokowski, who has her doctorate in art history from Yale—says that the greatest of all Renaissance artists was Albrecht Durer. So that should settle it: Durer was the greatest artist of the Renaissance period.

36. The defendant is guilty of breaking or entering only if she intended to commit a felony when she entered the house. Now certainly she had no intention of committing a felony when she opened the door and walked in: She saw the "for sale" sign in the yard and was simply looking the house over with the idea that she might like to buy it. Therefore, the defendant is not guilty of breaking or entering.

37. A recent study showed that people who drink at least two glasses of wine each day are generally healthier than people who do not drink wine. It's clear, then, that drinking wine every day is good for you.

38. If the United States had been a democracy in 1800, then all adult U.S. citizens would have had the right to vote. But certainly it was not the case that all U.S. citizens could vote: women, African Americans, and people without property were all denied the right to vote in 1800. So clearly the United States was not a democracy in 1800.

39. This whole debate about gay marriage is really very easy to settle. Certainly we do not want to deny all rights to gays: that would clearly be wrong. On the other hand, there's no need to go to the other extreme, and allow gays all the rights that heterosexuals enjoy, including the right to marry. Obviously the best solution is to allow civil unions for homosexual couples, but not allow homosexual marriage.

40. Bruce is guilty of check fraud only if he knew there was no money in his account. But Bruce certainly did not know that there was no money in his account: he is a complete idiot about everything related to finances. So Bruce is not guilty of check fraud.

41. Closing argument to the jury by the district attorney in a murder trial: "Counsel for the Defense has entertained us with the ever-popular defense that lawyers call SODDI: Some Other Dude Did It. But as you consider your verdict, keep this in mind: the defense lawyer never told you who that other dude is, and never gave you any evidence that he—whoever that dude is—is the murderer. So if the defense can't prove some other dude did it, you should find the defendant guilty as charged."

42. Almost every authority on health and smoking—the U.S. Environmental Protection Agency, the American Lung Association, the American Cancer Society, and health researchers throughout Europe and North America—agree that secondhand smoke (sometimes called passive smoke or environmental tobacco smoke) causes lung cancer. So we should acknowledge the fact that secondhand smoke causes lung cancer.

43. Almost every authority on health and smoking—the U.S. Environmental Protection Agency, the American Lung Association, the American Cancer Society, and health researchers throughout Europe and North America—agree that secondhand smoke (sometimes called passive smoke or environmental tobacco smoke) causes lung cancer. But there is an exception: Gary Huber was a professor at the University of Texas, where he ran a health research center. Professor Huber has published a number of articles on secondhand smoke, and Professor Huber maintains that secondhand smoke poses no health risks. But there's something you should know about Professor Huber: He receives enormous sums of money from the tobacco companies. During his few years at the University of Texas, he was paid $1.7 million by the tobacco companies—in secret payments—for writing and speaking against research showing links between secondhand smoke and health problems, and over the years he received more than $7 million in tobacco company funds. So Professor Huber is very well paid for his "expert opinion" that secondhand smoke does not cause health problems; so well paid that it casts doubts on his status as an objective expert (Information for this case drawn from Sheldon Rampton and John Stauber).

44. Look, we all agree that every child, rich or poor, should be provided with a decent education, since without a good education one does not have a real opportunity to succeed, right? So likewise, we should also make sure that every child has good health care, since lack of good health care also destroys a child's opportunity for success: a child who is sick or chronically unhealthy is deprived of opportunity, just like a child who is not taught to read or write.

45. Some people believe that we should legalize marijuana for medicinal purposes: for example, marijuana can be very effective in relieving severe nausea following certain types of cancer treatments. But it would be a mistake to legalize medicinal marijuana, because we should never legalize marijuana for any use whatsoever.

46. Critical thinking is obviously a worthless class, because either learning about critical thinking will make you wealthy or critical thinking is worthless. But it's perfectly clear that learning to think critically will not make you wealthy. After all, Bruce knows about critical thinking, and he's poor as a church mouse. And in fact if you look at the people who teach critical thinking, they all look pretty seedy: not a wealthy person in the bunch. Therefore, the critical thinking class is worthless.

47. The people who are pushing for increased airport security claim that they can make air travel completely safe from terrorist attacks. But of course they are sadly mistaken. After all, even if we have much better security checks in the airports, there's always a chance that terrorists could shoot down an airliner with a surface-to-air missile; or some terrorist might become a professional airline pilot and pass all security checks and then crash the plane; or even if we prevent any passenger from carrying weapons, some passenger who is a karate expert might overpower the crew and crash the plane. So obviously those people who want better airport security, and who believe that they can find fail-safe methods of stopping terrorist attacks against passenger planes, are just wrong.

48. Congressman Jim Traficant was recently convicted of taking kickbacks and payoffs while in office, and now he is serving a term in prison. But really, what he did wasn't so bad. Sure, he took some payoffs for helping people get government contracts, and he took kickbacks from some of the office staff he hired. But think of it this way: Suppose you were baking some cookies for a friend, and while you're mixing the cookie dough and spooning the cookies out on the baking sheet, you take just a few bites of the cookie dough. There's nothing wrong with that, is there? You're not stealing cookies, you're just taking a little taste. Well, that's really all Congressman Traficant was doing: he was just taking a little taste of the contracts, jobs, and deals that he was cooking up. Nothing to get excited about, and certainly not any reason to send him to prison.

49. There are those who want to allow the medicinal use of marijuana, especially for the relief of pain for those undergoing cancer treatments. It sounds like a good idea at first, but consider the longer view: If a cancer patient is allowed to use marijuana, then that patient's legal marijuana will be readily available to the family members and friends of the patient; and then cancer patients, in order to raise some extra money for their expensive treatments, will begin to sell the marijuana to non-patients. And once they start to sell marijuana, it's a very easy step to selling other drugs like cocaine and heroin. So if we want to avoid a major expansion of the market in illegal drugs, we must not allow the medicinal use of marijuana.

50. If the U.S. unemployment rate were over 10%, then the U.S. economy would not be healthy. So clearly the U.S. economy is in good shape, because the unemployment rate is certainly lower than 10%.

51. If Ohio did not have a lottery, then our schools would not have enough money. But Ohio does have a lottery. So obviously our schools do have sufficient money.

52. During this entire week of final exams, the University Library has been open extended hours, usually until midnight every night. And during the same period, it is obvious that university students have been more stressed, irritable, worried, and tired. Obviously having the library open for extended hours is causing greater stress, worry, and exhaustion for our students, and such extended library hours should be stopped immediately.

53. Martin Fielding argues that we should make a major investment in our transportation system, and make the needed repairs on our highways, railroads, and bridges. He notes that the federal budget provides lots of money for building new bridges and highways, but very little money for maintenance of existing bridges and highways; and that state budgets have been very tight for many years, and so states have not had enough money to make the needed repairs and do the essential upkeep. And Fielding points out that the bridge collapse in Minneapolis cost many lives and even more injuries, and that there are bridges in similar need of repair posing potential dangers all over the country, and that therefore we should spend the money needed to make extensive needed repairs. But before you accept Fielding's argument, consider this: Martin Fielding owns a major bridge construction and repair company, and if there is more money for bridge repairs then Fielding will probably make a bundle of money. When you factor in Fielding's financial stake in this question, his argument loses all plausibility.

54. If we have real doubts that the defendant committed the crime, then we should find the defendant not guilty. So clearly we should find the defendant not guilty, because we do have real doubts about whether he committed the crime.

55. If you do not make any mistakes on this exam, then obviously you are sober. So clearly you are not sober, since you did make a mistake.

56. Look, if you are in an auto accident and have to go to an emergency room, whatever you do, stay at our little local hospital, and don't let them transfer you to the big Capitol City Hospital Trauma Center. Because it turns out that the mortality rate at the Capitol City Trauma Center is much *higher* than at our local emergency room! That is, a *higher* percentage of Capitol City Trauma patients die than do patients at our local emergency room! So obviously you get better medical care at our local hospital emergency room than you would at Capitol City Trauma Center.

57. Allowing children to watch too much television is likely to have bad long-term effects. They watch passively, and thus get less exercise and tend to snack more, so they gain weight, become lethargic, are slower, and are less competent in sports. Then they may be ridiculed when they attempt sports or exercise, and that may cause them to avoid sports and perhaps turn to television and food for comfort. Thus when they start watching excessive television, the result may be a spiral of lethargy, increased weight, absence of exercise, and eventual depression that spins ever deeper.

58. Clearly the courts in London used to go too far in inflicting the death penalty: They hung people for the theft of a few scraps of food, for pickpocketing, for a whole host of minor crimes. But on the other hand, we should not go so far as to entirely eliminate the ultimate criminal penalty of capital punishment. The right policy, then, is to keep the death penalty, but only as punishment for the most awful and hideous crimes.

59. The Senate seat held by Senator Foghorn, who recently died, should be given to Senator Foghorn's wife. After all, if a person who owns a grocery store dies, the grocery store normally goes to the person's spouse. In the same way, now that Senator Foghorn has died, his Senate seat should go to his wife, at least for the remainder of his term.

60. Jill is guilty of breaking and entering only if she did not have Joan's permission to enter Joan's apartment. But Jill certainly did have Joan's permission, as Joan herself testified. Therefore, Jill is not guilty of breaking or entering.

61. We must either do random drug testing of all segments of society or abandon all efforts to stop the use of illegal drugs. Now certainly we cannot abandon our efforts against illegal drugs, for illegal drugs are causing addiction, increased crime, and, with alarming frequency, death. Thus, even though it may seem an extreme measure, we must do random drug testing of all segments of society.

62. It has often been claimed that the U.S. Air Force keeps a secret file—a top-secret "green book"—containing conclusive evidence of extraterrestrial visitations to Earth. Now of course the Air Force always denies such a secret file, but they have never provided one shred of hard evidence to prove that such a file does not exist. Until they offer such proof, it is only reasonable to conclude that there really is such a secret file.

63. Some people argue that capital punishment is necessary, because it is the only appropriate punishment for those who commit the most atrocious and depraved crimes. However, we should not pay any attention to such arguments. It is well established that those who argue for capital punishment are usually people who see themselves as helpless and inadequate in a changing, complex world, and subconsciously such people see capital punishment as a way of striking back at a confusing world.

64. No one who has really experienced faith healing ever doubts that a spiritual power, beyond anything in the natural world, genuinely exists and can miraculously heal the body and soul. Of course some claim to have had similar experiences that they try to explain away as merely natural psychological processes; but such persons obviously have never felt the real miraculous healing of true faith, since those who have that true experience can never doubt it.

65. Industrial pollution is not harming our environment. Pollution control devices are very expensive, and they raise the prices American consumers pay for manufactured products. Also, if American industry must spend money on pollution control, that will make American industrial products more costly, and will thus make it more difficult for American-made products to compete in the international market. Therefore, our environment is not being damaged by industrial pollution.

66. I had been wondering what would be a good nutritious breakfast, but now I know! Just yesterday I saw Michael Jordan, one of the finest basketball players of all time, on television, and he recommended eating Wheaties. Well, Michael Jordan is an NBA all-star, so if he says Wheaties are the right cereal to eat, then they must be, so I'm going to take his advice and eat Wheaties.

67. Meetings of the U.S. Senate Budget Committee should be closed and confidential, because obviously the discussion of the Budget Committee should not be open to the public.

68. Now that you are the manager of this store in our chain, you will have the opportunity—and the temptation—to "manipulate" the books: for example, to show more profit than the store really made during one quarter in order to impress the regional manager. But don't do it! For if you over-state the profits a bit this quarter, then the profits next quarter will seem especially low—and you'll be even more tempted to make larger exaggerations to keep the profits increasing; and having done it once, it will seem easier to do it a second time. And those exaggerations will have to be covered up with other falsifications. Before you know it, you are deeply enmeshed in a web of fraud-ulent accounting records from which you cannot extricate yourself. Better not to ever start with those small manipulations of the books.

69. It is sometimes claimed that an artist who creates a model for a sculpture and then has someone else actually do the sculpting is still really the artist: like a composer who writes a symphony and then has an orchestra perform it. The composer doesn't play the instruments, but is still the artist; and in a similar way, some people claim, the artist who creates the model doesn't actually use a hammer and chisel, but she is still the artist. But that's not a good comparison, because sculptors work with solid materials like marble or steel and composers work with sounds.

70. Janie Jenkins insists that we should avoid using drugs. She argues that nicotine, marijuana, cocaine, and amphetamines all are proven to be dangerous to health, that they can be addictive, and that at the very least they impair intellectual abilities. But then it turns out that Janie drinks a full bottle of Scotch whiskey every evening—and certainly alcohol is also a drug, and it can also be dangerous to health, and drinking large quantities of whiskey can certainly be detrimental to one's intellectual abilities. Janie has no business arguing against drugs if she can't get her own drinking problem under control.

71. There is currently a movement to raise the speed limit above 65 mph on interstate highways. But the program of those who want to raise the speed limit is quite absurd. They want to eliminate speed limits altogether—according to them, it would be perfectly alright for people to drive 90 mph through school zones and race through residential neighborhoods and drive as fast as their cars will run through busy downtown traffic. It's easy to see what sort of carnage would result, for drivers as well as for pedestrians. Obviously the position of those who are campaigning to raise speed limits is ridiculous.

72. There are those who are opposed to random drug testing of college athletes, because they say it violates the individual rights and liberties of the athletes. But that is just false. Random drug testing is the only means of reliably determining whether an athlete is using drugs; such random drug tests are an effective means of discouraging drug use among athletes; and, since college athletes are often role models and heroes for high school students, it is very important that we prevent drug use among college athletes. Therefore, such random drug tests are not a violation of the athletes' rights.

73. This painting is signed "Vincent van Gogh." It is certainly in the vivid post-impressionist style of van Gogh, and it is being offered at auction as the work of the great nineteenth-century Dutch artist Vincent van Gogh. So it must be either a genuine painting by van Gogh or a forgery. But it cannot be genuine: It uses a type of oil paint that was not developed until 1891, and van Gogh died in 1890. Therefore, the painting is a forgery.

74. Obviously there is controversy over the best way to handle the drug problem in the United States, and different experts on the issue are recommending different policies. But Ramsey Clark, former attorney general of the United States, says that we should decriminalize drugs such as cocaine and heroin, have doctors dispense them by prescription to addicts, not impose any criminal penalties on those who possess and use such drugs, and provide good medical treatment programs for any addicts who wish to overcome their drug addictions. Ramsey Clark is obviously an expert on law enforcement (since he once held the position of attorney general), and he has made a special study of the drug problem. Therefore, since Ramsey Clark recommends decriminalization as the most effective policy for dealing with our drug problem, it must certainly be the best policy.

75. I had a terrible cold last week, so I bought a bottle of Dr. Dogood's Miracle Fast Action Cold Medicine, and I took two tablespoonfuls every morning and every night all last week. Now my cold is completely gone, and I feel great. Dr. Dogood's Miracle Medicine is really an effective medicine for curing colds.

76. Donald Dobble should *not* be honored with selection as Central State's "Outstanding Graduate of '12." While it's true that he has superb grades and has been active in student government, those good qualities are more than offset by the fact that he has *twice* violated the honor code by cheating on exams, and twice while a student at the university he has been convicted of driving while intoxicated, and this very semester he pleaded guilty to shoplifting jewelry from Southern Park Mall. So when we look at his record as a whole, it is obvious that he does not deserve the honor of being named "outstanding graduate."

77. We should not place any government requirements on the energy efficiency of cars sold in the United States; that is, we should not require auto manufacturers to design their cars to exceed a minimum number of miles per gallon. For if we allow fuel-efficiency restrictions, then that will open the door to other restrictions, such as restrictions on the size of the engines; and then will come restrictions on the shape of the car; and before you know it, automobile design will be so completely regulated by the government that you will not even have a choice about what color of car you wish to buy.

78. We should not abolish capital punishment because we have had capital punishment in this country since the Colonial period. Even in the early days of Western expansion, the death penalty was imposed. In short, we have had capital punishment in the American colonies and the American nation for some 300 years, and we should not change now.

79. The position of those who push "soft energy" or "renewable energy use" is quite ridiculous. They want us to get all our energy from windmills! But it would require thousands and thousands of windmills to provide us with all the energy required by our highly industrialized society, and in some areas of the country there is not a sufficiently strong and steady wind to generate much electricity. In those areas, energy would have to be wired in from long distances, and at tremendous expense. When we look closely and soberly at the windmill schemes of the "alternative energy" people, we can see that they simply would not work.

80. On rare occasions all the planets, in traveling their respective orbits, wind up roughly in line on the same side of the Sun. In fact, that will happen sometime next year. Some people have claimed that the combined gravitational force of all the planets is likely to lead to cataclysmic events: tidal waves, floods, perhaps terrible earthquakes. But there is really no cause for alarm: Carl Sagan, a well-respected professor of astronomy, assures us that because of the enormous distances involved, the combined force of gravity of all the planets upon Earth will still be negligible, and certainly will not be enough to cause floods or tidal waves—not even a slightly higher tide. And in fact, all the astronomers at MIT, Oxford, and the University of Toronto agree with Sagan that there is no danger. Therefore, we have no need to worry about the claims of cataclysmic events caused by the alignment of the planets.

81. The cities of Boston, Chicago, and New York all have rapid transit systems (public subway systems) and they also have among the worst traffic and the most traffic jams of any cities in the country. Obviously, then, rapid rail transit systems cause traffic problems rather than solving them.

82. Some people say that building more nuclear weapons when we already have enough to kill everyone on Earth many times over is like standing knee-deep in gasoline and asking for more matches. But the cases aren't really analogous: A gasoline fire certainly is not the equal of a nuclear attack.

83. Critics of the pharmaceutical industry argue that pharmaceutical manufacturers overcharge for prescription drugs, taking advantage of their exclusive control over some vitally important drugs to set prices excessively high, thus making excessive profits. For example, critics note that (according to data compiled by *USA TODAY,* March 2, 1993) in 1991 the top 20 drug companies averaged over 15% profit; the average profit of all the Fortune 500 companies was just over 3%. This extremely high rate of profit indicates that perhaps the pharmaceutical manufacturers are setting prices too high.

    The Pharmaceutical Manufacturers Association countered with a series of glossy newspaper and magazine advertisements, offering the following counterargument:

    > When prescription drugs can save ulcer patients from surgery, it's obviously a good thing. What's not so apparent is how dramatically the same drugs reduce healthcare costs.
    >
    > In 1976, the year before the introduction of the first modern anti-ulcer drug, there were 155,000 ulcer operations. By 1987, the number had dropped to under 19,000.
    >
    > And today, while ulcer drug therapy costs a sizable $1,000 a year, it is far less expensive than surgery, which averages $25,000, resulting in an estimated savings of $3 billion a year.

84. There should not be any controversy over the teaching of evolution and the teaching of creationism in public schools. The correct solution to the problem is obvious. Certainly it would be excessive to ban the teaching of evolution and teach only the creationist view. And it would be going too far in the opposite direction to teach only evolution and totally neglect the creationist position. Obviously, then, the correct solution is to simply give equal time to both views.

85. Business is like playing poker. In poker it's OK to deceive someone with a bluff, if you can get away with it; and in the same way, if you can get away with a "bluff" in business, such as false advertising, then it's OK to do it.

86. Senator Scam has been tried on two charges of accepting bribes, and after a lengthy trial the jury returns a verdict of not guilty. Senator Scam offers the following argument:

> I am glad to have it proved once and for all that there is absolutely no substance to the charges that I accepted bribes. I have insisted all along that I am not guilty of those charges, and now a jury has also asserted their belief in my innocence by returning their verdict of not guilty.

87. We should adopt a policy of requiring drug tests for every high school athlete in Mahoning County. Some people may oppose such tests, but clearly such testing is a good idea. After all, the great majority of college and professional teams require drug testing for their athletes, and so does the Olympics. Besides, many businesses now require drug testing for all their employees. So drug testing, especially for athletes, is becoming more and more common. In fact, if Mahoning County does not require drug testing for all its high school athletes, it will soon be one of the few areas that does not require such testing. So obviously we ought to adopt a policy of required drug testing for all Mahoning County high school athletes.

88. There are those who argue that marijuana should be legalized, because, they say, we generally agree that alcohol should be legal; and marijuana is basically very similar in its effects to alcohol; so if alcohol should be legal, then marijuana should also be legal. But that is a lousy argument. It's silly to compare legalization of marijuana to legalization of alcohol, because the cases are not really similar: Alcohol is a beverage, and it can be mixed with soda, juices, and tonic; but you can't drink marijuana, and certainly it cannot be mixed with soda or fruit juice.

89. If Rachel is guilty of first-degree murder, then she must have intended to kill Ralph. And indeed she did intend to kill him, as she admitted in her own testimony. Therefore, Rachel is indeed guilty of first-degree murder.

90. In an article discussing the morality of fetal-tissue transplants (the use of tissue from aborted fetuses in the treatment of such diseases as Parkinson's and Alzheimer's), John A. Robertson claimed that using such aborted fetal tissue for research and treatment does *not* imply approval of abortion. Therefore (he argued), even those opposed to elective abortions should have no objection to fetal-tissue research and treatment. His argument goes like this:

> A researcher using fetal tissue from an elective abortion is not necessarily an accomplice with the abortionist and woman choosing abortion. The researcher and the recipient [of a fetal-tissue transplant] have no role in the abortion process. They will not have requested it, and may have no knowledge of who performed the abortion or where it occurred since a third-party intermediary will procure the tissue. They may be morally opposed to abortion, and surely are not compromised because they choose to salvage some good from an abortion that will occur regardless of their research or therapeutic goals.
>
> A useful analogy is transplant of organs and tissue from homicide victims. Families of murder victims are often asked to donate organs and bodies for research, therapy, and education. If they consent, organ procurement agencies retrieve the organs and distribute them to recipients. No one would seriously argue that the surgeon who transplants the victim's kidneys, heart, liver, or corneas, or the recipient of the organs, becomes an accomplice in the homicide that made the organs available, even if aware of the source.
>
> If organs from murder victims may be used without complicity in the murder that makes the organs available, then fetal remains could also be used without complicity in the abortion. (John A. Robertson, "Rights, Symbolism, and Public Policy in Fetal Tissue Transplants," *Hastings Center Report* [December 1988], p. 6.)

91. From "In Defense of a Little Virginity," an advertisement run in July 1992 by "Focus on the Family" (in order to raise money to "reach out to America's kids"):

> Condom distribution programs do not reduce the number of kids exposed to disease . . . they radically increase it!
>
> Want proof of that fact? Since the federal government began its major contraception program in 1970, unwed pregnancies have increased 87 percent among 15- to 19-year-olds. Likewise, abortions among teens rose 67 percent, unwed births went up 61 percent. And venereal disease has infected a generation of young people. Nice job, sex counselors. Good thinking, senators and congressmen. Nice nap, America.

92. I have the right to smoke cigarettes if I want to; therefore, it's right for me to smoke cigarettes if I so desire.

93. We should not place any waiting period requirement on the purchase of handguns. For if you first start with a required waiting period for handguns, then soon other restrictions on handguns will occur, and then the ban of handguns, and before too long there would be a ban on all private ownership of firearms—and you wouldn't even be able to own a shotgun for hunting or skeet shooting.

94. Obviously some people really do have genuine experiences of having lived previous lives. Of course there are some skeptics, who doubt the reports of those who claim to remember past lives. The skeptics suggest that those who claim to remember past lives are lying or have an overactive imagination. But we should keep in mind that those who can remember their past lives are in a spiritually advanced stage, for only those who achieve such spiritual advancement can recall their past lives. And certainly no one who has reached such a spiritually advanced state would lie or be deceived by his or her imagination.

95. You keep saying you don't want to vote guilty, because you still have doubts about whether the defendant is guilty. OK, Mr. Reasonable Doubt, you say you aren't convinced that the defendant murdered James Finn. Well, I know one thing: James Finn was murdered, and someone murdered him. And there are no other suspects, and the defendant does not have an alibi. So unless you can give me some reason to think that the defendant really is not guilty, then I have to conclude that the defendant is guilty as charged.

96. During a friendly basketball game, Joe trips and hurts his foot. The injury causes Joe a good deal of pain, and it appears that Joe's foot might be broken. You insist that Joe should go down to the emergency room and have his foot checked, and you volunteer to drive him to the hospital. On the way there, your speed slips up to 50 mph in a 35-mph zone; a city policeman pulls you over and proceeds to write you a speeding ticket. You protest as follows: "Look, Officer, this isn't fair. A week ago my wife's mother had a heart attack while driving to lunch with my wife, Sarah; Sarah immediately drove toward the hospital emergency room and was driving 55 mph in a 35 mph zone when a city policeman waved her over. When Sarah explained the situation and said that she was on her way to the emergency room with her mother, the policeman waved her on without giving her a speeding ticket. So it's not fair for you to ticket me for speeding on the way to the emergency room."

97. Ladies and gentlemen of the jury, you heard Dr. Greta Garringer testify that in her expert opinion the blood on the hands of the defendant certainly was type AB negative, the rare blood type of the murder victim. But remember this: Dr. Garringer—this "expert witness" that the prosecution case depends on—was recently barred from medical practice by the American Medical Association for falsifying treatment records, and last year she lost her license to practice medicine in Virginia because it was discovered that she had lied about her medical education. It turns out that Dr. Garringer's medical degree was not from Duke University, as she claimed, but instead came from a small college in Bolivia. And she was recently fired from her position at Western Hospital when it was discovered that she had been drinking heavily during working hours. So I ask you: Can you really trust her claims about the blood type?

98. The following is an argument by Thomas Aquinas to support belief in miracles:

> If you object that no one has seen miracles occurring, I can give an answer to that. It is well known, in fact, that the whole world used to worship idols and to persecute Christ's faith. To this even the histories written by pagans give testimony. Today, however, all are converted to Christ—the wise men, the nobles, the rich, the powerful, and the great—all are converted to the preaching of those who are simple and poor, of those few men who preach Christ. Now, this was either accomplished miraculously, or it was not. If done miraculously, the point is proved. If not, then I say that there could be no greater miracle than this fact, that the whole world was converted without miracles. So, we need not look for anything else.

99. If long prison sentences were actually effective in preventing crime, then the United States, by virtue of having the largest prison population in the world, would not have a high crime rate. But in fact the United States has a very high crime rate. So, clearly, long prison sentences are not effective in preventing crime.

100. Senator Zane claims that he has strong and conclusive evidence that his opponent, Lewis Clark, accepted bribes while he was governor. Senator Zane says he can't reveal his evidence, because that would undermine ongoing investigations. But he assures us that he has solid evidence, and he says that he will make it all public as soon as possible. But I see no reason to believe Senator Zane. He is a politician who is trying desperately to defeat Clark in the senatorial election. So given Senator

Zane's strong motives for lying, or at least exaggerating the "evidence" he claims to have against Clark, no one should have any faith in his unsubstantiated claims. Besides, Senator Zane has played this sort of game before. During his first campaign for the Senate, he claimed to have conclusive evidence of serious lawbreaking and moral depravity by his opponent, but he said he couldn't reveal the evidence. After he won the election, he finally revealed his "conclusive evidence": It showed that his opponent had once been ticketed for driving 10 mph over the speed limit, and had once paid a small tax penalty for filing his state income tax returns 3 days late! So we should ignore Senator Zane's claims of "secret evidence" against Clark: Senator Zane should put up or shut up.

101. Managed medical care systems sometimes have a rule that no physician in the system is allowed to say critical things about another physician in the system when talking with a patient. That is, if both Dr. Green and Dr. White are members of XYZ Managed Medical Care, Dr. Green cannot tell her patient that Dr. White is an incompetent surgeon and that the patient should not have surgery done by Dr. White. Some people claim that such rules are wrong, and that they undermine the relation of trust between physician and patient. But there is nothing wrong in such rules. After all, suppose you own a large department store: How would you like it if a salesperson in appliances went around telling her customers not to buy clothing at your store, because the clothing sold by the store is lousy? You would certainly have a rule against any of your employees telling customers negative things about other departments in your store, and there is nothing wrong with such a rule. Likewise, there is nothing wrong with a managed medical care company having a rule against allowing its physicians to tell patients negative things about other physicians in the practice.

102. Some people object to children dressing up as monsters and ghosts for Halloween, claiming that it glorifies violence and promotes superstition. But Halloween has been celebrated with monsters, ghosts, and costumes for decades, even for centuries: Our grandparents celebrated Halloween, and so did our parents; we dressed up in Halloween costumes when we were children. So obviously there's nothing wrong with our children celebrating Halloween with scary costumes.

103. Obviously we should not have unlimited violence and gore on television programs, especially during hours when children are likely to be watching. However, that doesn't mean that we have to completely eliminate violence from television. A workable solution is to allow unrestricted violent programming late at night, but to restrict violent programming during the hours when children are usually watching.

104. The laws protecting endangered species seem innocent enough. Let's protect endangered species: save the bald eagle and the whooping crane and the spotted owl. But of course that means protecting the natural habitats of those endangered animals, and that means restricting logging in some areas. And soon we find that not just the areas where the animals nest have to be protected, but also their foraging areas. And then that's not enough: We have to protect the habitats of the animals they feed on. And then we have to protect all the areas they fly over. But since bald eagles and whooping cranes fly over tremendous distances, that means that almost every place in the continental United States will become an endangered species habitat, with no construction, logging, road-building, or new houses allowed! So when you consider where these endangered species laws are really leading, it's clear that we should cut them off at the roots: We should drop all laws protecting endangered species, and not pass any new ones.

105. Ladies and gentlemen of the jury, the defendant, Alice Andrews, admits that she was in the apartment of Catherine Colvin on the night of December 15. Now, this case is really very simple. Either Alice had a right to be in that apartment, or she is guilty of breaking or entering. But certainly she had no right to be in the apartment: She was never invited in, she doesn't rent or own the apartment, and Catherine did not even know her. Obviously, then, the defendant had no right to be in the apartment, so we must conclude that she is guilty of breaking or entering.

106. Over the last 30 years in the United States, we have had a steady increase in the number of abortions performed. During the same period, there has also been a sharp increase in violent crime. The conclusion is inescapable: Abortion causes violent crime.

107. Some people claim that sending U.S. troops to the Middle East is like stepping into a deep swamp, filled with quicksand, where every step can pull the United States deeper and deeper into this terrible conflict. But that's ridiculous. After all, the Middle East is full of deserts, not swamps, and there probably isn't any quicksand in the whole area.

108. Columbus Day has been celebrated for many years in the United States, and became a federal holiday in 1937. While it celebrates the voyage of Christopher Columbus, for many years it has also

been a celebration of Italian American achievements and pride. But now some people want to elim-inate Columbus Day; they claim that it is wrong to celebrate Columbus, because in their view he is *not* worthy of celebration. They claim that he was particularly vicious toward the native peoples of the Americas, murdering many, and on at least one occasion burning alive a large group of Indians as part of a celebration. But we should reject the views of those who want to end Columbus Day: they seem to think that no Italians deserve to be honored, and that Italian American heritage is some-how disgraceful, and should not be celebrated.

109. During the 1996 election in the United States, Reform Party presidential candidate Ross Perot frequently made accusations against President Bill Clinton: that he was guilty of illegal campaign fundraising, that he had misused the powers of the presidency, that he had engaged in illegal real-estate deals. Clinton generally refused to comment on the charges, focusing instead on his plans for improving the U.S. economy and education. Perot attempted to use Clinton's silence on the charges as evidence against him, claiming that if someone was falsely accused of arson, auto theft, or bank robbery, then "every impulse in your body would be to speak out to clear your good name. If you were guilty, you would remain silent, knowing that anything you may say could be used later against you in a court of law."

110. You remember our old friend Spencer Garrett? He was a faithful fan of the Pittsburgh Steelers, and had bought season tickets every year for 40 years. Then when he got older, and trips to the stadium got to be just too much for him, he passed on his season tickets to his son, Arthur Garrett, and Arthur took his dad's seats at the stadium. Well, now our old senator, Ben Burgoyne, is getting too old to keep his Senate seat, and he wants to pass his seat on to his son, Ben Jr. And if that is Senator Burgoyne's choice, then I think it ought to be respected. After all, when Spencer wanted to pass on his Steelers seats to his son, we all thought that was fine; so now that Senator Burgoyne wants to pass on his Senate seat to his son, that also ought to be fine.

111. It is sometimes claimed that Christopher Columbus was a cruel and brutal man, who seemed to take pleasure in the torture and murder of many of the indigenous people whom he encoun-tered in his journeys of exploration. But those charges against Columbus are ridiculous. After all, Columbus was an extraordinarily brave explorer and a brilliant navigator and mariner, who took his small sailing ship on extraordinary voyages into uncharted oceans, risking his life in terrible storms and in unknown waters, and greatly increasing European knowledge of the American continents and islands. So clearly it is false that Columbus brutally mistreated the natives of those lands.

112. "It is absurd to deny money to religious schools on the grounds that it offends the rights of those who don't believe in such schools. Every other democratic society in the Western World sees no such violation of rights in partial support of denominational schools." (Andrew M. Greeley, Religion News Service, November 21, 1995)

113. Look, the defendant is charged with breaking or entering. The judge was very clear on what is required to be guilty of breaking or entering, and one of the necessary conditions for being guilty of breaking or entering is that the defendant must have intended to commit a felony when he broke into or entered the building. Now there's no question that the defendant broke into Jones house: The police caught him in the house, and he admitted that he broke down the door and entered the house. But he didn't intend to commit a felony. As he said, what he was intending to do was beat up Joe Jones, but he wasn't intending to commit a felony. In fact, I doubt that the defendant even knows what a felony is, so he certainly never intended to commit one.

114. Some people argue that capital punishment should be abolished because of the danger of making a mistake and executing an innocent person. But it would be ridiculous to stop capital punishment just because we sometimes make mistakes. If we applied that standard, then humans would never do anything!

Consider the U.S. program of space exploration. Mistakes were made, despite the best efforts of NASA scientists to avoid them: rockets exploded, satellites were lost, and in some tragic cases astronauts died. But just because mistakes were made, and innocent lives were lost, that did not mean that we should abandon the program of space exploration. NASA learned from its mistakes, and continued with its space program—and after all, NASA has had lots more successes than failures. Likewise, when we make mistakes in capital punishment, and innocent persons are executed, we must learn from those mistakes, and improve our capital punishment policies; but a few mistakes are no reason to abandon capital punishment altogether, no more than a few mistakes should lead us to abandon space exploration.

115. In order to properly consider health-care issues in the United States, we must start with a key question: Why is it that the United States has managed to develop the most efficient, fairest, and most economical health-care system in the entire world?

116. Members of the jury, the defendant, David Doyle, is charged with writing bad checks on an account he had closed a week before he wrote the checks. Now let's consider the possibilities. Either he wrote the bad checks by accident, or he did it on purpose. Of course we've all bounced a check now and then: We spend a bit more than we had in the account, we forget to write down one of the checks we wrote, or maybe we make a mistake in calculating the balance in our account. That sort of error or memory lapse happens to everyone. But when David Doyle wrote those bad checks, it was no accident, no error in calculation, no memory lapse. David Doyle had only one bank account; he himself closed it out, and took the entire balance of the account in cash just one week before he wrote the bad checks. And after closing the account, he himself wrote six checks, totaling over $3,000, on an account that he knew was empty. Members of the jury, either David Doyle wrote those checks because of forgetfulness and error, or he intentionally wrote bad checks on a closed account. And, as we just went over, he certainly didn't do it by error; so you must conclude that he did it intentionally.

117. There are those who favor guaranteed universal health care for every U.S. citizen. But their position is impossible and absurd. They want everyone in the United States to have complete and unlimited access to every medical procedure they want: not just vaccinations and basic health care and needed surgeries, but anything anyone wants in the way of medical services. So if you want seven pairs of designer eyeglasses—one for each day of the week—then that would be completely paid for. If you felt a bit tired, you could go and spend a week or two in a fancy health spa, again, completely paid for by the government, and guaranteed for everyone! And if you don't like the way your nose looks, you could have plastic surgery; and if you don't like your new nose, you could try another. How about a facelift? You could have one every year—twice a year, if you wish! But if you think medical costs are high now, just think of the incredible costs that would be involved in providing such services for everyone in the country. We are a wealthy nation, but no country could afford the costs of that kind of lavish and extravagant medical care. So the proposal of universal health care is obviously unworkable, impractical, and ridiculous.

118. It is sometimes claimed that if we start with *voluntary* active euthanasia—allowing the purposeful killing of a suffering, terminally ill patient at that patient's specific request—that will inevitably lead to *involuntary*, coerced killing of those who have no wish to be killed. But that is absurd. The gap between *voluntary* and *involuntary* is too wide to be bridged so easily. After all, when I ask someone to act as my agent in taking something from me that is mine to give, or in doing something to me that I am asking them to do, it does not lead to people taking things from me without my consent or doing things to me against my wishes. I voluntarily give my old truck to a charity, and ask the charity to collect the truck and take it away, and that doesn't mean that my voluntary act will increase the likelihood that the charity will move toward truck theft. I instruct my plastic surgeon to nip off the end of my nose, but that does not make it more likely that my surgeon will start slashing people against their wishes. It is one thing for my physician to act as my agent in giving me a drug that will cause the swift and painless death that I voluntarily request; it is something very different for my physician to kill me, against my own wishes, because he or she thinks I should be killed. There is no reason to think the former will lead to the latter.

119. "18,812,563 customers can't be wrong." Worldwide Auto Parts (billboard advertisement).

120. There is not a health-care crisis in the United States. If there were a severe shortage of hospitals and hospital beds, then the United States would have a health-care crisis. But there is no shortage of hospitals and hospital beds. If anything, there are too many.

121. DONNA: The way education is funded is just not fair to the children of our state. In some wealthy districts, schools spend more than three times as much on each student as in other, poorer districts. So the kids in the wealthier districts have smaller classes, better maintained and more modern school buildings, more computers, better libraries, newer books, more classes: In short, they get a better educational opportunity than the kids in the poorer districts. That's not equal education, it's not equal opportunity, it's not equal treatment—and it's not fair.

DANIEL: OK, so some students in some districts do have a lot more educational funding than do students in other districts. But that doesn't mean that they have unfair or unequal educational opportunities. After all, some students from the best-funded schools are dropouts, and students from the poorest schools sometimes do well in high school and then

> successfully finish college and even professional school. So there's nothing unfair about school funding.
>
> DONNA: Come on, Daniel, it is too unfair. Of course some of the kids from the poorer districts, who have unequal educational opportunities, wind up being more successful students than some of the kids from the wealthier districts. But that doesn't mean they both had fair educational opportunities. Look, suppose we have a race between the red team and the blue team. The red team is given perfectly fitted, light, and speedy track shoes; the blue team has to wear heavy, oversized combat boots. No doubt a few of the blue team racers may still finish ahead of some of the red team racers; but that doesn't change the fact that the race was unequal and unfair.

122. It would be wrong to require a specific prayer at graduation services, because we are a very diverse society and no prayer can satisfy everyone. However, it would also be a mistake to completely eliminate all opportunity for prayer from the graduation ceremony. A good, reasonable solution is to allow for a brief moment of silence at some point early in the ceremony, during which time people may pray or not, as they choose.

123. The problem with religion is that religion promotes intolerance and dogmatism. In Judaism, one of the basic principles is that "Thou shalt have no other God before Me"; and Christianity insists that salvation and truth come only through Jesus: "I am the way, the truth, and the light; no man cometh unto the Father but by me." Islam is just as bad: "There is one God, and Mohammed is His Prophet." All religions claim that they have a monopoly on the truth, and that all other religions and beliefs are wrong. Of course people may say that some religions are not like that: Hinduism, for example, teaches that there are many paths and approaches to God, and that we can learn from other religions; and Buddhism insists that each person must seek truth, and that religious doctrines should not be imposed on others. But Hinduism and Buddhism don't count: They aren't genuine religions, because all real religions claim to have the one and only truth, and all real religions insist that everyone must follow their specific doctrines and beliefs. Hinduism and Buddhism may be philosophies or thought systems, but they aren't real religions, because all real religions promote intolerance.

124. Recently, some states have passed laws requiring that teacher salaries be based on "merit," and in many of those cases the "merit" will be measured by the test scores of their students: Teachers whose students score highest on the standardized tests will receive raises; teachers whose students score lower do not get raises, may suffer pay cuts, and ultimately may be fired. Perhaps it makes sense to reward teachers on the basis of merit; but the proposed "merit" pay policies are terrible. Merit policies are like penalizing physicians who treat the most difficult cases: Linda is an outstanding cancer specialist who treats the most difficult cases, and manages to save a number of patients whose cancers were regarded as inevitably fatal, but who only has a "success" rate of 50%, may be the best oncologist in the state; Lawrence is a second-rate lazy physician, who does not keep up with research in the field and uses outdated treatment methods, but who treats only relatively healthy patients who are likely to eventually recover whether they get medical treatment or not, will have a very high "success" rate, even though he may well be the *worst* physician in the state. In the same manner, Andrew is a brilliant, creative, and dedicated teacher who teaches children in impoverished crime-ridden neighborhoods—children who may have very unstable family lives, who have never been read to, who have never had anyone help them or encourage them on their homework, where no one taught them colors or letters or numbers or the names of animals at a tender age, where they may not get good food and likely will suffer from inadequate health care and possibly from lead poisoning; and if Andrew manages to help 50% of his students pass the standardized tests, then he has done a splendid job. Anita teaches in a luxurious suburban school, and her students have been read to every day since they were toddlers, they have had the opportunity to travel, their parents expressed delight when they learned the names of colors and "what sound the cow makes" at a tender age, and taught them the alphabet song when they were three years old. Even if Anita is an abominable teacher, it is very likely that almost all her students will easily pass the same standardized tests. Just as we do not count the brilliant oncologist as a "bad doctor" because her "success rate" with her desperately ill patients is low, it is nonsense to judge teacher merit on standardized test scores without taking into account the condition of the students when they enter that teacher's classroom.

125. As use of the Internet by teenagers has steadily increased over the past decade, the teenage use of cocaine during the same period has steadily dropped. So whatever good or bad effects the Internet may have had, we should celebrate one very positive result: Internet use has reduced teenage drug abuse.

126. It is sometimes claimed that persons in prison have a right to private phone calls with their family and friends. But prisoners do not have a right to private phone calls, because people who have been convicted of crimes and are serving time in prison have no rights whatsoever.

127. Certainly there was no conspiracy to assassinate President John Kennedy. After all, the Warren Commission investigated the assassination of Kennedy, and they reported that Lee Harvey Oswald acted alone, and that there was no conspiracy. So either Oswald really did act alone, or the entire Warren Commission lied and purposefully covered up an assassination conspiracy. But it makes no sense to suppose that all the Warren Commission members would have lied and taken part in a massive cover-up, and that their lies and the cover-up would never have been exposed. So we must conclude that the Warren Commission report is true, and that there was no assassination conspiracy.

128. Some people in this country favor legalizing marijuana, but it would be a dreadful mistake to accept their proposals. They want to make marijuana use legal, and they want to remove all criminal penalties and all restrictions on the sale and use of marijuana. If they have their way, there would be no restrictions whatsoever on marijuana use: Vending machines would supply packs of marijuana cigarettes to anyone with a few quarters to feed the machines, and marijuana would be available without restriction to high school and even to elementary school students. Children would no longer have milk and cookies after school, but instead would light up a couple of joints. And marijuana sellers could legally offer free samples to children, and advertise their products during Saturday morning cartoons on TV. When we look closely, then, at the program of those who favor legalization of marijuana, it is obvious what a disastrous program it really is.

129. Rachel argues that it is wrong for humans to eat animals for food since meat-eating is a luxury and not a necessity for humans, and because such indulgence in luxury cannot justify the suffering imposed on the slaughtered animals. But Rachel is wearing leather shoes, a leather belt, and carrying a matching leather handbag: all luxuries, not necessities; and they are all made from slaughtered animals. So Rachel's arguments against eating meat are undermined by her own actions!

130. There are people who want to raise doubts about the reliability of eyewitness testimony. They note that eyewitness identifications are often erroneous, and that juries tend to give eyewitness testimony and identifications much more weight than they should, since jurors are often unaware of all the ways eyewitness testimony can go wrong. But it is a terrible mistake to cast doubts on the use of eyewitness testimony in court. Our courts and our juries have relied on eyewitness testimony for literally hundreds of years, and eyewitness testimony has been a central part of our justice system during all that time. Thus the testimony and identifications of eyewitnesses must keep their honored roles in our system of justice.

131. Everything that happens shows the generous loving hand of God in our midst. Of course sometimes there are events that seem harsh and terrible, and we can see no good coming out of them: the bombing in Oklahoma City, for example, or the crash of a jetliner. But those also show the loving and generous kindness of God, because they show that some of our infinite God's kindnesses are inscrutable to mere human understanding.

132. It is sometimes suggested that we should allow the buying and selling of body parts, such as kidneys and hearts, which are used in transplant surgery. At first glance it may sound like a fairly innocent way of increasing the supply of organs for transplant—organs that can save lives, and that are always in chronically short supply. Dear old Uncle Joe dies and Aunt Sarah sells his heart and kidneys to pay for the funeral and perhaps help their grandchildren get through college. Or Uncle Joe himself sells the organs, and gives the buyer the right to collect those organs after his death. But innocent as it sounds, we should never take that step of allowing the sale of body parts. For once we have done that, we are taking the view that the body and its parts can simply be treated as property. Maybe Uncle Joe had some loans that he didn't manage to repay before he died. Then the bank could come in and claim his property for repayment of those debts—Uncle Joe's car, but also Uncle Joe's heart and kidneys. And just as it wouldn't matter whether or not Uncle Joe (or his widow, Aunt Sarah) wanted his car taken, likewise it wouldn't matter whether he wanted his organs taken: the bank that held the loan could simply claim them. And it gets worse. Suppose you run up a credit card debt that you can't pay. The credit card company seizes your car, but that doesn't cover the debt. Now they can demand your heart and your kidneys and your corneas for payment of the debt. And it doesn't matter that you haven't finished using them. After all, you hadn't finished using your car, either. So once we see what the sale of organs could lead to—persons being butchered just for the price of their organs—it's clear that we should never allow the sale of body parts.

133. Ladies and gentlemen of the jury, the defendant is charged with attempted murder. You have listened to all the evidence that we have presented, and now we ask you to find the defendant, Pierre Boudreaux, guilty as charged. As you heard from several witnesses, Pierre became very angry when his girlfriend dropped him and started seeing Jean Arbonne. Pierre swore that he would kill Jean, and he went to a shop that sells voodoo materials. He bought a doll to represent Jean, and even put some of Jean's hair on the doll. And then he went through an elaborate voodoo ritual and curse that was supposed to cause Jean to suddenly die. Of course, the curse didn't work, and we are not really surprised that it didn't work: we don't believe that voodoo rituals have any power. But what we believe doesn't matter here. The point is that Pierre Boudreaux *did* believe that the curse would work, and that it would kill Jean; and so Pierre did attempt to murder Jean, and you must find him guilty of attempted murder.

You remember that Pierre's defense attorney argued that since the voodoo ritual had no real power to kill, Pierre should not be found guilty of attempted murder. But just because Pierre's murder attempt was faulty, that doesn't change the fact that it was still an attempted murder. Look, suppose I plan to kill you, and I go out and get a pistol. I think the pistol is loaded, and I believe that it will cause your death, and I aim the pistol at you and pull the trigger. Now in fact the pistol is not loaded, so of course it doesn't fire. But I still *attempted* to murder you, even though my attempt was flawed. I can't murder you with an empty pistol, and Pierre couldn't murder Jean with a voodoo curse, but we can both *attempt* to murder. So you should find Pierre guilty of the crime he committed: the attempted murder of Jean Arbonne.

134. The United States spends an enormous amount of money on health care: far more than any other country in the world. Now, *if* the United States had an *efficient* health-care system, then we would *not* have a high infant mortality rate. But the United States *does* have a high infant mortality rate (one of the highest in the industrialized world). So obviously the United States does not have an efficient health-care system.

135. We should not give students credit for taking online courses. Education has always involved personal, face-to-face contact between teacher and student. From the time that Plato taught Aristotle, and Aristotle taught Alexander, right through to the medieval universities, and all the way up to the present, we have always had students actually meeting with their professors, with questions and answers going back and forth, in situations where the students and teachers can see, hear, and even touch one another. And now people want to abandon all that, and have students take courses online, without ever actually meeting their professor or even their fellow students. We've had face-to-face education for well over 2,000 years, and I don't think we should let online courses change that.

136. Well, researchers in England have now cloned a sheep! We must put a total stop to this cloning business right now: all cloning must be banned. Just consider what will happen if we allow cloning to continue. It won't stop with cloning sheep, cows, and mice. It's an easy step from there to cloning humans. And once we begin cloning humans, it will lead to all sorts of terrible abuses. Basketball coaches will be hiring biologists to clone whole teams of Michael Jordans and Shaquille O'Neals; orchestras will clone copies of Isaac Stern. And lots of parents will want "their" kids to grow up to be famous political leaders, so you'll see thousands of duplicate Bill Clintons, George Bushes, Jesse Jacksons, and Margaret Thatchers; other parents will want their kids to be outstanding lawyers, so there will be a huge crop of Marcia Clarks and Johnnie Cochrans. Soon the entire population will be made up of copies of a few "ideal types"; and then we will have lost the genetic diversity that makes successful evolutionary development and adaptation possible. So we must stop all cloning immediately.

137. Now that President Hazim has announced his upcoming retirement, Western State University will soon begin the search for a new president. Some WSU students are pushing for more student involvement on the search committee, in the evaluation of candidates, and in the final selection of WSU's new president. But what they are asking for is completely unreasonable. What they want is total student control of the selection of a new president, with no input from faculty, administration, or the board of trustees. They want the student government to have complete control over how the position is advertised, who is interviewed, and who is finally hired. But they are obviously forgetting that they are not the only ones who have an interest in who the new president will be. If they have their way, the faculty, administration, and trustees will be left out of the search process altogether, and that's obviously not fair.

138. Since the United States is no longer locked in a nuclear arms race, it would be silly to keep building more and more nuclear weapons. But of course, that's no reason to go to the other extreme and start dismantling our nuclear arsenal. The right course, obviously, is to simply maintain our current nuclear warheads in good working order, but not build more.

139. The North State University Board of Trustees should be allowed to hold closed meetings when they wish, because obviously the board of trustees should be able to meet confidentially when that is their preference.

140. Criminal acts by juveniles are a serious problem in our country. Children who are 12, 13, or 14 years old—and often younger!—are committing assaults, robberies, even murders. Either we must prosecute those juveniles as full adults, and when they are convicted lock them up in maximum-security prisons, and perhaps even execute them; or we have to just ignore the problem of juvenile crime, and do nothing at all to control violent crime by juvenile offenders. Since we obviously cannot ignore the problem of violent crimes committed by juveniles, it follows that we must start treating juvenile offenders just like adults.

141. Joan claims that health care is like education: that a decent education is essential for equal opportunity, and likewise that decent health care is also essential for equal opportunity. So, since we believe that there should be universal access to a decent education for every citizen, we must conclude that there should be universal access to decent health care for every citizen. But Joan's analogy is ridiculous. After all, decent health care often involves prescribing drugs; and you can't educate people by giving them drugs.

142. As unemployment rates in the United States and Europe remain high, there is much controversy about how to create new jobs for all the people who desperately need them, and a wide variety of economics and financial experts are proposing a wide variety of solutions. Some believe that we should cut government spending and regulation, and then private employers will create many new jobs. Others claim that the big problem is that jobs are being shipped to other countries with lower wages, and that we should restrict trade in order to prevent such job losses. But Paul Krugman, who teaches economics at Princeton University and won the Nobel Prize in Economics, maintains that in order to increase the number of jobs we need to make a bigger investment in education and in public works projects that rebuild our bridges and highways and rail system. Professor Krugman is one of the top authorities on economics and the economic system, so clearly his solution to the problem of creating more jobs is the path we should follow.

143. Some animal rights advocates insist that it is wrong to inflict suffering on animals such as chimpanzees in order to conduct medical research that might provide benefits to humans. But the animal rights position is obviously wrong, since it can never be wrong to cause the suffering or even death of an animal in order to provide medical benefits for humans.

144. Some people think that the Cleveland Indians' logo (the "Chief Wahoo" cartoon of an Indian with a huge grin) is offensive to Native Americans, and that the Cleveland team should find another logo and change their team name. But obviously it would be going too far to demand that the Cleveland team completely change both its name and its logo, uniforms and all. On the other hand, we should not be completely insensitive to the demands of Native Americans who find the name and logo offensive. A good, reasonable solution is to allow the team to use "Indians" as a name, but get rid of the "Chief Wahoo" logo, which many Native Americans find particularly offensive.

145. In 1999, Senator Mitch McConnell, chairman of the National Republican Senatorial Committee, mailed a fundraising letter to several thousand people. The letter conducted a "survey" on how people felt about the danger of nuclear attack by North Korea on cities of the United States (presumably most thought it was a bad idea), and asked for donations to "protect our country from a potentially devastating nuclear attack."

    Some advocates of campaign-finance reform expressed outrage that the specter of nuclear war was being used for political fundraising, calling it an effort to play on people's fears in order to increase political donations. Steven Law, the executive director of the committee that mailed the fundraising letter, responded to the criticisms:

    This is standard fare for direct mail, and it is a good deal less incendiary than some mailings I've seen. These letters have been a staple of direct mail fund-raising drives for years. (Based on an article by Don van Natta, Jr., *New York Times*, September 4, 1999)

146. Some people criticize the United States for its huge and still increasing gap between rich and poor—a gap that is now the largest of any industrialized nation. But if we tried to make all U.S. citizens exactly equal in wealth and income, then that would have terrible effects on the U.S. economy, and probably leave everyone worse off; and the sort of government interference and oversight

that would be required to enforce strict equality of wealth and income would be intolerable. So obviously the citizens of the United States are better off leaving our economic system and wealth distribution as it is.

147. Recently Congressman Peter King, New York Republican, held a congressional hearing on the dangers of terrorism among American Muslims. The hearings were very controversial, because they seemed to imply that American Muslims posed a special terrorist threat, and that we should be suspicious of American citizens who are Muslims. Critics of the hearings pointed out that American Muslims have not supported terrorism, and that in fact American Muslims—like other American citizens—have worked hard to combat terrorism, and have sometimes been the victims of terrorism (such as Mohammed Salman Hamdani, a medical technician who lost his life in heroic efforts to save victims of the World Trade Center attack). Other critics argued that it was wrong to focus a terrorism hearing on American Muslims, when in fact the white supremacist groups have been by far the greatest source of terrorist acts by American citizens. Representative Dan Lungren, a California Republican, insisted that there was nothing wrong with focusing a terrorism hearing on American Muslims, rather than on the broader threat of terrorist groups such as white supremacists; Lungren pointed out that when there was a House hearing on youth gang violence, "We didn't talk about non-youth gang violence," and so in a hearing on the threat of American Muslim terrorism we shouldn't talk about threats from non-Muslims.

148. It would be a grave mistake to pass a constitutional amendment banning the burning of the American flag. Now obviously many of us are deeply disturbed when a protester burns the American flag; but there is no doubt that that is a form of political protest, a voicing of deep disgust with American policies—and unpopular and distasteful as that protest may be, we have always held fast to the principle that all citizens have a right to express even the most offensive and disgusting political views with protests: It is part of our basic commitment to freedom of speech, protected by the First Amendment of our Bill of Rights. But if we pass an amendment to the Constitution that bans the burning of the American flag, then we are making a basic exception to the principle of freedom of speech. And once we have made one exception, it will be easier to make others: Some people are, understandably, deeply offended by pro-Nazi propaganda, and may wish to ban such speech. Others will want to silence those who advocate communism. And once we make one exception to our principle of freedom of speech, it will be difficult to stop there. If we pass laws banning the burning of the American flag, why not also a law banning the burning of the U.S. Constitution? Or a law banning any satirical use of our national anthem? The problem is, once the basic principle of freedom of speech is compromised, it is more tempting to try to ban any speech that we don't like. And in our highly diverse society, there will always be views that are extremely unpopular, and that some people want to ban. The dangerous, long-term result of a constitutional amendment banning flag-burning is likely to be a threat to the freedom to express any unpopular political view; and when that happens, freedom of speech will no longer be one of our cherished liberties.

149. There are some people who believe we should stop killing animals for food and become vegetarians. But asking humans to stop eating meat really doesn't make sense. After all, humans have been meat-eaters for thousands of years. The earliest recorded dietary laws placed some restrictions on what *type* of meat could and could not be eaten, but they clearly approved of meat eating. And obviously, for thousands of years before any written history or formalized dietary rules, humans had been eating meat from a wide variety of animals. And in the thousands of years since those dietary laws, humans have continued to eat meats from many different animals, prepared in many different styles. As we look through human history, we find many different cooking styles, but almost always one of the main items that was cooked and eaten—the most important and most valued thing on the menu—was the meat dish. Sometimes the meat dish has been wild boar, and sometimes meat from a deer or a water buffalo or a rabbit or an alligator, and sometimes the meat is a thick juicy burger; but humans have always eaten meat, and we should continue to do so.

150. For our trip to the critical thinking conference in Toronto, we should certainly leave all the driving to Janice. She grew up in Toronto, so she knows the city well; and she did both her undergraduate and graduate work in Los Angeles, so she is certainly familiar with driving in heavy city traffic. Furthermore, she has been driving for over 20 years, and she has *never* been involved in an accident, and never received a ticket! She has excellent eyesight, good reflexes, and she would absolutely never drink and drive: she refuses to drink even a small glass of wine if she has to drive anywhere in the next hour. She is committed to safe driving, and will not talk on a cell phone while she drives—

much less text while driving! Janice is a safe, conscientious driver, and she should be the person driving our van to Toronto.

151. The governors and legislatures in a number of states have recently passed laws that block collective bargaining by state and local government employees, such as firefighters, police officers, and teachers. Many people complain that denying public employees the right to form unions and bargain collectively is a violation of human rights, in particular the right to join together to have some voice in their own working conditions and to protect themselves against exploitation; they point out that Article 23 of the United Nations Universal Human Rights Declaration recognizes collective bargaining as a basic human right. But it is simply not true that state laws blocking collective bargaining undercut human rights. Many states are in severe financial difficulties, and must find ways to reduce their costs. By blocking collective bargaining, it becomes easier for states to reduce wages and cut pension benefits of state workers, and that is one way that states can save money and balance their budgets. Cutting collective bargaining is a useful step toward balancing state budgets, not an attack on human rights.

152. Drug companies sometimes run multiple studies of a drug they are proposing for market, and if a study indicates that the drug is ineffective or harmful they simply put the study back in their files and never publish it, and instead only release studies that indicate the drug is safe and effective. Critics have complained about this practice, but there is really nothing wrong with it. Suppose that you are trying to come up with a new recipe for a cake, and you try half a dozen recipes, and five of the recipes give you a cake that tastes awful, but the sixth recipe gives you a cake that tastes delicious. In that case, you wouldn't be obligated to tell everyone about all the bad recipes; you would only publish the recipe that produces a good result. Likewise, there is nothing wrong with the drug company publishing only the studies that yield good results, and hiding the other studies.

153. Increasing taxes to balance the federal budget is a bad economic policy, because economic policies that raise taxes are policies that harm the economic well-being of the country.

154. Ladies and gentlemen of the jury, consider the case against my client. He is accused of hiring John Jefferson to plant a bomb in the car of Waylon Wiley. Now, there's no doubt that John Jefferson did indeed plant a bomb in the car of Wiley, and that the bomb exploded and killed Wiley. Jefferson admits that he planted the bomb. But what reason is there to believe that the defendant hired Jefferson? Just this: the testimony of John Jefferson. Now, how reliable is that testimony? How reliable is the testimony of a man who admits that he has lied under oath on many occasions, who is now testifying against the defendant in the hope of receiving a reduced sentence for his own crime, and who has lived his whole life dedicated to crime, deceit, and money, and who has never shown the least regard for decency and honesty? You wouldn't trust John Jefferson to sell you a used car; don't trust him to sell you these desperate lies against the defendant. You can't take the word of a man like John Jefferson; and since you can't trust John Jefferson, you have no grounds for finding the defendant guilty.

155. Certainly Jones is not guilty of breaking or entering into West Building. After all, as a registered student at the University, Jones had permission to be in West Building. And if Jones had permission to be in West Building, then he cannot be guilty of breaking or entering into West Building.

156. Recently the voters in our county passed a law requiring a Christian prayer at all public school graduation ceremonies. Some people claim that the law is fair because it was passed democratically. And it was passed democratically—a majority of the voters favored it—but that doesn't make it fair. Just because something is done democratically is no indication of its fairness. After all, the vast majority of us are right-handed. Now suppose that we right-handers began to develop a deep dislike of left-handers. It gets so bad we propose a law banning all left-handers from attending public schools and colleges, and banning all left-handers from holding public office. That law would be passed *democratically*—but it certainly would not be *fair*. So maybe the law requiring a Christian prayer at graduation is fair, or maybe it's unfair, but one thing is clear: Just because it was passed democratically, and a majority of people favor it, certainly doesn't make it fair.

157. Thomas Jefferson always insisted on the vital importance of small farmers and small merchants to the well-being of American democracy. Jefferson argued that small farmers and small merchants would have a strong stake in the success of the country, that they would be independent thinkers who would not be controlled by special interests and so they could critically evaluate government policies, and that they would give long-term stability to both the economy and the government.

But before you sign on to Jefferson's argument for small farmers and small business owners, you should know this: for many years Jefferson had sexual relations with one of his slaves, Sally Hemings, who had several children by Jefferson; and Jefferson actually kept his *own children*—the children born to Sally Hemings—as *slaves*. Anyone who could enslave his own children is not someone whose arguments can be taken seriously.

158. Some people have criticized our new children's cereal, Cotton Candy Crunch. They say that Cotton Candy Crunch is not a good children's cereal because it is loaded with sugar, high in salt, and contains no fiber. But Cotton Candy Crunch is in fact a very good cereal. Kids love it, and there are many adults who find it very tasty.

159. Some people suggest that distributing condoms to high schools students encourages them to be sexually active. But of course it doesn't; instead, it only encourages those who decide to be sexually active to practice safe sex. Claiming that condoms encourage students to be sexually active is like claiming that seatbelts encourage students to ride in cars.

160. This person is surely a true messenger from God, because he performs wonderful miracles. And clearly the works he performs are genuine miracles, and not cheap, deceitful tricks, for no true messenger of God would stoop to using cheap tricks.

161. There is a lot of debate over whether we should have a large tax cut, and whether such a tax cut would be good for our economy. But recently Dr. Lynn Akkad, a biochemistry professor at MIT who was recently awarded the Nobel Prize for her work on genetic links to cancer, stated that she firmly believes that a large tax cut is the best way to keep our economy from sliding into a recession. That should settle the issue: if the brilliant Dr. Akkad favors a tax cut, it must be a good idea.

162. Look, it's not at all fair for you guys to raise my insurance rates; after all, I'm a very safe and cautious driver. OK, it's true that I was responsible for four small traffic accidents during the last 2 years, and have received several tickets for reckless driving. But all those things happened when I wasn't really driving: I was distracted by something, or I was daydreaming or talking on my cellular phone. So those don't really count as driving. So when I drive, I am always a very safe and cautious driver.

163. Teenagers who attend religious services with their parents every week are much less likely to commit crimes than are teenagers who rarely or never attend religious services with their parents. The evidence is clear: When parents take their teenagers to religious services regularly, it prevents teenage crime.

164. Look, we were faced with a tough choice. Either we carry out a full-scale military attack on Iraq and occupy the country, or we allow Saddam Hussein to build nuclear weapons, biological weapons, and any other weapons of mass destruction that he pleases. But of course we could not allow Saddam to build such weapons of mass destruction. That would have posed a threat to the United States, and also would have destabilized the Middle East. So we were forced to launch a military attack against Iraq.

165. John Walker Lindh was accused of fighting against the U.S. in Afghanistan, a charge he denied. But just remember this: he was an armed fighter in Afghanistan. And either he was fighting *for* the U.S. forces, or he was fighting against them. Now certainly he was not fighting in support of the U.S. forces. So obviously we must conclude that he was indeed fighting against the United States.

166. I recommend we hire Dr. Ruth Salidas as the new dean of Arts and Sciences. Dr Salidas has a brilliant publication record, and recently won a national book award. Also, she has excellent administrative experience as Chair of the English Department at Michigan State, and both her colleagues and her students at Michigan State agree that she is a person of great integrity and warmth who has innovative ideas and a cooperative spirit. Dr. Salidas is bright, articulate, energetic, and well organized, and she would be the perfect person to lead our School of Arts and Sciences.

167. Okay, so Bill now says that he has turned over a new leaf, and he's through with Barbara, and he'll never cheat on you again. But girl, if you take that man back, you're crazy. That's exactly the same thing that he said last month when you caught him with Julie, and 2 months before that, when he spent the night with Ginger. And you remember after he had that affair with Sandra, he swore that was the last time, and that he would be faithful and true forever. That guy is a liar and a cheat, and you're better off without him.

168. Some people suggest that chimpanzees have higher intelligence: that they can make plans, solve problems, and even use language. But clearly chimps do not have higher intelligence, because humans are the only animals that have higher intelligence.

169. Some students claim that when a professor cancels a class—due to sickness, or whatever—students should receive a tuition refund for that class. If a rock concert is cancelled because the lead guitarist is sick, those who bought tickets get a refund; so students should likewise get a refund when their classes are cancelled. But that's a bad comparison: professors are lousy guitarists, and no one would buy a ticket to hear a bunch of professors play a rock concert.

170. Some people want to guarantee health care for every citizen of the United States. It may sound like a good idea at first glance, but when you think about it carefully, it would obviously have terrible consequences. Because if you start by guaranteeing every citizen health care, then next people will want a guarantee of decent housing, and then a guarantee of food, and soon a guarantee of a good job, a new car, a beautiful lawn, a yearly vacation cruise, and stylish clothes, and before you know it everyone will expect to be given everything, and no one will want to work for anything.

171. Some students think that if they suffer a special hardship during the semester—a prolonged illness, for example—that makes it impossible for them to complete their coursework successfully on time, then they should be allowed to drop the course without any penalties. But what they want is clearly wrong. After all, if you hire a construction company to build a building for you, and they agree to complete the building by a specific date, then if someone at the construction company gets sick and the building is not completed on time, they can't just drop their contract: they have to pay a penalty. Likewise, students who don't complete their coursework on time should be penalized, even if they couldn't complete the work because they were sick.

172. There are several U.S. citizens suspected of planning terrorist acts who are being held in U.S. prisons—and they have not been charged with any crime, they are not allowed to see a lawyer or judge, they do not get to hear the evidence against them, and they are being held in prison indefinitely (perhaps for many years) without any real proof of guilt. Some people complain that this violates basic principles of the U.S. Constitution, and that it is simply wrong to imprison citizens without a fair trial. Apparently those people who complain about such practices believe that we should just let the terrorists do whatever they like and kill as many people as they want without taking any action to stop them.

173. Philosophy has been a central and prominent area of study since the earliest universities were started many centuries ago, and during all that time university studies have included philosophy. So it is clearly desirable that we continue to make courses in philosophy a central part of the university curriculum.

174. Obviously priests should not be allowed to sexually abuse children repeatedly and continue in the priesthood. But we shouldn't go to the other extreme and force people out of the priesthood for a single case of sexual abuse. Clearly the best policy, then, is to allow priests to continue in the priesthood if they have been guilty of only one case of sexual abuse, but remove them if they are repeat offenders.

175. Alyssa Squires is a candidate for Common Pleas Judge. She holds a law degree from Yale University, and she has been a leading attorney in the Mahoning Valley for many years. She has donated her valuable time and expertise to United Way, the Sierra Club, and the Mahoning Public Legal Foundation; and she has frequently taken on cases, without pay, for impoverished people who needed legal help. She has been endorsed by the Bar Association, and she has fought against corruption in the Valley for many years. She is brilliant, dedicated, and honest; and if elected she will be a fair, just, and hard-working judge for the people of Mahoning County. I strongly urge you to vote for Alyssa Squires for Judge.

176. If Homer Simpson works at the Springfield Nuclear Power Plant, then the Springfield Nuclear Power Plant is not safe. So clearly the Springfield Nuclear Power Plant is not safe, because Homer Simpson does work there.

177. JOE: Spring in the Mahoning Valley is wonderful: warm spring days, bright sunshine, birds singing, and flowers blooming.
JOAN: Are you crazy? Spring in the Mahoning Valley is cold, grey, rainy, muddy, windy, and often snowy—and any flowers foolish enough to bloom are quickly frost-bitten.
JOE: Well, sure there are some days like that; but those cold rainy days aren't real spring days. The real spring days are the warm sunny days, filled with birds and flowers, and the real spring is wonderful in the Mahoning Valley.

178. There is now controversy about sending children ages 10–12 to adult prisons. But when you think about it, locking children up in high-security prisons is not as bad as it sounds. After all, parents have long punished their children by requiring them to stay in their rooms, or "grounding" them. And if we think it's OK for a parent to force a misbehaving child to stay in his or her room, then we should have no objection to a judge forcing a misbehaving child to stay in a prison cell.

179. Why is critical thinking the best course offered at the university? Is it the witty and charming professor? Or perhaps the fascinating textbook? Or the high quality of the students who enroll in the class?

180. Robert is guilty of negligent homicide only if he did not exercise due caution. But Robert is a careful driver, and he was exercising due caution. So we must find Robert not guilty of negligent homicide.

181. Stan Stohlmeyer has argued that we should have a very strict policy against plagiarism at North State University. He argues that plagiarism cheats students who actually do their own work, because their original work is then graded in comparison to high-quality stolen work. And he says that when plagiarism is not punished, it becomes more widespread, and that puts pressure on more and more students to cheat in order to compete. And finally, he argues that if it becomes known that plagiarism is common at North State, employers will be more suspicious of all North State students, and so even the honest students will be under suspicion and have a harder time getting jobs. His arguments sounded pretty good, until I learned from one of Stan's roommates that Stan buys all of his term papers from an online term paper service! So much for Stan's arguments against plagiarism!

182. Some people are concerned that the U.S. balance of payments is so large; that is, they are concerned because the United States spends much more on imported goods than we are paid for our exported goods. They suggest that we restrict imports in order to reduce the balance of payments. But Michael Kinsley claims that we should not be so concerned with the balance of payments, for that is not the real problem:

    The balance of payments is a measure of economic health, not a cause of it; restricting imports to reduce the deficit is like sticking the thermometer in ice water to bring down a feverish temperature. (This example is from Michael Kinsley, "Keep Trade Free," *The New Republic,* Vol. 188, no. 14 [April 11, 1983], p. 11.)

183. Christianity is a religion of peace, tolerance, kindness, and mercy, and Christians are tolerant and peaceful people. Of course some Christians participated in the Inquisition, in which Jews, nonbelievers, and heretics were tortured and killed. At other times Christians went on Crusades into the Middle East, and slaughtered thousands of Muslims. And then there was the period when Christians were burning or hanging people suspected of witchcraft, and there were also decades of brutal war between Protestants and Catholics. But the Christians who did such things were not really Christians, because genuine Christians would never commit such warlike and brutal acts.

184. Some critics have claimed that the current tax cut is unfair because by far the largest share of the tax cut goes to the wealthiest 5% of Americans, while the lower and middle classes just get crumbs. But the tax cut is certainly *not* unfair! After all, we have been in an economic slump for over a year, and a tax cut will help stimulate the economy. And tax cuts can also help simplify the tax code, and make it easier to file tax returns. And when the tax cuts were passed, the government had a budget surplus, so it was a good time for a tax cut. So obviously there is nothing unfair about the current tax cut.

185. Recently there have been arguments about abolishing the inheritance tax, as some politicians want to do. But Bill Gates has recently argued that the United States should *increase* the inheritance tax. Gates argues that by having a larger tax on inherited wealth, we could provide fair opportunities for those children who suffer the severe disadvantages of inadequate health care and inferior education; and Gates also argues that allowing people to inherit enormous wealth that they haven't earned makes them lazy and less ambitious. And notice this: Bill Gates is one of the richest people in the world, and an increase in the inheritance tax would greatly increase his *own* taxes. So when Bill Gates argues that we should increase the inheritance tax, we must count that as a very strong argument.

186. Some critical thinking students think that they should be able to use a list of all the argument forms on the exam. Professor Adams says they should *not* be allowed to use such a list: She insists that students having a list of the argument forms would be like a surgeon using a list of steps and instructions during surgery. But Professor Adams's analogy doesn't work. After all, surgery is a matter of life and death, and critical thinking exams aren't life-and-death activities.

187. Janice argues that instead of electing judges, they should be appointed by a special judicial commission: a commission of nine distinguished former judges, attorneys, and good, honest citizens who have been selected by the governor, the state Senate, and the state House. That way, Janice says, we could get away from the nasty attacks made on judicial candidates and people would have more confidence in our judges; and furthermore, she argues, judges could be more fair and impartial and pass judgments they believe are just and right, rather than worrying about how their judgments will play on Election Day. But Janice's arguments about justice and impartiality are just a smoke screen. Actually, she worked hard for a judicial candidate who got trounced in the general election, and she's really bitter about the whole election process. Her only real reason for wanting judges appointed by a special commission instead of being elected is because she's angry about this candidate losing the election. If her candidate had won, she would be singing the praises of judicial elections.

17

❖ ❖ ❖

Thinking Critically about Statistics

Statistical reasoning is vitally important. Without statistical calculations, medicine would be at the mercy of quacks who promote useless or harmful "cures." Snake oil promoters can always tell dramatic stories of a few people who "recovered" (probably from placebo effect, perhaps by natural remission) while under their "treatment." Only by making exact statistical analyses can we determine that any new treatment (perhaps successful in 75% of the cases) is significantly more promising than some old treatment, which perhaps works for only 60% of patients. Without careful statistical study a few dramatic "successes" for an old treatment, coupled with touching accounts of the failures of a new treatment, might lead us to reject a promising new therapy.

Unfortunately, many people, particularly politicians and advertisers, lean on statistics the way a drunk leans on a streetlamp: for support, rather than illumination. Often we must sift out the chaff before finding the valuable grain of truth in statistical reasoning. This chapter is not intended as a substitute for a good course in statistics, but it should help you see through some common statistical deceptions. If you have had the benefit of a statistics course, you may still discover some subtle statistical tricks that sometimes deceive even knowledgeable statisticians.

ALL CHILDREN ARE ABOVE AVERAGE

Averages are a common source of statistical confusion. Professor Longstreet has a 10-point grading scale: 60–69 is a D, 70–79 a C, 80–89 a B, and above 90 is an A. I squeaked by with a 70 on the first exam, soared up to a 71 on the second exam, and then the bottom fell out: a 40 on the final. Professor Longstreet informs me that I have a D for the course. "That's not fair, Professor," I reply. "After all, my average grade was a C. So obviously I have a C average, and I should get a C in the course." And in fact, I do have a C average, in *two* senses of the term: a grade of C is both the *median* and the *mode* of my test scores. That is, speaking of "the average" is *ambiguous* (as discussed in Chapter 9) since there are three different things that it might mean.[1] First, there is the *arithmetic mean*, or just "mean," for short. The mean is what

Skewed Averages

Several years ago, there was some very interesting data about graduates of the University of North Carolina at Chapel Hill. If we look at UNC alumni who graduated 20 years earlier, which undergraduate major do you suppose had the highest average income? I guessed philosophy, but that was wrong. Finance, maybe? Or possibly chemistry? Perhaps economics? None of the above. It was *geography*. But before you switch majors, you should consider one thing: Geography is a relatively small department at Chapel Hill, with few majors, and it produces very few graduates. And the year in question happened to be the graduation year for one of the better known geography majors: Michael Jordan. When you add in his annual income of several million dollars, and then divide it by the small number of graduates for that year, you get a *very* high—and very misleading—average: the *mean*, in this case, is not very helpful. The median would be considerably more informative.

you get when you add all the values together, and then divide by the number of values. If there are seven people in the class, and they scored 100, 95, 90, 85, 80, 80, and 16 on the exam, then the arithmetic mean is 78. That is the mean, but in this case the mean is not very helpful: It makes the grades on the exam look somewhat lower than they actually were. In fact, most people did quite well on the exam, while one poor sod had a rough day. When the distribution of values is skewed—as it is in this example, in which one score is much lower—the arithmetic mean can be deceptive. It would be more informative to report the *median* as the "average": that is, the value in the middle, in this case 85 (three students scored higher, and three scored lower). Or the *mode* might be a useful measure: the score that occurred most often (in this case, the score of 80).

While it is convenient to have these three measures, there is also great potential for deception. In 1999, the Republicans in the U.S. House of Representatives proposed an "across the board" tax cut, which would have provided several hundred dollars in annual tax cuts to the "average American." True, if you use the arithmetic mean; true, but very misleading, for almost half the tax cut would go to the top 1%, those with incomes over $300,000 a year: they would have received annual tax cuts of $40,000 a year, often more; while the working poor, who work for minimum wage with no benefits, would have received a tax cut of only $15 a year. When a distribution is tilted so heavily in one direction, claims about the "average" can hide that tilt. Information about the median or mode would be much more helpful; but then, if you are trying to pass a tax package in which half the money would go to the richest 1%, you aren't eager to help most people understand it.

Though the mean is the measure most often abused, the others also offer possibilities of distortion. For example, imagine a small company whose workers make the following incomes: $900,000, $850,000, $800,000, $750,000, $50,000, $15,000, $12,000, $12,000, and $12,000. If they report that their "average" salary is $50,000 (and that their workers thereby receive good, solid, comfortable, middle-class incomes), this will

A Misleading "Average"

George W. Bush pushed the huge tax cut package in his "economic growth package" by claiming that: "Under this plan 92 million Americans receive an average tax cut of $1,083. That's fair. Twenty-three million small-business owners across America will receive an average income tax rate cut of $2,042. That matters." Literally true, but a very misleading use of averages, since the tax cut is weighted heavily toward the wealthy, which brings the "average tax cut" way up. It turns out that those in the middle fifth of the income spectrum would receive a tax cut of only $256. But the "average" is much higher, since the top 1% would receive tax cuts of $24,100, and those with annual incomes above $1 million would receive tax cuts averaging $90,200. And that $2,042 "average tax cut" for small-business owners is also heavily tilted toward the wealthiest, with the majority of small-business owners actually receiving less than $500.[2]

certainly be a deceptive use of the *median*. Suppose the worker making $15,000 complains about her salary, and is told to count her blessings, since she makes well above the *average* salary of $12,000: that would be a deceptive use of the *mode*. (In fact, the salary distribution for this company is so skewed, there is probably no use of "average" that would be very helpful.)

So reports of "averages" may be informative, but they can also cover deceptive *ambiguity*, since "average" may indicate mean, median, or mode; and depending on which measure is selected, the results can be easily manipulated.

EMPTY STATISTICS

Claims about averages can be misleading, but at least when you sort things out you are usually left with something meaningful. Some statistical assertions have no substance at all: for example, claims like "New Plate Glow dishwashing detergent gets your dishes 43% cleaner!" Certainly it makes sense to talk about some things being cleaner than others. For example, adolescent boys often become significantly cleaner after they become interested in adolescent girls. (I mean physically cleaner, not morally more wholesome.) And we can compare two plates, and say that one is cleaner than another. But 43% cleaner? I'm not sure what such precise plate cleanliness data could possibly be measuring.

In addition to the problem of trying to pin a precise number on a measure that does not lend itself to such quantification, there is also the problem of 43% cleaner than *what*? The older version of Plate Glow detergent? The leading competitor detergent? Or is it supposed to get dishes 43% cleaner than washing with no detergent at all? Or perhaps 43% cleaner than the dishes were before they were washed? Unless the comparison base is specified, the statistical claim is meaningless.

FINDING THE APPROPRIATE CONTEXT

Sometimes data can be accurate, but misleading in the context in which it is used. The assault victim remembers that her assailant was wearing a Cleveland Browns stocking cap. The police spot Jones walking a few blocks away, wearing a Cleveland Browns stocking cap. Is it reasonable to conclude that Jones is a likely suspect? (Obviously we could not reasonably conclude that Jones is the assailant on such flimsy evidence, but does his wearing of the cap give reasonable grounds to identify him as a suspect?)

Consider the fact that less than .01% (less than one in 10,000) of men in the world wear Cleveland Browns stocking caps. And Jones is one of those rare birds wearing such a cap. That makes him a likely suspect, right?

Maybe if the crime occurred in Cairo, Mumbai, or Peking, where Cleveland Browns stocking caps are unusual headgear; but if the assault occurred in Cleveland or Akron during the month of November, then there would be much less reason to consider Jones a likely suspect.

Swift Singer has won 70% of his races over his lifetime; so we should bet on Swift Singer. He's got a great chance of winning this race, right?

Not necessarily. Before we can conclude that, we need a better context for that 70% winning percentage. Were those winning races against competition similar to the horses Swift Singer is facing today? (If he dominated his races against very inferior competition at small tracks, but is now facing top-stakes horses at Saratoga, then that winning percentage may not be very reassuring.)

Sluggo has a lifetime batting average of .333, so there's a one in three chance that he will get a hit. Well, true, so far as it goes. Over his career he has 2,000 official at-bats, and has gotten hits 667 times; so he has a one in three chance of getting a hit this time. But lots of factors can complicate this calculation. Suppose Sluggo has been in a terrible slump this year, and is only hitting .195 (most of his hits came in the early years of his career, and now his skills are eroding). In that case, the more recent data would give a better indication of his likelihood of getting a hit. Or suppose that Sluggo is great when he plays at home (where he consistently hits over .400) but is mediocre on the road (where he hits about .250), and this game is on the road. Or perhaps Sluggo has a great batting average against right-handed pitchers, but can't hit lefties with a tennis racquet, and this pitcher is left-handed. Or maybe Sluggo does hit .333, but today he is facing Tim Lincecum, who is a much tougher pitcher than average.

In short, determining the appropriate sample can be tricky, and very important. For example, suppose someone is trying to decide whether to undergo a very expensive and debilitating treatment that her doctor recommends as her only chance of surviving cancer. Before embarking on this treatment program, she would want to know its chance of success. She is told that this treatment has a 60% 5-year survival rate. That sounds promising, but she needs more details. What's the survival rate for cancer detected at the stage she is in (e.g., if the cancer has already metastasized, the survival rate may decrease dramatically)? What's the survival rate for people over age 70, which is her category? (Some treatments are more successful with younger patients.) What's the survival rate for patients who also suffer from diabetes and emphysema, as she does? (Of course there is also the problem that if we narrow down the sample too far, the sample will become so small that the results are meaningless: What's the survival rate for 72-year-old Italian mothers of four who have diabetes and emphysema, and smoke two packs a day, drink dry martinis, and live in Buffalo?)

Caught Off Base

Even when the base of comparison *is* specified, that does not always clear things up. One way to manipulate statistics is by using a favorable comparison base. For example, "Over the past 5 years, our mutual fund has outperformed the market index by 14%." This can be helpful if the fund has been a poor performer during the last 2 years, but made strong gains the 3 years before that. Funds tend to have good years and bad years, as their investment specialties flourish or falter. But by picking the right base year for comparison, almost any fund can put a positive spin on the numbers.

Finally, there is another way of manipulating the base that is sometimes used by retailers. An automobile dealership says that its markup on a particular model is only 10%: We are selling the car for $20,000, and it cost us $18,000. Two thousand is 10% of 20,000, so our markup is 10%. In one sense that's true. But the customer may point out that the actual markup on the car is over 11%: the cost of the car is $18,000, and the dealer is selling it for $20,000, a markup of $2,000; and a markup of $2,000 is a little over 11% of the $18,000 base. To see the difference, suppose that you are making $50,000 a year, and your employer comes to you with a plan: things are tough for the company this year, so we have to cut your salary by 20%; but don't worry, next year things will turn around, and we'll *raise* your salary by 20%, and you'll be back where you started. Well, not quite. The 20% cut drops your salary to $40,000. When you now receive a raise, 20% of $40,000 is only $8,000, and you wind up with only $48,000.

Statistical Apples and Oranges

A special kind of deception occurs when statistical comparisons are made between groups that are not comparable.

"Some people claim that snowmobiles are dangerous, because there have been dozens of deaths and severe injuries to people who were riding on snowmobiles. But before you jump to the conclusion that snowmobiles are dangerous, consider the thousands of people who are killed and injured in automobiles. Of course there is some danger from riding snowmobiles, but obviously not nearly so much danger as riding in your automobile. In fact, when you add up the numbers, you will find that over a hundred times more people are killed in automobile crashes than in snowmobile crashes; so we have to recognize that while snowmobiles do pose some risk, they are at least a hundred times safer than cars." It's not too difficult to see through that comparison. It's obvious that more people will be killed and injured in cars, because people ride in cars a lot more than they ride in snowmobiles. It compares apples and oranges. (It's like saying that riding your car is more dangerous than playing Russian roulette, because more people are killed in cars than by playing Russian roulette.) To make this a legitimate comparison, we would have to have a comparison of how many people are killed or injured in cars *for each hour of driving*, compared to how many are killed or injured on snowmobiles during each hour of riding.

The faulty comparison of cars to snowmobiles is rather obvious, but faulty statistical comparisons are often more subtle. For example, suppose someone offers the following argument: "Ninety-eight percent of all smokers live past age 25; only 97% of the population as a whole reaches age 25. So perhaps smoking actually *increases* your chances for avoiding an early and untimely death!"

Suppose this data is correct. It shows nothing at all about whether smoking helps you survive past age 25, because this is an example of comparing apples and oranges. Fortunately, very few infants take up smoking. So the comparison is between people age 14 or 15 (when they start smoking) and people at birth: Obviously if you are age 14, you have a much better chance of living to age 25 than does a newborn infant (the 14-year-old has already avoided all the infant and early childhood mortality risks that the newborn must now face). Instead of comparing the mortality rate of smokers for a 10-year period (ages 15–25) with the mortality rate of nonsmokers from a 25-year period, it would be more helpful to compare the mortality rates of smokers aged 15–25 with the mortality rates of nonsmokers in the same age period.

Uncritical use of such comparisons can lead to absurd conclusions. For example, it was reported some years ago (around the time that the movie *Jaws* came out) that shark attacks on men were much more common than shark attacks on women. Some people started to wonder why sharks apparently found men tastier than women. But there was really no mystery to solve. It's just that a large proportion of shark attacks were on surfers, whose search for the "perfect wave" had drawn them a good distance away from shore, and there were more men surfers than women.

In a 1978 study of male symphony conductors in the United States, a medical researcher discovered that their mean length of life was 73.4 years. The mean length of life for the overall U.S. male population was only 69.5. The researcher looked for what caused symphony conductors to live longer, and concluded that their increased life span was probably due to their unusual talent, drive, and sense of accomplishment. Nice theory. But in fact there was nothing to explain. Even the most talented musicians rarely become symphony conductors before age 32 (very few symphony conductors take that job at birth). But the researcher used life expectancy from birth; the appropriate comparison would be to examine the life expectancies of those who have already lived to be age 32. In 1978, a U.S. male, age 32, had a life expectancy of an additional 40.5 years, until age 72.5. The sample of symphony conductors averaged 73.4, which indicates there is actually very little difference to be explained. The researcher was comparing baby apples to adult oranges.

In 1981, the District of Columbia reported a wonderful and amazing drop in the number of tuberculosis cases reported: from 341 in 1980 to 239 in 1981, a drop of 30%. What caused this encouragingly steep decline? Better treatments? An improved environment? Before answering, make sure there was really a decline to explain. In 1980, all suspected cases of TB (that were not definitely ruled *out*) were reported to the TB control clinic as tuberculosis; in 1981, the reporting changed: Only cases that were definitely *confirmed* as TB were reported. Again, a comparison of doubtful oranges with certain apples.[3]

STATISTICAL HALF-TRUTHS

Chapter 9 noted that sometimes what is not stated is more important than the narrowly true statement that is actually made. Statistics are not infrequently used for such deception and obfuscation. "Some people complain that the income of the top executives at Strato Manufacturing is too high, while most of the workers get low wages and lousy benefits. But that claim is simply untrue. In fact, the CEO at Strato receives an annual salary of $600,000, and he has the highest salary at the company. Certainly that's a decent salary, but it's not out of line; in fact, it is considerably less than the salary of most top executives at similar companies." The statement is literally true, but only half the truth is being told. The CEO does make a *salary* of $600,000, but most of his money does not come from his salary but instead from bonuses and stock options (not to mention memberships in country clubs and a very generous retirement program). When those are added in, his actual annual pay may be several times his salary.

Half-truths can also be employed to manipulate a company's level of profits. There are complaints that the XYZ nursing-home chain employs staffs that are too small to care adequately for their residents, and that their workers are underpaid (usually minimum wage, or just over minimum wage). But the XYZ nursing-home chain opens its books, and shows that its profits are so low that it simply can't afford to hire more caregivers or pay them better. True, the profits at XYZ were low, but XYZ owns several subsidiary companies: X nursing supply company, Y maintenance company, and Z therapy specialists staffing company. XYZ gets all its supplies from X, pays Y for all its maintenance, and contracts with Z for therapy services: and it pays all those companies very generously (well above market rates) and those companies make handsome profits. So now XYZ can open its books and show that its profits are minimal, while not mentioning the profits that are being funnelled into these other companies they own. (It's an old trick, but it never goes out of fashion. Some states allow private operators to run bingo gambling games, so long as a high percentage of the profits from the games goes to legitimate charities. So private operators run games, and give 80% of the profits to charity. But, unfortunately, their profits are never very high, because they have high expenses: For example, hiring a janitorial service to clean the facility. The janitorial service is paid a king's ransom for its services, and so the bingo company makes very low profits; but the janitorial service happens to be owned by the guy who owns the bingo company.)

A variation on this game is sometimes played by large corporations that wish to portray their profits as very low. A huge petroleum company acknowledges that its overall profits are huge, but claims that it makes a very small profit on each gallon of gas sold. "Sure, Scrooge International Oil made several hundred million dollars in profits last year; but we made a profit of only 3 cents on each gallon of gas we sold. That's hardly excessive, right?" The trick is that Scrooge Oil may have "sold" that gallon of gasoline several times before it finally comes out of the pump to your car: Scrooge International sold the gallon of gas to Scrooge North American, who sold it to Scrooge U.S., who sold it to Scrooge East Coast, who sold it to Scrooge Pennsylvania, who finally sold it to you. The gallon of gas never left the possession of Scrooge Oil, but it is "sold" five times, through paper transactions within the company. And so they make a profit of "only 3 cents per gallon sold," but you ultimately pay them a profit of 15 cents when you pump the gallon into your car.

Sample Size and "Statistical Significance"

In the popular image of medical research, the researcher administers the new experimental drug to patients dying of some terrible disease (such as pancreatic cancer) and they all recover, and the researchers rejoice. It hardly ever happens that way. Instead, researchers compare patients in the *experimental* group (patients who are actually taking the experimental drug) with patients in a *control* group (who are usually taking whatever treatment is standard treatment for this disease) and look to see if the patients in the experimental group recover faster or (in the case of a disease such as pancreatic cancer, which is almost invariably fatal) live a little longer than the patients who received the standard treatment. If enough of the patients in the experimental group live longer than the patients in the control group, then the researchers have found a *statistically significant* difference between the two groups; and while they will not have found a *cure* for pancreatic cancer, they will have discovered a better treatment method—and they will have some indication that their research is heading in the right direction, and might eventually lead to a cure. Basically, a *statistically significant* result is a result that statisticians determine was very unlikely (less than one chance in 20) to occur by chance. Suppose I'm testing a new drug to prevent colds. Of the 10 people in the experimental group (who received the new drug), four develop a cold over the next 3 months; of the 10 people in the control group (who received a placebo), six people suffered a cold during the same period. Have I found a drug that is at least *slightly* effective in preventing colds? Probably not. That difference does not rise to the level of statistical significance; the result is more than likely just the result of chance. On the other hand, if I run the same study with 10,000 subjects in each group, and 4,000 people in the experimental group develop colds while 6,000 in the control group suffer colds, then it is unlikely those results were the product of chance: those results are at least 95% likely to be the result of a difference between the medication and the placebo, and so the results are statistically significant. I may not have found the cure for the common cold, but at least I have likely found a medication that does *some* good. So the *larger* your study, the more likely that you will gain a statistically significant result. (There's nothing strange about that: Flip a coin 10 times, most of the time—by chance—it will not come out exactly five heads and five tails; in fact, if you do that several times, you are likely to get some runs of only one or two heads, and some with heads coming up eight or nine times. But if you flip a coin 10,000 times—and the coin is not specially weighted, and no trickery is involved—then it is *very* unlikely that you will get heads showing up less than 4,000 or more than 6,000 times.) So suppose there are some reports about the bad effects of studying critical thinking: Several critical thinking students have experienced insomnia, and some people are concerned that the study of critical thinking may disrupt sleep patterns and cause insomnia. (I think it's very doubtful: The students in my critical thinking classes never seem to have any difficulty sleeping.) Anyway, I want to run a study that shows that there is *no* evidence that studying critical thinking causes insomnia. If I keep my study very *small*, then even if the study shows that the experimental group (who study critical thinking) have more instances of insomnia than do the "placebo" control group (who are studying something else), that difference will probably not be great enough to yield a statistically significant result. Those who want to claim that a product—such as a herbicide or pesticide—is *not* harmful have taken this lesson to heart: if you keep your studies very small, the results will hardly ever be statistically significant (even if your product is in fact quite harmful).

How to Make Your Study Yield the Results You Want

When your goal is to get a result, rather than discover the truth, there are ways to manipulate your study to get that result. The pharmaceutical companies are awash in cash, and they are quite willing to spread it around in order to increase their profits. Unfortunately, the temptations of the billions of dollars they can make from a popular drug can sometimes lead them to very questionable practices: practices that are scientifically flawed and morally bankrupt. The problem is not so much with consciously and purposefully falsified research—though that happens, especially when there is money to be made. Rather, the more common problem is in responding to pressures and hopes and profits that lead one to interpret research results—or even subtly shape research results—to reach the desired conclusion. Certainly there are some researchers who cannot be bought or influenced; unfortunately, there are some who can be. Suppose MegaPharma corporation has given me a very generous contract for testing the safety and effectiveness of their new arthritis drug: a research contract that has brought in lots of money and prestige to the university, and made my dean very happy; has allowed me to hire several assistant professors and generously fund a large number of graduate students; and has also paid me very handsomely for my own efforts. It's not like MegaPharma came to me and said, "Look, here's several million dollars; your job is to create a research study that makes our new drug look very effective and wonderfully safe." But the pressures are certainly there: I know this is potentially a blockbuster drug that could bring in billions in profits to MegaPharma; they have given me—as "part of the MegaPharma family"—large stock options that will be worth lots of money, *if* my research shows positive results and makes MegaPharma stock shoot up; and I know that if I want to receive additional research contracts from MegaPharma, then my chances will be much better if the research results are positive. So I run the study, and now I have to evaluate those in the control group (who are taking a placebo) and those taking new MPX (the experimental group). Do those arthritis sufferers taking MPX experience less joint pain? Do they show gains in flexibility? Are they— my great fear—more *likely* to experience depression, or severe indigestion, or even heart attacks or liver failure? Let's see, here's Joe, he's in the experimental group who are taking MPX; and it looks to me as if he is feeling substantially better, and he seems to have less trouble walking around; maybe he seems a little down, but that's just normal mood swing, not really depression. On the other hand, when I observe Jim—from the control group, so taking a placebo rather than MPX—it seems to me that he is suffering increased loss of flexibility; he says he is not, but in my judgment he is. But my judgment is obviously influenced by what I *want* (and perhaps expect) to see: dramatic improvement in the patients taking MPX. That is the problem of *confirmation bias*, and that is why good medical researchers use *double-blind* research—in which *neither* the test subjects nor the researchers interacting with the subjects know who is taking the drug and who is taking the placebo. If my goal is to carry out accurate research, controlling confirmation bias— through double-blind testing—is essential; but if my goal is to get the "right result," confirmation bias can be very useful. (All scientists recognize that confirmation bias is a major problem, and therefore—whenever possible—double-blind experiments are a basic requirement of good medical science. But a recent study of 192 randomized trials, at least half of which were funded by drug companies, found that almost half the trials were not double-blind and thus did not control for confirmation bias. The study also found that industry-sponsored research was much more likely to report favorable outcomes for the tested drug than were the studies not funded by the drug companies; and the company-sponsored studies that *were* double-blind were less likely to reach conclusions favorable to the company.[4])

If my "confirmation bias" is not enough to push the results for MPX into the positive column, then there are other possibilities: the results weren't very good after 6 months; but maybe if we extend the study another 3 months, things will look better (and if I'm getting positive results after 7 months, that would be a good stopping point). Or maybe I can go back to the data from 4 months: If the study showed positive results then, perhaps we can just make that the end point. Or possibly the test showed positive results for those 55–60, but no one else, then we can report the positive results for that group ("That was the group we really wanted to study anyway, right?"). If we look hard enough at the data, we can almost always find *some* group during *some* time period that had positive test results from MPX. After all, if we study enough people for long enough, eventually chance will give us a positive result even if the drug we are testing is useless. That is called *cherry-picking* or *data-dredging*. We dredge through all the data until we can cherry-pick something positive, and we leave everything else out of the report. (And if nothing I can do can turn the results of this study into something positive, MPX won't despair. They may have other researchers running similar studies; if my study fails to show a positive result—or reveals that the drug may cause harmful results—then MPX can decide not to publish my study, and instead publish one that looks more positive.)

Suppressing Unfavorable Results

In the mid-1990s, GlaxoSmithKline wanted to market Paxil, an antidepressant drug with huge sales, for the treatment of children. It ran three clinical trials in an effort to show that Paxil was safe and effective for the treatment of depressed children. The results were terrible: Paxil didn't work for treating childhood depression; worse, significantly more children on Paxil attempted suicide than did those in the control group. In an internal memo to senior executives at GlaxoSmithKline, the director of the studies made this report:

> The results of the studies were disappointing. The possibility of obtaining a safety statement from this data was considered but rejected. Consultation of the marketing teams confirmed that this would be unacceptable commercially.

In fact the marketing people, in internal memos, were quite clear that they did not want this study released:

> Originally we had planned to do extensive media relations surrounding this study until we actually viewed the results. Essentially the study did not really show paroxetine [Paxil] was effective in treating adolescent depression, which is not something we want to publicize.

Not only did the study show Paxil was ineffective for treating adolescent depression; it also indicated that Paxil was likely to increase the risk of adolescent suicide. So GSK buried the study, for several years; and rather than marketing directly, they paid doctors to act as spokespersons, reporting that their adolescent patients had experienced positive results when treated with Paxil (as no doubt some had: but the studies indicate it was probably a placebo effect).[5]

Suppose my study shows a problem: turns out more of the subjects in the experimental group had heart attacks than did those in the control group—that's the kind of bad result that damages sales, and maybe even keeps the drug off the market. But let's look really closely at that result: The increased number of heart attacks occur only when we compare experimental and control group subjects who were over 75; and now that I think more carefully about the experimental design, it seems to me that we should limit the experiment to people under 75, and drop all the data from subjects over 75; and when we do that, the heart attack results disappear. Or if that doesn't work, let's look again at the people we enrolled in the study: you know, several of those people who suffered the heart attacks while taking MPX probably shouldn't have been in the study in the first place; now that we look really closely, we find they didn't fit the experimental design (maybe one of them drank a bit more than he admitted when he was enrolled; another didn't really fit, because her arthritic condition wasn't really as severe as the testing protocol required; and a third doesn't really fit, because his work environment posed special hazards). And once those "unsuitable" subjects are eliminated from the study, now we find there was no significant difference in heart attack rates. (In an early study of Paxil— a drug widely used for treatment of depression—suicide rates for those taking Paxil were substantially higher than for those taking a placebo; but GlaxoSmithKline, the pharmaceutical giant that produces Paxil, apparently added to the study a number of suicides that occurred to members of the control group during the "washout" period: the period *before* the actual study starts, when subjects take *no* drugs so that any previously taken drugs could *washout* of their systems and not affect the study. When those *pretest* cases were added, the suicide rates for the Paxil experimental group and the control groups were similar. Harvard psychiatrist Joseph Glenmullen, a researcher who analyzed the Paxil study, claimed that if the research results had been reported correctly—without adding the suicides that occurred *prior* to running the study—they would have shown the suicide risk for those taking Paxil to be eight times the risk on a placebo.) If you suggest that I am deliberately manipulating the research results—much less falsifying the research—I shall reject and resent your accusation. And, in fact, I may not even be aware—or at least not admit to myself—that such manipulation is occurring; but the pressure to produce positive results can have a profound effect on how tests are run—and can result in "cutting corners" on careful controlled objective testing, leading to results that are unreliable. Of course eventually MPX will be found to be useless—and even dangerous—to arthritis sufferers, but that will take a long time (the placebo effects will carry us for quite a while). And in the meantime, my stock option will make me wealthy, MegaPharma will make billions of dollars off MPX, and arthritis sufferers will pay a lot of money for a useless drug—and some will die of heart attacks caused by the drug. Will my reputation as a scientist suffer? Perhaps, but not with the drug companies that hand out the huge contracts and big bonuses. When other drug companies see that I was able to make a silk purse out of an MPX sow's ear that was not only useless but actually harmful, my attractiveness as a "researcher" will be greatly enhanced.

Exercise 17-1

What additional information would you need in order to know whether the following claims are meaningful and useful, or misleading (or perhaps empty)? Explain what sort of statistical *deception* might be involved in each of these claims.

1. Over the last 7 years, the average tuition increase at Home State University has been only 4%.
2. It is sometimes claimed that heavy smoking poses a severe health hazard. But, in fact, in the United States over 50% of people who smoke live past age 70.
3. I pay my employees very fairly. In fact, my average employee makes $50,000 a year; and that's not bad.
4. Skydiving is really much less dangerous than soccer: Last year in Canada, there were fewer than 100 serious injuries from skydiving, and more than 300 serious injuries from playing soccer.
5. Chromo cars are wonderfully durable and reliable. In fact, over 80% of Chromo cars sold in the United States during the past 10 years are still on the road.
6. You will get superb, careful, quality care at GreenBriar Hospital, and the data prove it. At GreenBriar, we have a mortality rate of only 1%: fewer than 1 out of every 100 GreenBriar admissions dies in our hospital. University Hospital, by comparison, has a mortality rate of 3%, *triple* the GreenBriar rate. So for the best in care, go to GreenBriar.
7. Super Cleano gets your dishes 30% cleaner!
8. Enrollment at Home State University has increased by 20% over the past 5 years. Obviously Home State is doing something right!

SURVEYS

Since public opinion surveys play such a prominent part in contemporary political life—surveys on how many people want restrictions on abortion rights, what percentage of the population favors capital punishment, how many people would vote for Senator Scam if the election were held tomorrow—it is important to recognize some of the ways that surveys can be hazardous to the truth.

The first difficulty with drawing conclusions from samples—including survey samples—is making sure that the sample is sufficiently large to support a reliable conclusion. We are all tempted to make faulty generalizations on the basis of inadequate samples. I get lost while driving through Winnipeg, and stop to ask directions. The person I ask spends 10 minutes giving me detailed directions, and even draws a map to help me. "The people in Winnipeg sure are friendly," I say to myself. The next day I am again lost, on this occasion in Edmonton. The person from whom I request guidance answers rather abruptly that he is in a hurry, telling me I should buy a map. "Edmonton residents certainly are a rude and surly lot," I conclude. We are all tempted to such faulty inductive conclusions on the basis of ridiculously small samples. If I ask directions of another

Edmonton citizen who also brusquely refuses, I may conclude that the people of Edmonton are among the nastiest on Earth. But obviously it is impossible to draw an accurate conclusion about the people of a large city on the basis of a two-person sample.

The toughest and most common challenge for surveys—a problem that can bedevil even honest efforts to secure reliable survey results—is drawing the survey from a *representative sample.* If you want to do an accurate survey of Canadian citizens, then you must be sure that your survey covers all ethnic groups, all age groups, new immigrants as well as longtime citizens, urban and rural and suburban citizens, rich and poor and middle class, citizens from every province, from all education levels, from a broad spectrum of employment categories (bankers and oil field workers, physicians and the unemployed, secretaries and farmers); and on top of that, you have to be sure that your sample is *proportionate* to the entire target population (it won't work to include 20 French Canadians in your sample of 1,000, if the actual proportion of French Canadians in the population as a whole is much greater). Also, you must be sure that the people interviewed are randomly selected. If you mail survey letters all across Canada, and base your survey on the responses of the 10% who went to the trouble to fill out the survey and mail it back, then you are not getting a *representative* sample. The people who feel strongly enough to complete the survey may have stronger opinions about the issues than those who did not complete the survey; they may be more (or less) educated; they have more leisure time than the population as a whole. The problem is even worse if you do a "survey" based on self-selected respondents (and worst of all if respondents actually have to pay for the privilege of being included, such as "surveys" that require respondents to call a 900 toll number). For example, Ann Landers did a "survey" on how parents felt about having children: If they had it to do over again, would they have children?

Dear Ann Landers:
Saw another letter in your column from a complaining woman—bogged down by two children—sorry she can't live the same kind of life as before. Travel! Fun! Such happy days! Now she is "dead-tired" and "tied-down." Then you, Ann Landers, bring up your survey again—the one where you asked, "If you had it to do over again, would you have had children?" You said 70 percent replied, "No." I ask you, Ann, when did you survey this 70 percent? When the children were babies? One year old? Six years old? Teenagers? College graduates? Or after they had children of their own? I found the time raising my children the most exciting and fun years of my life. I wouldn't have missed them for anything. I don't believe your survey. Anyone can publish a "survey," and the public will believe it if it is printed in the newspaper—

Suspicious in Palo Alto

Dear Palo:
That 70 percent represented parents from every group you mentioned. The majority of "No" responses came from (1) young parents with babies and (2) parents of teenagers. I am not surprised that you are suspicious about the survey. I wouldn't have believed it either, except for the evidence right there in huge piles on my desk. I still haven't recovered from it.[6]

Ann Landers claims that this is a reliable survey because it has a huge sample and it covers parents of children of all ages. But that is far from sufficient to make it reliable. We must be sure that it includes wealthy, middle-class, and poor parents; single parents; parents who had children at a very early age, and parents who had children late in life; well-educated parents and poorly educated parents; conservative parents and liberal parents; parents from west Texas and Long Island and Seattle; fathers as well as mothers. And it's not enough just to include survey respondents from each of those groups: They must respond to the survey in numbers *proportionate* to their actual size. (If 10% of the *target population*—the group that the survey is supposed to tell us about—have household incomes under $15,000, then approximately 10% of the survey respondents must share that characteristic.) It's easy to see that one group of parents will be badly underrepresented in Ann's sample: namely, parents who rarely read newspapers. And there is also a group that is heavily overrepresented in the sample: parents who like to participate in surveys. In order to be a part of the sample, a parent had to write a letter, address an envelope, buy a first-class stamp—and only a small and unrepresentative fraction of parents would go to that much bother to participate in Ann's "survey." Thus even if Ann's sample includes a tremendous diversity of responses, it still will not provide a reliable survey. The moral of the story: It is very difficult to obtain a genuinely representative sample of a large and diverse population. If you see a "survey" in which people are invited to fill out a magazine questionnaire and mail it in, then you should treat that "survey" as exactly what it is: public entertainment rather than a reliable survey.

In addition to the problems of small sample and unrepresentative sample, there can be problems with the survey questions. Suppose we are conducting a survey on whether the people of our state favor a ban on dove hunting. The phrasing of the question may influence the survey results. If we ask, "Should hunters be allowed to shoot doves?" then the question appeals to our general preference to let people do as they wish. If we ask instead, "Should doves be protected from hunters?" we tap the desire to protect the innocent. Even more obviously, we might get the answer we want by asking, "Should gentle mourning doves be protected from being stalked and gunned down by hunters?" or, for the opposite result, "Should the dove population be regulated and kept in check by allowing hunters to harvest a limited number of doves?"

Rigged "surveys" often used rigged questions: "Do you favor a tax cut that will stimulate investment, increase personal savings, and boost the economy?" And from the other side: "Do you favor a tax cut that will increase inflation, take needed money from medicare and social security, and threaten our healthy economy?" When such "survey questions" are mailed out to a "sample" that probably already favors the side sending the mailing, it is not surprising when it turns out that "almost 70% of the American people favor" a tax cut and simultaneously "more than two-thirds of the American people oppose" the same tax cut. Another example (given by Joel Best, in *Stat-Spotting: A Field Guide to Identifying Dubious Data*) comes from competing surveys concerning school voucher programs. The National Education Association (which represents public school teachers, and opposes vouchers) included this question in their survey: "Do you think tax dollars should be used to assist parents who send their children to private, parochial, or religious schools, or should tax dollars be spent to improve public schools?" The Center for Education Reform (a pro-voucher organization) ran their own survey, with this question: "How much do you support providing parents with the option of sending their children to the school of their choice—public, private, or parochial—rather than only to

Getting the Survey Results You Want

If you are simply interested in getting survey results that *support* your position—rather than *accurate* survey results—there are many ways of doing that. One way, as already mentioned, is to rig the questions to get favorable answers; for example, one "survey" that was designed to get a result opposing sex education in schools posed the question this way: "Do you favor providing school children with pornographic material in the guise of sex education?" Not surprisingly, most people "surveyed" objected to sex education.

There is another method that is also effective in producing slanted results: simply "survey" people you are confident will agree with your views. If you want a survey that opposes handgun registration, survey members of the National Rifle Association. If you are looking for survey results opposing legalized abortion, survey active members of the Catholic Church. If you want a survey opposing oil drilling in Alaskan Wilderness areas, survey members of the Sierra Club. Or if you want a survey favoring public funding for a new football stadium, survey subscribers to *Pro Football Weekly*.

the school to which they are assigned?" Not surprisingly, the two surveys yielded very different results.

Another source of survey problems is the subtle (and sometimes not so subtle) influence of the surveyor. A sweet old lady, who reminds me of my grandmother, arrives at the door wearing her Daughters of the American Revolution pin. She wants to ask a single survey question: "Do you favor a constitutional amendment that would outlaw the burning of the American flag?" "Well, I love Old Glory, and I hate it when our flag is burned. I'm a bit worried about restricting free speech, but surely there are other ways of protesting. So yes, I suppose I would favor an amendment banning flag burning." Later, a pleasant surveyor arrives on my doorstep wearing a button from the American Civil Liberties Union, and asks exactly the same question: "Do you favor a constitutional amendment that would outlaw the burning of the American flag?" "Well, I'm not really in favor of flag burning, but I don't like the idea of placing restrictions on free speech. And after all, flag burning is a very rare occurrence. Overall, I would have to say that such an amendment is not a good idea." So what's going on? Am I just being two-faced? Not really; well, maybe a little. It's just that I, like many people, would rather make people happy than upset them, and I suspect that the surveyor wearing the DAR pin supports the amendment, and the ACLU surveyor opposes it. My views on the issue aren't that strong one way or the other, so I'm willing to go along with what the surveyor wants. Obviously there are many people who do have strong feelings about the subject, and their survey opinions would not change from interviewer to interviewer. But if only one in five are undecided, and will go along with whoever happens to be asking the question, then it should not be surprising when one group reports their survey shows that Americans favor the amendment, with 60% in favor and 40% opposed; and the other group reports a survey showing exactly the opposite result. For a legitimate survey, it is essential that those surveyed do *not* know the views of the surveyors.

Politicians sometimes use "surveys" that abandon even the pretense of objectivity. Called "push polls," these are designed to sound like surveys but are actually an attempt to influence those who are "surveyed." For example, "If you knew that candidate Joe Jones wants to increase the tax burden on the middle class, would you vote for him for Senate?" "If you knew that candidate Joan Salter favors destroying social security, would you vote for her as your member of the House of Representatives?" Such "surveys" pull out all the tricks: loaded questions, obvious identification of the source of the "survey," and probably unrepresentative samples as well.

Exercise 17-2

1. We want to know what proportion of the graduates of Home State University are pleased with the education they received. Which of these would be the best source for a sample, and why? Which would not yield a representative sample?
   a. The names and addresses of graduates supplied by the alumni affairs office.
   b. The homecoming football game.
   c. The registrar's records of graduates.
2. Do most baseball fans favor the use of a designated hitter? Which of the following samples would be most representative?
   a. A call-in survey during a televised major league baseball game.
   b. A survey included in programs sold at major league baseball parks.
   c. A survey included in the sports sections of several major daily newspapers. (None of the above are very good. How would you get a representative sample? You must think carefully about exactly who your target group is.)

3. If you wanted to find out whether most students at your college favor banning smoking in class-rooms, how would you go about setting up a reliable survey to answer that question? In particular, what would you do to make sure your sample was representative?

4. Suppose we are trying to obtain a representative sample of all adult residents of the United States. The samples below are becoming progressively more representative (i.e., B is more representative than A and C is more representative than B). Explain why.

   a. Interviewing from randomly selected residential telephone numbers.

   b. Interviewing from randomly selected residences.

   c. Random selection of individuals from census records.

5. Suppose that you want to do a survey that you can release to the press showing that most citizens favor (or oppose, you can take your choice) a ban on private ownership of assault weapons. How would you manipulate such a survey?

 Study and **Review** on **mythinkinglab.com**

REVIEW QUESTIONS

1. What are the three measures that fall under the heading of "average"?
2. Give an example of an "empty" statistic.
3. Give an example of statistical "apples and oranges."
4. What is "statistical significance"?
5. What is "confirmation bias," and how can it be prevented?
6. Describe some of the problems that can result in inaccurate surveys.

NOTES

1. Actually, there are five, including the geometric mean and the harmonic mean, but those measures are less common.

2. Figures from an analysis by the Urban Institute-Brookings Institution Tax Policy Center.

3. The last two examples were drawn from an excellent book by Abram J. Jaffee and Herbert F. Spirer, *Misused Statistics: Straight Talk for Twisted Numbers.* See the additional readings at the end of this chapter for more details.

4. Lisa Bero, Fieke Oostvogel, Peter Bacchetti, and Kirby Lee, "Factors Associated with Findings of Published Trials of Drug-Drug Comparisons: Why Some Statins Appear More Efficacious Than Others," *PLoS Medicine,* June 5, 2007.

5. Information taken from "GlaxoSmithKline's Deadly Cover-Up," by Shelley Jofre, posted on Alternet, August 8, 2007.

6. Reprinted by permission of Ann Landers and News America Syndicate.

INTERNET RESOURCES

A superb source for extensive, clearly presented information on surveys and polls is at *www.publicagenda.org*. This is the site for "Public Agenda Online: The Inside Source for Public Opinion and Policy Analysis." It is a treasure trove of accurate and useful information on almost any major political or social issue, from abortion to euthanasia to welfare reform. Be sure to check their "Cautionary notes about survey findings," included in the material on each issue.

An informative, very interactive site with clear information on political polling and its pitfalls is *www.learner.org/exhibits/statistics* (part of the Annenberg/CPB Projects). It is presented in the form of planning an ongoing political campaign.

ADDITIONAL READING

For a more extensive introductory treatment of induction, see Brian Skyrms, *Choice and Chance: An Introduction to Inductive Logic* (Belmont, CA: Dickenson, 1966). A book that raises some of the most famous questions concerning inductive logic is *Fact, Fiction and Forecast* by Nelson Goodman (Cambridge, MA: Harvard University Press, 1955).

A very readable book on the difficulties involved in surveys is Michael Wheeler, *Lies, Damn Lies, and Statistics* (New York: W. W. Norton, 1976).

A slightly dated but still entertaining look at statistical skullduggery is offered by Darrell Huff, *How to Lie with Statistics* (New York: W. W. Norton, 1954). A more recent book along the same lines is *A Mathematician Reads the Newspaper* by John Allen Paulos (New York: Harper-Collins, 1995). My favorite of the books on statistical fallacies is perhaps Herbert F. Spirer, Louise Spirer, and Abram J. Jaffee, *Misused Statistics: Straight Talk for Twisted Numbers*, 2nd ed. (New York: Marcel Dekker, 1998). Another excellent book on statistical errors and deceptions—aimed at journalists, but readable and interesting for anyone interested in the subject—is *Statistical Deception at Work* by John Mauro (Mahwah, NJ: Lawrence Erlbaum, 1992). Still another is Joel Best, *Stat-Spotting: A Field Guide to Identifying Dubious Data* (Berkeley, CA: University of California Press, 2008).

An excellent and very readable book on everyday statistical reasoning, and on the confusions that can arise from common misconceptions concerning probability, is Robyn M. Dawes, *Everyday Rationality: How Pseudo-Scientists, Lunatics, and the Rest Systematically Fail to Think Rationally* (Boulder, CO: Westview Press, 2001).

▶ Read the Document on mythinkinglab.com

Matrixx Initiatives v. James Siracusano, U.S. Supreme Court (2011). This case focuses on questions related to statistical significance, lack of statistical significance, and their implications.

Castaneda v. Partida, 430 U.S. 482 (1977). This Supreme Court case examines statistical studies and their significance for drawing conclusions concerning racial and ethnic discrimination.

18

❖ ❖ ❖

Symbolic Sentential Logic

In Chapter 14, we talked about the valid deductive argument forms *modus ponens* and *modus tollens* (and about their scurrilous invalid impostors, affirming the consequent and denying the antecedent). *Modus ponens* and *modus tollens* arguments intuitively appear to be valid; the problem is, denying the antecedent and affirming the consequent also appear to be valid, and they are not. We know that they are invalid, because we can find examples of arguments having that logical form, but having premises we know are true and a conclusion that is false: If Michael Jordan scored 100 points in every game, then the Chicago Bulls won the NBA championship; Michael Jordan did not score 100 points in every game; therefore, the Chicago Bulls did not win the NBA championship. True premises, false conclusion, invalid argument.

But there's got to be an easier way of determining whether a deductive argument is valid or invalid. After all, it requires considerable imagination to come up with such examples—especially as arguments become more complicated—and on most mornings my imagination gutters. Even worse, while finding an example of true premises and false conclusion will always prove an argument form invalid, the *failure* to find such an example does *not* prove that an argument is *valid* (it may prove only the poverty of one's imagination). So we need some means of proving arguments valid and a more convenient method of proving arguments invalid: a method that imposes less stress and strain on the imaginative capacities.

TRUTH-FUNCTIONAL DEFINITIONS

Fortunately, such a method is readily available, it is simple to use, and it does both jobs with equal facility. It's called the *truth-table* method of determining validity and invalidity.

Negation

To use this method, we have to think carefully about the conditions under which statements are true, as well as when they are false. Let's start with a simple statement: The Chicago Bulls won the 1993 NBA championship. That statement happens to be true.

(Being a Cleveland Cavs fan, I'm not particularly pleased that it's true; it is true, nonetheless.) So let's consider what happens when we apply negation to that statement. Symbolize "The Chicago Bulls won the 1993 NBA championship" as *B* (for Bulls).

$$B \qquad \sim B$$

TRUE   FALSE

Now consider a false statement: The Cleveland Cavs won the 1993 NBA championship. (Call it *C* for Cavs.)

$$C \qquad \sim C$$

FALSE   TRUE

Since it is *not* the case that the Cavs won the 1993 NBA championship, the *negation* of *C* is true; and of course *C*—the Cavs won the 1993 NBA championship—is, sadly, false.

By combining these, we can give a *truth-functional definition* for negation, by means of a *truth table*. Let *D* stand for any statement you like ("The Bulls won the championship," "The Cavs won the championship," "Surf's up," "Bananas are high in potassium," "Eating spinach causes flat feet," or whatever). The truth-functional definition for negation can be given by:

$$D \qquad \sim D$$

TRUE   FALSE
FALSE   TRUE

That is, if "the Bulls won" is true, then "it is not the case that the Bulls won" is false; and if "the Bulls won" is false, then "it is not the case that the Bulls won" is true. Since any statement must be true or false, that covers all the possibilities and provides a full truth-functional definition for negation (for $\sim$).

As noted in Chapter 14, the same thing applies if we negate a negation. Suppose that you greet me with a cheery smile and announce that it is a beautiful morning. Since I am not a morning person, I shall certainly deny your claim: "It is *not* a beautiful morning," I will respond. (If your statement is true, and it is indeed a beautiful morning, then my negation of your statement is false; if you lied to me, and it is in fact false that it is a beautiful morning, then my statement—the negation of your false statement—is true.) If you are really adamant, you may continue to insist: "It is *not* the case that it is *not* a beautiful morning." And that, of course, is the logical equivalent of saying that it *is* a beautiful morning; that is, $\sim\sim B$ is logically equivalent to *B*. And we could go on with the argument. I might answer, "It is *not* the case that it is *not* the case that it is *not* a beautiful morning." ($\sim\sim\sim B$ is logically equivalent to $\sim B$.) And you might respond (again with the logical equivalent of "It is a beautiful morning") by asserting that "It is *not* the case that it is *not* the case that it is *not* the case that it is *not* a beautiful morning." But by this time the conversation has lost all interest for anyone other than logicians and Oscar the Grouch.

Disjunction

Once you have the hang of truth-functional definitions—and how they are defined by truth tables, like the one above for negation—it's easy to learn truth-functional definitions for other logical connectives. Consider the *disjunction,* which functions in either–or statements. The statement "Either Joan is at the party or Bill is at the party" is a disjunction. As we shall use it, it will always mean "either–or, and *maybe both*." That is, we shall interpret it as an *inclusive* disjunction. Sometimes, of course, in ordinary language, we use either–or as an *exclusive* disjunction, meaning "either–or, but *not* both." For example, if Joan and Bill have recently been feuding, then when we say, "Either Joan is at the party or Bill is at the party," that may be understood as meaning one of them—but certainly not both—is present. But the more ordinary usage of either–or is inclusive: At least one is at the party, and possibly both. And that is how we'll use disjunction: as inclusive, not exclusive. The symbol we shall use is ∨: Thus $D \vee G$ means: "Either D or G, and maybe both." While the whole statement is called a disjunction, each *part* is called—not very originally—a *disjunct*. "Either Joan is at the party or Bill is at the party" is a *disjunction*; "Joan is at the party" is one *disjunct* of that disjunction; "Bill is at the party" is also a disjunct.

The truth-functional definition of disjunction is thus:

D	G	$D \vee G$
TRUE	TRUE	TRUE
TRUE	FALSE	TRUE
FALSE	TRUE	TRUE
FALSE	FALSE	FALSE

That is, if both disjuncts are true, then the entire disjunction is true; if one disjunct is true and the other is false, the disjunction is still true; in fact, the *only* way the disjunction can be false is if *all* the disjuncts (in this case, *both* of the disjuncts) are false. Or another way of putting it: If at least one disjunct is true, then the disjunction is true.

Conjunction

With disjunction in hand, *conjunction* is simple. A conjunction is a "both–and" statement: Both Mars and Jupiter are planets in our solar system. For that to be true, it must be the case *both* that Mars is a planet in our solar system *and* that Jupiter is a planet in our solar system. (If Jupiter decided to leave our solar system, then the conjunction would become false.) Since we called the parts of a disjunction *disjuncts*, it does not require psychic powers to guess that the parts of a conjunction will be called *conjuncts*. Thus "Mars is a planet in our solar system" and "Jupiter is a planet in our solar system" are both *conjuncts* of that conjunction. And *all* the conjuncts must be true in order for the entire *conjunction* to be true. The symbol for conjunction that we shall use is &. Thus the truth table for conjunction—the *truth-functional definition of conjunction*—looks like this:

D	G	$D \& G$
TRUE	TRUE	TRUE
TRUE	FALSE	FALSE
FALSE	TRUE	FALSE
FALSE	FALSE	FALSE

Just as in the truth-functional definitions of negation and disjunction, the truth-functional definition of conjunction covers all the possibilities: D may be true while G is true, D may be true while G is false, D may be false while G is true, and both D and G may be false. Those are all the possible truth-value assignments, and the truth-functional definition tells what the truth value of the conjunction is for each and every one of those possible truth-value assignments.

Conditional

There's just one more truth-functional definition to examine (actually, there are more, but this is the last one we'll use), and I've saved the best for last. Consider the conditional.

If *A* then *B*. If Drew Brees has a good game, then the Saints will win. If I ace this exam, I'll pass the course. If more people smoke, cancer deaths will increase. If Batman is captured, then evil will triumph. If wishes were horses, then beggars would ride. It's a type of statement with which you are already quite familiar; and from your extensive study of necessary and sufficient conditions, you are on especially intimate terms with conditional statements. So you already know that in the statement "If the sun shines, then we'll go on a picnic," the *antecedent* is "the sun shines" and the *consequent* is "we'll go on a picnic." So developing a truth-functional definition—by means of a truth table—for the conditional is a simple matter:

D	*G*	*D* → *G*
TRUE	TRUE	TRUE
TRUE	FALSE	FALSE
FALSE	TRUE	TRUE
FALSE	FALSE	TRUE

Some of this may seem a bit strange, so let's go through each truth-value assignment. When the antecedent and the consequent are both true, then the conditional statement is true. That's obvious enough, right? The sun shines, and we do go on the picnic; the statement is true. But suppose the antecedent is true and the consequent is false: the sun shines, but no picnic. In that case, I lied to you. I promised that "If the sun shines, then we'll go on a picnic"; the sun is shining, no picnic is forthcoming, the conditional statement is false. In fact, that is the *only* way the conditional statement can be false: true antecedent, false consequent. Now suppose that the antecedent is false: that is, it is *not* the case that the sun shines. Well, then, all bets are off; there's no way I can be accused of deceiving you. What I said was strictly about what would happen *if* the sun shines; I made *no* promises about what would happen if the sun did *not* shine. So if the antecedent is false, and the consequent is *true*—the sun doesn't shine, but so what, we go on a picnic anyway—then I certainly haven't broken any promises, right? My statement is not false, so it must be true. And of course if the sun does not shine (the antecedent is false) and we do *not* go on a picnic (the consequent is also false), then that's rather sad, but again I certainly can't be accused of deceiving you; again, the truth value of the conditional will have to be true. (If you can run a mile in under 3 minutes, then you'll win an Olympic gold medal; that's true, even though you can't run a mile in under 3 minutes and you will not win an Olympic gold medal.) It seems simple, doesn't it?

Maybe it's not that simple. There's a problem. Consider this statement: "If I play LeBron James one-on-one in basketball, then I'll beat him." Now that is a perfectly ridiculous statement. LeBron James could be suffering from the worst game of his career, and I could be playing wildly over my head, and LeBron would still beat me without raising a sweat: LeBron can soar, and I can barely get off the court; LeBron is a fabulous ball-handler, and I have trouble getting the ball to midcourt in your average pick-up game at the gymn. You get the picture. Still, that conditional statement is *true*. For while the consequent is certainly false, so is the antecedent: It is *not* the case that I play LeBron James one-on-one in basketball; LeBron prefers to play against more worthy opponents. Yet—according to the truth-table definition given above—that statement must be true. But if our truth table assigns *true* to a statement that is obviously and absurdly *false*, then something is wrong.

Material Implication

Actually it's not as bad as all that. Conditionals with false antecedents can be bothersome, but they rarely cause a lot of difficulty. But because of the problems with false antecedents, it's not quite accurate to say we are developing a truth-functional definition for our ordinary notion of *conditional,* because as the above example shows, we are not. So instead of a truth-functional definition for *conditional,* we shall substitute *material implication.* That is a relation that is very similar to the conditional, but without any claims of real connection between the antecedent and the consequent. Thus while the *conditional* "If I play LeBron James, I will win" is false, as a *material implication* it will count as true. That's because the *material implication* doesn't imply any real connection between the antecedent and the consequent; it implies only that when the antecedent is true the consequent must be true: that the consequent will not be false when the antecedent is true. And since that is the case here (the antecedent will *not* be true and the consequent false, simply because the antecedent will not be true—I'm not playing LeBron James) the material implication is true.

So what we shall actually do is translate conditional statements as statements of material implication; and the truth-functional definition given above for conditional is not really for conditional statements; rather, it is for material implication:

D	G	$D \rightarrow G$
TRUE	TRUE	TRUE
TRUE	FALSE	FALSE
FALSE	TRUE	TRUE
FALSE	FALSE	TRUE

So in sum, we shall treat conditionals as if they were statements of material implication, and we shall use the truth-functional definition of material implication when checking the truth value of conditionals. Since we are primarily interested in testing validity, that should not cause much difficulty, because treating conditionals as if they were statements of material implication will generally not affect the validity or invalidity of the arguments we shall be examining. So while I shall continue to call if–then statements *conditionals,* those who insist on being logically scrupulous will remember that they are really statements of material implication.

Exercise 18-1

First diagram the following statements; then, using the truth tables for negation, disjunction, conjunction, and conditional (material implication truth table), tell whether each one is true or false. (You will have to use knowledge of the real world as well as your knowledge of the truth tables.)

Examples:

a. Either Barack Obama was elected president of the United States in 2008 or the chickadee is the national bird of the United States.

> $B \vee C$; B is true, C is false; thus (by the second line of the truth-functional definition of disjunction) the statement is true.

b. If Venus is the largest planet in the solar system, then there is intelligent life elsewhere in our universe.

> $\vee \rightarrow I$ (I stands for: there is intelligent life elsewhere in our universe). The antecedent is false (Jupiter is largest). Is the consequent true, or is it false? Who knows? But for our purposes, who cares? We don't need to know, since we already know that the conditional statement must be true: Since the antecedent is false, the statement will be true no matter what the truth value of the consequent.

1. Orange juice contains vitamin C and baseball is played with a round ball.
2. If some apples are red, then the Earth is flat.
3. Either the Earth is flat or Barcelona is in Spain.
4. If the Earth is flat, then all apples are orange.

5. Either Jupiter is the largest planet in our solar system or Paris is in France.

6. If Republicans support universal health coverage, then Oprah Winfrey is the Queen of England.

7. Iraq had weapons of mass destruction and George Bush won the Nobel Prize for physics.

8. The Earth orbits around the Sun, and Mars orbits around Jupiter.

9. If a basketball is square, then Jupiter is the largest planet in our solar system.

10. Either it is not the case that Jupiter is the largest planet in our solar system or Egypt is in South America.

11. Jupiter is the largest planet in our solar system, and it is not the case that Egypt is in South America.

12. If Jupiter is the largest planet in our solar system, then it is not the case that the Danube River flows through Africa.

13. Either Jupiter is the largest planet in our solar system or Plato's maternal grandfather was an only child.

14. If it is not the case that Jupiter is the largest planet in our solar system, then Plato's maternal grandfather was an only child.

TESTING FOR VALIDITY AND INVALIDITY

Once you've learned to use truth tables to determine the truth value of statements, it's an easy step to apply that knowledge to the testing of deductive arguments for validity or invalidity. Think back to the definition of a valid argument: In a valid argument, if all its premises are true then its conclusion *must* be true; or alternatively, in a valid argument, it is *impossible* for all its premises to be true and its conclusion false. So let's examine a couple of arguments—our old friends *modus ponens* and affirming the consequent—using the truth-table definitions to test validity.

Modus ponens, as you vividly recall, has this form:

$$A \rightarrow B$$
$$\underline{A}$$
$$\therefore B$$

In this argument, there are two variables, *A* and *B*, and they can *vary* in truth value: Each may be either true or false. That gives us a total of four possibilities:

A	*B*
TRUE	TRUE
TRUE	FALSE
FALSE	TRUE
FALSE	FALSE

Now all we have to do is try out each of those four possibilities. Validity requires that in *every* case in which *all* the premises are true, the conclusion is *also* true. That is, we shall be checking to be sure that it is *impossible* for all the premises to be true and the conclusion false: Under *every possible* truth-value assignment that makes all the premises true, the conclusion must also be true.

So, let's try it out (using T for true and F for false). We'll number the lines to make it a bit easier.

	A	*B*	*A* → *B*/	A/∴ *B*
1.	T	T	T T T	T T
2.	T	F	T F F	T F
3.	F	T	F T T	F T
4.	F	F	F T F	F F

Let's take a careful look at this diagram, since we'll be using a lot of them. The first two columns (with *A* and *B* at the top) represent all the possible truth values of the variables. *A* may be true while *B* is also true (the first line); *A* may be true while *B* is false (second line); *A* may be false while *B* is true (third line); and finally, both *A* and *B* might be false. That covers all the possibilities. Then in the rest of the diagram, we work through each of those truth-value assignments. For example, in the third line *A* is false. That makes the antecedent of the first premise false (*A* is the antecedent of the conditional *A → B*, which is the first premise). Since *B* is true in this line, the consequent of the first premise (which is *B*) is true. Thus in the third line the first premise (*A → B*) is true, because when a conditional statement has a false antecedent and a true consequent, the conditional is true. Look next at the second premise: it is *A*, and since *A* is false in this line, that premise obviously is false. The conclusion is just as simple: it is true, since the conclusion is *B*, and *B* is assigned true in the third line.

Now we can examine the diagram in more depth to determine whether the diagrammed argument is valid or invalid. The diagram represents all the possible truth-value assignments, and we shall go through each one to see if there is a case—a truth-value assignment—in which all the premises are true and the conclusion is false. If we find even one, then the argument is invalid, and we need look no further; if there is not even one, then—since we have gone through all the possible truth-value assignments—we shall know that the argument is valid.

What about the first line? The premises are both true under that truth-value assignment; but so is the conclusion. In the second line, the conclusion is false; but so is the first premise. In the third line, the second premise is false, and, besides, the conclusion is true: That is obviously not a truth-value assignment that makes all the premises true and the conclusion false. The fourth line has a false conclusion, and the first premise is true; but the second premise is false. So we have gone through all the possibilities and have discovered that *no* possible truth-value assignment makes *all* the premises true *and* the conclusion false. It is impossible for an argument of this form to have a false conclusion while all its premises are true; therefore, *modus ponens* is a valid argument form.

Now let's look at affirming the consequent. (We already know it's invalid; but let's pretend we don't.) As you recall, it looks a lot like *modus ponens*, only with the second premise and the conclusion switched:

$A → B$
B
$∴A$

We'll set it up just as we did the *modus ponens* argument; and again, we are checking to see if there is any truth-value assignment that will make all the premises true and the conclusion false. If such a truth-value assignment exists, the argument is invalid; if it is *impossible* to make all the premises true and the conclusion false, the argument is valid. As in the *modus ponens* case, there are only two variables, so again there are only four possibilities:

	A	B	A → B/B/	∴A
1.	T	T	T T T T	T
2.	T	F	T F F F	T
3.	F	T	F T T T	F
4.	F	F	F T F F	F

In line 1, the premises are both true, but so is the conclusion. Line 2 certainly will not show that affirming the consequent is invalid: Both the premises are false, and the conclusion is true; to show that the argument is invalid, we need all *true* premises and a *false* conclusion. But look at line 3: The first premise is true, since the antecedent is false and the consequent is true; the second premise is also true under that truth-value assignment; but the conclusion is false. That does it; our quest is ended, our quandary is settled: Affirming the consequent is *invalid,* because—as line 3 clearly demonstrates—it *is* possible to have a truth-value assignment that makes *all* its premises true and its conclusion false. In the fourth line we also find a false conclusion, but there one of the premises is false; so that line doesn't prove anything about the validity or the invalidity of the argument. But it doesn't matter; the invalidity of the argument has already been established by examining line 3; we don't even have to bother with the other lines.

Throwing in a negation doesn't change anything. Suppose you were considering an argument that looked like this:

$$A \to \sim B$$
$$\underline{A}$$
$$\therefore \sim B$$

Of course that's just *modus ponens,* embellished a bit with a negation of one of the variables. The negation doesn't change the form, as long as it is applied throughout the argument. But let's suppose we didn't know that, and we wanted to test to see whether this argument is valid. We do it the same way:

	A	B	$A \to \sim B/A/$	$\therefore \sim B$
1.	T	T	T F FT T	FT
2.	T	F	T T TF T	TF
3.	F	T	F T FT F	FT
4.	F	F	F T TF F	TF

In this case, the conclusion is the *negation* of B; so when B is assigned true (as in the first line) the *conclusion* is false; and when B is assigned false (as in line 2) the *conclusion* is true. And the same applies to the consequent in the first premise: The consequent is the *negation* of B; so when B is assigned true (as in the first line) the *consequent* is false, and since in that line the antecedent is assigned true, the conditional statement (the first premise) is false; and when B is assigned false (as in line 2) the *consequent* is true, making the conditional true.

Now we simply examine each line to see if we can find a case in which all the premises are true and the conclusion is false. The first line obviously will not give us such a case, since the first premise is false. The second line has all true premises, but also a true conclusion. The third line has a false conclusion, but the second premise is false. And the fourth line has neither all true premises nor a false conclusion. So there is no truth-value assignment that will make all the premises true and the conclusion false, and this argument— surprise, surprise—is valid.

Exercise 18-2

Now it's your turn. Use the method of examining all possible truth-value assignments to determine the validity or invalidity of the following argument forms.

1. $P \to Q$
         $\underline{\sim Q}$
         $\therefore \sim P$

   2. $P \to Q$
          $\sim P$
          $\overline{\therefore \sim Q}$

   3. $P \lor Q$
          $\sim P$
          $\overline{\therefore Q}$

   4. $P \lor Q$
          P
          $\overline{\therefore \sim Q}$

   5. $\underline{P \,\&\, Q}$
          $\therefore Q$

PUNCTUATION

So now you are running swiftly and surely through proofs of validity and invalidity; but you may wish to apply this method to arguments that are more complex. To do that, we must deal with punctuation. How can we arrange compound statements so that we can tell what the logical operators cover? There's nothing really new or strange about doing this. Suppose I ask, "What is the total of 2 plus 3 times 4?" One person might answer 20; another, 14. Both answers would have to be accepted, because the question is ambiguous: It might be asking for the product of 5 (the sum of 2 plus 3) times 4, which would give an answer of 20, or for the sum of 2 plus 12 (the product of 3 times 4), for an answer of 14. Or consider the phone call you get from the Beautiful Beachfront Florida Condominium Sales Office. YOU have won a WONDERFUL prize! Of course you must claim your prize in person. You simply stop by their office, watch a BRIEF presentation on the advantages and joys of owning a custom-made Beautiful Beachfront Florida Condominium, and then you can claim your FREE PRIZE: YOU have won a *PORSCHE* and $10,000 or dinner at Joe's. Well, that's not so bad, right? I've won a Porsche, and maybe $10,000 besides. So you find a pair of clean socks and hustle to the sales office to claim your prize. But of course there's been a small misunderstanding. It was NOT: You won a Porsche, and also either $10,000 or dinner at Joe's. Rather, EITHER you won both a Porsche and $10,000, OR you won dinner at Joe's. And you happen to be one of the hundred thousand lucky winners of dinner at Joe's. (But while you're here, why don't we talk some more about that easy payment plan on your very own Beautiful Beachfront Florida Condominium.)

So punctuation is important. In conversation, we punctuate with pauses and inflections and emphasis; in written communication, through commas and colons and parentheses. In logic, we'll use parentheses—()—and brackets—[]—and braces—{}; and if we need more, we'll start over with more parentheses, and so forth. So instead of the ambiguous compound statement:

     Porsche & $10,000 ∨ Dinner at Joe's

we have the much clearer statement:

     (Porsche & $10,000) ∨ Dinner at Joe's

With the statement in that form—$(P \,\&\, T) \lor D$—its real form is quite clear: It is a disjunction. The second disjunct is D; the first disjunct is a conjunction: $P \,\&\, T$. Your mistake—when you rushed down to pick up the keys to your new Porsche—was to interpret the statement as a conjunction: $P \& (T \vee D)$.

With punctuation, plus disjunction, conjunction, conditional, and negation, there is no end to the statements and arguments we can symbolize. Consider this statement:

> If Jupiter is the largest planet and Saturn has rings, then either there is intelligent life on Earth or the moon is made of green cheese.

It could be symbolized like this:

$$(J \& S) \rightarrow (I \vee M)$$

That statement is a conditional (or if you insist, a statement of material implication): Its antecedent is a conjunction and its consequent is a disjunction. And you would have little trouble determining the truth value of that statement. The antecedent is true, because both conjuncts of the conjunction that forms the antecedent are true; and the consequent (the disjunction) is also true, since the first disjunct (there is intelligent life on Earth) is true, and that makes the entire disjunction true (even though I have it on good authority that the moon is not made of green cheese, and so the second disjunct is false). And a conditional statement with true antecedent and true consequent is true.

Suppose we added one more twist to that silly conditional statement:

> *It is not the case that* if Jupiter is the largest planet and Saturn has rings, then either there is intelligent life on Earth or the moon is made of green cheese.

In that case, the statement becomes a negation, and it is symbolized thus:

$$\sim[(J \& S) \rightarrow (I \vee M)]$$

Since without the negation the conditional statement was true, the statement—as a negation—is false. That is, since it is *true* that "If Jupiter is the largest planet and Saturn has rings, then either there is intelligent life on Earth or the moon is made of green cheese," it must be *false* that "*It is not the case that* if Jupiter is the largest planet and Saturn has rings, then either there is intelligent life on Earth or the moon is made of green cheese." Notice that the brackets must go around the *entire* conditional: The negation is of the entire conditional; it is *not* a negation of the antecedent. It would thus be *wrong* to symbolize the statement as:

$$\sim(J \& S) \rightarrow (I \vee M)$$

Try another example:

> If it is not the case that both the Earth contains water and Jupiter is not the largest planet, then Saturn does not have rings.

That one should test your symbolizing mettle. Try it yourself, being careful of the *negations* and of exactly where the parentheses should go.

What's the shape of that statement? In the first place, it does of course contain negations; but the statement itself is *not* a negation. To be a negation, it would have to be something like *this:* "It is *not* the case that *if* . . ." But instead, it started: "*If* it is not the case that both . . ." So what we have is a conditional rather than a negation. The antecedent of that conditional *is* a negation: the *negation* of a conjunction. And the consequent is simply a negation: Saturn does not have rings; that is, it is not the case that Saturn has rings. So put all together, the statement is symbolized thus:

$$\sim(E \& \sim J) \rightarrow \sim S$$

Notice exactly what that first negation covers: It does not apply to the entire statement, nor does it apply just to *E*; it applies to the *conjunction E & ~J*.

What's the truth value of that conditional? It may be easier to see if we set it up step by step. First, fill in the truth values of *E*, *J*, and *S*.

$$\sim(E \,\&\, \sim J) \rightarrow \sim S$$
$$\text{T} \quad\quad \text{T} \quad\quad\quad \text{T}$$

That's easy, right? The Earth does have water, Jupiter is the largest planet, and Saturn does have rings. So now let's add the *negations* of the simple statements *J* and *S*:

$$\sim(E \,\&\, \sim J) \rightarrow \sim S$$
$$\text{T} \quad\quad \text{FT} \quad\quad \text{FT}$$

Since *J* is true (it's true that Jupiter is the largest planet), *~J* (it is not the case that Jupiter is the largest planet) is false; same thing for *S* and *~S*. So now we have a conjunction (*E & ~J*) in which one conjunct (*~J*) is false; and that makes the whole conjunction false:

$$\sim(E \,\&\, \sim J) \rightarrow \sim S$$
$$\text{TF} \quad \text{FT} \quad\quad \text{FT}$$

But the antecedent is not the conjunction; rather, it is the *negation* of the conjunction. Since the conjunction is false, the antecedent (the negation of the conjunction) is true:

$$\sim(E \,\&\, \sim J) \rightarrow \sim S$$
$$\text{T TF} \quad \text{FT} \quad\quad \text{FT}$$

That gives us a conditional statement with a true antecedent and a false consequent; and under that truth-value assignment, the conditional is false:

$$\sim(E \,\&\, \sim J) \rightarrow \sim S$$
$$\text{T TF} \quad \text{FTF} \quad\quad \text{FT}$$

Now that's the sort of fun you can have for hours, without gaining weight, spending money, or risking infection.

There are a couple of perils. Look back at the negation of that conjunction. You remember that the negation applies to the *conjunction*, and *not* to each of the conjuncts. That's important to note, because it is tempting to suppose that ~(*A* & *B*) simply means ~*A* and ~*B*; tempting, but like temptations are supposed to be, terribly, grievously, horrendously wrong. For consider this perfectly true statement: It is not the case that both Jupiter is the largest planet in the solar system and cobras make good pets. That would be symbolized as ~(*J* & *C*), and it is true, as we can easily see by assigning truth values. Since it is true that Jupiter is the largest planet, *J* is true; since it is false that cobras make good pets, *C* is false:

$$\sim(J \,\&\, C)$$
$$\text{T} \quad\ \text{F}$$

So we have a conjunction with a false conjunct; and that—as you remember vividly from the truth-functional definition of conjunction—makes the conjunction false:

~(*J* & *C*)

   TF F

But since the conjunction is false, the *negation* of the conjunction is true:

~(*J* & *C*)

 T TF F

Actually, we don't even need to go through all that, do we? You already knew—even though you probably haven't thought about it all that much—that it is *true* that it is *not* the case that *both* Jupiter is the largest planet *and* cobras make good pets. But look at what happens if we—mistakenly—apply the negation of the conjunction to each of the conjuncts. We get this result: Jupiter is *not* the largest planet *and* cobras do *not* make good pets. And that is a very different claim indeed; in fact, it is false. For Jupiter *is* the largest planet, and so one conjunct of the conjunction is false, making the entire conjunction false. So the moral of the story is just this: The negation of a conjunction applies to the *whole conjunction* and *not* to the conjuncts.

An analogous rule applies to the negation of *dis*junctions. Consider this statement: It is *not* the case that either Jupiter is the largest planet or cobras make good pets. That is a false statement: Jupiter *is* the largest planet, so the first disjunct is true, and that makes the disjunction true—and so the *negation* of the disjunction is false. But if we apply the negation directly to both of the disjuncts, we get this: Either Jupiter is not the largest planet or cobras do not make good pets. That disjunction (unlike the original negation of the disjunction) is *true,* since one disjunct is true: Cobras do not make good pets. *So,* if you try to apply the negation of a disjunction directly to the disjuncts, you get a very different claim. Just as with the negation of a conjunction, the negation of a disjunction applies to the entire disjunction, *not* to the individual disjuncts.

You cannot apply the negation of a conjunction directly to the conjuncts, nor can you apply the negation of a disjunction directly to the disjuncts. However, if you think carefully about what the negation of a conjunction and the negation of a disjunction actually mean, there is a way to remove the parentheses and apply the negation to the conjuncts and disjuncts. Think about *exactly* what you mean when you say: "It is *not* the case *both* that the butler lied and the gardener is guilty." Well, obviously you do *not* mean—as we noted above—that *both* the butler did not lie *and* the gardener is not guilty. What you mean, instead, is that *at least one* of those is *not* the case. That is, you mean that *either* it is not the case that the butler lied *or* it is not the case that the gardener is guilty. Which is to say that ~(*B* & *G*) is the same as (is the logical equivalent of) ~*B* ∨ ~*G*. Notice that it is a *disjunction* and *not* a conjunction. In short, ~(*A* & *B*) is the same as ~*A* ∨ ~*B*; but it is *not* the same as ~*A* & ~*B*.

Something similar can be done with the negation of disjunctions. If I say that it is not the case that I attended Harvard or Yale, I do *not* mean that either I did not attend Harvard or I did not attend Yale. Saying either I did not attend Harvard or I did not attend Yale is compatible with having attended *one* of those universities; what I said, instead, is that I attended *neither.* So saying that it is *not* the case that I attended either Harvard or Yale means that I did not attend Harvard *and* I did not attend Yale. That is, ~(*H* ∨ *Y*) is logically equivalent to ~*H* & ~*Y*. Notice that it is a *conjunction*, in which both of the conjuncts are negated. So now we have a couple of rules—called "DeMorgan's Theorems"—for dealing with the negations of conjunctions and disjunctions. The rules are these:

~(*P* & *Q*) is logically equivalent to ~*P* ∨ ~*Q*.
~(*P* ∨ *Q*) is logically equivalent to ~*P* & ~*Q*.

(Of course, if you had something like ~(~P & Q), that would be logically equivalent to ~~P ∨ ~Q, which—as you recall—is the same as P ∨ ~Q.)

    Now you know a tremendous amount about punctuation and about determining the truth value of rather complicated statements. So try analyzing some statements on your own; or perhaps with a few friends.

Exercise 18-3

First symbolize the following statements and then tell whether the statements are true or false.

Example:

If London is in England, then either New York is in Argentina or Toronto is in Canada.

$$L \to (N \lor T)$$

  TT F T T

The antecedent is true, and the consequent (which is a disjunction) is true (because one disjunct is true), and so the entire conditional statement is true.

1. It is not the case both that Jupiter is the largest planet and the Sun is a planet.
2. Either the Sun is a planet, or, if Earth is a planet then there is intelligent life on Mars.
3. If frogs can hop and cheetahs can run, then penguins can fly.
4. If Barcelona is in Spain, then, if Paris is not in Portugal then Boston is in Canada.
5. If either Ottawa is in Canada or Paris is in Portugal, then Los Angeles is not in the United States.
6. If sharks can swim and eagles can fly, then it is not the case that either lobsters can play basketball or penguins can program computers.
7. It is not the case that if penguins pay taxes then either walruses love Mozart or giraffes play tennis.
8. Either rhinoceroses love classical ballet or both whales can swim and swallows can fly.
        You *can* determine the truth value of the following statements, but it may require a bit of thought (it will *not* require you to look up anything in your encyclopedia).
9. If jabberwockies have sharp teeth, then either Aristotle had brown eyes or eagles can fly.
10. Either slimey toves have scales, or, if tigers do not have stripes then Socrates was an only child.

THE TRUTH-TABLE METHOD OF TESTING FOR VALIDITY

Now that you've mastered punctuation and determining the truth value of statements, we're ready for the fun stuff. As you recall, we've already done some simple cases of proving arguments valid or invalid by means of truth-value assignments; now we're ready for slightly more complicated cases. But remember, when we are determining the *validity* or *invalidity* of an argument, we are not worried about whether any of the statements—the premises and conclusion—of the argument are actually true; what we want to know is this: *If* the premises are true (whether they are or not) would the conclusion *have* to be true? If it is *possible* for all the premises to be true while the conclusion is false, then the argument is invalid; if instead there is *no consistent truth-value assignment* that will make all the premises true and the conclusion false, then the argument is *valid*. (That doesn't mean that the argument is *sound;* the soundness of an argument is a different matter.)

Consider this argument:

> If the butler was polishing silver and the cook was making scones, then the Major murdered Lord Twinkletoes. The cook was not making scones. Therefore, the Major did not murder Lord Twinkletoes.

I'm sure you've been longing to be able to prove that sort of argument either valid or invalid; and now you can. It's a simple matter of making truth-value assignments. Let B stand for the butler was polishing the silver, C stand for the cook was making scones, and M for the Major murdered Lord Twinkletoes. That means we have three variables B, C, and M; and with three variables, there are eight possible truth-value assignments, thus:

B	C	M
T	T	T
T	T	F
T	F	T
T	F	F
F	T	T
F	T	F
F	F	T
F	F	F

That covers all the possibilities; and now all we have to do is try each of those truth-value assignments in the argument, to see if it is possible to find a truth-value assignment that makes all the premises true and the conclusion false. If that *is* possible, then we know that the argument is invalid; if we try *all* the possible truth-value assignments, and *none* of them make all the premises true *and* the conclusion false, then we know it is *not possible* for the premises to be true and the conclusion false, and we'll know that this is a valid argument.

The argument, you recall, goes like this:

> If the butler was polishing silver and the cook was making scones, then the Major murdered Lord Twinkletoes. The cook was not making scones. Therefore, the Major did not murder Lord Twinkletoes.

With B for butler, C for cook, and M for Major, the argument can be represented thus:

$$(B \& C) \to M$$
$$\underline{\sim C }$$
$$\therefore \sim M$$

When we assign truth values, we get this:

B	C	M	$(B \& C)$	$\to$	M /	$\sim C$ /	$\therefore \sim M$
T	T	T	T	T	T	T	T
T	T	F	T	T	F	T	F
T	F	T	T	F	T	F	T
T	F	F	T	F	F	F	F
F	T	T	F	T	T	T	T
F	T	F	F	T	F	T	F
F	F	T	F	F	T	F	T
F	F	F	F	F	F	F	F

For the next step, let's determine the truth values of the negations. That's easy enough: Wherever *C* is assigned true, ~*C* will be false; and wherever *C* is assigned false, ~*C* will be true; and the same applies for *M*.

B	C	M	(B & C)	→ M/~C/∴ ~M
T	T	T	T T T	FT FT
T	T	F	T T F	FT TF
T	F	T	T F T	TF FT
T	F	F	T F F	TF TF
F	T	T	F T T	FT FT
F	T	F	F T F	FT TF
F	F	T	F F T	TF FT
F	F	F	F F F	TF TF

Now consider the first premise. It's a conditional, with a conjunction as the antecedent. So next we must determine the truth values of the conjunction under every truth-value assignment. As you remember, the conjunction is true when *both* of its conjuncts are true; all other truth-value assignments make the conjunction false. So in the first two lines of the truth table the conjunction is true; in the remaining lines, it is false.

B	C	M	(B & C)	→ M/~C/∴ ~M
T	T	T	T T T	T FT FT
T	T	F	T T T	F FT TF
T	F	T	T F F	T TF FT
T	F	F	T F F	F TF TF
F	T	T	F F T	T FT FT
F	T	F	F F T	F FT TF
F	F	T	F F F	T TF FT
F	F	F	F F F	F TF TF

Now all that remains is the truth value of the conditional (the first premise). As is burned into your memory, the *only* way a conditional (a statement of material implication) can be false is when the antecedent is true and the consequent is false; all other truth-value assignments make the conditional true. (Remember, in the premise we are examining, the *antecedent* is a *conjunction*.) There are only two lines in which the antecedent is true: the first two lines. In the first line, the antecedent is true and the consequent is true, so the conditional statement is true; but in the second line, the antecedent (the conjunction) is true and the consequent is false; so the second line is the only line in which the truth-value assignment makes the conditional statement false.

B	C	M	(B & C)	→ M/~C/∴ ~M
T	T	T	T T T	T T FT F T
T	T	F	T T T	F F FT T F
T	F	T	T F F	T T TF F T
T	F	F	T F F	T F TF T F
F	T	T	F F T	T T FT F T
F	T	F	F F T	T F FT T F
F	F	T	F F F	T T TF F T
F	F	F	F F F	T F TF T F

Now we've done all the hard work; all that's left is to look down the lines of truth-value assignments to see if there is one that makes all the premises true and the conclusion false (if there is one, then the argument is invalid; if there is no possible truth-value assignment that makes all the premises true and the conclusion false, then the argument is valid). In the first line, the first premise is true but the second premise is false; but we are looking for a line in which *all* the premises are true (and the conclusion is false), so that line won't help. In the second line, both premises are false, so we can eliminate that line also. Skip down to the fourth line. (We'll return to the third line in a moment.) The first premise is true; and the second premise is also true. So in the fourth line, all the premises are true; however, the conclusion is also true. Since we are seeking a line in which all the premises are true and the conclusion is *false*, we must continue our quest. Look at the line we skipped, the third line. *Both* premises are true, *and* the conclusion is false. On that truth-value assignment, we get all the premises true and the conclusion false. That proves that it *is* possible for all premises to be true and the conclusion false; and that proves that this is an *invalid* argument. We need look no further; it doesn't matter about the other lines of the truth table; once we have found *one* truth-value assignment that makes all the premises true and the conclusion false, we know that the argument is invalid. (It turns out that the truth-value assignments in the seventh line also make all the premises true and the conclusion false. But, having found one line that makes the premises true and the conclusion false, we already know that the argument is invalid.)

Exercise 18-4

Use the truth-table method of determining the validity or invalidity of the following argument forms.

1. $\sim P \rightarrow \sim Q$
     Q
     $\therefore P$

2. $P \rightarrow \sim Q$
     $\sim P$
     $\therefore Q$

3. $\sim P \vee (P \,\&\, Q)$
     $\sim Q$
     $\therefore \sim P$

4. $P \vee (Q \rightarrow R)$
     $\sim R \,\&\, \sim P$
     $\therefore \sim Q$

5. $(P \,\&\, \sim R) \rightarrow Q$
     $\sim P \vee R$
     $\therefore \sim Q$

6. $R \vee (Q \,\&\, \sim R)$
     $\sim Q$
     $\sim P \rightarrow \sim R$
     $\therefore P$

7. $Q \rightarrow \sim (P \rightarrow R)$
     R
     $P \rightarrow \sim Q$
     $\therefore P$

8. $\sim R$
        $Q \rightarrow \sim(P \& \sim R)$
        P
        $\overline{\quad\quad\quad\quad\quad\quad}$
        $\therefore \sim Q$

9. $\sim[P \& \sim(Q \vee R)]$
        $P \rightarrow Q$
        R
        $\overline{\quad\quad\quad\quad\quad\quad}$
        $\therefore \sim Q$

10. $\sim[P \& (Q \vee \sim R)]$
        $P \rightarrow R$
        Q
        $\overline{\quad\quad\quad\quad\quad\quad}$
        $\therefore \sim R$

THE SHORT-CUT METHOD FOR DETERMINING VALIDITY OR INVALIDITY

The truth-table method is great, so long as we are dealing with only two or three variables. If we have arguments with P, Q, and R, it's not much bother to do eight lines of truth-value assignments. But if we have arguments with more variables, things can get out of hand. Consider this argument:

> If it is not the case that either the butler lied or the cook has an alibi, then either Lord Horsefeathers is the murderer or Lady Sweatsuit is an adulterer. If the cook has an alibi, then it is not the case that both the gardener is guilty and the nanny is an impostor. Lord Horsefeathers is not the murderer. Either Lady Sweatsuit is not an adulterer or the duke drinks too much. If the duke drinks too much then Margery gets huffy. Margery does not get huffy. The butler did not lie, and the nanny is an impostor. Therefore, the gardener is not guilty.

The diagram of that argument looks like this:

$\sim(B \vee C) \rightarrow (H \vee S)$
$C \rightarrow \sim(G \& N)$
$\sim H$
$\sim S \vee D$
$D \rightarrow M$
$\sim M$
$\underline{\sim B \& N}$
$\therefore \sim G$

Now—to use the standard truth-value assignment method—all we have to do is go through every possible truth-value assignment and see if there is a truth-value assignment that will make *all* the premises true and the conclusion false. If there is, the argument is invalid; if there is not, it is valid. So how many truth-value assignments will that require?

Well, how many variables are there? B, C, H, S, G, N, D, and M. That's a total of eight variables. If there were only two variables, we would need four lines of truth-value assignments:

X	Y
TRUE	TRUE
TRUE	FALSE
FALSE	TRUE
FALSE	FALSE

With three variables (as we saw in the argument about the Major not murdering Lord Twinkletoes), eight lines are required. And it doubles with each additional variable. Four variables yield 16 different possible truth-value assignments; five variables, 32; six variables, 64 different truth-value assignments; seven variables, 128; and for our eight variables, we would need to examine 256 different and distinct truth-value assignments to determine if there is *one* that will make all the premises true and the conclusion false. While working through 256 lines of truth-value assignments is a wonderful diversion for a winter's evening, it may be a bit time consuming for the hustle of contemporary life. Fortunately, we don't have to go through all those truth-value assignments (though of course you may do so if you wish); there's a shorter, quicker, and to my taste more elegant method of determining the validity or invalidity of an argument.

In order to understand the shorter method of determining validity or invalidity, you must keep in mind *exactly* what we are trying to do when we check truth-value assignments: We are going through all the possible truth-value assignments to see if there is *one* that makes all the premises true and the conclusion false. If we find one, then we know that the argument is invalid; if we cover *all* the possible truth-value assignments, and *not one* will make *all* the premises true *and* the conclusion false—it is impossible to make all the premises true and the conclusion false—then we know that the argument is valid. If we keep in mind exactly what we're seeking, finding it will be much easier.

Consider a short argument:

$$A \rightarrow B$$
$$\underline{B}$$
$$\therefore A$$

How can we test this argument for validity? We can of course do the old truth-value assignments:

A	B	$A \rightarrow B/B/\therefore A$
T	T	T T T T
T	F	T F F T
F	T	F T T F
F	F	F T F F

And now we check all the possible truth-value assignments, and lo, there in the third line is what we're after: true premises and a false conclusion; so this is an invalid argument. But by focusing on exactly what we're after—a truth-value assignment that yields true premises and a false conclusion—we can move a lot faster. We don't need to check *every* truth-value assignment, only the truth-value assignments that have a *chance* of giving us all true premises *and* a false conclusion. That means, in the first place, we don't have to check any truth-value assignments that make A true (as in the first two lines); for A is the conclusion, and when A is assigned true, the conclusion is automatically true, and what we are seeking is a truth-value assignment that will make the conclusion *false* and the premises true. Truth-value assignments that make A true are sending us down a dead end, and we can eliminate them. In like manner, we aren't interested in truth-value assignments that make B false: the second premise is just B, and when B is assigned false, that premise is false; and we are in search of all *true* premises and a false conclusion. So that last line of truth-value assignments can be eliminated. And that leaves just the one truth-value assignment: the third line, the one that proves the argument invalid.

So the *shorter* (and sweeter) truth-value assignment method looks like this:

$$A \rightarrow B/B/\therefore A$$
$$$$
F

Start by assigning the conclusion false. Now at this point, of course, we don't know whether we'll be able to make all the premises true *and* the conclusion false; but we do know that if there is *any* possibility of making all the premises true and the conclusion false, then it will have to be when A (the conclusion) is assigned the truth value of false. Since A has been assigned false in the conclusion, we next must assign A false wherever it appears in the argument:

$A \rightarrow B/B/\therefore A$

  F   F

Now we turn to the premises. What truth-value assignment will make the premises true? Well, the first premise is a conditional, with a false antecedent. What truth value should we assign in order to make that conditional statement true? It doesn't matter. Since the antecedent is false, the conditional will be true *no matter what* truth value we assign the consequent. So we don't know what truth value to assign the consequent. Don't assign it *any* truth value; instead, look for a place at which you have *no choice* about what truth value to assign, and that place is not far to seek: the second premise, B. What truth-value assignment will make B true? That's sort of like asking who is buried in Grant's tomb. Obviously to make the second premise (B) true, we must assign B true.

$A \rightarrow B/B/\therefore A$

  F   T   F

And again, we must assign the same truth value to B wherever it occurs in the argument:

$A \rightarrow B/B/\therefore A$

  F   T T   F

But as already noted, the first premise will be true no matter what we assign B:

$A \rightarrow B/B/\therefore A$

  F T T T   F

And there we have it: All the premises are true and the conclusion is false, and the result is quick, neat, and easy proof that the argument is invalid. And it's just as easy to prove an argument valid. Consider this argument:

$A \rightarrow B/A/\therefore B$

Again, start by making the conclusion (B) false:

$A \rightarrow B/A/\therefore B$

                F

And as before, we do not yet know whether we will be able to make all the premises true and the conclusion false; but we know that if there is any possibility of that, it must be when B (the conclusion) has the truth-value assignment false.
Now make B false wherever it occurs in the argument:

$A \rightarrow B/A/\therefore B$

       F   F

Next we turn to the premises, and we attempt to find a truth-value assignment that will make them *all* true. The first premise is a conditional, with a false consequent; in order to make the conditional true, we *must* make the antecedent *false* (because a true antecedent and a false consequent would make the conditional statement false):

$A \rightarrow B/A/\therefore B$

   F T F   F

But now we must make *A* false wherever it occurs in the argument; and that means that we are *forced* to make the second premise (which is *A*) false; thus it is *impossible* to make all the premises true and the conclusion false. The *only* way to make both the conclusion false and the first premise true resulted in the second premise being false. Therefore, this is a *valid* argument.

     Notice that we could reach the same result by a slightly different route. Instead of making the first premise true, we might have skipped to the second premise and made it true by assigning *A* true:

$A \rightarrow B/A/\therefore B$

   F   T   F

That would make the conclusion false and the second premise true, but it would make the first premise false (with a true antecedent and a false consequent); again, the result is that it is impossible for all the premises to be true and the conclusion false, which is as it should be, since this is a valid argument.

     Incidentally, there is yet another way to assign truth values to prove the argument valid. We could start with the premises, and start by making the second premise true:

$A \rightarrow B/A/\therefore B$

          T

Then we assign *A* true throughout the argument:

$A \rightarrow B/A/\therefore B$

   T   T

And thus in order to make the first premise ($A \rightarrow B$) true, we *must* assign *B* true (since the antecedent is true, the consequent must be true in order for the entire conditional statement to be true).

$A \rightarrow B/A/\therefore B$

   T   T T

That truth-value assignment is the *only* way of making all the premises true; so in order to make all the premises true, we were *compelled* to assign *B* true. But of course *B* is also the conclusion. Thus *if* the premises are true, then the conclusion *must* be true; and that's precisely our definition of a *valid* argument.

     When we turn back to our longer argument, nothing really changes; there are just more steps. In case you don't remember every line in that argument, it goes like this:

$\sim(B \vee C) \rightarrow (H \vee S)$
$C \rightarrow \sim(G \& N)$
$\sim H$
$\sim S \vee D$
$D \rightarrow M$
$\sim M$
$\underline{\sim B \& N}$
$\therefore \sim G$

Writing it in a form that will make it easy to apply the short-cut method of truth-value assignment validity testing, we start with the argument in this form:

$$\sim(B \lor C) \to (H \lor S)/C \to \sim(G \& N)/\sim H/\sim S \lor D/D \to M/\sim M/\sim B \& N/\therefore \sim G$$

Now we just go through the same steps we did with the shorter argument; the only difference is that there are more steps. Keep in mind what we're after: a truth-value assignment that will make the conclusion false and all the premises true. If we find just one such assignment, then we know that the argument is invalid; if we find instead that it is *impossible* to make all the premises true and the conclusion false, then we know that the argument is valid. Let's start by trying to make the conclusion false. The conclusion is ~*G*; assign it false, being sure to place the *F* under the ~: we are *not G* making false; rather, we are making the *conclusion*, which is ~*G*, false.

$$\sim(B \lor C) \to (H \lor S)/C \to \sim(G \& N)/\sim H/\sim S \lor D/D \to M/\sim M/\sim B \& N/\therefore \sim G$$
$$\text{F}$$

Next, in order for ~*G* to be false, *G* must be true, right? So we assign *G* true.

$$\sim(B \lor C) \to (H \lor S)/C \to \sim(G \& N)/\sim H/\sim S \lor D/D \to M/\sim M/\sim B \& N/\therefore \sim G$$
$$\text{FT}$$

And now we assign *G* the truth value *true* wherever it appears in the argument (being sure ·to assign true to *G*, *not* to the conjunction in which it occurs).

$$\sim(B \lor C) \to (H \lor S)/C \to \sim(G \& N)/\sim H/\sim S \lor D/D \to M/\sim M/\sim B \& N/\therefore \sim G$$
$$\text{T}\text{FT}$$

OK, where are we now? We've made the conclusion false, and the truth-value assignment we used (assigning *G* true) is the only possible way of making the conclusion false. Will we be able to make all the premises true and the conclusion false? I have no idea. But I do know that *if* that is possible, it will have to be done by assigning *G* true. (If *G* is assigned false, that will make the conclusion *true*, and our quest for a truth-value assignment that will make all the premises true and the conclusion false won't even get started.) So now the conclusion is false. In the next step, we try to find a truth-value assignment that will make all the premises true. So what truth-value assignments should we make next?

We could start with the first premise: What should we assign *B*, *C*, *H*, and *S* in order to make that conditional statement true? There are lots of truth-value assignments that would do the job: If we make *H* true, then the disjunction (*H* ∨ *S*) is automatically true; and since that disjunction is the consequent of a conditional, that would make the entire conditional automatically true (since the only way a conditional can be false is when the antecedent is true and the consequent is *false*). We could get the same result by making *S* true (and then we could assign *H* false). Or we could make both *H* and *S* false (making the disjunction (*H* ∨ *S*) false), but then make the antecedent ~(*B* ∨ *C*) false: A false antecedent and a false consequent would make the conditional true. So in short, there are many different truth-value assignments that would make the first premise true; how do we choose among them?

We don't. Instead, look for a premise where there is only *one* truth-value assignment that will make it true. And there are three premises of that sort: ~*H*, ~*M*, and the last premise, ~*B* & *N*. Which one should we do? It doesn't matter. Once we have found a place where we are *forced* to make a single truth-value assignment—it's our *only* chance of getting all true premises and a false conclusion—we can go ahead and make the assignment.

If instead we assigned truth values to the first premise (the conditional) in order to make *that* premise true, that wouldn't really be wrong: There are lots of different truth-value assignments that will make that premise true, but if we happen to be lucky and get a truth-value assignment that makes all the premises true and the conclusion false, then we know that the argument is invalid. The problems occur if the truth-value assignment we use to make that conditional statement true does *not* result in all true premises and a false conclusion; then we would have to go back and try *all the other* possible truth-value assignments that would make that premise true, to see if *any* of them would yield all true premises and a false conclusion (because to be sure that an argument is *valid*, we must be sure that there is *no possible* truth-value assignment that would make all the premises true and the conclusion false). And if we have to go through all those possible truth-value assignments, then our short-cut method for determining validity becomes much less of a shortcut. So, whenever possible, make truth-value assignments where you have *no choice* about what truth-value assignment to make. (*If* you should reach a point at which there is *no* forced truth-value assignment—a very rare occurrence, but not impossible—then go ahead and make *one* of the truth-value assignments that will work at that point, and if it leads to all true premises and a false conclusion, then you know that the argument is invalid, and you can rest from your labors; but if it is impossible on *that* truth-value assignment to get all true premises and a false conclusion, *then* you must remember to go back and check all the other possible truth-value assignments to see if one of those other options would have led to all true premises and a false conclusion; of course, if *none* of them do, you know the argument is valid.)

Let's get back to where we were. In the argument we are testing, there are several premises where we have *no choice* about what truth-value assignments to make in order to make those premises true. As noted, those premises are: $\sim H$, $\sim M$, and the last premise, $\sim B$ & N. (The only way that $\sim H$ can be true is to assign H false, and so on.) And as we noted, so long as we have found a place where we have *no choice* about what truth-value assignments to make (in order to keep open the possibility of getting all true premises and a false conclusion) we can go ahead and make the truth-value assignment. It doesn't matter which one we do: $\sim H$, $\sim M$, or $\sim B$ & N. So let's do the first one: $\sim H$. We have to make $\sim H$ true, in order to have any chance of making all the premises true and the conclusion false.

$$\sim(B \vee C) \to (H \vee S)/C \to \sim(G \,\&\, N)/\sim H/\sim S \vee D/D \to M/\sim M/\sim B \,\&\, N/\therefore \sim G$$
$$\qquad\qquad\qquad\qquad \text{T} \qquad\qquad \text{T} \qquad\qquad\qquad\qquad\qquad\qquad\qquad \text{FT}$$

And as noted before, in order for $\sim H$ to be true, we *must* assign H the truth value false.

$$\sim(B \vee C) \to (H \vee S)/C \to \sim(G \,\&\, N)/\sim H/\sim S \vee D/D \to M/\sim M/\sim B \,\&\, N/\therefore \sim G$$
$$\qquad\qquad\qquad\qquad\qquad \text{T} \qquad \text{TF} \qquad\qquad\qquad\qquad\qquad\qquad \text{FT}$$

And now we simply assign H false wherever it occurs in the argument:

$$\sim(B \vee C) \to (H \vee S)/C \to \sim(G \,\&\, N)/\sim H/\sim S \vee D/D \to M/\sim M/\sim B \,\&\, N/\therefore \sim G$$
$$\qquad\qquad \text{F} \qquad\qquad\qquad \text{T} \qquad \text{TF} \qquad\qquad\qquad\qquad\qquad\qquad \text{FT}$$

Now we look for another place at which we are *forced* into a single truth-value assignment; and we don't have far to look. There's the premise $\sim M$; and to make that premise true, we must assign M false. Combining those steps, now our short-cut truth-value assignment looks like this:

$$\sim(B \vee C) \to (H \vee S)/C \to \sim(G \,\&\, N)/\sim H/\sim S \vee D/D \to M/\sim M/\sim B \,\&\, N/\therefore \sim G$$
$$\qquad\qquad \text{F} \qquad\qquad\qquad \text{T} \qquad \text{TF} \qquad\qquad\qquad\qquad \text{TF} \qquad\qquad \text{FT}$$

And again, we make *M* false wherever we find it:

$$\sim(B \lor C) \to (H \lor S)/C \to \sim(G \& N)/\sim H/\sim S \lor D/D \to M/\sim M/\sim B \& N/\therefore \sim G$$

               F   T   TF   F TF   FT

Now what? We're still trying to make all the premises true and the conclusion false; and we still don't know whether that will be possible, but we *do* know that *if* it's possible, this is the only truth-value assignment that has a chance of working (so if this truth-value assignment doesn't make all the premises true and the conclusion false, then it's not possible to do so, and the argument is valid). We get another choice about what truth-value assignments to make: There's still the last premise, ~*B* & *N*; to make that conjunction true, we must make both conjuncts true (we would have to then assign *N* true and *B* false). Or we could turn our attention to *D* → *M*: Since *M* (the consequent) has been assigned false, we must assign the antecedent (*D*) false, in order to make the conditional true. Again, since in both cases the choices of truth-value assignment are *forced*, it doesn't matter which one we do. Let's do the conditional (there's no reason for choosing that over the conjunction; I'm just more in the mood for a conditional). In order to make that conditional (with its false consequent) true, we *must* make the antecedent false; and that's easy: The antecedent is *D*, so we assign *D* false:

$$\sim(B \lor C) \to (H \lor S)/C \to \sim(G \& N)/\sim H/\sim S \lor D/D \to M/\sim M/\sim B \& N/\therefore \sim G$$

                 F   T   TF   FT F TF   FT

And next we assign all *D*s everywhere the truth value false:

$$\sim(B \lor C) \to (H \lor S)/C \to \sim(G \& N)/\sim H/\sim S \lor D/D \to M/\sim M/\sim B \& N/\therefore \sim G$$

                 F   T   TF   F F   T F TF   FT

Suddenly we recognize that in the fourth premise—the disjunction, ~*S* ∨ *D*—there is a forced truth-value assignment. Having made *D* (the second disjunct) false, we *must* make the remaining disjunct, ~*S*, *true* in order to make that premise true. So to make ~*S* true, we must assign *S* the truth value of false; and that truth-value assignment makes the premise true.

$$\sim(B \lor C) \to (H \lor S)/C \to \sim(G \& N)/\sim H/\sim S \lor D/D \to M/\sim M/\sim B \& N/\therefore \sim G$$

                 F   T   TF TFTF F T F TF   FT

And then we assign *S* false wherever it occurs (namely, in the first premise):

$$\sim(B \lor C) \to (H \lor S)/C \to \sim(G \& N)/\sim H/\sim S \lor D/D \to M/\sim M/\sim B \& N/\therefore \sim G$$

   F   F   T   TF TFTF F F T F TF   FT

So where do we go next? Well, there now remains only one place where we are *forced* to make a specific truth-value assignment: the last premise, ~*B* & *N*. Since we are trying to make all the premises true (and the conclusion false), and since for a conjunction to be true both of its conjuncts must be true, it follows that we must assign truth values that will make both conjuncts true. Obviously, to make the second conjunct, *N*, true, we must assign *N* the truth value true:

$$\sim(B \lor C) \to (H \lor S)/C \to \sim(G \& N)/\sim H/\sim S \lor D/D \to M/\sim M/\sim B \& N/\therefore \sim G$$

   F   F   T   TFTF TF F T FTF T   FT

And almost as obviously, in order to make the first conjunct (~*B*) true, we must assign *B* false:

$$\sim(B \vee C) \to (H \vee S)/C \to \sim(G \& N)/\sim H/\sim S \vee D/D \to M/\sim M/\sim B \& N/\therefore \sim G$$

$$ F F T TF TFTF\ F\ T\ F TF TFT\ T FT$$

And again, we assign *N* true wherever it occurs, and *B* false wherever it occurs:

$$\sim(B \vee C) \to (H \vee S)/C \to \sim(G \& N)/\sim H/\sim S \vee D/D \to M/\sim M/\sim B \& N/\therefore \sim G$$

$$F F\ F T\ T TF TFTF\ F\ T\ F TF TFT\ T FT$$

Having done that, we again look over the premises to see if there is now any place where we are forced to assign truth values in order to make all the premises true; and our attention falls on the second premise, $C \to \sim(G \& N)$. As *G* and *N* have both been assigned true, that makes the conjunction in which they occur true:

$$\sim C \to \sim(G \& N)$$

$$T T$$
$$T$$

But then the *negation* of that conjunction will be false.

$$C \to \sim(G \& N)$$

$$T T$$
$$T$$
$$F$$

The entire statement is a conditional, and its consequent is false; thus in order to make that premise true, we must assign the antecedent—*C*—false. When we put this into the truth table, the truth-value assignments now look like this:

$$\sim(B \vee C) \to (H \vee S)/C \to \sim(G \& N)/\sim H/\sim S \vee D/D \to M/\sim M/\sim B \& N/\therefore \sim G$$

$$F F F\ FTF TTT TF TFTF\ F\ T\ F TF TFT\ T FT$$

And once again, we assign false to *C* wherever it occurs in the argument:

$$\sim(B \vee C) \to (H \vee S)/C \to \sim(G \& N)/\sim H/\sim S \vee D/D \to M/\sim M/\sim B \& N/\therefore \sim G$$

$$F\ F F F FT FTTT TF TFTF\ F\ T\ F TF TFT\ T FT$$

At last we arrive at the last premise (actually, the first premise). All the other premises have been assigned truth values that made them true and also made the conclusion false. We still don't know whether this argument is valid or invalid; but we know that if there is any possible truth-value assignment that will make all the premises true and the conclusion false, then this is the one: If we cannot make all the premises true and the conclusion false on this truth-value assignment, then it cannot be done, and the argument is valid. Actually, at this point there are no more truth-value assignments to be made: Now it's just a matter of checking the first premise to see if the *only* possible truth-value assignment that makes all the other premises true and the conclusion false will *also* make the first premise true.

The first premise—with its assigned truth values—looks like this:

$$\sim(B \vee C) \to (H \vee S)$$

$$F\ F F F$$

It's a conditional, with the antecedent being the negation of a disjunction, and the consequent being a disjunction. Obviously, both of the disjunctions are false (since both disjuncts are false in both disjunctions):

$$\sim(B \vee C) \rightarrow (H \vee S)$$
$$\quad\ \text{F F F} \qquad \text{F F F}$$

In the antecedent, the *negation* of the false disjunction is true:

$$\sim(B \vee C) \rightarrow (H \vee S)$$
$$\text{T F F F} \qquad \text{F F F}$$

But that leaves us with a true antecedent and a false consequent; and thus the conditional statement—the first premise—is *false* under that truth-value assignment.

We were unable to find a truth-value assignment that made all the premises true and the conclusion false; but you can't say we didn't try. In fact, we tried *every possible* truth-value assignment that had a *chance* of making all the premises true and the conclusion false. Every truth-value assignment we made was the *only one* that could possibly work to make all the premises true and the conclusion false; and in the end, the only possible truth-value assignment that could make all the other premises true and the conclusion false yielded a *false* premise; therefore, we now know that it is *impossible* to find a truth-value assignment that will make *all* the premises true and the conclusion false; and thus we now know, and have proved, that that argument is *valid*.

I've gone through a rather lengthy example to show how the short-cut method of determining validity works, how it can be applied to arguments with many premises and a multitude of variables, and how much fun it is. There's nothing difficult about doing long arguments; it involves the same steps you follow with shorter arguments, but you do more of those steps. Having done this argument, you should have no trouble doing the shorter exercises.

Let's look at one more example—a short one—of how the short-cut method of determining validity or invalidity works:

> Either Anthony is a liar or Bert is a thief. If Anthony is not a liar, then Carol is the brains of the outfit. Carol is not the brains of the outfit. Therefore, Bert is not a thief.

The argument could be represented thus:

$$A \vee B$$
$$\sim A \rightarrow C$$
$$\underline{\sim C}$$
$$\therefore \sim B$$

And when written across the page, in a form that makes it easier to apply the short-cut method of testing validity, it looks like this:

$$A \vee B / \sim A \rightarrow C / \sim C / \therefore \ \sim B$$

As always, we shall try to find a truth-value assignment that makes all the premises true and the conclusion false, thus proving the argument *invalid*. If we find such a truth-value assignment to be impossible, then we know that the argument is *valid*. Suppose we start by making the conclusion false. (We could also start by making the third premise true; but the conclusion is *usually* a nice starting point. Of course if the conclusion were a *conjunction*, then it would not be a good idea to start with the conclusion: Too many truth-value assignment options would make the conjunction false.) There is only one way to make the conclusion false: *B* must be assigned true, so that ~*B* can be false.

$$A \vee B / \sim A \rightarrow C / \sim C / \therefore \sim B$$
$$ \text{FT}$$

Next we assign the other occurrences of *B* true:

$$A \vee B / \sim A \rightarrow C / \sim C / \therefore \sim B$$
$$ \text{T} \text{FT}$$

Now we look for a place where we are forced to make a truth-value assignment, and the only such place is the third premise. (There are several different truth-value assignments that would make the second premise true; and in the first premise, since one disjunct is already true, the disjunction will be true no matter what truth value is assigned to A, so we certainly are not forced to make a specific truth-value assignment there.) The third premise is ~*C*; and of course there is only one way for ~*C* to be true: *C* must be assigned false.

$$A \vee B / \sim A \rightarrow C / \sim C / \therefore \sim B$$
$$ \text{T} \text{TF} \text{FT}$$

And then to maintain consistency we must assign *C* false in the second premise:

$$A \vee B / \sim A \rightarrow C / \sim C / \therefore \sim B$$
$$ \text{T} \text{F TF} \text{FT}$$

But now we have—as the second premise—a conditional with a false consequent; and in order to make that premise true, we will have to make the antecedent (~*A*) false, which means that *A* will have to be true:

$$A \vee B / \sim A \rightarrow C / \sim C / \therefore \sim B$$
$$ \text{T FT T F TF} \text{FT}$$

So we must assign *A* true in the first premise also:

$$A \vee B / \sim A \rightarrow C / \sim C / \therefore \sim B$$
$$\text{T T FTT F TF} \text{FT}$$

That truth-value assignment makes the disjunction (the first premise) true:

$$A \vee B / \sim A \rightarrow C / \sim C / \therefore \sim B$$
$$\text{T T T FT T F TF} \text{FT}$$

So on this truth-value assignment, all the premises are true, and the conclusion is false; and that proves that the argument is invalid.

When using the short-cut method of proving an argument valid or invalid, you should start by trying to find a truth-value assignment that makes all the premises true and the conclusion false. Thus—as in the examples we examined—you should always try to make truth-value assignments where you have no real choice about what truth-value assignments to make; that is, if the conclusion is *A*, then you should assign *A* false. And if the conclusion is *A* & *B*, then you should probably *not* start with the conclusion (there are too many ways to make that conjunction false: make *A* true and *B* false, *B* true and *A* false, or make both false); instead, look at the premises, and see if there is some truth-value assignment that is *forced*: a place where you *must* assign a specific truth value if you are to have any chance of making all the premises true. But what if you come to a point at which there is *no* forced truth-value assignment in either the premises or the conclusion? In that case, you simply assign a truth value arbitrarily, and see if it works; that is, assign one of the variables true (or false), and see if that assignment will lead you to a result in which all the premises are true and the conclusion false. If it does, then you know that the argument is invalid, and you are done. But if it does *not*—if that truth-value assignment does *not* result in all true premises and a false conclusion—then you must go back to the point at which you made the arbitrary truth-value assignment, and try the *other* truth value (if you initially assigned a truth value of true, now try assigning false); because before you can declare an argument valid, you must be certain that there is *no possible truth-value assignment* that will make all the premises true and the conclusion false.

Exercise 18-5

Use the short-cut truth-value assignment method to prove the following arguments valid or invalid.

1. $\sim Q \vee R$
       $\sim Q$
       _____
       $\therefore \sim R$

2. $P \rightarrow \sim Q$
       $\sim P$
       _____
       $\therefore Q$

3. $\sim Q \rightarrow \sim R$
       R
       _____
       $\therefore Q$

4. $P \vee (Q \rightarrow R)$
       $\sim R \,\&\, \sim P$
       _____
       $\therefore \sim Q$

5. $R \vee (Q \,\&\, \sim R)$
       $\sim Q$
       $\sim P \rightarrow \sim R$
       _____
       $\therefore P$

6. $\sim(\sim P \,\&\, Q)$
       $\sim P \rightarrow R$
       $\sim R$
       _____
       $\therefore Q$

7. $\sim R$
       $\sim(P \,\&\, \sim R)$
       _____
       $\therefore P \rightarrow \sim Q$

8. $Q \rightarrow \sim(P \rightarrow R)$
    R
    $\underline{P \rightarrow \sim Q}$
    $\therefore P$

9. $\sim[P \,\&\, (Q \vee \sim R)]$
    $P \rightarrow R$
    $\underline{Q}$
    $\therefore \sim R$

10. $\sim[P \,\&\, \sim(Q \vee R)]$
    $P \rightarrow Q$
    $\underline{R}$
    $\therefore \sim Q$

11. $\sim(P \vee Q) \rightarrow \sim R)$
    $S \vee R$
    $\underline{\sim S \,\&\, \sim Q}$
    $\therefore P$

12. $R \rightarrow (\sim S \rightarrow \sim P)$
    $S \rightarrow \sim Q$
    $\underline{Q \,\&\, R}$
    $\therefore P \vee \sim Q$

13. $\sim[P \rightarrow (Q \,\&\, R)]$
    $Q \rightarrow \sim S$
    $\underline{\sim S \vee \sim P}$
    $\therefore \sim R$

14. $S \rightarrow \sim P$
    $Q \vee R$
    $\underline{\sim[Q \,\&\, (P \rightarrow \sim R)]}$
    $\therefore R$

Exercise 18-6

Now it's time to put it all together. We'll start with some arguments, which you must write in symbolic form. You will have to think carefully about punctuation (parentheses and brackets). Notice that— as occurs in many real-life arguments—the conclusion will *not* always be the *last* statement; it may be first, last, or in the middle; it might even be combined with a premise, which will require that the conclusion and that premise be separated. [Included in brackets are the suggested symbols; notice that these symbols do *not* include negations, which you must supply on your own.] You know how to do these; but let's start with an example anyway, to be sure everyone is on the same wavelength.

Examples:

Penguins do not write bad checks [*P*]. For if penguins write bad checks, then either seals will lose their credit cards [*S*] or walruses will not be able to obtain credit [*W*]. But walruses will certainly be able to obtain credit, and if walruses will be able to obtain credit, then seals will not lose their credit cards.

When you analyze the structure of arguments, it is always a good idea to *start* by determining the *conclusion*. In this argument, the conclusion is stated first in the argument: Penguins do not write bad checks. (Notice that it is a negation, and should be represented as ~*P*.) So we start with that:

$$\therefore \sim P$$

The first premise (in abbreviated form) is: If penguins, then either seals or not walruses. And that is represented as: $P \rightarrow (S \vee \sim W)$. When that premise is added, the argument looks like this:

$$P \rightarrow (S \vee \sim W)$$
$$\overline{\therefore \sim P}$$

The final premise is a conjunction: Walruses, *and* if walruses then not seals. That is: $W \& (W \rightarrow \sim S)$. When we stick that in as the second premise, the diagrammed argument looks like this:

$$P \rightarrow (S \vee \sim W)$$
$$W \& (W \rightarrow \sim S)$$
$$\overline{\therefore \sim P}$$

Now you do a few:

1. Either studying logic improves your love life [I], or studying logic is a waste of time [W]. If you graduate [G], then your mother will be proud of you [M] and you will become rich [R]. If studying logic improves your love life, then you will graduate. Your mother will be proud of you, but [and] you will not become rich. Therefore, studying logic is a waste of time.

2. If cats enjoy Stravinsky [C], then dogs like progressive jazz [D]. It is not the case that if anteaters prefer to tango [A], then penguins favor polkas [P]. Therefore, anteaters do prefer to tango; because either cats enjoy Stravinsky or penguins favor polkas, and dogs do not like progressive jazz.

3. If sausage is good for you, [S], then pizza is a health food [P]. If cholesterol is bad for the heart [C], then sausage is not good for you. If cholesterol is not bad for the heart, then either medical researchers have lied [M] or doctors are very confused [D]. It follows, then, that pizza is not a health food; because it is not the case that either medical researchers have lied or doctors are very confused.

4. Either the judge will be lenient [J], or the sentence will be severe [S] and the case will be appealed [A]. If the case is appealed, then the defense lawyers will withdraw from the case [W] and the bar association will investigate [B]. The defense lawyers will not withdraw from the case, but the bar association will investigate. Therefore, the judge will be lenient.

5. If the defendant is not guilty [G], then either the alibi witness told the truth [A] or both the police accepted a bribe [P] and the jury was duped [J]. Either the jury was duped or the criminal justice system is corrupt [C]. The defendant is guilty and the criminal justice system is not corrupt. Therefore, the police did accept a bribe, and the alibi witness lied.

6. The jury must have been prejudiced against the defendant [P]. For if the jury returned a verdict of guilty [G], then either they were prejudiced against the defendant or they were confused about the law [C]. If the judge explained the law carefully [E], then it is not the case both that the jury members were intelligent [I] and that the jury members were confused about the law. The judge did explain the law carefully and the jury members were intelligent, and the jury returned a verdict of guilty.

Exercise 18-7

For questions 1–6 in Exercise 18-6, use the short-cut truth-value assignment method to determine the validity or invalidity of the arguments; then do the same for the following arguments:

7. $\sim E \rightarrow (A \vee \sim B)$
             $G \vee \sim E$
             $\sim (G \& \sim A) \rightarrow \sim H$
             H
             $\overline{\therefore \sim B}$

8. $(M \vee N) \rightarrow \sim(P \& Q)$
    $R \vee (P \& \sim M)$
    $\sim R \& (\sim M \rightarrow Q)$
    _____
    $\therefore \sim N$

9. $\sim E \vee G$
    $E \rightarrow (A \vee B)$
    $(G \vee A) \rightarrow \sim H$
    _____
    $\therefore H \rightarrow \sim B$

10. $B \rightarrow [D \rightarrow (E \vee \sim G)]$
    $H \rightarrow [\sim(B \vee E) \& G]$
    H
    _____
    $\therefore \sim D$

11. $B \rightarrow E$
    $\sim(\sim A \& \sim B) \vee D$
    $\sim(E \vee D)$
    _____
    $\therefore \sim A$

✔●—|**Study** and **Review** on **mythinkinglab.com**

REVIEW QUESTIONS

1. Give the truth-functional definition for disjunction and for conjunction.
2. Give the truth-functional definition for conditional (or more precisely, for material implication).
3. What sort of truth-value assignent must you find in order to prove that an argument is invalid?
4. Why is it that simply finding a truth-value assignment that makes all the premises true and the conclusion also true is *not* enough to prove that an argument is *valid?* What is actually required to prove an argument valid?

▯●—|**Read** the **Document** on **mythinkinglab.com**

For much more detail on the material covered in this chapter, see Chapters 3, 4, and 5 of Virginia Klenk, *Understanding Symbolic Logic*, 5th Ed. (Upper Saddle River, NJ: Prentice Hall, 2008.

19
❖ ❖ ❖

Arguments about Classes

))•▬ **Listen** to the **Chapter Audio** on **mythinkinglab.com**

Truth tables and the short-cut truth-value assignment method enable us to determine the validity or invalidity of a variety of complex arguments. But for one species of argument those methods won't work. That species of argument is not a rare or exotic one; it includes such workaday, run-of-the-mill arguments as this:

> All lions are mammals. All mammals are friendly. Therefore, all lions are friendly.

And also this:

> No penguin is fond of walruses. Some penguins are psychics. Therefore, some psychics are not fond of walruses.

And again:

> All rock stars are wealthy. No logicians are wealthy. Therefore, no logicians are rock stars.

Of course we don't want to just ignore such arguments; sometimes it may be quite important to determine whether they are valid or invalid—and their validity or invalidity may not be intuitively obvious. Indeed, it is notoriously true that such arguments may often sound valid when they are invalid. For example:

> All dogs have fur. All cats have fur. Therefore, all dogs are cats.

That somehow sounds right, even though we know it can't be (its premises may be true, but its conclusion is certainly false). And at times, the invalidity of such arguments may be even less obvious:

> All projects that are really valuable require sacrifices. Fighting this war certainly requires sacrifices. So fighting this war must be really valuable.

That argument is invalid, of course; but it sounds valid and may well pass for valid—especially in the U.S. Senate. In any case, it is not immediately obvious *why* it is invalid. So how are we to prove that such arguments are invalid and that valid arguments—such as the following—really are valid?

> All lions are mammals. All mammals are friendly. Therefore, all lions are friendly.

Certainly not by means of truth-value assignments. For we would have to diagram it thus:

> *L* (for "All lions are mammals")
> *M* (for "All mammals are friendly")
> ∴ *P* (for "All lions are friendly")

And that argument obviously would be invalid: It is a simple matter to assign *P* false, *L* true, and *M* true, resulting in all true premises and a false conclusion. But the argument is valid, not invalid. So that representation of the argument leaves a lot out. In this chapter, we work on a way to analyze what was omitted.

Arguments like the examples above deal with *classes,* with *categories.* "All lions are mammals": That means that the class of lions is contained in the class of mammals; everything that is a member of the lions class is also a member of the mammals class. We call such statements *categorical propositions.* We call them that because that is what they are: propositions that make claims about categories and the members of categories.

In order to facilitate our discussion of categorical logic, it will be convenient to have some common terminology. First, we need terms for the parts of a categorical proposition. When we have a statement such as "All lions are mammals," we want to be able to refer to the lions part of the statement and to distinguish it from the mammals part. In that statement, "lions" is the *subject* term; "mammals" is the *predicate* term. And it is important not to mix them up. It's one thing to say that all lions are mammals; it's something quite different to claim that all mammals are lions.

TYPES OF CATEGORICAL PROPOSITIONS

It will also be useful to divide categorical propositions into four sorts. The first is the *universal affirmative (UA):* All lions are mammals, all college students are wealthy, all men are pigs, all the children in Lake Wobegon are above average, all lovers are star-crossed, all bridges in Idaho are structurally sound. These are *universal* because the subject term deals with *all* members of its class: all lions, all college students, all the children in Lake Wobegon, all bridges in Idaho. Notice that the class may be rather narrowly defined. The last proposition does not say something about all bridges; rather, it makes a claim about a narrower class: bridges-in-Idaho. The class might be narrower still: railroad-bridges-in-Idaho, or railroad-bridges-in-Idaho-constructed-since-1970. The proposition is still *universal* if it makes a claim about *all* members of the class (however small or limited that class might be): "All U.S. Presidents named Barack like basketball" is a universal proposition, though the subject class has only one member. In fact, the subject class of a universal proposition may be empty: "All students over 12 feet tall are psychology majors." It is universal *affirmative,* simply because it is an affirmative rather than a negative statement. All college students *are* wealthy. A universal affirmative proposition states that all members of the subject class are also members of the predicate class: All members of the class of college students are also members of the class of wealthy persons.

The second type of categorical proposition is the *universal negative (UN):* No college students are wealthy. It is a *universal,* because it makes a claim about *all* members of the subject class: In the entire class of college students, *not one*—not a single member of that whole class—is wealthy. And of course it is negative because it claims that *no* (rather than all) college students are wealthy.

The third type of categorical statement is the *particular affirmative (PA): Some* (particular) college students *are* (affirmative) wealthy. Perhaps all college students are wealthy, or perhaps not; the particular affirmative asserts only that at least *some* college students are wealthy (actually, at least *one*). And you have probably already guessed that the fourth type of categorical proposition is the *particular negative (PN): Some* college students are *not* wealthy (perhaps none of them are; this particular negative statement asserts only that at least *one* college student is *not* wealthy).

Exercise 19-1

For each of the following categorical propositions, first specify—*exactly*—both the subject and the predicate terms; and then tell what form the proposition is.

Example:

No real cowboy eats brussel sprouts.

The subject is: real cowboys. The predicate is: eats brussel sprouts (or persons-who-eat-brussel-sprouts, since that actually defines the class). And of course it is a universal negative (UN) proposition.

1. Some penguins wear red bow ties.
2. No tomatoes are purple.
3. Some Olympic athletes are quite wealthy.
4. No painting is more beautiful than a flower.
5. Some defendants are not guilty.
6. All children in Lake Wobegon are above average.

RELATIONS AMONG CATEGORICAL PROPOSITIONS

With the four types of categorical propositions in mind, we can begin to think about the relations among them. If a universal affirmative (UA) statement is true, what does that imply? Suppose that it's true that all college students are wealthy. Then the corresponding particular negative (PN) statement—some college students are not wealthy—must be false. And going in the other direction, if the PN statement is true (*some* college students are *not* wealthy), then the corresponding UA (*all* college students *are* wealthy) statement must be false. That is, UA and PN are *contradictories:* If one is true, the other must be false; if one is false, the other must be true. The same relation holds between universal negative (UN) statements and particular affirmative (PA) statements: They are contradictories. If it is true that no college students are wealthy, then it must be false that some college students are wealthy. If it is true that some college students are wealthy, then it must be false that no college students are wealthy.

What about some other relations among UA, UN, PA, and PN propositions? Well, it would seem that if (UA) all college students are wealthy, then it must also be true that (PA) some college students are wealthy; and that if (UN) no college students are wealthy, then (PN) some college students are not wealthy. Do those implications hold? That is a vexed question. Its answer depends on what sort of *existential presupposition* we ascribe to universal statements. By "existential presupposition," we do not mean that universal statements are experiencing bad faith or are worried about their essences or their place in the cosmos. Rather, the question concerns whether a universal statement implies actual existence of members of the subject class. That is, if we say "All college students are wealthy," does that imply that any college students really *exist* (i.e., does it imply that there *exist* some members of the subject class)? And if we say "No college students are wealthy," does that imply that there *are some* college students?

That question gets a trifle thorny. Universal statements *usually*—in ordinary conversation—do seem to carry existential presuppositions. Suppose, for example, I played baseball yesterday, and you are inquiring about my performance: "Did you have a good day at bat?" I reply, with zest: "All my hits were home runs!" Very impressive, right? But when you inquire further about how many hits I had, you discover that in fact I had *no* hits at all. You might suggest that I had been a bit deceitful: Saying that *all* my hits were home runs would *seem* to suggest the presence of at least *one* hit. On the other hand, some of our universal statements do *not* seem to carry existential presuppositions. At the beginning of a baseball game, the announcer warns: All persons throwing objects onto the playing field will be immediately ejected. But that does not imply that there are such persons; in fact, it is hoped that there are *not*. And (to borrow an excellent example from I. M. Copi) when a physicist asserts Newton's law that "all bodies not acted upon by external forces persevere in their state of rest or of uniform motion in a straight line," certainly the physicist is *not* suggesting that there actually exist any bodies-not-acted-upon-by-external-forces; indeed, they would claim that there are *no* such bodies. (Incidentally, that statement *is* a universal *affirmative:* The *subject* is bodies-not-acted-upon-by-external-forces. The subject class is defined by a negative characteristic; but the statement makes an affirmative statement about all members of the class so defined.) So contemporary logicians have usually found it easier to say that *universal* propositions do *not* carry an existential presupposition. Particular propositions do imply existence of members of the subject class; universal propositions do *not*. As noted above, that is not always exactly consistent with ordinary usage; but on the whole, for logical analysis, it is better *not* to assume that universal propositions have existential presuppositions. (After all, if we *want* to assert an existence claim *along with* a universal proposition, we can always add the appropriate particular proposition: "All ducks have feathers, *and some* ducks have feathers.")

VENN DIAGRAMS

Now let's get to the fun part: Venn diagrams, developed by John Venn, an English mathematician. By using them, we can not only visualize the implications of categorical propositions, but also determine the validity or invalidity of many arguments using categorical propositions, and we can have a lot of fun doing so.

Diagramming Statements

Let's start with a universal affirmative proposition: All seals are pessimists. What does that really mean? It means that the class of seals is fully contained within the class of pessimists. That's a mouthful. But using Venn diagrams, we can illustrate it clearly and elegantly: Venn's pictures may not be worth a thousand words, but they are worth at least a few dozen.

To start with, let's represent the class of seals, as shown in Figure 19-1. That's easy enough, right? Everything in the circle is a seal, and all seals are in the circle; and

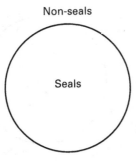

Figure 19-1   The class of seals and its complement, non-seals.

anything that is *not* in the circle is not in the class of seals: it is non-seal. Another way of describing the class of non-seals is to say that it is the *complement* of the class of seals. Every class has a complement; the complement of class A is simply the class of all things that are not members of class A. (Incidentally, the complement of class A—the class of non-A—also has a complement: the class of everything that is *not non*-A, in other words, A. That is, the complement of the complement of class A is simply class A.) We'll use a special symbol to represent class complements: a bar over the symbol used for the class. Thus the complement of A is "A bar" ($\bar{A}$). (Walruses, volcanoes, skateboards, and U.N. ambassadors all fall into the realm of non-seal; they are members of the complement of S; they are members of $\bar{S}$.) Within the circle, there may still be a lot of variety: pessimistic seals and optimistic seals, friendly seals and haughty seals, clever seals and dull seals. But what all members of the class have in common is that they are seals.

So we've got the subject term represented, now for the predicate. The predicate deals with the class of things that are pessimistic: pessimistic seals, pessimistic football coaches, pessimistic taxpayers; pessimistic pine trees, if there are such. And we represent the predicate class just as we did the subject (see Figure 19-2). Everything within the circle is a pessimist; everything outside the circle is a *non*-pessimist. (Notice that everything outside the circle need not be an *optimist;* many people and seals—and almost all rocks, turnips, volcanoes, and radioactive isotopes—are neither pessimistic nor optimistic; but they are still *non*-pessimists.)

So now we have a circle representing the class of seals and another representing the class of pessimists. How do we put them together?

There are several possibilities. We could just draw two circles as shown in Figure 19-3. That may be esthetically appealing, but it has some problems: the two classes are completely separate, and that makes it impossible for any seals to be pessimists. We need some way for the classes to overlap. So we could try another arrangement (Figure 19-4). Now we have the opposite problem: With these concentric circles, the class of seals is wholly contained within the class of pessimists, and we may want to represent the claim that some seals are *not* pessimists. The solution is a Venn diagram to overlap the circles

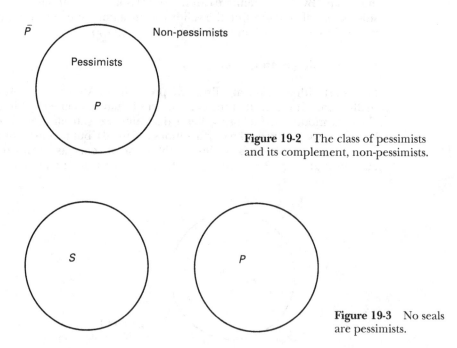

Figure 19-2   The class of pessimists and its complement, non-pessimists.

Figure 19-3   No seals are pessimists.

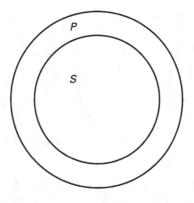

Figure 19-4 All seals are pessimists.

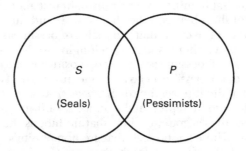

Figure 19-5

(see Figure 19-5). With this arrangement, we can represent all manner of wonderful class relationships.

First, it is essential to understand what each part of this picture represents. With all the labels applied, the diagram looks like Figure 19-6. What does all that mean? We already know that everything in the circle on the left is a seal, and everything in the circle on the right is a pessimist. But those circles overlap; and so now we must discuss the *intersection* of the two circles. That intersection, or *product*, represents everything that is a member of *both* classes; that is, the intersection represents pessimistic seals, or the class of pessimistic seals: things that are *both* seals *and* pessimistic, and it is written as simply *SP.* The part of the *S* circle that does *not* intersect *P* represents all members of the class that are *not* members of *P.* that is, all seals that are *not* pessimistic. That part of the circle represents the *product* (the intersection) of *S* and the *complement* of *P.* the product of the classes *seal* and *non-pessimist.* And it is written as *S$\bar{P}$* The pattern is repeated in the other circle. The part of the *P* circle that does *not* intersect the *S* circle represents all pessimists that are not seals: all members of the class *P* that are not members of *S.* That is, it represents the product of *P* and non-*S*: $\bar{S}P$. Finally, there is that part of the diagram that falls outside both circles; and indeed, I imagine that's where most of us fall, since we are

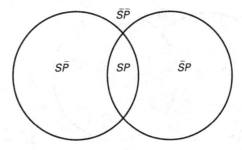

Figure 19-6

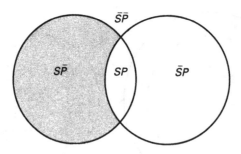

Figure 19-7   All seals are pessimists.

neither seals nor pessimists. That represents everything that is non-seal *and* non-pessimist: the product or intersection of the complements of *S* and of *P*, which *is* $\bar{S}\bar{P}$.

With that in mind, we can represent just about anything we might wish to say about the relationships between the class of seals and the class of pessimists. We can, for example, represent the claim that: All seals are pessimists. *Exactly* what does that claim assert? Simply this: that there is *nothing* belonging to the class of seals that does not *also* belong to the class of pessimists; or more positively, *all* members of the seal class are *also* members of the pessimist class. Or one more way of stating the same thing: There are *no* members of the intersection of *S$\bar{P}$*; *nothing exists* in *that* section of circle *S*.

So how do we represent that universal affirmative proposition? Easy; we just shade out that part of the diagram, to show that nothing is there (Figure 19-7). Notice exactly what that means. There are no seals that are non-pessimists; all seals are members of the class of pessimists. But it does *not* imply that there *really exist* any pessimistic seals (any members of *SP*), *or* that there exist any pessimists who are *not* seals ($\bar{S}P$), or that anything exists that is a non-pessimistic non-seal ($\bar{S}\bar{P}$). It says only that any seals that do exist (if there should be any) are all pessimists. (As you recall, universal propositions do *not* carry existential presuppositions. Remember the signs your high school coach put up on the walls of the locker room? Things like "All quitters are losers." But coach certainly was not suggesting that any quitters really exist—at least not in *his* locker room.) So this diagram implies *only* that there is *nothing* in *S$\bar{P}$*; it doesn't make any claims about what might or might not exist anywhere else.

What about a universal *negative* proposition, such as: *No* seals are pessimists. "No seals are pessimists" simply means that there is *nothing* that is *both* a seal *and* a pessimist; no members of the class of seals are also members of the class of pessimists; *nothing exists* in the intersection of those two classes; *SP* is empty. And so we just shade out that section of the diagram (Figure 19-8). Again, just as with the universal affirmative proposition, this says nothing about what actually exists or does not exist *anywhere else* in the diagram; it says *only* that there is nothing in *SP*.

Suppose we now want to represent a *particular* affirmative proposition: *Some* seals are pessimists. That statement asserts that there really does exist something that is *both* a seal *and* a pessimist: There exists something that is a member of the class of seals and also a member of the class of pessimists; something exists in the *intersection* of the class of seals

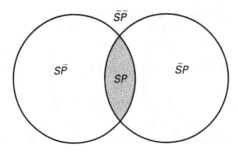

Figure 19-8   No seals are pessimists.

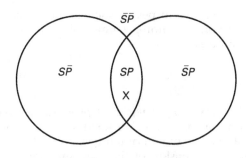

Figure 19-9   Some seals are pessimists.

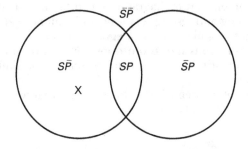

Figure 19-10   Some seals are not pessimists.

and the class of pessimists. How do we represent that? We can simply place an X in that *SP* section of the diagram, as shown in Figure 19-9. That means there is at least *one* seal that is also pessimistic; at least one member of the class of seals is also a member of the class of pessimists. Maybe there are lots of pessimistic seals, maybe just one, but there is at least one really existing individual occupying the intersection of the seal and pessimist classes. Are there some seals that are *non*-pessimists? Are there some pessimists that are *non*-seals? Maybe, maybe not; *no* claim is made about any other part of the diagram.

That leaves only *negative* particular statements, such as: Some seals are *not* pessimistic. That means that something really exists that is a seal *and* is *non*-pessimistic; there is at least one member of the intersection of the class of seals and the *complement* of the class of pessimists; something is $S\bar{P}$. And that is represented by placing an X in the appropriate section of the diagram (Figure 19-10). Again, this statement makes no claims

---

Another Way of Representing Categorical Propositions

There's another useful way of representing categorical propositions: in terms of their existence claims. For example, we might say, There are no passenger pigeons. Unfortunately, passenger pigeons are now extinct: That class has no members; the class is empty. That fact could be represented (using P to stand for passenger pigeons) thusly: $P = 0$. If we should be so fortunate as to discover that in some remote area there remains a small population of passenger pigeons, we would then say, There are some passenger pigeons; that would mean that the class of passenger pigeons is *not* empty, which would be represented as: $P \neq 0$. Taking this process a step further, we can represent standard-form categorical propositions—all seals are pessimists, no seals are pessimists, some seals are pessimists, some seals are not pessimists—using this technique. The universal affirmative proposition—all seals are pessimists—

implies (as shown in Figure 19-7) that the intersection of $S\bar{P}$ is empty; that is, $S\bar{P} = 0$. The universal negative proposition—no seals are pessimists—implies that the intersection of S and P is empty: $SP = 0$. The particular propositions are just as simple. The particular affirmative proposition—some seals are pessimists—means that there does exist something that is a seal *and* is also a pessimist: The intersection of the class of seals and the class of pessimists is *not* empty. Thus the particular affirmative is represented as: $SP \neq 0$. And finally, a particular negative proposition (some seals are *not* pessimists) means that there does exist something that is a member of the class of seals and is *not* a member of the class of pessimists: The intersection, or product, of the class of seals and the complement of the class of pessimists is *not* empty. That is represented as $S\bar{P} \neq 0$.

about whether there are or are not any pessimistic seals or any non-seal pessimists; it says only that there exists at least one seal non-pessimist: The intersection of the class of seals and the class of non-pessimists is *occupied*.

Diagramming Arguments

So we now have ways of representing categorical propositions, but a single categorical proposition does not an argument make. We need a way to represent *arguments* using categorical propositions and a way of determining whether those arguments are valid or invalid. Fortunately, a simple extension of the diagrams used to represent categorical propositions will speed us on our way to diagramming and testing such arguments. It may not be handy for diagramming and testing very long and complex categorical arguments, but we can use it on the most popular sort of categorical argument: the famous *categorical syllogism*. Categorical syllogisms consist of two propositions as premises, a third as conclusion, and three terms or categories or classes (such as seals or pessimists), each of which occurs twice in the argument.

Consider an example of a categorical syllogism: one that we shall now be able to diagram and analyze with amazing alacrity.

> All seals are pessimists.
> All pessimists cheat at cribbage.
> _____
> Therefore, all seals cheat at cribbage.

Here we have three categorical propositions, each of which we can represent with a two-circle diagram, thusly:

All seals are pessimists (Figure 19-11).
All pessimists cheat at cribbage (i.e., All pessimists are cribbage-cheaters) (Figure 19-12).
All seals are cribbage-cheaters (Figure 19-13).

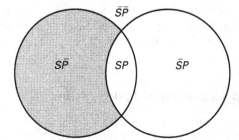

Figure 19-11   All seals are pessimists.

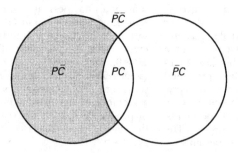

Figure 19-12   All pessimists are cribbage-cheaters.

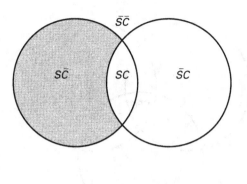

Figure 19-13 All seals are cribbage-cheaters.

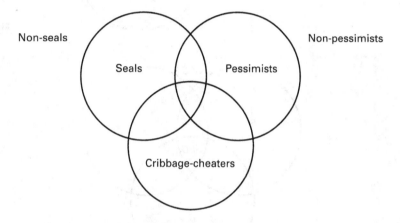

Figure 19-14 Seals, pessimists, and cribbage-cheaters.

Now how do we represent and analyze the *argument?* Simply by putting the circles together. We are discussing the classes of seals, pessimists, and cribbage-cheaters, so we require three overlapping circles rather than two. But the basic principles remain the same. Let's start with three overlapping circles, *S*, *P*, and *C*, representing the classes of seals, pessimists, and cribbage-cheaters (Figure 19-14). What does each section of those circles actually represent? Well, the area *outside* of *all* the circles represents the *intersection* of the *complements* of *S*, *P*, and *C*. (Anything outside all three circles is non-*S*, non-*P*, and non-*C*: It is a non-seal, non-pessimist, non-cribbage-cheater. And I trust that most of us—with perhaps a few unsavory exceptions—fall into that category.) That is, it represents $\bar{S}\bar{P}\bar{C}$. In contrast, there is the area where all three circles overlap, and that area represents the intersection or product of the three classes. That little area where all three circles overlap is home to (and only to) all pessimistic seals who cheat at cribbage. And that intersection is labeled *SPC*. So let's add *SPC* and $\bar{S}\bar{P}\bar{C}$ to the picture, as shown in Figure 19-15. Where is the area of residence for the seals who are pessimists but who do *not* cheat at cribbage ($SP\bar{C}$, for short)? Obviously it must fall within the seal class, and, also, it must fall within the pessimist class. And finally, it must fall *outside* the class of cribbage-cheaters. There is only one spot that fits those criteria (Figure 19-16).

Now what about the cribbage-cheaters who are *non*-seals and *non*-pessimists (indeed, there may be some in our midst; they are known as $\bar{S}\bar{P}C$ to their friends). They must fall

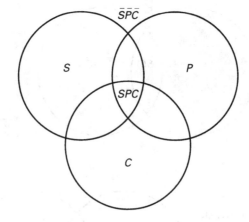

Figure 19-15

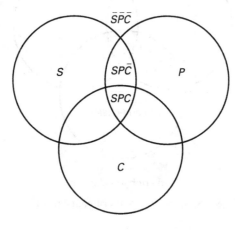

Figure 19-16 $SP\bar{C}$, where there are pessimistic seals who do not cheat at cribbage (if any exist).

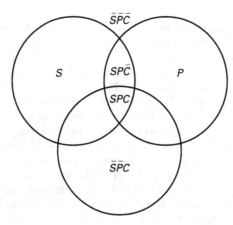

Figure 19-17 $\bar{S}\bar{P}C$, cribbage-cheaters who are non-seal and non-pessimist.

within the cribbage-cheater circle, but outside the seal circle and outside the pessimist circle, as shown in Figure 19-17.

You get the idea, right? So let's fill in all the blanks, and you can study Figure 19-18 a bit until you are comfortable with all those intersections of classes and complements of classes and where they fit.

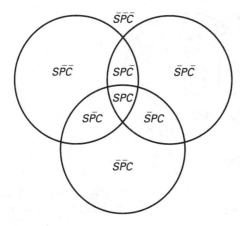

Figure 19-18 All the areas are identified.

With all of that done, mapping out the categorical syllogism is easy. Lest you have forgotten, the argument we were examining was this:

All seals are pessimists.
All pessimists cheat at cribbage.
———————————————————
Therefore, all seals cheat at cribbage.

Consider the first premise: All seals are pessimists. How shall we diagram that in the three-circle diagram? The proposition asserts that all members of the class of seals are contained in the class of pessimists; that is, *no* seals fall outside the pessimist class. So we shall have to shade out *all* parts of the seal circle that fall *outside* the pessimist circle, as shown in Figure 19-19.

That was easy, right? Just be sure that you get *all* the parts shaded; you've got to cover *both SP̄C̄ and SP̄C* (and try to stay within the lines with your shading; those skills you honed in kindergarten should serve you well).

Now we add the second premise to the diagram: All pessimists cheat at cribbage. That means that all members of the pessimist class are also members of the cribbage-cheaters class: There are *no* pessimists outside the cribbage-cheaters circle. So next we shade out all parts of the pessimist circle that fall outside the cribbage-cheaters circle (notice that again there are *two* sections to shade: *SPC̄* and *S̄PC̄*; that shouldn't

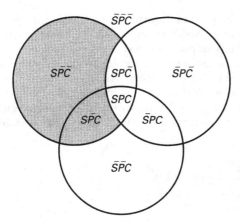

Figure 19-19 All seals are pessimists.

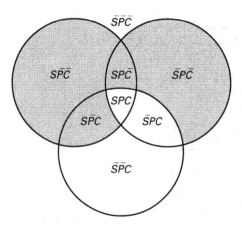

Figure 19-20 All seals are pessimists, and all pessimists cheat at cribbage.

give you any trouble; just focus on shading out *all* of *P* that is outside *C*), as shown in Figure 19-20.

Now we've diagrammed all (both) the premises, and this may be a good moment to pause from our labors and reflect on exactly what we are doing, and why. What we want to know is whether the argument is *valid;* that is, we want to know if the truth of the premises would *guarantee* the truth of the conclusion: If the premises are true, will the conclusion *have* to be true? If it is in any way *possible* for all the premises to be true and the conclusion false, then the argument is *invalid;* if that is *not* possible, then the argument is valid. We are trying to determine whether this argument is valid; if it is valid, then, if its premises are true, its conclusion *must* be true. We have the premises diagrammed into the Venn diagram; now all we have to do is *scrutinize* that diagram to see if according to that diagram the conclusion *must* be true.

The conclusion is, All seals are cribbage-cheaters. That is, the conclusion asserts that *all* members of the class of seals are *also* members of the class of cribbage-cheaters. Of course if any section of our diagram is shaded out, that means that there is *nothing* in that section. The question, then, is this: Are *all* *non*shaded parts of the seal circle completely contained *within* the cribbage-cheaters circle? If they are, then that means that *all* possible seals *must* be cribbage-cheaters; that would make the argument *valid.* But if there is any unshaded section of the seals circle that is *not* contained in the cribbage-cheaters circle, then there might *possibly* be a seal lurking there who does *not* cheat at cribbage; that possibility would be enough to make the argument *invalid.*

Look back at the diagram in Figure 19-20: *Is* there any *un*shaded part of circle *S* that does *not* fall within circle *C?* No! The only unshaded part of circle *S* is *SPC;* and *SPC* falls within circle *C.* So there is *no* place for a seal that does *not* cheat at cribbage; *if* there are any seals (and remember, universal propositions do *not* carry an existence presupposition), then they *must* be cribbage-cheaters. Therefore, the argument is *valid:* The truth of the premises makes it *impossible* for the conclusion to be false.

Now you try one. *Diagram* the premises of this argument onto a Venn diagram, and then *examine* your diagram to determine the validity or invalidity of the argument:

All seals are pessimists.
All cribbage-cheaters are pessimists.

Therefore, all seals cheat at cribbage.

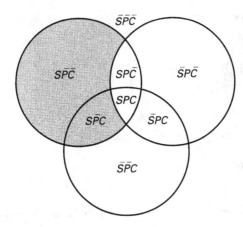

Figure 19-21   All seals are pessimists.

I'm going to try to work this one out also; but *do it yourself* before you peek further down the page.

What's your answer? Invalid, right? First you diagrammed the first premise, "All seals are pessimists"; the resulting diagram looked like Figure 19-21.

Then you added the second premise: All cribbage-cheaters are pessimists. That premise required you to shade all parts of circle *C* that are *not* contained in circle *P*, so you shaded out section $\bar{S}\bar{P}C$. You *would* have shaded section $S\bar{P}C$, but it was already shaded by the first premise, so you didn't have to shade it again. (Of course, some of you are so compulsive that you could not resist reshading section $S\bar{P}C$, so now that part of your diagram is double-shaded; that's OK: compulsive people make great logicians.) Your final diagram looked like Figure 19-22. Then you looked at that diagram to see if there was any way that the conclusion could still be false (after the premises are diagrammed in). The conclusion is, All seals are cribbage-cheaters. Does that follow? Or is it instead *possible* that the conclusion is *false:* that there *might possibly* be some seals who are *not* cribbage-cheaters? When we examine the diagram, we see that there *is* such a possibility: Section $SP\bar{C}$ is *not* shaded, so there *might* be some seals there; since that section of the seal circle falls *outside* the cribbage-cheater circle, it *is* possible for there to be some seals that are *not* cribbage-cheaters. So when the premises of the argument are true, it is still possible for the conclusion to be false; therefore, this argument is *invalid.*

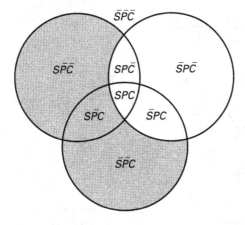

Figure 19-22   All cribbage-cheaters are pessimists is added to the diagram.

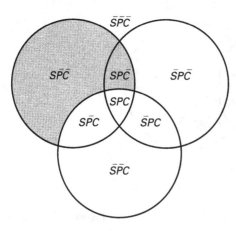

Figure 19-23   All seals are cribbage-cheaters.

Now we need to do some arguments with *particular* propositions. Consider this argument:

Some seals are pessimists.
All seals are cheaters-at-cribbage.
_____

Therefore, some pessimists are cheaters-at-cribbage.

We do this in basically the same fashion as we did the other categorical syllogisms. Let's start with the universal affirmative: the second premise. It states that *all* members of the seal class fall within the cribbage-cheaters class; to represent that proposition in our Venn diagram, we shade out all parts of the seal circle that fall outside the cribbage-cheaters circle, as shown in Figure 19-23. Next we add the first premise: It is a *particular* proposition, and so it asserts that something actually exists. Specifically, it asserts that there exist some (at least one) pessimistic seals. That is, there *is something* in the intersection of the classes of seals and pessimists. To represent that premise in our Venn diagram, we place an X at the appropriate place in the diagram. But exactly where? There are two sections of the Venn diagram where seal-pessimists might dwell: $SP\bar{C}$ and SPC. But we already know—from the second premise—that there is *nothing* in the $SP\bar{C}$ section (that is why that section is shaded out); so the seal-pessimists—whose existence is affirmed by the first premise—must be lodged in the only section that remains open to seal-pessimists: SPC. And it is there that we place an X, as shown in Figure 19-24. Now we simply look at the completed

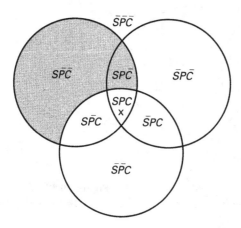

Figure 19-24   Some seals are pessimists is added to the diagram.

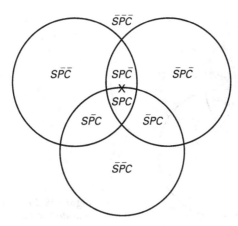

Figure 19-25 Some seals are pessimists.

Venn diagram to see if the argument is valid: That is, when all the premises are drawn in, *must* the conclusion be true? The conclusion is that some pessimists are cribbage-cheaters; that is certainly guaranteed by our Venn diagram, since there is an X squarely within the intersection of P and C, signifying that there *is* something that is both a pessimist and a cribbage-cheater. When all the premises are true, it is impossible for the conclusion to be false. So this argument is valid.

In diagramming that argument, we started with the universal rather than the particular premise, and there's a good reason for doing so. Look what would have happened had we started with the particular premise: Some seals are pessimists. To represent that in our Venn diagram, we must place an X within the intersection of the class of seals and the class of pessimists. But that intersection is made up of *two* sections: $SP\bar{C}$ and SPC. In which of those sections do our pessimistic seals belong? The premise doesn't tell us, and we must be very careful *not* to put any information in the diagram that is *not* contained in the premises. If we placed the X in $SP\bar{C}$, that would assert that there are some seals that are pessimists and are *not* cribbage-cheaters. But the premise doesn't say that: It says only that some seals are pessimists; it says *nothing* about whether those seal-pessimists do or do not cheat at cribbage. So obviously we can't just place our X in the SPC section, either: It is one thing to say (as the premise does) that some seals are pessimists; it is quite another thing to say—and that premise does *not* say—that those seal-pessimists are cribbage-cheaters. So where do we place the X? Look at Figure 19-25.

The X is on the fence, in the middle, right on the line between sections $SP\bar{C}$ and SPC. And that fence-sitting X indicates that there is something in at least one of those sections (possibly both), but we do *not* know which. That is, there is at least one pessimistic seal; but we do not know whether it cheats at cribbage.

Suppose, then, that we had started our Venn diagram by diagramming the first premise: the particular proposition "Some seals are pessimists." Our Venn diagram would now look like Figure 19-25, with its fence-sitting X. Next we turn to the second premise—all seals are cribbage-cheaters—and insert it into the diagram; to do so, we shade out all parts of S that are not contained in C, and the resulting diagram looks like Figure 19-26. But when we do that, our X gets jolted off the fence. Section $SP\bar{C}$ is closed. Since we have an X that must be lodged in either $SP\bar{C}$ or SPC, we now know that that X belongs to SPC (we don't have to change it on the diagram; we just have to think about it and realize where it must fall). And so the final Venn diagram looks just like the one we got when we started by diagramming the universal premise; of course, that's precisely as it should be. The moral of this story is this: If you start with the particular premise (rather than the universal premise) you can *still* get the right answer; it's just a bit *easier* if you start with the universal premise. You may do as you wish, but I prefer the easiest way of doing Venn diagrams.

Figure 19-26   All seals are cribbage-cheaters is added to the diagram.

Now you do one. Represent this argument by means of a Venn diagram, and tell whether it is valid or invalid.

Some pessimists are seals.
All cribbage-cheaters are seals.

Therefore, some cribbage-cheaters are pessimists.

Now that you've finished the problem, let's see if we got the same answer. You started, I hope, with the universal proposition (if some of you started instead with the particular premise, then you'll have to trudge along on your own: I'm taking the easy way). To diagram "All cribbage-cheaters are seals," we simply shade out all the parts of the cribbage-cheaters circle that fall *outside* the seal circle, as shown in Figure 19-27. Next we toss the first premise—some pessimists are seals—into the diagram. To do that, we have to place an X *somewhere* in the pessimist–seal intersection, made up of sections $SP\bar{C}$ and SPC; but exactly where, and in which section? Are the pessimistic seals cribbage-cheaters or non-cribbage-cheaters? We don't know, and we can't say. So we must put the X on the line dividing section $SP\bar{C}$ from section SPC to indicate that there *is* something in at least *one* of those sections, but we do not know which one. (Notice, in Figure 19-28, that the X falls *completely within* the intersection of *S* and *P*. It is completely within *both* circle *S and* circle *P*.

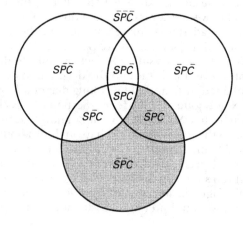

Figure 19-27   All cribbage-cheaters are seals.

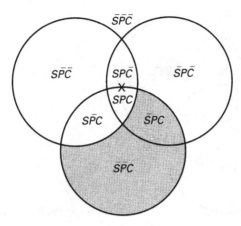

Figure 19-28 Some pessimists are seals is
added to the diagram.

That is as it should be, since the premise asserts that there *are* pessimistic seals; what we
don't know is whether those pessimistic seals are cribbage-cheaters.) Now we examine our
diagram of the premises to see if the diagram makes it *impossible* for the conclusion to be
false (if so, the argument is valid; if it *is* possible for the conclusion to be false, then the
argument is invalid). The conclusion is: Some cribbage-cheaters are pessimists. Does our
diagram of the premises show that there *must* be some cribbage-cheaters that are pessimists? It shows that it is *possible* that some cribbage-cheaters are pessimists, but it does *not*
show that to be necessary, for—according to our Venn diagram of the premises—there
certainly are some pessimists (there is an X squarely within the *P* circle); but we can *not*
tell whether any cribbage-cheaters are pessimists (because the X in the *P* circle is *on the
line* of the cribbage-cheaters circle, and not inside the circle; so we don't know which way
it falls). So this argument is invalid.

Let's do one more, together, and this one is about as hard as these get, which, as you
will quickly gather, is not very hard at all.

> Some seals are not pessimists.
> Some pessimists are not cribbage-cheaters.
> _____
> Therefore, some seals are not cribbage-cheaters.

In diagramming this argument, we don't have a universal proposition to do first; so let's just
start with the first premise: a particular negative proposition, "some seals are not pessimists," like all the propositions in this argument. That means that there is something in
the seal class that is *not* a member of the pessimist class; so we have to place our X *completely
inside* the seal circle and *completely outside* the pessimist circle. But we don't know whether
our non-pessimistic seals are cribbage-cheaters; so the X must fall *on* the line of the
cribbage-cheaters circle (and inside *S*, and outside *P*), as in Figure 19-29. Now we turn to the
second premise: Some pessimists are not cribbage-cheaters. To diagram this premise,
we must put the X completely *inside* the pessimist circle and completely *outside* the cribbage-
cheaters circle; since we do not know whether our pessimistic cribbage-cheaters are seals or
not, the X must straddle the line dividing seals from non-seals, as in Figure 19-30.

Now we examine the diagram, to see if those premises make it *impossible* for the
conclusion—some seals are not cribbage-cheaters—to be false. *Must* it be the case that
some seals are not cribbage-cheaters? Well, no. It's *possible* that some seals are not cribbage-cheaters; but it is also possible that there are *no* seals that are not cribbage-cheaters.
To see that, look closely at both Xs. One X shows that there *are* seals, but we don't know if
those seals are cribbage-cheaters or not (for that falls *on the line* of the cribbage-cheater
circle). The seals represented by that X *might* not be cribbage-cheaters, but then again,

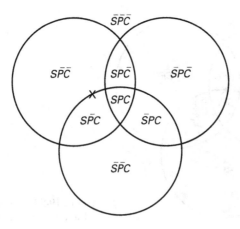

Figure 19-29   Some seals are not pessimists.

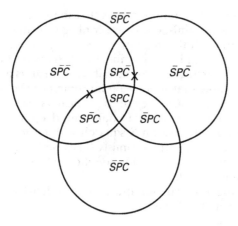

Figure 19-30   Some pessimists are not cribbage-cheaters is added to the diagram.

they might be. The other X definitely represents *non*-cribbage-cheaters, since it falls completely outside the *C* circle. The problem is, we don't know whether those non-cribbage-cheaters are *seals* or not, since the X straddles the line of the seals circle. Thus if all the premises are true, the conclusion may still be *false;* so this is an *invalid* argument.

Exercise 19-2

For these exercises, use Venn diagrams to determine the validity or invalidity of the arguments.

1. All seals are pessimists.
   No pessimist is a cribbage-cheater.
   Therefore, no seal is a cribbage-cheater.

2. All seals are pessimists.
   No pessimist is a cribbage-cheater.
   Therefore, some seals are not cribbage-cheaters.

   (Don't let this argument give you trouble. Remember, universal propositions do *not* carry any existential presupposition.)

In the remainder of the exercises, we shall stray from this unseemly obsession with pessimistic seals that cheat at cribbage. So you will probably wish to label the circles as something other than *S, P,* and *C.* In each of the following arguments, I have capitalized the *letter* that I think would be most convenient as a circle label (e.g., *Superhero, Villain,* and *Leap* in the next argument). Also, you'll have to line up the premises and conclusion for yourself (there might even be an argument in which the conclusion is *not* stated last).

3. No Superhero is a Villain. Some Villains are able to Leap tall buildings. Therefore, some who are able to Leap tall buildings are not Superheroes.

4. No Bridges are made out of Pasta. Nothing made out of Pasta Tastes good with champagne. So all Bridges Taste good with champagne.

5. No Ninja warriors are good Psychiatrists, because all Ninja warriors Scream "cowabunga," and nothing that Screams "cowabunga" is a good Psychiatrist.

6. Some Penguins are great Lovers. All Penguins Hate walruses. So some great Lovers Hate walruses.

7. All Cajuns eat Jambalaya. All Jambalaya-eaters Wrestle alligators. Therefore, all Cajuns Wrestle alligators.

8. Some Ninja warriors do not eat Ice cream, and some Ice cream–eaters do not play the Accordion; therefore, some Ninja warriors are not Accordion players.

9. All Stamp collectors Howl at the moon. No Tyrannosaurus is a Stamp collector. So no Tyrannosaurus Howls at the moon.

10. All Extraterrestrials are Shifty-eyed. Some Politicians are Shifty-eyed. Therefore, some Politicians are Extraterrestrials.

11. Some Students are not Beer drinkers. All Students are Cheerful. Therefore, some Cheerful people do not drink Beer.

TRANSLATING ORDINARY-LANGUAGE STATEMENTS INTO STANDARD-FORM CATEGORICAL PROPOSITIONS

OK, you are now about as good at working Venn diagrams as anyone should ever wish to be. But in order to use them effectively—and to get maximum enjoyment out of your Venn diagramming—you must be able to translate ordinary language into a form that makes it possible to apply Venn diagrams. You've already been doing that, of course, in the exercises in this chapter. But some ordinary language propositions can be a trifle tricky. For example: Only high school graduates are eligible. How would you write that in such a way that you could easily place it in a Venn diagram? That is, how would you translate that into a standard-form categorical proposition, such as All *A* are *B*?

First, you must think about exactly what that statement means. It cannot be translated as: All high school graduates are eligible. After all, the proposition states that you must be a high school graduate to be eligible; it doesn't say that you are automatically eligible if you are a high school graduate: Being a high school graduate is a minimum requirement for eligibility. There's another reason that "All high school graduates are eligible" will not work: It leaves open the possibility of non–high school graduates also being eligible. So what should we do with "Only high school graduates are eligible"? What does it really mean?

It means that: All eligible persons are high school graduates. (That is, the class of eligible persons is contained within—is a subset of—the class of high school graduates. That doesn't imply that all members of the class of high school graduates are eligible; it does imply that the only eligible persons are members of the class of high school graduates.) A simple two-circle diagram of that statement might make it a bit more obvious: As the diagram in Figure 19-31 shows, all members of the class of eligible persons (*E*) fall within the class of high school graduates (*G*) (but of course not all graduates need be eligible); that is, the only members of the class of eligible persons are in the intersection of *E* and *G*.

There are many common expressions that we easily understand but that may be a bit puzzling when we try to convert them into standard-form categorical propositions that can fit snugly within the confines of a Venn diagram. Consider this sentence: "There are no rich philosophers." That sounds simple, but how should it be represented? Simply as: "No philosophers are rich." (No members of the philosopher class are members of the

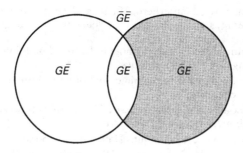

Figure 19-31   All eligible persons are high school graduates.

rich class.) "There are some tigers who change their stripes" would be: "Some tigers are stripe-changers." "The poor deserve our help" means, "All poor persons are persons deserving of our help." When working on these types of statements, you must *think* about exactly what they mean. For example, it may be tempting to write "Not all defendants are guilty" as "No defendants are guilty." But a moment's reflection shows the error. When we say that not all defendants are guilty, we do not mean that none of them are guilty; we mean instead that some defendants are not guilty. "Not all clouds have a silver lining" means that "Some clouds are not in the class of things having silver linings." (That seemed to lose something in translation.)

Another tricky sort of proposition is the exclusive proposition, such as, "Only those who study hard will pass," or "No one except registered students is allowed to attend." The first is just: "All who pass are hard-studiers"; the second, "All who are allowed to attend are registered students." So in general, when you are translating ordinary sentences into standard-form categorical propositions, stop and think carefully about *exactly* what the sentence means, and be sure that your translation does not imply *more* than what is stated in that sentence.

Exercise 19-3

Translate the following sentences into standard-form categorical propositions that can be diagrammed within a Venn diagram.

Examples:

a. There are some pessimistic walruses.
    Some walruses are pessimistic.
b. Only those over age 65 are eligible.
    All eligible people (all in the class of eligible) are over age 65 (are in the class of over age 65).
c. Philosophers are ineligible for sainthood.
    No philosopher is eligible for sainthood.

1. There are some innocent prisoners.
2. There are no atheists in foxholes.
3. Smokers are not great marathoners.
4. Not everyone with a weak chin is a criminal.
5. No one except employees is allowed to enter the kitchen.
6. There really are extraterrestrials who visit Earth.
7. Not all dolphins are friendly.
8. Only hard workers can be on the team.
9. There are innocent defendants who appear nervous.
10. You must be good at critical thinking to find happiness.

Reducing the Number of Terms

One other problem may arise when there appear to be too many terms. Sometimes there really are too many terms, and the argument cannot be conveniently represented by means of a single Venn diagram (and somewhat heavier logical artillery must be brought to bear). But sometimes arguments appear to have more than three terms, when in fact the number of terms can be reduced. For example:

> No philosophers are very wealthy. All industrialists are rich. Therefore, no philosophers are industrialists.

At first glance, this argument seems to involve four classes: philosophers, the very wealthy, industrialists, and the rich. But "very wealthy" and "rich" designate the same class-defining characteristic; so the number of terms is reduced to three, and the argument takes this form:

> No philosophers are rich.
> All industrialists are rich.
> ──────────────────────────────
> Therefore, no philosophers are industrialists.

Exercise 19-4

The following arguments may require a bit of mental dexterity in order to represent them in standard-form categorical propositions; use all your wiles—and all you have learned concerning categorical propositions and Venn diagrams—to turn the following arguments into standard-form categorical propositions, and then determine their validity or invalidity by means of Venn diagrams.

Examples:

a. A thing of beauty is a joy forever. So Michael Jordan's jump shots are an eternal joy, since Jordan's jumpers are beautiful.

The conclusion is at the beginning of the second sentence (indicated by "*so* Michael Jordan's jump shots"). The first premise (A thing of beauty is a joy forever) sounds as if it is talking about *a* single thing of beauty and *a* joy forever; but of course what it means is that *All* things of beauty are joys forever: It is a *universal* affirmative proposition. Likewise, we aren't talking about a particular jump shot made by Michael Jordan; rather, we are discussing the entire class of Michael Jordan jump shots: All Jordan's jump shots are beautiful. And then we have to reduce the number of terms: "Jordan's jumpers" is the same as "Michael Jordan's jump shots"; "a joy forever" is "an eternal joy"; and the class designated as beautiful is simply all those things that are things of beauty. So the argument goes:

All things of beauty are joys forever.
All Michael Jordan jump shots are things of beauty.
Therefore, all Michael Jordan jump shots are joys forever.

You can do the diagramming yourself to determine that the argument is valid (incidentally, it's also sound, as everyone knows who has seen Jordan shoot a jump shot).

b. No criminals are honest. Some lawyers are honest people. Therefore, there are some attorneys who are not criminals.

We're dealing with criminals, lawyers, honest people, and attorneys. But lawyers are the same as attorneys; so we can reduce that to three classes: criminals, honest people, and lawyers. The argument is:

No criminals are honest.
Some lawyers are honest.
Therefore, some lawyers are not criminals.

And it's easy to use a Venn diagram to show that that argument is valid.

1. Only royalty are permitted to wear the crown jewels.
   No penguin is allowed to wear the crown jewels.
   Therefore, no penguin is a member of the royal family.
2. No student dislikes parties.
   Penguins do not like parties.
   Therefore, no penguins are students.
3. Sick people are morose.
   Some firefighters are suffering from illness.
   Therefore, some members of the fire department are gloomy.

Exercise 19-5

The following arguments require all your accumulated knowledge of categorical propositions. You will have to translate the sentences into standard-form categorical propositions, reducing the number of terms in some cases, and thinking carefully to translate ordinary language expressions such as "not all" and "only." Write these arguments as standard-form categorical propositions, and then determine their validity or invalidity by means of Venn diagrams.

1. Only cribbage-cheaters eat liver.
   Some liver-eaters are drinkers.
   Therefore, some dishonest cribbage players are not teetotalers.
2. Anyone who is guilty of burglary must have intended to steal.
   No one who is demented could really intend to steal anything.
   So everyone guilty of burglary is sane.
3. All accused persons are entitled to the presumption of innocence.
   Some defendants are unpopular.
   Therefore, some people who are not popular are entitled to the presumption of innocence.
4. Some jewels aren't worth much; so some jewels aren't beautiful, since everything that is beautiful is valuable.
5. Anything that is the result of coercion is worthless as evidence.
   Some confessions have no evidentiary value.
   Therefore, some confessions are forced.

✓•─ **Study** and **Review** on **mythinkinglab.com**

REVIEW QUESTIONS

1. Give an example of a universal affirmative categorical proposition.
2. Give an example of a particular negative categorical proposition.
3. Which sorts of categorical propositions have existential import? Which sorts do *not*?
4. In a Venn diagram, if a section is not shaded and also does not contain an X, what should you conclude about whether or not it contains any members?

ADDITIONAL READING

For more details and exercises on the material covered in this chapter, see Chapter 12 of Virginia Klenk, *Understanding* *Symbolic Logic*, 5th ed. (Upper Saddle River, NJ: Prentice Hall, 2008).

Consider Your Verdict:
Comprehensive Critical
Thinking in the Jury Room

The following is a fictional case. Consider whether you would vote guilty or not guilty, and *why*. Effective critical consideration of this case will require all the skills you have developed in your study of critical thinking, from how to determine the conclusion and operate with necessary and sufficient conditions to placing the burden of proof and detecting fallacies and weighing evidence.

State v. *Ransom*

> *Prosecution Witnesses:* Dr. Arthur Hamilton
> Robert Andrews, forensics expert
> Lester Liggin, eyewitness
> Allen Arnold, friend of the defendant
> Detective Ross Reynolds, Lincoln County Sheriff's Department
> Scott Guyonovich, bartender
> *Defense Witnesses:* Alice Lawrence
> *Judge:* Jennifer Schwebel
> *District Attorney:* Wendell Warren
> *Defense Attorney:* Lisa West

JUDGE: Is the State ready?
DISTRICT ATTORNEY: Yes, Your Honor.
JUDGE: Is the Defense ready?
DEFENSE ATTORNEY: We are, Your Honor.
JUDGE: Does the State wish to make any opening remarks?

Opening Statement, DISTRICT ATTORNEY: Thank you, Your Honor. Ladies and Gentlemen of the Jury, just after midnight, in the early hours of last September 10, Jim Larkin was brutally murdered in a drive-by shooting. As is often the case in brutal murders, no one actually saw the gunman: Murderers typically do their foul deeds under cover of darkness or in some other way hide their murderous designs from public observation. But that

411

does not mean that they can always escape justice, for sometimes there is conclusive evidence—often a web of compelling facts—that points to the murderer just as certainly as an eyewitness standing and pointing a finger. And this is just such a case. The facts that we will bring before you will show, beyond even a shadow of doubt, that Robert Ransom brutally murdered Jim Larkin; and the vile nature of this crime, together with your certainty of its perpetrator, will lead you to one inescapable conclusion: Robert Ransom is guilty of murder, and must be found guilty of murder, and must pay for his crime.

JUDGE: Does the Defense have opening remarks?

Opening statement, DEFENSE ATTORNEY: Yes, thank you, Your Honor. Ladies and Gentlemen, my learned friend just described for you a web of evidence. That is an accurate description: The web that the prosecution will weave is as flimsy and thin as the gossamer strands of the spider's web. But don't you be caught in it. Stick to the facts, and you will avoid its entanglements. The fact is that a terrible murder has been committed, a murder that does indeed cry out for justice. But convicting the wrong person will not bring justice; it will only compound the injustice. And so we must be very sure before we find anyone guilty of this terrible crime: sure beyond a reasonable doubt. The flimsy web spun by the prosecution cannot support such weight. A terrible murder was committed, yes; but if you find an innocent person guilty of that murder, then injustice will be piled upon injustice, and the actual murderer will escape justice. And as you fairly and critically examine the case against Robert Ransom, I think you must conclude that there is no good reason to think that he committed this terrible crime. Thus you must return a verdict of not guilty and send the District Attorney and the police out to find the real killer; only in that way can justice be served.

JUDGE: The State can call its first witness.
DISTRICT ATTORNEY WARREN: The State calls Dr. Arthur Hamilton.

Dr. Hamilton enters the witness box and is sworn in.

WARREN: Dr. Hamilton, could you tell us your position and your qualifications?
HAMILTON: I am Chief Coroner for Lincoln County; I have an MD degree from Duke University Medical School, and I have done training in forensic medicine at several universities.
WARREN: Your Honor, I ask that Dr. Hamilton be qualified as an expert witness.
WEST: The defense has no objection, Your Honor; we certainly respect the expertise of Dr. Hamilton.
JUDGE: Without objection, so ruled.
WARREN: Dr. Hamilton, did you perform an autopsy on Jim Larkin?
HAMILTON: I did.
WARREN: Could you describe your findings?
HAMILTON: The deceased had been struck by three bullets from a .38 caliber handgun; one had struck him in the left thigh, another had passed through his body, penetrating his heart; another had entered his skull and lodged in his brain. Either of the last two wounds would have been sufficient to cause immediate death.
WARREN: So it is your conclusion that Jim Larkin was killed by shots fired from a handgun?
HAMILTON: That is correct.
WARREN: Thank you, no further questions.
JUDGE: The defense may cross-examine.
JUDGE: The defense has no questions of this witness, Your Honor.
JUDGE: Thank you, Dr. Hamilton; you may step down. The State may call its next witness.
WARREN: The State calls Robert Andrews.

Robert Andrews takes the stand and is sworn in.

WARREN: Mr. Andrews, could you describe your position and your qualifications for the court?

ANDREWS: I am the director of the forensics laboratory for the Lincoln County Sheriff's Office; I studied forensic science at Ohio State University, where I received my Master's degree in forensic science; I have since completed a number of in-service training institutes in forensic science.

WARREN: Your Honor, the State asks that Mr. Andrews be qualified as an expert witness.

JUDGE: Does the defense have any objections?

WEST: The defense has no hesitation in recognizing the expertise of Mr. Andrews.

JUDGE: Without objection, Mr. Andrews is qualified as expert.

WARREN: Mr. Andrews, did you examine the bullets taken from the body of Jim Larkin?

ANDREWS: I did.

WARREN: And could you tell the jury what you concluded?

ANDREWS: The bullets had been fired from a .38 caliber pistol.

WARREN: Are you sure of that?

ANDREWS: Positive. The markings on the bullets were quite clear; and those, when combined with the size and weight of the slugs, were all consistent with their being from only one type of weapon: a .38 caliber handgun. Furthermore, because of the distinctive markings of the slugs, it is clear that they were all fired from the same weapon.

WARREN: So it is your expert conclusion that all three bullets that struck the murder victim were fired from the same .38 caliber pistol?

ANDREWS: That's right.

WARREN: No further questions.

JUDGE: Ms. West?

WEST: Thank you, Your Honor. Mr. Andrews, you have no hesitation in saying that the bullets were fired from a .38 caliber handgun, right?

ANDREWS: Right.

WEST: And that conclusion is based on your excellent training and the number of years you have spent making such investigations?

ANDREWS: Yes.

WEST: How many years have you worked at the county forensics lab?

ANDREWS: Fourteen years.

WEST: I guess you've examined a lot of bullets over the course of those years.

ANDREWS: A *lot* of bullets, yes.

WEST: And a lot of bullets from .38 caliber handguns, right?

ANDREWS: Yes.

WEST: In fact, that's a pretty common handgun, isn't it? Don't the county deputies carry .38 caliber revolvers?

ANDREWS: Yes, that is the standard issue sidearm.

WEST: In fact, that's a very popular weapon, in Lincoln County and elsewhere, right?

WARREN: Your Honor, these questions are taking us off the track. The number of handguns in Lincoln County is not the issue, and besides, Mr. Andrews is an expert in forensics, not an expert in how many handguns there are in the area.

WEST: Your Honor, the fact that .38 caliber pistols are widely owned and easily available in Lincoln County has obvious relevance to this case; and Mr. Andrews, through the experiences of his office, is uniquely qualified to testify on that issue.

JUDGE: I'm going to allow this question, but I think this will just about reach the limit of the questions that can be put to Mr. Andrews on this issue of the number of .38 caliber weapons in the area. If the defense wishes to pursue this line beyond this question, you will have to call an expert more directly related to the issue.

Consider Your Verdict: Comprehensive Critical Thinking in the Jury Room

WEST: Thank you, Your Honor. Now, Mr. Andrews, would you say, on the basis of your long experience in the Lincoln County forensics laboratory, that .38 caliber handguns are fairly common in this area?

ANDREWS: There do seem to be a number of .38 caliber pistols, that's correct.

WEST: A number of them, thank you. And would you say that a number of those weapons are owned by people who are active in selling and distributing illegal drugs?

WARREN: Your Honor, I object to that question. It falls completely outside the expertise of this witness, and calls for speculation.

JUDGE: That question is out of order. Ms. West, you have reached the limits of this line of questioning with this witness.

WEST: Yes, thank you, Your Honor. And thank you, Mr. Andrews. We have no further questions.

JUDGE: Mr. District Attorney, do you wish to redirect?

WARREN: We have no further questions, Your Honor.

JUDGE: Thank you, Mr. Andrews; you may step down. The State may call its next witness.

WARREN: Your Honor, if it please the court, at this time the State wishes to enter People's Exhibit 1. It is a copy of the vehicle registration for a car owned by Robert Ransom.

JUDGE: Does the Defense have any objections?

WEST: No objections, Your Honor.

JUDGE: Without objection, enter People's Exhibit 1.

The bailiff marks the exhibit.

WARREN: Ladies and Gentlemen of the Jury, I am handing you a copy of the registration papers issued to Robert Ransom. As you will note, they are for the New Virginia registration of a Jaguar automobile, 2008 model, white in color.

The jury passes the registration among themselves.

WARREN: The State calls Lester Liggin.

Lester Liggin enters the witness box, and is sworn in.

WARREN: Would you state your full name and address?

LIGGIN: Lester Howard Liggin, 788 Fairlawn Drive, Silverton.

WARREN: Mr. Liggin, could you tell the jury where you were at just after midnight in the early morning of September 10?

LIGGIN: I was on the corner, at 12th and Church; I had just left the Sideways Lounge, and was lighting a cigarette, and was walking toward where my car was parked on 12th Street.

WARREN: Was there anyone else on the corner near you?

LIGGIN: Jim Larkin was walking about 50 yards from me, on the sidewalk going up Church Street.

WARREN: Did you recognize him?

LIGGIN: Yes, I recognized him. I had seen him before at the Sideways, and he had walked out just ahead of me. I didn't know who he was then, but I recognized him.

WARREN: Could you describe for us what happened?

LIGGIN: Well, while I was lighting my cigarette, I heard this car come roaring up the street. I don't know where it came from, but it had its lights off, and the engine was revved up high. When it got even with Jim Larkin, it hit the brakes, and then there were four or five shots from the car, and Jim fell over, and I ducked down, and the car roared off.

WARREN: Did you get a good look at the car?

LIGGIN: Yes, I did.

WARREN: Could you describe it for us?

LIGGIN: It was a white, late-model Jaguar; a convertible, with the top up.

WARREN: You're sure it was a Jaguar?

LIGGIN: Yes, I recognize a Jaguar; I was thinking about buying one a couple of years ago, so I looked at a lot of them. I can tell a Jaguar when I see one.

WARREN: How far would you say the car was from Jim Larkin when the shots were fired?

LIGGIN: Oh, maybe 20 feet; not more than 30 feet.

WARREN: Thank you, no further questions.

WEST: Mr. Liggin, you thought it was unusual that the car didn't have its lights on, is that right?

LIGGIN: Yes, I did.

WEST: Why was that?

LIGGIN: Why? Well, it was the middle of the night; it was dark; cars usually have their lights on when it's dark.

WEST: So it was quite dark on the street there?

LIGGIN: Well, there's a streetlight, but it is dark.

WEST: You say you were leaving the Sideways just after midnight, is that correct?

LIGGIN: Yes.

WEST: That's sort of a favorite hangout, right? A lot of your friends stop by the Sideways to have a couple of drinks, talk about football, maybe play a game of darts, is that right?

LIGGIN: Yeah, that's about it.

WEST: So you sometimes go there after work, see your friends there?

LIGGIN: Yes.

WEST: On the evening of September 9, do you remember what time you arrived at the Sideways?

LIGGIN: I think I went over after work; I get off at 8:00, I probably got to the Sideways about 9:00.

WEST: Saw your friends there?

LIGGIN: Yeah.

WEST: Had a couple of drinks with some friends?

LIGGIN: Couple of beers.

WEST: Well, let's see, you were there about 3 hours, maybe a little more, right? Maybe more than a couple of beers?

LIGGIN: Maybe.

WEST: Maybe substantially more than a couple?

LIGGIN: I wasn't drunk.

WEST: But you had had a good deal to drink, right? You had been sitting in the tavern for 3 hours drinking, isn't that right?

LIGGIN: I drank some beer, but I wasn't drunk.

WEST: In fact, you don't have any idea what sort of car you saw, do you? You were standing on the corner trying to get your balance and bearings, and a car roars by, and shots ring out, and you're ducking behind a car, and you really don't know what sort of car you saw, isn't that right?

LIGGIN: I saw a white Jaguar, I know that.

WARREN: Your Honor, the Defense is badgering the witness.

WEST: I have no further questions of this witness, Your Honor.

JUDGE: Mr. Warren, you may reexamine the witness if you wish.

WARREN: Mr. Liggin, it was dark there; but in the light from the streetlight, do you have any doubt whatsoever that the car you saw was a white Jaguar?

LIGGIN: No, I'm sure; it was a white Jaguar, alright.

WARREN: Thank you, no further questions.

JUDGE: You may step down. Call your next witness.

WARREN: The State calls Allen Arnold.

Allen Arnold takes the witness stand and is sworn in.

WARREN: Would you please state your full name?

ARNOLD: Allen Barron Arnold.

WARREN: Mr. Arnold, are you acquainted with the defendant, Robert Ransom?

ARNOLD: I know Robert, yes.

WARREN: Have you ever had occasion to go target shooting with the defendant?

ARNOLD: Yeah, a couple of times Bob and I have driven out to my grandfather's farm and shot at bottles and cans.

WARREN: On those occasions, did the defendant bring a weapon with him?

ARNOLD: Yes.

WARREN: Would you describe the weapon.

ARNOLD: It was a .38 revolver; silver barrel, I think the grip was some sort of brown or tan wood.

WARREN: On those occasions, did the defendant fire the .38 revolver?

ARNOLD: Yes, he did.

WARREN: Was the defendant a good shot?

ARNOLD: Yeah, he was pretty good.

WARREN: Could you be a bit more specific? Was he able to consistently hit a target, what sort of target, what distance?

ARNOLD: Well, shooting at, say, a beer can, from maybe 50 or 60 feet, he would hit it maybe one time in three, maybe a little better.

WARREN: Did you ever see the pistol other than on those occasions when you went target shooting?

ARNOLD: Once I was riding with Bob, and I opened the glove compartment to get a tape, and it was in there; and I've seen it at his apartment a couple of times.

WARREN: When was the last time you saw the pistol?

ARNOLD: I guess maybe about 3 months ago, at his apartment.

WARREN: Thank you, Mr. Arnold; no further questions.

WEST: Mr. Arnold, you say you and Robert went target shooting on a couple of occasions.

ARNOLD: Right.

WEST: How would you describe Robert's handling of the pistol? Was he careful? Reckless? Or what?

ARNOLD: He was very careful; he wasn't waving it around and shooting wildly or anything.

WEST: Did he ever fire the pistol while you were anywhere near the target?

ARNOLD: No, he always made real sure that no one was anywhere near the target before he fired.

WEST: Did he ever point the pistol at you?

ARNOLD: No, of course not.

WEST: Did you ever see him point a pistol at anyone?

ARNOLD: No.

WEST: Did you ever hear him threaten anyone with a pistol, or threaten to shoot anyone?

ARNOLD: Never.

WEST: So in all your experiences with Robert Ransom, you found that he used his pistol in a safe, cautious manner, purely for target shooting, and never threatened anyone with it or brandished it about or aimed it at anyone, is that right?

ARNOLD: That's right.

WEST: Thank you, no further questions.

WARREN: No further questions, Your Honor.

JUDGE: You may step down. Mr. Warren, you may call your next witness.

WARREN: The State calls Detective Ross Reynolds.

Ross Reynolds takes the stand and is sworn in.

WARREN: Would you state your full name and your position?

REYNOLDS: Ross Reynolds, detective with the Lincoln County Sheriff's Office.

WARREN: Detective Reynolds, were you involved in the investigation of the Jim Larkin homicide?

REYNOLDS: Yes.

WARREN: In the course of your investigation, did you have occasion to search the apartment and car of the defendant?

REYNOLDS: Yes.

WARREN: Was this an extensive search?

REYNOLDS: Yes, very thorough and extensive.

WARREN: In the course of your search, did you find any type of firearm?

REYNOLDS: No, I did not.

WARREN: Thank you, no further questions.

JUDGE: Ms. West, your witness.

WEST: Thank you, Your Honor. Detective Reynolds, prior to your homicide investigation, had you had occasion to visit the Westgate Apartment complex in the course of your work as a detective?

WARREN: Your Honor, I object to this question; it's obviously irrelevant to this case.

JUDGE: Approach the Bench.

The following is a sidebar conference, out of hearing of the jury.

WARREN: Your Honor, earlier investigations by Detective Reynolds cannot be relevant to this homicide case.

WEST: Your Honor, the prosecution is obviously suggesting through this witness that my client purposefully disposed of his pistol in order to eliminate incriminating evidence; I believe we have a right to bring up other possibilities, such as the possibility of the pistol being stolen; Detective Reynolds's investigation of burglaries at Westgate Apartments is thus certainly relevant.

JUDGE: I'll allow the questions. Step back.

WEST: Detective Reynolds, had you conducted any earlier investigations at Westgate Apartments, within the period of 2 years prior to your visit in connection with this case?

REYNOLDS: Yes, I had.

WEST: For what purpose did you previously visit Westgate Apartments?

REYNOLDS: To investigate a burglary.

WEST: Was that the burglary of a single apartment?

REYNOLDS: No, there had been two apartments burglarized during one weekend, when their occupants had been away.

WEST: Among the items stolen during those burglaries, were there any firearms?

REYNOLDS: Yes; a 12 gauge shotgun and a .22 caliber pistol were reported missing from one apartment.

WEST: Thank you, Detective Reynolds, no further questions.

WARREN: Did you ever investigate a burglary at the apartment of the defendant, Robert Ransom?

REYNOLDS: No, I did not.

WARREN: To your knowledge, did Robert Ransom ever report a burglary or any other theft from his apartment?

REYNOLDS: Not to my knowledge.

WARREN: Thank you, no further questions.

JUDGE: Thank you, Detective, you may step down. Mr. Warren, you may call your next witness.

WARREN: The State calls Scott Guyonovich.

Scott Guyonovich enters the witness box and is sworn in.

WARREN: State your full name.

GUYONOVICH: Scott Garrison Guyonovich.

WARREN: Mr. Guyonovich, where do you work?

GUYONOVICH: I tend bar at the Wayward Inn.

WARREN: Do you know the defendant, Robert Ransom?

GUYONOVICH: I'm acquainted with him; he would sometimes come to the Inn when I was working, have a few drinks. We'd talk about baseball, that sort of stuff. I knew his first name, knew that he usually drank vodka tonics, that's about it.

WARREN: But you knew him, and would have no doubt about identifying him?

GUYONOVICH: Oh, I could recognize him, certainly.

WARREN: Did you see the defendant on the night of July 4?

GUYONOVICH: Yes, I did.

WARREN: Would you tell us what you observed?

GUYONOVICH: Well, Bob was in the Wayward, had been there most of the evening; he was with a woman named Laura, she was usually with him when he came there. He had been drinking some, and while he was in the men's room, this guy—I didn't know him—came over to where Laura was standing at the bar, and asked to buy her a drink. I guess Laura was flirting a little, and she said OK. So I mixed drinks for both of them, and this guy picked up his drink, and raised it, and said something like "To your beautiful eyes." About that time Bob came back to the bar, and sort of grabbed the guy by the arm, and said "Who are you?" or maybe "Who the hell are you?" And this guy said, "I'm the guy who is buying this lady a drink. Who the hell are you?" And then Bob said something like "I'm the guy who's going to kick your butt," and he took a swing at this guy, and knocked his drink out of his hand.

WARREN: What happened next?

GUYONOVICH: Well, Joe—he clears tables, and sort of keeps order in the place—grabbed Bob, and I got a hand on the other guy; and Joe—he's a huge man, very powerful—got between them, and made it clear to both of them that there wasn't going to be any fighting there. Then Laura was sort of embarrassed about the whole thing, and she got Bob out of there; anyway, they left.

WARREN: As he was leaving, did the defendant say anything to the fellow at the bar?

GUYONOVICH: Oh, the usual sort of barroom stuff.

WARREN: Answer my question, please, as specifically as you can: What, if anything, did the defendant say to the man at the bar?

GUYONOVICH: He was just sort of blowing off steam, you know.

WARREN: Your Honor, would you please instruct the witness to answer my question?

JUDGE: Mr. Guyonovich, the District Attorney has asked you a clear, specific question. He did not ask for your speculation about what the defendant may or may not have intended; he asked specifically what the defendant said. You must answer that question, as directly and accurately as you can.

GUYONOVICH: He said "I'll get you, I'll blow your head off."

WARREN: "I'll get you, I'll blow your head off." That's what he said?

WEST: Objection, Your Honor; asked and answered.

JUDGE: Sustained.

WARREN: Mr. Guyonovich, did you know the deceased, Jim Larkin?

GUYONOVICH: Yes, he stopped by the Inn maybe a couple of times a week.

WARREN: Do you know a woman by the name of Laura Larue?

GUYONOVICH: Yeah; as I said, she used to come in with Bob; she was with him on the night we were just talking about.

WARREN: Did you ever see Jim Larkin and Laura Larue together?

GUYONOVICH: Yes, I don't remember the dates, but I think twice, in late August, they came in to the Wayward together.

WARREN: They had a drink together?

GUYONOVICH: Yes.

WARREN: Did they leave together?

GUYONOVICH: Yes.

WARREN: Mr. Guyonovich, where were you on the night of September 9?

GUYONOVICH: I was at work, at the Wayward Inn.

WARREN: Did you have occasion to see Robert Ransom?

GUYONOVICH: Yes, he came in about 9:00 P.M.

WARREN: What, if anything, did he say to you?

GUYONOVICH: He asked if I had seen Laura that night, and he asked if I had ever seen Laura with Jim Larkin; and then he wanted to know if I had seen Jim that evening.

WARREN: What did you tell him?

GUYONOVICH: I told him I had not seen Laura, and that I hadn't seen Jim that evening; and, well, you know, a bartender has to keep secrets, right? So I told him I hadn't seen Laura with Jim.

WARREN: What did Robert say after that?

GUYONOVICH: He sort of sneered, said something like, uh, "Yeah, right"; then he left.

WARREN: No further questions.

JUDGE: Your witness, Ms. West.

WEST: Thank you, Your Honor. Mr. Guyonovich, how long have you tended bar?

GUYONOVICH: About 4 years.

WEST: During that time, have you seen any fights at the bar?

GUYONOVICH: A few.

WEST: Maybe more than a few?

GUYONOVICH: Several, I guess.

WEST: In these fights, usually someone's had a bit too much to drink, there's a punch or two thrown, it's broken up, and then there's a lot of wild talk and threats, is that the way it usually goes?

WARREN: Your Honor, I must object; Counsel for the Defense is asking questions about the folkways and patterns of bar fighting and arguing, and this man is surely not qualified as an expert in that area; if she wishes to pursue this line of reasoning, she should bring in a tavern anthropologist to testify.

JUDGE: Given the earlier testimony by this witness, I will allow him to answer the question. You may answer, Mr. Guyonovich.

GUYONOVICH: Yes, that's about it. They throw a punch or two, and then threaten to kill each other, and smash faces, and so forth; usually they're back drinking together the next night.

WEST: So you don't take these drunken threats very seriously?

WARREN: Your Honor . . .

JUDGE: Objection sustained; that's about as far as that line of questioning can go.

WEST: Mr. Guyonovich, you said that you knew Jim Larkin, that he came into the tavern perhaps twice a week, is that correct?

GUYONOVICH: Right.

WEST: During that period, did you ever have any trouble with him? Did he ever cause any trouble at the tavern?

GUYONOVICH: No, not really.

WEST: Didn't you have to ask him to leave the tavern on at least one occasion?

GUYONOVICH: Yes.

WEST: Had he been drinking too much?

GUYONOVICH: No; he, uh, was sitting in the back, in a booth in the back; and I saw him put his hand in his jacket pocket, and then put his hand to his nose and sniff, and I thought he might be using cocaine, and so I asked him to leave; actually, I told Joe to tell him to leave.

WEST: What happened?

GUYONOVICH: He left.

WEST: He didn't protest, didn't deny he was using cocaine, he just left.

GUYONOVICH: That's right.

WEST: While he was in the tavern, sitting in the back booth, did you ever see him pass anything to anyone, anything that might have been a packet of cocaine, for instance?

WARREN: Your Honor, that question is completely out of line. There is no evidence whatsoever that the deceased ever passed illegal drugs, and the defense is using a leading question in a most improper manner to suggest something that is without any foundation, and is in any case totally irrelevant to this case.

WEST: Your Honor, the witness has just testified that Jim Larkin used cocaine in the tavern; it is perfectly legitimate to inquire as to whether he might have also dealt the stuff he used; that is certainly relevant, since this sort of activity might have motivated his murder.

JUDGE: I will allow the question, but I will caution the jury: Ladies and Gentlemen of the Jury, the mere fact that a question is allowed and asked should not be construed as suggesting anything whatsoever as to the subject of the question; allowing Ms. West to ask this question does not imply that Jim Larkin did deal drugs, nor does it imply that there is evidence that he did deal drugs. This is simply a question, nothing more: It is not an assertion, nor even a suggestion, of fact. Ms. West, you may ask your question.

WEST: Mr. Guyonovich, while Jim Larkin was sitting in his booth at the back of the tavern, did you see him pass anything to anyone that might have been cocaine or some other illegal drug?

GUYONOVICH: No, I did not.

WEST: You never *saw* him pass cocaine; no further questions.

JUDGE: Does the State have any more witnesses?

WARREN: No, Your Honor; that concludes the case for the State.

JUDGE: The Defense may call its first witness.

WEST: The Defense calls Mrs. Alice Lawrence.

Mrs. Lawrence enters the witness box and is sworn in.

WEST: Mrs. Lawrence, would you state your full name and tell us where you live.

LAWRENCE: My name is Alice Ellen Winslow Lawrence. I live at the Westgate Apartments in Silverton, Apartment 7-B.

WEST: Do you live alone?

LAWRENCE: Yes, since my husband died 12 years ago.

WEST: You certainly appear to be in excellent health; how are your vision and your hearing?

LAWRENCE: Well, I'm in real good health, can still look after myself, my hearing is excellent, and with my bifocals I can see real well.

WEST: Could you describe the location of your apartment in the complex?

LAWRENCE: I live on the second floor, a corner apartment, near the entrance of the apartment complex, overlooking the apartment drive.

WEST: So you can see the driveway from your living room window?

LAWRENCE: Yes.

WEST: And you can hear cars pass in and out of the complex?

LAWRENCE: That's right.

WEST: Do you know the defendant, Robert Ransom?

LAWRENCE: Well, I recognize him. I just know him to say hello. I know he lives in the next building, because I've seen him when I take my walk in the morning, and I've seen him coming in and going out in his car.

WEST: So you recognize his car?

LAWRENCE: Certainly; it's white, a real sporty little thing; he drives it with the top down in the summertime.

WEST: Mrs. Lawrence, from where you sit in your living room to watch television, can you see the driveway into and out of the apartment complex?

LAWRENCE: Well, I have to stretch my neck a little bit, but I can see it.

WEST: And you can hear cars pass from there?

LAWRENCE: Sure can; sometimes in the summer it gets a little noisy.

WEST: And is that the only driveway entering or leaving the apartment complex?

LAWRENCE: That's right.

WEST: Now Mrs. Lawrence, on the night of September 9, were you at home?

LAWRENCE: Yes, I was; I remember because I watched *My Fair Lady* on television, and I had been looking forward to seeing it; it's one of my favorite movies, and I hadn't seen it in years.

WEST: Do you remember what time that was?

LAWRENCE: Well, I believe the movie started at 10:00, and it was after midnight before it ended, because of all the commercials; that's a little later than I usually go to bed.

WEST: Did you see or hear Mr. Ransom's car at any time during that evening?

LAWRENCE: Yes, about the time the movie was starting, I remember I heard his car coming into the driveway—it makes kind of a special fast roar, that sports car—and I looked over and saw his car.

WEST: You're sure about that?

LAWRENCE: Yes, I'm certain. I couldn't really see him, because the streetlight wasn't that bright; but it was his car, alright. I remember thinking that he was going a little too fast for that driveway.

WEST: So you saw him coming into the apartment complex about 10:00 P.M., right?

LAWRENCE: That's right; at least, I saw his car coming in, and so I guess he must have been the one driving it.

WEST: You're sure his *car* came in. Now Mrs. Lawrence, was that the only time you saw his car that evening?

LAWRENCE: Yes, it was.

WEST: During the whole time you watched your movie, from 10:00 P.M. until after midnight, you never saw the defendant's white sports car go out again?

LAWRENCE: That's right, I didn't.

WEST: And from where you were sitting watching the movie, you would have seen it if it had gone out, wouldn't you?

WARREN: Objection; that question calls for speculation on the part of the witness.

WEST: No speculation is involved, Your Honor; I'm simply asking whether the witness was in a position to see a car if it had gone out of the driveway.

JUDGE: The witness has already testified that she could see cars in the driveway from where she was sitting; that is all she can testify to: She can't say whether she *would* have seen a car, in some hypothetical circumstances. Objection sustained.

LAWRENCE: Yes, I would have seen it.

WARREN: Your Honor . . .

JUDGE: Mrs. Lawrence, I have ruled against that question; you are not allowed to answer it. Members of the jury, please disregard anything that the witness might have said in answer to that question. Continue, Ms. West.

WEST: So during the time from 10:00 P.M. until after midnight, while you were sitting overlooking the driveway and watching the movie, you did *not* see the defendant's car leave?

WARREN: Objection, Your Honor; that question has been asked and answered.

WEST: No further questions.

JUDGE: The State may examine the witness.

WARREN: Mrs. Lawrence, *My Fair Lady* is one of my favorites also. Do you watch many movies?

LAWRENCE: Yes, I do, especially musicals.

WARREN: Now I imagine that like most folks, when you watch a movie, you don't make it a point to watch all the commercials, do you?

LAWRENCE: I certainly don't.

WARREN: And I believe you said that this particular movie had a lot of commercials?

LAWRENCE: They all do; sometimes it just takes forever to watch a movie because of all those commercials, and they just go on and on with them.

WARREN: There are a lot of commercials, aren't there? And like most folks, you probably take advantage of the commercials to get up, stretch your legs, maybe pop some popcorn, or get a drink, or refresh yourself in the powder room, or even tidy up the dinner dishes, is that right? You don't sit there glued to the television set during those long commercial breaks, do you?

LAWRENCE: No, I sometimes get up, get a glass of milk, freshen up; I might get a treat for my cat, Whiskers.

WARREN: Now your kitchen and pantry and bathroom, they aren't right by the window, are they? They are over on the other side of your apartment, away from the driveway?

LAWRENCE: That's right.

WARREN: And Mrs. Lawrence, you're certainly not a nosy neighbor, are you? You don't keep your nose out the window all the time, looking for who is going in and coming out, right? Of course you can't avoid seeing and hearing cars pass when you are sitting by the window; but you wouldn't run from the kitchen to make sure that a car doesn't pass without your seeing it, would you?

WEST: Your Honor, the District Attorney is leading the witness.

JUDGE: Mr. Warren, I will grant some latitude during cross-examination; but your last question overstepped the bounds. Do not lead the witness.

WARREN: I'll rephrase the question. Mrs. Lawrence, do you exert yourself to make sure you see every car that enters or leaves the apartment complex?

LAWRENCE: Certainly not; I can't help seeing most of the cars that come and go, but I certainly don't make any special effort to do so.

WARREN: Thank you, Mrs. Lawrence; no further questions.

WEST: Mrs. Lawrence, are you a member of the Citizen's Watch group at your apartment complex?

LAWRENCE: Yes, I am.

WEST: And so as a member of that group, do you consider it your responsibility to keep your eyes and ears open for cars that don't belong in the apartment complex, that might belong to burglars?

WARREN: Objection; leading question.

JUDGE: Sustained.

WEST: Does being a member of your Citizen's Watch group carry any special obligations for you?

LAWRENCE: Well, it makes me more aware of the need to watch carefully about any strange cars that might be coming into the apartment complex, in case they belong to burglars.

WEST: Burglary has been a problem there, hasn't it?

LAWRENCE: We did have some break-ins, yes, made me real nervous.

WEST: Thank you, Mrs. Lawrence; no further questions.

JUDGE: You may step down. Ms. West, do you have any other witnesses?

WEST: No, Your Honor.

JUDGE: The State may make its closing argument.

Closing statement, DISTRICT ATTORNEY WARREN: Ladies and Gentlemen of the Jury, we said at the outset of this case that we would show you strands of proof that would weave together to form a powerful and inescapable web of proof: proof that the defendant is the person who stalked Jim Larkin, drove a white Jaguar past the victim, and killed him with several shots from a .38 revolver. These are the ropes of that proof. First, consider who had a motive for killing Jim Larkin: who else but Robert Ransom? The lovely Laura Larue, who had been Robert's girlfriend, was slipping into the same taverns where she had gone with Robert. But now she was on the arm of Jim Larkin, sipping drinks beside him, laughing at his jokes: and at the very same places where she once had gone with Robert! Not only would Robert be jealous of Laura's new romantic interest, he would also be humiliated by having the two of them seen by his friends. And Robert Ransom has the potential: He is not a man to suffer jealousy patiently. When a man bought Laura one drink, he challenged the man to a fight, and then threatened to kill him. That's the sort of reaction that jealousy provokes in Robert Ransom: "I'll get you." And the very night of Jim Larkin's murder, Robert Ransom was looking for Jim, and for Jim with Laura; Robert Ransom was *looking* for Jim Larkin just 3 hours before Jim was murdered. Robert had the motive; Robert had the violent personality; did Robert have the means to *get* Jim Larkin? Certainly. He had the means of carrying out a murder, for he had a .38 revolver and he knew how to use it. And Jim Larkin was murdered by slugs accurately fired from a .38 revolver. Now Robert Ransom's .38 revolver is missing. Not in his house, not in his car, nowhere to be found. And finally, Robert had the means of transportation to track down his victim: a white Jaguar. And it was a white Jaguar that was used in the killing. So wrap these cords together: Robert Ransom had the motive, the violent temper, a .38 revolver like the one used to fire the fatal shots, and a white Jaguar like the one used to hunt down Jim Larkin, drive by him, and murder him. Wrap those cords together, and they bind Robert Ransom to the murder of Jim Larkin. They bind his guilt with a certainty that eliminates any possibility of reasonable doubt. And they demand a verdict of guilty. The evidence points conclusively to Robert Ransom as the murderer of Jim Larkin; and that same evidence convicts him of first-degree murder: You cannot find him guilty of less. For when someone stalks his victim, waits for him in the night, drives into close firing range, and methodically pumps bullets from a .38 caliber pistol into his victim's heart and brain, then there can be no doubt that this was a coldly calculated premeditated murder. The State asks that you weigh the evidence carefully, follow the law conscientiously, and return a verdict of guilty: guilty of murder in the first degree. Thank you.

JUDGE: Is the Defense ready to present its closing arguments?

Closing statement, DEFENSE ATTORNEY: Yes, thank you, Your Honor; and thank you, Ladies and Gentlemen of the Jury, for your careful attention throughout this entire case. The defendant has a right to your fair, careful consideration of all the evidence and all the arguments; and that is all we ask. For when you scrutinize the case offered against Robert Ransom, its flimsiness is readily apparent. What is the case against Robert Ransom? That he is jealous when his girlfriend goes out with another man; well, if that is the charge, then he is guilty. But then, who is innocent? Of course he becomes jealous, as any of us would. But *that* is no grounds for thinking Robert guilty of murder: you know it, I know it, and the *prosecution* knows it, and that is why they try to prop it up with all these other things. What other things? Well, that Robert Ransom once took a swing at a guy in a bar. True enough: Robert was celebrating our national holiday, had perhaps a bit too much to drink, was provoked when his girlfriend teased him a bit with another man, and took a wild swing. And from that flimsy episode, the prosecution hopes to persuade intelligent jurors that Robert Ransom has the sort of violent, vindictive personality that would turn him into a cool, calculating, stalking killer. It just doesn't add up; it's too big a jump, from one small tavern altercation to cool, methodical murder. So what evidence does the prosecution have to offer you? Jim Larkin was killed with a .38 pistol; Robert Ransom owns a .38 pistol. So what? What does that prove? There are .38 caliber pistols all over this city! Walk in any gun shop, and ask to see a .38 caliber pistol: They'll bring out whole *cases* of them. Go to any target-shooting range, and *count* the number of people taking target practice with a .38 caliber pistol. Check the holsters of the policemen in this very courtroom! If owning a .38 caliber handgun is proof of guilt, then there are lots and lots of guilty people in this city! The prosecution wants to make something of the fact that Robert's pistol is missing. But Robert lives in an apartment complex where things go missing not infrequently, where dear old ladies like Mrs. Lawrence join crime watchers to struggle against theft and burglary. And of course, as we all know, what is one of the favorite theft targets? Firearms, and particularly pistols. So what remains of this powerful prosecution case against Robert? Well, there's the white Jaguar: The murderer drove a white Jaguar—or perhaps, in the darkness of the street, some other model of sportscar, or a Jaguar of a different shade, or a different sort of car altogether; it's hard to be sure. And Robert owns a white Jaguar. But what sort of evidence is that? Even if the murderer did drive a white Jaguar, there are plenty of white Jaguars—and *lots* of cars that closely resemble white Jaguars, especially on a city street at a bleary-eyed midnight after a few drinks. And Robert's white Jaguar was safe at home, parked next to its owner's apartment, from approximately 10:00 P.M.—when, according to Mrs. Lawrence, Robert drove it home—until well after midnight. Now the prosecutor wants you to believe that maybe that loud sportscar slipped past under Mrs. Lawrence's window without her noticing, but I don't think so. In fact, God bless her, I don't think you could slip a skateboard past Mrs. Lawrence's window without her noticing. I doubt that a single sparrow falls in the Westgate Apartment complex without Mrs. Lawrence taking note of it. So even if the murderer did drive a white Jaguar, there's no reason to think that it was Robert's; and there is excellent reason—the good, honest testimony of Mrs. Lawrence—to believe that it was *not*.

So who did kill Jim Larkin? I don't know, and Robert doesn't know; and unfortunately, the police don't know: They simply charged the person who was easiest to find. We can guess about who might have done so. Was Jim perhaps involved in cocaine to the point that he sold some to support his habit? If so, he was entering into a very hazardous occupation, with a low life expectancy, especially if he started to edge into another dealer's market. That is one of the frustrating things about being wrongly accused: You don't *know* what happened, you can't tell who committed the crime. But then, that is also one of the glories of our system of justice: The defendant does not have to prove someone else did it, because the burden of proving who killed Jim Larkin is on the prosecution. We have no idea who murdered Jim Larkin, or why. But one thing is perfectly clear: The prosecution has certainly failed to prove beyond a reasonable doubt that Robert Ransom is guilty; in fact, the whole case against Robert is a tragic tissue of happenstance. Robert should never have been charged with this terrible crime; but I am confident, that as you consider the facts carefully and impartially, you will end his awful nightmare with a verdict of not guilty.

Judge Schwebel's Summation and Charge to the Jury

LADIES AND GENTLEMEN OF THE JURY:

Soon you will retire to the jury room to consider your verdict. All the evidence has been presented. It is now your duty to decide from the evidence what the facts are. You must then apply the law to those facts. It is essential that you understand and apply the law as it is, and not as you *think* it is, and not as you might like it to be. This is important, because justice requires that everyone tried for the same crime be tried under the same law.

The defendant has entered a plea of "not guilty." The fact that he has been indicted is no evidence of guilt. Under our system of justice, when a defendant pleads "not guilty," he is not required to prove his innocence; he is presumed to be innocent. The State must prove to you that the defendant is guilty beyond a reasonable doubt.

The defendant in this case has not testified. The law of New Virginia gives him this privilege. This same law also assures him that his decision not to testify creates no presumption against him. Therefore, his silence is not to influence your decision in any way.

The defendant is charged with first-degree murder in the death of Jim Larkin. It is alleged that the defendant fatally shot Jim Larkin in the early morning hours of September 10. Under the law of New Virginia, a person is guilty of first-degree murder if he purposely or knowingly causes the death of another human being. If you find—beyond a reasonable doubt—that the defendant, Robert Ransom, did purposely or knowingly cause the death of Jim Larkin, then you must return a verdict of guilty of first-degree murder. If, however, you have a reasonable doubt that Robert Ransom purposely or knowingly caused the death of Jim Larkin, then you must return a verdict of not guilty. It is your exclusive province to find the true facts of the case and to render a verdict reflecting the truth as you find it.

I instruct you that a verdict is not a verdict until all 12 jurors agree unanimously as to what your decision shall be. You may *not* render a verdict by majority vote.

Now, members of the jury, you may retire to your deliberations and consider your verdict.[1]

Note

[1]Some parts of the judge's instructions to the jury were drawn (in edited form) from the North Carolina Conference of Superior Court Judges and North Carolina Bar Association Foundation, *North Carolina Pattern Instructions—Criminal.*

Internet Resources

Professor David Linder has put together a fascinating site containing details of many famous trials, from the trial of Socrates in ancient Athens to the trial of O. J. Simpson. It can be found at http://law2.umkc.edu/faculty/projects/ftrials/ftrials.htm.

Additional Reading

If you enjoyed thinking about these courtroom exercises, you might also enjoy a book by Judge Norbert Ehrenfreund and Lawrence Treat, *You're the Jury* (New York: Henry Holt, 1992). As it says on the cover of the book, "Solve Twelve Real-Life Court Cases Along with the Juries Who Decided Them," it presents a variety of authentic cases, edited into readable and interesting form.

Key Terms

Ad hominem. "Ad hominem" literally means "to the person." An ad hominem argument is an argument that focuses on a person (or group of people), typically attacking the person. For example, "Joe is a liar," "Sandra is a hypocrite," "Republicans are cold-hearted." Ad hominem arguments are *fallacious* only when they attack the source of an *argument* in order to discredit the argument; for example, "Joe's argument against drinking and driving doesn't carry much weight, because Joe himself is a lush." When *not* attacking the source of an *argument,* ad hominem arguments do *not* commit the ad hominem *fallacy,* and can often be valuable and legitimate arguments. For example, an ad hominem attack on someone giving *testimony* ("Don't believe Sally's testimony, she's a notorious liar") is relevant, and *not* an ad hominem fallacy; likewise, it is a legitimate use of ad hominem argument (*not* an ad hominem *fallacy*) if you are attacking a job applicant ("Don't hire Bruce, he's a crook"), a politician ("Don't vote for Sandra, she's in the pocket of the tobacco industry"), and in many other circumstances ("Don't go out with Bill, he's a cheat and a creep").

Affirming the consequent. Always *fallacious,* it is any argument of this form:

$$P \rightarrow Q$$
$$\frac{Q}{\therefore P}$$

It is fallacious because it treats a necessary condition (the consequent) as if it were a sufficient condition.

Ambiguity. The fallacious use of two different word meanings in premises and conclusion. For example, if we argue (premise) that the witness was "testifying *truthfully*" (in the sense of testifying *honestly*), therefore (conclusion) the testimony of the witness was the *truth* (in the sense of being *accurate*), then "truth" is being used ambiguously, and that argument commits the fallacy of ambiguity.

Analogical literalism fallacy. The fallacy of treating an analogy too literally; attacking the analogy on a point of irrelevant difference between the two cases.

Analogy. A comparison between two different cases. See *Deductive analogy, Figurative analogy, Inductive analogy.*

Antecedent. The part of a conditional statement that sets the condition for something else. In "If you study hard, you will pass," "you study hard" is the antecedent. When a conditional statement is represented symbolically, as in P → Q, P is the antecedent.

Appeal to authority. Any attempt to establish a claim by appealing to an expert or to someone who supposedly has special expertise. If the authority to whom the appeal is made is a genuine expert or authority in the *relevant area,* and there is *consensus* among authorities, then appeal to authority is legitimate; otherwise, it is fallacious.

Appeal to ignorance. A fallacious argument that attempts to shift the burden of proof from the person making the claim or assertion, by asserting that a claim should be believed because no one has been able to prove it false.

Appeal to popularity fallacy. A special form of appeal to authority fallacy that appeals to the false authority of popular opinion or popular acceptance.

Appeal to tradition fallacy. A special form of appeal to authority fallacy that appeals to the false authority of traditional practice or long-standing belief.

Average. Usually designates the *mean,* which is the number derived by adding together all the numeric members in a set, and dividing the total by the number of members in the set. However, "average" is sometimes used to refer to the *median,* or the *middle* value; and sometimes refers to the *mode,* or number that occurs most frequently. For example, in the set of numbers 1, 2, 2, 3, 5, 6, and 9, the *mean* is 4, the *median* is 3, and the *mode* is 2.

Begging the question fallacy. The fallacy of using the conclusion of an argument as a premise.

Camel's nose is in the tent argument. See *Slippery slope argument.*

Cogent argument. An inductive argument that is *strong* and has all true premises. If an inductive argument is not strong, *or* it has a false premise, then it is *uncogent.*

Complex question fallacy. A question that contains a controversial assumption, for example, "Why are philosophy majors so smart?" Sometimes called a loaded question.

Conclusion. What an argument aims at proving; the statement that is supposedly proved by the premises of an argument.

Conditional statement. A statement asserting that *if* one condition is met, then something else will follow; for example, "If you study hard, you will pass." It is represented symbolically using an arrow, as in P → Q.

Consequent. The part of a conditional statement that states what will follow if a condition is met. In "If you study hard you will pass," "you will pass" is the consequent. When a conditional statement is represented symbolically, as in P → Q, Q is the consequent.

Convergent argument. An argument in which each premise supports the conclusion independently of the other premises; if one premise fails, the other premises may still offer significant reasons for accepting the conclusion.

Deductive argument. An argument that draws its conclusion from the premises by logical operations; it extracts from the premises a conclusion that is logically implied by the premises, or already contained in the premises (in contrast to an *inductive* argument).

Denying the antecedent. Always *fallacious,* it is any argument of this form:

$$P \rightarrow Q$$
$$\sim P$$
$$\therefore \sim Q$$

It is fallacious because it treats a sufficient condition (the antecedent) as if it were a necessary condition.

Dilemma arguments. Any argument that contains a premise asserting that there are a limited number of options (usually two) that we must choose from. If there are actually more options than are named in the dilemma, then it is a *false* dilemma fallacy. If the dilemma poses the only genuine alternatives, then it is a *genuine* or legitimate dilemma.

Enthymeme.   An argument in which a premise (or sometimes the conclusion) is regarded as so obvious that it is left unstated.

Fallacy.   An argument error; usually a standard or common argument error.

False dilemma.   See *Dilemma.*

Golden mean fallacy.   An argument that presents its conclusion as the moderate or middle-of-the-road or compromise position, *and* claims that because the conclusion is moderate, that is a good reason for accepting the conclusion. (It is *not* a fallacy to advocate a moderate position; rather, it is fallacious to claim that one's position is right *because* it is moderate.)

Half-truth.   A claim that is literally true, but which leaves out important information that would alter the significance of the claim.

Inductive argument.   An argument that uses the premises to draw a conclusion that goes beyond the premises; an inductive argument may make its conclusion highly probable, but since the conclusion is not logically extracted from the premises (as in a *deductive* argument), the conclusion is not established with logical certainty.

Inverse ad hominem.   This is the mirror image of ad hominem arguments. Ad hominem arguments are arguments *to the person,* that is, they attack the person. Inverse ad hominem arguments *praise* the person. Inverse ad hominem arguments are legitimate whenever ad hominem arguments would be legitimate, and are fallacious whenever ad hominem arguments would be fallacious. The *inverse ad hominem fallacy* is committed *only* when someone praises or commends the source of an *argument,* and maintains that because the argument *source* is good or courageous or self-sacrificing (or whatever virtue you like), that person's *argument* must be a good argument. But there are also many circumstances in which inverse ad hominem arguments are *legitimate* and *not* fallacious. For example, if Joan is giving *testimony,* it is certainly relevant that she is unbiased, objective, and a person of deep integrity. If Arthur is applying for graduate school, it is perfectly legitimate for the author of his letter of reference to make the *inverse ad hominem* assertion that Arthur is a brilliant, dedicated, creative, and hard-working student. And if Sabrina is running for Congress, it is certainly relevant and nonfallacious to assert that Sabrina is a dedicated public servant who is not motivated by greed.

Irrelevant reason fallacy.   An argument that uses premises that have no bearing on the conclusion, but only distract from the real issue. Also known as the *red herring* fallacy.

Linked argument.   An argument in which the premises link together in such a way that if one premise fails, the entire argument fails.

Loaded question fallacy.   See *Complex question fallacy.*

Mean.   See *Average.*

Median.   See *Average.*

Mode.   See *Average.*

Modus ponens.   Always *valid,* it is any argument of this form:

$$P \rightarrow Q$$
$$P$$
$$\therefore Q$$

Modus tollens.   Always *valid,* it is any argument of this form:

$$P \rightarrow Q$$
$$\sim Q$$
$$\therefore \sim P$$

Necessary condition.   An essential condition for some event or circumstance. For example, oxygen is a *necessary condition* of human life; passing logic is a *necessary condition* for a degree in philosophy. In a conditional statement, the consequent is always a necessary condition of the antecedent.

No true Scotsman fallacy.   See *Self-sealing fallacy.*

Parade of horribles argument.   See *Slippery slope argument.*

Post hoc, ergo propter hoc.   See *Questionable cause fallacy.*

Premise.   In an argument, a premise is a statement that supports or provides justification for the conclusion.

Prospective studies.   Scientific studies in which the *control* group (which does *not* receive the drug, procedure, or product being tested) is *matched* as closely as possible with the *experimental* group (which *does* receive the test product). For example, in a test of the health effects of smoking, it would be unethical to use a *randomized* experimental design, since that would involve *assigning* test subjects to a smoking group, when we already have reason to believe that smoking is a severe hazard to health. So we might use a prospective design, in which we start with an experimental group who are already habitual smokers, and *compare* them with a control group that we match as closely as possible with the characteristics of the smokers (in diet, exercise habits, work environment, etc.) except that the control group are nonsmokers. Though not quite as reliable as a randomized control experiment, the prospective study gives us good grounds for concluding that any difference in health outcomes between the two groups is caused by smoking.

Questionable cause fallacy.   The fallacy of supposing that because event A is followed by event B, or because there is a *correlation* between two phenomena, the second is caused by the first; sometimes called the *post hoc* fallacy, or the fallacy of *post hoc ergo propter hoc.*

Randomized controlled experiment.   An experiment in which the experimental subjects are *randomly* divided into two groups: the *experimental* group, who actually receive whatever is being tested (such as a drug, or some therapy process); and the *control* group, who are similar in every way to the experimental group except that they do *not* receive the experimental treatment (but otherwise are treated exactly as the experimental group is treated). Any difference in outcome between the two groups can be attributed to the effect of the experimental product or process.

Red herring fallacy.   See *Irrelevant reason fallacy.*

Representative sample.   A sample that accurately reflects the character of the population being sampled.

Self-sealing fallacy.   The fallacy of modifying a claim in such a way that it is made empty of real content—transforming an empirical claim into a claim that is true by definition, or vacuously true. Sometimes called the *no true Scotsman* fallacy.

Slippery slope argument.   An argument claiming that a proposed act or policy that looks harmless may lead to very undesirable consequences. If adequate reasons are given to support the claim of risk, then it is a legitimate slippery slope argument; if the argument merely suggests a future peril, or merely notes steps that could lead to that bad result without giving reasons to suppose those steps would occur, then it is a slippery slope *fallacy.* Also known as the *wedge* argument, the *domino* argument, the *camel's nose is in the tent* argument (particularly among politicians), and the *parade of horribles* argument (by lawyers).

Slippery slope fallacy.   See *Slippery slope argument.*

Sound argument.   A deductive argument that is both valid and has all true premises.

Strawman fallacy.   The fallacy of distorting, exaggerating, or misrepresenting an opponent's position in order to make it easier to attack.

Strong argument.   An inductive argument the premises of which (*if* they were true) would make the conclusion very probably true. (An inductive argument may be *strong* even though its premises are false; if it is strong and its premises are actually true, then the inductive argument is *cogent*.)

Sufficient condition. A condition the existence of which guarantees an outcome. For example, if passing the final exam is a *sufficient condition* for passing the course, then all who pass the final exam pass the course, no matter what else they have or have not done in the course. In a conditional statement, the antecedent is always a sufficient condition of the consequent.

Target population. In a survey, the population that the survey is supposed to represent.

Truth table. A table that represents all the possible truth values for a statement or argument.

Uncogent argument. See *Cogent argument*.

Unsound argument. See *Sound argument*.

Valid argument. A deductive argument in which the truth of the premises guarantees the truth of the conclusion; in a valid argument, *if* the premises are true, then the conclusion *must* be true.

Venn diagram. A set of interlocking circles used to determine validity or invalidity of arguments containing universal and/or particular statements.

Voir dire. The process of questioning potential jurors in order to select a jury.

Weak inductive argument. See *Strong inductive argument*.

Wedge argument. See *Slippery slope argument*.

Answers to Selected Exercises

Chapter 2

Exercise 2-1

1. No
4. No
7. Yes
10. Yes
13. Yes
16. Yes
19. Yes
22. Yes (a statement about one's feelings may be difficult to verify, but it certainly makes a claim that can be either true or false).
25. No
28. No
31. Yes
34. No
37. Yes
40. No
43. Yes
46. Yes

Exercise 2-2

1. Argument; there are mice on the moon.
4. Argument; Wheaties is a nutritious cereal.
7. Argument; the New York Mets will win the World Series.
10. Argument; my critical thinking professor owns a private jet.
13. No.
16. Argument; gasoline prices will increase in July.
19. Argument; Brenda must hate the Steelers.

22. Argument; federal disaster relief was not well-organized.
25. Argument; you should vote.

Exercise 2-3

1. Deductive argument; Ralph is not a licensed physician in the United States.
4. Not an argument.
7. Inductive argument; the team with the best pitching will win the World Series.
10. Deductive argument; Smith was lying.
13. Inductive argument; Mighty Casey will almost certainly strike out.
16. Inductive argument; the Toronto Blue Jays will probably win the World Series.
19. Inductive argument; if you attend every class, you will pass the course.
22. Inductive argument; Bruce will be late for class tomorrow.

Exercise 2-4

1. c
4. b
7. e
10. a
13. c
16. e

Exercise 2-5

1. b
4. c

7. c
10. a
13. c

Chapter 3

Exercise 3-1

1. Fallacy.
4. Legitimate (even if we decide that Bill is giving argument, it is clear that some of the key premises of Bill's argument depend on his testimony, and that makes him a legitimate ad hominem target).
7. Legitimate (Webster is not giving argument, but being considered for a position).

How Do You Rule?

This is a legitimate question; the witness (Mr. Candor) is giving testimony, and it is legitimate to question the motivation of the witness.

Exercise 3-2

1. Legitimate ad hominem.
4. Inverse ad hominem, fallacious.
7. Neither ad hominem nor inverse ad hominem: simply an attack on the argument, which is legitimate.
10. Ad hominem fallacy.
13. Legitimate ad hominem.
16. Ad hominem fallacy.
19. Legitimate ad hominem.
22. Ad hominem fallacy.
25. Legitimate inverse ad hominem.

Chapter 4

Exercise 4-1

1. While there are a few people who would like to compel everyone in the United States to practice Christianity, that is certainly a much more extreme position than the position taken by most of those who advocate school prayer, who want at most a "generic" prayer fitting almost any conception of God, or more likely a "moment of silence" in which one could pray or not.
4. Almost no one wants a total ban on the private ownership of guns; rather, the goal is typically much stricter regulation and registration and the ban of weapons such as assault rifles, and at most a ban on handguns.

Chapter 5

Exercise 5-1

The verdict of not guilty is not based on the jury's judgment that the defendant did not commit the crime, but instead on the judgment that the defendant's guilt was not proved beyond a reasonable doubt. The jury may well believe that there is strong evidence and substantial probability that the accused politician is guilty, but that the evidence does not establish guilt beyond a reasonable doubt.

Exercise 5-2

1. God exists.
4. We should develop solar power.
7. There should not be laws restricting abortion.

Chapter 6

Consider the Verdict exercise

2. Relevant. I think it is *false*—Reid did have the capacity to know that he possessed a firearm—but the question is not whether the claim is true, but whether it *matters* whether it is true or false; and it certainly matters, for *if* it were true, then Reid would not be guilty under the law.
4. Irrelevant.

Exercise 6-1

1. Irrelevant.
4. Relevant.
7. Irrelevant.
10. Irrelevant.
13. Irrelevant. The question is not whether they get back more than they pay in taxes, but whether they have any *voice* or representation in the setting of tax policy. Even if they get back one hundred times more in services than they pay in taxes, it would still be taxation without representation.

Chapter 7

Exercise 7-1

1. You are suffering from the Wyoming Gollywobbles virus; linked argument.
4. The United States should reduce its stockpile of nuclear weapons; convergent.
7. The defendant is guilty of murder; convergent.

10. Elaine Slevert is guilty of fraud; linked argument (with linked subarguments).
13. We should require unanimous verdicts; convergent argument.
16. Gwendolyn stole the collected works; linked argument.
19. Bruce is guilty of the robbery; a convergent argument, but each of the converging subarguments are linked arguments.
22. Bart is guilty: overall a convergent argument, but the first converging subargument is an extensive linked argument.

Exercise 7-4

1. There is an unstated assumption that when there is reasonable doubt of guilt the jury should find the defendant not guilty.

Chapter 8

Exercise 8-1

1. The burden of proof is on the manufacturer (by offering the mouthwash for sale, the manufacturer is making an implied claim that the product is safe for use as directed).
4. The burden of proof was on the Copernicans, who were proposing a theory that contradicts our commonsense beliefs and observations (the Sun certainly *looks* as if it is moving, and it certainly feels as if we are on a *stationary* Earth).
7. The burden of proof was on the U.S. government, which was making the claim that Iraq possessed such weapons (obviously it would be impossible for anyone to prove that he or she does *not* possess such weapons, for there is always some other place they could be hidden).

Chapter 9

Exercise 9-1

The testimony of the witness is *truthful*, but truthful is ambiguous, and the prosecutor is switching between the different meanings of "truthful." The witness is telling the truth in the sense of being *honest* (she is not lying) but it does not follow that she is telling the truth in the sense of being *accurate*. She may be honestly mistaken about the identification of the person she saw (eyewitnesses are often honestly mistaken); so she is truthful in the sense of being honest (no one disputes that), but the real question is whether she is being truthful in the sense of making an *accurate* identification.

Exercise 9-2

1. Ambiguity. "Theory" is being used in two ways. When we speak of the Darwinian *theory*, we mean a system of scientific hypotheses (that system may be very well established, such as the Copernican theory or the germ theory of disease); the second sense of "theory" means "idle speculation, without proof," as in "I have a *theory* about that, but it's really only a guess."
4. Amphiboly. The 100% can modify only the *corn oil* in the bottle, or it can apply to the total contents of the bottle.
7. Ambiguity. "Democracy" can mean either the form of government we *actually* live under (which we call a democracy, even though in practice it is obvious that not everyone has equal influence or voice in government) or the *ideal* of democracy, in which each citizen has an equal voice.
10. Ambiguity. The fact that this issue is *irrelevant* to a specific argument or issue (in this case, whether the defendant committed the crime) does not mean it is *irrelevant* in the larger sense of having no importance, of being trivial.

Chapter 10

Exercise 10-1

1a. Fallacious.
1d. Legitimate.
1g. Fallacious.
3. Even if one counts Aristotle as an authority on ethics, there is certainly no agreement among those who could be considered authorities on ethics (thus this cannot be a legitimate appeal to authority). And arguing that because many people have believed it for a long time it must be correct combines the fallacies of appeal to tradition and appeal to popularity. (Of course if we are examining Aristotle's *arguments* about ethics—rather than appealing to him as an authority—then the arguments have to stand or fall on their own merits.)
6. A legitimate line of questioning (it raises questions concerning a possible bias of someone giving expert testimony).

Cumulative Exercises One

1. Irrelevant reason fallacy.
4. Inverse ad hominem, legitimate.
7. Appeal to tradition, fallacy.
10. Ad hominem, legitimate.
13. Irrelevant reason, fallacy.

16. Straw man, fallacy.
19. Ad hominem, legitimate.
22. Inverse ad hominem, fallacy.
25. Irrelevant reason, fallacy.
28. Appeal to authority, legitimate.
31. Irrelevant reason, fallacy.
34. Appeal to ignorance, fallacy.
37. Appeal to ignorance, fallacy.
40. Appeal to ignorance, fallacy.
43. Ad hominem, fallacy.
46. Ad hominem, legitimate.
49. Appeal to authority, fallacy.
52. Appeal to authority, legitimate.
55. Appeal to authority, legitimate.
58. Appeal to authority, legitimate.

Chapter 11

Exercise 11-1

1. Attacking the principle, one would say, I disagree, I believe we *should* require people to exercise. Attacking the analogy, one would argue that requiring people to wear seatbelts is *not* like requiring people to exercise (they do not fit under the same principle); for example, I believe that we should require people to do things for their own good so long as it is not intrusive on their privacy: requiring people to wear seatbelts on public highways is not an intrusive measure, but checking to make sure that they exercise regularly would be intrusive. (You may believe the analogy is a good one; the point here is only that this is what would be required in order to attack the analogy, even if you think that attack fails.)

4. To attack the principle: I believe season ticket holders *should* be required to attend every game. There are several ways to attack the analogy; for example, attending class is part of getting a certificate (a diploma) certifying that one has completed various educational requirements; attending a sporting event does not certify any special level of accomplishment.

7. To attack the principle, one would have to assert that no measures should be taken to prevent death. To attack the analogy, one must argue that there is a difference between interfering in nature to prevent death and interfering to hasten death (e.g., the former is a natural survival instinct—we naturally attempt to avoid death, as when we spontaneously jump out of the way of a speeding car—but hastening death is not a natural process).

10. To attack the principle, one would deny that anyone should have the right to place a nativity scene on private property. To attack the analogy, one would argue that placing restrictions on what one can do on one's own private property is very different from placing restrictions on the use of public shared property.

Exercise 11-2

1. Figurative analogy; there may be room for disagreement, but it seems legitimate to me.
4. Figurative analogy, though you could read it as a deductive argument by analogy; a good analogy, by my lights.
7. Deductive analogy; legitimate.
10. Figurative analogy; I would count it as legitimate.

Exercise 11-4

1. Deductive argument by analogy. The principle is that mildly addictive "intoxicating" drugs (comparable to alcohol in dangers and effects) should not be banned. In arguing against that analogy, one could reject the principle: Perhaps marijuana is similar to alcohol, but I believe *both* alcohol and marijuana should be prohibited. Second, one could attack the analogy (claiming that marijuana is much more harmful or addictive than alcohol).
4. Faulty deductive argument by analogy.
7. Inductive argument by analogy.
10. A deductive argument by analogy, and I would judge it a good argument.

Exercise 11-5

1. Figurative analogy; legitimate.
4. Could read this as either a figurative analogy or a deductive argument by analogy; it seems to me legitimate.
7. A figurative analogy; there can be debate over whether it is legitimate or faulty.
10. Figurative analogy; legitimate.
13. Deductive analogy; legitimate (though it could be disputed).
16. Figurative analogy; legitimate.
19. Figurative analogy; whether legitimate or faulty will be controversial.
22. Can be read as either figurative or deductive; legitimate, in either case.
25. Faulty figurative analogy.
28. Good figurative analogy.
31. Inductive analogy; fairly strong (though it could be stronger), and I would count it as legitimate.

Exercise 11-6

1. The defense will interpret the principle broadly: The principle might be that giving a warning of any known hazards on your property is an adequate safeguard. The plaintiff will interpret the *Whittle* v. *Cox* principle

narrowly: A posted sign is a required warning for a vicious dog (but that says nothing about verbal warnings, nor does it imply that the warning is a *sufficient* safeguard).

2. The city attorney (interpreting the piano lesson precedent narrowly) can argue that the principle is that home businesses are permitted so long as they do not produce any material product for sale (or, perhaps, home businesses are permitted so long as they are exclusively educational in nature). The plaintiff might argue that the precedent implies that businesses are permitted so long as they operate out of the primary residence.

3. When the Torelli precedent is added, the city attorney must narrow the precedent still further: the principle is that home businesses are permitted so long as they do not produce *and sell* any material product.

Chapter 12

Exercise 12-1

1. Fallacy.
4. Fallacy.
7. Fallacy.
10. Legitimate.
13. Legitimate.

Exercise 12-2

1. Straw man.
4. Straw man.

Exercise 12-3

1. False dilemma; it might not cause cancer, but might cause damage to the heart, lungs, or nervous system.
4. Genuine dilemma.
7. False dilemma; some good upright Scots might be honestly mistaken.
10. Genuine dilemma.
13. False dilemma; she might be indifferent to him.
16. False dilemma; it could be a case of self-defense.
19. False dilemma; we could raise taxes, or make cuts elsewhere.

Exercise 12-4

1a. Smoking in public restaurants should be banned. It would be a mistake to try to enact a total prohibition against smoking. On the other hand, we shouldn't just allow people to smoke anywhere, with no consideration of others. Therefore, there should be no smoking in any situation where it is likely to bother others, such as in restaurants or airplanes or offices.

b. Smoking in public restaurants should not be banned. It would be wrong to allow smoking in areas where it poses a major threat or annoyance, such as in hospitals or in elevators. On the other hand, we shouldn't take the extreme stance of banning all smoking in public places, such as restaurants.

2a. Passive euthanasia should be permitted. Obviously we should not go to the extreme of allowing the purposeful causing of death by active euthanasia; but on the other hand, it would be wrong to require that treatment continue even when the dying patient does not want it. Therefore, allowing passive euthanasia is a good and reasonable policy.

b. Passive euthanasia should not be permitted. That is not to suggest that we go to the extreme of requiring all possible treatment—even experimental and burdensome treatments—for every patient; but we should not go to the other extreme and allow standard treatments to be stopped for terminally ill patients. So the good, moderate position is this: We do not always require extraordinary treatment measures, but we should also never allow passive euthanasia.

Chapter 13

Exercise 13-1

1. Begging the question.
4. Complex question.
7. Begging the question.
10. Does not beg the question.
14. Self-sealing.

Exercise 13-2

1. The assumption is that women think less analytically than men.
4. Assumes the existence of such a plan.
7. Assumes that the mind does cause the body to do things; and more basically, assumes that the mind and the body are distinct (assumes that materialism is false, that the mind is something different from the brain).
10. Did he, or did Leif Ericson? More to the point, how could he "discover" a continent on which people were already living? If an Iroquois sailor had landed in London, would we say that he "discovered Europe"?

Cumulative Exercises Two

1. Irrelevant reason, fallacy.
4. False dilemma, fallacy.
7. Appeal to authority, legitimate.

10. Ambiguity, fallacy ("good argument" is being used in two different senses; one, in the sense that it *worked*—it sold a lot of cereal—and the other in the sense of actually giving good reasons in support of the conclusion).
13. Golden mean, fallacy.
16. Ad hominem, legitimate.
19. Inverse ad hominem, fallacy.
22. Begging the question, fallacy.
25. Appeal to ignorance, fallacy.
28. Ad hominem, fallacy; followed by straw man, fallacy.
31. Appeal to tradition, fallacy.
34. False dilemma, fallacy.
37. Begging the question, fallacy.
40. Ad hominem, legitimate.
43. Golden mean, fallacy.
46. Complex question, fallacy.
49. Ad hominem, fallacy.
52. Irrelevant reason, fallacy.
55. Inverse ad hominem, fallacy.
58. Genuine dilemma, legitimate.
61. Appeal to popularity, fallacy.
64. Slippery slope, fallacy.
67. Appeal to tradition, fallacy.
70. Appeal to authority, fallacy.
73. Slippery slope, legitimate.
76. Begging the question, fallacy.
79. Straw man, fallacy.
82. Self-sealing, fallacy.
85. Ambiguity ("made with real fruit" implies that they are primarily fruit, when it is likely that they are primarily sugar with a tiny amount of fruit flavoring).
88. Ad hominem, legitimate.
91. Appeal to authority, fallacy.
94. False dilemma, fallacy.
97. Self-sealing, fallacy.
100. False dilemma, fallacy (could have been a case of self-defense).
103. Ad hominem, legitimate.
106. Slippery slope, fallacy.
109. False dilemma, fallacy.
112. Ambiguity (something can be "desirable" in the sense of actually being desired without being "desirable" in the sense of being *worthy* of desire).
115. Faulty analogy, fallacy.
118. Straw man, fallacy (in the response by Annas).

Chapter 14

Exercise 14-1

1. Against. He may be guilty of some other crime, but if he had permission to be there, he cannot be guilty of breaking or entering (not having permission is a necessary condition of guilt).

Exercise 14-2

1. a
4. a

Exercise 14-4

1. a
4. b
7. b
10. b
13. a
16. a
19. c
22. c
25. c
28. b
31. b
34. a

Exercise 14-5

1. No permission is a necessary condition of Joe's guilt.

   Joe's guilt is a sufficient condition of no permission.
   $G \rightarrow {\sim} P$

4. Mighty Casey striking out is a sufficient condition for no joy.

   No joy is a necessary condition of Mighty Casey striking out.
   $SO \rightarrow {\sim} J$

7. Playing is a necessary condition of winning.

   Winning is a sufficient condition of playing.
   $W \rightarrow P$

10. Answering correctly is a necessary condition of passing.

    Passing is a sufficient condition of answering correctly.
    $P \rightarrow AC$

13. Seeing is a sufficient condition for believing.

    Believing is a necessary condition for seeing.
    $S \rightarrow B$

Exercise 14-6

1. Affirming the consequent.
4. *Modus ponens.*
7. Denying the antecedent.

Exercise 14-7

1. *Modus tollens*, valid.
4. Affirming the consequent, invalid.
7. Denying the antecedent, invalid.

10. Affirming the consequent, invalid.
13. *Modus tollens*, valid.
16. *Modus tollens*, valid.
19. *Modus tollens*, valid.
22. *Modus tollens*, valid.
25. Affirming the consequent, invalid.
28. *Modus tollens*, valid.
31. *Modus ponens*, valid.
34. Denying the antecedent, invalid.

Chapter 15

Exercise 15-1

1. One, if an elderly person can afford a pet, that person is more likely to be able to afford medications and better health care; two, it's likely that the cause is coming from the other direction: healthier people are more likely to be able to take care of pets, so it's being healthy that causes them to keep a pet, rather than the pet causing them to be healthy; and finally, the results in this study might have occurred by chance.

4. One, people have to be fairly healthy in order to go gambling, so it is probably being healthy that increases the likelihood of gambling, rather than gambling causing good health; two, if one can afford to gamble, one can also afford other health-enhancing benefits such as healthy food and better living conditions. And finally, this result might have occurred by chance in this study, and another study might give different results.

Exercise 15-2

1. Another difference is that the team has an additional year of experience; and there is always the possibility that the other teams in the league have become much worse. Hard to tell, but this is probably just a chance result: the added player was just a coincidence, having nothing to do with the changed record.

4. In this case, it is not the stopping smoking that causes death; rather, it runs in reverse: being very sick and close to death finally causes people to stop smoking.

7. There are too many other factors: the closeness of the community, with the social pressures and social management that brings, is probably the decisive factor.

10. In this case, there is probably a decisive factor that is associated with playing Mozart for babies; namely, parents who are eager to seize every possibility of pushing their children ahead academically (that's why they play Mozart for them as babies) also are more likely to encourage their children to do homework, get them tutoring when they need help, enroll them in special summer academic camps, and so on.

13. It's not the size of the stadium, but something associated with stadium size: the top football programs, that spend the most on their athletic programs and hire the best coaches, are also the programs with the huge stadiums.

Exercise 15-3

1. It may be that sicker patients (who need longer to recover) are placed in interior rooms, with no windows (e.g., the intensive care unit often is in the center of the hospital, and has no windows). Also, the patients who have windowed rooms may be paying more for those rooms, and thus have significantly better health insurance and more money, and thus have access to the top medical care from the most expensive specialists (access that poorer patients do not have).

Chapter 16

Exercise 16-1

1a. Someone who is supportive of the rally may—in his or her enthusiasm—draw an exaggerated impression of the size of the rally.

d. If this is someone who recently bought the car, it is very likely that the owner will be pleased; after all, that person picked out the car, and would not have chosen it if he or she had not liked it; and if the car is quite new, then it is unlikely that it has had serious mechanical problems.

g. Is this a person who already disliked the defendant? Is this a person who stands to gain by his or her testimony against the defendant?

Exercise 16-2

1. Do any apple juices contain added sugar? (None that I know of, since apple juice is naturally quite sweet, and adding sugar would make it undrinkable.)

4. How close to impossible is "all but"? And might dangerous levels of radiation escape elsewhere (into the water table, for example)?

7. Perhaps most of the people who receive tax cuts will be middle class (not surprising, since there are more middle-class people than rich people); but will most of the tax cuts go to the middle class? That is, will lots of middle-class people receive very small tax cuts, while a few rich people receive enormous tax cuts? In the U.S. presidential campaign of 1996, the Republicans noted that most of the people who would receive tax cuts from their proposed reduction of the

capital gains tax would be middle class. That was true. However, most of the tax cut dollars were destined for the wealthy, with the bulk of the tax cut money going to the extremely wealthy.

9. The number of deaths from cancer is declining; but the number of *cancer cases* is increasing. The decline in cancer deaths is due to better cancer treatment methods, *not* because the cancer rate is decreasing. So the continuing *increase* in cancer rates—the important half of the truth that the article omits—raises legitimate concerns about increasing carcinogenic hazards in our environment.

Cumulative Exercises Three

1. Ad hominem, fallacy.
4. Deductive argument by analogy; whether it is a good analogy or a faulty analogy would be a matter of dispute.
7. Ad hominem, legitimate (Art Sinn may be giving an argument, but at least part of that argument seems to depend on his own testimony).
10. Analogical literalism, fallacy.
13. Faulty analogy, fallacy.
16. Appeal to tradition, fallacy.
19. Fallacy of denying the antecedent.
22. Ad hominem, legitimate.
25. Slippery slope, fallacy.
28. Ambiguity, fallacy.
31. *Modus tollens*, legitimate.
34. Inverse ad hominem, fallacy.
37. Questionable cause, fallacy.
40. *Modus tollens*, legitimate.
43. Ad hominem, legitimate.
46. False dilemma, fallacy.
49. Slippery slope, fallacy.
52. Questionable cause, fallacy.
55. Denying the antecedent, fallacy.
58. Golden mean, fallacy.
61. False dilemma, fallacy.
64. Begging the question (or possibly self-sealing), fallacy.
67. Begging the question, fallacy.
70. Ad hominem, fallacy.
73. Genuine dilemma, legitimate.
76. Ad hominem, legitimate.
79. Straw man, fallacy.
82. Analogical literalism, fallacy (and it starts with a figurative analogy).
85. Faulty analogy, fallacy.
88. Analogical literalism, fallacy.
91. Questionable cause, fallacy.
94. Begging the question, fallacy.
97. Ad hominem, legitimate.
100. Ad hominem, legitimate.

103. Golden mean, fallacy.
106. Questionable cause, fallacy.
109. Appeal to ignorance, fallacy.
112. Appeal to popularity, fallacy.
115. Complex question, fallacy.
118. Analogy (could be read as either figurative or deductive), legitimate.
121. Deductive argument by analogy (*might* be read as figurative), legitimate.
124. Deductive argument by analogy; there could be dispute over its legitimacy, but I would count it as legitimate.
127. False dilemma, fallacy.
130. Appeal to tradition, fallacy.
133. Deductive argument by analogy; you will have to judge whether it is legitimate or fallacious; either way, it will be controversial.
136. Slippery slope, fallacy.
139. Begging the question, fallacy.
142. Appeal to authority, fallacy (Krugman is a genuine authority, but there is no agreement among authorities).
145. Appeal to popularity, fallacy.
148. Slippery slope, legitimate.
151. Irrelevant reason.
154. Ad hominem, legitimate.
157. Ad hominem, fallacy.
160. Begging the question, fallacy.
163. Questionable cause, fallacy.
166. Inverse ad hominem, legitimate.
169. Alice offers a legitimate deductive argument by analogy, which is followed by an attack which commits the fallacy of analogical literalism.
172. Straw man, fallacy.
175. Inverse ad hominem, legitimate.
178. Faulty analogy, fallacy.
181. Ad hominem, fallacy.
184. Irrelevant reason (red herring), fallacy.
187. Ad hominem, fallacy.

Chapter 17

Exercise 17-1

1. You need to know what sense of "average" is being used; for example, if there have been tuition increases of these percentages: 4, 4, 9, 11, 12, 15, and 18, then the *mode* (one sense of "average") is only 4 percent, but that is not a very helpful measure in this case.
2. That sounds like important data; in fact, the claim is outside of any context of reference. To make it meaningful, we need to know what percentage of the population as a whole (or what population of *non*smokers) live past 70. Also, there is a comparison of apples and

oranges: Don't compare smokers with the population as a whole (for that includes all the people who died in infancy or childhood); instead, compare those who smoked with those who didn't, starting with perhaps age 16.

4. Obviously such a comparison shows nothing, since there is no information concerning the number of skydivers and the numbers of soccer players. If there are 30,000 soccer players who play twice a week, and 1000 skydivers who jump twice a *month*, then certainly skydiving will pose a greater risk than a game of soccer.

7. This is a detached and meaningless statistic; first, it does not tell you what is used in comparison (Cleaner than using water alone? Cleaner than using a competing brand? Cleaner than using mud?). But the basic problem is that it puts a number on something that is not really quantifiable: one thing may be cleaner than another, but it's not clear that something can be 30% clearer (rather than, say, 32% cleaner).

Exercise 17-2

1. C. is the best.

Chapter 18

Exercise 18-1

1. C & B, true.
4. F → O, true.
7. W & B, false.
10. ~J ∨ E, false.
13. J ∨ P, true. (Since J is true, the truth or falsity of the second disjunct does not matter; one disjunct is true, so the entire disjunction must be true.)

Exercise 18-2

1.

	P	Q	P → Q/~Q/∴ ~P
1.	T	T	T T T FT FT
2.	T	F	T F F TF FT
3.	F	T	F T T FT TF
4.	F	F	F T F TF TF

Valid argument; there is no line in which all the premises are true and the conclusion is false.

2.

	P	Q	P → Q/~Q/∴ ~P
1.	T	T	T T T FT FT
2.	T	F	T F F FT TF
3.	F	T	F T T TF FT
4.	F	F	F T F TF TF

Invalid argument; in the third line all the premises are true and the conclusion is false.

Exercise 18-3

1. ~(J & S)

   (T & F)
   (T F F)
   T F

   Since one conjunct of the conjunction is false (it is false that the sun is a planet), the conjunction is false; so the negation of the conjunction is true.

2. S ∨ (E → M)

   F (T   F)
   F (T F F)
   F   F

   False.

4. S → (~P → C)

   T (~F   F)
   T (TF   F)
   T (TF F F)
   TF (TF F F)

   False.

8. R ∨ (W & S)

   F ∨ (T & T)
   F ∨   T
      T

   True.

9. J → (A ∨ E)
   ? → (? ∨ T)
   ? → (T   )

   True.
   (Since the consequent is true, the conditional will be true no matter what the truth value of the antecedent.)

Exercise 18-4

1.

P Q ~P	→ ~Q/Q/∴ P
T T FT T	FT T T
T F FT T	TF F T
F T TF F	FT T F
F F TF T	TF F F

Valid argument, since there is no truth-value assignment that makes all the premises true and the conclusion false.

4.

P Q R	P ∨ (Q → R)/~R & ~P/∴ ~Q
T T T	TT (TT T) FT F FT FT
T T F	TT (T F F) TF F FT FT
T F T	TT (FT T) FT F FT TF
T F F	TT (FT F) TF F FT TF
F T T	FT (TT T) FT FTF FT

FT F	F F (T F F)	TFTTF	FT
F FT	FT (FTT)	FT FTF	TF
F F F	FT (FT F)	TFTTF	TF

Valid.

9. $P\ Q\ R$ ~[P & ~(Q ∨ R)]/P → Q/R/∴ ~Q

TTT	T T F F(T T T)	T T T T	FT
TT F	T T F F(T T F)	T T T F	FT
T FT	T T F F(F T T)	T F F T	TF
T FF	F TT T(F F F)	T F F F	TF
FTT	T F F F(T T T)	F T T T	FT
FT F	T F F F(T T F)	F T T F	FT
F FT	T F F F(F T T)	F T F T	TF
F F F	T F F T(F F F)	F T F F	TF

Invalid, as shown by the first line (all the premises are true and the conclusion false) and also by the fifth line.

Exercise 18-5

1. ~Q ∨ R/~Q/∴ ~R

T	FT
TT	FT
TT TF	FT

Start with the conclusion false: In order for ~R to be false, R must be assigned true. That means that R must be true in the first premise, and that automatically makes the first premise true (it's a disjunction, with one true disjunct). Now we simply assign a truth value that makes the second premise true (make Q false, so that ~Q is true), and the result is that both premises are true and the conclusion is false; so the argument is invalid.

2. P → ~Q/~P/∴ Q

	F
T TF	F
T TF TF	F

We have found a truth-value assignment that makes both premises true and the conclusion false; therefore, this argument is invalid.

3. ~Q → ~R/R ∴ Q

	F
TF	F
TF	T	F
TF	FTT	F
TF F	FTT	F

We had to make Q false in order to make the conclusion false. That made the antecedent of the first premise true. Then we had to make R true in order to make the second premise true. But that made the consequent of the first premise (~R) false. But with a true antecedent and a false consequent, the first premise was false. So it's impossible to make all the premises true and the conclusion false; therefore, the argument is valid.

6. ~(~P & Q)/~P → R/~R/ ∴ Q

	F
(F)	F
(F F)	F
T(F F)	F

(Since the conjunction is false, the negation of the conjunction is automatically true.)

T(F F)	TF	F
T(F F)	F TF	F
T(F F)	FTT F TF	F

The premises are all true, and the conclusion false; the argument is invalid.

9. ~[P & (Q ∨ ~R)]/P → R/Q/ ∴ ~R

[( )]/	/ /	FT
[(FT)]/	T/ /	FT
[(FT)]/ T	T/ /	FT
[(FT)]/ T	T/T/	FT
[(TT FT)]/ T	T/T/	FT
T[F F (TT FT)]/ T	T/T/	FT

(In order for the first premise—which is a negation of a conjunction—to be true, the conjunction must be false. The second conjunct—a disjunction—is true; therefore, the other conjunct—P—must be assigned false.) That makes all the premises true, and the conclusion false; the argument is proved to be invalid.

13. Invalid. (Start with R true, in order to make the conclusion false. Then turn to the first premise: for that negation to be true, the conditional must be false; for the conditional to be false, the antecedent—P—must be true and the consequent false. The consequent is a conjunction—Q & R—and R has already been assigned true, so Q must be assigned false in order to make that conjunction false. Then take it from there.)

Exercise 18-6

1. I ∨ W
    G → (M & R)
    I → G
    M & ~R
    _____
    ∴ W

3. S → P
    C → ~S
    ~C → (M ∨ D)
    ~(M ∨ D)
    _____
    ∴ ~P

5. ~G → [A ∨ (P & J)]
    J ∨ C
    G & ~C
    _____
    ∴ P & ~A

Notice that the conclusion is P & ~A; the alibi witness lied: The alibi witness did not tell the truth.

Exercise 18-7

1. Valid (though obviously unsound, since the conclusion is false).
3. Invalid. The key is the fourth premise: to make that negation true, you must make the disjunction false, and that means that both disjuncts must be false.
5. Invalid. It is usually best to start by making the conclusion false, but not in this case. Since the conclusion is a conjunction, there are too many different truth-value assignments that would make it false. Start instead with the third premise: There is only one way to make it true (*G* must be assigned true, and *C* must be assigned false). And then move to the second premise. Since *C* is false, *J* (the other disjunct) must be assigned true in order to make that premise true. Now look at the first premise: since *G* is assigned true, ~*G* is false; and that makes the entire premise automatically true, since the antecedent is false. So now you can assign any truth value you wish to *A*, and also to *P*. All the premises will still be true. Drop down to the conclusion and make it false (you can make one conjunct true and the other false or make both false: whatever you prefer).
7. Invalid.

$$\sim E \to (A \vee \sim B) / G \vee \sim E / \sim (G \,\&\, \sim A) \to \sim H / H \,\therefore\, \sim B$$

(	)	(	)			FT
(	FT)	(	)			FT
(	FT)	(	)		T	FT
(	FT)	(	)	FT	T	FT
(	FT)	F(	)	FT	T	FT

Since the consequent of the third premise is false, the antecedent—the negation of the conjunction—must be false in order for the conditional statement to be true.

(	FT)	F(T)	FT	T	FT
(	FT)	F(T T TF)	FT	T	FT
(F	FT) T	F(T T TF)	FT	T	FT
(F F FT) TT		F(T T TF)T	FT	T	FT

At this point we have a truth-value assignment that makes the conclusion false and the second, third, and fourth premises true. The consequent of the first premise is false, so we have to try to make the antecedent false in order to make the first premise true. That's easy: We just assign *E* true in order to make ~*E* false. And that completes the truth-value assignment: All the premises are true and the conclusion is false, and so the argument is proved invalid.

FTT (T F FT)TT FT F(TTTF)T FTT FT

9. Invalid. Notice that there is only one truth-value assignment that will make the conclusion false. Since the conclusion is a conditional, the only way it can be false is for the antecedent to be true and the consequent false. So *H* must be assigned true, and *B* must also be true (in order to make ~*B* false).

11. Valid. *A* must be false to make the conclusion false. Then in order for the third premise to be true, both *E* and *D* must be assigned false. With *E* false, however, *B* must be false in order to make the first premise true. But then it's impossible to make the second premise true: The second disjunct (*D*) has already been assigned false, but the first disjunct (the negation of a conjunction) is also false.

Chapter 19

Exercise 19-1

1. Subject term: Penguins (*not some* penguins).
   Predicate term: Wear red bow ties (or wearers of red bow ties).
   Form: PA (particular affirmative).
3. Subject term: Olympic athletes.
   Predicate term: Quite wealthy (or people who are quite wealthy).
   Form: PA (particular affirmative).
5. Subject term: Defendants.
   Predicate term: Guilty (The predicate is *guilty*, rather than *not guilty*).
   Form: PN.

Exercise 19-2

1. Valid.
2. Invalid. If there are any seals, they are not cribbage-cheats; but since there is no *X* in *SPC*, we can't be sure that any seals really exist. So the argument is invalid.
5. Valid. (Note that the conclusion is: "No Ninja warriors are good psychiatrists.")
8. Invalid.

Exercise 19-3

1. Some prisoners are innocent people (or, Some innocent people are prisoners).
4. Some weak-chinned persons are not criminals.
6. Some extraterrestrials are Earth visitors. (This does not suggest that *all* extraterrestrials visit Earth; Earth may be a hot vacation spot for extraterrestrials, but it is not a mandatory stop on the extraterrestrial itinerary.)
8. All people-who-can-be-on-the-team are hardworkers.

Exercise 19-4

1. "Royalty" is "a member of the royal family." So the argument goes:
   Only royalty are permitted to wear the crown jewels.
      That is: All permitted to wear the crown jewels are royalty.
   No penguin is permitted to wear the crown jewels.
   Therefore, no penguin is royalty.
   And a simple Venn diagram shows that to be invalid.

3.
>   All sick-people are morose.
>   Some firefighters are sick people.
>   Therefore, some firefighters are morose.

   Valid.

Exercise 9-5

1. All liver-eaters are cribbage-cheaters.
   Some liver-eaters are drinkers.
>   Therefore, some cribbage-cheaters are drinkers.

   Valid.

3.
>   All accused are entitled.
>   Some accused are unpopular.
>   Therefore, some unpopular are entitled.

Or you could write it like this:
>   All accused are entitled.
>   Some accused are not popular.
>   Therefore, some entitled are not popular.

Either way, it's valid.

5.

All results-of-coercion are worthless.
Some confessions are worthless.
Therefore, some confessions are results-of-coercion.
Invalid. (The *X* in your Venn diagram is inside the Confessions circle, but it is on the line of the Results-of-Force class; so we cannot conclude that there must be confessions that are the results-of-force.)

Index

Note: Page numbers followed by n.refer note numbers.

DeMorgan's Theorems, 369
Denying the antecedent, fallacy of, 269–270
Diderot, Denis, 202
Dilemma arguments, 211–217
  conditional form of, 215–216
  false dilemma, fallacy of, 212–217
    with strawman, 216
  genuine dilemma, 212
DiNicola, Ralph, 242
DiPerna, Paula, 12, 13n.
Dirck, Joe, 163
Disjunction, 359
Dispositive facts, 171
Dixon, Jeane, 291
Donohue, Brian, 13n.
Double-blind experiments, 286, 294, 350
Doublespeak, 132, 139
Dowden, Bradley, 55
Drosnin, Michael, 281
Du Cann, Richard, 55n.
Duhem, Pierre, 114
Dunagin, Ralph, 280
Dworkin, Ronald, 126, 128n., 168
Dwyer, Jim, 317
Dwyer, William L., 12

E
Eckardt, Robert, 189
Eddleman, David, trial of, 34
Epidemiological study, 288
Ehrenfreund, Norbert, 224n., 225, 425
Enthymemes, 111
Euphemism, 132
Evidence-driven deliberation, 9
Ewen, Stuart, 317
Expert witnesses. *See* Testimony, expert
Eyewitnesses. *See* Testimony, eyewitness
Ezzell, Carol, 225

F
Factcheck.org, 316
False dilemma. *See* Dilemma, false
Faulty analogy, 170–171
Fenton, Andrew, 155
Filling-in memories, 307
Fischer, John Martin, 177–178, 201n.
Fleming, Peggy, 34
Flew, Antony, 231, 238n.
Folger Coffee Company, 134
Fontes, Norman E., 316n.
Forer, Lois G., 297n.
Foster, Kenneth R., 154
Frank, Barney, 64
Frazier, Kendrick, 297n., 315n.

Frankfurter, Felix, 128n.
French Declaration of the Rights of Man and of the Citizen, 118
Frontline, 91n., 316
Frye v. *United States*, 154n.
Fuller, Lon L., 192, 202n.

G
Gaskins, Richard H., 128, 128n.
Gates, Bill, 187
Gay-Williams, J., 209, 224n.
Giago, Tim, 191, 202n.
Gideon, Clarence Earl, trial of, 61–62
Giere, Ronald N., 298
Giles, F. T., 55n.
Ginsburg, Justice Ruth Bader, 167
GlaxoSmithKline, 351
Glenmullen, Joseph, 351
Golden mean fallacy, 220–223
  and jury deliberations, 222–223
Golding, Martin P., 114, 202
Goodman, Nelson, 357
Grassley, Charles, 296
Greeley, Andrew M., 331
Greensboro Daily News, 50, 55n., 86, 139n., 201n., 202n., 229, 285
Greider, William, 317
Griffin v. *Illinois*, 202
Groopman, Jerome, 298
Gross, Samuel R., 6, 13n.
Guilt not proven, 119
Gupta, Anil, 139

H
"Hagar the Horrible," 213
Half-truths, 311
Halley, Edmond, 289
Hans, Valerie, 9, 12, 13n., 297n.
Hardin, Garrett, 225
Harris, Carlyle, trial of, 230
Harrisburg Seven, 2
Hart, Betsy, 251
Hart, H. L. A., 298
Hart, Johnny, 234, 277
Hastorf, Albert, 302, 315n.
Hightower, Jim, 222
Hill, Betty, 51
Hinckley, John Jr., trial of, 144
Hocking, John E., 316n.
Hoffer, Marilyn Mona, 316n.
Hoffer, William, 316n.
Holland, Barbara, 13n.
Holland v. *Illinois*, 66, 74, 225